Object-Oriented ActionScript 3.0

Peter Elst
Sas Jacobs
Todd Yard

Object-Oriented ActionScript 3.0

ISBN-13 (pbk): 978-1-59059-845-0

ISBN-10 (pbk): 1-59059-845-8

Printed and bound in the United States of America 9 8 7 6 5 4 3 2 1

Distributed to the book trade worldwide by Springer-Verlag New York, Inc., 233 Spring Street, 6th Floor, New York, NY 10013. Phone 1-800-SPRINGER, fax 201-348-4505, e-mail `orders-ny@springer-sbm.com`, or visit `www.springeronline.com`.

For information on translations, please contact Apress directly at 2855 Telegraph Avenue, Suite 600, Berkeley, CA 94705. Phone 510-549-5930, fax 510-549-5939, e-mail `info@apress.com`, or visit `www.apress.com`.

The source code for this book is freely available to readers at `www.friendsofed.com` in the Downloads section.

Cover images courtesy of NASA.

Credits

Lead Editor
Chris Mills

Technical Reviewer
Crystal West

Editorial Board
Steve Anglin, Ewan Buckingham, Gary Cornell, Jonathan Gennick, Jason Gilmore, Jonathan Hassell, Chris Mills, Matthew Moodie, Jeffrey Pepper, Ben Renow-Clarke, Dominic Shakeshaft, Matt Wade, Tom Welsh

Project Manager
Denise Santoro Lincoln

Copy Edit Manager
Nicole Flores

Copy Editor
Ami Knox

Assistant Production Director
Kari Brooks-Copony

Production Editor
Laura Esterman

Compositor
Dina Quan

Proofreader
Linda Seifert

Indexer
Broccoli Information Management

Interior and Cover Designer
Kurt Krames

Manufacturing Director
Tom Debolski

CONTENTS AT A GLANCE

PART THREE: CORE OOP CONCEPTS

PART FOUR: BUILDING AND EXTENDING DYNAMIC FRAMEWORKS

PART FIVE: DATA INTEGRATION

CONTENTS

PART THREE: CORE OOP CONCEPTS

PART FIVE: DATA INTEGRATION

FOREWORD

If there's one thing I've learned as a developer, it's this: complexity happens; simplicity, you have to strive for. Nowhere is this truer than in education. Our role as teachers, by definition, is to simplify subjects so that they can be easily understood. A good teacher dispels trepidation with anecdote, abstraction with analogy, superstition and magic with knowledge.

Simplicity, however, is not easily attained. In order to simplify, you must first gain an encompassing understanding of the complex. It is a rare person who can simultaneously exist in both the simple and complex plains of a problem domain and communicate effectively at both levels. It is, however, these same people who make the best teachers.

Object-oriented programming (OOP) is a subject that many Flash developers do not approach due to a widespread erroneous perception of its enormous scope and complexity. Nothing could be further from the truth. The core concepts behind OOP are simple enough for a primary school student with a particularly nasty case of Hynerian flu to understand in a single sitting.

It must be because OOP is essentially such a simple concept that we sometimes feel the need to protect ourselves with important-sounding words the length of major rivers in order to explain it. Because, hey, if we said that OOP involves the interaction of objects, each of which is an instance of a certain blueprint and has certain traits and behaviors—well, that would just be too simple. Who'd respect our geeky prowess then? Instead, we lock ourselves in ivory towers guarded by the frightening monsters we call Inheritance, Composition, Polymorphism, and Encapsulation, and hope that the FlashKit masses will tend to their tweens and leave us to meditate quietly on the path to programming nirvana.

But object-oriented programming is easy. All right, it's easy just like chess is easy. You can pick up the basics in an hour and start playing the game but it can take years to fully master. This book teaches you the basics to get you started on the right foot.

What you may not know is that if you have done any Flash development at all, you have already used at least some object-based programming. Each time you set the x and y coordinates of a movie clip or you tell it to `gotoAndPlay()`, you are interacting with the properties and methods of an object (a movie clip, just like everything else in Flash, is an object). However, your applications do not magically become object oriented just because you use objects. You can very easily use objects in a procedural manner without practicing object-oriented programming. What this book teaches you is to go beyond a mixture of procedural and object-based programming to understand how to structure your Flash applications in an object-oriented manner. It goes beyond the mere use of existing objects to teach you how to model your own objects and structure the communication between objects using good practices.

OOP is so often presented in such pretentious prose so as to be illegible to all but a handful of PhDs. If grandiose, self-important passages of academic rambling are what you're after, you should put this book down and walk away now. I'm sure you'll find an 800-page hardback elsewhere to satisfy your thirst for confusion. If, however, you are looking for a pragmatic guide to OOP and ActionScript 3.0 (AS3) that is simply written and easy to understand, you could do far worse than to look through these pages more closely.

Aral Balkan
June 4, 2007
Brighton, United Kingdom

ABOUT THE AUTHORS

Peter Elst is a certified Flash instructor, an Adobe Community Expert, and an active member of the Belgian Adobe user group. As the managing director of MindStudio, a freelance Flash platform consultant, and a respected member of the online community, Peter has spoken at various international industry events and published his work in leading journals. He regularly posts his views on emerging trends in Rich Internet Application development on his blog: `www.peterelst.com`.

Sas Jacobs is a web developer who loves working with Flash and Flex applications. She set up her business, Anything Is Possible, in 1994, working in the areas of web development, IT training, and technical writing. The business works with large and small clients building web applications with Flash, Flex, ASP.NET, XML, and databases. Sas has spoken at many international conferences on topics relating to XML and dynamic content in Flash. In her spare time, she is passionate about traveling, photography, running, and enjoying life. You can find out more about her at `www.sasjacobs.com`.

Todd Yard is a senior software engineer at Brightcove in Cambridge, Massachusetts, leading the development of their Flash video players and templating system. He has contributed as an author to over ten friends of ED books and as a technical reviewer for several others. His personal site, `www.27Bobs.com`, really needs updating, but he's a busy guy.

ABOUT THE TECHNICAL REVIEWER

Crystal West has been using Flash and ActionScript to build Rich Internet Applications since 2002. She is currently working as a software engineer at Brightcove (`www.brightcove.com`) in Cambridge, Massachusetts, helping to build the future of Internet TV. When she is not coding or problem solving, you'll most likely find her in dance class, hanging out with her husband, Jeffrey, and their dog, Gus, or pining for the next *LOST* episode. She and her husband currently reside in Boston, Massachusetts.

ACKNOWLEDGMENTS

Special thanks to friends and family for their support; Tink and Crystal for their help and technical expertise; Serge, Koen, and the local Adobe community for the inspiration; and, last but not least, coauthors Sas and Todd, and the friends of ED team for making this book a reality.

Peter Elst

INTRODUCTION

Hello and welcome to *Object-Oriented ActionScript 3.0*. We've written this book to guide you through the world of object-oriented programming in ActionScript 3.0.

As you'll no doubt know, Adobe revolutionized ActionScript when it introduced ActionScript 3.0. Far from being a minor overhaul, it's a complete update—we think it's fair to say that the language has been reinvented as a full-scale proper programming language, with many things vastly improved, such as the way it handles events and XML, and some very cool additions, such as regular expressions, a standardized event model, and a new Display List API for working with visual objects much more effectively. But one of the biggest overriding things to note involves object orientation: whereas with ActionScript 2.0, it was possible, and certainly beneficial, to code your applications the OO way, with ActionScript 3.0 it is completely mandatory.

But there's no need to go running for cover—object-oriented programming is not something to be scared about. What it really comes down to is best practices for structuring your code and finding techniques dealing with common problems that arise when building applications.

And this book takes you through those best practices and techniques from the ground up. After a quick introduction to the area, and a run-through of essential ActionScript 3.0 syntax, we jump into OOP best practices (including workflow and planning) and cover OOP principles in detail—inheritance, classes, encapsulation, interfaces, design patterns, and polymorphism—showing how to apply these to ActionScript 3.0 most effectively. In this edition of our book, examples are provided in both the Flash IDE and Flex Builder. Flex Builder has an entire chapter devoted to it to show you how best to code OO applications with it.

The first three parts of the book cover the topics just described. This should get you comfortable enough to start mastering OOP ActionScript 3.0 applications, no matter what development environment you choose to use to work with them.

The last two parts of the book (which cover dynamic frameworks and data integration) take all the concepts covered in the first three parts and apply them to building lots of real-word examples that solve different problems you might encounter in your professional work. We recommend you follow through all the examples attentively, as there is a lot of learning and inspiration to be taken from them. Specific cases range from manager classes and OOP animation and effects frameworks, to communication between Flash and the browser and XML and Web Services.

All too often, object-oriented programming and design patterns are presented as some sort of religious edict; the aim of this book is to present these topics to you in a way that is pragmatic, practical, and down to earth, giving you the inspiration to start developing well-maintained, reusable, and well-structured code.

Onward!

Mac or PC?

This book supports both PC and Mac platforms. During the writing of this book, both operating systems were used, and differences in how the platforms support certain features were taken into account. These are highlighted throughout the chapters in relevant places.

Development environment?

As alluded to earlier, there are numerous ways to author ActionScript 3.0 content. The two most common ways are through Flash CS3 and Flex Builder, but you could also use the free Flex SDK, available at `www.adobe.com/products/flex/sdk/`, or even open source tools that support development of ActionScript 3.0. One specifically worth mentioning is FlashDevelop (PC only), available at `www.flashdevelop.org`. There is also a large, vibrant community of open source Flash developers who have created a wealth of open source tools—see `http://osflash.org` for more.

Intended audience

This book is aimed at readers who have some previous experience developing in ActionScript and are looking to broaden their knowledge on the latest syntax introduced in ActionScript 3.0 and start writing object-oriented code. Some familiarity with the Flash or Flex authoring environments is recommended to be able to easily follow along with the example code.

Layout conventions

To keep this book as clear and easy to follow as possible, the following text conventions are used throughout:

Important words or concepts are normally highlighted on the first appearance in *italic type*.

Code is presented in `fixed-width font`.

New or changed code is normally presented in **`bold fixed-width font`**.

Menu commands are written in the form Menu ➤ Submenu ➤ Submenu.

Where we want to draw your attention to something, we've highlighted it like this:

> *Ahem, don't say I didn't warn you.*

Sometimes code won't fit on a single line in a book. Where this happens, we use an arrow like this: ➥.

```
This is a very, very long section of code that should be written all ➥
on the same line without a break.
```

PART ONE **OOP AND ACTIONSCRIPT**

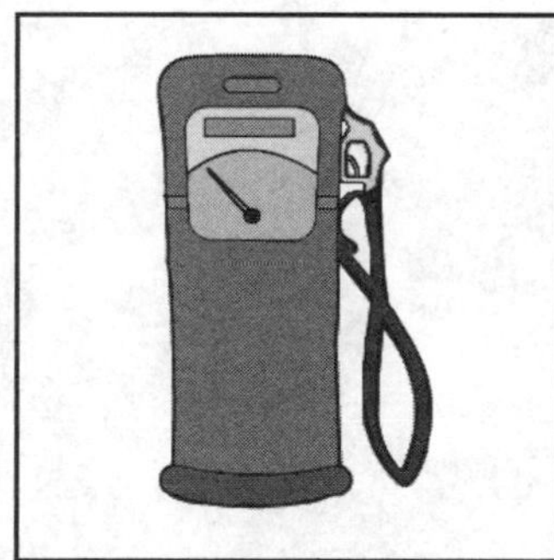

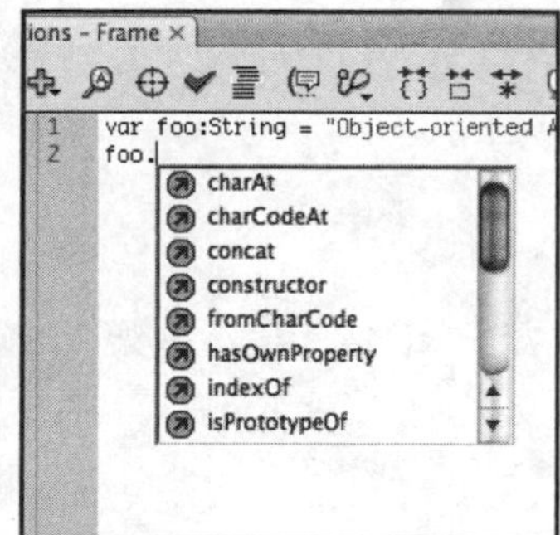

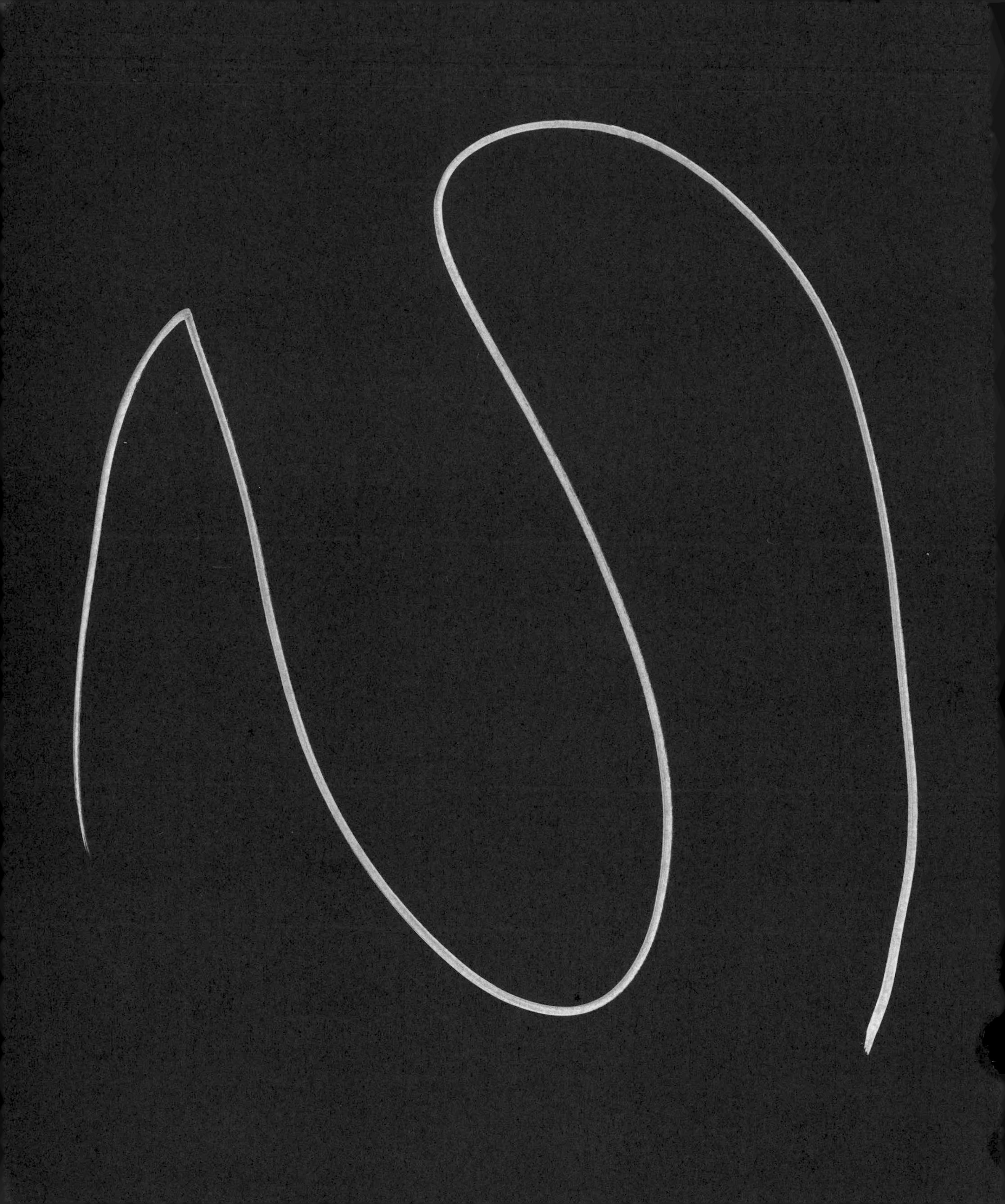

1 INTRODUCTION TO OOP

Object-oriented programming (OOP) sounds much scarier than it actually is. Essentially OOP is nothing more than a way of looking at a particular problem and breaking it down into smaller pieces called *objects*. These objects form the building blocks of object-oriented applications, and when designed properly they help form a solid framework on which to build your project.

The scoop with OOP

Before OOP became commonplace, we had something called *procedural programming*, which often required developers to write very complex and highly interdependent code. A minor change to any part of the code could spell disaster for the entire application. Debugging that type of application was a terribly painful and time-consuming task that often resulted in the need to completely rebuild large pieces of code.

When more and more user interaction got introduced in applications, it became apparent that procedural programming wouldn't cut it. Object-oriented programming was born as an attempt to solve these very problems. Although it certainly isn't the be-all and end-all of successful programming, OOP does give developers a great tool for handling any kind of application development.

The wonderful thing about object-oriented thinking is that you can look at practically any item in terms of a collection of objects. Let's look at a car for example. To the average Joe, a car is simply a vehicle (or object) that gets you places. If you ask a mechanic about a car, he'll most likely tell you about the engine, the exhaust, and all sorts of other parts. All these car parts can also be thought of as individual objects that work together to form a larger object, "the car." None of these parts actually know the inner workings of the other parts, and yet they work (or should work) together seamlessly.

Understanding the object-oriented approach

> *"'See that bird?' he says. 'It's a Spencer's warbler. (I knew he didn't know the real name.) Well, in Italian, it's a Chutto Lapittida. In Portuguese, it's a Bom da Peida. In Chinese, it's a Chung-long-tah, and in Japanese, it's a Katano Tekeda. You can know the name of that bird in all the languages of the world, but when you're finished, you'll know absolutely nothing whatever about the bird. You'll only know about humans in different places, and what they call the bird. So let's look at the bird and see what it's doing, that's what counts.'"*
>
> *—Richard Feynman*

When studying OOP, you'll come across a *plethora* of big words like *encapsulation*, *polymorphism*, and *inheritance*. Truth be told the ideas behind them are often quite simple, and there's no real need to memorize those terms unless you'd like to use them for showing off at your next family get-together.

Knowing the theory behind this terminology is, however, essential, and that's just what we'll be discussing next.

Classes and objects

When studying OOP, you cannot ignore classes and objects, as those are the fundamental building blocks of any project. A good understanding of what classes and objects are and the roles they play will help you get on track to understanding OOP.

There's a subtle difference between a class and an object. A *class* is a self-contained description for a set of related services and data. Classes list the services they provide without revealing how they work internally. Classes aren't generally able to work on their own; they need to instantiate at least one object that is then able to act on the services and data described in the class.

Suppose you want to build a house. Unless you build it yourself, you need an architect and a builder. The architect drafts a blueprint, and the builder uses it to construct your house. Software developers are architects, and classes are their blueprints. You cannot use a class directly, any more than you could move your family into a blueprint. Classes only describe the final product. To actually do something you need an *object*.

If a class is a blueprint, then an object is a house. Builders create houses from blueprints; OOP creates objects from classes. OOP is efficient. You write the class once and create as many objects as needed.

Because classes can be used to *create* multiple objects, objects are often referred to as *class instances*.

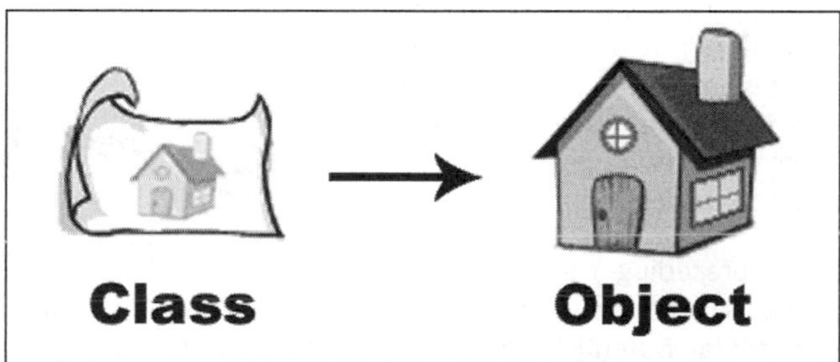

Properties

Properties give individual objects unique qualities. Without properties, each house (from the previous example) would remain identical to its neighbors (all constructed from the same blueprint). With properties, each house is unique, from its exterior color to the style of its windows.

Let's look at a Ball class for example. From that one class you can create multiple ball instances; however, not all balls look identical to one another. By providing your Ball class with properties such as color, weight, and shape, you can create instances that describe balls as diverse as a basketball, bowling ball, or rugby ball just by assigning different values to properties in each instance of the class.

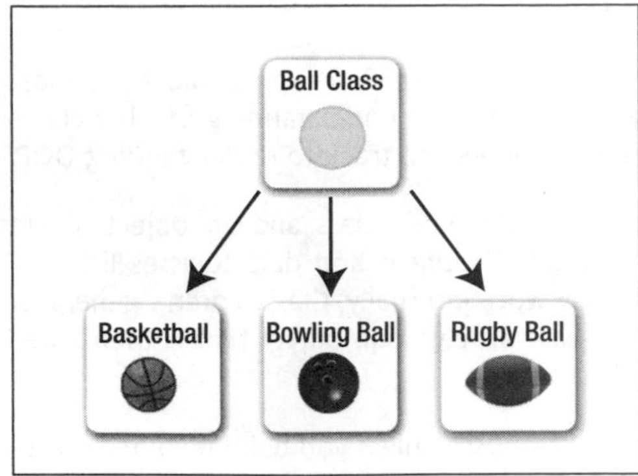

In OOP, you write classes to offer predefined behaviors and maybe hold some data. Next, you create one or more objects from a class. Finally, you endow objects with their own individual property values. The progression from classes to objects to objects with unique properties is the essence of OOP.

Encapsulation: Hiding the details

When you get into your car, you turn the key, the car starts, and off you go. You don't need to understand how the car parts work to find yourself in rush-hour traffic. The car starts when you turn the key. Car designers hide the messy internal details so you can concentrate on important things like finding another radio station. OOP calls this concept *encapsulation*.

Analogies like the preceding car example are very useful to explain concepts such as encapsulation, but it is no doubt more appealing to take an in-depth look at potential real-world scenarios like, for example, an accounting office.

Accountants love details (all the numbers, receipts, and invoices). The accountant's boss, however, is interested in the bottom line. If the bottom line is zero, the company is debt-free. If the bottom line is positive, the company is profitable. She is happy to ignore all the messy details and focus on other things. Encapsulation is about ignoring or hiding internal details. In business, this is delegation. Without it, the boss may need to deal with accounting, tax law, and international trading at a level beyond her ability.

OOP loves encapsulation. With encapsulation, classes hide their own internal details. Users of a class (yourself, other developers, or other applications) are not required to know or care why it works. Class users just need the available service names and what to provide to use them. Building classes is an abstraction process; you start with a complex problem, and then reduce it down (abstracting it) to a list of related services. Encapsulation simplifies software development and increases the potential for code reuse.

To demonstrate, I'll present some pseudo-code (false code). You can't enter pseudo-code into a computer, but it's great for previewing ideas. First, you need an Accounting class:

```
Start Of Accounting Class
End Of Accounting Class
```

Everything between the start and end line is the Accounting class. A useless class so far, because it's empty. Let's give the Accounting class something to do:

```
Start Of Accounting Class
    Start Of Bottom Line Service
        (Internal Details Of Bottom Line Service)
    End Of Bottom Line Service
End Of Accounting Class
```

Now the Accounting class has a Bottom Line service. How does that service work? Well, I know (because I wrote the code), but you (as a user of my class) have no idea. That's exactly how it should be. You don't know or care how my class works. You just use the Bottom Line service to see if the company is profitable. As long as my class is accurate and dependable, you can go about your business. You want to see the details anyway? OK, here they are:

```
Start Of Accounting Class
    Start Of Bottom Line Service
        Do Invoice Service
        Do Display Answer Service
    End Of Bottom Line Service
End Of Accounting Class
```

Where did the Invoice and Display Answer services come from? They're part of the class too, but encapsulation is hiding them. Here they are:

```
Start Of Accounting Class
    Start Of Bottom Line Service
        Do Invoice Service
        Do Display Answer Service
    End Of Bottom Line Service

    Start Of Invoice Service
        (Internal Details Of Invoice Service)
    End Of Invoice Service

    Start Of Display Answer Service
        (Internal Details Of Display Answer Service)
    End Of Display Answer Service
End Of Accounting Class
```

The Bottom Line service has no idea how the Invoice service works, nor does it care. You don't know the details, and neither does the Bottom Line service. This type of simplification is the primary benefit of encapsulation. Finally, how do you request an answer from the Bottom Line service? Easy, just do this:

```
Do Bottom Line Service
```

That's all. You're happy, because you only need to deal with a single line of code, which is essentially the interface that the class exposes. The Bottom Line service (and encapsulation) handles the details for you.

When I speak of hiding code details, I'm speaking conceptually. I don't mean to mislead you. This is just a mental tool to help you understand the importance of abstracting the details. With encapsulation, you're not actually hiding code (physically). If you were to view the full Accounting class, you'd see the same code that I see.

```
Start Of Accounting Class
    Start Of Bottom Line Service
        Do Invoice Service
        Do Display Answer Service
    End Of Bottom Line Service

    Start Of Invoice Service
        Gather Invoices
        Return Sum
    End Of Invoice Service

    Start Of Display Answer Service
        Display Sum
    End Of Display Answer Service
End Of Accounting Class
```

If you're wondering why some of the lines are indented, this is standard practice (that is not followed often enough). It shows, at a glance, the natural hierarchy of the code (of what belongs to what). Please adopt this practice when you write computer code.

Polymorphism: Exhibiting similar features

Are you old enough to remember fuel stations before the self-service era? You could drive into these places and somebody else would fill up your tank. The station attendant knew about OOP long before you did. He put the fuel nozzle into the tank (any tank) and pumped the fuel! It didn't matter if you drove a Ford, a Chrysler, or a Datsun. All cars have fuel tanks, so this behavior is easy to repeat for any car. OOP calls this concept *polymorphism*.

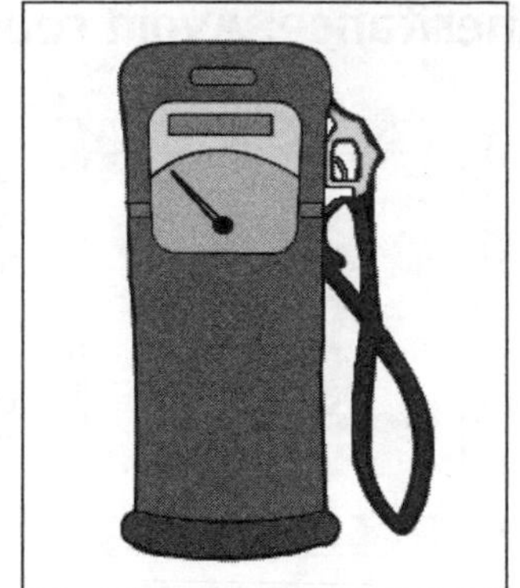

Much like cars need fuel to run, I take my daily dose of vitamins by drinking a glass of orange juice at breakfast. This incidentally brings me to a great example showing the concept of polymorphism.

Oranges have pulp. Lemons have pulp. Grapefruits have pulp. Cut any of these fruit open, I dare you, and try to scoop out the fruit with a spoon. Chances are you'll get a squirt of citrus juice in your eye. Citrus fruits know exactly where your eye is, but you don't have to spoon them out to know they share this talent (they're all acid-based juice-squirters). Look at the following Citrus class:

```
Start Of Citrus Class
    Start Of Taste Service
        (Internal Details Of Taste Service)
    End Of Taste Service

    Start Of Squirt Service
        (Internal Details Of Squirt Service)
    End Of Squirt Service
End Of Citrus Class
```

You can use the Citrus class as a base to define other classes:

```
Start Of Orange Class
    Using Citrus Class
    Property Named Juice
End Of Orange Class

Start Of Lemon Class
    Using Citrus Class
    Property Named Juice
End Of Lemon Class

Start Of Grapefruit Class
    Using Citrus Class
    Property Named Juice
End Of Grapefruit Class
```

Besides demonstrating inheritance again, the Orange, Lemon, and Grapefruit classes also exhibit similar behaviors. This is polymorphism. You know that the Orange, Lemon, and Grapefruit classes have the ability to squirt (inherited from the Citrus class), but each class has a Juice property. So the orange can squirt orange juice, the lemon can squirt lemon juice, and the grapefruit can squirt grapefruit juice. You don't have to know in advance which type of fruit, because they all squirt. In fact, you could taste the juice (inherited from the Citrus class) to know which fruit you're dealing with. That's polymorphism: multiple objects exhibiting similar features in different ways.

Inheritance: Avoid rebuilding the wheel

Grog roll wheel. Wheel good. Grog doesn't like rebuilding wheels. They're heavy, made of stone, and tend to crush feet when they fall over. Grog likes the wheel that his stone-age neighbor built last week. Sneaky Grog. Maybe he'll carve some holes into the wheel to store rocks, twigs, or a tasty snack. If Grog does this, he'll have added something new to the existing wheel (demonstrating inheritance long before the existence of computers).

Inheritance in OOP is a real timesaver. You don't need to modify your neighbor's wheel. You only need to tell the computer, "Build a replica of my neighbor's wheel, and then add this, and this, and this." The result is a custom wheel, but you didn't modify the original. Now you have two wheels, each unique. To clarify, here's some more pseudo-code:

```
Start Of Wheel Class
    Start Of Roll Service
        (Internal Details Of Roll Service)
    End Of Roll Service
End Of Wheel Class
```

The Wheel class provides a single service named Roll. That's a good start, but what if you want to make a tire? Do you build a new Tire class from scratch? No, you just use inheritance to build a Tire class, like this:

```
Start Of Tire Class
    Using Wheel Class
End Of Tire Class
```

By using the Wheel class as a starting point, the Tire class already knows how to roll (the tire is a type of wheel). Here's the next logical step:

```
Start Of Tire Class
    Using Wheel Class
    Property Named Size
End Of Tire Class
```

Now the Tire class has a property named size. That means you could create many unique Tire objects. All of the tires can roll (behavior inherited from the Wheel class), but each tire has its own unique size. You could add other properties to the Tire class too. With very little work, you could have small car tires that roll, big truck tires that roll, and bigger bus tires that roll.

What's next?

Now that wasn't too difficult, was it? In this chapter, I covered the basic idea of OOP as well as an introduction to some of its key features, including encapsulation, polymorphism, and inheritance. I'll explain those ideas in much greater detail in Part 3 of this book.

Coming up next, I will focus on the general programming concepts common to modern high-level computer languages.

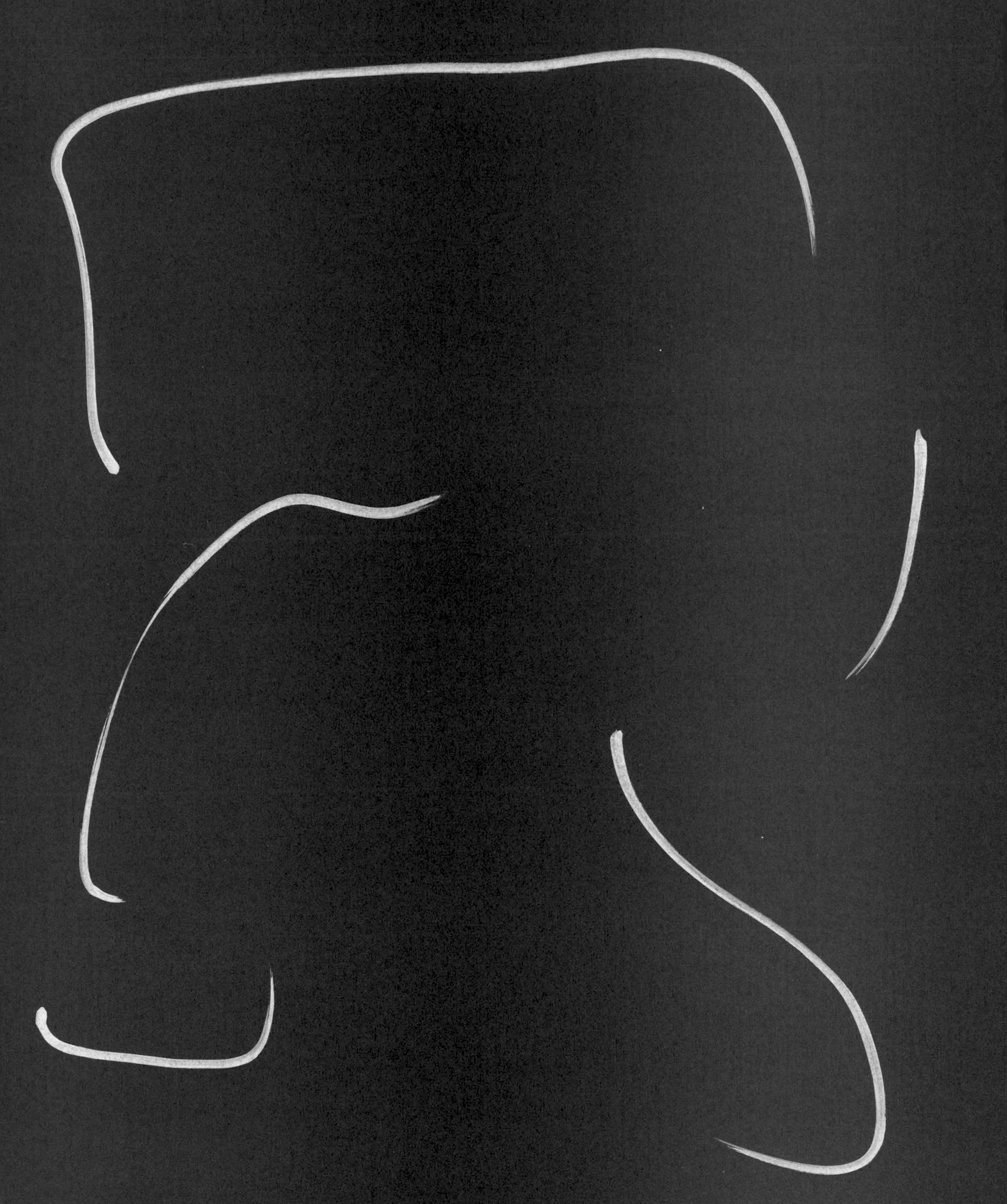

2 PROGRAMMING CONCEPTS

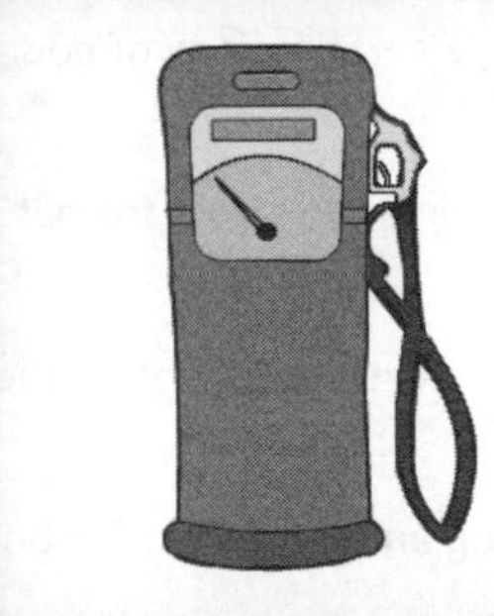

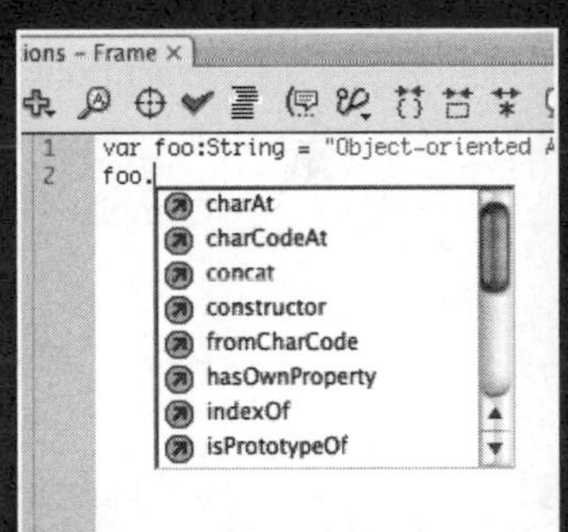

In this chapter, I'll introduce you to some common programming concepts you'll want to know about before starting to program with ActionScript 3.0 (AS3).

When working closely with computer programmers, you no doubt get slapped round the head with acronyms and techno-babble at regular intervals. If you are new to the game, don't fear, I'll soon have you joining in with this typical bonding ritual, thus affirming your newly acquired position in the office tribe.

In all seriousness, though, learning some basic terminology is really very useful. You'll come across many of the terms discussed in this chapter when reading articles, tutorials, or talking to fellow developers. Let's get started by looking at common programming slang.

About programming slang

Slang	Meaning
IDE	Integrated Development Environment, the software in which you develop an application
The code	The entire body of source code found in a computer application
Writing code	The process of creating the computer program (entering the code)
Run, running	Starting, using, or testing an application or self-contained piece of code
Runtime	When the application runs, and the things that occur during the run
Execution	The process of running a certain piece of code during runtime
Compile, compilation	The process of assembling code into a format usable for executing the code
Design time	When the application is developed (writing the code and so on)
Debugging	The process of reviewing an application for bugs in the code

In general, application development shifts continuously between design time and runtime (between creating and testing) until the computer application is "finished." Some computer languages (such as ActionScript) may require compilation before the code can be previewed, run, or deployed to another machine.

Building blocks of programming

Computer languages consist of certain building blocks that store data and determine the way an application needs to run. These building blocks are very similar across different languages, but the way in which they are implemented may differ. Certain languages are better equipped to deal with certain tasks, but there's no single one that's perfect for all types of applications. The following table lists the major building blocks of programming:

Building Block	Purpose
Variables	For storing temporary data
Arrays	For storing lists of temporary data
Functions	For grouping and reusing instructions
Loops	For repeating instructions
Conditionals	For making decisions

Let's consider variables first.

Variables

When you write down what a typical application needs to do, you immediately think of storing and retrieving data. The role of data in an application is temporary; you need to have a placeholder for information you get from the keyboard and mouse, a database, the Web, on a network drive, etc.

These placeholders in your application are called *variables*. For every single piece of data you'll want to work with in your application, you'll declare a variable, give it a name, and assign a value to it. Any time you want to retrieve, modify, or delete a variable, you'll just use that very name you gave it. To write this in English, I might use the following:

```
The number of paper clips in the box is 500.
```

To write this in ActionScript 3.0, I might use this:

```
var paperClipsPerBox:Number = 500;
```

The name of the variable is paperClipsPerBox. It holds numeric data, specifically 500. Variables can hold many kinds of data (more than just numbers). The different values that can be assigned to a variable are called *data types*, and we'll discuss those next.

About variable data

What kind of data may variables hold? It depends upon the computer language, but in practice, most languages accommodate a similar set of data types (numbers, text, true/false values, and more). Some computer languages handle variables with a strict set of rules, while others do not. The strict languages demand that a single variable stores one type of data, so numeric variables can store numbers, but nothing else.

The not-so-strict languages (such as ActionScript 1.0) allow variables to hold any type of data, even to the point that a single variable may hold a number first and then maybe a sentence of text later. If you think this is good, think again. When the developer makes a mistake, the computer has far less power to help spot the error.

Luckily, from ActionScript 2.0 onward you can use strong typing, which greatly increases the ease of debugging Flash applications. ActionScript 3.0 is much stricter with regards to the use of strong typing, and you'll want to make it part of your coding practice if you want to avoid compile-time warnings and errors. Important to know is that strong typing is also a big contributing factor to the performance increase of ActionScript 3.0 running in the new virtual machine of the Flash Player.

Arrays

Arrays are like variables, but they're a little different. Other variables store a single piece of data per variable, like a number in this case:

```
var paperClipsPerBox:Number = 500;
```

The variable paperClipsPerBox can only hold one value at a given time; that value may change while the application is running, but at no point will you be able to assign two values to that single variable.

Arrays on the other hand allow you to store multiple values in a single instance. This is great for storing related items, such as a list of personal phone numbers. To write this in English, I might use the following:

```
1. Jenny (555) 867-5309
2. Pauly (555) 422-4281
3. Ricky (555) 383-9287
...
25. Benny (555) 954-2921
```

To write this in ActionScript 3.0, I might use this:

```
myPhoneList[0] = "Jenny (555) 867-5309";
myPhoneList[1] = "Pauly (555) 422-4281";
myPhoneList[2] = "Ricky (555) 383-9287";
...
myPhoneList[24] = "Benny (555) 954-2921";
```


With arrays, you have a single variable named myPhoneList and you access the data by number. If you need the third phone number in the list, you ask for myPhoneList[2] and the computer answers

```
Ricky (555) 383-9287
```

Arrays combine the convenience of simple variables with the power to access data in an ordered list. Arrays are dynamic objects in most computer languages, which means you can insert or remove array items as often as needed. It is even possible to add arrays inside arrays to create more complex data structures called *multidimensional arrays*. Building on the previous example, we could, instead of simply storing a phone number, create an array for each item in myPhoneList that holds their additional information such as e-mail address, location, date of birth, etc.

Functions

Functions provide a means to call a specific set of instructions that achieve a single, specific task in your application. When first starting to program, you might be tempted to put too much into a function. Just remember: one (and only one) task per function. The function may include 10, 20, 30, or more separate instructions to achieve its task. That's fine, as long as the whole group maintains a single and focused purpose. While this practice is by no means enforced by OOP, it is strongly recommended, and I believe it will help you build reusable and more effective code.

About calling functions

Calling a function means *using* a function. Once you declare a function, you may call its name from elsewhere in the application. Once called, the application carries out the instructions defined by the function. You declare a function once, but call it as needed.

Suppose you have an application to convert distances. You don't have to retype the conversion instructions every time you need them. Instead, you can create a single function named milesToKilometers and call it from elsewhere in the application. The milesToKilometer function returns the resulting data once it has finished its calculation. The resulting data from a function is typically stored in a variable that you can use later on in your application.

About function parameters

Functions can accept additional (agreed upon) information called *function parameters*. Using function parameters, the `milesToKilometers` function can accept a variable for miles. That way, the function can calculate an answer for 15 miles, 500 miles, 600 miles, and so on. Function parameters make functions reusable and flexible.

As with variables, in some computer languages these function parameters are assigned a particular data type and only allow that particular type of value to be used when a function is called.

Loops

Loops repeat a specific set of instructions. The number of times a loop may repeat depends on the situation. The loop may repeat a fixed number of times, or perhaps a condition determines when it expires.

A good example of where you'd use a loop is when working with arrays. Doing this allows you to easily go through each and every item stored in the array and retrieve those values for use in your application.

Conditionals

Conditionals are a major building block of any type of programming. Conditional instructions let applications make decisions; they're the actual logic and control the flow of your code.

Think of the last time you used a vending machine. You put some money in and choose your particular flavor of soft drink. The machine then uses some programming logic to determine if you put in an exact amount, too little, or too much cash. If you use exact change, the vending machine will immediately give you your soft drink; if you put in too little, it won't give you the drink and will wait for you to put more money in or press the refund button. Finally, if you put in too much money (and the machine detects that it has enough spare change), you'll get the drink and the remaining money.

Computer languages call this conditional structure an *if-then-else* statement. You can read it like this: "if a condition is met, *then* do this, otherwise (*else*) do this instead." You'll find if-then-else logic in every piece of software you can imagine. Similar to *if-then-else* is the *switch* statement, which allows you to evaluate a variable or condition and run a block of code based on its value. You'll see more examples of these conditional statements throughout the code in this book.

OOP concepts

OOP really is a methodology, a way of using the building blocks of programming to create dynamic, flexible, and reusable applications. Here's a brief review of what I discussed:

Classes. From a code-centric view, a class is a collection of functions and variables working together to support a common goal. When you get to the heart of it, though, classes handle custom data. The variables in a class store the data and functions manipulate the data. Classes provide a powerful and self-contained way of organizing and processing every type of custom data you can possibly think of.

Objects. Classes cannot do any real work themselves—for that they need to be instantiated as objects. Classes are merely templates that provide a blueprint for multiple objects. Every object automatically contains the data (variables) and behaviors (functions) described by the class. Just remember: one class can have very many objects.

Properties. Properties allow objects to be customized. Suppose you use a class named House to build 25 House objects. All houses based on the House class will look identical because they are built from the same master plan. However, House objects can individually change their own properties they got from the House class and make themselves unique from their neighbors.

What's next?

Now that we've covered the basic programming concepts, let's get started with the real work. I will discuss ActionScript 3.0, the latest incarnation of the Flash scripting language, show you how it relates to ActionScript 2.0, and run you through the new syntax. Before you know it, you'll be coding your first AS3 classes.

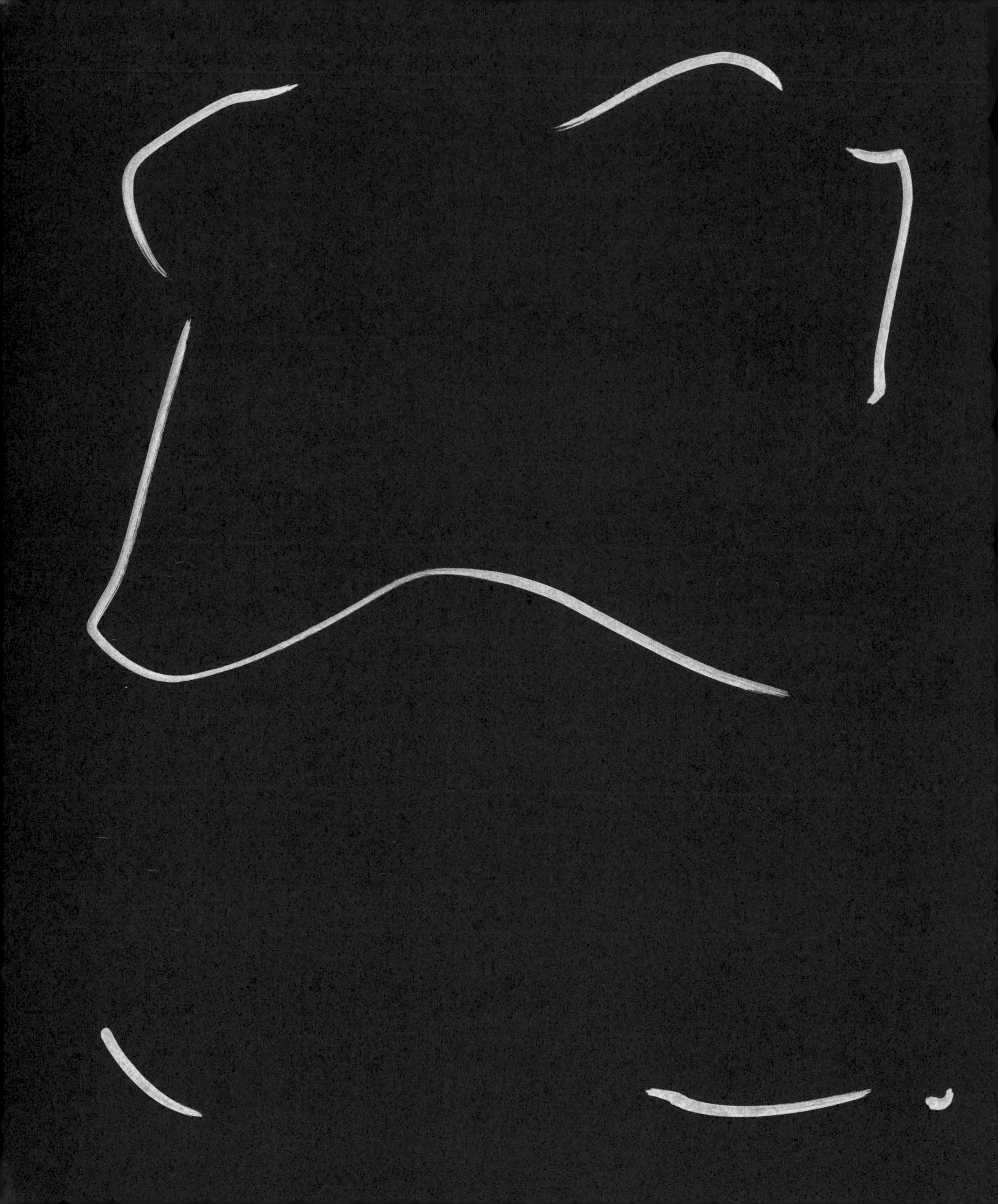

3 ACTIONSCRIPT 3.0 PROGRAMMING

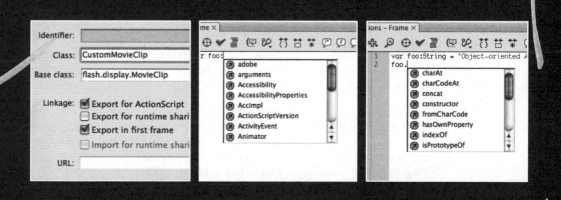

Identifier:
Class: CustomMovieClip
Base class: flash.display.MovieClip
Linkage: Export for ActionScript
Export for runtime shari
Export in first frame
Import for runtime shari
URL:

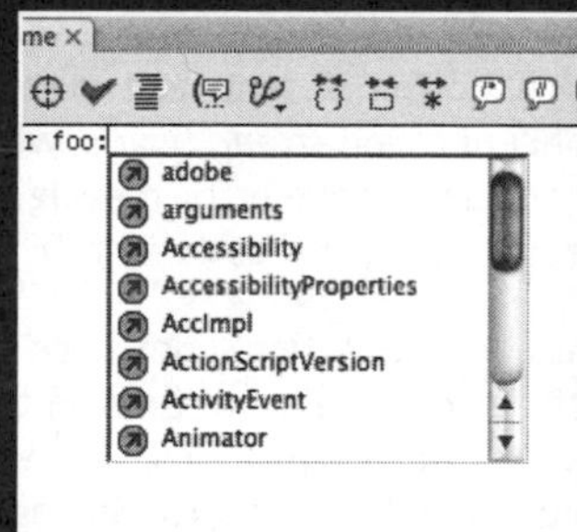

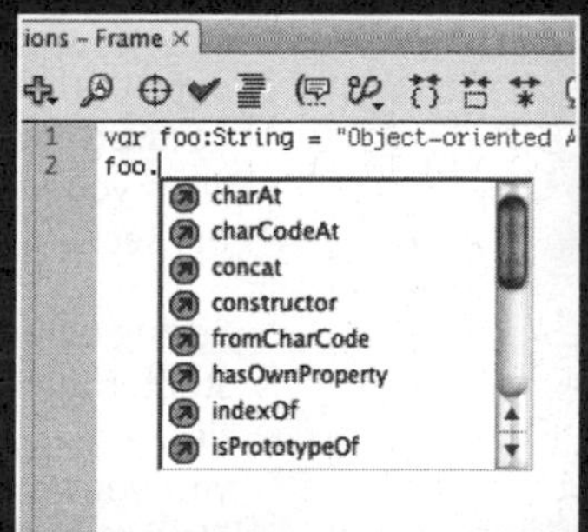

In this chapter, I'll introduce you to programming with ActionScript 3.0, the latest version of the language that you can use with Flash CS3 and Flex Builder 2 (or in fact any text editor of your choice, but more about that later).

If you were already familiar with programming in a version of ActionScript prior to this release, you were probably using ActionScript 2.0—which was the first version to include true object-oriented syntax—or further back, you may have done procedural programming or prototype hacking with ActionScript 1.0. Don't worry though, whatever version you used or haven't used, there is no need to worry: I'll walk you through it in this chapter. In terms of syntax, fairly little has changed between ActionScript 2.0 and 3.0; but the bulk of the learning curve will be learning about new features supported in the language and getting used to new package names. If you're moving over directly from ActionScript 1.0 and this is your first exposure to object-oriented programming, you'll pick up the basic principles in the following few chapters.

Let's get started by looking at the key differences between ActionScript 2.0 and 3.0 so you can familiarize yourself with what's new under the sun.

ActionScript 2.0 vs. ActionScript 3.0

You've probably been wondering how ActionScript 2.0 differs from ActionScript 3.0 and whether you should really be bothering to learn it—after all, they both involve object-oriented code, right?

There are actually numerous advantages to using ActionScript 3.0 over ActionScript 2.0, the main one being you'll be writing code that runs in a brand-spanking-new virtual machine dubbed AVM2. This new virtual machine was written from scratch and added onto the Flash Player specifically for running ActionScript 3.0 content: it is considerably faster and has a lower memory footprint. The biggest problem usually is that developers (not in the least including myself) are inherently lazy: we don't like to type longer code, we don't like to comment every function—heck, we don't even like to get out of our chairs to get a cup of coffee. Important to realize is that the process of building an application often consists of about 20% writing code, 10% tweaking that code, and 70% debugging. By using object-oriented ActionScript, you can greatly reduce that time needed for debugging because of a concept called *strong typing*, which helps you detect type mismatch bugs and gives you far more descriptive error messages (more about this later on in this chapter in the section "Strong typing and code hints").

Strong typing has been in ActionScript since version 2.0, but in this latest release it's much stricter than before: you might not be able to get away with not typing your class properties, arguments, or return types, or in the very least you'll get compiler warnings telling you you've been a bad boy (or girl). Strong typing also contributes greatly to the Flash Player running faster in the new virtual machine. Unlike in ActionScript 2.0, strong typing actually changes the bytecode when your code gets compiled to ActionScript 3.0, which allows for this tremendous performance increase.

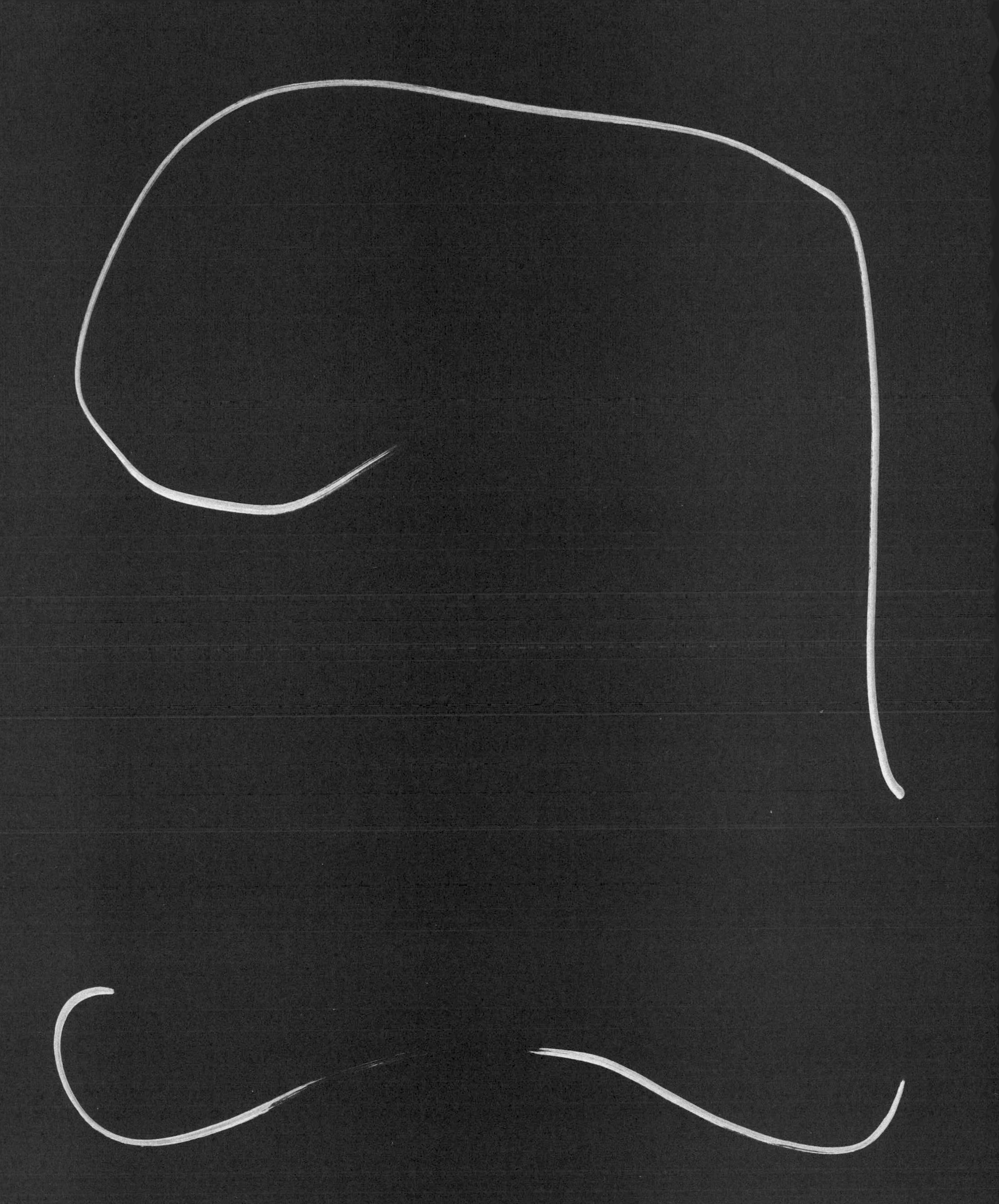

4 PLANNING

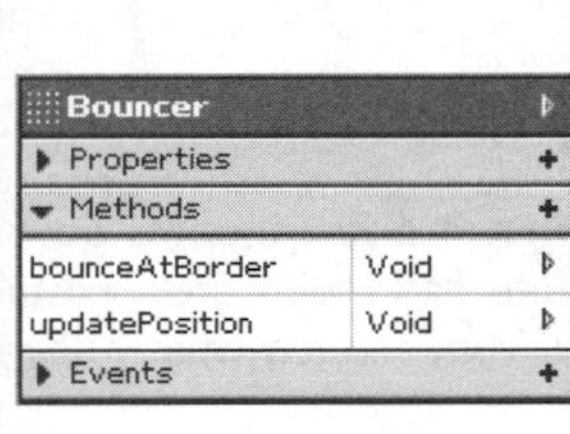
Bouncer
Properties
Methods
bounceAtBorder
Void
updatePosition
Void
Events

Ball
Properties
+color
+shape
+weight
-bounceCount
Methods
+bounce
+getBounceCount

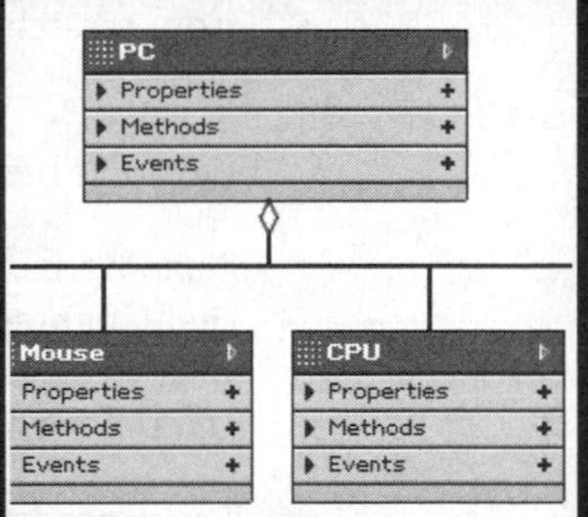
PC
Properties
Methods
Events
Mouse
Properties
Methods
Events
CPU
Properties
Methods
Events

Another thing to note is that unlike ActionScript 2.0, anything written in ActionScript 3.0 doesn't compile down to ActionScript 1.0 bytecode and can only run in this new virtual machine. As a nasty side effect, this does make it slightly difficult to have ActionScript 3.0 and 2.0 code communicate with each other, and you'll have to resort to using something like the `LocalConnection` class. Not every single project you do will need to make use of ActionScript 3.0, so don't feel you must build everything in the new syntax. There are, however, some major advantages going with ActionScript 3.0, and at the time of writing Flash Player 9 already has well over 80% worldwide adoption, so that should not be an obstacle in starting to develop with AS3.

Note that a lot of the code comparison in this chapter is between ActionScript 1.0 and version 3.0. This was done intentionally to highlight the differences between the old prototype-hack way to do OOP and the new true OOP syntax in ActionScript 3.0. The actual syntax differences between ActionScript 2.0 and 3.0 are minimal and are highlighted throughout the chapter where applicable.

Declaring variables

If in some distant past you were already using ActionScript 1.0, you know that declaring a variable was very easy indeed, and it's not that much different from how it's done in ActionScript 3.0.

```
foo = "Object Oriented ActionScript 3.0"; // ActionScript 1.0
```

The only time you'd use a `var` keyword was when you wanted to declare a variable to be of a local scope inside a function, which ensured it was removed from memory after the function had finished its task. *Scope* is the range of visibility for a particular variable; not all variables are available throughout an entire project. You'll learn more about this later on in this chapter. When declaring a variable using ActionScript 2.0 or 3.0, however, you'll always want to use that `var` keyword as a best practice.

```
var foo = "Object Oriented ActionScript 3.0"; // ActionScript 3.0
```

The preceding example shows you how a basic variable is declared in ActionScript 3.0. Important to know is that this variable is not yet strongly typed, and the compiler will complain with a warning if you try to run it. To avoid this, you can type a variable as *, which indicates that this particular variable can take on any datatype. As defined in the ECMAScript 4 standard, this enables the language to have a dynamic typing feature and not require it to be strictly defined.

```
var foo:* = true; // ActionScript 3.0
```

Now, as a best practice, you'll always want to assign datatypes to your variables wherever possible rather than type them as * unless there is some compelling reason to do so. So in the preceding example, the correct way would be to type the `foo` variable is as a Boolean.

```
var foo:Boolean = true;
```

Important to know is that you only use the var keyword the first time you declare your variable; from then on you just assign values to it by referring to its name. The value you assign to the property must be of the same type you assigned to it, so a Number type, for example, can't get a String assigned.

```
foo = "ActionScript 3.0"; // ActionScript 3.0
```

Classes vs. prototypes

ActionScript, like quite a few other languages, is based on ECMAScript standards. These standards are taken very seriously, as is underscored by Adobe's spearheading the ECMAScript 4 draft as a member of the ECMA consortium.

ActionScript 1.0 made use of a prototype-based syntax for building classes. Using a so-called prototype chain, you could modify or extend classes as well as simulate a form of inheritance that is a crucial aspect of OOP. There was no clear-cut way to see whether you were dealing with a simple function or an actual class apart from the this keyword and the prototype keyword.

ActionScript 1.0

```
function Ball(color, weight, shape) {
  this.color = color;
  this.size = size;
  this.weight = weight;
}
basketBall = new Ball("orange","light","round");
bowlingBall = new Ball("blue","heavy","round");
rugbyBall = new Ball("brown","light","oval");
```

Extending built-in classes using a prototype object became very popular in ActionScript 1.0; you can find an example of this in the following code:

```
MovieClip.prototype.setPosition = function(x,y) {
  this._x = x;
  this._y = y;
}
```

The preceding code adds to the blueprint of the MovieClip class, which makes the setPosition function available to all instances of MovieClip in your project. The setPosition function allows you to set both the x and y position of a movie clip on stage using a single function call. Let's say you've got two movie clips in your project with instance names mc1 and mc2; you could use the following function calls to position them:

```
mc1.setPosition(10,50);
mc2.setPosition(50,70);
```

Now let's look at building classes in ActionScript 3.0. The most obvious new requirement is that you need to use external files for each of your classes. If you build a class named Ball, you are required to save that in a file named `Ball.as`. You can save that file in either the folder where the Flash FLA source file is stored or in the `First Run/Classes` directory of your Flash CS3 installation.

Since ActionScript 2.0, the language also supports something called *packages*, which are a way to call classes by their folder structure. Let's say you save the `Ball.as` file in a subfolder called `sports`; you can instantiate that Ball class by using its fully qualified classpath: `sport.Ball`. Using class packages has a number of advantages; first, it prevents any possible name conflicts and also allows for easy importing of a series of classes. The `import` keyword can be used to include all classes in the sports package for use in your project:


```
import sports.*;
```

If you had more classes than just Ball placed in that directory, you'd have those all included for use inside your project.

By default, Flash looks for classes in the install directory, and if not found there moves on to the folder in which you saved the FLA. If you want, you can also add your own locations for Flash to look for classes. This could be handy if you'd like to store your ActionScript classes in a central custom location.

To add a custom classpath location, you go to Edit ➤ Preferences on a PC or Flash ➤ Preferences on a Mac and select the ActionScript tab. You'll notice there is an ActionScript 2.0 Settings button and an ActionScript 3.0 Settings button available. As you might have guessed, these allow you to set different classpaths to your ActionScript 2.0 and 3.0 classes.

When you click the ActionScript 3.0 Settings button and the dialog box shown in Figure 3-1 pops up, you can use the plus button to manually add a new location, the minus button to remove one, or the target button to browse for a location. The up and down arrow buttons can be used to set the priority for each of the locations, the topmost being the first place Flash looks.

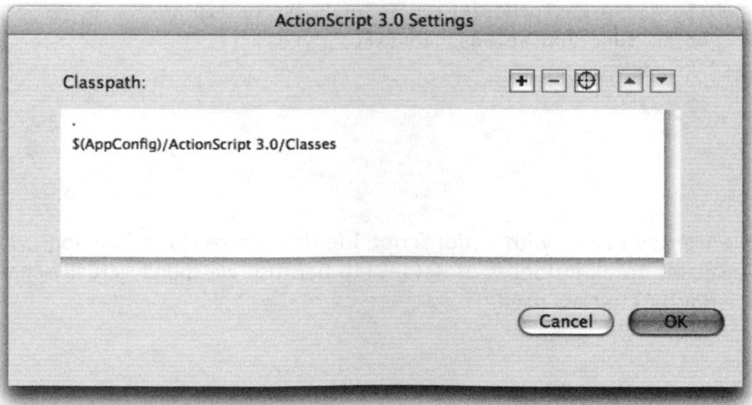

Figure 3-1. ActionScript 3.0 settings

ActionScript 3.0: Ball.as

```
package sports {
  public class Ball {
    function Ball(color,size,weight) {
      trace("Ball created");
      color = color;
      size = size;
      weight = weight;
    }
  }
}
```

The preceding code should be saved as a file called Ball.as and in a subfolder called sports. (Note that both the class filename and package name are case sensitive!) In that same folder where you created the subfolder, you save a new FLA that contains the following lines of code on Frame 1 of the main timeline:

```
import sports.Ball;

var basketBall:Ball = new Ball("orange","light","round");
var bowlingBall:Ball = new Ball("blue","heavy","round");
var rugbyBall:Ball = new Ball("brown","light","oval");
```

By using the import keyword, you can simply instantiate the class by using its class name and not giving its full path. If you test the project, you'll see Ball created listed three times in the Output panel.

Just like I showed you with ActionScript 1.0, ActionScript 3.0 also allows you to add your own custom functionality to a class. Instead of using prototype as you'd do in ActionScript 1.0, you now use the extends keyword in an external class file named CustomMovieClip.as.

```
package {
  import flash.display.MovieClip;
  public class CustomMovieClip extends MovieClip {
    public function setPosition(xPos, yPos) {
      x = xPos;
      y = yPos;
    }
  }
}
```

Now, unlike we saw before with ActionScript 1.0, the setPosition function is not automatically available to all instances of MovieClip because we didn't actually change anything to the MovieClip class itself.

What we did was create our own subclass that inherits all functionality from the `MovieClip` class and adds its own. To have this all work, we need to associate a movie clip with our new ActionScript 3.0 class. The way you handle that in Flash is quite easy. In the Library panel of the Flash IDE, you choose the movie clip object you'd like to associate this class with. You then right-click that particular movie clip and choose Linkage, which pops up a dialog box (see Figure 3-2).

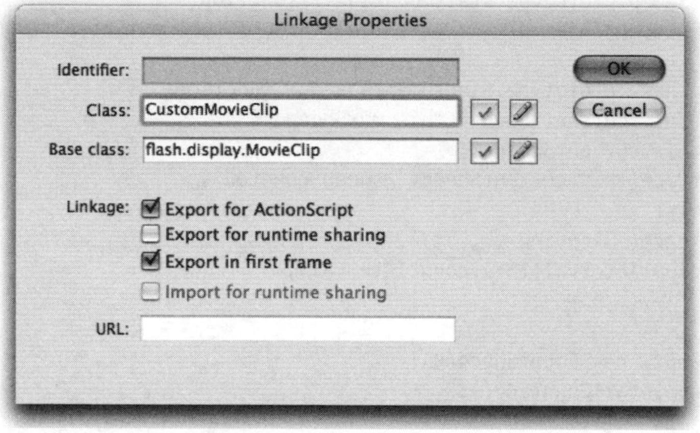

Figure 3-2. Linkage Properties dialog box

In this dialog box, you check the Export for ActionScript check box and enter CustomMovieClip in the Class text field. Flash CS3 is intelligent enough to create a class for you if it can't find the one you're referring to in the classpath; as you can see from Figure 3-2, you can even specify the class it should extend (leave it to `flash.display.MovieClip` here). Now, it doesn't save it on your hard drive, but it is in fact compiled into the SWF when you export. This way of auto-generating classes can be really helpful to allow you to use a Library asset for scripting without needing to necessarily create a class file for it.

When you click OK to close the dialog box, you've just associated that `MovieClip` object with the custom class. You can now start using the `setPosition` function with all instances of that object. Drag two instances of the `MovieClip` on stage and name them `mc1` and `mc2`. Just like with the ActionScript 1.0 example, you can now use the following code:

```
mc1.setPosition(10,50);
mc2.setPosition(50,70);
```

Public and private scope

In ActionScript 1.0, you had no real means of enforcing private scope, that is to say, all functions of a class could be called outside the scope of that class. What would usually happen was that developers used either the $ or _ sign to prefix a private class function so as to indicate that it was not supposed to be used as a publicly available function.

ActionScript 1.0

```
function CountSheep(maxSheep) {
  this.currentSheep = 0;
  this.maxSheep = maxSheep;
}
CountSheep.prototype.startCounting = function() {
  this.countInterval = setInterval(this,"$incrementSheep",1000);
}
CountSheep.prototype.$incrementSheep = function() {
  if(this.currentSheep < this.maxSheep) {
    this.currentSheep++;
    trace(this.currentSheep+" sheep counted");
  } else {
    trace("Sleeping ...");
    clearInterval(this.countInterval);
  }
}
mySleep = new CountSheep(5);
mySleep.startCounting();
```

In the preceding example, you can see a simple ActionScript 1.0 prototype class that helps you count sheep to fall asleep. The constructor takes one parameter, which is the amount of sheep you want to count. I personally am an easy sleeper, so I've just specified to count five sheep.

If you look at the way the code is structured, you'll notice that there really is only one function that you'll want to have called outside the scope of this class and that is `startCounting()`. The `incrementSheep()` function is only useful inside the class and would be a good candidate to give a private scope. Having the function called outside the class scope might in fact even break our code (take a look at Chapter 8, which covers the concept of encapsulation, if you want to read more about the theory behind this in object-oriented programming). You can see I prefixed the code with a $ sign to indicate that it shouldn't be considered a public function. As I explained before, no enforcement occurs there whatsoever. In ActionScript 1.0, you can only indicate private scope by naming convention.

ActionScript 3.0: CountSheep.as

```
package {
  import flash.utils.*;
  public class CountSheep {
   var currentSheep:uint;
   var maxSheep:uint;
   var countInterval:uint;
   function CountSheep(maxSheep:uint) {
```

```
      this.currentSheep = 0;
      this.maxSheep = maxSheep;
    }
    public function startCounting():void {
      countInterval = setInterval(incrementSheep,1000);
    }
    private function incrementSheep():void {
     if(this.currentSheep < this.maxSheep) {
        this.currentSheep++;
        trace(this.currentSheep+" sheep counted");
      } else {
        trace("Sleeping ...");
        clearInterval(this.countInterval);
      }
    }
  }
}
```


As you can see, this is largely the same as any other ActionScript 3.0 class, with the only difference being that we've got a public and private keyword in front of the class functions. One important note is that you would typically use the new `flash.utils.Timer` class in ActionScript 3.0 instead of `setInterval`—but for this example, we'll keep it simple. It's pretty obvious what those public and private keywords will do for you, so you'd expect the following code to work in an FLA that you've saved in the same location as this class:

```
var mySleep = new CountSheep(5);
mySleep.startCounting();
```

Hoorah, it works! But wait a minute—let's see if our private function really is private:

```
var mySleep = new CountSheep(5);
mySleep.incrementSheep();
```

As expected, the compiler now throws an error when you try to compile: it can't find the `incrementSheep` method we are trying to reference.

```
ReferenceError: Error #1069: Property incrementSheep not found on ➥
CountSheep and there is no default value.
at CountSheep_fla::MainTimeline/CountSheep_fla::frame1()
```

Isn't this cool—having the possibility to prevent methods from being accessed outside of the class scope allows for more control over how your class gets used.

ActionScript 3.0 now also gives us the opportunity to set a protected scope for methods and properties. The difference between protected and private scope is that the first still allows access to the methods from subclasses, but you'll see that in context later on in the book when I cover OOP concepts such as inheritance, encapsulation, and polymorphism in Part 3.

This about wraps up my comparison between ActionScript versions 1.0, 2.0, and 3.0. Important to note is that all examples in this section until now have not used any form of strong typing. I'll soon set that right and discuss strong typing and its benefits in ActionScript 3.0 next.

Strong typing and code hints

Strong typing is a very useful feature and not that difficult to implement. I discussed declaring variables in ActionScript 3.0 earlier in this chapter; the only difference when it comes to strong typing is you add a colon and then type the class you want it to be an instance of.

Flash CS3 and Flex Builder 2 automatically pop up a list of all available built-in classes as soon as you type a colon when declaring a variable (see Figure 3-3).

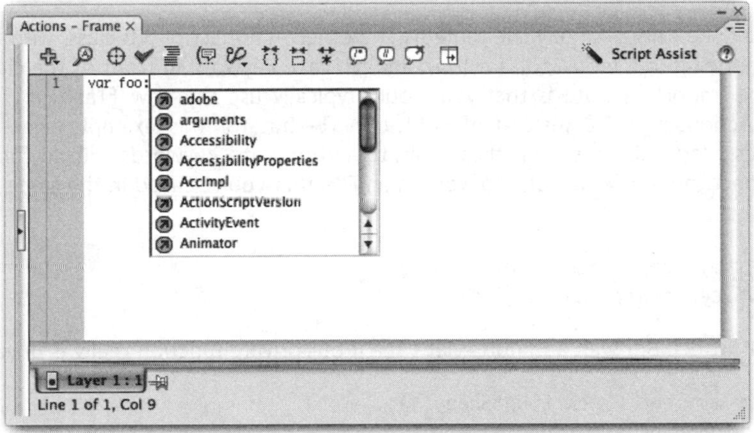

Figure 3-3. Class code hints

In this example, we'll declare our variable as a `String` type and give it the value `"Object-Oriented ActionScript 3.0"`.

```
var foo:String = "Object-Oriented ActionScript 3.0";
```

Now anytime we use this particular variable, we automatically get context-sensitive code hints listing all available functions for variables of that type. In this example, we get all functions available for the `String` datatype (see Figure 3-4).

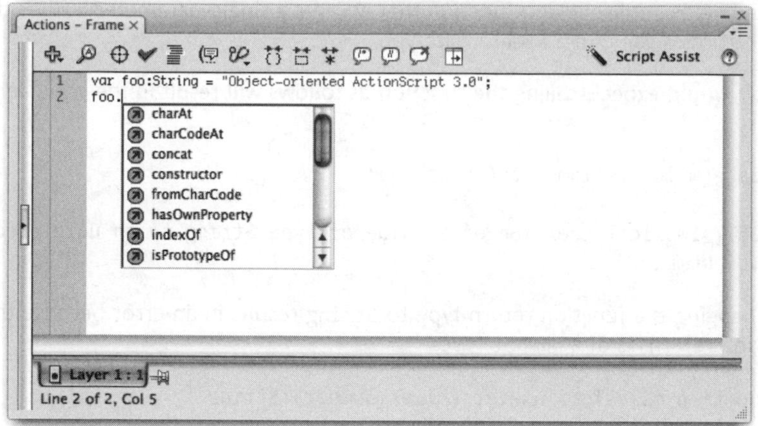

Figure 3-4. Context-sensitive code hints

Code hints are all well and good, but the most important advantage of using strong typing is that it allows for easy debugging.

If you declare a variable of type String and try to assign another datatype to it, the compiler will send out an error warning you of a type mismatch:

```
var foo:String = "Object-Oriented Flash CS3";
foo = true;
```

```
1067: Implicit coercion of a value of type Boolean to an ➥
unrelated type String.
```

You can see that strong typing in ActionScript gives you useful detailed and descriptive error messages. In this case, the Compile Errors panel states that we have a type mismatch and are trying to coerce a Boolean value into a variable where a String is defined as its datatype.

Apart from using strong typing to enforce datatypes on variables, it also allows us to assign types to both function parameters and function return values.

```
function milesToKilometers(miles:Number):Number {
  var ratio:Number = 1.609344;
  return miles*ratio;
}

trace(milesToKilometers(200)); // outputs 321.8688
```

The preceding example shows a function that accepts a single-parameter Number datatype and also returns a value of a Number datatype.

Just as you would expect, calling the function as follows will result in the compiler throwing an error:

```
trace(milesToKilometers("Flash"));

1067: Implicit coercion of a value of type String to an unrelated ➥
type Number.
```

Equally changing the function return type to String results in an error because the value the function returns is of a Number type:

```
function milesToKilometers(miles:Number):String {
  var ratio:Number = 1.609344;
  return miles*ratio;
}
trace(milesToKilometers(200));'


1067: Implicit coercion of a value of type Number to an unrelated ➥
type String.
```

As you can see, strong typing and code hints are very useful features you'll have available when doing application development with ActionScript 3.0. In the end it is well worth the effort of applying it to your variables, function parameters, and return types. This small additional effort will help you out when it comes to debugging the application in the long run.

ActionScript gotchas

ActionScript 3.0 does have a few things you will want to watch out for. In this section, I'll discuss some interesting tidbits you'll want to pay attention to when writing ActionScript 3.0 code.

Case sensitivity

Unlike way back in ActionScript 1.0, ActionScript 3.0 is case sensitive as the following example shows:

```
var myVariable:String = "Object-Oriented ActionScript 3.0";
trace(myvariable); // outputs undefined
trace(myVariable); // outputs Object-Oriented ActionScript 3.0
```

Declaring variables

When you initially declare a variable, you use the var keyword. You used to need to watch out in ActionScript 2.0 that you didn't use that keyword later on in the application when referring to the variable. Doing that would overwrite any datatype that you applied to it using strong typing.

```
var myVariable:String = " Object-Oriented ActionScript 3.0";
var myVariable = true;
```

Now, if you use a var keyword on that second line that assigns a Boolean true value to the variable, you get the compiler complaining about a namespace conflict error.


```
1151: A conflict exists with definition myVariable ➥
in namespace internal.
```

Use of the this keyword

When building classes in ActionScript 2.0 or 3.0, there is theoretically no need to use the this keyword to refer to variables of the class scope (though it can make your code more readable, and in specific situations prevent code from breaking).

```
package {
 public class MyClass {
   var myString:String;
   public function MyClass(param:String):void {
     myString = param;
     outputString();
   }
   public function outputString():void {
     trace(myString);
   }
 }
}
```

As you can see in the preceding example, there is a variable named myString that is of a class scope, and we can refer to it without use of the this keyword. The same thing can be seen when the outputString function is called.

Although you can safely remove the this keyword, I would advise you to keep using it, for example, to make the distinction between variables of a class scope (myString) and a local scope (param). The same code with the this keyword looks like this:

```
package {
  public class MyClass {
    var myString:String;
    public function MyClass(param:String):void {
      this.myString = param;
      this.outputString();
```

```
        }
        public function outputString():void {
          trace(this.myString);
        }
      }
    }
```

What's next?

I covered quite a bit of information in this chapter, and you'll have learned the differences you see from ActionScript 1.0 through 3.0 and the benefits of using strong typing. If you want to learn more about specific changes between ActionScript 2.0 and ActionScript 3.0, Adobe has an interesting article that gives an excellent overview of this: `http://livedocs.adobe.com/flex/2/langref/migration.html`.

For a more thorough introduction to ActionScript 3.0, *Foundation ActionScript 3.0 with Flash CS3 and Flex 2* by Steve Webster and Sean McSharry (friends of ED, 2007) covers this in detail.

This chapter closes Part 1 of this book. We now move on to discuss OOP guidelines, best practices, and planning. Even if you are already familiar with programming concepts, I'd highly recommend that you read the following chapters to start off on the right foot before we get to the in-depth OOP concepts and put theory into practice.

PART TWO **FLASH OOP GUIDELINES**

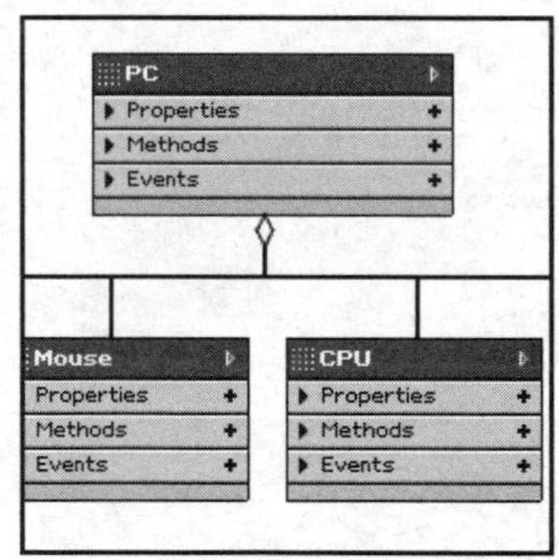

Ah, the magic word "planning," where would we all be without it? Most likely out of a job, that's for sure!

When you think of it, planning is nothing more than an object-oriented way of scheduling a project. You divide the project up into tasks, look at the task dependencies, and try to get those pieces to fit together within a predefined deadline.

Your initial impulse might be to skip this chapter and go right for the information on in-depth OOP, but I'd like to convince you to do otherwise. In this chapter, I'll discuss the importance of planning as an integral part of object-oriented projects and run you through the process of analyzing and modeling your application.

The importance of planning

If you've ever been in a situation where your entire project lacks any form of planning, you're working in a team with both remote and local developers, and the client keeps calling you every 10 minutes with an ever increasingly loud voice warning you that the deadline is coming ever closer—you'll soon know what you're missing.

Of course, not all projects are like the one just described, and there are numerous situations in which you could think the planning stage is obsolete. Let's look at some of these possible scenarios and see why it is not:

We don't have time for planning (deadline is next month).

The time you'll spend planning a project will greatly decrease development time and time needed for debugging. In that sense, you'll notice that the planning stage will help you better manage projects with a tight deadline.

We don't have a budget for planning (we need to begin today).

Planning will enable you to save money on development costs. At the end of the day, what's the cost of a few pieces of paper compared to possibly rebuilding your application from scratch because nobody thought of taking that one critical parameter into consideration?

We don't need planning (this is just a quick little project).

Planning is useful for any type of application. What if a few months down the line the client figures out that the application doesn't quite fit in with their existing data infrastructure? Wouldn't you be frustrated to rebuild from scratch what a few simple notes could have avoided?

The preceding situations are some of the most common reasons why people tend to think that planning is not necessary. These examples show that even in these circumstances planning is a very important part of the development process.

As I briefly discussed in the introduction to this chapter, you can look at planning as an object-oriented process. The different sections of your planning can be handled just like objects in OOP, and each have their own particular role to play in the bigger whole. The tasks of the project can be considered as self-contained objects, project dependencies are comparable to interaction between classes, etc.—in that sense, planning should not be handled much differently than writing actual code. This object-oriented nature of planning makes it very suitable to be written down in a structural model, which is what we'll do later on in this chapter. Next, I'll discuss the various steps involved with the process of planning and walk you through various examples.

Initial phase: Planning reusability!

Long-term reusability for your applications doesn't just happen by accident; it needs to be carefully planned. A first step in this planning process is getting the various tasks of your application down on paper.

Doing initial planning on paper is usually best because it allows you to *focus* on the issues at hand without getting distracted by details like what font and color scheme to use, which line style to use, etc. It's often a good thing to turn off your computer at this stage to help you stay focused on the bigger scheme of things rather than get involved with exactly how you want the presentation and layout to look.

The first question you'll need to ask yourself is *what* the application needs to do, not *how* it does it. We'll look at the ways in which the necessary tasks will be achieved at a later stage, but to start with you need to be clear on what exactly it is you need.

Suppose you need to build a car. In itself that is a rather generic term; you could come up with various solutions that cover the load. You could build something resembling a car with a whole bunch of clay. You could build a car from a kit. If you have way too much money, you could commission BMW to build a prototype car for you. As you can see, just knowing a car is what you want to build isn't really enough information to know enough about *what* you need.

In the initial phases of planning, you repeatedly ask *what* until it is extremely clear what the final product should be (but you can still leave most of the difficult, technical how-to questions for later).

Planning encapsulation

After reading through Chapter 1, you know that encapsulation is a key feature in OOP and serves to *hide the internal workings of a class*. I'll run you through planning encapsulation for your project with the following example:

Let's say we're faced with a ball and want to have it bounce. If we abstract this in object-oriented terms, we come up with a Ball class and a Bounce or, in more general terms, Mover class.

If you're not that familiar with OO concepts, you might not have considered creating that Mover class, instead adding the functionality directly to the Ball class. Think about it, what would be the benefit of making it a separate class? The answer is quite simple: you want to avoid duplicate code and increase reusability.

The Ball class is a special case in our example; it is in fact an instance of the Sprite class. No need to worry about this just now, it'll be explained in more detail in Chapters 8 through 11.

Now, how does this work in Flash? If you've worked with ActionScript before, you know that there are quite a few events that the built-in objects broadcast. One commonly used event is `EnterFrame`, which runs once every frame. Let's say we've got a frame rate of 30 frames per second that would have the `EnterFrame` event, and thus the event handler we attached to that event, broadcast 30 times every second. You can see that using this event you can quite easily simulate movement using ActionScript.

An event handler is a function that you apply to an event; how exactly that event handler code looks is not important in this example—we'll just focus on how it is set up.

Figure 4-1 shows the class diagram for Mover.

Mover	
Properties	
Methods	
startMoving	Void
updatePosition	Void
Events	

Figure 4-1.
Mover class diagram

The Ball class calls the `startMoving` method in the Mover class. This `startMoving` method then sets the `EnterFrame` event that calls the `updatePosition` method. The internal details of the Mover class and the `updatePosition` method aren't important from the event handler's point of view (think encapsulation).

That completes the circle any time the `EnterFrame` event is broadcast and the `updatePosition` method is executed, which results in the simulated motion we wanted.

Planning inheritance

Let's expand on that encapsulation plan; without knowing exactly how the Mover class works, we want to add additional functionality. To achieve just that, we'll be using inheritance.

Inheritance allows you to extend or enhance classes that already exist, without altering existing behavior. Inheritance allows new classes to *inherit* the services of some other existing class. When you use the new class, you get the features of the existing class too (as if they were both merged into a single bigger class).

Inheritance is more than simply an organized way to add new features—it also prevents you from breaking applications that already use existing classes (because you're not modifying the existing classes one single bit).

Let's build on our example. This time I'm adding another new class named Bouncer. The Bouncer class will inherit from the Mover class, and will consequently be able to do everything the Mover class can do, but add its own additional functionality. In particular, I want the class to bounce the ball whenever it hits a border.

Just like before, we're not concerned with the details of how the ball will bounce or how the borders are determined. Right now, I only need to invent the proper method names to cover the behavior I want to provide.

Figure 4-2 shows the class diagram for Bouncer.

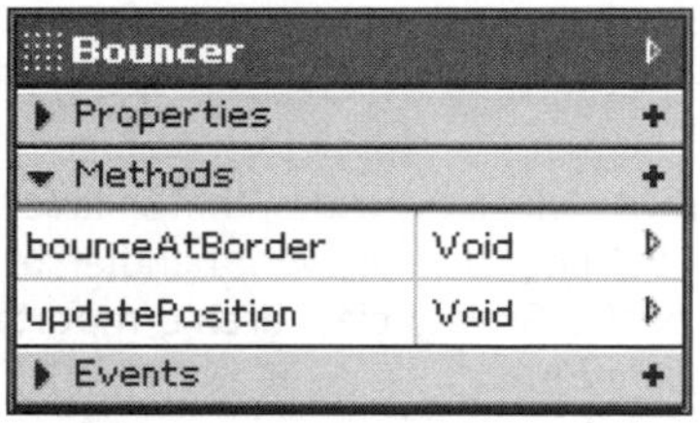

Bouncer	
Properties	
Methods	
bounceAtBorder	Void
updatePosition	Void
Events	

Figure 4-2.
Bouncer class diagram

1. The `updatePosition` method in the Bouncer class overrides the original `updatePosition` method in the Mover class. The internal details of the Bouncer class aren't important from the event handler's point of view (encapsulation).
2. The Mover class doesn't know it, but the Bouncer class has an additional behavior (the `bounceAtBorder` method), which gets referenced in the Bouncer class `updatePosition` method. The Bouncer class thus uses this behavior without revealing it to the Mover class.
3. The Ball class doesn't know it, but the Bouncer class has inherited the Mover class. Indeed, the Ball class has no idea that the Mover class even exists. The Bouncer class initiated the request to inherit; it doesn't need permission from the Ball class to do so. The Ball class has no idea that any of this is happening, and that's just the way it should be. The Bouncer class can do anything the Mover class can do, plus it contains a `bounceAtBorder` method.

This completes another code sequence that *somehow* (we haven't looked at a single line of code yet) moves the ball instance and bounces it back any time it hits a border.

While we're at it, let's go one step further and add a class that simulates friction and gravity to give our ball some more natural movement. I'll name this class Gravity and have it inherit from the Bouncer class so it can use all functionality that is already defined in there.

Remember, the Bouncer class itself inherits from the Mover class so we've really got a great inheritance chain going on here. One thing to note is that a class can inherit methods from many classes down but can only interact directly with its parent class (for the Gravity class that is the Bouncer class).

We're still not bothered about the workings of our new Gravity class but simply add two methods called applyFriction and applyGravity. Let's look at the setup of this new class. Figure 4-3 shows the class diagram for Gravity.

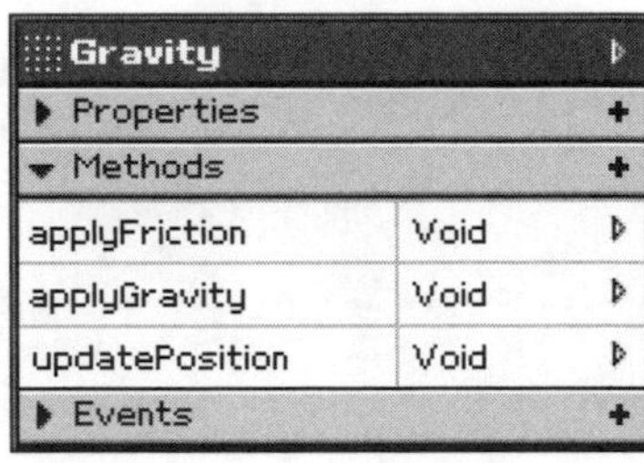

Figure 4-3.
Gravity class diagram

1. The updatePosition method in the Gravity class overrides the updatePosition method in the Bouncer class and acts as the EnterFrame event handler, as defined in the Mover class. The internal details of the Gravity class aren't important from the event handler's point of view (encapsulation).
2. The Ball class doesn't know it, but the Gravity class has inherited from the Bouncer class. The Gravity class can do anything that the Bouncer class can do, plus it provides its own unique methods named applyFriction and applyGravity.
3. The Bouncer class inherits from the Mover class. This implies that the Gravity class has also inherited (albeit indirectly) the functionality of the Mover class (without it even knowing that the Mover class exists).

This wraps up another sequence that is still just triggered by the Ball class calling the startMoving method. The entire series of events that we added from the Mover class, through the Bouncer class, down to the Gravity class is executed every time the EnterFrame event triggers the updatePosition method and any additional methods the class provides.

I've covered a lot of information in this example that will have helped you get an idea of how to model your project with encapsulation and inheritance in place.

If you've lost your way in the class setup, take a look at Figure 4-4.

Next, I'll walk you through the specifics of applying the planning techniques we just discussed on an ActionScript 3.0 project.

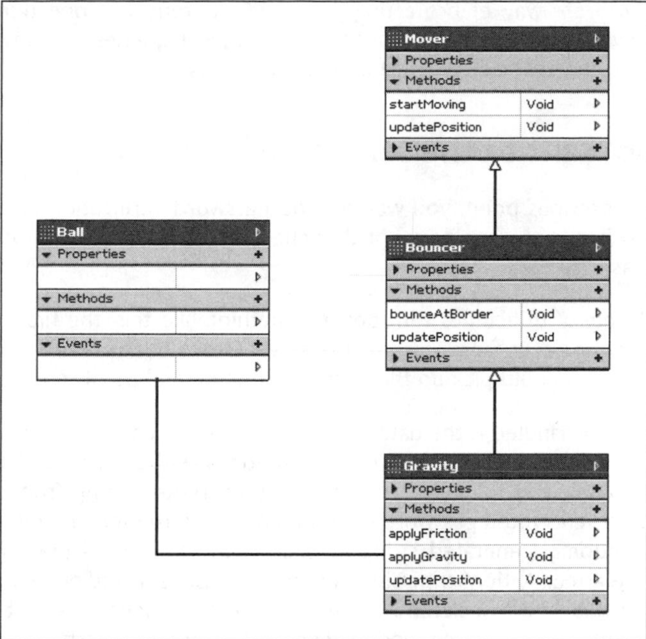

Figure 4-4. Mover class inheritance diagram

Analyzing a Flash ActionScript project

For a long time, serious developers have shied away from using Flash and ActionScript, not because they weren't impressed by its functionality, but mostly because of its *unconventional timeline metaphor* and cluttered coding practices. Up until quite recently, Flash was mainly classified as a tool for the creative and the odd few experimental developers. Luckily, this is all changing rapidly; technologies like Flex 2 provide a framework that allows the creation of Rich Internet Applications (RIA), and more and more developers are venturing into this field.

When analyzing projects that are to be built in ActionScript, it is important to take certain things into consideration. I'll discuss some of these trouble spots here and offer you some ideas on how to approach those when planning your application.

Flash files run on the client

When you deploy your Flash file on the Web, the SWF file is not run on the server but is cached and displayed in the browser using the Flash player plug-in. This brings up certain risks with what you include in your project file. There are several SWF decompilers available on the Web these days, and it is very easy for anyone to decompile your file and extract sensitive information (password information, high score submission URL, etc.).

There is no foolproof way of protecting your SWF content, but one thing you should always do is move all your database connection details, SQL queries, and anything else that you don't want to be public knowledge on the server.

Securing data sent to the server

Building on the previous point, you wouldn't do password verification on the client side but rather send it to a server-side script that checks this for you and returns whether or not the user was validated.

There are a couple of difficulties with doing something like this, the first one being that the login information sent from Flash to the server is not encrypted in any way. Anyone using a packet sniffer could pick up the login information and use it to get access illegally.

How this is typically handled is the data entered into Flash is concatenated to the user's IP and encrypted using an ActionScript implementation of either MD5 or SHA1, which are algorithms that allow you to create an irreversibly encrypted string from whatever data you pass to it. This encrypted password data is then sent to the server along with the username and a randomly generated string in plain text. The server-side script now does exactly the same as our ActionScript did. It detects the user's IP and encrypts that with the password in the database associated with the login that was sent. Finally, it returns a true or false value along with the same randomly generated string to Flash.

You can see that this is a useful way to secure login information but doesn't really help you out with data you can't compare on the server. Other types of data transfer are harder to secure with Flash; in most cases the best bet there is to use a Secure Socket Layer (SSL) connection.

Parsing data in Flash

Despite some incredible increases in Flash Player performance with parsing XML and text data in recent years, specifically since Flash Player 9, it isn't equipped to handle large data loads very well. The key is to organize your data transfers as efficiently as possible; you want to avoid long waits when the application initializes and don't want to trigger too many calls to the server to make the user experience as fluent as possible.

Let's take a train schedule for example. If you were to write an application that allows users to look up train schedule information, you obviously wouldn't load all the departure times, trains, and platform number information in at the same time. Yet at the same time just loading information for one particular train might not be the best thing to do. You could predict that a user might want to know about the previous and next train, and returning this information from your call to the server makes the whole experience much more enjoyable. Balancing out data load with task workflow is what you'll have to bear in mind.

For applications like the one discussed previously, you might want to consider using Flash Remoting technology, which uses binary AMF files to communicate directly with Flash from the server. Using this technology allows your server-side data to keep its datatype intact when loaded into Flash so that it doesn't require any further parsing (see Chapter 18 for more information).

As you'll have noticed, most concerns you'll have to deal with when planning a Flash project are related to data security and performance issues. Now, how does this affect the planning process?

From my own experience, I've seen that back-end development and Flash applications are often designed and modeled as totally different processes. The consequence there is that it brings all the stress of your application to the middle scripting layer, which is forced to do extensive data manipulation to get it molded into shape for use with the Flash application. It's not easy to have a square peg fit into a round hole.

Ideally the scripting layer should simply act as a *gateway* for presenting the back-end data to the Flash client. To achieve this, it is important to look at the data flow between the server and the client and model in a way that allows for easy integration.

Introduction to UML modeling

The Unified Modeling Language (UML) is an incredibly useful for tool for modeling applications. The language was first introduced in 1997 as a way to visually represent object-oriented projects and has become the de facto means to visually represent object-oriented structures and processes.

When building a model of your application, you typically have multiple views that are mapped in diagrams. UML supports nine different diagrams that can be applied to create different views: class, object, use case, sequence, collaboration, statechart, activity, component, and deployment diagrams. Following is a short overview with a description of the different diagrams:

Diagram	Description
Class	Describes the static class structure of an application
Object	Describes the static structure of class instances at a certain point in time
Use case	Describes application functionality using actors and use cases
Sequence	Describes data interaction between individual classes
Collaboration	Describes class interaction in the application as a whole
Statechart	Describes class behavior in response to external data
Activity	Describes the flow between different tasks of the application
Component	Describes dependencies between components of the application
Deployment	Describes physical resources used for deploying the application

In the scope of this book, I'm not able to provide you a full and in-depth reference for UML modeling, but I will introduce you to the concepts that will help you get started modeling ActionScript 3.0 projects.

I'll first run you through the reasons for choosing UML and then move on to discussing building a class diagram, which is without doubt the most essential diagram to have from a code-centric point of view.

Why use UML?

Why would you use UML to model your application? There are several reasons why UML is the way to go, and I'll discuss a couple of those right now.

UML offers standardized notation and has a language-neutral syntax

Standards are very important when modeling an application; you want to have something that everyone can understand. If you model an application using UML and a different developer is assigned to its development, that developer should easily be able to take over the project.

UML can be used to model anything

You can model anything from a business process down to a software class structure. The various diagrams that are supported by UML allow you to visually represent just about anything you might need.

Aside from the advantages discussed previously, you'll soon notice that using UML helps you out tremendously in the planning process. Being able to visualize concepts and application structure helps you to easily point out any possible weaknesses or imperfections unlike any other method you might have used before. I personally find that using UML in the planning process improves the overall development workflow and decreases the amount of time you'll need to spend on debugging and tweaking the application.

Class diagram

The UML class diagram is without doubt the most important diagram you'll be using when planning your Flash ActionScript project. Class diagrams describe the static structure of your application, the classes with their attributes and methods and relationships between them.

Let's look at some basic notation you'll need when creating a class diagram. The first thing you'll notice is that classes are shown as a rectangle that contains its name. Note that the Ball class I'll use as an example in Figure 4-5 is not related to the Ball class discussed earlier in this chapter when looking at planning your project.

Figure 4-5. UML class notation

All classes in your project will be shown in such a rectangle; this is the minimal state in which they need to appear in the class diagram. More often though, you'll want to have the properties and methods of that class showing as well. To do this, the UML notation extends the class rectangle symbol with two other areas: the topmost is used for properties and the bottom one for methods (see Figure 4-6).

Ball	
Properties	
+color	Color
+shape	String
+weight	Number
-bounceCount	Number
Methods	
+bounce	Void
+getBounceCount	Number
-incrementBounceCount	Boolean
Events	

Figure 4-6. UML class attributes and methods

You might have noticed that the properties and methods in the Ball class have plus or minus signs before their names. Those signs indicate whether the property or method is of a public (+) or private (-) scope. The hash sign (#) is used to specify a property or method as being assigned a protected scope. Property and method scopes aren't always provided when drawing a UML class diagram, but I find it very useful to do so as it helps with visualizing class interaction.

In the preceding example, we see three public properties: `shape`, `weight`, and `color`, which means those values are available outside the class. There also is a `bounceCount` property that is set to private; it cannot be accessed outside the class, but if you look closely there is a public `getBounceCount` method that returns this value. I'll discuss getter and setter methods in greater detail in later chapters, but it's important to note how this helps you achieve encapsulation and prevent properties from being altered outside the class, which could cause problems with the internal workings. Also notice that the properties and methods are followed by a datatype written after their names; this shows you the particular datatype of the property, or in the case of methods the datatype of the value it returns.

When you've drawn all classes for your project, you're all set to define their relationships to each other. I'll discuss the most important relationships you'll need when working on an ActionScript 3.0 project next.

Association and generalization

Association is the simplest link you can have between two classes; it describes two classes working together on a conceptual level (see Figure 4-7).

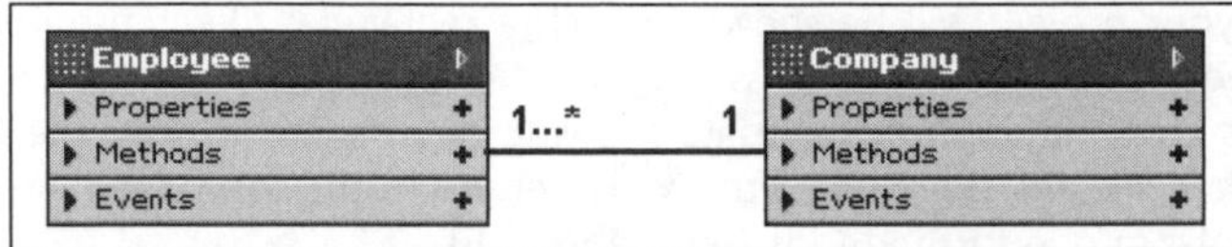

Figure 4-7. UML association relationship

This example shows an association between an Employee class and a Company class. You can clearly see that those two classes are separate entities, and yet there is a link between the two concepts.

In UML notation, we show this by connecting the classes with a line; you can optionally write a description of the relationship above the line, in this example "works in." There are situations in which associations will deal with a concept called *multiplicity*. Multiplicity determines the type of association the classes are dealing with. Some types of multiplicity are one to one, one to many, one to one or more, etc.

In the example of our Employee and Company classes, the Company has a one-to-one-or-more association. A company can have one or more employees; that sounds about right.

Generalization is nothing more than a UML term for what we've been calling class inheritance. Using generalization in a class diagram shows what classes inherit from other classes. Let's look at the example shown in Figure 4-8.

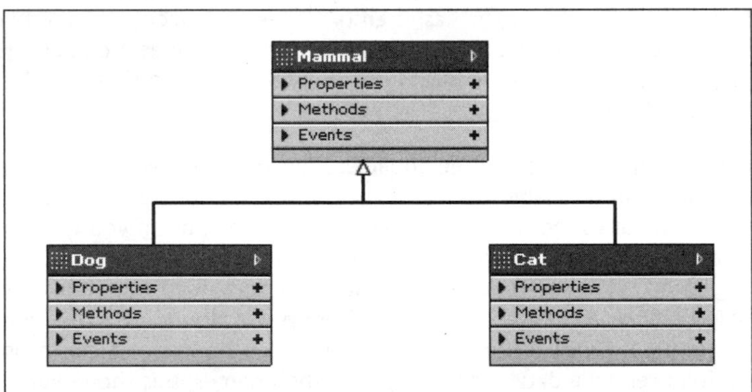

Figure 4-8. UML generalization relationship

As you can see, we've got a Dog and Cat class that both inherit from a Mammal superclass. A *superclass* or *base class* is the class that you use to base your new class on. You'll learn more about this in Chapter 10. The notation is not that much different from a class association apart from the fact that the line that connects the classes has an open-ended arrow facing the class from which it inherits. Both the Dog and Cat class will inherit everything that was defined in the Mammal class.

If you look at a UML class diagram and trace the class back in the direction the empty arrows are pointing, you automatically arrive at one or more base classes for the application from which it all started.

Aggregation and composition

There will quite often be situations in which you need to model a class that consists of multiple components. The way UML handles this is by relationships called *aggregation* and *composition*.

Let's take a PC for example. As shown in Figure 4-9, the way you would visualize this is by creating class elements for each of the components and a class that represents the whole. The components are connected to the whole with a solid line, and an empty diamond shape is added at the end to represent an aggregation-type relationship.

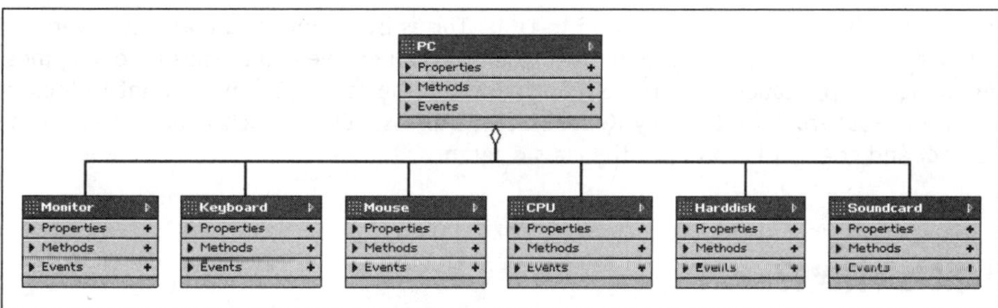

Figure 4-9. UML aggregation relationship

The model shown in Figure 4-9 is a limited representation of a PC that consists of components like a monitor, keyboard, mouse, etc. Now, what exactly is the difference between aggregation and composition? It's not always an easy distinction to make, but a good rule of thumb is the following:

> *In aggregation the whole cannot exist without its components, while in a composition the components cannot exist without the whole.*

A good example of composition is a human being. If the human dies, its parts die with it. If we look at our PC aggregation example, while the PC might not continue working, the monitor, keyboard, and mouse components will all remain functional as stand-alone parts and can be used in another PC.

UML notation for composition is very similar to that of aggregation except for the fact that it uses a filled diamond shape at the connection between the component and the whole, as you can see in Figure 4-10.

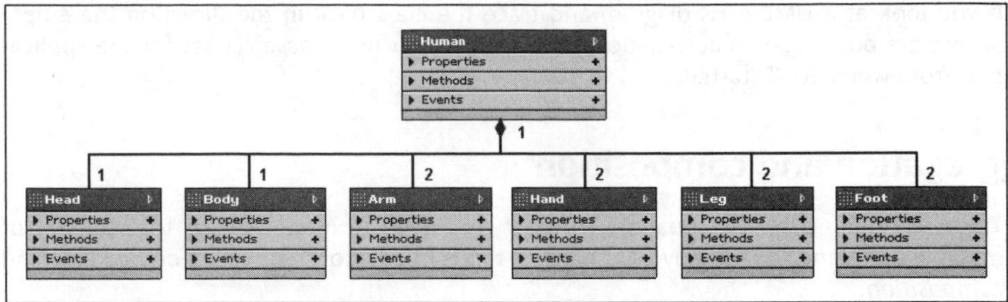

Figure 4-10. UML composition relationship

The difference between aggregation and composition is mostly conceptual for ActionScript 3.0 projects; it just shows you whether or not the components need to be destroyed when the whole is destroyed.

This concludes my short introduction to UML. This is by no means a complete overview, but it should have taught you some basic skills that will enable you to start modeling most ActionScript applications. For more information on the topic, you might want to look at the book *Fast Track UML 2.0* by Kendall Scott (Apress, 2004), which is dedicated to the subject and goes far beyond just the class diagram.

What's next?

Be sure not to underestimate the importance of this chapter; I've covered some essential information here that will help you work more efficiently and productively. The introduction to UML is a must-read if you're interested in pursuing application development in ActionScript 3.0.

Coming up in the next chapter, I'll discuss project workflow, versioning control, and usability testing, which are all very important topics to read up on before embarking on actual application development.

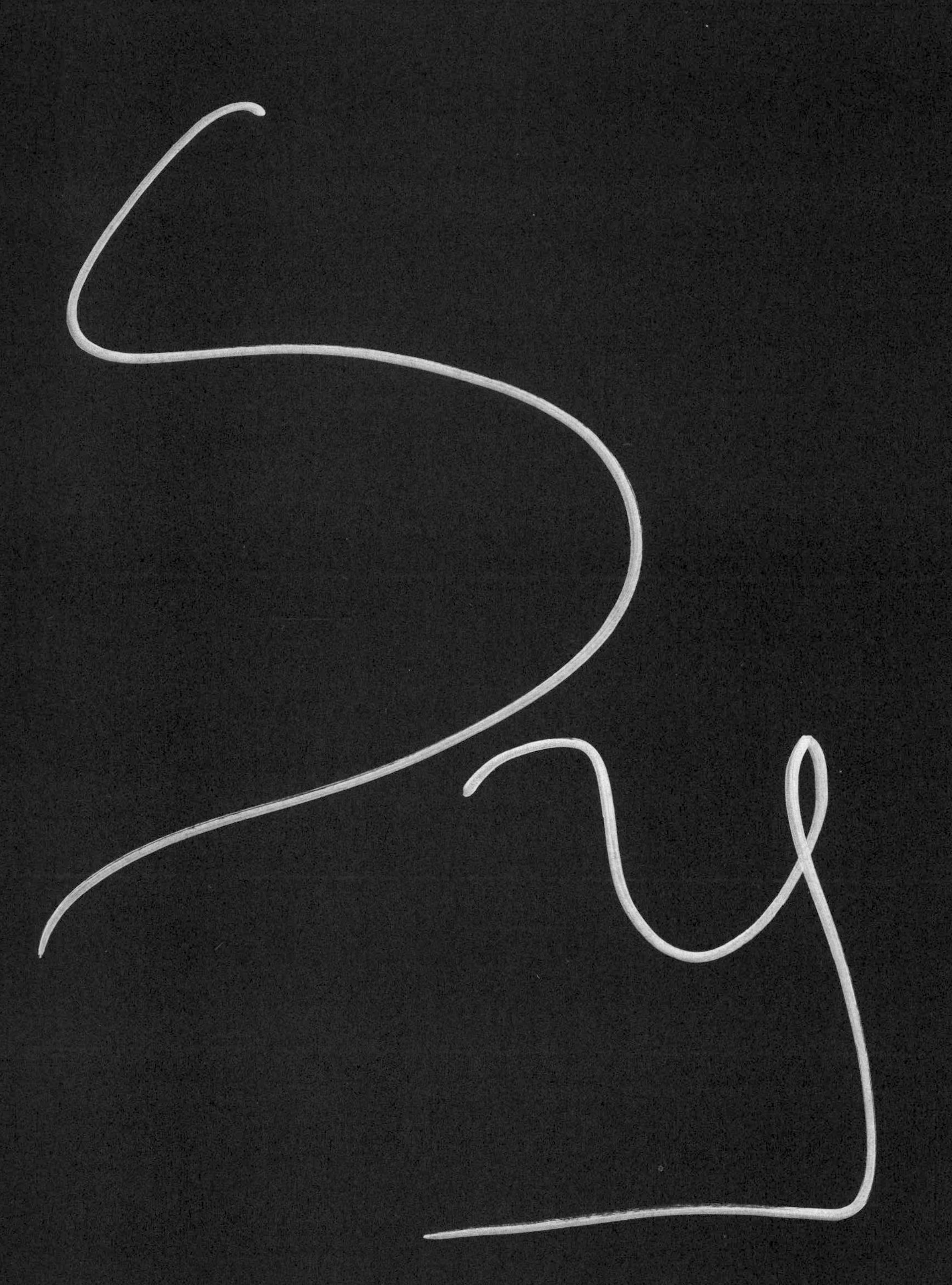

5 PROJECT WORKFLOW

We've certainly covered quite a number of topics by now; you've learned about programming concepts, using ActionScript 3.0, and how to plan and model your applications. Now it's time to look at how you can take all those things and integrate them in your project workflow.

Project workflow describes the process by which you most efficiently handle applications from start to finish. In Chapter 6, I'll discuss best practices for coding in ActionScript 3.0, but first I want to introduce you to some topics that are essential to painlessly completing your projects. One of those topics is version control, which has no doubt saved many developers from chronic insanity. Be sure to read up on this, if you're not already using it!

After covering the basics of version control, I'll move on to discussing some important approaches to programming that will help you be more productive in the way you work.

Introducing version control

Version control is a system that allows you to keep track of multiple versions of source code. It provides you with a history of your development process and supports some advanced features that simple backup files just can't match.

You might think that it is all well and good to track the history of your code, but wouldn't that take an enormous amount of disk space storing all those copies of the project? No it won't; version control is smart enough to store only the actual changes that were made to files, not the entire files themselves. Which is, when you think about it, much more efficient than the way we usually back up our code.

Whether you're working in a team or as a single developer, it is imperative that you use a form of version control to prevent any loss of code or wasted hours of coding trying to revert to a version you might have created days earlier. Not using version control is probably the single biggest risk you can take when developing an application.

I'll be discussing the benefits of using a version control system as well as running you through the basics of setting up and managing a local *Concurrent Versions System* (CVS) repository for your project in the following few sections of this chapter.

Worth noting is that an alternative to Concurrent Versions System, called Subversion (SVN), has become a popular choice for version control in the Flash community. There are some clear advantages to this newer system such as the following:

- **SVN is faster**: Less information gets transmitted back and forth to the server.
- **Directories are under version control**: You can delete, rename, and move directories in SVN.
- **Commits are atomic**: A set of files can get committed as one transaction as opposed to file by file like in CVS. This ensures that, if something goes wrong while committing the set of files, they are all rolled back to the original version, and no code breaks.

Nonetheless, you'll find that at the moment, Concurrent Versions System, having been the uncontested favorite for years, is still more widely supported in any development environments you'll want to use. If you are interested in using Subversion for version control of your ActionScript 3.0 projects, there is a plug-in called Subclipse (available at `http://subclipse.tigris.org`) that works for Flex Builder.

About Concurrent Versions System

Concurrent Versions System is without doubt the most well-known open source implementation of version control. Using CVS, your source code gets maintained in a code *repository* where it generates a branched tree structure based on the different versions of a file you (or colleagues) submitted. The reason why CVS uses a tree structure is because that allows developers not just to work in a linear sequence, but also to build out different branches of code based on a particular revision of a file.

The application uses a client/server model that hosts your code repositories. It also uses a nonexclusive process whereby multiple developers can simultaneously work on the same file without breaking each others' code—isn't that just brilliant!

> *When I look back at my early web developer days, there were many occasions when some very last-minute changes needed to be made to a website before it could be pushed live. This resulted in the entire team (often project manager included) frantically typing code to get all the tweaks done on time. About half an hour before deadline, we usually managed to get it all finished up only to realize that some of us were working on the very same page and had overwritten each others' work, resulting in a lot of shouting, finger pointing, and even more frantic typing.*

Those days are luckily in the past. Using CVS, you can now have developers working on the same file by *checking out* that file from the code repository and *committing* changes back to repository when they've finished. If another developer made changes to the file and committed it to the repository before you did, you'll be asked to *update* your file, which automatically *merges* your changes with the latest copy from the repository. If by any chance multiple developers were working on the same line of code, CVS will not be able to merge the files, and you'll be prompted to manually correct that line before it gets merged.

Getting confused? You shouldn't be; let's recapitulate and look at some basic CVS terminology in the following table:

Term	Description
Repository	Directory in which all CVS files are stored.
Module	Files in the repository are grouped in modules.

Continued

Term	Description
Add	Add a local file to a module in the CVS repository.
Remove	Remove a file from a module in the CVS repository.
Check out	Get a local copy of a file from the CVS repository.
Update	Merge the latest version of the file in the CVS repository with your local copy.
Commit	Add or merge the local copy of a file with the CVS repository.
Release	Remove the local copy of a file retrieved from the CVS repository.
Revision	Number indicating the version of particular file.
Tag	Give a common version name to all files in a module.
Diff	Retrieve the difference between a local file and the one in the CVS repository.
History	Retrieve the revision history for a file in the CVS repository.

The commands as listed in the preceding table are those you'll most commonly use. This by no means attempts to be a full and comprehensive list, but it should give you a good idea of what to expect.

The way you would usually work with CVS is to walk through the following steps for each file you want to make changes to:

1. Check out a file from the CVS repository.
2. Make the necessary changes to that file.
3. Execute an update command on that file.
4. Commit your changes to that file back to the CVS repository.

Now what does that mean in plain English? Well, it's not very difficult: you get a file from the CVS server, make changes to it, and before submitting your changes back to the CVS server, you check whether there is a more recent version available on the server (someone might have submitted a newer version while you were working). If there is a newer version available on the CVS server, it will merge with your file, which you can then safely submit back to the server.

All those goodies do come at a price. A CVS server can be quite hard to install and configure and has a small but relatively steep learning curve. Luckily for us, there is software out there that makes this all much easier for us. My personal favorite is the *TortoiseCVS* client, which actually gives you CVS control at the click of a mouse right from within Windows Explorer.

TortoiseCVS is unfortunately not available for Mac. The following section discusses how this stand-alone client can be used on the PC platform. If you want to implement version control in your Flex projects, then you'll be interested to know that Flex can be integrated seamlessly with CVS. For more information on this topic, check out the bonus material available for download at `http://www.friendsofed.com/book.html?isbn=1590598458`.

Using TortoiseCVS

TortoiseCVS is an easy-to-use CVS client that supports common CVS tasks. It allows you to check out, update, and commit files right from within your familiar Windows Explorer interface. More importantly, it won't cost you a cent; the client software is open source and available as a free download at `www.tortoiseCVS.org`.

One of the key benefits of TortoiseCVS is that it supports local repositories, which is perfect if you're a single developer working on a project and don't want to go to the trouble of installing a CVS server. It's complete enough for most enterprise projects and basic enough for your basic programming needs.

Charlie Vernon Smythe (CVS for short) is the lovable mascot for TortoiseCVS (see Figure 5-1) and, despite the reputation of its species, will have your local repository set up by the time you're back from the bathroom. OK, well that's not entirely true . . . you will have to do some actual work yourself. Not to worry, though, I'll walk you through it in a couple of easy steps.

Figure 5-1. Charlie the TortoiseCVS mascot

First, the obvious: you download a copy of TortoiseCVS from the website (`www.tortoiseCVS.org`) and install it on your PC. You'll be prompted to restart your system; be sure to do that to make sure the icons in Windows Explorer will work properly.

The next thing you'll want to do is create a repository for your code. Open up Windows Explorer and browse to the folder you'd like to have act as your repository. You right-click that folder and choose CVS ➤ Make New Module, which brings up the dialog box shown in Figure 5-2.

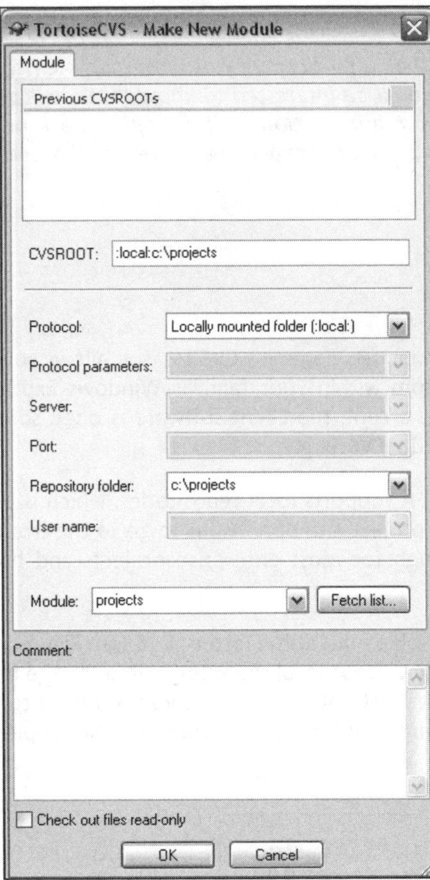

Figure 5-2.
TortoiseCVS Make New Module dialog box

In this dialog box, you set the protocol to Locally Mounted Folder and specify the full path to the folder (including the folder name itself) in the Repository folder field. Next, you click the OK button, which brings up the Import dialog box. Wait for another dialog box to pop up telling you no repository was found and asking you whether or not you want to initialize one (see Figure 5-3). You select the check box option and again click OK to continue.

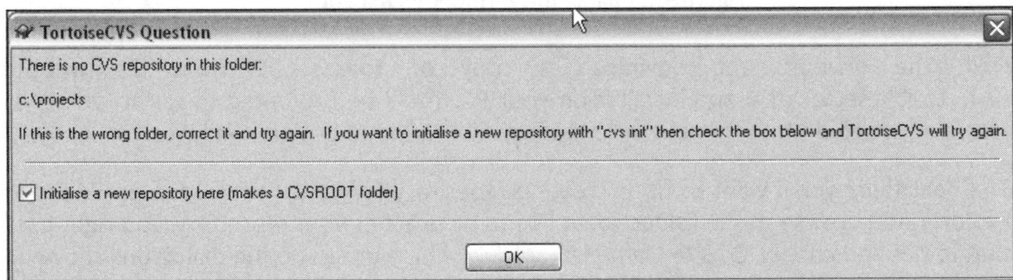

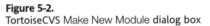

Figure 5-3. Initializing the repository in TortoiseCVS

Now that the repository is initialized, wait for the module dialog box to finish and click OK to close it (see Figure 5-4).

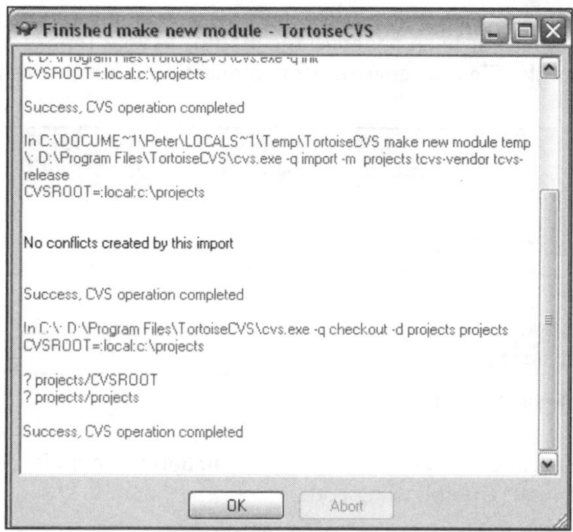

Figure 5-4. TortoiseCVS Finished make new module dialog box

That's not bad, is it? It probably took you longer to read this than to actually do it. Well this is it, you've got yourself a local CVS repository and module to work in. You'll notice that the folder now has a green overlay indicating that it is controlled by CVS.

Now, let's go one step further and add some actual source code to this local repository. Create a new file in that folder and name it `SomeClass.as`. As soon as you've created that file, you'll notice that you see a big question mark sign on top of the normal icon associated with an ActionScript file. The question mark shows you that the file is not yet added to the repository; to do this you right-click the file and choose CVS add, which brings up the dialog box you see in Figure 5-5.

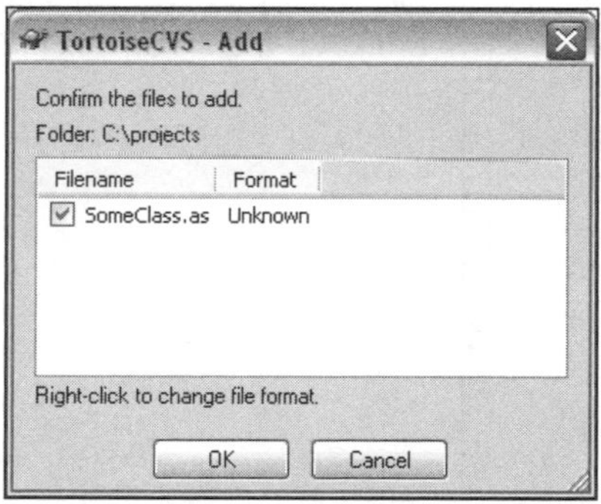

Figure 5-5. TortoiseCVS Add dialog box

Notice that the dialog box shows your SomeClass.as file but isn't able to determine the filetype format. You just right-click the file and choose Text/ASCII. Good to note is that TortoiseCVS also supports binary files, which allows you to keep a version history for images or even your FLA source files. When you click the OK button, you get a dialog box confirming that your file has been added to the module in your repository (see Figure 5-6). The overlay icon for the file now changes from a question mark to a red mesh.

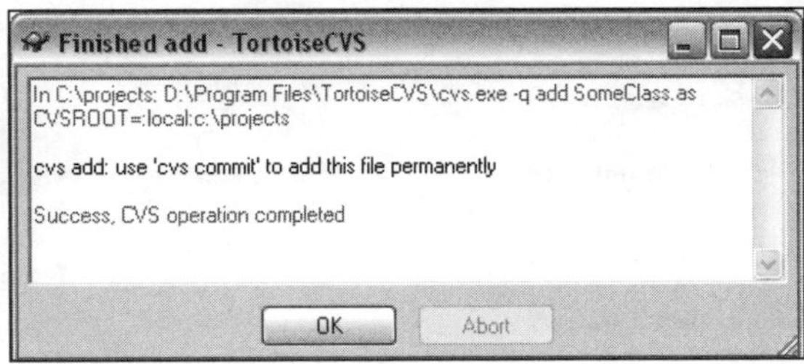

Figure 5-6. TortoiseCVS Finished add dialog box

Now that your file is added to the repository, you can add some initial code to it. Open up SomeClass.as and insert the following code:

```
package {
  class SomeClass {
    function SomeClass() {
    }
  }
}
```

You've just added a basic class structure to the file and can now save it. What you do now is commit the file to the local *repository*. Because you are working in a local repository, you only deal with one developer and do not have to worry about *updating* your code first. Back in Windows Explorer, right-click the file SomeClass.as and choose CVS commit, which brings up the dialog box in Figure 5-7.

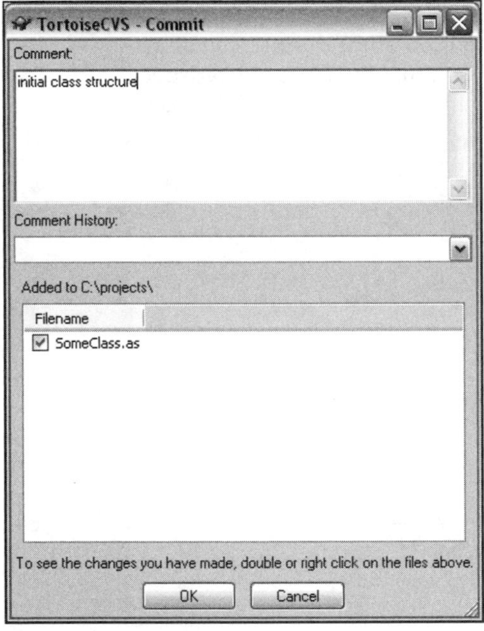

Figure 5-7.
TortoiseCVS Commit dialog box

In the Commit dialog box, notice a Comment field; I'd advise you always to include something in this field. Doing so allows you to easily see what particular review you made; a time and date doesn't do as much to refresh your memory. Add initial class structure as the comment for your first SomeClass.as revision. After clicking the OK button, a dialog box pops up telling you that the file has been committed to the repository (see Figure 5-8).

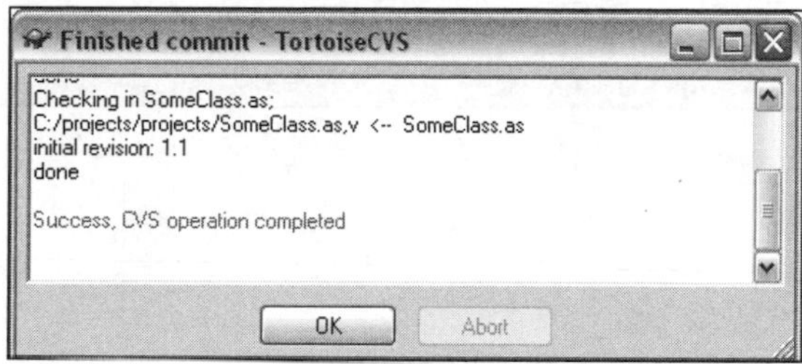

Figure 5-8. TortoiseCVS Finished commit dialog box

After you close the Finished commit dialog box, the overlay icon for SomeClass.as will change from a red to a green mesh, confirming that the revision has been posted to the repository.

Let's do one more basic revision to the file so you can see how the version history works and how to revert to an earlier version. Make the following changes to SomeClass.as:

```
package {
  class SomeClass {
    function SomeClass() {
      trace("constructor called");
    }
    private function someMethod():void {
    }
  }
}
```

In a real-world situation, you would obviously not commit a file back to the repository for such a minor revision. Save the file and again right-click the file in Windows Explorer, choose CVS commit, follow the steps as described earlier, and set the comment field to added someMethod method. You will have noticed that once you saved your changes, the icon overlay changed back from green to red, indicating that there were changes that have not yet been committed to the repository.

Now that you've got two revisions to your file, you can look at the version history. To do this, you right-click SomeClass.as and choose CVS ➤ History, which brings up a dialog box showing you all revisions (see Figure 5-9).

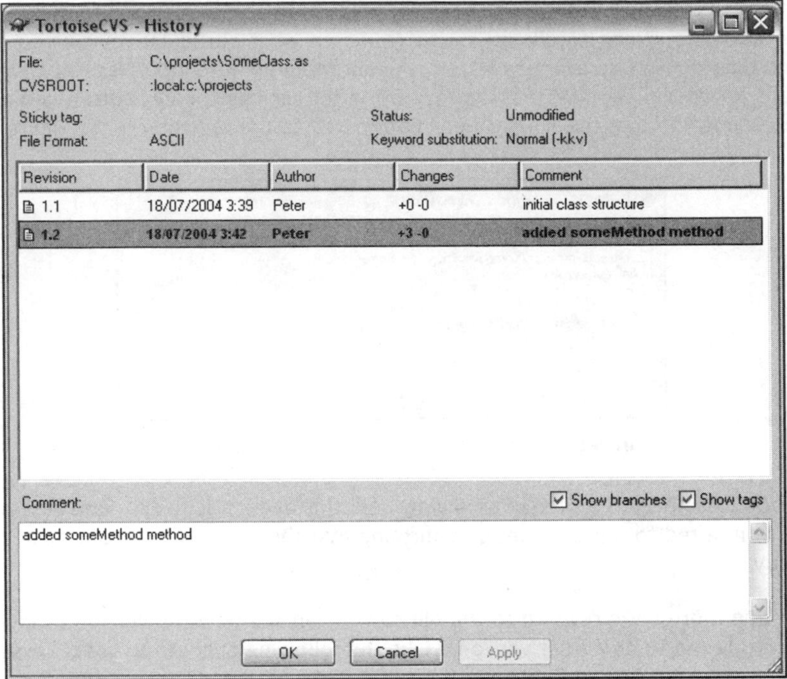

Figure 5-9. TortoiseCVS History dialog box

You'll notice that the History dialog box shows you the revision number, date and time, and author for that specific file. It also shows you how many lines of code were added and how many removed. In this case it shows you that three lines of code were added and none removed between revision 1.1 and 1.2 and the comments you added for those revisions.

To revert to an earlier version of a file, you just right-click that revision in the History dialog box and choose Get this revision (sticky). When you close the History panel, that particular revision will be saved back to your local file. Don't worry about losing any changes you made later on; those are still tracked in the History panel, and you can always get that revision should you need it.

Another very nice feature in TortoiseCVS is the ability to get a graph showing your revisions. You do this by right-clicking the file and choosing CVS ➤ Revision graph (see Figure 5-10).

The revision graph gives you a nice overview of the history of a file. By clicking any of the revisions, you'll be presented with information about the author, changes made, and comments. This is a very handy feature to use if you want to look back at the development path of your files.

This concludes my brief introduction to the TortoiseCVS client. I'm sure it has shown you some powerful features that will undoubtedly make life a lot easier for you when doing object-oriented programming with ActionScript 3.0.

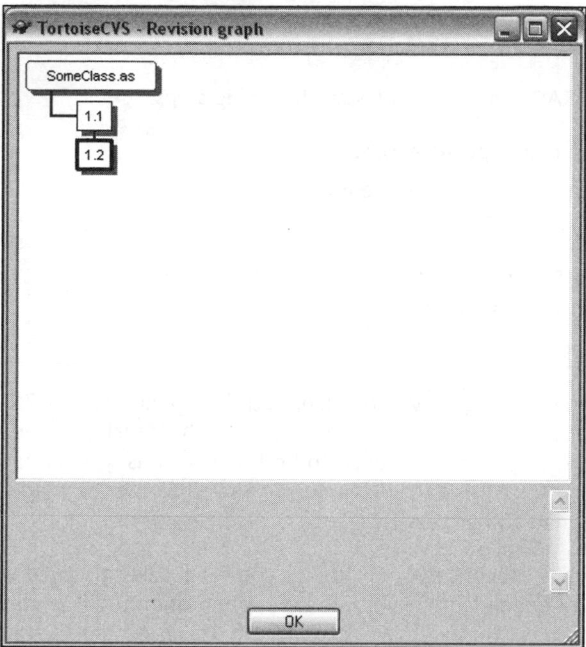

Figure 5-10. TortoiseCVS revision graph

Approaches to programming

Over the last few years, we've heard a lot about various approaches to programming. No, these aren't just buzzwords for cunning marketeers. Both you and your client can actually benefit from choosing an effective and complementary way to work on a particular project.

Whatever acronym you decide to call it is of little importance, but more importantly you need to have the rules for your way of working clearly outlined and consistently used. I'll briefly be discussing two programming concepts that have become quite popular recently, especially for projects that use Flash or Flex and ActionScript: Rapid Application Development and Extreme Programming.

Rapid Application Development

Rapid Application Development (RAD) is a popular programming methodology that allows applications to be built under a tight deadline and often limited budget. It lends itself well to applications that don't have very specific requirements to start with, providing you're able to get good user feedback throughout the development cycle.

To achieve this, there often needs to be some compromises made, which is highlighted in one of the key principles of RAD, the 80-20 rule:

In certain situations, a usable 80% solution can be produced in 20% of the time that would be required to produce a total solution.

In a nutshell, the RAD process includes the following steps:

1. Brainstorm initial specifications.
2. Prototype system and have client review.
3. Update application.
4. Conduct user reviews (repeat step 3 as necessary).
5. Create project analysis (optional).
6. Finalize application.

Now this, of course, sounds very compelling, but is it really possible? Bringing RAD into practice requires quite some discipline on the part of the developer, specifically in regards to scheduling reviewing user comments. To best achieve this, you should work with milestones for your project. After an initial brainstorm session with the client, provisional specifications are outlined and implemented in a *prototype system*.

You can't expect a nontechnical client to give you feedback on source code, so you need to have a basic working prototype version of the application (be it limited in functionality) for them to play around with and give feedback on. This prototype system is the first milestone of your project and is typically just reviewed by the client to finalize the requirements and feature set and start the actual application development.

At this stage, scheduling becomes increasingly important, and you need to bring out application updates at a regular interval for users to review. The development cycle is driven by feedback, so it is very important that you can get timely and complete feedback from your users. The cycle of update and review is repeated as long as is deemed necessary and feasible given the deadline. Ideally, reviewing the application would not happen by the client or yourself but by the actual user the application is targeting, which always gives you the most useful feedback on the flow of the application.

Once the development cycle is closed, you can move on to an optional analysis stage. Analysis of the project gives your client the opportunity for a final review. While the analysis stage is not a requirement in RAD, it certainly is recommended practice when the project relies on tight integration with another application or a degree of security needs to be implemented.

After the development cycle or project analysis, the code is finalized and prepared for deployment. If no analysis was done before this final stage, it is important that no further changes to the source code are made; if there was an analysis stage, changes to the code should be limited to any problems that came up.

RAD is a very useful programming methodology that you'll no doubt be using quite a lot for typical ActionScript 3.0 projects. If you think about it, Flash and particularly Flex are really great tools for doing RAD. RAD allows you to perform quick prototyping, design and code are managed using the best IDE for the job, it has a relatively low learning curve, and it is a highly portable, which helps tremendously with the testing and reviewing process.

Extreme Programming

Extreme Programming (XP) is another interesting programming methodology and is, far more so than RAD, applicable when working with a team of developers.

Breaking down the XP development process into steps is not as straightforward as with RAD, but roughly translates into the following sequence:

1. Define an initial release plan.
2. Put together an iteration plan based on user stories.
3. Use pair programming to develop an iteration.
4. Run acceptance tests on the completed iteration (repeat step 3 as necessary).
5. Project is finished when the code has passed all acceptance tests.

Throughout XP, there are a number of practices that all rely on principles of *simplicity* and *communication*. One of the most obvious differences the XP methodology introduces is the way it handles a team. The client is actually part of the team and works with the developers on a daily basis, helping to steer everything in the right direction, defining priorities, and further outlining the requirements for the project.

There are no strict roles in the team but rather personal expertise; everyone can contribute to the project within their area of expertise. A team can consist of anywhere from 2 to 15 people, though this methodology generally works better with small teams. As you can well imagine, this type of setup can be prone to a mild form of anarchy when not focused properly, and it is therefore often advisable to have a person designated to coordinate the process.

Another major part of XP is planning. There are two types of planning that XP uses, *release planning* and *iteration planning*. The release planning outlines the schedule for the overall project, while iteration planning uses this release plan for scheduling individual iterations of the project during the development process. The way release plans are created is by evaluating *user stories* that the client in the team supplies.

Each user story is basically a short description of a task that the application needs to perform. Those user stories are basic nontechnical and user-centric descriptions of a task that will need to be reviewed by developers in the team to ascertain how much development time it would need. As an alternative to a long requirement document, these user stories are used to make up iterations and plans that fall within the constraints of the release plan.

User stories are used to compile an iteration and to base *acceptance tests* on. Acceptance tests are scenarios outlined by the client and are used to verify whether the application returns the expected result based on the input. If these acceptance tests are passed, the user story is considered complete; if not, the issue will need to be addressed in the following iteration. If an iteration becomes too heavy to handle (usually due to failed acceptance tests in earlier iterations), you can meet with the client and reschedule the user stories in following iterations.

The way development works in an XP environment is using *pair development*. Two developers sit side by side at the same machine and work. The idea behind this is that you get better code because it is continuously monitored by a second developer. Recent studies have also confirmed that 1 + 1 > 2 when it comes to programming. Pair development takes a while to get used to and requires the developers in question to work well together; if that is not the case, this technique can cause accelerated production of gray hair.

Refactoring, another concept that XP strongly supports, involves breaking down code to the simplest level possible, only keeping the necessary functionality in there. Doing this avoids bloated and difficultly managed code down the line. Repeating the refactoring process might look very harsh, but it will definitely pay off in the end.

So far, so good. You'll notice that with XP the team setup is open and dynamic, while the project itself is scheduled and monitored very strictly. This certainly helps keep the project on track along with automated *unit testing*. Automated tests are very important in XP; they help monitor your code and run objective tests independent of anyone in the team. Based on the results of the automated tests, the development process is tweaked until all user stories are addressed and the application is considered final.

XP goes beyond simply being a programming methodology in that it requires you to not only follow a certain project workflow, but also actually organize practical aspects of your business to have them fit in with an XP development environment.

Throughout these various steps, members in the team might take on various roles and contribute in a variety of ways. Communication and planning are very important to have this work properly and should not be ignored at any stage of the development process.

Applying XP techniques to your programming workflow is certainly a good idea. While you might not be able to go for the full package, individual techniques like pair programming or unit testing are certainly worth considering!

I myself recently started using a remote form of pair programming for a number of ActionScript projects. While it may not be as effective as physically sitting at the same computer with a co-developer, I've had great experiences with getting specific code issues worked out.

One instance I can remember was when writing a Flash application that handles shared calendars. There were some problems getting recurring events validated for all users subscribed to the same group calendar. Another developer and I were initially working separately on finding a solution for this and just compared notes. Unfortunately, that didn't really resolve the issue until we started to do a couple of shared coding sessions.

Using Flash Communication Server (now known as Flash Media Server), we set up a little application through which we could in turn work on the same piece of ActionScript code while the other one checked syntax and comments on the approach. After just a couple of those sessions, and what could not have been more than half a day's work, we found the key to solving the problem on what had earlier took us several days to work on individually. It's quite amazing how effective pair programming can be in some instances, even with your fellow developer located all the way across the ocean.

Usability testing

Usability testing is an often underestimated process that allows you to get real-world information about the way a target user handles your application.

What do you attempt to find out with usability tests? That is a valid question—not all information you can get from users is relevant for evaluating a project. One thing you do know is that you want to make sure users are able to independently perform the tasks that the application was built for. Building on that information, you can find out how easy it was for a user to navigate through the application and complete various required steps.

Often usability tests are thought of as a means of evaluating a project near the end of its development cycle. Nothing is further from the truth. Usability tests can (or dare I say should) be used throughout the entire project workflow. All too often this step is neglected, resulting in bad user experience, which in turn influences *return on investment* for the project.

Usability tests during the development cycle don't have to be very elaborate, but they do differ from simple reviews of your application. Remember, the tests serve to get feedback from actual users; it would be bad practice for you or the client to take part. When working with multiple user tests, make sure not all people participating in the test have taken part in one or an earlier version. It is important to have users test an application without any prior knowledge, so while it may be interesting to see how previous testers handle the new version, the information you need to act upon is always that of the new people in the test group.

So how do you put together a usability test? First, make sure you have clearly defined the target audience and try to represent that as closely as possible in your test group. Each user represents multiple users in the usability test—for example, 1 user represents 100 users with a target audience of 1,000. While you might think that an application that reaches 1,000 users will need more usability testers than 1 for 100 people, this doesn't appear to be the case. In fact, statistics indicate that groups of just 5 people give the best overall results. What that means in practical terms is that it's more effective to invest in multiple limited usability tests than a couple of large ones.

When you've got your user test group together, you need to address the questions that you want answered with the usability test. Tests can include questions based on *information* users can get from the application; you can also ask about their *experience* of using the application or have them perform *tasks* with the application to time how efficiently they can get to the desired information.

Let's say we've got a car configurator application that we're running a usability test on. The application lets users choose a model car and customize it to their liking with any accessories, finally to be presented with the total price of their ideal car. Questions and tasks for this type of project might be

- What colors can you get the latest model of a BMW in?
- How much does it cost to include a GPS system with the car?
- What model car would you first look at when searching for a family vehicle?

- Would you be more likely to buy a particular model car after trying the car configurator?
- Locate the car dealer closest to your home.
- Find all car models that come with built-in air conditioning.

Important with asking these questions is that you don't guide users through it. Try not to suggest an answer with the way you ask your question, and before having users take the test, simply explain what the application is without discussing how to use it. Monitor users objectively and compare statistics between different releases. Doing that gives you a good indication of how far the changes you made based on prior feedback have been successful.

When handled properly, usability tests are an invaluable tool to make sure your applications do what you want them to do and increase user experience. In the end, that's what it's all about. An application is not just a collection of features, but a way for you to present data in a format that is most efficient and enjoyable for the end user.

For more information on usability, be sure to check out *Flash Application Design Solutions: The Flash Usability Handbook* by Craig Bryant and Ka Wai Cheung (friends of ED, 2006), which is an excellent guide on the topic and goes a lot more in depth than the scope of this chapter allows.

What's next?

This chapter discussed aspects of the project workflow that will help you organize and handle your projects most effectively. In the next chapter, I'll discuss some more practical considerations when working with ActionScript 3.0, such as commenting, naming conventions, and other best practices.

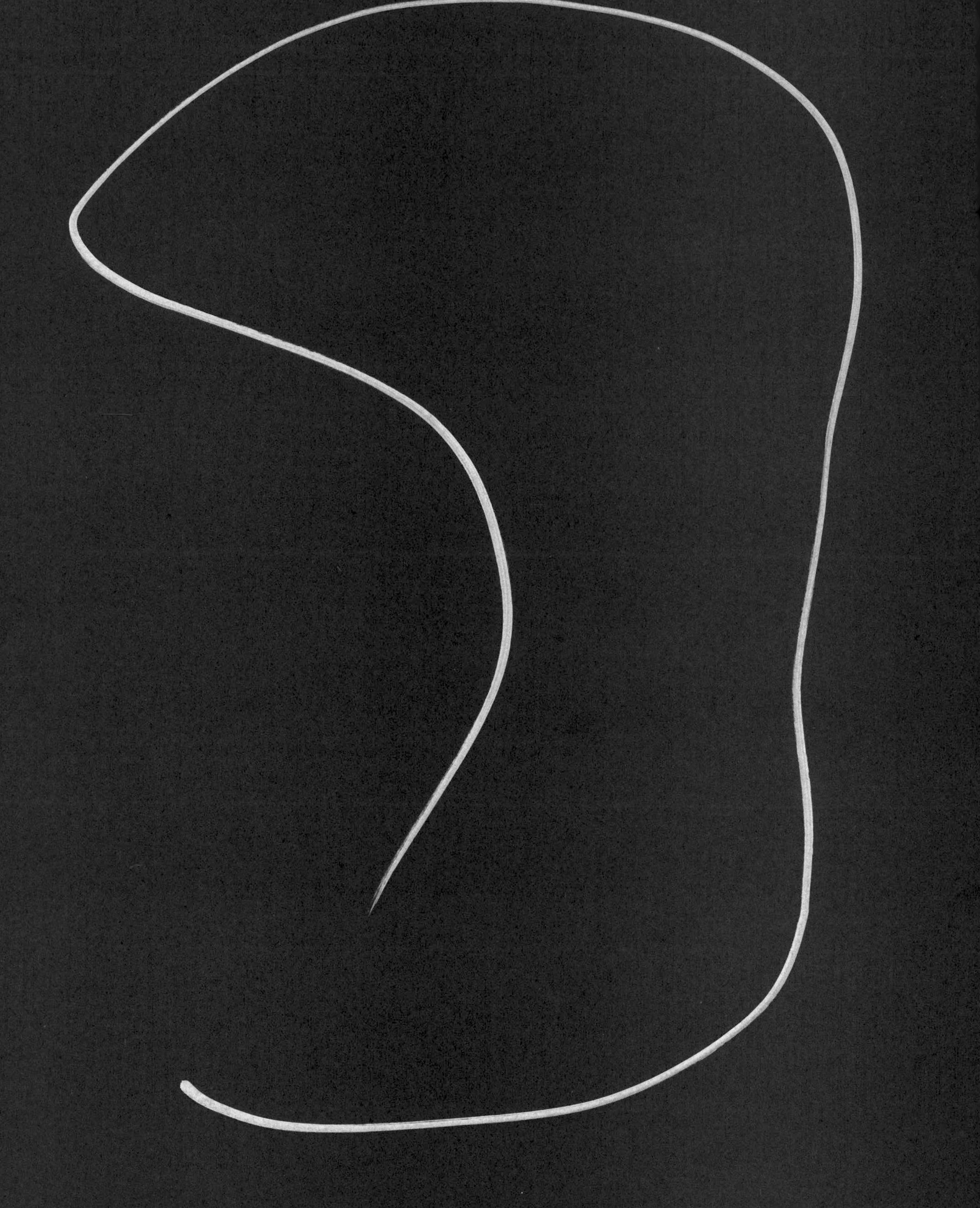

6 BEST PRACTICES

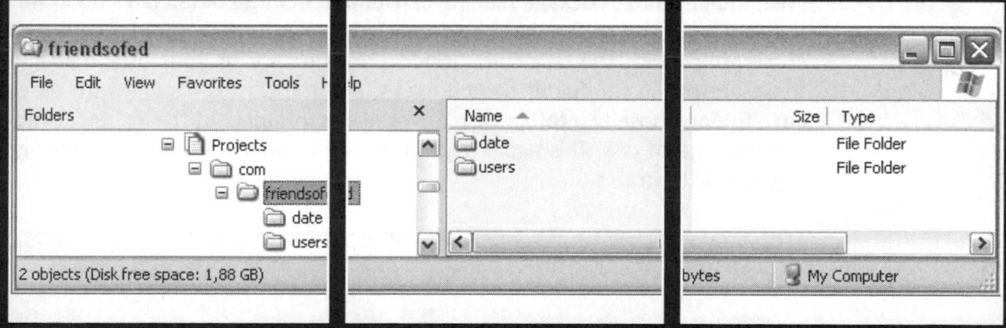

In the previous chapter, we looked at some important aspects of managing a project workflow. Now we'll specifically explore best practices for working with ActionScript. Best practices aim to make your programming experience as comfortable as possible and outline some standardized methods to structuring and managing code.

The coding practices and naming conventions that will be discussed here are in no way legally binding (I promise I won't sue—unless of course you forget to comment your code!), but I can't stress enough the importance of writing consistent and readable code. What you'll find here can be thought of as the common denominator of best programming practices; be sure to read through these best practices and apply them as much as possible to your project.

External ActionScript

As you know after reading Chapter 3, which covers ActionScript 3.0 programming, all ActionScript classes you code must be placed in external `.as` files. You might think of this as a bit of an annoyance, but it actually does have a number of advantages such as the ability to work with class packages.

Class packages allow you to organize classes in a folder structure and organize by the specific tasks they perform. One of the main reasons you use class packages is to help avoid naming conflicts; by "packaging" classes in a unique folder structure, you can be sure that you don't accidentally use a class with the same name in the classpath.

Let's say you've written a bunch of classes that deal with user management. Putting those classes in the same folder with classes that handle date functions would not be the most efficient approach. Rather than doing that, you would make two class packages and structure those as follows:

```
com.friendsofed.users
com.friendsofed.date
```

We'll look into this package naming convention in more detail later on in this chapter, but for now it is good to see that you organized your classes in a folder with a name that best corresponds with the task they perform. In the case of your user management classes, those are put in the folder named `users`, and the classes dealing with dates are put in a `date` folder. Those two folders are themselves subfolders of the `friendsofed` package that is a package of `com`. This again might look a bit convoluted, but it makes good sense, as Figure 6-1 illustrates.

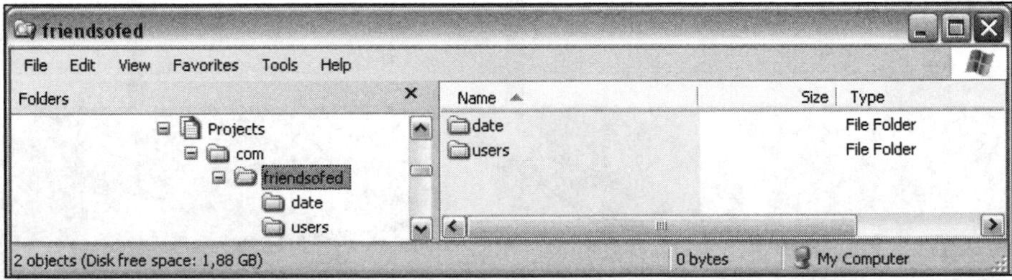

Figure 6-1. Package folder structure

Since ActionScript 2.0, there's an import keyword that can use a wildcard character (*) to load an entire class package in with a single statement. The com.friendsofed.users package might contain 20 different classes, but a single line of code will do all that work for you:

```
import com.friendsofed.users.*
```

Now, don't get too excited—there are a couple of "buts" that you should take into consideration. Let's say you wanted to import both the com.friendsofed.users and com.friendsofed.date packages. Trying to avoid RSI, my inherent developer instinct would tell me to make that into one import statement:

```
import com.friendsofed.*
```

No such luck, however; that statement will load all classes in the com.friendsofed package but no classes that are located in a folder below that. If you need both packages, you will need to use

```
import com.friendsofed.users.*
import com.friendsofed.date.*
```


Another point to make is that import statements only make temporary references to the package in question. If you have an import statement on Frame 1 of your timeline, and you wanted to use it again in the next frame, it would not work. To achieve that, you'd need to use the import statement again. Of course, when doing class-based development, you're not dealing with the constraints of frames.

That's all well and good, but keeping in mind the limitations, is it really necessary to use class packages? The answer there is a definite YES! Working with class packages in itself is perfect when doing OOP because it helps you work in a more organized and structured way. Whether you should use import statements is a different question altogether.

Here's an example of using the import statement:

```
import com.friendsofed.users.*
var userInfo:UserProfile = new UserProfile();
```

And now an example of using the full package name:

```
var userInfo:UserProfile = new com.friendsofed.users.UserProfile();
```

The preceding examples assume we have a class called UserProfile in the com.friendsofed.users package and clearly show that when you're not extensively instantiating classes, there is no real use to the import statement (in fact, in this case it will give you slightly more code to write). Of course, there will be situations where you're dealing with more complex scripts that will require you to make lots more class instances, and in those cases you could certainly consider using the import keyword.

I would, however, recommend always using import when coding your ActionScript 3.0 classes; adding the import statement on top of your class file will allow you to find all class dependencies at a single glance as soon as you open up the file. Also worth noting is if you ever change class packages, you can simply change the `import` statement to update your application rather than having to do a complete find and replace.

You might even want to import each class individually rather than using the wildcard character to give you a quick overview of what classes you use in that particular class package.

Let's move on to another very important subject that is often underestimated and happily ignored: commenting your code.

About commenting

Comments are notes that programmers insert into their code to clarify important aspects of the application. With all the new technology these days, comments seldom get the attention they deserve. Many trainers assume that if you can write a simple program, you must know how to write comments. Not true. I want to bring comments back to the foreground and tell you the correct way to use them.

Some programmers don't write comments. Ever. Others write so many comments, it's nearly impossible to read their code. There's a better way, with neither too few nor too many comments. To maintain the middle course, just remember the word *why*.

Ideally, comments should answer the question *why* (not *what*). The code already demonstrates *what* it is doing, but it may not be clear *why*. When you need to explain *why* in your code, consider including a comment.

> *Some programmers write comments that restate (in their spoken language) what the code already demonstrates. If your code reads* `n = 10`*, there's no need to write a comment that reads "Setting the variable named n equal to 10." The real comment should be "n represents the number of seconds until the rocket launches." Ultimately, strive to write naturally self-descriptive code. If you write code such as* `secondsToLaunch = 10`*, you don't need to include a comment in the first place.*

Comments in ActionScript are ignored when your project is compiled down to a `.swf` file, so you definitely don't need to worry about bloating file size of the finished application. There are two ways by which you can add comments to your ActionScript code. The first one is used for small notes that take no more than a single line.

```
// This is a single-line comment
```

When you need multiple lines of comments, it's best to use a comment block by using a combination of the /* and */ characters.

```
/**
  *  This is a comment block.
  *  Everything in here is a comment.
  */
```

Now that you know how to add comments to your code, let's consider when you should add them. I personally use the following commenting style when writing classes:

```
/**
  * UserProfile
  * Author: Peter Elst
  * Revision: 1.2
  * Description: The UserProfile class manages
  * personal user information
  * To-do: add method for deleting a profile property
  */
```

The preceding example shows what I add on top of all my classes: the class name, author, revision number, and description. The to-do information is optional and helps you remember what functionality you planned on adding. If you're faced with a nasty bug, you might also want to flag that up in this comment block.

There is no need to go overboard with commenting; not every method in a class needs additional info. This is certainly the case if you make use of the naming conventions that I'll discuss in the next section. In theory, your code should be fairly legible if you have naming conventions in place as well as keep to the advice that I gave in the introduction to OOP, which is strictly to have one task for one method.

Classes do usually have a couple of methods that are worth commenting. Those are typically the ones in which a lot of the data processing happens or those that rely on very specific information to be passed to them. In those instances, I use another short comment block that describes a method's specific task.

```
/**
  * buildProfile builds an XML document from the user profile
  * information stored in the userData object
  */
```

I generally don't like adding inline comments (comments within functions) because those clutter the code. The only times I use them is when flagging bug locations or development notes.

```
function buildProfile() {
  // Note: for-in loops do not necessarily go through
  // objects in reverse order in AS3
  for(var i in userProfile) {
    ...
  }
}
```

Development notes are just small single-line comments that I put in as reminders when I know I'll be tweaking a specific method. They usually pertain to a very specific part of code and are better placed inline than above the method. The next time I open up the class, I'll find what functions need my attention in the to-do list comment block at the top of the file, and when I move down to that function, there will likely be some notes there that help me get started.

The commenting styles I use are not based on any particular guideline but have grown from my own experience with coding ActionScript 3.0 classes. You might well want to use a slightly different approach, and of course you're free to do so. There are a few benchmarks you can use to check how effective your commenting style is:

1. Do your comments increase readability of the code?
2. Is your commenting style consistent throughout all classes?
3. Do your comments help you be more productive when revising a class?

Those are three very basic questions that will help you determine the quality of your comments. If one or more answers to these questions is no, you should really consider changing the way you document your code. If they're all a big fat yes, sit back and relax—you've just earned yourself a cup of coffee.

Comments are finally getting the recognition they deserve. Over the last few years, several initiatives have been set up that have given commenting best practices a new lease on life. One such initiative is Javadoc, a tool developed by Sun Microsystems for automatically generating HTML documentation by extracting comments from class source files. This type of commenting has gained ground with many Flash developers ever since the release of ActionScript 2.0. To read more about this, be sure to visit `http://java.sun.com/j2se/javadoc/`.

Adobe now has its own solution available called ASDoc, which does a great job for automatically generating documentation from your AS3 and Flex projects. ASDoc is available for download from the following web page: `http://labs.adobe.com/wiki/index.php/ASDoc`.

If you're using Flex Builder for doing ActionScript 3.0 development, there is a great extension that adds support for `/TODO` and `/FIXME` comments. It goes through your project and adds those items to the Task panel so you can easily see what still needs to be done. You can download the extension from the following website: `www.richinternet.de/blog/index.cfm?entry=911D4B57-0F0D-5A73-AF6F4D4D04099757`.

Naming conventions

I remember following a discussion on naming conventions back when ActionScript 2.0 first came out. Many people were wondering whether strong typing and context-sensitive code hints would make naming conventions obsolete. Definitely not! If anything, naming conventions have become more important with the introduction of things like private and public scope, and now in ActionScript 3.0 I still consider them invaluable. Aside from private and public scope, we also have protected and internal scope to deal with. Personally, I treat these as I would private scope, but you might want to consider your own convention if that makes your code more readable.

Imagine being faced with a property called "foo" in a class with several hundred lines of code with no idea what type it is (unless you cheat and try to use code hints on it), whether it is a public or private property, etc. I've had to deal with classes like that before and let me tell you, it's not a pretty sight. If there's one way to get a fellow developer to lose his nerve, this is it.

After a while, reading ActionScript code becomes like a second language. Naming conventions play a big part in this; they provide developers with a lot of background information on properties and method names that allow them to work in a much more convenient and productive way.

Enough promotion, let's get to it! The naming conventions discussed here are very common throughout most programming languages and are ideal for working with ActionScript 3.0.

Variables

Variables are namespaces to which you can assign a particular datatype and values. Names for variables can contain letters, numbers, the dollar sign ($), or an underscore (_). Things to consider are that variable names cannot start with a number, and there are a number of reserved words such as `class` and `import` that are also not allowed.

In general, variable names consisting of more than one word are written in *camel case*, starting with a lowercase letter and using an uppercase letter for every new word like so: `thisIsMyVariable`. This is by far the most common practice, and I would certainly recommend using this.

An example of a variable declaration is `var countSheep:uint = 500;`.

Constants

A constant is a variable whose value does not change after it has been initialized. Examples of constants are the event names you'll find prevalent in ActionScript 3.0 projects, such as `MouseEvent.MOUSE_DOWN`, `KeyBoardEvent.KEY_DOWN`, or `LoadEvent.LOAD`.

The naming convention for constants is to use all uppercase and separate words with underscores. An example of a constant declaration is `const MAX_SHEEP:uint = 500;`.

Notice that there is a new keyword in ActionScript 3.0, `const`, for explicitly setting a variable as a constant.

Functions

Functions are reusable containers for code; they can be used throughout an application and optionally return a value that is often based on one or more parameters passed to them.

Function names follow the same convention as variables do. Names for functions usually consist of two parts; the first is a verb that describes the task it performs, and the second is a noun that defines the object it applies that task to. This sounds much more difficult than it actually is; here are a few examples:

```
getProfile();
validateEmail();
parseFeed();
```

Classes

Classes are essential building blocks for doing object-oriented programming. They provide a collection of variables and functions (respectively called *properties* and *methods* in this context) from which multiple independent instances can be created.

The naming convention for classes is camel case, but with an initial uppercase letter. Usually names for classes just consist of a single nonplural noun. It is important to keep your class names as descriptive as possible; try to avoid too generic terms.

Some example of class names are

```
Ball
Sheep
UserProfile
```

Methods

Methods are essentially functions defined inside a class, and as such they use largely the same naming convention. The difference with methods is that they can have a public, private, protected, or internal scope, and some developers like to prefix the name with an underscore sign to designate it as private. This naming convention is not essential, but it can make your classes more readable, which is always a good thing.

Some examples of method names are

```
buildTable()
_parseFeed();
```

Properties

Properties are variables defined inside a class, and as such use the same naming convention. Just like methods, properties can be assigned a public, private, protected, or internal scope. To show what properties are private, you can optionally use the underscore sign.

Some examples of property names are

```
profileID
_indexCounter
```

Packages

Packages, as discussed earlier in this chapter, are folder namespaces that you can store classes in to give them a unique identifier, and you can use them to sort classes by function and make importing classes easier.

There is a very common naming convention with packages that originally came from languages such as Java. Typically, the class path is made up of your domain name in reverse order; this makes sure the class path is unique to your own code.

```
Example: com.friendsofed
```

Once you've got this basis for your package name, you can go on and add your own folders and extend the package name as far as you find necessary.

Some examples of package names are

```
com.friendsofed.sports
com.friendsofed.animals
com.friendsofed.users
```

As discussed earlier, class names are written in camel case and start with an uppercase letter, which might result in the following class `import` statements:

```
import com.friendsofed.sports.Ball;
import com.friendsofed.animals.Sheep;
import com.friendsofed.users.UserProfile;
```


Applying naming conventions should, just like commenting your code, become an essential part of your ActionScript 3.0 programming practice. I'm sure you'll have noticed how consistent names for the different elements in your application make a huge difference in understanding what they represent and are used for. We'll explore some further aspects of good coding practices next by discussing good programming styles.

Programming styles

There's more to writing code than typing instructions from this (or any other) computer book. There's also programming style, which is really essential as you'll notice from the example of sloppy programming that follows.

> *I've mentioned earlier that it is important to remember that it's likely at some stage other developers will be using your code. Being faced with unreadable and/or badly written code is not very pleasant and will only result in frustration. Just a few tweaks and good coding practice will make life easier for everyone involved.*

Sloppy pseudo-code

```
Start of Application
Variable
  Variable
Variable
Start of Function
    Instruction
Instruction
  Instruction
       End of Function
Start of Function
 Instruction
Instruction
   Instruction
End of Function
  End of Application
```

Cleaning up the preceding example is not that difficult; the things to keep in mind are *consistency* and *spacing*. Just take a look at the improvement when this very same code is spaced consistently in the following example. I put *at least* one blank line between so-called paragraphs of code (groups of related code). I use consistent indentation to illustrate the code's natural hierarchy (what belongs to what).

Cleaned-up pseudo-code

```
Start of Application

    Variable
    Variable
    Variable

    Start of Function
        Instruction
        Instruction
        Instruction
    End of Function

    Start of Function
        Instruction
        Instruction
        Instruction
    End of Function

End of Application
```

The code just discussed is a very generic overview of how to structure an application. Let's bring this into perspective for use with ActionScript 3.0 classes.

Sloppy ActionScript 3.0 class

```
    package {
import flash.net.*;
public class myClass {
  function myClass() {
    var TextColor:Color = 0x003366;
trace("Constructor");
  }
var userName:String = "Peter";
  var maxcount:uint = 5;
    var base_url:String = "http://www.friendsofed.com";
private function reverseString(str):String {
    var tmp:Array = str.split("").reverse();
    return tmp.join("");
  }
function set URL(url:String) {
var base_url:String = url;
}
      function loadSite(){
    navigateToURL(new URLRequest(base_url),"_blank");
  }
  private var _foundNumber:Boolean;
function $isEvenNumber(num:Number) {
return (num % 2 == 0);
}
private var _countIndex;
  function countLoop(){
    for(var i=1; i<=maxcount; i++) {
      trace("Loop "+i+" of "+maxcount);
    }
  }
  function get URL():String {
return base_url;
}
}}
```

The preceding example is rather extreme, but you can see how inconsistent code and lack of spacing and indentation can cause a lot of issues with readability. Now, how difficult is it really to clean that up? Just take a look for yourself; this very same class is listed next, and just a few tweaks have made a huge difference.

Cleaned-up ActionScript 3.0 class

```
package {

import flash.net.*;

public class MyClass {

  // Constants
  private const MAX_COUNT:uint = 5;
  private const BASE_URL:String = "http://www.friendsofed.com";

  // public properties
  public var textColor:Number = 0x003366;
  public var userName:String = "Peter";

  // private properties
  private var _countIndex:uint;
  private var _foundNumber:Boolean;

  // constructor
  public function MyClass() {
    trace("Constructor called");
  }

  // public methods
  public function loadSite():void {
    navigateToURL(new URLRequest(BASE_URL),"_blank");
  }
  public function countLoop():void {
    for(var i:uint=1; i<=MAX_COUNT; i++) {
      trace("loop "+i+" of "+MAX_COUNT);
    }
  }

  // private methods
  private function _reverseString(str:String):String {
    var tmp:Array = str.split("").reverse();
    return tmp.join("");
  }
  private function _isEvenNumber(num:Number):Boolean {
    return (num % 2 == 0);
  }
```

```
    // getter/setter methods
    public function get URL():String {
      return BASE_URL;
    }

  }

}
```

If you look at the preceding code, you'll notice something very important to a clean programming style, which is *grouping*. By grouping properties and methods according to their scope and function within the class, you can quickly find whatever you're looking for, and this increases the overall readability of your code. Just like with our pseudo-code earlier, a couple of blank lines between these various sections of code make it even easier to navigate through. The example shown previously is the way I usually structure my ActionScript 3.0 classes; it is not set in stone, and you can certainly tweak it to your own style and preference.

The key to successful programming is often hidden in the details. You can teach any old monkey OOP (well, at least smart, genetically modified monkeys), but that does not guarantee good and readable code. Never underestimate what things like comments, naming conventions, and good programming styles can do for you.

Alternative programming styles

Coding practices: Peter Elst

As mentioned earlier, developers often have their own distinctive guidelines and best practices for writing their code and defend those with their life. There's nothing wrong with this, and thinking about how to best structure code can only lead to a more efficient development process.

When in the process of writing this book, we discovered that myself, Todd, and Sas have slightly different code styles and best practices for coding ActionScript 3.0. Rather than force each other to adhere to a style we don't particularly agree or feel comfortable with, we opted to each outline our best practices and code style and explain why we use them.

You've read about my practices for ActionScript 3.0 development earlier on in this chapter, so I'll leave it up to Todd and Sas to show you theirs here. This should hopefully spark some ideas of your own on how you want to structure application code.

Coding practices: Todd Yard

I would first start off by saying that there is a difference in my mind between good coding techniques and code formatting. I believe it is in the latter issue where many, or even most, developers disagree. For instance, a debate could continue for years on how code should best be indented or whether a space should appear between a `for` or `if` keyword and its following parenthesis, but this does not really affect the quality of the code. One developer may use the following format for a function:

```
function myFunction()
{
}
```

while another developer uses the following:

```
function myFunction() {
}
```

Neither in my opinion is more correct than the other. As long as the intention of the code is clear, and it is done in a way that balances both optimal performance and readability, then it is good code. Everything that Peter has laid out for good practices in this chapter does just that. What is left then is differing opinion on naming conventions and formatting.

In the code I present later in this book, I use the following conventions that might at times differ from those of either Peter or Sas:

1. Private and protected properties have a single underscore prefix. No distinction is made between a protected property defined in a child class versus a superclass (e.g., if I defined a Shape class with a protected property `_fillColor`, a Rectangle class that inherited from Shape would access `_fillColor` and not use some distinction to note that the property was defined in the superclass).
2. I begin local variables with a lowercase p and continue in camel case (e.g., `pWidth` or `pLineColor`).
3. I do not normally use public properties in a class and instead expose private and protected properties through getter/setter methods. Because of this, no distinction usually needs to be made for the naming of public properties.
4. I do not use the keyword `this` in a class file. This is done mostly for readability's sake, as a color-coded file peppered with `this` distracts from the unique code around it. For instance, of the following two lines, I feel the second one is much easier to digest when perusing code:

   ```
   this._area = this._width * this._height;

   _area = _width * _height;
   ```

   With the single underscore denoting private and protected properties and the lowercase *p* denoting local variables, I feel the `this` becomes redundant.

5. Though perhaps a somewhat controversial opinion, personally I'm not a big fan of comments, and when not writing for a book or in a team, I must admit I don't use them all that often. This probably stems from the fact that too often comments are overused and distract from the actual code, which, if written with descriptive method, property, class, and instance names in a clear and straightforward manner, should be fairly readable without the extra comments. Whenever it is NOT possible to accomplish this with the code, for instance, in lines of complex mathematical calculations, or where there is some backwards logic that needs to be applied for a case not readily apparent, then comments become useful or even necessary. Now that comments can be collapsed in Flash, or if you are using Flex Builder or another application with that functionality, thankfully comments can be tucked away until they are needed; so I have taken advantage of adding Javadoc-style comments to methods themselves in order to generate documentation, as I have done for all the downloaded code for my chapters, but I rarely write inline comments.

6. I do not use `super()` in my constructor unless it is necessary to pass variables to the superclass's constructor, since the line is already implied. If there is a question about whether a class inherits from another, I need only look to the class definition a few lines above, which gives better information as to what the superclass is.

7. I usually choose to use shorthand for the creation of `Object` and `Array` instances, using the syntax more often of the first of the following two lines:

   ```
   var myArray:Array = [];

   var myArray:Array = new Array();
   ```

   Again, I feel if the code is readable and clear in intent and accomplishes its purpose, it is hard to argue with. There is nothing confusing about the intent of that first line, even if it uses the shortcut.

All of these points, though, are completely subjective, and alternative viewpoints and arguments may be equally valid (or even more so in the mind of the person with the alternative viewpoint!).

Coding practices: Sas Jacobs

I follow many of the coding best practices that Peter outlines in this chapter. Like Peter, I prefer to use `import` statements so that I can avoid using fully qualified class package names. I think it makes my code much easier to read. I always locate the statements together at the top of the class file so I can easily find them again later. I am also very particular about writing properly indented code blocks because I think it makes the lines much easier to read.

I have a couple of different coding styles from Peter. These differences are in my commenting and naming conventions.

Commenting code

I also like to comment blocks of code and, unlike Peter, I'm happy to use inline comments. . In fact, I'll often write the class structure and pseudo-code using comments. Then, when I write the code, it is already commented by my pseudo-code lines. For example, I might start my class file by writing the following:

```
class ClassName {

  //declare private properties

..//constructor
  function ClassName() {

  }

  //public methods:
  //init
    //create components
    //size components
    //position on stage

  //loadFile
    //create LoadVars
    //parse and assign to arrays
....//loop through arrays and populate components

  //private methods
    //format date - returns a long date string from a date object
}
```

I'd then start writing the code under the comments, testing as I go. For me, this provides a roadmap when I'm writing code. The comments serve as markers to specific blocks of code, and they help to refresh my memory when I come back to a project that I haven't seen for months.

From the preceding code, you can see that I also like to organize my class file into sections. I start by declaring my private variables, then write the constructor function and public methods, and finish with private methods.

Naming conventions

I use the following naming conventions because they make my code easier to understand:

1. Private properties start with a double underscore, for example, `__parentContainer_mc`. I don't preface these variables with this (e.g., `this.__parentContainer_mc`) because I think it makes the variable names harder to read.
2. Variable names are descriptive, start with a lowercase letter, and use camel case (e.g., `var returnValue:Number`).

3. When referring to components, I usually use a name that indicates the component type (e.g., `product_txt` or `__item_lbl`).
4. Function names use a verb and noun (e.g., `createBinding`, `loadProduct`).
5. Class names are descriptive, start with an uppercase letter, and use camel case (e.g., `FeaturedProduct`).
6. Package names start with `com`, include the company name, and use a descriptive name (e.g., `com.aip.products`). Feel free to use a different top-level domain if you feel that it will cut down further on any chances of naming conflicts, or simply suit your projects better.

Looking through my conventions, I realize that I don't have a standard for distinguishing between public and private method names. I guess that shows that even experienced coders are inconsistent at times!

What's next?

In the last few chapters, we covered object-oriented programming guidelines. You've learned how to plan, model, and manage projects. I covered an introduction to version control, some common programming methodologies, usability testing, and best practices for ActionScript 3.0.

The next chapter will introduce you to Flex Builder 2, a great development environment for working with ActionScript 3.0 and a good alternative to the Flash authoring environment. Now that we're getting serious about code, this is something you definitely will want to look at.

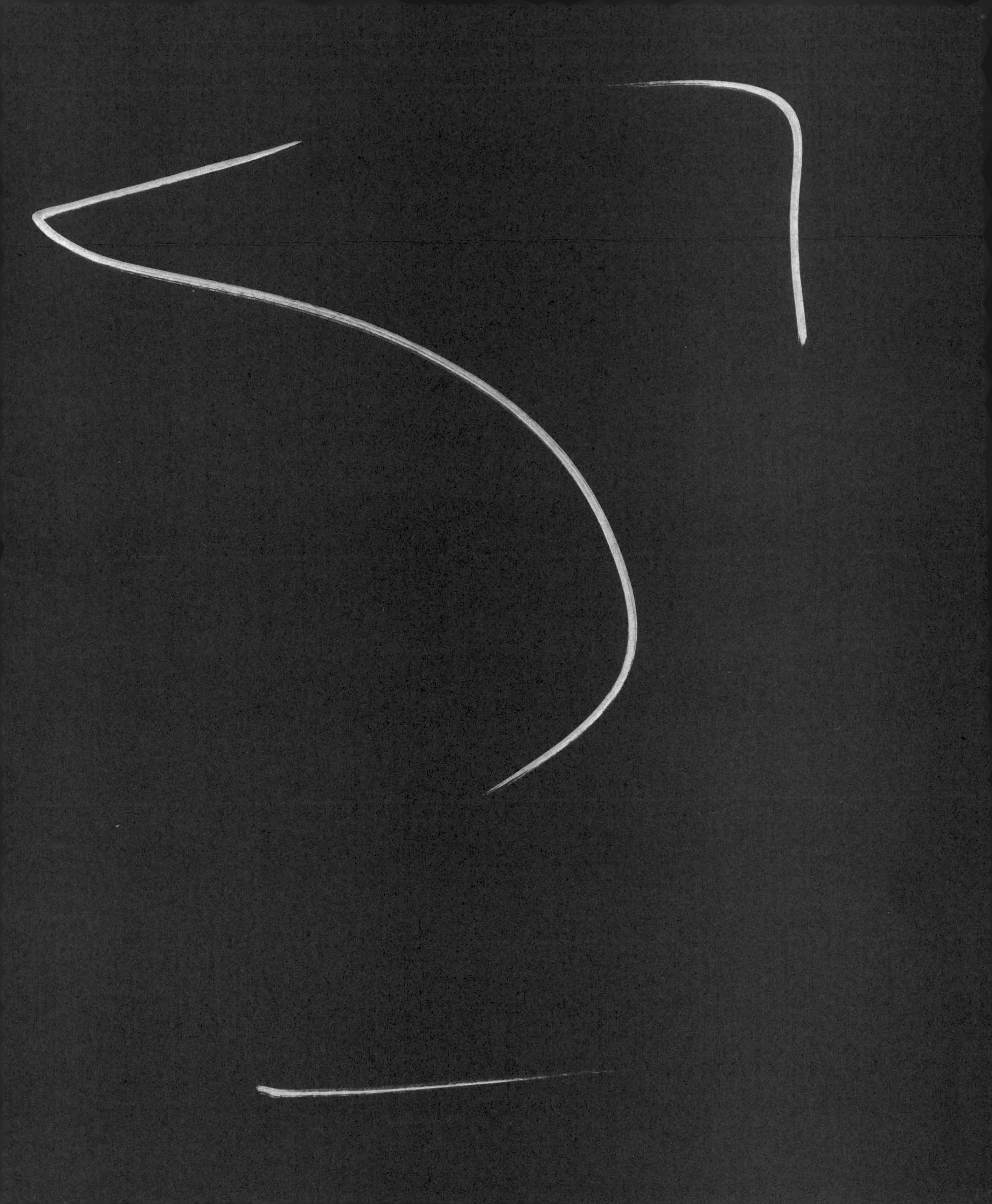

7 WORKING WITH FLEX 2

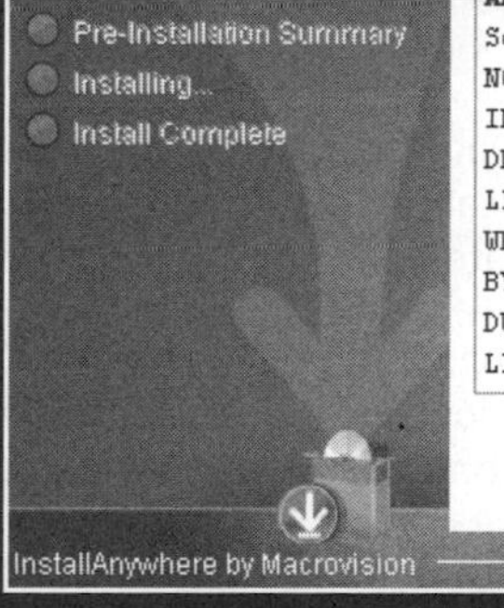

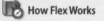

Flex 2 allows you to build rich Internet applications suitable for Flash Player 9. Like Flash, it creates SWF files capable of being played with Flash Player, but as you'll see in this chapter, that's where the similarity ends.

Flex allows you to create user interfaces using an Extensible Markup Language (XML) vocabulary called *MXML*. You can then add functionality to the interface by writing ActionScript 3.0. You can also create the interface solely in ActionScript. If you've used the Visual Studio .NET IDE, you'll find that Flex uses a very similar approach.

The Flex framework consists of

- The Flex 2 Software Development Kit (SDK)
- Flex Builder 2
- Flex Data Services (FDS)
- Flex Charting 2

The Flex 2 SDK is at the core of the Flex framework. This SDK is free to download from the Adobe website. It provides access to a library of ActionScript classes that can be used to create applications. Each class relates to an MXML tag, and you can add tags to work with these classes, directly address them in ActionScript 3.0, or use a combination of the two approaches.

Flex Builder 2 is a commercial development environment specifically created for writing MXML and ActionScript 3.0. It is based on Eclipse, an open source development environment. Flex Builder 2 provides features such as code hinting and completion so that you can easily add and configure user interface components and nonvisual elements like data connections and data bindings. You can download a free 30-day trial of this software from the Adobe website.

While Flex Builder may make creating Flex applications easier, it is by no means the only way to do so. Because MXML is a vocabulary of XML, you can write it using other tools, even text editors. You can also write ActionScript 3.0 in the same way. The Flex SDK comes with a command-line compiler that allows you to create SWF files without installing Flex Builder. You'll see how to work with the compiler in the section "Compiling SWF files from the command line" at the end of the chapter.

Another component in the Flex framework is Flex Data Services, which allows applications to connect with server-side data. FDS is a J2EE application that extends the way Flex applications work with data, and it is available as a separate download from the Adobe website.

The final part of the Flex framework is Flex Charting, which adds charting capabilities to Flex applications. Again, it is available as a discrete download that is purchased separately. Flex Charting adds access to a range of charting components that developers can easily customize.

This chapter focuses on Flex Builder 2, the commercial software package that allows you to build Flex applications. If you already have Eclipse, you can install Flex Builder as a plug-in. Otherwise, you can install both Eclipse and Flex Builder at the same time in a custom package. I'll focus on the second option here and guide you through the installation process as well as take you through a simple Flex project.

This chapter is designed to give you a grounding in Flex 2 so you can get started with working with it. For a more thorough treatment of the topic, check out The Essential Guide to Flex 2 with ActionScript 3.0 *by Charles E. Brown (friends of ED, 2007).*

Working with Flex Builder 2

If you're used to working with Flash, you'll find it a big change to create applications using Flex Builder 2. There is no timeline, no keyframes, and no library. The process of creating applications focuses on building interfaces that respond to user interactions. Developers can do this using MXML, ActionScript, or a combination of the two. You can work visually in Design view and drag and drop components onto a work area. You can also work directly with MXML tags and ActionScript 3.0 in Source view.

When working with Flex Builder, you can work with different file types and projects. For example, Flex Builder allows you to create Flex projects as well as pure ActionScript projects. In addition to editing MXML and AS files, you can also use Flex Builder as a text editor for working with file types such as XML and CSS. In this chapter, I want to focus on creating a Flex project.

Flex Builder automatically compiles projects into SWF files and generates the relevant HTML document as well. The first time you run the application and each time you save, Flex Builder generates the SWF files for you. If you're not working in Flex Builder 2, you can use the command-line compiler to carry out this task.

Let's start by downloading and setting up Flex Builder 2.

Downloading Flex Builder 2

You can download a trial version of Flex Builder 2, as well as any of the other components of the Flex framework, from `www.adobe.com/products/flex`. Trial versions are valid for 30 days for evaluation purposes. You'll need to log in with your Adobe ID or register at the site before you can start the download.

You'll have a choice between downloading the stand-alone Flex Builder 2 package that includes Eclipse and downloading just the Flex Builder 2 Eclipse plug-in. You can choose the second option if you already have Eclipse installed, but in some instances you may want to keep Flex Builder separate from your other development tools and choose the full package installation anyway.

You can choose either the PC or Macintosh version of the software as well as the English or Japanese version. The English PC download version was 168.78MB at the time of this writing. In the next section, I cover how to install the stand-alone installation version of Flex Builder 2 for Windows.

Installing Flex Builder 2 Windows version

After you've downloaded the Flex Builder Windows installer, double-click it and you'll be prompted for a save location for the temporary installer files as shown in Figure 7-1.

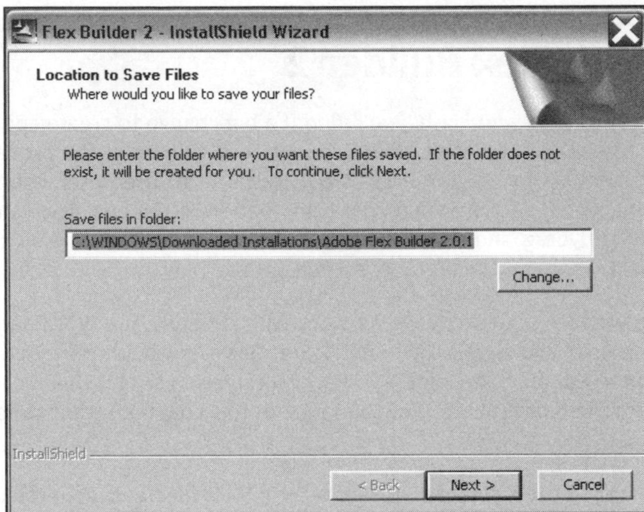

Figure 7-1. The installer prompts for the temporary file location.

The installer will then extract the temporary files to this location. During this process, you'll see the window shown in Figure 7-2. If you have a slow computer, the process can take a little while.

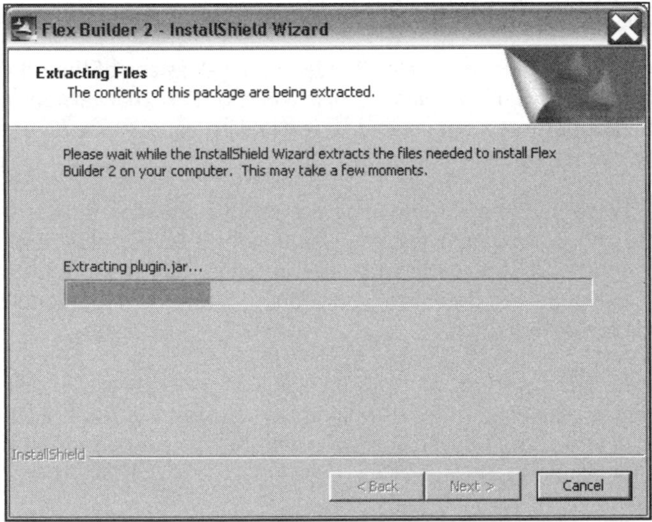

Figure 7-2. The installer extracts temporary files.

You'll then be prompted to choose either the full installation of Flex Builder 2 or the plug-in for Eclipse. You may want to choose the second option if you've already installed Eclipse on your computer. Figure 7-3 shows the prompt.

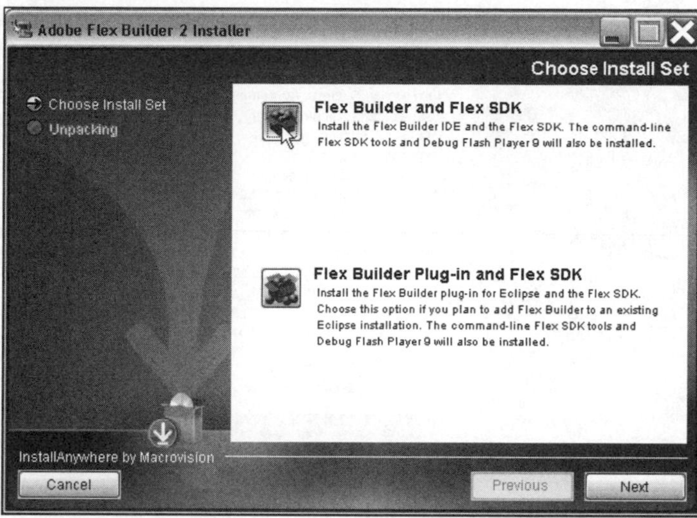

Figure 7-3. Choosing the installation set

In this case, I've chosen the full install as I don't already have Eclipse on my computer. Once you've made your selection, click the Next button. The unpacking process will then begin, after which installation starts.

Figure 7-4 shows the start of the installation process.

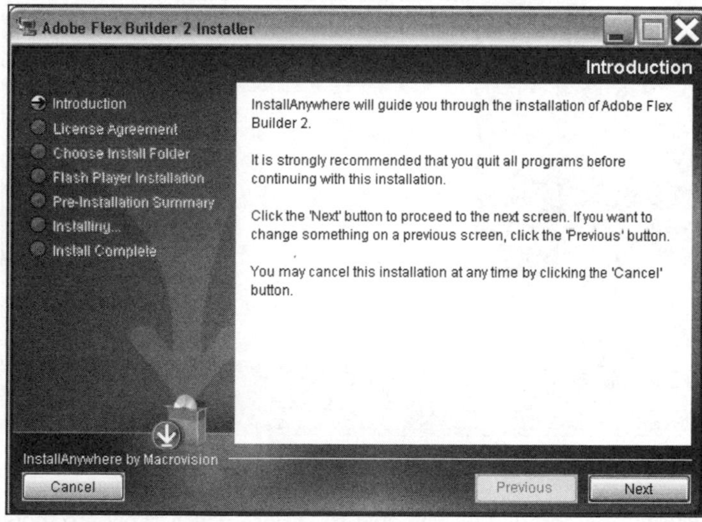

Figure 7-4. Introducing the installation process

At this point, you need to click Next, accept the license agreement shown in Figure 7-5, and click Next again.

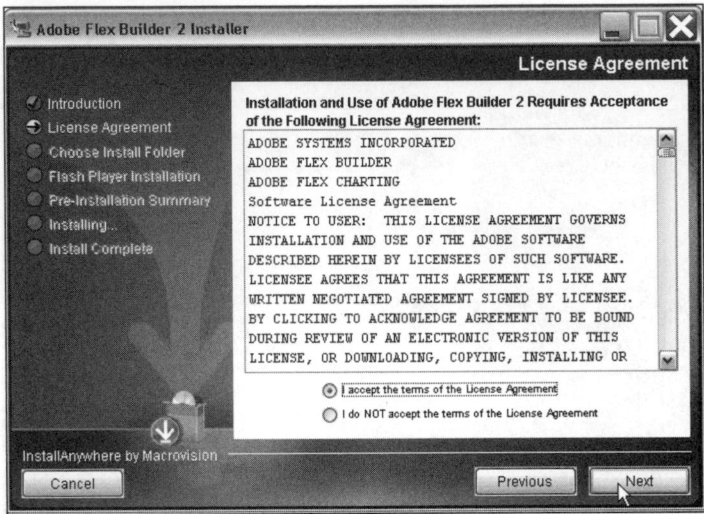

Figure 7-5. Accepting the license agreement

The installer will then prompt you for the install location. Figure 7-6 shows the default stand-alone location for Windows. On a Macintosh computer, the installer saves the application file in the `\Applications\Adobe Flex Builder 2` folder.

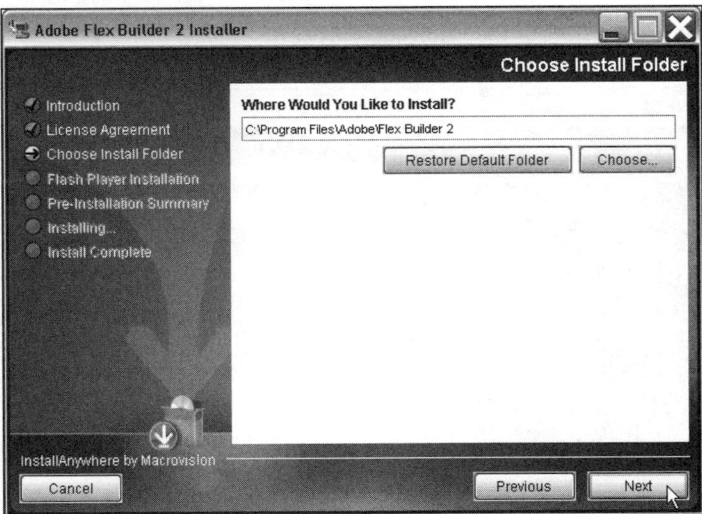

Figure 7-6. Choosing the installation location

Click the Next button and you will be able to choose which browsers should have the debug version of Flash Player 9 installed as shown in Figure 7-7. Flex developers work with a special version of Flash Player 9 that allows for debugging. It's vital that you install this version if you want to carry out debugging in your Flex applications.

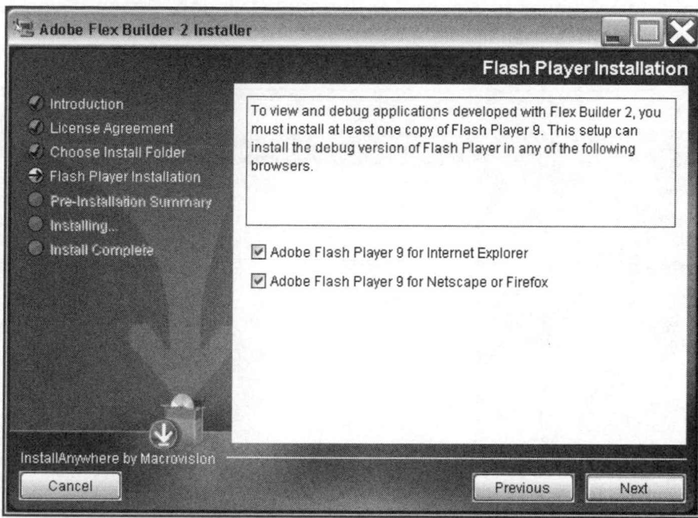

Figure 7-7. Selecting which browser will install the debug version of Flash Player 9

Make sure that the selected web browsers are closed before you proceed with the installation; otherwise, the process will halt.

Once you've made your selection, click Next. You'll have a chance to review the installation options as shown in Figure 7-8.

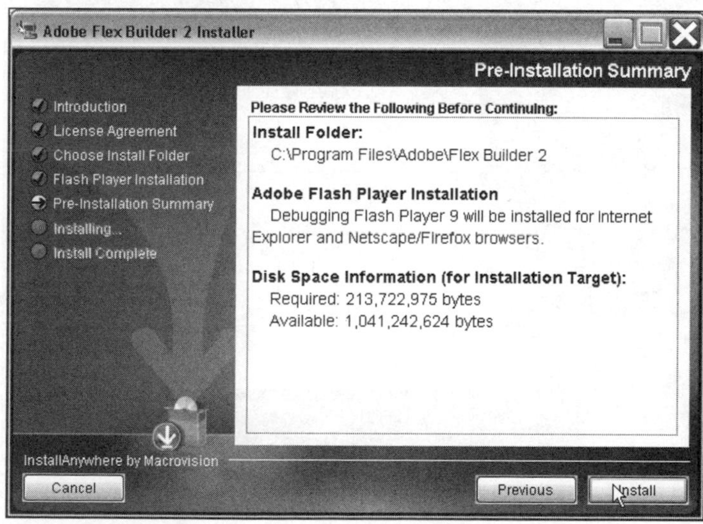

Figure 7-8. The installation options summary

If anything is incorrect at this point, click the Previous button to return to an earlier step in the process. You can proceed with the installation by clicking Install.

You'll see something similar to Figure 7-9 during installation. Again, if you have a slow computer, this process can take quite a while.

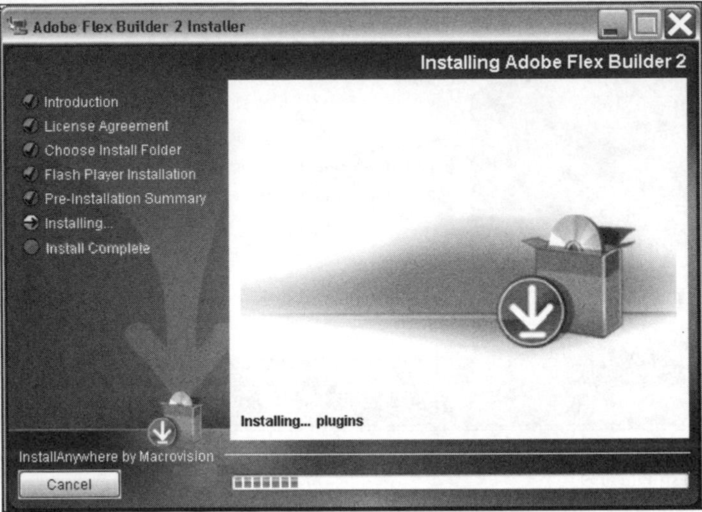

Figure 7-9. The installation process

Once the installation is complete, you'll see a window similar to that shown in Figure 7-10.

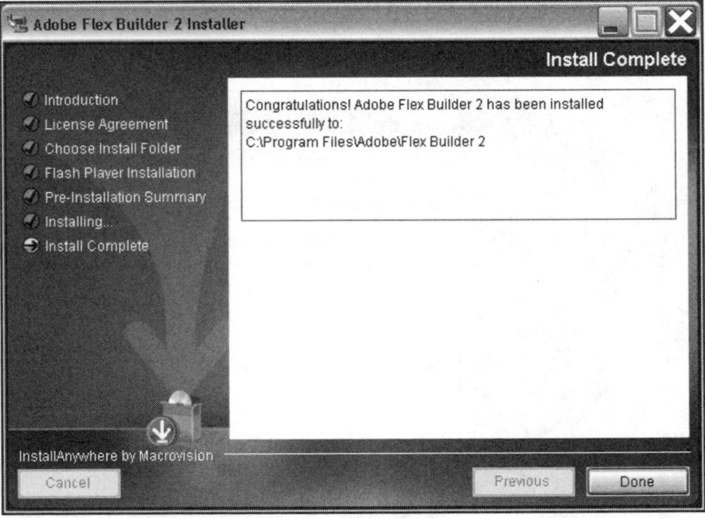

Figure 7-10. Installation is complete.

You'll then be prompted about whether you'd like to see installation instructions for ColdFusion Extensions as shown in Figure 7-11.

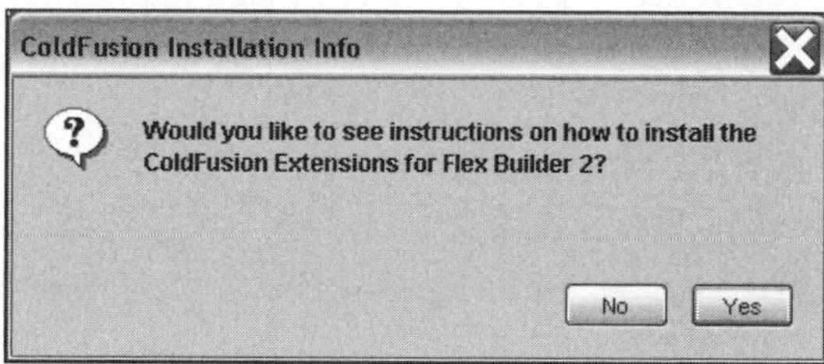

Figure 7-11. Prompting for ColdFusion Extensions installation instructions

If you click Yes at this prompt, the installer will open a folder containing the extensions and instructions for their installation. You can follow these instructions if you plan on using ColdFusion with Flex Builder, but I won't go through them here.

Your installation is complete, and you're ready to start working with Flex Builder 2.

Starting Flex Builder 2

When you start Flex Builder for the first time, the software will prompt you to enter your Flex Builder 2 serial number as shown in Figure 7-12. You'll see this prompt for the duration of the 30-day trial period.

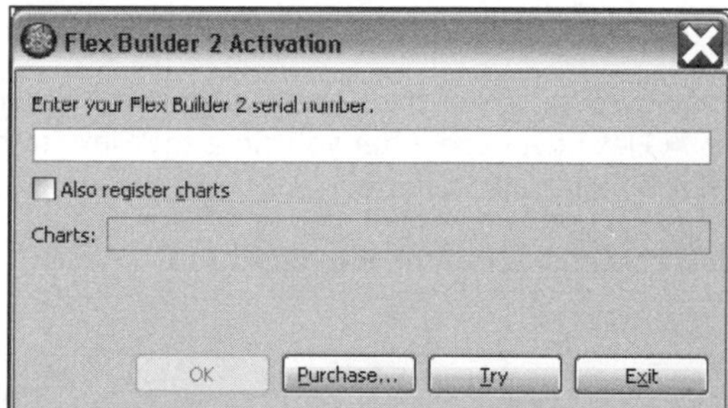

Figure 7-12. Flex Builder 2 will prompt for a serial number.

If you have purchased Flex Builder 2, enter the serial number and click OK. You can also click Purchase to buy a copy of Flex Builder 2 online; otherwise, click the Try button to evaluate the Flex Builder 2 software for 30 days.

Once you've chosen your option, you'll see the Flex Builder interface (see Figure 7-13).

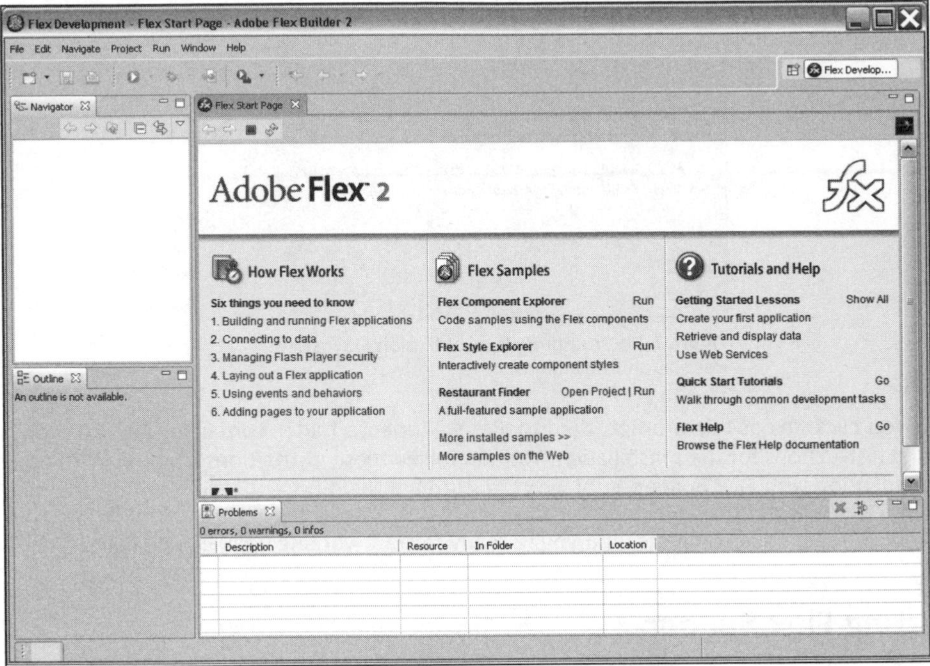

Figure 7-13. The Flex Start Page

When you first open Flex Builder 2, you'll see the Flex Start Page, which allows you to choose from a range of options. As you can see from Figure 7-13, these options include tutorials and sample applications, and these can be a great guide to getting started.

Close the Flex Start Page by clicking the cross on the page tab. You can return to it at any time by choosing Help ➤ Flex Start Page. After you close the Flex Start Page, the real work begins and you can start building applications.

In the next section, you'll take a tour of the interface.

Understanding the Flex Builder 2 interface

Figure 7-14 shows the Flex Builder 2 interface before you've done any work. The screen will look busier after you've created an application.

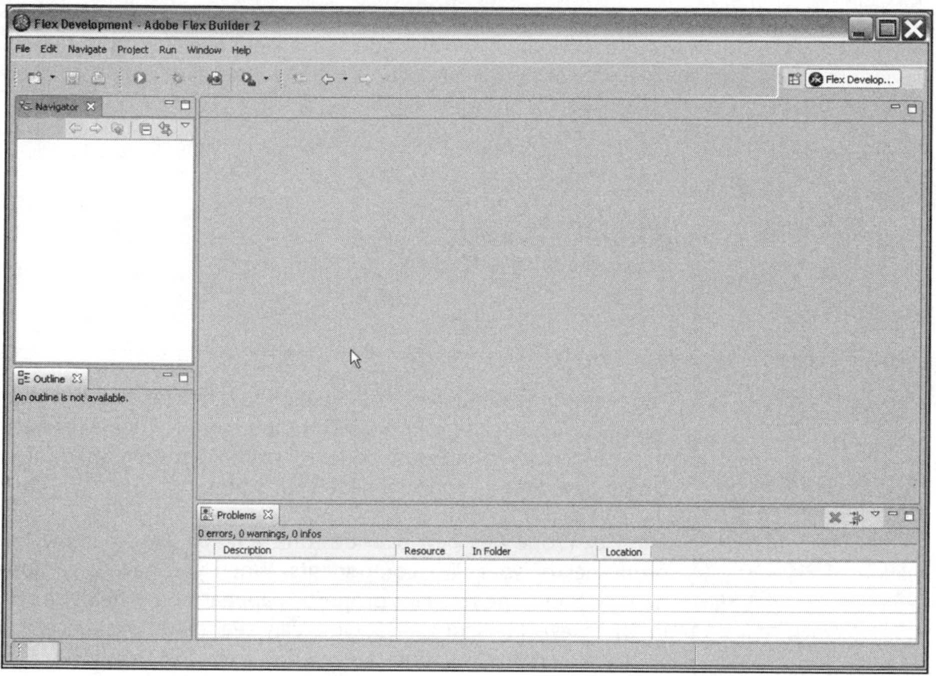

Figure 7-14. The Flex Builder 2 interface

To start, you can see a menu bar across the top with a toolbar underneath. On the left, there is the Navigator or Project Navigator view, which shows all the files and folders in your applications. At the moment, nothing appears there, but the view will fill up as soon as we get to work.

At the bottom left, you can see the Outline view. This area displays the structure of your application components. It will list the script elements, any containers, and other user interface controls that are present in the selected file.

The blank area in the middle will house your documents. These may be MXML, ActionScript, or other document types. If you have multiple documents open, you'll see one tab for each.

At the top right, you can see the Perspective bar. This bar allows you to switch between different perspectives of the current application. For example, while developing, you may be working in the Flex Development perspective, but this will change to the Flex Debugging perspective when you start to debug your applications. Flex Builder normally manages these perspectives for you, but you can use the Perspective bar to change them manually. You can also create your own custom perspectives.

At the bottom of the screen, you'll see the Problems view. This view is very useful as it displays errors and warnings about your current application. Keep an eye on this area of the screen as you build your application.

You'll be able to interact with your application files in two ways: Source view and Design view. Source view allows you to work directly with code, while Design view provides visual development options. As you work in Design view, you'll see the States and Flex Properties views on the right side of the screen as shown in Figure 7-15.

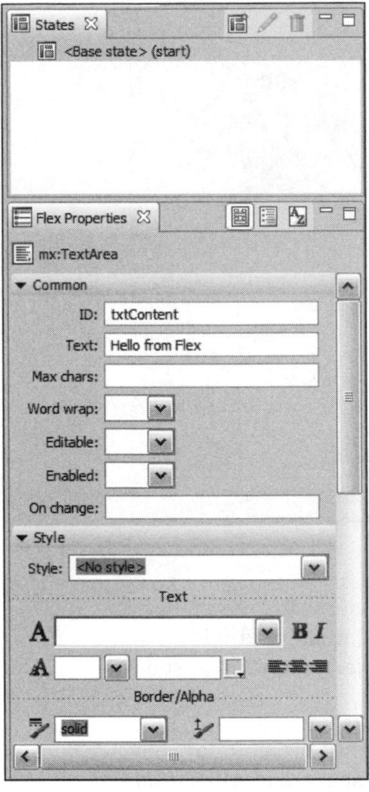

Figure 7-15.
Views available when working in Design view of an application

The States view allows you to manage the different states in your application. You can include different interface elements for each state and use ActionScript code to switch between them. The States view allows you to manage your states.

The Flex Properties view provides one way for you to define the properties of your Flex components. When you have a component selected, the relevant properties appear in the fields shown in this view. In Figure 7-15, you can see that I've selected a `TextArea` control as the panel shows mx:TextArea. The Flex Properties view shows that I've set the ID and Text values for this control.

Flex Builder includes other views that can help with debugging: Breakpoints, Console, Debug, Expressions, and Variables. You can display these views by choosing them from the Window menu. The views will display automatically when you start debugging, and you can find out more about this topic in the section "Debugging applications" later in the chapter.

Getting started with Flex Builder 2

Before we build our first Flex application, it's important to understand the structure of a Flex application.

Working with controls

Flex allows you to describe a user interface using controls. In Model-View-Controller application architecture, these elements represent the View. In Flex Builder, controls are added either declaratively by writing MXML tags in Source view or by dragging them into the application area in Design view. Developers can also write classes that add controls programmatically.

Controls can be divided into user interface components and containers. User interface components allow users to interact with the application. These components consist of standard user interface elements like buttons, text input boxes, and combo boxes. Flex includes other user interface controls with additional functionality like the `NumericStepper`, `ProgressBar`, and `RichTextEditor`. In addition, Flex Builder 2 includes a range of navigation controls to simplify the process of navigating through an application. If you have installed Flex Charting 2, you'll also have access to a range of chart components.

Containers are components that encompass user interface controls and other container elements. Containers visually organize the other components in the application. The advantage of containers is that they can group and position other components.

There are also a number of nonvisual elements within the Flex framework that developers can add to a Flex application. These include items like data models, connections to information stored on a web server, and data bindings.

Now that you understand how Flex applications are built, let's get started by creating a simple application.

Building a Flex application

When you build Flex applications, you'll usually work through the following steps:

1. Create a project for the application including the main application file.
2. Insert the controls for the user interface, either by dragging them in Design view or by adding MXML tags in Source view.
3. Add ActionScript code that responds to user interactions.
4. Optionally add data connections.
5. Run the application to compile a SWF and HTML file for the application.

So that you can learn how to use Flex Builder 2, we'll create a basic Flex application: a simple calculator that determines how many calories are burned through various types of exercise. The calculator will allow you to work with different types of controls and to see some simple ActionScript. It won't use data from any external sources.

Creating a Flex project

The starting point for your application is to create a project. Each project normally contains a single MXML application file that corresponds to the application interface. There may be a range of supporting files for the application, including ActionScript classes, XML, CSS, and custom component MXML files.

To create a project, choose File ➤ New ➤ Flex Project from the top menu. As you can see in Figure 7-16, you can choose from a number of different file and project types. In this example, we'll create a Flex Project, so choose this option.

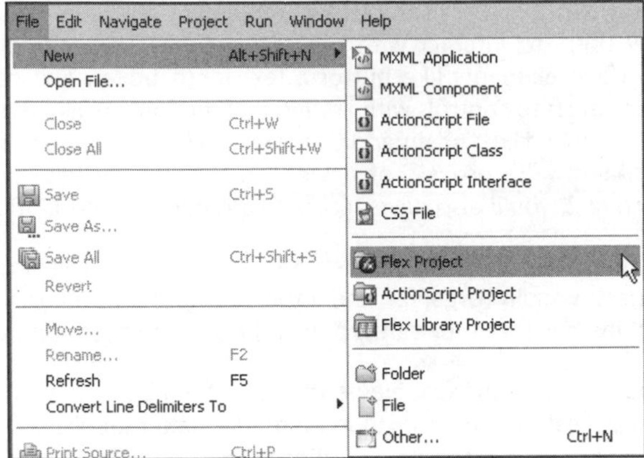

Figure 7-16. The options available in the File ➤ New menu

Once you've chosen the Flex Project option, you need to specify how the application will access data as shown in Figure 7-17.

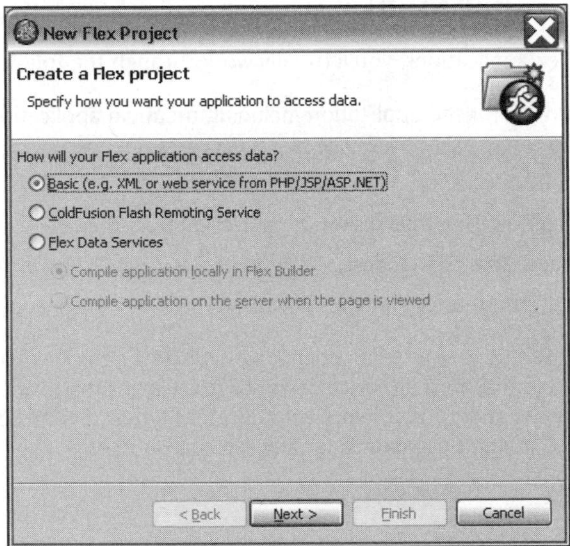

Figure 7-17. Specifying how the application will access data

If you want to create a client-side application that doesn't access remote data, or you want to make only simple calls to remote procedures, you'll choose the first option. You can take advantage of ColdFusion Flash Remoting if you have installed the ColdFusion Extensions. If you have installed Flex Data Services, you can choose that option. In our case, because we're creating a very simple client-side application, we'll leave the first option selected and click Next.

The next step is to specify a name for the application as well as its location. The default location for project folders is C:\Documents and Settings\<username>\My Documents\Flex Builder 2 for Windows-based computers. For Macintosh computers, the default location is /Users/<username>/Documents/FlexBuilder. In this example, we'll leave the default option selected, although you could uncheck the option and click Browse to select an alternative location.

Enter the name CalorieCalculator and click Next as shown in Figure 7-18.

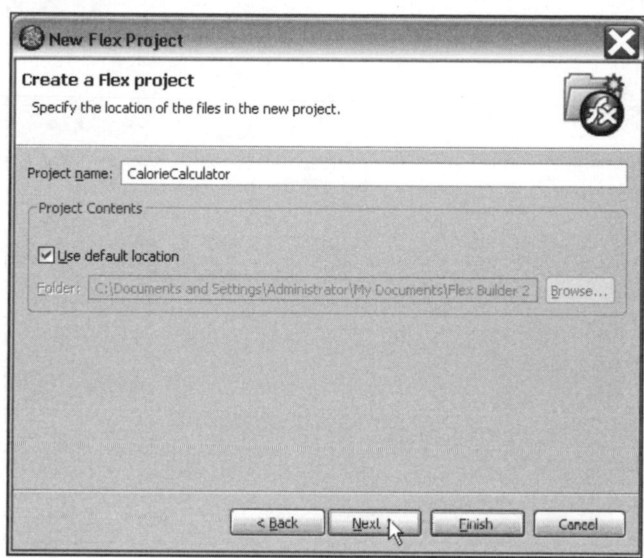

Figure 7-18. Specifying a name and location for the project

You could have clicked Finish at this point, but it's worth looking at the last option in the creation process, so click Next instead. Figure 7-19 shows this option.

The last step allows you to choose additional options like adding folder references from different locations and changing the name of the main application file. You'll notice that this file, by default, takes its name from the name of the project. You can also specify an alternative output folder. By default, all compiled SWF files will appear in the bin folder of your application folder. Finally, you can use this step to add references to external packages, classes, and libraries compiled as SWC files.

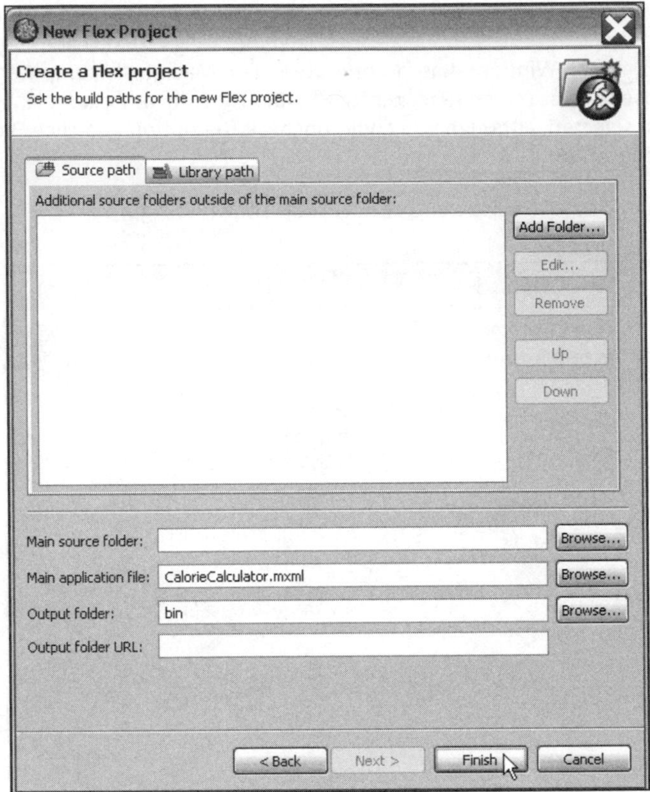

Figure 7-19. Additional project options

Click Finish to create the project. You'll see the Navigator view update with the project folders as shown in Figure 7-20. The `bin` folder will store all compiled files and their supporting HTML documents. These files include any created debug SWF files. The `html-template` folder contains the HTML templates used in the application. You'll also see the starting structure of the MXML tags in the `CalorieCalculator.mxml` file.

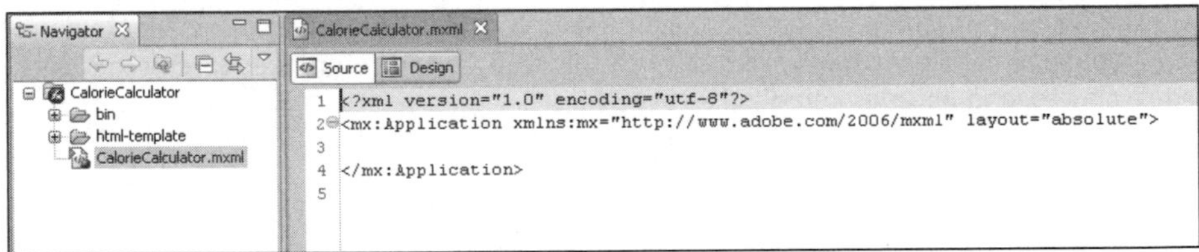

Figure 7-20. The calorie calculator application

Before we move on, you'll need to understand the structure of MXML files a little better, so let's take a look at that next.

Understanding MXML files

MXML is a vocabulary of XML, so it follows all of the same construction rules. I've summarized these rules as follows:

- The document must contain one or more elements.
- The document must contain a single root element that may contain other nested elements.
- Each element must close properly.
- Elements must nest correctly.
- Attribute values must be contained in quotes, either single or double.

An MXML application document must contain at least one element, usually the root element, `<mx:Application>`. This element surrounds all other content in the document except for the XML declaration, which must appear on the first line of the application file. Other types of MXML files, such as custom components, may use other MXML tags as their root element. The root element corresponds to the base class for the MXML document.

You'll notice that all MXML tags start with the prefix `mx:`. The root element of the file contains an XML namespace declaration that specifies that all Adobe tags must be prefixed by `mx:`.


```
<mx:Application xmlns:mx=http://www.adobe.com/2006/mxml ➥
layout="absolute">
```

You can use this tag to specify other namespaces, for example, those that correspond with custom components that you create.

Each MXML tag has a range of attributes that correspond to the properties, methods, and events of the associated class. The preceding `<mx:Application>` tag contains the `layout` attribute with a value of `absolute`. If you're typing the tag declaratively, a list of relevant members will pop up as you type. Figure 7-21 shows this list. If it fails to appear, backspace and type a space within the element, and you should see the pop-up list. You can also press Ctrl+spacebar to bring up this list.

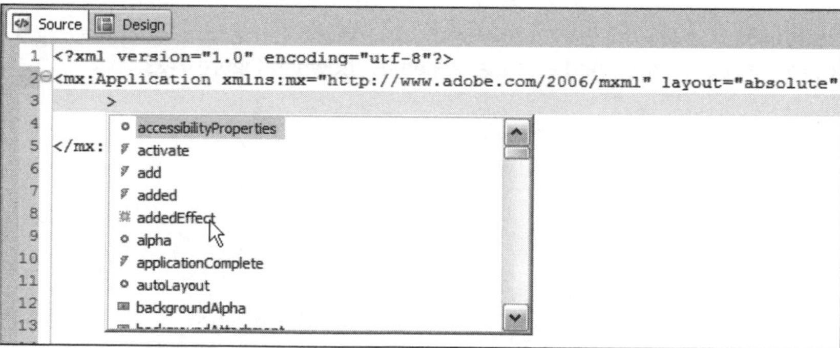

Figure 7-21. Displaying a list of class members in the Source pane

You can also set many of these values in Design view by entering values in the fields in the Flex Properties view.

You need to compile the MXML file to generate the SWF file and corresponding HTML document. You can compile it by either running the application from within Flex Builder 2 or using the Flex compiler from the command prompt. You'll see how to do this a little later in the chapter in the section called "Compiling SWF files from the command line."

Creating the interface

The interface in a Flex application is made up of a series of controls. Within the Flex Builder interface, you can either drag a control onto the application in Design view or add it by writing the appropriate MXML language declaratively in Source view. In the next section, you'll see both methods as we build the application interface. As an aside, you can also create the interface by writing ActionScript 3.0. For simplicity, we'll focus on the first two approaches.

Adding controls to the application

Now that we've created the application file, we'll add some controls. All controls must appear between the opening and closing `<mx:Application>` tags. We'll start by adding the controls visually. Click the Design button to switch to Design view. Figure 7-22 shows this button.

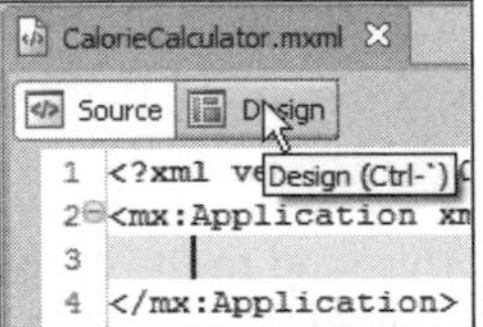

Figure 7-22.
Clicking the Design button

We'll place the user interface controls into a `Panel` container control. It is useful to group controls together in a single container so you control overall positioning easily. Some container controls such as the `HBox` and `VBox` also handle automatic layout of their child controls.

Open the `Layout` folder in the Components view at the left of the screen. Drag a `Panel` control to the area in the middle of the screen as shown in Figure 7-23.

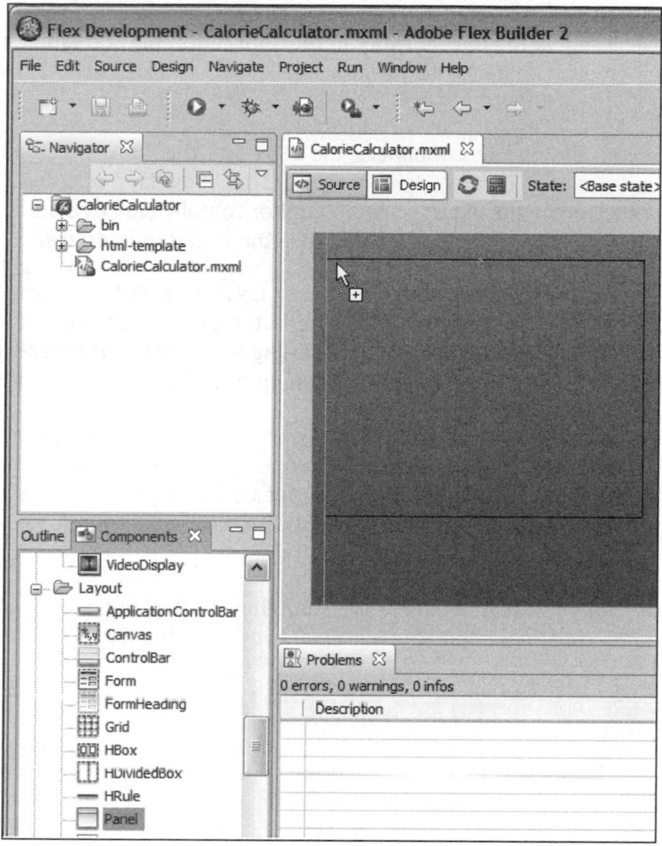

Figure 7-23. Dragging a Panel control into the application

In the Flex Properties view at the right of the workspace, enter the title Calorie Calculator. You should see these words appear at the top of the Panel control. Switch back to Source view and the code will have been updated to something similar to the following:

```
<?xml version="1.0" encoding="utf-8"?>
<mx:Application xmlns:mx="http://www.adobe.com/2006/mxml"
  layout="absolute">
  <mx:Panel x="10" y="10" width="250" height="200" layout="absolute"
    title="Calorie Calculator">
  </mx:Panel>
</mx:Application>
```

You can see that Flex Builder has created the <mx:Panel> tag and that it has generated values for the x, y, width, height, layout, and title attributes. The x and y positions in your <mx:Panel> tag may be a little different from mine.

We have just added a control by dragging in Design view. We can also add components in Source view by clicking at the relevant spot in the application file and typing the tag name. We'll use some layout containers to position the other controls, and we'll add these in Source view.

Flex includes two useful layout containers, the VBox and the HBox, which allow for automatic positioning of the controls within them. The VBox lays out controls vertically beneath each other, while the HBox lays them out horizontally, side by side. It's common to nest these containers inside each other to achieve the required interface.

Click between the opening and closing `<mx:Panel>` tags and start typing <mx:VBox or even just <Vbox. Once you see the tag name selected in the pop-up list, you can press the Tab or Enter key to add it into your file. Enter a closing > character. We'll add an HBox container inside the VBox, so click between the opening and closing tags and start typing.

Add an `<mx:Label` to the HBox and, once you've added the tag name, press the spacebar and start typing text. Again, you can select the property from the list with either the mouse or by pressing the Tab or Enter key when it appears highlighted. Enter the text Weight between the quotes. Type the attribute width and enter a value of 100. Type /> to close the tag.

If you switch to Design view, you should see something similar to Figure 7-24. Notice that the VBox and HBox containers don't appear unless you click them.

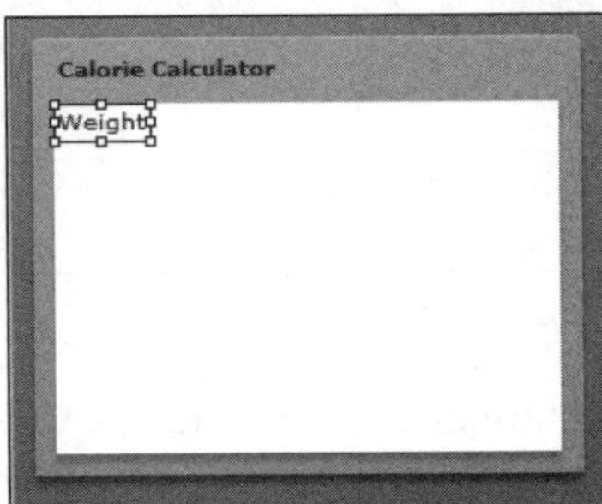

Figure 7-24.
The application interface

The `Label` control appears to the left of the panel and contains the word Weight. You can change any of the style properties of the `Label` control in the Flex Properties panel. For example, you may wish to add bolding to the text. You can also change the properties in Source view.

Add a `TextInput` control next to the Weight label, inside the HBox control. If you switch to Design view, you'll notice that the control appears next to the label.

In either Design or Source view, add another HBox below the first and add a second `Label` control with the text Exercise type and a width of 100, and a ComboBox control. In Design view, you'll see that the HBox containers are stacked on top of each other within the VBox. Add a third HBox container with a `Label` control that is 100 wide showing the word Duration and a `TextInput`.

Add a fourth HBox container and add an <mx:Spacer> tag with a width of 200. Spacers are useful to add space in an application. Place two radio buttons next to the spacer and give them the labels Pounds and Kilograms respectively by entering the text into the Flex Properties view. Use this view to give the radio buttons the same group name, rdoWeight, and set the Pounds radio button to be selected. Enter rdoPounds as the ID for this radio button and add the ID of rdoKilograms for the other.

Finish the interface by adding a button that shows the text Calculate underneath the last HBox, but inside the VBox. Add another spacer above the first HBox inside the VBox with a height of 10. You may need to resize the Panel control and rearrange the other controls so that everything fits properly. Figure 7-25 shows my finished interface. Notice that I've made the text in the labels appear in bold.

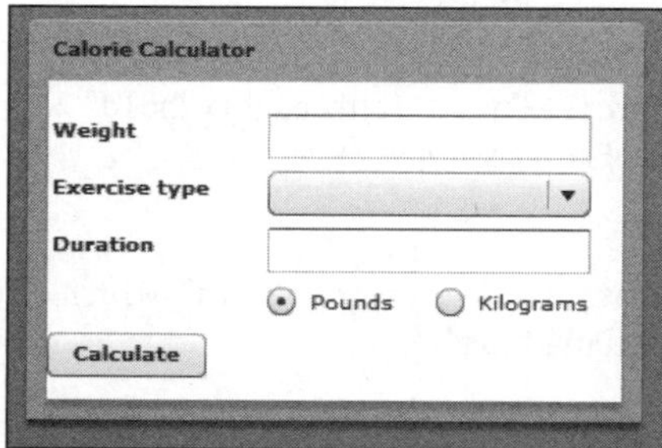

Figure 7-25.
The finished interface

I created this interface using a combination of HBox and VBox containers to control the flow of elements in the interface. Maybe you'd like to experiment with using these containers to change the layout of the interface.

Adding ID attributes

We'll need to address the TextInput, ComboBox, and RadioButton controls programmatically, so they'll need to have a value entered for their ID attributes. Enter the ID values shown in Table 7-1 in the Flex Properties view.

Table 7-1. The ID attributes for the user interface controls

Control	ID
First TextInput (next to Weight)	tiWeight
ComboBox component	cboExerciseType
Second TextInput (next to Duration)	tiDuration

Switch to Source view, and the MXML code to create the application interface should look similar to the following:

```
<?xml version="1.0" encoding="utf-8"?>
<mx:Application xmlns:mx="http://www.adobe.com/2006/mxml"
  layout="absolute">
  <mx:Panel x="10" y="10" width="304" height="197" layout="absolute"
    title="Calorie Calculator" id="panel1">
    <mx:VBox>
      <mx:Spacer height="10"/>
      <mx:HBox>
        <mx:Label text="Weight" fontWeight="bold" width="100"/>
        <mx:TextInput id="tiWeight"/>
      </mx:HBox>
      <mx:HBox>
        <mx:Label text="Exercise type" fontWeight="bold" width="100"/>
        <mx:ComboBox id="cboExerciseType"/>
      </mx:HBox>
      <mx:HBox>
        <mx:Label text="Duration" fontWeight="bold" width="100"/>
        <mx:TextInput id="tiDuration"/>
      </mx:HBox>
      <mx:HBox>
        <mx:Spacer width="100"/>
        <mx:RadioButton label="Pounds" groupName="rdoWeight"
          selected="true" id="rdoPounds"/>
        <mx:RadioButton label="Kilograms" groupName="rdoWeight"
          id="rdoKilograms"/>
      </mx:HBox>
      <mx:Button label="Calculate"/>
    </mx:VBox>
    </mx:Panel>
</mx:Application>
```

Don't worry if your placement attributes on the Panel control have different values from the ones shown here. Incidentally, I could have made this application a little more robust by restricting the type of entries possible in each of the TextInput controls. However, the purpose here is simply to get you started. You'll learn more about these topics later in the book.

Now we need to populate the ComboBox control. We could do this by loading external data but, for simplicity, we'll add some ActionScript to handle the population of the control.

Populating the ComboBox

We can populate the ComboBox control using the dataProvider property. We'll write ActionScript that creates an array of objects with label and data properties. We could also do this by adding an MXML <mx:dataProvider> tag containing the data in an <mx:Array> or <mx:ArrayCollection> element.

Start by adding an <mx:Script> tag immediately below the <mx:Application> tag. When you've finished, you'll notice that the script block is written in the following way:

```
<mx:Script>
  <![CDATA[

  ]]>
</mx:Script>
```

You need to enter ActionScript statements as blocks of CDATA so that Flex doesn't interpret them as MXML code. This approach is the same one used by developers when adding JavaScript to a strict XHTML document.

Add the following private function to the CDATA block:

```
private function populateCombo(e:FlexEvent):void {
  var dp:Array = new Array();
  dp.push({label:"Choose exercise...",data:0});
  dp.push({label:"Aerobics (high impact)",data:0.07142});
  dp.push({label:"Aerobics (low impact)",data:0.0333});
  dp.push({label:"Basketball",data:0.0779});
  dp.push({label:"Cycling",data:0.0779});
  dp.push({label:"Jogging (slow)",data:0.0666});
  dp.push({label:"Jogging (moderate)",data:0.0974});
  dp.push({label:"Jogging (fast)",data:0.1});
  dp.push({label:"Soccer",data:0.07142});
  dp.push({label:"Swimming (moderate)",data:0.05844});
  dp.push({label:"Tennis",data:0.06666});
  dp.push({label:"Walking (brisk)",data:0.0666});
  cboExerciseType.dataProvider = dp;
}
```

This function creates a new array called dp and populates it with objects containing label and data properties. The last line sets the dataProvider property for the ComboBox to the array.

The label property will display in the ComboBox control. The data property indicates the number of calories burned per pound of weight for each minute of the exercise. I can't vouch for the accuracy of the figures, but at least they give us something to use in our calculations.

You'll also need to include the relevant import statement as we have a reference here to the passed FlexEvent without the fully qualified path. Add the following statement below your opening CDATA declaration:

```
import mx.events.FlexEvent;
```

We need to populate the ComboBox after the application interface has been created. We can do this by setting the creationComplete attribute in the <mx:Application> tag as shown in bold. It's a bit like using the onload handler in the <body> tag to call a JavaScript function in a web page.

7

```
<mx:Application xmlns:mx="http://www.adobe.com/2006/mxml"
  layout="absolute" creationComplete="populateCombo(event)">
```

Note that the values won't appear in the ComboBox control until we compile the application, so don't switch to Design view and expect them to appear. We'll run the application shortly.

We still need to add a handler to the Calculate button and change the interface to display the number of calories burned. While we're at it, we may as well display the kilojoules. We'll handle the interface change by creating another state in the application. This state will be the same as the initial state, but it will show the calculated values in an extra Label control.

Creating a new application state

Switch to Design view, and you'll see the States view at the top right of the workspace. It shows one state, the Base state. The word start indicates that this is the initial state for the application. Click the New State button to create a second state in the application as shown in Figure 7-26.

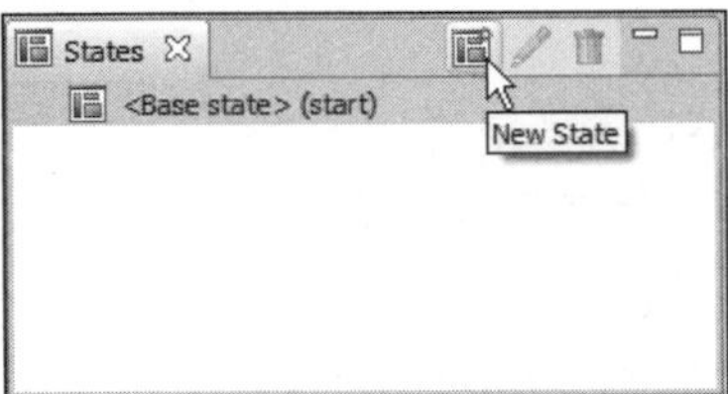

Figure 7-26.
The New State button in the States panel

Create a state called results based on the Base state as shown in Figure 7-27.

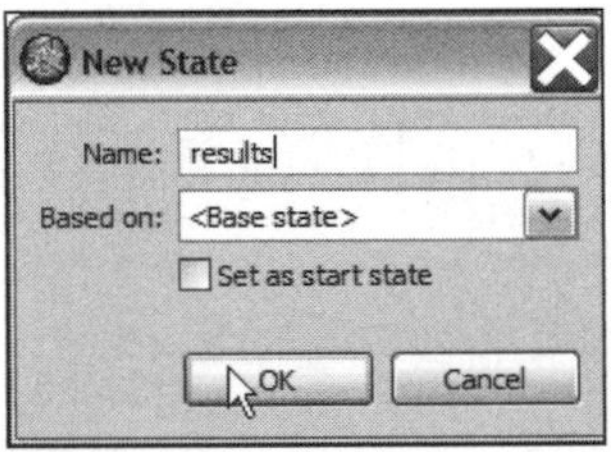

Figure 7-27.
Creating the new application state

When you click OK, you should see the results state selected in the States view. The interface will look unchanged.

Drag a Label control underneath the button, inside the VBox, and expand it to the width of the Panel control. You should be able to toggle between the two states in the States panel to see the change in the interface. Give the Label control an ID of lblResults and remove the text. You may also want to make it wider.

If you switch to Source view, you'll see the following added MXML tags underneath the <mx:Application> tag:

```
<mx:states>
  <mx:State name="results">
    <mx:AddChild relativeTo="{vbox1}" position="lastChild">
      <mx:Label id="lblResults" width="270"/>
    </mx:AddChild>
  </mx:State>
</mx:states>
```

The `<mx:states>` tag contains the additional states for the application, and each state is in an `<mx:State>` tag. Notice that the `<mx:states>` tag starts with a lowercase letter in the word `states` unlike the other tags. Flex changes the interface by using the `<mx:AddChild>` tag to create a new `<mx:Label>` control relative to the `VBox`, which it has given the ID `vbox1`.

Performing the calculation

We'll set up the Calculate button so that when a user clicks it, the application performs the calculation and changes states, displaying the results in the new `Label` control. Add a `click` handler to the button in Source view as shown in bold in the following code:

```
<mx:Button label="Calculate"
  click="getCalories(event)"/>
```


When users click the button, they'll call the `getCalories()` function.

Save the application now, and you should see an error in the Problems view at the bottom of the screen. Figure 7-28 shows the error.

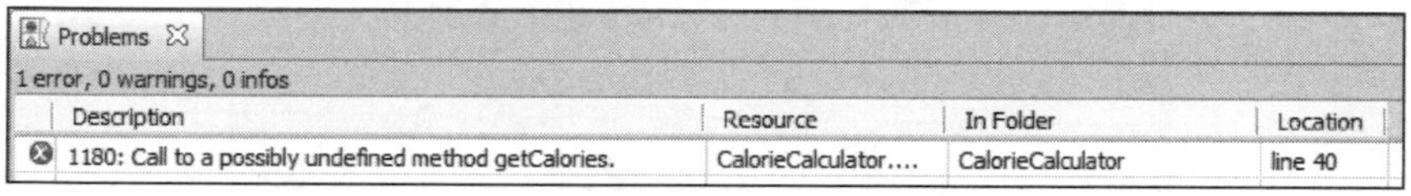

Problems

1 error, 0 warnings, 0 infos

Description	Resource	In Folder	Location
1180: Call to a possibly undefined method getCalories.	CalorieCalculator....	CalorieCalculator	line 40

Figure 7-28. An error in the Problems panel

It's worthwhile keeping an eye on this view each time you save your application, as it will display error and warning messages. In this case, the error occurs because we haven't yet created the function `getCalories()`. We'll do this now.

Add the following function inside the CDATA section. For simplicity, I haven't dealt with validation of the `TextInput` or `ComboBox` entries.

```
private function getCalories(e:MouseEvent):void {
  var calsBurned:Number = Number(cboExerciseType.value);
  var kjBurned:Number;
  var duration:Number = Number(tiDuration.text);
  var weightLBS:Number;
  if (rdoKilograms.selected == true) {
    weightLBS = 2.2 * Number(tiWeight.text);
  }
  else {
```

```
        weightLBS = Number(tiWeight.text);
      }
      calsBurned *= weightLBS * duration;
      currentState="results";
      kjBurned = calsBurned * 4.2;
      lblResults.text = "You burned " + String(Math.floor(calsBurned)) +➥
      " calories or " + String(Math.floor(kjBurned)) + " kilojoules";
    }
```

The function retrieves the values from the TextInput and ComboBox controls and carries out the relevant calculations. It determines the calories and kilojoules burned and displays the results in the lblResults control. Notice that we set the state of the application to display this control by using currentState = "results".

You'll also need to import the MouseEvent reference as we didn't use the fully qualified name. Add the following import statement:

```
import flash.events.MouseEvent;
```

You're probably itching to see this application in action now. I'll cover that next.

Running your application

You can run the application to create a SWF and HTML file. This action will display the output in a web browser. Simply click the Run button as shown in Figure 7-29.

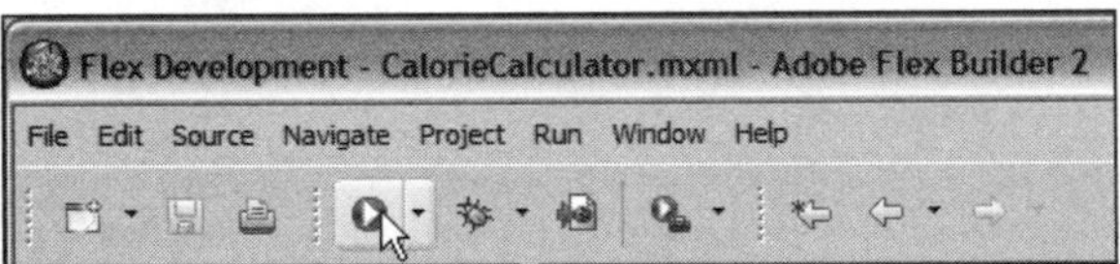

Figure 7-29. Clicking the Run button

After you've clicked the Run button, a browser window will open, showing the compiled application. Test that it works correctly by entering values in the fields. When you click the Calculate button, you should see something similar to the window shown in Figure 7-30.

Remember that there's no validation, so if you add nonnumeric values, you won't be able to perform the calculation.

We created this simple application so that I could introduce you to some of the basic features of Flex Builder 2 and so that you could see the different ways available for working with the IDE. You can find the finished CalorieCalculator.mxml file saved with the resources for this chapter. You might want to download the resources from www.friendsofed.com and compare your code. I'll show you shortly how you can import files into an existing Flex application.

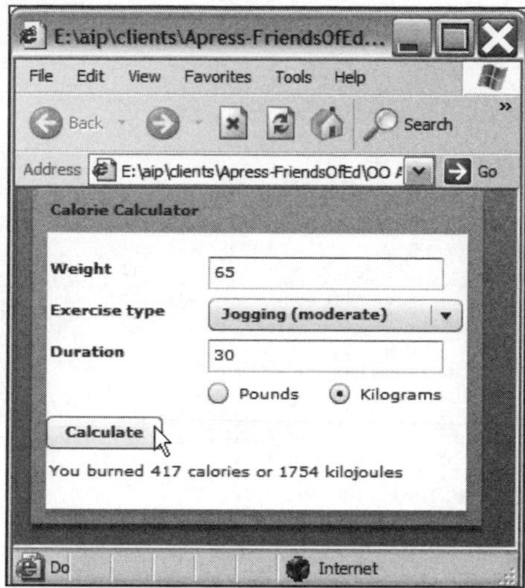

Figure 7-30. The completed application

Debugging applications

Flex Builder contains all the debugging tools that you'd expect in any development environment. You can work with breakpoints; suspend, resume, and terminate an application; step into the code; watch variables; and evaluate expressions.

Debugging occurs with the debug version of Flash Player 9, so you must make sure that this is installed before you can use these tools. If you don't have the debug version installed, download and install it from `www.adobe.com/support/flashplayer/downloads.html`. You'll need this if you want to see any output from `trace` statements, as these work a little differently in Flex Builder compared with Flash.

To debug a Flex application, you need to click the Debug button, shown in Figure 7-31, instead of Run.

Figure 7-31. Debugging an application

Clicking the Debug button runs the application in debug mode in a web browser. When the application reaches a breakpoint, Flex Builder activates the Flex Debugging perspective, which you can see in Figure 7-32. You'll be switched from the web browser back to the Flex Builder interface so you can interact with the debugger. You can also manually switch to the Flex Debugging perspective using the Perspective bar as shown in Figure 7-32.

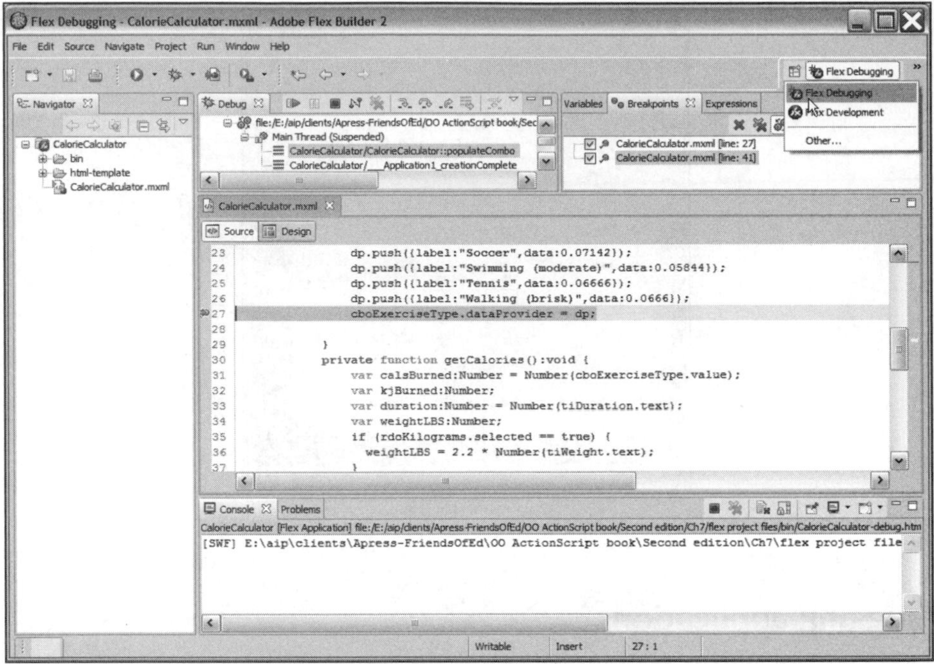

Figure 7-32. The Flex Debugging perspective

In Figure 7-32, debugging has been triggered by a breakpoint at line 27.

The Debug view at the top left of the screen allows you to manage the debugging process. Click the buttons at the top of the panel to perform debugging actions. I've listed the buttons and their actions from left to right in the following list:

- Resume: Resumes a suspended application
- Suspend: Suspends an application
- Terminate: Terminates the debugging session
- Disconnect: Disconnects the debugger when using remote debugging
- Remove All Terminated Launches: Clears all terminated debugging sessions
- Step Into: Steps into a function, stopping at the first line
- Step Over: Runs the current line of code
- Step Return: Continues running the current function
- Drop to Frame: Represents an Eclipse function not supported in Flex Builder
- Use Step Filters/Step Debug: Represents an Eclipse function not supported in Flex Builder

You can add breakpoints in Source view wherever you want the application to stop. Double-click to the left of the line number in the gray gutter on the left or right-click and choose Toggle Breakpoint. Either way, you'll see a blue dot at the appropriate point as in Figure 7-33.

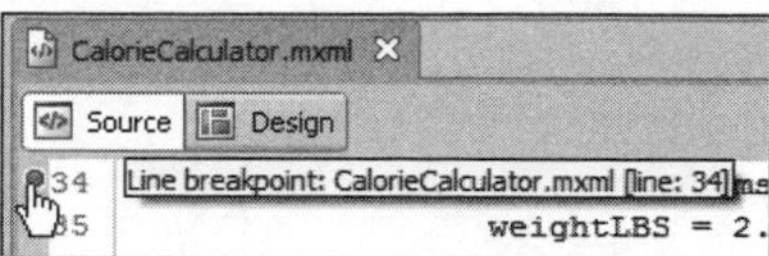

Figure 7-33. Setting a breakpoint

You can remove the breakpoint by double-clicking again or by right-clicking and choosing Toggle Breakpoint.

Breakpoints can only stop the application on one of the following conditions:

- Where there is an event handler in an MXML tag
- On a line of ActionScript in a script block
- On a line of code in an ActionScript file

You can manage breakpoints in the Breakpoints view. This view appears at the top right of the Flex Debugging perspective as shown in Figure 7-34.

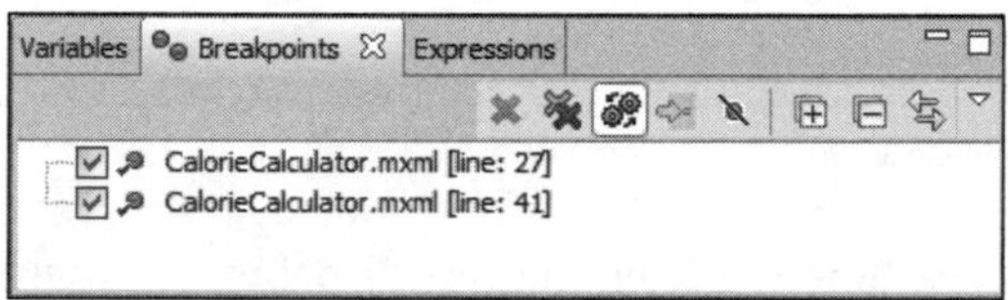

Figure 7-34. The Breakpoints panel

You can remove a single breakpoint by selecting it and clicking the cross button at the top of the panel. Clicking the button with two crosses removes all breakpoints in the file. If you want to skip a single breakpoint during debugging, uncheck the box in the window.

The Variables view, to the left of Breakpoints, allows you to watch the values of variables. Simple variables appear as a single line in the panel, while more complicated variables appear over several lines. Figure 7-35 shows the dp array variable in the Variables view.

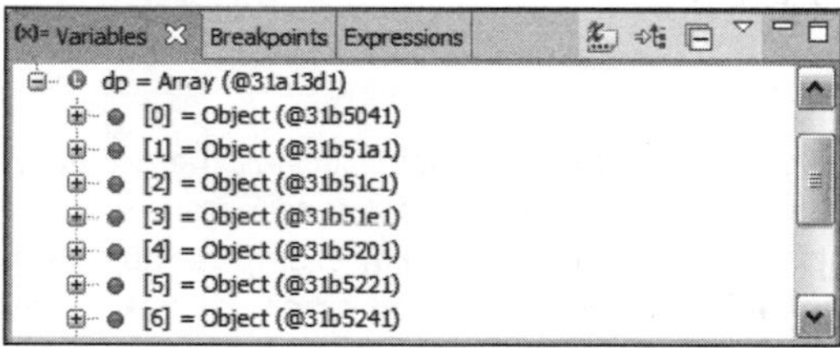

Figure 7-35. The Variables view

You can watch a variable by right-clicking it and selecting the Watch option. You'll then add the variable to the Expressions view as shown in Figure 7-36. This view allows you to track the values of variables within the application.

Figure 7-36. A watched variable in the Expressions view

The Console view at the bottom of the window displays the output from `trace` statements in ActionScript 3.0 code. It also displays messages from the debugger, and an example appears in Figure 7-37.

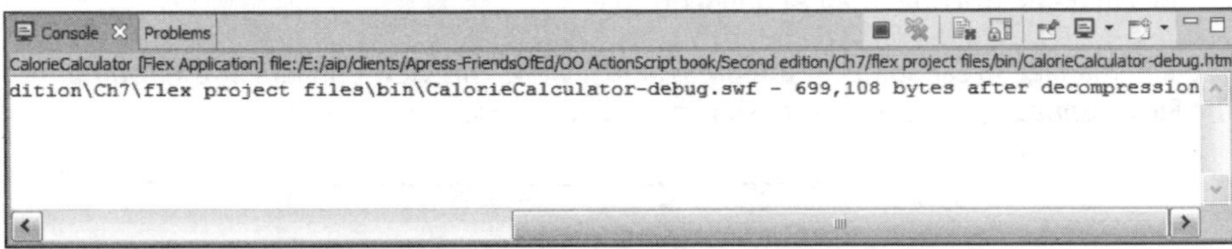

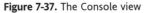

Figure 7-37. The Console view

It's worthwhile spending time exploring the various debugging options in Flex Builder 2. You can switch back to the Flex Development perspective by choosing the option from the Perspective bar. Don't forget to stop the debugger though, or you'll still be operating in debug mode.

The next section provides an overview of a few handy features in Flex Builder 2.

Tips for working with Flex Builder 2

In this section, I'll run through some tips that will make your life easier when working with various aspects of Flex Builder 2.

Creating folders

Create a new folder in your Flex project by right-clicking the project in Navigator view and choosing New ➤ Folder. Adding folders helps you to organize your projects and creates the folders for storing ActionScript packages. For example, you may want to separate your images into an `images` folder and your XML and other documents into an `assets` folder.

It's also a good idea to create classes within their own folders in your project. Adobe doesn't recommend that you create them in the default package, the top-level folder in the project.

Exporting projects

Right-click a Flex project and choose Export to export all of the files from your project to another location. If you choose the Archive File option, you can automatically add the files to a ZIP or TAR file.

Importing files

You can import files from other locations into your Flex project by right-clicking in Navigator view and choosing Import. Select the import location and follow the prompts. You can import a ZIP or TAR archive file that you previously exported, and this can be an easy way to share projects with other developers.

Collapsing code

Source view allows you to collapse blocks of code by providing plus and minus signs to the right of line numbers. Click a minus sign to collapse a block of code. Click the plus sign to expand it again.

Viewing a quick outline

Press Ctrl+O to view a quick outline of your application. The outline displays as a pop-up window as shown in Figure 7-38. You can double-click an item in the outline to jump directly to it in Source view.

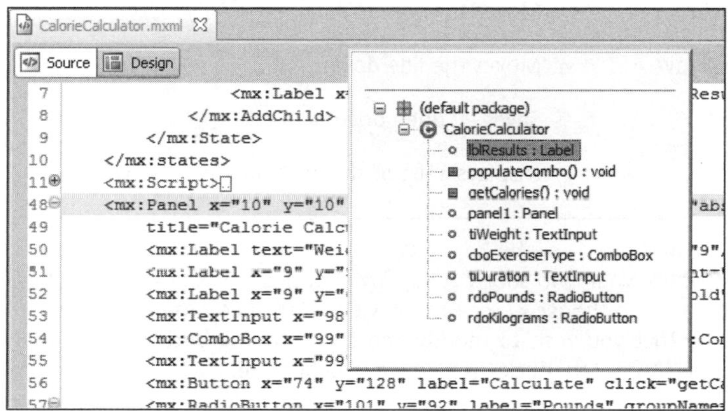

Figure 7-38. Displaying the Quick Outline view

Displaying line numbers

In Source view, right-click the left gray bar to bring up the context menu. You can show and hide line numbers by toggling the Show Line Numbers option.

Adding tasks

You can add tasks to your Flex project through the Tasks view. Choose Window ➤ Other Views ➤ Basic ➤ Tasks to see the Tasks view at the bottom of the workspace. You can then add and delete tasks as you need them.

Listing useful shortcuts

Table 7-2 contains a list of shortcuts that you might find useful for working in Flex Builder 2.

Table 7-2. Useful Flex Builder shortcuts

Shortcut	Action
F1	Displays help on the selected element
Shift+F2	Displays details of the currently selected code element in the language reference
Ctrl+Shift+C	Adds a code block
Ctrl+Shift+D	Adds a CDATA block
Ctrl+Alt+down arrow	Copies a line of code
Ctrl+L	Goes to a line number
Ctrl+Q	Jumps to the last edited line of code
Alt+up arrow	Moves the line up
Alt+down arrow	Moves the line down
Ctrl+Shift+S	Saves all open documents
Ctrl+Shift+L	Displays a list of shortcuts in a pop-up window

You can customize your own shortcut keys by choosing Window ➤ Preferences. Expand the General category and choose Keys. You can view a list of commands in the View tab. Select the command that you wish to modify and click the Edit button. You can assign a new shortcut in the Modify tab. Click OK when you've finished.

Before I finish this chapter, I want to provide some information on compiling SWF files for people who don't own a copy of Flex Builder 2. In that case, it's still possible to generate SWF files from the command line.

Compiling SWF files from the command line

If you don't own Flex Builder, you can still write MXML and ActionScript 3.0 code and compile it into an application by using the command-line compiler. You will need to have Flash Player 9 installed to view the compiled output.

The compiler file, `mxmlc.exe`, comes with the full Flex Builder 2 install, but you can also get it with the Flex SDK, which is free to download from the Adobe website. You need to have a Java runtime in your system path to use the compiler. The Adobe TechNote "Using the command line compiler on Mac OS 10" (`www.adobe.com/cfusion/knowledgebase/index.cfm?id=tn_19244`) describes how to use this tool with Macintosh OS 10.

Flex Builder 2 installs the compiler in `C:\Program Files\Adobe\Flex Builder 2\Flex SDK 2\bin\mxmlc.exe` on Windows computers and in `/Applications/Adobe Flex Builder 2/Flex SDK/bin/mxmlc.exe` on Macintosh computers. If you download the Flex SDK, you can locate the same file wherever you saved the downloaded files.

We'll create a very simple MXML file in a text editor and use the command line to compile it with `mxmlc.exe`. Open a text editor and enter the following code:

```
<?xml version="1.0" encoding="utf-8"?>
<mx:Application xmlns:mx="http://www.adobe.com/2006/mxml"
  layout="absolute">
  <mx:Label x="10" y="10" id="lblMessage" text="Hello World"/>
</mx:Application>
```

This code block creates a `Label` control that displays the text Hello World. Save the file as `helloWorld.mxml` in the location of your choice. I chose `C:\Temp` as an easy-to-remember folder.

Note that you can't double-click the compiler to run it. The easiest way to use it is to drag the MXML application file onto the compiler's icon. You'll briefly see the Command Prompt window, and if you check your `MXML` folder, you should see a compiled SWF file. If there are errors in the application, the Command Prompt window will briefly show an error message before closing.

You can also open a Command Prompt window and enter the parameters for the compile process. Either choose Start ➤ All Programs ➤ Accessories ➤ Command Prompt or press Windows+R, type the text command, and click OK. You'll then see a Command Prompt window.

You then need to specify the location of the `mxmlc.exe` file and pass to it the location of the MXML file that you want to compile. The easiest way to add the location of the compiler is to drag and drop it on the Command Prompt window. You can also type in the path, but if it includes spaces, you'll need to enclose the text inside quotation marks.

Type a space after the location of the compiler and enter the location of the MXML file. You can also drag the MXML file to the Command Prompt window to add the location automatically. Figure 7-39 shows how my Command Prompt window appears after I enter the paths.

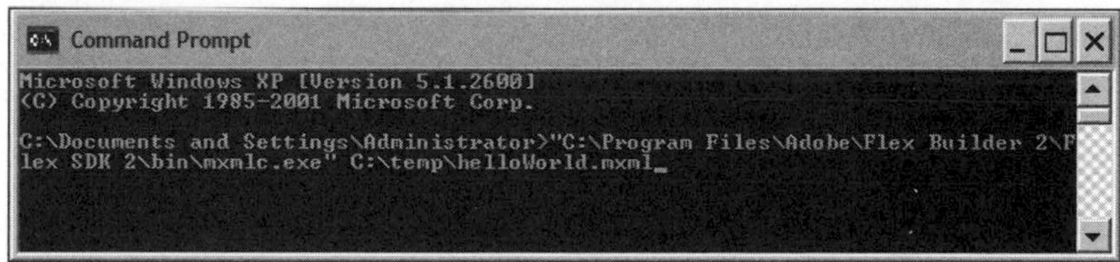

Figure 7-39. Compiling an application from the command prompt

Press Enter to compile the SWF file. When the processing completes, you'll see the size and location of the completed file as shown in Figure 7-40. You can type exit and press Enter to close the Command Prompt window.

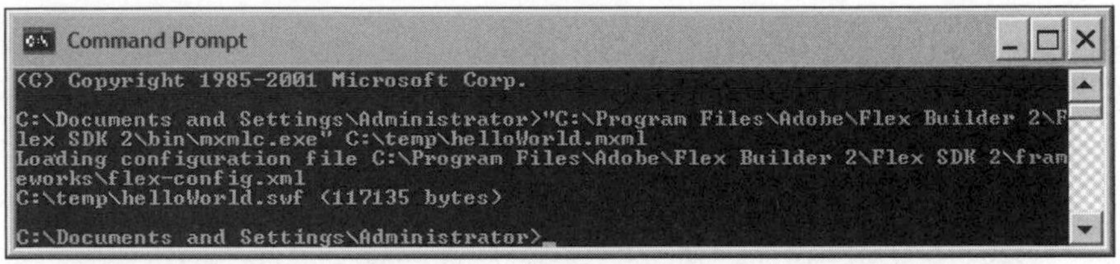

```
(C) Copyright 1985-2001 Microsoft Corp.

C:\Documents and Settings\Administrator>"C:\Program Files\Adobe\Flex Builder 2\F
lex SDK 2\bin\mxmlc.exe" C:\temp\helloWorld.mxml
Loading configuration file C:\Program Files\Adobe\Flex Builder 2\Flex SDK 2\fram
eworks\flex-config.xml
C:\temp\helloWorld.swf (117135 bytes)

C:\Documents and Settings\Administrator>_
```

Figure 7-40. Command-line compilation is complete.

The command line compiler has a number of other options that you can include as part of the compilation process. Check the online help at the Adobe website for more information. At the time of this writing, the reference to this information was at `http://livedocs.macromedia.com/flex/201/html/wwhelp/wwhimpl/js/html/wwhelp.htm?href=Part7_Build_Deploy_112_1.html`.

What's next?

This chapter introduced you to Flex Builder 2. You learned how to install the software, and you worked through a simple application so you could start to use Flex Builder. During the process, you looked at some of the common controls that you can use to create an interface. You learned how to add simple ActionScript to make the application work, and you ran the application in a web browser.

In the chapter, you also used the Flex debugger to locate errors in your application. Flex Builder has a range of standard debugging tools that you can use with any Flex application, and the chapter presented some tips for working with Flex Builder.

The final section of the chapter showed how to compile SWF files from the command line using the Flex compiler. This process allows you to create SWF files using MXML and ActionScript code created in a text editor without the need for Flex Builder 2.

Starting with the next chapter, you'll be introduced to the core concepts of object-oriented programming, such as encapsulation, inheritance, and polymorphism.

PART THREE **CORE OOP CONCEPTS**

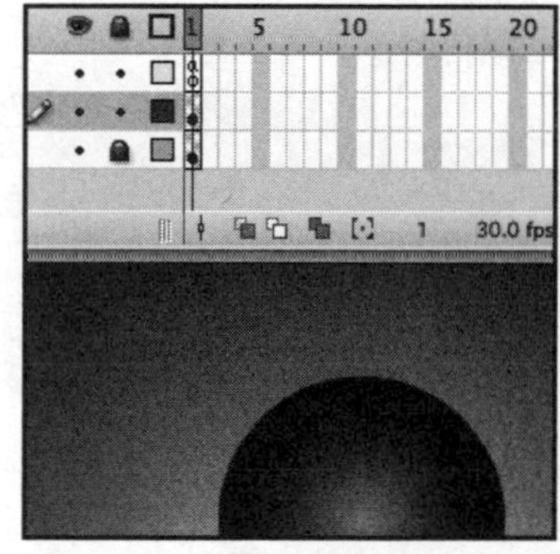

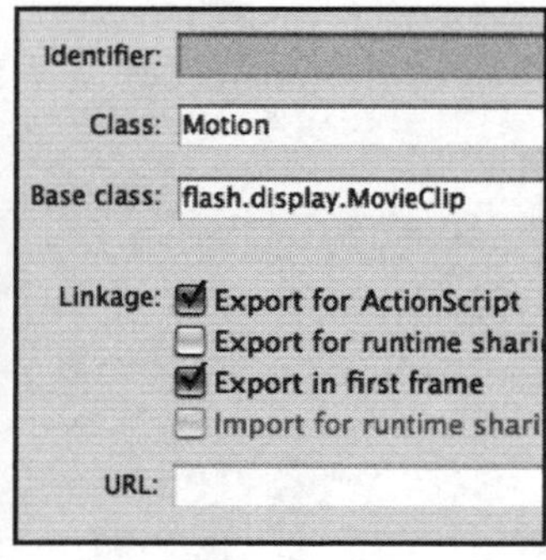

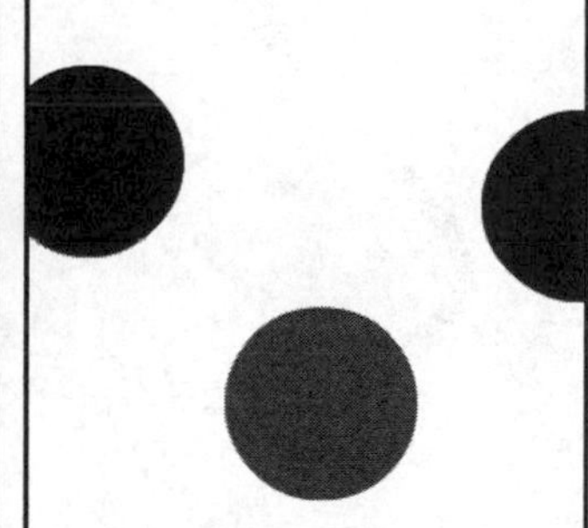

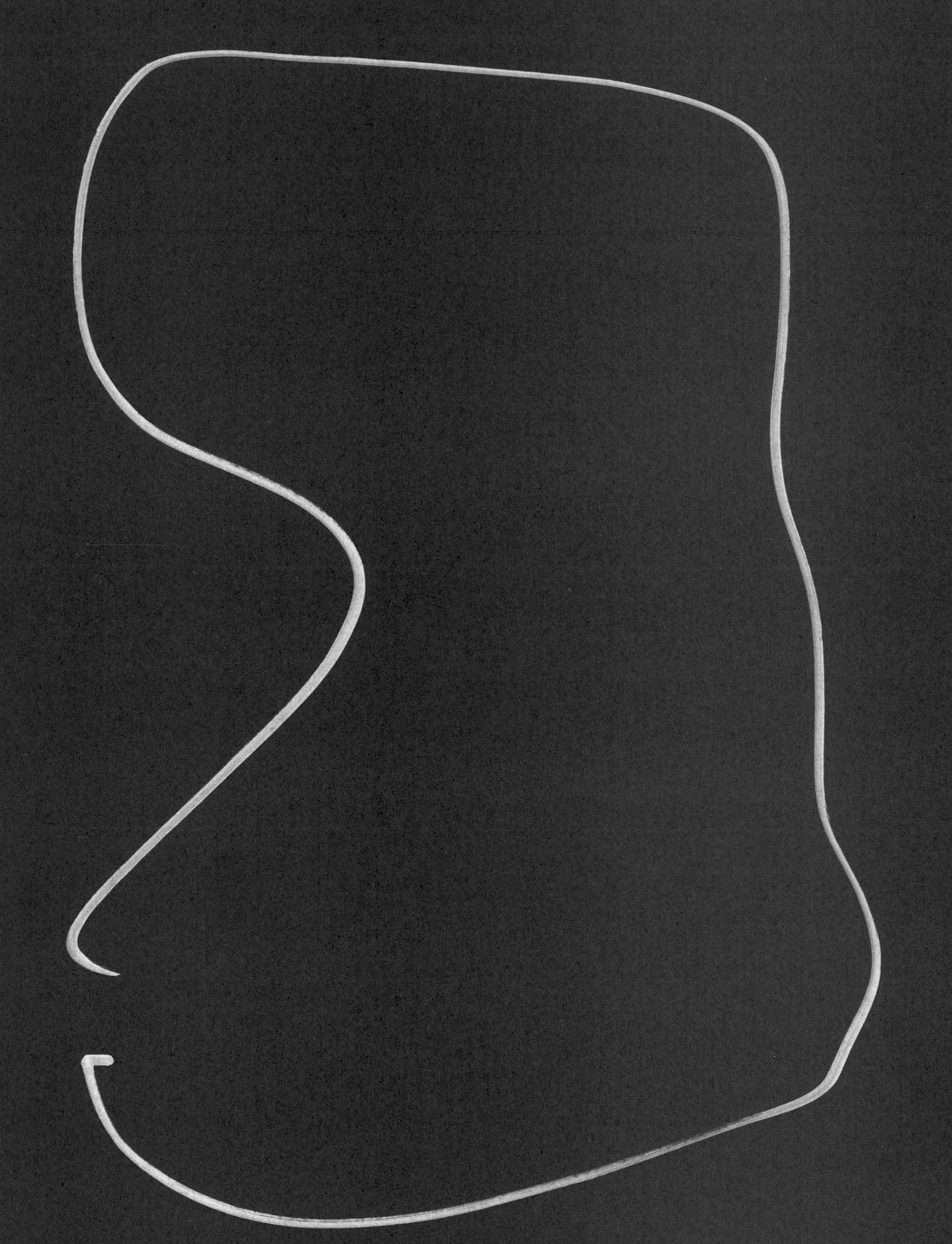

8 ENCAPSULATION

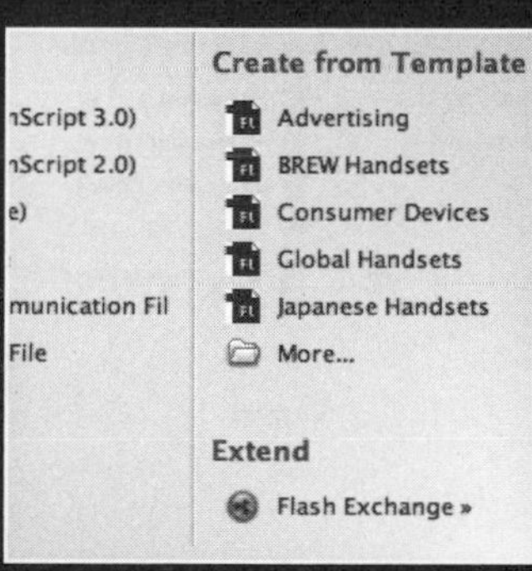

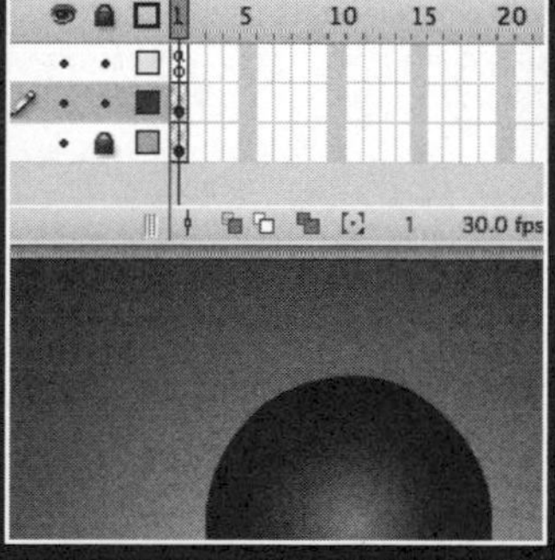

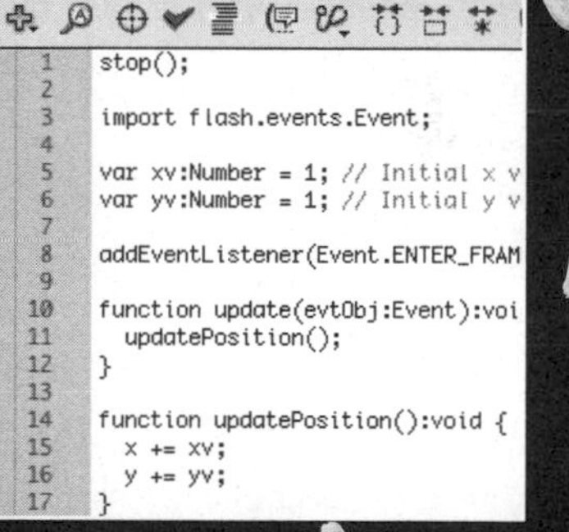

In this chapter, I create an example to demonstrate encapsulation in ActionScript 3.0. This is the first of four chapters that demonstrate encapsulation, classes, inheritance, and polymorphism using step-by-step instructions. Please note that the code shown in these chapters is mostly timeline based to quickly show you the OOP concepts discussed; for real-world projects, you would of course use classes, as you'll see used in the case study chapters in this book.

If you haven't read the introduction to encapsulation in Chapter 1, I would advise you to do so now before we get into the practicalities of applying the concept to an ActionScript 3.0 project. Just to recap, encapsulation helps you to hide the details of your object-oriented code. You just provide the methods that do the job and don't require any other classes to know the internal workings of your code.

I'll show you an example of encapsulation in action next, and start off by setting up the graphics.

Setting up encapsulation

This section describes the manual work—drawing the shapes and parts needed in the encapsulation example. Let's start with a blank FLA:

1. Launch Flash CS3.
2. Choose Flash File (ActionScript 3.0) from the Create New menu on the Start Page (see Figure 8-1).
3. Save the blank document as `Encapsulation.fla`.

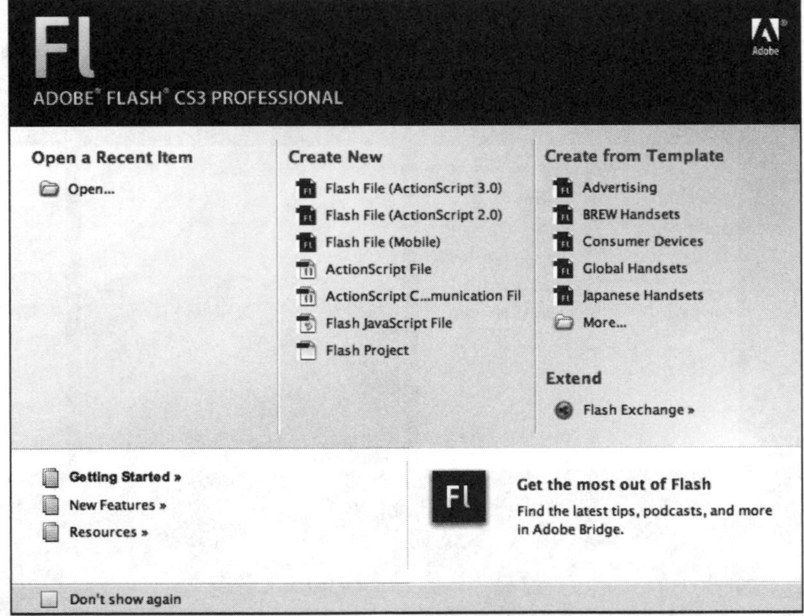

Figure 8-1. Flash CS3 Start Page

If you have the Start Page in Flash CS3 disabled, you should—depending on your settings—be presented with either a new blank FLA, last edited FLAs, or nothing at all when you launch the application. If it gives you a blank FLA, simply follow step 3 and save it as `Encapsulation.fla`; in the other cases, you create a new blank FLA by going to File ➤ New and choosing Flash File (ActionScript 3.0) from the General tab. The source files for this example are also available from the friends of ED website (`www.friendsofed.com`) if you don't feel like setting it up yourself.

Creating new layers

In previous chapters, I often referred to the idea of a bouncing ball. Let's now put this into practice and start by drawing a ball and a simple background. First, create two new layers in the timeline to hold them:

1. Display the timeline (select Window ➤ Timeline) if it isn't visible.
2. Double-click Layer 1 and rename it Background.
3. Create a new layer in the timeline (select Insert ➤ Timeline ➤ Layer), as shown in Figure 8-2.

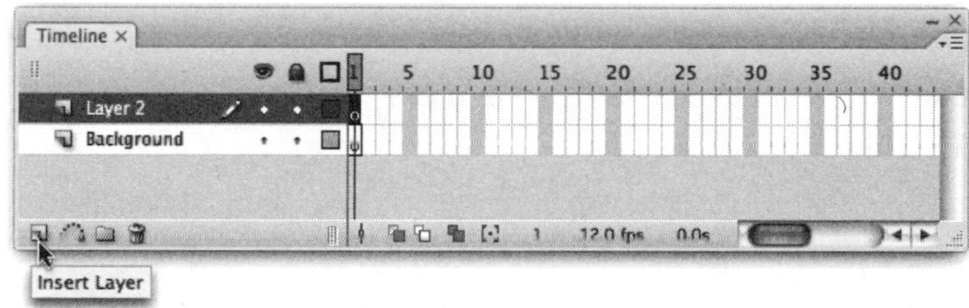

Figure 8-2. Creating a layer in the Timeline panel

4. Double-click Layer 2 and rename it Ball.
5. Create a new layer in the timeline (select Insert ➤ Timeline ➤ Layer).
6. Double-click Layer 3 and rename it ActionScript (see Figure 8-3).

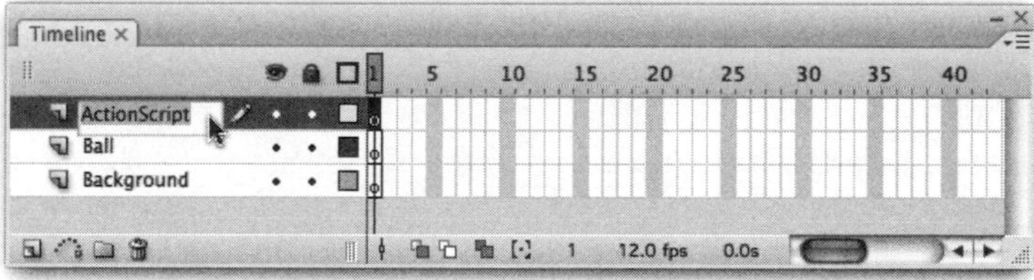

Figure 8-3. Renaming the layer in the Timeline panel

7. Select Frame 1 of the ActionScript layer.
8. Open the Actions panel (select Window ➤ Actions).

8

9. Add the following ActionScript code in the Actions panel (see Figure 8-4):

```
stop();
```

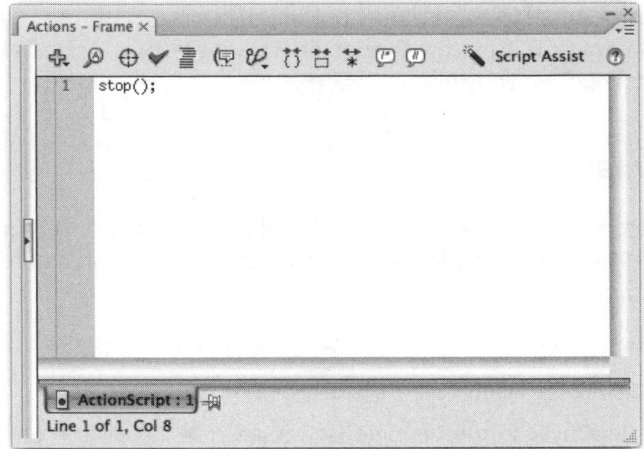

Figure 8-4. Adding code in the ActionScript panel

10. Open the Document Properties panel (select Modify ➤ Document).
11. Set the frame rate to 30 (see Figure 8-5).

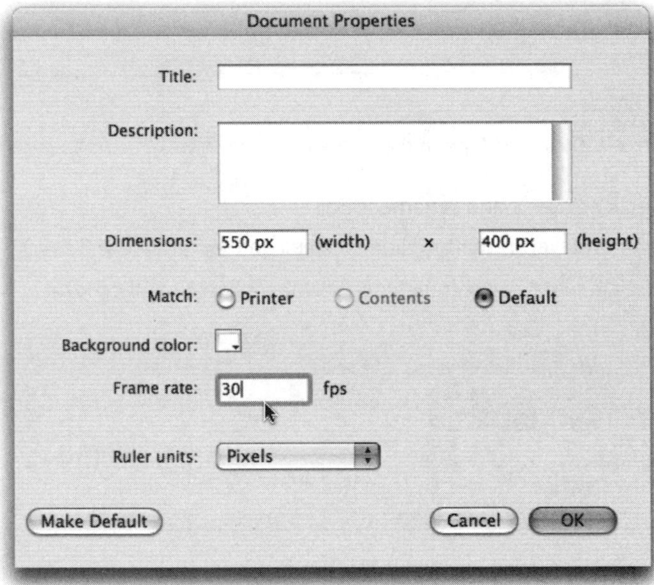

Figure 8-5. Setting the timeline frame rate

12. Click OK.

You'll now have three layers in your timeline. From top to bottom, the layers should read ActionScript, Ball, and Background (see Figure 8-6).

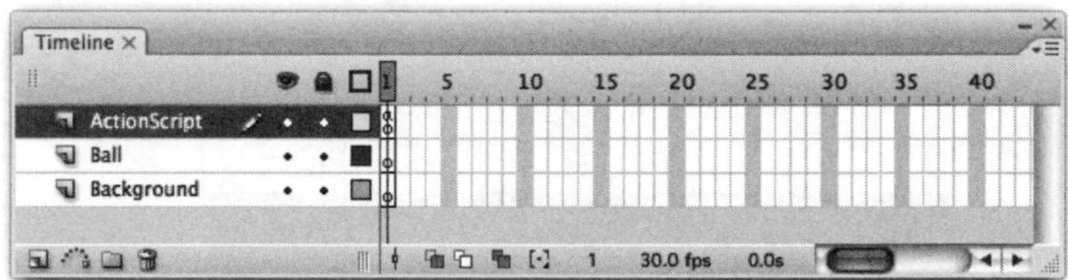

Figure 8-6. Your timeline after creating and organizing layers

Drawing a background

Let's put a filled rectangle into the Background layer:

1. In the Tools panel (select Window ➤ Tools), click the Rectangle tool (see Figure 8-7).

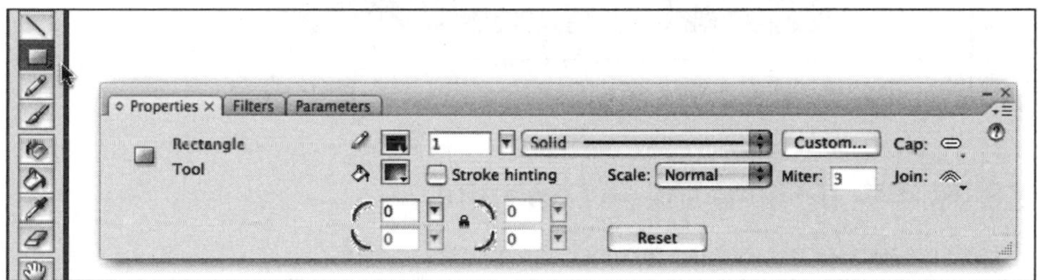

Figure 8-7. Anatomy of a filled rectangle

2. In the Properties panel (select Window ➤ Properties ➤ Properties), select hairline for the line style, select black for the line color, and select the black-to-white radial fill for the fill color (see Figure 8-7).
3. In the timeline, click Frame 1 of the Background layer.
4. Draw a rectangle somewhere on the stage. When you release the mouse button, a filled rectangle appears. Your stage should look something like the one in Figure 8-8.

8

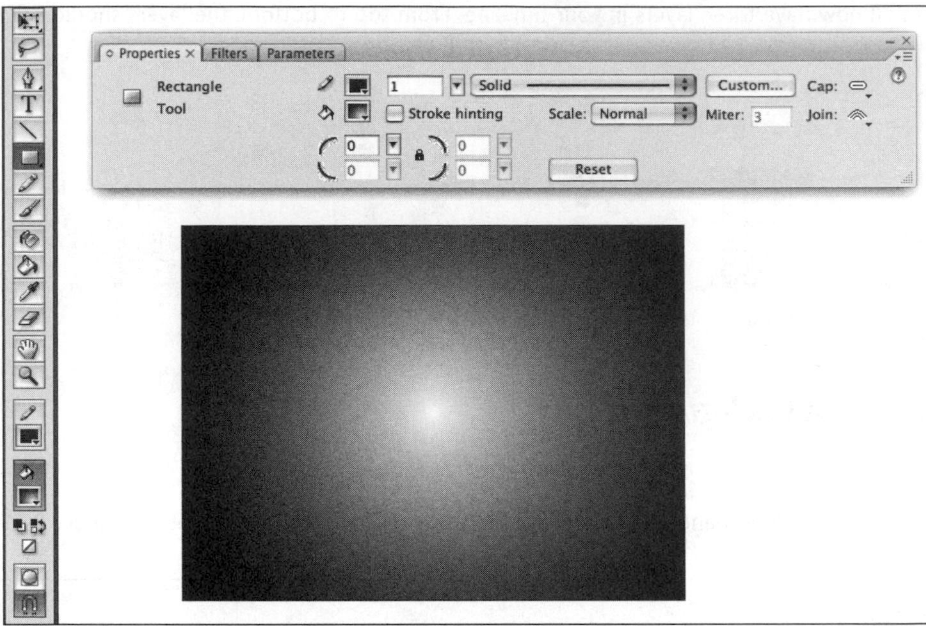

Figure 8-8. The stage after drawing a filled rectangle on the Background layer

Aligning and locking the background

Here's an easy way to make the rectangle fill the stage perfectly:

1. In the timeline, click Frame 1 of the Background layer (this selects the rectangle you just drew).
2. In the Align panel (select Window ➤ Align), click the To stage button (see Figure 8-9). This is a toggle button. Clicking it once presses it down. Clicking it again releases it. It appears white when it is pressed down and gray when it is released. It must be pressed down for the next step.

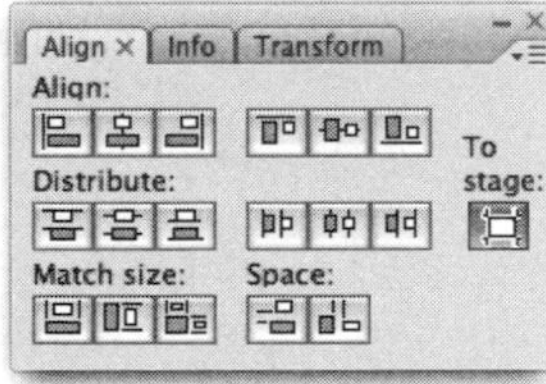

Figure 8-9. The Align panel

3. In the Align panel, click three buttons: the Match width and height button (the third button under Match size), and the Align left and Align top buttons (the first and fourth buttons under Align).

4. Lock the Background layer to protect it while you draw on other layers. Click the Background layer's lock column (see Figure 8-10). When the padlock icon is visible, the layer is locked (clicking the lock column repeatedly locks and unlocks a layer).

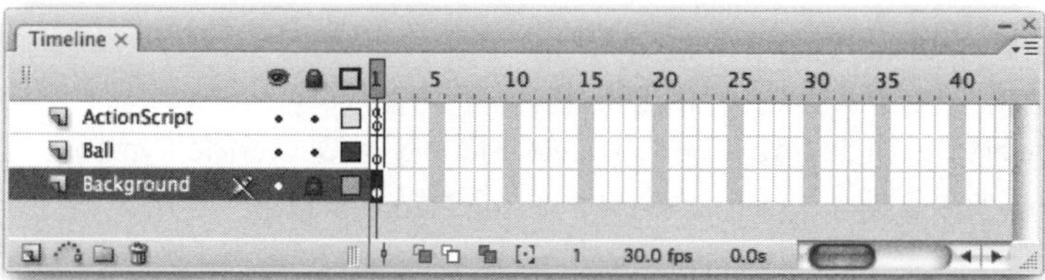

Figure 8-10. Locking the Background layer

Drawing a ball

Let's draw a filled circle to represent the ball. The steps are just like those you performed to draw the background, except you'll use the Oval tool instead of the Rectangle tool:

1. In the timeline, click Frame 1 of the Ball layer.
2. In the Tools panel, click the Oval tool.
3. In the Properties panel, select hairline for the line style, select black for the line color, and select the black-to-green radial fill for the fill color.
4. While you hold down the Shift key on your keyboard, draw an oval in the center of the stage (the Shift key yields a perfect circle). Try to match the size shown in Figure 8-11.

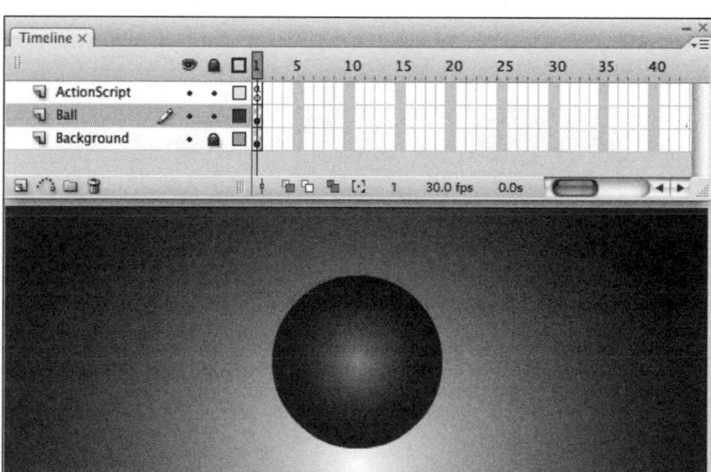

Figure 8-11. The stage after drawing a filled circle (black to green) on the Ball layer

Converting the ball into a Library symbol

Symbols are reusable content stored in the Library (every Flash document has its own internal Library for storage). Let's convert the ball into a symbol:

1. In the timeline, click Frame 1 of the Ball layer (this selects the circle). Another option is to double-click the ball shape on the stage.
2. Convert the circle into a symbol (select Modify ➤ Convert To Symbol).
3. In the Name field, type the word Ball (see Figure 8-12).

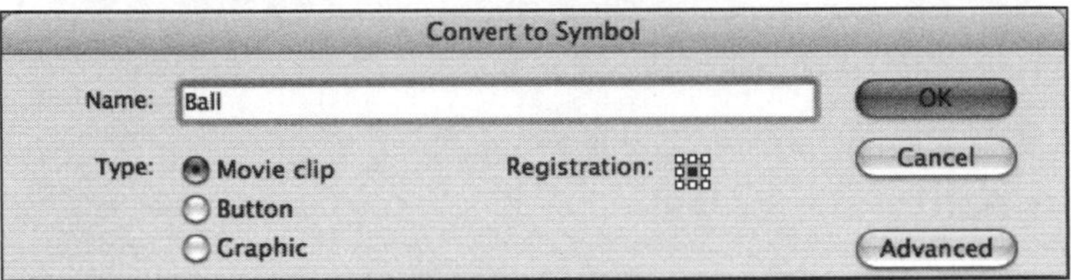

Figure 8-12. Entering a name in the Convert to Symbol dialog box

4. For Type, select Movie Clip (see Figure 8-12).
5. Ensure the black registration mark is in the center (see Figure 8-12).
6. Click OK.

> *Symbols are reusable. You can use multiple copies (instances) of any symbol in the Library, without increasing the size of the final published document.*

7. Confirm that the Ball symbol is stored in the Library (select Window ➤ Library), as shown in Figure 8-13.

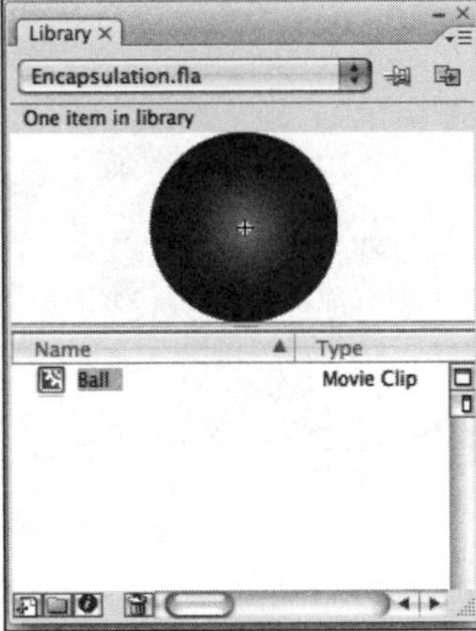

Figure 8-13. The Ball symbol

8. Save the document (select File ➤ Save).

Content summary

There are three layers in the timeline. The following table summarizes the existing content:

Timeline Layer Name	Content Description
ActionScript	This is the top layer in the timeline. It contains ActionScript code to prevent the timeline from advancing to the next frame.
Ball	This is the middle layer in the timeline. It contains an instance (an on-screen copy) of the Ball movie clip (the Ball movie clip is a symbol stored in the Library).
Background	This is the bottom layer in the timeline. It contains a simple filled rectangle that acts as a decorative background.

That completes the manual work for `Encapsulation.fla`. Next, you'll write ActionScript code to control the ball.

Writing the code

The Ball is a movie clip symbol stored in the Library (you chose Movie Clip for the Ball's type when you converted it to a symbol). For all practical purposes, *movie clips* are independent little Flash movies. Every movie clip has its own timeline and plays independently no matter what happens on the document's timeline.

Movie clips are object oriented; they have their own dedicated properties and functions. Suppose a movie clip named *George* is located at 100, 200 (stage coordinates), and another named *John* is at 300, 400. You could type the following ActionScript code:

```
trace("George is located at "+ George.x +", "+ George.y);
trace("John is located at "+ John.x +", "+ John.y);
```

The output would be as shown in Figure 8-14.

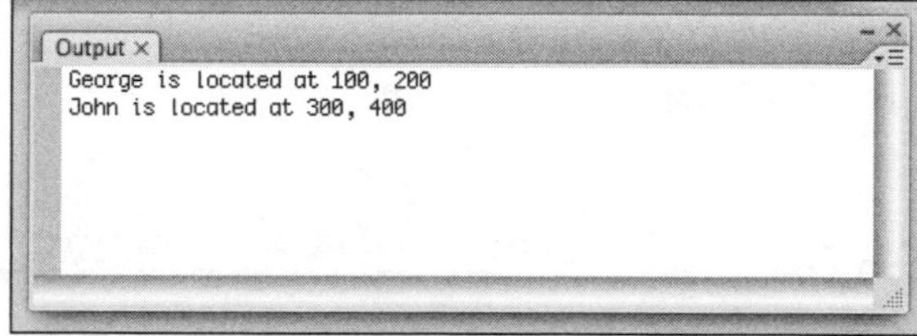

Figure 8-14. The Output panel

All movie clips contain the built-in properties x and y (note that unlike in ActionScript 2.0, there is no underscore prefix for these properties). The x property is the horizontal stage location of the movie clip, and y is the vertical stage location. Movie clips contain other properties too; you'll see more of them later.

Creating an event handler

You were briefly introduced to event handlers in Chapter 4. We'll now be using an event handler to control the Ball instance. In this document, Flash will attempt to broadcast 30 `enterFrame` messages per second (because the document's frame rate is 30). If the Ball instance listens for `enterFrame` messages, you can create the illusion of movement by changing its position each time it receives a message.

> *Setting the document's frame rate to 30 doesn't guarantee 30 frames per second (if that were true, you could just set the frame rate to 8,000 and write a fancy 3D game). It really depends on the computer's performance and how many actions run concurrently.*

Let's put an event handler into the Ball instance. Notice that the layers in the timeline are currently Background, Ball, and ActionScript. When you edit the Ball symbol in just a moment, the timeline will appear to change:

1. In the Library panel, click the Ball symbol to select it.
2. Edit the Ball symbol (select Edit ➤ Edit Symbols).

Now the timeline contains a single layer named Layer 1. That's because you're viewing the Ball instance's timeline (not the document's timeline). The Ball instance is a movie clip with its own independent timeline. Let's prepare it for the event handler:

1. In the timeline, click Layer 1 to select it.
2. Rename Layer 1 to Circle.
3. Create a new layer (select Insert ➤ Layer).
4. Rename the new layer ActionScript (select Modify ➤ Layer).
5. The Ball instance's timeline should match the one shown in Figure 8-15.

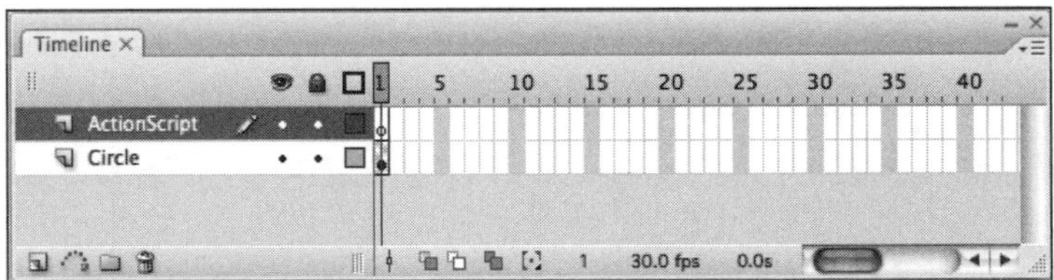

Figure 8-15. The Ball instance's timeline

Now you're ready to create the event handler:

1. Click Frame 1 of the ActionScript layer.
2. Display the Actions panel (select Window ➤ Actions) if it isn't visible.
3. Type the following code into the Actions panel:

```
stop();

import flash.events.Event;

addEventListener(Event.ENTER_FRAME, onEnterFrame)

function onEnterFrame(evtObj:Event):void {
  trace("Hello from onEnterFrame");
}
```

4. Save the document (select File ➤ Save).

The Actions panel should match the one shown in Figure 8-16.

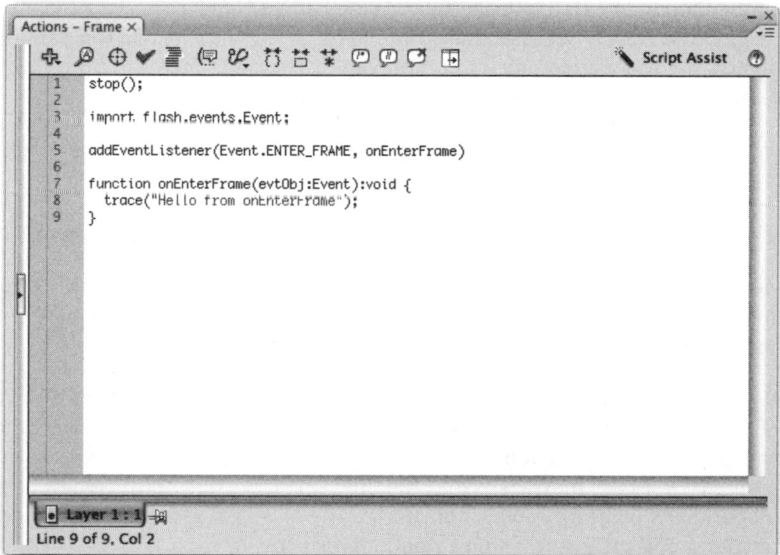

Figure 8-16. The Ball instance's event handler

The preceding code is used to easily illustrate a simple event handler in action; it is not the way you would typically handle objects in your applications. Once the code gets more complex, you'd start looking at writing ActionScript 3.0 classes and associating that to your movie clip, or set it as the document class for your project.

What about encapsulation?

If you're wondering what happened to the main topic of this chapter (a fair question), it's right in front of you in the code listing of step 3 in the preceding example. Conceptually, encapsulation is shielding (hiding) the internal details of the onEnterFrame function from the Ball instance's event handler. Here are the details:

```
01. stop();
02.
03. import flash.events.Event;
04.
05. addEventListener(Event.ENTER_FRAME, onEnterFrame)
06. function onEnterFrame(evtObj:Event):void {
07.  trace("Hello from onEnterFrame");
08. }
```

Line 01 calls the stop function (stop is a built-in function—you don't have to define it, you just use it), line 03 imports the event constants class (more about this concept later), and lines 05 through 08 set up the event listener and define the onEnterFrame function.

The stop function at line 01 prevents the timeline from advancing to the next frame (you don't want it to advance because there's no content after Frame 1). The stop function does not stop the application, nor does it prevent the code in Frame 1 from finishing (all the code in Frame 1 runs, no matter where you put the stop function).

The event handler begins and ends at line 05. To create a movie clip event handler in Flash, you can use the following syntax (as line 03 demonstrates):

```
addEventListener(MyEventClass.EVENT_CONSTANT, myEventListenerFunction);
```

All movie clips support the ENTER_FRAME event; to use it, you need to provide your own function name. The net result: every time this movie clip receives an ENTER_FRAME message from Flash, the event handler calls the onEnterFrame function.

The onEnterFrame function at line 05 is simple enough—it displays "Hello from onEnterFrame." It doesn't matter how simple or complex the onEnterFrame function is. That's the point of encapsulation! The event handler calls onEnterFrame whenever it receives an ENTER_FRAME message. What the onEnterFrame function actually does (from the event handler's point of view) is immaterial. The onEnterFrame function could call 50 other functions, and the event handler would never know it.

This type of encapsulation is very narrow (existing only at the function level). Encapsulation also exists at wider levels (in a single class or multiple classes, sometimes called *services* or *components*). The concept, however, is identical: the internal behavior of a function, class, or service is hidden (encapsulated) from the caller. The caller is only responsible for knowing which functions, classes, or services are available, not how they operate internally.

Testing the event handler

Test the movie by selecting Control ➤ Test Movie. The output is an endless stream of "Hello from onEnterFrame" messages (see Figure 8-17). Each "Hello from onEnterFrame" represents a call to the `onEnterFrame` function (so the event handler is calling the `onEnterFrame` function properly).

```
Hello from onEnterFrame
Hello from onEnterFrame
Hello from onEnterFrame
Hello from onEnterFrame
Hello from onEnterFrame
Hello from onEnterFrame
Hello from onEnterFrame
Hello from onEnterFrame
```

Figure 8-17. Testing the event handler

When you've seen enough `onEnterFrame` messages, close the test file (select File ➤ Close) to return to Flash.

> *Whenever you test a movie, you're actually viewing a published file. You must close it to return to Flash.*

Updating the ball

Movie clips have x and y properties to describe their location on the stage. The Ball instance is a movie clip, so what happens when you change these properties? Update your code to match the following listing:

```
stop();

import flash.events.Event;

addEventListener(Event.ENTER_FRAME, onEnterFrame)

function onEnterFrame(evtObj:Event):void {
  x++; // Same as x = x+1;
  y++;
}
```

The Actions panel should match Figure 8-18.

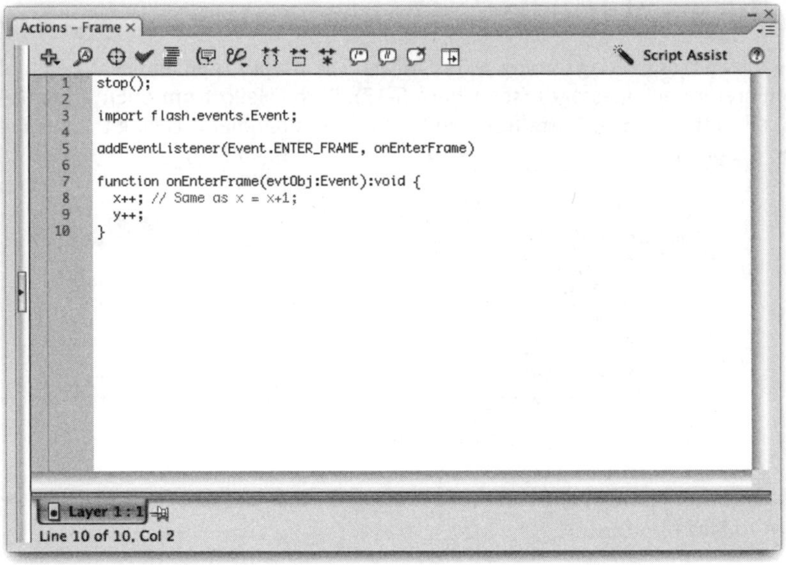

Actions - Frame

Script Assist

```
stop();

import flash.events.Event;

addEventListener(Event.ENTER_FRAME, onEnterFrame)

function onEnterFrame(evtObj:Event):void {
  x++; // Same as x = x+1;
  y++;
}
```

Layer 1 : 1

Line 10 of 10, Col 2

Figure 8-18. Updated code in the Actions panel

Test the movie by selecting Control ➤ Test Movie. The Ball instance moves 1 pixel down and 1 pixel to the right each time the event handler calls the `onEnterFrame` function. Close the test file (select File ➤ Close) to return to Flash.

The ++ in x++ is an increment operator (it increases the value of the variable by 1). This is a shorter way of writing `x = x + 1` or `x += 1`. This is how the Ball instance moves 1 pixel at a time (there's nothing preventing the Ball instance from moving off the screen, so it will).

Save your document by selecting File ➤ Save.

Improving the code

The Ball instance has a working event handler. That's a good start, but you can get the code closer to the plans from the last chapter. First, rename the `onEnterFrame` function to update (make sure you change the event handler *and* the function) like this:

```
stop();

import flash.events.Event;

addEventListener(Event.ENTER_FRAME, update);

function update(evtObj:Event):void {
  x++;
  y++;
}
```

The Actions panel should match Figure 8-19.

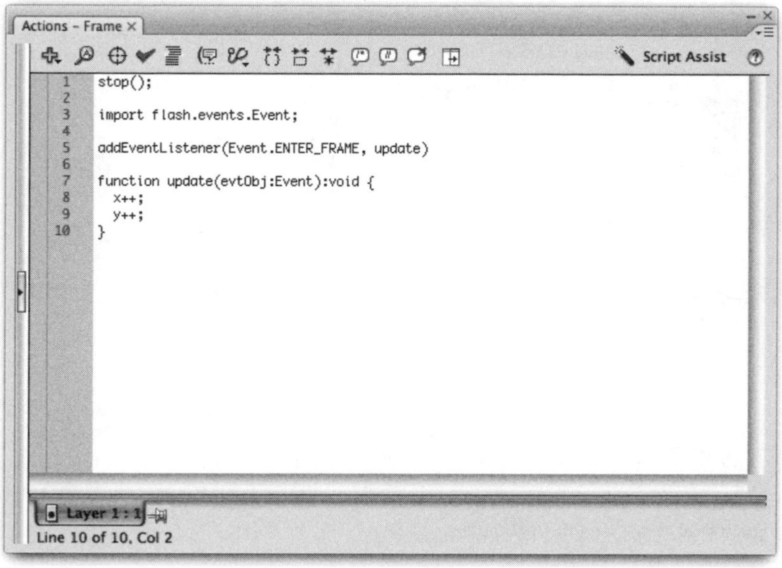

Figure 8-19. The Actions panel after renaming `onEnterFrame` as `update`

Enhancing behavior with properties

All movie clips have properties (you've seen x and y so far). *Properties* are variables dedicated to a specific instance of a given object. Currently, there's one instance of the Ball instance, but what if there were 50? Doesn't matter. Every instance has its own independent copy of x and y. You aren't limited, however, to the built-in movie clip properties—you can invent your own. Please modify your code to match the following listing:

```
stop();

import flash.events.Event;

var xv:Number = 1; // Initial x velocity.
var yv:Number = 1; // Initial y velocity.

addEventListener(Event.ENTER_FRAME, update);

function update(evtObj:Event):void {
  x+=xv;
  y+=yv;
}
```

The Actions panel should match Figure 8-20.

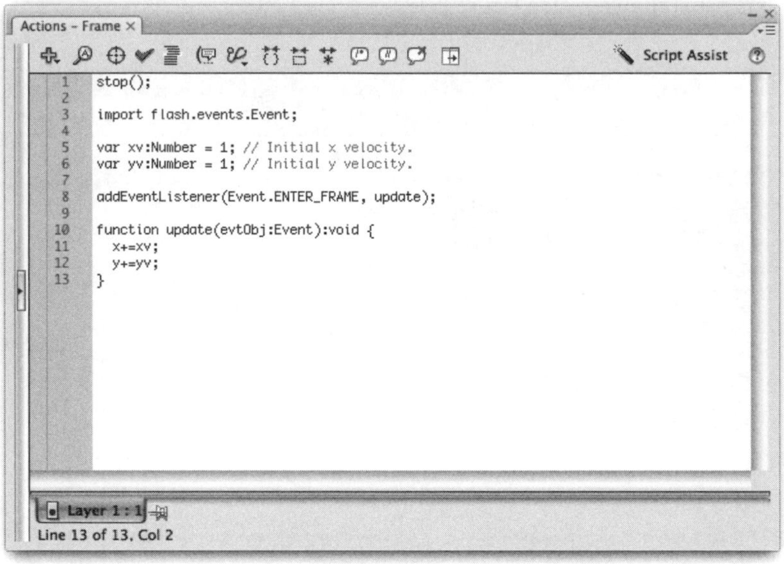

Actions - Frame

Script Assist

```
stop();

import flash.events.Event;

var xv:Number = 1; // Initial x velocity.
var yv:Number = 1; // Initial y velocity.

addEventListener(Event.ENTER_FRAME, update);

function update(evtObj:Event):void {
  x+=xv;
  y+=yv;
}
```

Layer 1 : 1

Line 13 of 13, Col 2

Figure 8-20. Using custom properties

Test the movie by selecting Control ➤ Test Movie. It behaves exactly as it did before. Instead of hard-coding the velocity directly inside the update function, you can store it in a property. This may not seem like an advantage right now, but trust me. Close the test file (select File ➤ Close) to return to Flash.

> *Portability is another advantage of encapsulation. Remember, the event handler doesn't care what the* update *function does or how it works (as long as there's an* update *function to call, it's happy). This will become even more apparent when I introduce classes in the next chapter.*

Narrowing the focus with functions

The golden rule of functions is this: one task per function. Right now, the update function is rather vague. What does it update? To clarify, update your code to match the following listing:

```
stop();

import flash.events.Event;

var xv:Number = 1; // Initial x velocity.
var yv:Number = 1; // Initial y velocity.
```

```
addEventListener(Event.ENTER_FRAME, update);

function update(evtObj:Event):void {
  updatePosition();
}

function updatePosition():void {
  x += xv;
  y += yv;
}
```

The Actions panel should match Figure 8-21.

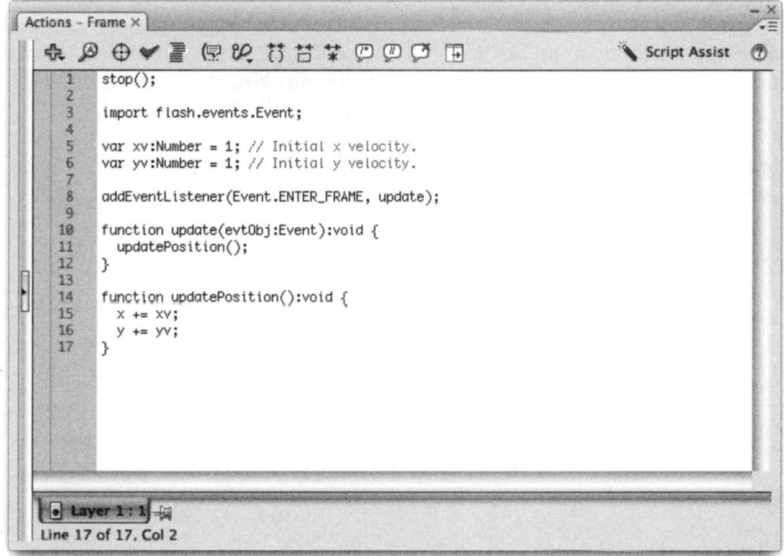

Figure 8-21. Narrowing the focus with functions

Save the document (select File ➤ Save) and test the movie (select Control ➤ Test Movie). The behavior is the same as before, but you've introduced a more descriptive function named updatePosition. Close the test file (select File ➤ Close) to return to Flash.

The name updatePosition is more descriptive than update. The code is now more self-descriptive than before, but was it worth creating another new function? Shouldn't you just rename the update function to updatePosition (and be done with it)?

In OOP, a group of simple functions is better than a single complex function. Think of the update function as an umbrella function. You could write a series of simple functions (updatePosition, updateVelocity, updateFriction). Each function handles one (and only one) task. Eventually, you could have this kind of update function:

```
function update():void {
  updatePosition();
  updateVelocity();
  updateFriction();
}
```

Now you know what the update function does, but you don't need to know how the details work. It's a nice overview, and you don't even need to see the rest of the code. Encapsulation simplifies development and makes the code naturally self-descriptive. The byproduct is easy-to-read code.

Encapsulation summary

Encapsulation is all about simplification, hiding the details, and distributing the workload. *Abstraction* is another way to describe encapsulation. You can take a complex set of behaviors and *abstract* them into a series of simple functions. For example:

```
import flash.events.Event;
addEventListener(Event.ENTER_FRAME. update);

function update(evtObj:Event):void {
  updatePosition();
  updateVelocity();
  updateFriction();
}

function updatePosition():void {
  // internal details of updatePosition
}

function updateVelocity():void {
  // internal details of updateVelocity
}

function updateFriction():void {
  // internal details of updateFriction
}
```

In this case, the event handler depends only on a function named update. Beyond that, the event handler doesn't know or care what the details are. It has no idea how the update function works or how many other function calls may be involved. That's encapsulation.

> *Consistency is another great benefit of encapsulation. All objects using the* update *function will either succeed or fail in exactly the same way. If there's a bug in the application, I can fix it in exactly one place. With encapsulation, the application behaves consistently—bugs or not.*

In generic terms, encapsulation involves the abstraction of various tasks into one entity. Functions are an example of this as they can contain a series of instructions that you need not know anything about to use them.

Just like in the real world, simple actions can be much more difficult than you'd expect. Let's take opening a door, for example:

```
function openDoor():void {
  approachDoor();
  grabDoorKnob();
  twistDoorKnob();
  pushDoorOpen();
}
function approachDoor():void {
  // internal details of approachDoor
}
function grabDoorKnob():void {
  // internal details of grabDoorKnob
}
function twistDoorKnob():void {
  // internal details of twistDoorKnob
}
function pushDoorOpen():void {
  // internal details of pushDoorOpen
}
```


We've all been conditioned to see the task of opening the door as one simple action, though as you can clearly see from this example, it is not. This is a form of abstraction and encapsulation we use in our daily lives; the same applies to object-oriented programming.

When communicating between different blocks of code or classes, as you'll see in the next chapters, you try to keep the message very straightforward. In this case, you just want the door to be opened, which is why there is a generic `openDoor` function. Your code should not be required to know what actions are needed to open the door, or care how this is done. For all you know, the door is opened by using a key, swiping an electronic badge, performing some silly little magic dance, or forcing it with a crowbar. All that matters to your code is that the door is "somehow" opened.

Encapsulation may look like a very simple concept, but it is tremendously powerful when doing object-oriented programming to create clean and easily reusable code. The aim with encapsulation is to provide an interface through which other classes can communicate without them needing to know anything else about the internal workings; for example, a Car class could have the method `startEngine`, a NuclearPlant class could have the method `generateElectricity`, and so on.

Thank heavens for that. This same encapsulation allows me to use complex Math classes without having to wreck my brain figuring out how to get the required result. I don't know about you, but anything that helps me to focus on the actual tasks rather than the intricate details when writing code gets my stamp of approval!

What's next?

There's nothing wrong with the current version of this document, but before I add more functionality, you should understand classes. Next, I introduce ActionScript 3.0 classes and upgrade the encapsulation example at the same time. Please save your document if you haven't already.

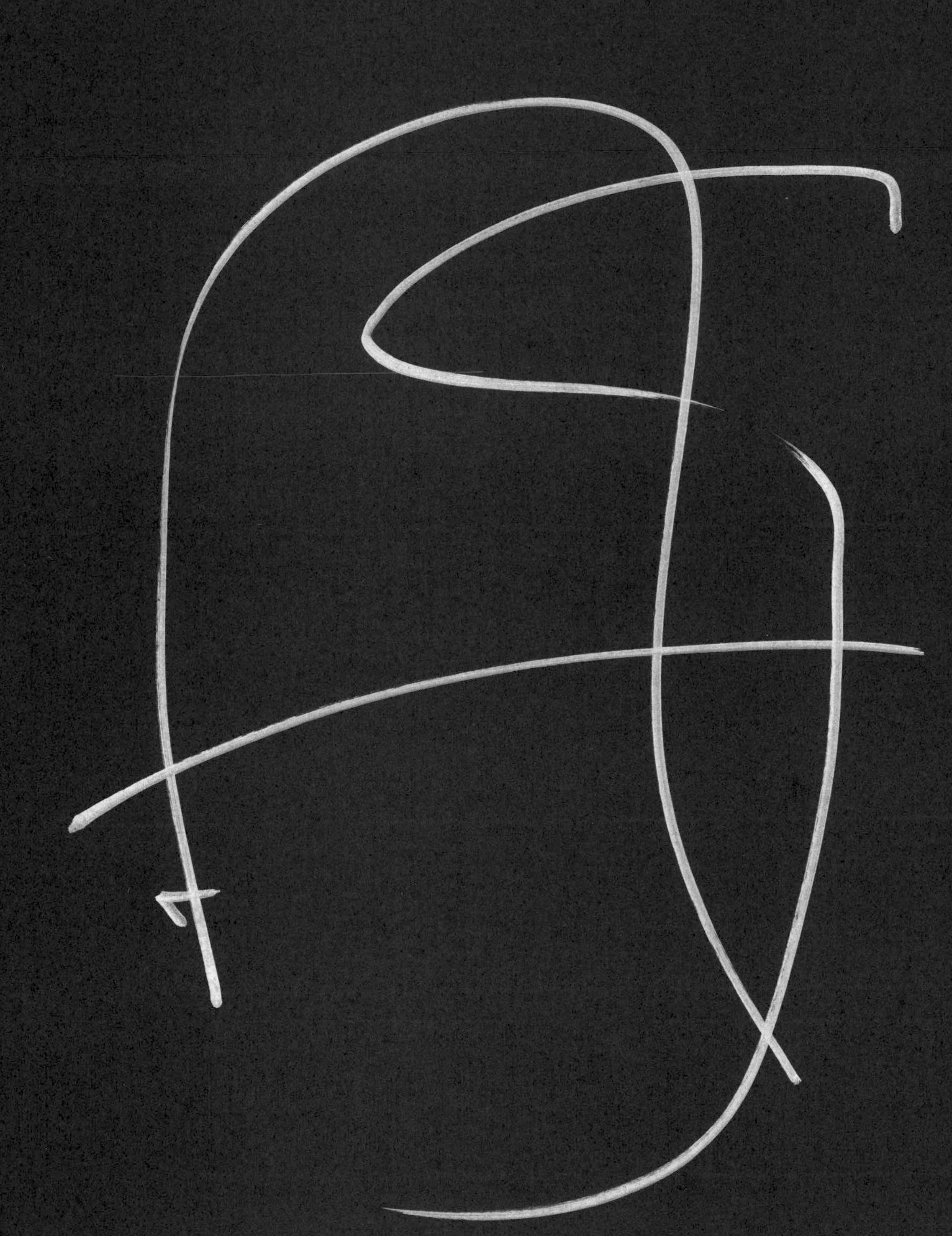

9 CLASSES

I want to update the encapsulation example from the last chapter, so this is the perfect time to introduce ActionScript 3.0 classes. Classes were briefly discussed in Chapter 3 in comparison with the prototype-based approach of ActionScript 1.0. We'll look at that difference again, but focus here on the differences in syntax. Just like languages such as C# or Java, ActionScript (since version 2.0) supports a class-based approach that makes it much more consistent with other languages that typically use OOP techniques.

Classes vs. prototypes

Prior to the 2.0 release of ActionScript, the language used a prototype-based syntax that was able to simulate classes but didn't have the formal syntax to show this. In many ways this method was a bit of a fraud; you would manipulate the prototype object to do inheritance, there was no support for public and private scope, etc. This is not to say that it wasn't effective. In many ways the prototype-based approach was a good way to quickly and easily extend built-in and custom classes.

Let's see how a `Motion` class would look in a prototype-based language such as ActionScript 1.0:

```
function Motion() {
}
Motion.prototype.updatePosition = function() {
  this._x++;
  this._y++;
}
```

You can see that by adding the `prototype` keyword before setting the function name, you actually add it to every instance that is instantiated from the `Motion` *prototype class* through the new keyword (see the following code).

```
ballMotion = new Motion();
onEnterFrame = ballMotion.updatePosition;
```

Now, how does ActionScript 3.0 handle classes? Take a look at the following syntax:

```
package {

  import flash.display.MovieClip;
  import flash.events.Event;

  public class Motion extends MovieClip {
    public function Motion() {
       this.addEventListener(Event.ENTER_FRAME, update);
    }
    private function updatePosition():void {
      this.x++;
      this.y++;
    }
```

```
        private function update(evtObj:Event):void {
          this.updatePosition();
        }
      }
    }
```

Nice. You can immediately see that this ActionScript 3.0 class looks quite a bit different from the ActionScript 1.0 prototype version. Don't worry, I'll walk you through it. First of all, the code for our Motion class shown previously should be saved as the file Motion.as.

The most important difference is that we now have a formal class keyword, which is very useful as it shows you what exactly is part of your class. Everything that you'll find between the curly braces of the class statement is part of that class.

Because our Motion class is going to make use of some properties (x and y) and an event handler for the ENTER_FRAME event of the built-in MovieClip class, we need to use the extends keyword which allows us—yes, you've guessed it!—to extend the MovieClip class. This behavior is called *inheritance*, and I'll discuss it in greater detail in the next chapter.

You'll notice an empty function in our class called Motion (notice it uses the same name as our class). This is the constructor for our class (more about this later on in this chapter).

The next function we defined in the Motion class is updatePosition. Just like in the prototype example, we just increment the built-in x and y properties that position the movie clip on the stage.

Finally, we define the update function and call updatePosition from there. Remember, the update event handler gets called as the event listener for the ENTER_FRAME event inherited from the MovieClip class, so it will still be called once every frame.

OK, so far so good—you'll have noticed that the ActionScript 3.0 class does exactly what our prototype class did. Now we only need to instantiate it. One way to do this is by associating a movie clip with a class, although if you wanted to do it purely through code, the drawing API is there to help you. From reading Chapter 3, you probably know how this is done, but I'll recap and run you through it again.

1. Launch Flash.
2. Choose Flash Document from the Create New menu on the Start Page (or select File ➤ New and click Flash File (ActionScript 3.0) if the Start Page is disabled).
3. Save the blank document as Motion.fla in the folder where you saved Motion.as.
4. Rename Layer 1 as Shape.
5. Draw any shape you want on the Shape layer.
6. Convert your shape on the Shape layer to a movie clip (Modify ➤ Convert to Symbol).
7. Set the Type to Movie clip and give it the name MotionShape.
8. If the Linkage area isn't visible in the Convert to Symbol panel, click the Advanced button.
9. Select the check box Export for ActionScript.

10. Set the class for this movie clip to Motion.
11. Click OK.
12. Test the Flash movie (Control ➤ Test Movie).

If all went well, you should now see your shape moving across the screen. Now, that wasn't too difficult, was it? In a nutshell, what you did was simply associate a movie clip with a class. The settings for the symbol we created should look like Figure 9-1.

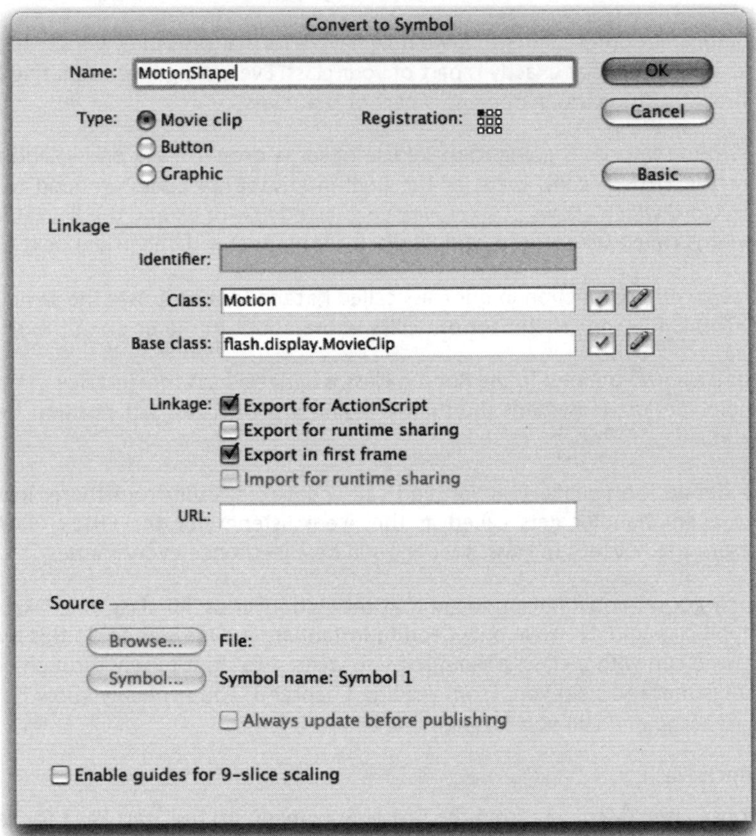

Figure 9-1. The Convert to Symbol panel

Now that you've seen that ActionScript 3.0 supports a class-based syntax, there are a couple of concepts you'll need to learn about to write your own custom classes: constructors, methods, and events. That is exactly what I'll be discussing next.

Constructors

A constructor is a function just like any other with the exception that it is called automatically when a class instance is instantiated. Let's look at an example:

```
var myPhoneList:Array = new Array();
```

The class is Array. The instance of the Array class is myPhoneList. The constructor function is Array(). If you could look at the source code for the built-in classes, you would find an Array class constructor function similar to this:

```
package {
  public class Array {
    public function Array() {
      // Internal details of Array class constructor.
    }
  }
}
```

As you can see, there's nothing to discern a constructor function from any other function. There's not a special keyword to mark the start of a constructor function. The only giveaway is that the class name (Array in this case) has the exact same name as the constructor function. So, if you'd look at the constructor for the built-in Date class, you would also see a function called Date. Also worth mentioning is that, although ActionScript 3.0 does not enforce this, the constructor is generally the first function in a class.

Let me put this into context. The following code shows a Motion class.

```
package {
 import flash.display.MovieClip;
 import flash.events.Event;
 public class Motion extends MovieClip {
   public function Motion() {
     trace("Motion class instantiated");
     addEventListener(Event.ENTER_FRAME, update);
   }
   private function updatePosition():void {
     this.x++;
     this.y++;
   }
   private function update(evtObj:Event):void {
     this.updatePosition();
   }
 }
}
```


To show that the constructor function gets called automatically any time that particular class is instantiated, I added a trace statement. Now let's make a couple of instances and see what that does.

```
var spaceship:Motion = new Motion();
var rocket:Motion = new Motion();
```

If we test this movie with the Motion class in place in the same directory, the items shown in Figure 9-2 get displayed in the Output panel.

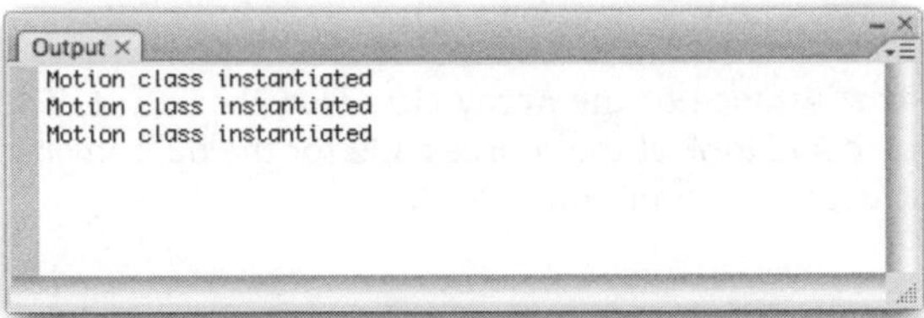

Figure 9-2. Motion class Output panel

We created two instances of the Motion class, and the constructor was called once for each instance. That makes sense, but where does the third line come from? Easy, because we have a movie clip on the stage associated with the Motion class, that itself is also an instance of the class that gets instantiated. Now, of course, the class doesn't do anything because we didn't associate it with a movie clip, but it does show you what we were after.

The class is Motion. The objects are spaceship and rocket. The constructor function is Motion(). All Motion objects have an x property and a y property and an event handler for the ENTER_FRAME event that they've inherited from the MovieClip class that it extends.

Constructors are functions, so you'd think there would be nothing stopping you from adding parameters to the constructor. Unfortunately, when using classes that are associated with movie clips, you cannot pass anything to the constructor. The way you would bypass this is by adding an init method that handles this as the following example shows you:

```
package {
  import flash.display.MovieClip;
  import flash.events.Event;
  public class Motion extends MovieClip {
    function Motion() {
    }
    public function init(xVal:Number,yVal:Number):void {
      this.x = xVal;
      this.y = yVal;
      addEventListener(Event.ENTER_FRAME, update);
    }
    private function updatePosition():void {
      this.x++;
      this.y++;
    }
    private function update(evtObj:Event):void {
      this.updatePosition();
    }
  }
)
```

You'll notice that the only thing I did was add a function, init, that sets the x and y properties of the movie clip to the xVal and yVal parameters that are passed to it. What you'll have to do next is give the movie clip you associated with the Motion class the instance name motionShape in the Properties panel (select Window ➤ Properties), after which you can add the following code to the main timeline of your document to call the init function:

```
motionShape.init(100,50);
```

What this code does is call the init method for the motionShape instance of the Motion class and pass x and y parameters that determine the initial position our movie clip starts moving from.

Classes that are not associated to movie clips can have parameters passed to the constructor. I'll show a quick example of this here:

```
package {
  public class MultiplyNumbers {
    public function MultiplyNumbers(num1:Number,num2:Number):void {
      trace(num1*num2);
    }
  }
}
```

The preceding class should be saved in a file called MultiplyNumbers.as, and in a blank FLA in the same directory you could add the following code:

```
var myMaths:MultiplyNumbers = new MultiplyNumbers(5,4);
```

When you test this movie, the output will show 20.

So far so good—you've just learned about constructors. Next, let's discuss the use of methods in your ActionScript 3.0 classes.

Methods

A class is more than a template for potential data; it's also a template for potential data *handling*. You've seen class properties (they describe the data). To provide data handling, you need to attach functions to the class. That is where the class methods come in. Here's the syntax:

```
package {
  public class Car {
    public function intendedFunctionName():void {
      // Function instructions go here.
    }
  }
}
```

9

Suppose you want to attach a crash function to a Car class. Here's how:

```
package {
  public class Car {
    public function crash():void {
      trace("Boom!");
    }
  }
}
```

The code that follows shows a complete example:

Car.as

```
package {
  public class Car {
    private var speed:Number;
    private var direction:String;

    public function Car(speed:Number,direction:String) {
      this.speed = speed;
      this.direction = direction;
    }

    public function showVelocity():void {
      trace("The car's velocity is "+this.speed
      +" KPH "+this.direction);
    }

    public function crash():void {
      trace("Boom!");
    }

  }
}
```

The preceding code needs to be saved as `Car.as` and can be instantiated by using the code that follows in an FLA located in the same folder:

```
var yugo:Car = new Car(10, "North");
yugo.showVelocity();
```

If you run the preceding code, the output shown in Figure 9-3 is generated.

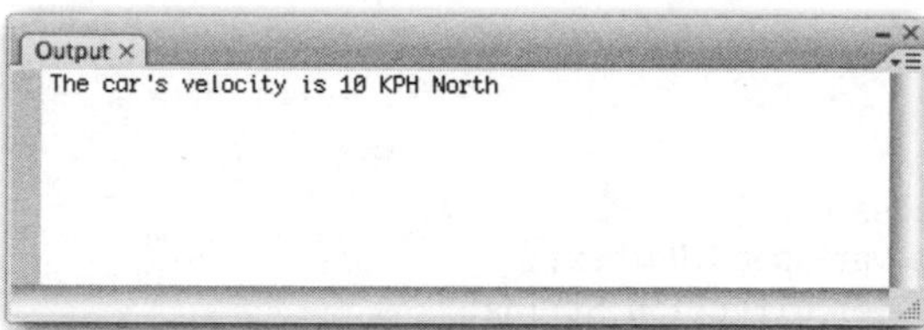

Figure 9-3. Car class Output panel

Aside from these normal class methods, you can actually have something called *anonymous functions*, which are mostly used for event handlers. We'll look at these next.

Anonymous functions

An anonymous function is a temporary function without a name. Wait. How can there be a function without a name? How would you call it? You can't . . . at least not directly. Take a look at this simple example:

```
myFunction = function():void {
  trace("This function is called");
}
```

If you think about it, in the preceding example what we really assign to myVariable is the following code:

```
function():void {
  trace("This function is called");
}
```

The function we assign to myFunction has no reference by which we can call it; if we were to write the same code with a named function, it would look like this:

```
function myFunction():void {
  trace("This function is called");
}
```

Now, what is the difference between the two? When you overwrite a variable using anonymous functions, that previous function is lost forever; there is no way you can retrieve it because there is no reference by which to call it.

Anonymous functions (though not always recommended) are often used for assigning functions to event handlers. They also provide a quick and easy way to add events to a class.

Car.as

```
package {
  public class Car {
    private var speed:Number;
    private var direction:String;
    public var onSpeedChange:Function;
    public var onDirectionChange:Function;

    public function Car(speed:Number,direction:String) {
      this.speed = speed;
      this.direction = direction;
    }

    public function increaseSpeed():void {
      this.speed += 10;
      this.onSpeedChange();
    }

    public function setDirection(direction:String):void {
      this.direction = direction;
      this.onDirectionChange();
    }
  }
}
```

The preceding code needs to be saved as Car.as, and the following code needs to be used in an FLA in the same folder:

```
var ferrari:Car = new Car(50, "West");
ferrari.onSpeedChange = function():void {
  trace("The car now has a speed of "+this.speed+" KMH");
}
ferrari.onDirectionChange = function():void {
  trace("Now driving in the following direction: "+this.direction);
}
ferrari.increaseSpeed();
ferrari.setDirection("East");
```

If you run this code, you'll see the output shown in Figure 9-4.

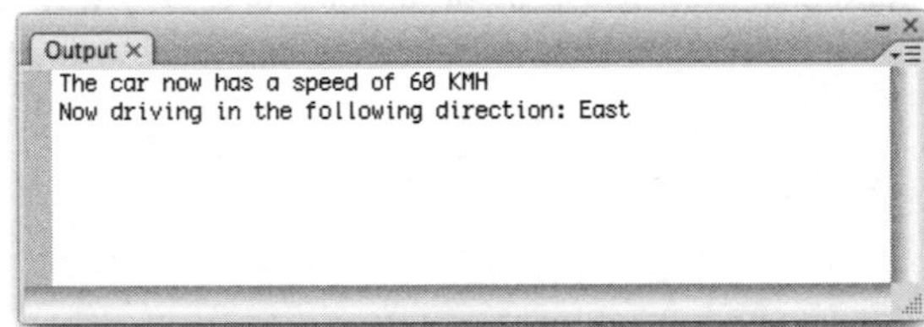

Figure 9-4. Car class Output panel

The code in our Car class is very interesting in that we initialize two variables of a Function type (onSpeedChange, onDirectionChange) but don't specify them as being a method in our class. Instead, we define anonymous functions in the FLA for these function references:

```
function():void {
  trace("The car now has a speed of "+this.speed+" KMH");
}
```

and

```
function():void {
  trace("Now driving in the following direction: "+this.direction);
}
```

By triggering the onSpeedChange and onDirectionChange references in the class, we're actually running the code that we associate with it from outside the class.

The method discussed previously is an easy way to simulate events, though there are certainly more flexible and generally accepted methods of handling events through the latest ActionScript 3.0 class framework, as I'll show in Chapter 15.

That completes the initial tour of classes. Right now, let's use classes to update the encapsulation example from the last chapter.

Implementing a class

When you think about the Motion class we discussed at the beginning of this chapter, there are a couple of difficulties with applying it to movie clips. For example, the class needs to be associated with a particular movie clip, and there is no easy way to start or stop the movement.

The way around this is to make a more abstract class that can handle this by passing parameters to its constructor method. I'll show how to handle this next by introducing the Mover class.

The Mover class

Every class needs a constructor. Since you're creating a Mover class, you need to have a constructor function named Mover.

```
package {
  import flash.display.MovieClip;
  import flash.events.Event;
  public class Mover extends MovieClip {
```

```
        private var targetMC:MovieClip;

        public function Mover(targetMC:MovieClip) {
          this.targetMC = targetMC;
        }

        private function updatePosition(evtObj:Event):void {
          this.targetMC. x++;
          this. targetMC.y++;
        }

        public function startMoving():void {
          this.targetMC.addEventListener(Event.ENTER_FRAME, ➥
          this.updatePosition);
        }

        public function stopMoving():void {
          this.targetMC.removeEventListener(Event.ENTER_FRAME, ➥
          this.updatePosition);
        }
      }
    }
```

The preceding code needs to be saved as `Mover.as` and the following steps need to be done to see the class in action:

1. Launch Flash.
2. Choose Flash File (ActionScript 3.0) from the Create New menu on the Start Page (or select File ➤ New and click Flash File (ActionScript 3.0) if the Start Page is disabled).
3. Save the blank document as `Mover.fla` in the folder where you saved `Mover.as`.
4. Set the frame rate to 30.
5. Draw a circle on stage and convert it to a symbol (Modify ➤ Convert to Symbol).
6. Select Movie clip as the type and give it a name of circle.
7. Draw a rectangle on stage and convert it to a symbol (Modify ➤ Convert to Symbol).
8. Give the circle instance on stage the instance name circle.
9. Give the rectangle instance on stage the instance name rectangle.
10. Rename Layer 1 as Stage.
11. Add a new layer to the timeline and rename it as ActionScript.
12. Add the following code to Frame 1 of the ActionScript layer:

```
var myMover:Mover = new Mover(circle);
myMover.startMoving();
```

If you run Test Movie (Control ➤ Test Movie), you'll see the circle movie clip moving across the screen. The beauty about this version of our class is that we can start and stop the movement at any time by using the `startMoving` and `stopMoving` methods.

Now we can easily apply our class to any movie clip without having to associate it in the Flash IDE. It's just as easy to apply it to our rectangle as it was to the circle as you'll see from the following code:

```
var myMover:Mover = new Mover(rectangle);
myMover.startMoving();
```

If you run Test Movie now (Control ➤ Test Movie), you'll see the rectangle movie clip moving across the screen instead. Of course, it's also possible to use multiple instances of this Mover class to apply it to multiple movie clips at the same time. You'll find an example of this here:

```
var circleMover:Mover = new Mover(circle);
var rectangleMover:Mover = new Mover(rectangle);
circleMover.startMoving();
rectangleMover.startMoving();
```

Running the preceding code, and you've got both movie clips on stage moving at the same time. Enough examples of the class in action—let's look at how it handles this movement.

The constructor of our Mover class accepts a single parameter that references a movie clip. The movie clip reference is stored in a class parameter called targetMC. Next up we've got our updatePosition method that handles the actual movie clip positioning by using its x and y properties.

Now we have two functions (startMoving and stopMoving) that respectively add and remove our updatePosition method from the targetMC movie clip ENTER_FRAME event handler.

By calling the startMoving method, we assign updatePosition to an event listener for the target movie clip ENTER_FRAME event, which consequently starts moving; by calling the stopMoving method, we remove the event listener for the target movie clip ENTER_FRAME event, which makes it stop moving.

This class is still a work in progress and could do with another couple of updates. That is exactly what I'll be doing throughout the following chapters.

What's next?

Now you know the basics of encapsulation and classes. Next, I cover class inheritance. Using inheritance, you can add new capabilities and extend the current code without even touching the Mover class.

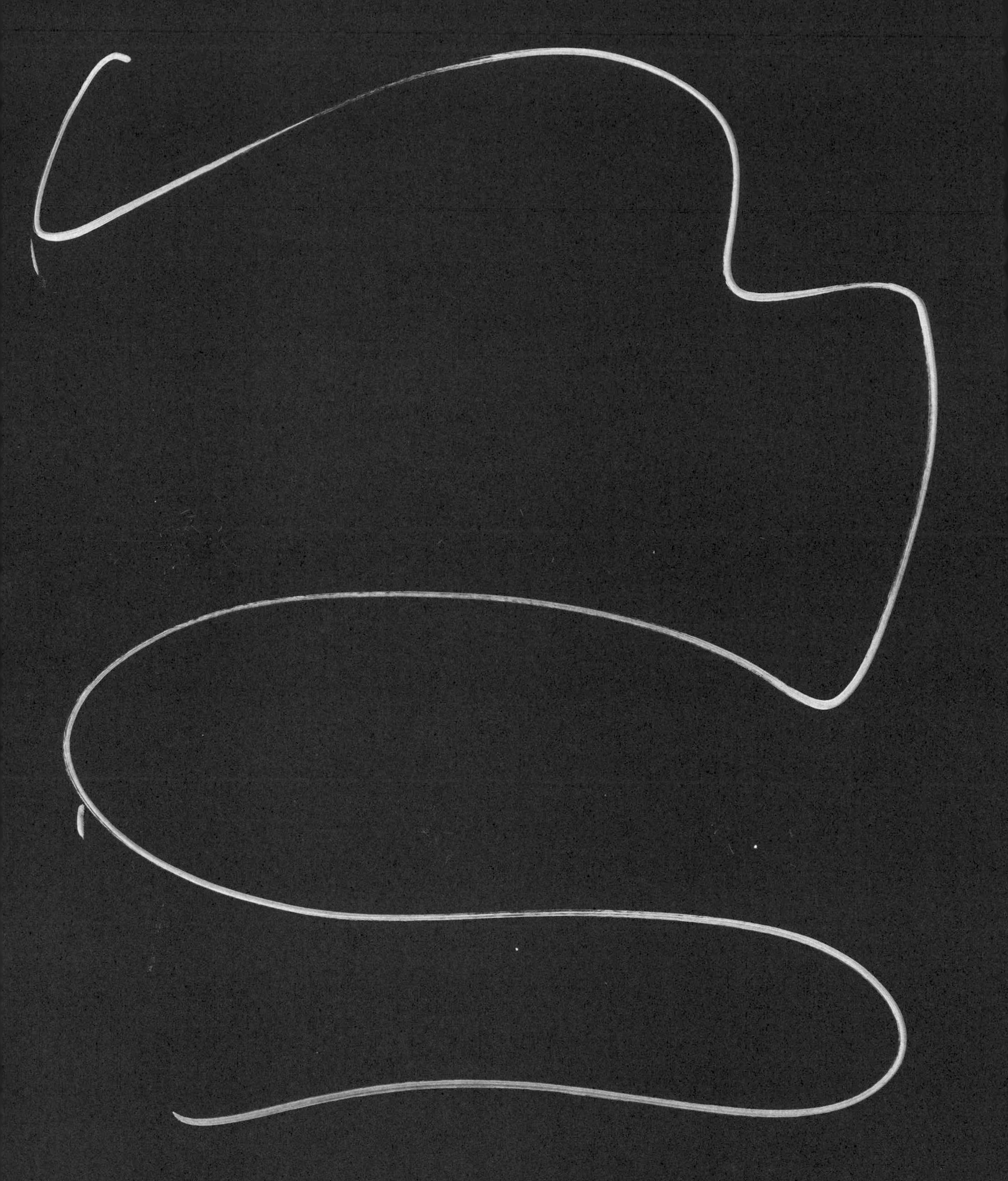

10 INHERITANCE

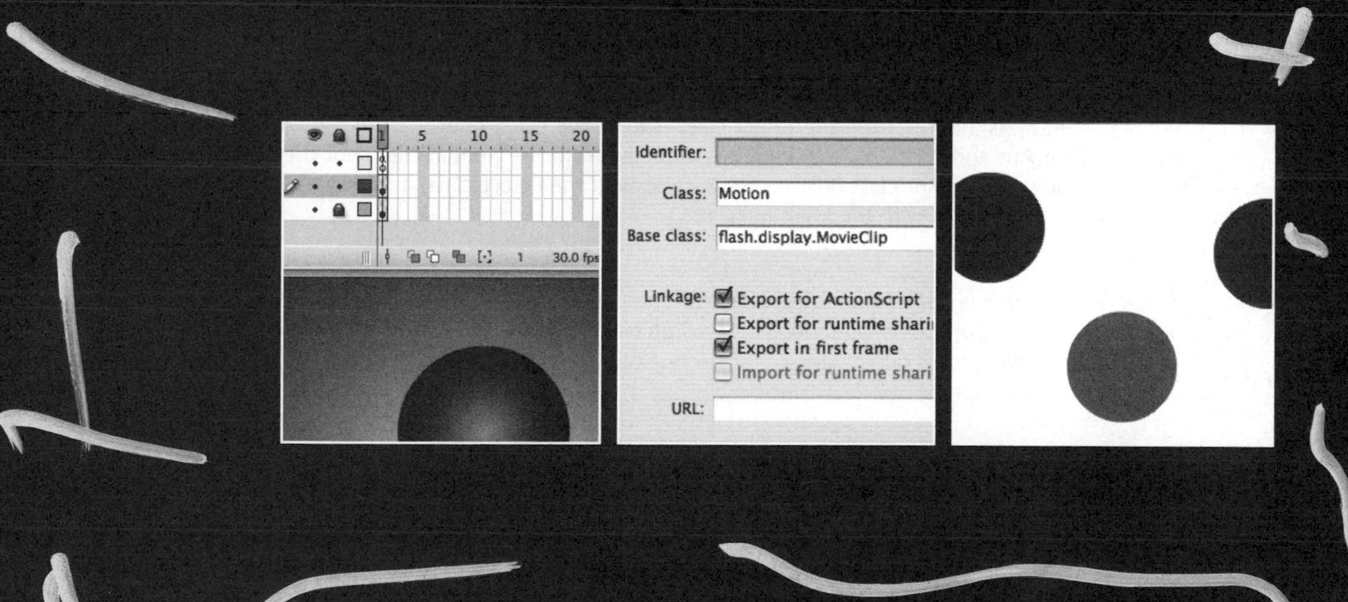

In this chapter, I'll walk you through an example to demonstrate inheritance in ActionScript 3.0. Whenever you write a new class to extend or enhance an existing class (without actually altering the existing class), you're using inheritance. Inheritance can introduce new capabilities without the fear of breaking existing applications.

About class hierarchy

Inheritance groups two or more classes together into a hierarchy (much like the folder structure on your computer). The first class in the hierarchy is the base class (like a top-level folder). The next class is a subclass (like a subfolder). Each subsequent class inherits from the previous one, so every subclass has a definite parent.

Look at the following class hierarchy:

Animal Class (this is the base class; it has no parent; its subclass is Mammal)

Mammal Class (this is a subclass; its parent is Animal; its subclass is Whale)

Whale Class (this is a subclass; its parent is Mammal; it has no subclasses)

Classes range from general to specific. The base class is the most general; subclasses are more specific (for example, a whale is a specific mammal). Class hierarchies can be simple or complex. Here's another example:

Life Class

Plant Class **Animal Class**

Tropical Class **Desert Class** **Insect Class** **Mammal Class**

Banana Class **Cactus Class** **Ant Class** **Whale Class**

Life is the base class (the most general); everything else is a subclass (more specific). The Ant class inherits from the Insect class. The Whale class inherits from the Mammal class. The Ant and Whale classes inherit (indirectly) from the Animal class, but they don't even know it! The Ant class only communicates with the Insect class, and the Whale class only communicates with the Mammal class.

> *This is natural inherited behavior in OOP—a class inherits from its parent (not its grandparent). ActionScript 3.0 provides a special keyword,* `super`*, as a reference to its parent class.*

A quick inheritance test

Let's do a quick inheritance test. Using the Mover class we built in the previous chapter, let's now extend it to include some bounce behavior. Just to remind ourselves, this is the code for the Mover class:

```
package {

  import flash.display.MovieClip;
  import flash.events.Event;

  public class Mover {

    public var targetMC:MovieClip;

    public function Mover(targetMC:MovieClip) {
      this.targetMC = targetMC;
    }
    protected function updatePosition(evtObj:Event):void {
      this.targetMC.x++;
      this.targetMC.y++;
    }
    public function startMoving():void {
      this.targetMC.addEventListener(Event.ENTER_FRAME,➥
      this.updatePosition);
    }
    public function stopMoving():void {
      this.targetMC.removeEventListener(Event.ENTER_FRAME,➥
      this.updatePosition);
    }

  }
}
```


Before we move any further, it is important to add a little functionality that allows our Mover class to do something more than just move at the same speed both horizontally and vertically. To do this, we'll add two properties: xVel and yVel, which store the velocity at which our targetMC moves in any given direction.

```
public var xVel:Number;
public var yVel:Number;
```

Next, we add two additional parameters to the constructor method:

```
function Mover(targetMC:MovieClip, xVel:Number, yVel:Number) {
  this.targetMC = targetMC;
  this.xVel = xVel;
  this.yVel = yVel;
}
```

Finally, the updatePosition method needs to be tweaked to read as follows:

```
protected function updatePosition(evtObj:Event):void {
  this.targetMC.x += this.xVel;
  this.targetMC.y += this.yVel;
}
```

Having made these tweaks, we can now have our Mover class move any movie clip with any given horizontal and vertical velocity. Pretty neat! The full code of the Mover class now looks as follows:

```
package {

  import flash.events.Event;
  import flash.display.MovieClip;

  public class Mover {

    public var targetMC:MovieClip;
    public var xVel:Number;
    public var yVel:Number;

    function Mover(targetMC:MovieClip, xVel:Number, yVel:Number) {
      this.targetMC = targetMC;
      this.xVel = xVel;
      this.yVel = yVel;
    }
    protected function updatePosition(evtObj:Event):void {
      this.targetMC.x += this.xVel;
      this.targetMC.y += this.yVel;
    }
    public function startMoving():void {
      this.targetMC.addEventListener(Event.ENTER_FRAME,➥
      this.updatePosition);
    }
    public function stopMoving():void {
      this.targetMC.removeEventListener(Event.ENTER_FRAME,➥
      this.updatePosition);
    }

  }
}
```

When you want to create an instance of this new Mover class, you would use the following code:

```
var myMover:Mover = new Mover(circle, 2, 3);
var myMover.startMoving();
```

This code moves our circle movie clip at a velocity of 2 pixels horizontally and 3 pixels vertically once every frame.

Now, the next step is writing our Bouncer class, which extends (or inherits) the new Mover class code. The code for this is listed here:

Bouncer.as

```
package {

  import flash.display.MovieClip;
  import Mover;

  public class Bouncer extends Mover {
    public function Bouncer(targetMC:MovieClip, xVel:Number,➥
    yVel:Number) {
      super(targetMC,xVel,yVel);
    }
  }
}
```

The preceding code needs to be saved in a file called `Bouncer.as` in the same folder as `Mover.as`.

What you'll need to do next is get a copy of `Mover.fla` and save it as `Inheritance.fla` in the folder where `Bouncer.as` and `Mover.as` are located. Open up `Inheritance.fla` and on Frame 1 of the ActionScript layer change the code to

```
var myBouncer:Bouncer = new Bouncer(circle, 2, 3);
myBouncer.startMoving();
```

Feel free to delete the rectangle movie clip from the stage, as we'll not be using this just now. Test the movie (select Control ➤ Test Movie) and you'll see that the circle on stage is now moving, just as was the case with the Mover class. Nothing spectacular, you say? Well, remember, you're now instantiating the Bouncer class, which shows you that it has inherited the functionality of the Mover class by its ability to use the `startMoving` method and the `targetMC` property. Inheritance in action, what an awe-inspiring sight!

About inheritance syntax

Let's look at what syntax we used to initiate class inheritance in ActionScript 3.0. First of all, you'll need to have the extends keyword when defining the class.

```
public class Bouncer extends Mover {
  ...
}
```

After the extends keyword, you define what class it inherits from, in this case Mover. Important to note is that a class can extend only one class at a time, and this class needs to be imported first.

As soon as this extends syntax is added to the class statement, all nonprivate methods and properties of that inherited class are available in the current class. This brings up an important point: what if we define a method or property with the same name in the Bouncer class? It's easy enough to give this a try—add the following code to the Bouncer class with the override keyword:

```
override public function startMoving():void {
  trace("startMoving function called in Bouncer class");
}
```

If we use Test Movie now, we get the following line in the Output panel, but our circle movie clip does not move at all:

startMoving function called in Bouncer class

That's not good at all. We also want to have access to the startMoving method that was defined in the Mover class. This is where the super keyword comes in; it specifically tells a class to look for a method or property in its parent class, our superclass. Using this keyword, we can tweak the startMoving method in the Bouncer class to read as follows:

```
override public function startMoving():void {
  trace("startMoving function called in Bouncer class");
  super.startMoving();
}
```

Testing our movie now gives us a much better response: we get both the trace statement in the Output panel and our circle is moving on the stage. It's getting more and more interesting by the minute—we've just extended a method and in the process used an important concept in OOP called **polymorphism** (more about this in the next chapter).

When you look at the code of our Bouncer class, you'll notice that the constructor also uses the super keyword but actually calls it as you would with any other method. It passes the targetMC, xVel, and yVel parameters we got in the Bouncer class down to the constructor of the Mover class.

In other words, a call to super() calls the superclass constructor; in this case, it was needed because Mover required a targetMC property to be passed to its constructor.

The Bouncer class

Using inheritance, you can safely extend existing classes with new or alternative behavior without breaking existing applications. Existing applications continue to work because they do not interact with (or even know about) the newer classes (they use the existing classes as always).

Currently, the Bouncer class behaves just like the Mover class. Next, we'll add new behavior to the Bouncer class. This new behavior will consist of a bounceAtBorder method that bounces our movie clip when it hits the end of the stage.

```
private function bounceAtBorder():void {
  if (this.targetMC.x > this.targetMC.stage.stageWidth-➥
   (this.targetMC.width/2)) {
    trace("Bounce at right edge");
    this.targetMC.x = this.targetMC.stage.stageWidth-➥
     (this.targetMC.width/2);
    this.xVel *= -1;
  }
  if (this.targetMC.y > this.targetMC.stage.stageHeight-➥
   (this.targetMC.height/2)) {
    trace("Bounce at bottom edge");
    this.targetMC.y = this.targetMC.stage.stageHeight-➥
     (this.targetMC.height/2);
    this.yVel *= -1;
  }
  if (this.targetMC.x < this.targetMC.width/2) {
    trace("Bounce at left edge");
    this.targetMC.x = this.targetMC.width/2;
    this.xVel *= -1;
  }
  if (this.targetMC.y < this.targetMC.height/2) {
    trace("Bounce at top edge");
    this.targetMC.y = this.targetMC.height/2;
    this.yVel *= -1;
  }
}
```

When you look at the bounceAtBorder method, you'll find that it has four if statements, one for each edge of the screen. Each of the if statements checks the x or y position of targetMC against the minimum or maximum width and height. To do this, we use the built-in stage object of the movie clip and its stageWidth and stageHeight properties that return the available width and height of the stage. Because the registration point of our movie clip is in the center, we need to accommodate the maximum and minimum width with the targetMC's width and height properties. Take a look at the following table to see how these minimum and maximum positions are calculated:

Edge	Calculation
Right edge	Width of the stage minus half the width of the targetMC movie clip
Bottom edge	Height of the stage minus half the height of the targetMC movie clip
Left edge	Half the width of the targetMC movie clip
Top edge	Half the height of the targetMC movie clip

10

The only thing that's left for us to do now is tweak the updatePosition method; along with the original code, it should now call the bounceAtBorder method as well.

```
override protected function updatePosition(evtObj:Event):void {
  super.updatePosition(evtObj);
  this.bounceAtBorder();
}
```

The preceding code overrides the updatePosition event listener that was originally defined in the Mover class. In this new updatePosition method in the Bouncer class, the original updatePosition method is called using the super keyword as well as the bounceAtBorder method in the Bouncer class. The complete code for our Bouncer class now looks as follows:

```
package {

  import flash.display.MovieClip;
  import Mover;
  import flash.events.Event;

  public class Bouncer extends Mover {

    public function Bouncer(targetMC:MovieClip, xVel:Number,➥
    yVel:Number) {
      super(targetMC,xVel,yVel);
    }

    private function bounceAtBorder():void {
      if (this.targetMC.x > this.targetMC.stage.stageWidth-➥
       (this.targetMC.width/2)) {
        trace("Bounce at right edge");
        this.targetMC.x = this.targetMC.stage.stageWidth-➥
         (this.targetMC.width/2);
        this.xVel *= -1;
      }
      if (this.targetMC.y > this.targetMC.stage.stageHeight-➥
       (this.targetMC.height/2)) {
        trace("Bounce at bottom edge");
        this.targetMC.y = this.targetMC.stage.stageHeight-➥
         (this.targetMC.height/2);
        this.yVel *= -1;
      }
      if (this.targetMC.x < this.targetMC.width/2) {
        trace("Bounce at left edge");
        this.targetMC.x = this.targetMC.width/2;
        this.xVel *= -1;
      }
      if (this.targetMC.y < this.targetMC.height/2) {
        trace("Bounce at top edge");
        this.targetMC.y = this.targetMC.height/2;
```

```
            this.yVel *= -1;
          }
        }

        override protected function updatePosition(evtObj:Event):void {
          super.updatePosition(evtObj);
          this.bounceAtBorder();
        }

      }
    }
```

You can now save Bouncer.as and take a look at Inheritance.fla. Make sure Frame 1 of the ActionScript layer reads as follows:

```
var myBouncer:Bouncer = new Bouncer(circle,2,3);
myBouncer.startMoving();
```

Save Inheritance.fla and run Test Movie, and you should now see the circle movie clip moving across the screen with a horizontal velocity of 2 pixels per frame and 3 pixels per frame vertically. As soon as the movie clip hits an edge, a trace statement is executed showing that in the Output panel, and it bounces off in the opposite direction.

Great work—you've just seen inheritance in action and built your very own Bouncer class by extending the Mover class!

The Gravity class

Let's create a Gravity class to help the Ball move in a natural manner. You'll use inheritance again, but this time you'll extend the Bouncer class.

Create a new file called Gravity.as and save it in the same folder as the Bouncer and Mover classes. We'll start off with the basic code as follows:

Gravity.as

```
package {

  import flash.display.MovieClip;
  import Bouncer;
  import flash.events.Event;

  public class Gravity extends Bouncer {

    private var strength: Number;
```

```
      public function Gravity(targetMC:MovieClip, xVel:Number,➥
      yVel:Number, strength:Number=1):void {
        super(targetMC, xVel, yVel);
        this.strength = strength;
      }
    }
  }
```

The Gravity class constructor takes the three parameters we know are needed for the Bouncer class as well as a strength parameter that defines the strength of the gravitational pull. We pass the first three parameters to the superclass, and the third is assigned to our class scope using the following syntax:

```
this.strength = strength ;
```

You'll have noticed that we set a default value of 1 in case no strength parameter gets passed to the Gravity class. The next thing we'll do is override the updatePosition method in the Gravity class, which will now point to two new methods, applyGravity and applyFriction (we'll be writing those in a minute), in the ENTER_FRAME event listener. You can see how that updatePosition method now looks:

```
override protected function updatePosition(evtObj:Event):void {
  super.updatePosition(evtObj);
  this.applyGravity();
  this.applyFriction();
}
```

Just like we did in the Bouncer class, we're now calling the applyGravity and applyFriction functions in the ENTER_FRAME event handler.

Now that we've got that sorted, let's focus on these two new methods. The first one we'll look at is applyGravity:

```
private function applyGravity():void {
  this.yVel += this.strength;
}
```

Doesn't that look easy? That code adds more pull to the vertical movement of our targetMC movie clip. As you'll see, the applyFriction method will not be much more difficult:

```
private function applyFriction():void {
  this.xVel *= 0.98;
  this.yVel *= 0.98;
}
```

In this method, we're adding friction to both the horizontal and vertical velocity by decreasing the velocity slightly every frame. We're using 0.98 here because it gives us the best effect. You could add this friction factor as an additional parameter for your Gravity class. Whatever the number is you'll use for this, it should be below 1; otherwise, it would in fact increase velocity.

It's nice to think about the friction coefficient as a percentage of the previous velocity. For example, with a coefficient of 0.98, our Mover moves only 98% the speed it did the frame before. Eventually, friction will slow the movement to nothing, just as in the physical world.

Save the Gravity class and turn your attention to `Inheritance.fla`. Make sure the code in Frame 1 of the ActionScript layer looks as follows:

```
var myGravity:Gravity = new Gravity(circle, 2, 3, 5);
myGravity.startMoving();
```

If you save the document and run Test Movie, you'll see the circle movie clip, moving with a horizontal velocity of 2 pixels and a vertical velocity of 3 pixels per frame, bounce off the edges of the stage and slow down as if gravity were pulling it to the ground, and eventually the targetMC will rest on the bottom of the stage. In this case, the amount of gravity we applied is 5 pixels per frame.

One thing you will notice is that even when the movie clip has come to a standstill at the bottom of the stage, the `ENTER_FRAME` event handler continuously keeps firing the "Bounce at bottom edge" `trace` statement to the Output panel. To optimize our code and stop this from happening, we'll add a method that monitors the `yVel` property, and if that is zero, we stop listening to the `EVENT_FRAME` event on our targetMC movie clip. This method, which we'll call checkForStop, needs the following code:

```
private function checkForStop():void {
  if(this.targetMC.y == this.targetMC.stage.stageHeight ➥
    (this.targetMC.height/2)) {
    if(this.targetMC.x == this.lastPosX &&➥
      this.targetMC.y == this.lastPosY) {
      this.stopMoving();
    }
  }
  this.lastPosX = this.targetMC.x;
  this.lastPosY = this.targetMC.y;
}
```

That's quite a bit of code just to check whether our targetMC is still moving or not, but you'll see what it does in a minute. The first `if` statement in the `checkForStop` method checks whether the movie clip is on the bottom edge of the stage. If that is the case, it moves on to an `if` statement that checks the current x and y position of the targetMC against the last position. To do this, two new private class properties are introduced: `lastPosX` and `lastPosY`, which hold the latest x and y position of targetMC. If the current x and y position is the same as the last x and y position, and the targetMC is on the bottom edge, we can be sure that our movie clip has stopped moving. In that case, we call the `stopMoving` function in the superclass, which removes the `ENTER_FRAME` event listener and stops the animation.

That's it—we've just completed the Gravity class! Be sure to save Gravity.as and run Test Movie on Inheritance.fla. You'll see that the previous problem with the ENTER_FRAME event handler not stopping after the movie clip finished moving is now solved. The following is the full code of the Gravity class:

Gravity.as

```
package {

  import flash.display.MovieClip;
  import flash.events.Event;

  public class Gravity extends Bouncer {

    private var strength: Number;
    private var lastPosX: Number;
    private var lastPosY: Number;

    public function Gravity(targetMC:MovieClip, xVel:Number,➥
    yVel:Number, strength:Number=1) {
      super(targetMC, xVel, yVel);
      this.strength = strength;
    }

    override protected function updatePosition(evtObj:Event):void {
      super.updatePosition(evtObj);
      this.applyGravity();
      this.applyFriction();
      this.checkForStop();
    }

    private function applyGravity():void {
      this.yVel += this.strength;
    }

    private function applyFriction():void {
      this.xVel *= 0.98;
      this.yVel *= 0.98;
    }

    private function checkForStop():void {
      if(this.targetMC.y == this.targetMC.stage.stageHeight-➥
        (this.targetMC.height/2)) {
        if(this.targetMC.x == this.lastPosX &&➥
          this.targetMC.y == this.lastPosY) {
          this.stopMoving();
        }
      }
```

```
      this.lastPosX = this.targetMC.x;
      this.lastPosY = this.targetMC.y;
    }

  }

}
```

You might remember that we hard-coded the value of 0.98 in the `applyFriction` *method of the Gravity class. As an exercise, try updating the code so people can specify the amount of friction when instantiating the class. Be sure to have a default value for friction. (Hint: study the* `strength` *property in the constructor of the Gravity class.)*

Inheritance summary

Inheritance extends existing classes with new and alternative behaviors without breaking existing applications. Existing applications continue to work because they do not interact with (or even know about) the newer classes. Inheritance adds capability without breaking compatibility. Look at this sample code:

Animal.as

```
package {
  public class Animal {
    public function Animal() {
    }
    public function speak(sound:String):void {
      trace(sound);
    }
  }
}
```

Cat.as

```
package {
  import Animal;

  public class Cat extends Animal {
    public function Cat() {
    }
    public function cryBaby():void {
      for(var i:uint = 0; i < 100; i++) {
        super.speak("Meow! Meow! Meow!");
```

10

```
            }
        }
    }
}
```

```
var suki:Cat = new Cat();
suki.cryBaby();
```

With just one statement

```
public class Cat extends Animal {
  ...
}
```

the Cat class inherits from the Animal class. The Cat class has all the capabilities and characteristics of the Animal class, plus its own unique capabilities. The super keyword enables child classes (such as Cat) to talk to parent classes (such as Animal). If you try the previous code, you'll find out that you can use ActionScript 3.0 to code a very noisy cat.

What's next?

This chapter introduced the major features and benefits of class inheritance. Next, we'll look at the final building block of OOP: polymorphism.

11 POLYMORPHISM

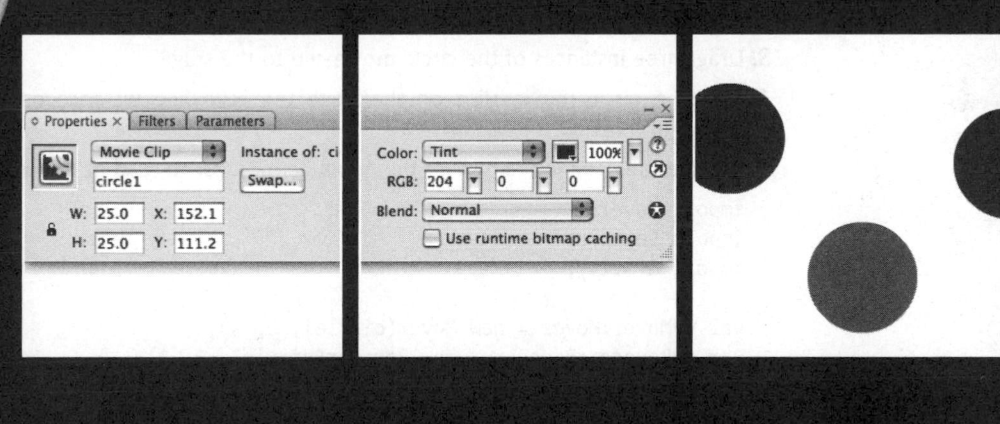

The concept of *polymorphism* implies having certain functionality appear in multiple forms throughout your application, but having a unified way to call it. Doing this allows different classes throughout the project to be easily interchangeable.

In this chapter, we'll create some examples to demonstrate polymorphism in ActionScript 3.0. In a visual environment such as Flash, polymorphism is best observed when multiple objects exhibit similar behavior. Behind the scenes, this usually means multiple classes implementing functions of the same name.

I didn't mention this in detail in the previous chapters, but things like the `startMoving` method that you can call for the Mover, Bouncer, and Gravity classes are excellent examples of *polymorphic design*. You could create many different objects from these classes and know that any of them could fulfill the `startMoving` request (because they're all based on classes that implement that same method). At random, you could request any of them to start moving. With polymorphism, you don't care how things happen, just that they happen. (That sure reminds me of some project managers I've worked with in the past!)

Building a polymorphism example

This section presents a brief, visual demonstration of polymorphism. We're not going to spend a great deal of time creating a complex example right now; the idea is to get you acquainted with the concept of polymorphism and how you can take advantage of it in your own projects.

To start off, make a copy of `Inheritance.fla` and name it `Polymorphism.fla`. Double-click `Polymorphism.fla` to launch Flash.

The next thing we'll do is populate the stage so we have some movie clips to work with:

1. Delete all items on the stage.
2. Display the Library panel (select Window ➤ Library).
3. Drag three instances of the circle movie clip to the stage.
4. Give the circle movie clips on the stage the following instance names: circle1, circle2, and circle3.
5. Change the code in Frame 1 of the ActionScript layer to read as follows:

```
import Mover;
import Bouncer;
import Gravity;

var myMover:Mover = new Mover(circle1, 2, 3);
var myBouncer:Bouncer = new Bouncer(circle2, 2, 3);
var myGravity:Gravity = new Gravity(circle3, 2, 3, 5);

function startClassInstanceMoving(className:Mover):void {
  className.startMoving();
}
```

The preceding code does not differ much from the code used for instantiating the Mover, Bouncer, and Gravity classes in the previous chapters. The one thing I added is a function, `startClassInstanceMoving`, that accepts a parameter, `className`. The function itself tries to call a `startMoving` function on whatever object is passed to it.

To make the difference between all the circle instances more obvious, let's make each a different color. First select the `circle1` instance on the stage by clicking it and opening up the Properties panel (Window ➤ Properties). In the Properties panel, select `Tint` from the `Color` drop-down menu and choose red with the color picker tool (see Figure 11-1).

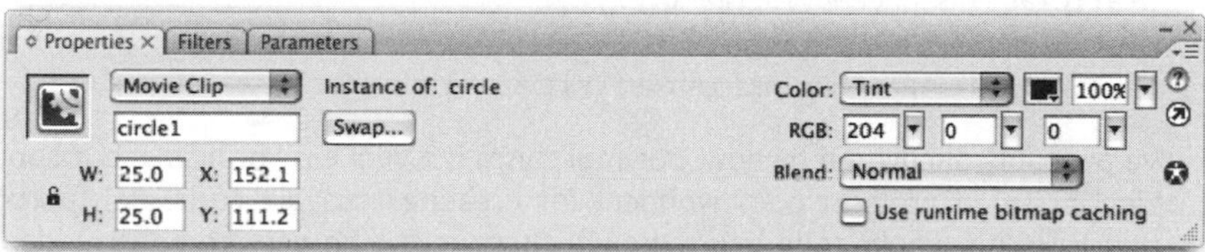

Figure 11-1. Setting the tint color in the Properties panel

Repeat the same for the `circle2` and `circle3` instances, giving them a blue and green color tint, respectively. When you've finished, `Polymorphism.fla`'s stage should look something like Figure 11-2.

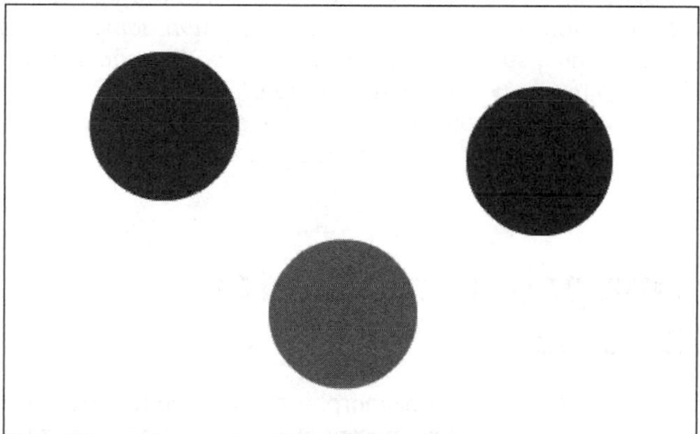

Figure 11-2. The circle instances on the stage

You've probably guessed by now what you'll be doing: passing the names of our class instances to this function should start them moving. Add the following line of code before testing this movie:

```
startClassInstanceMoving(myMover);
```

Save the document and run Test Movie (Control ➤ Test Movie) to see this code in action. If all went well, you should now see the `circle1` instance moving across the stage. When you change that last line of code to read as follows, you get a different result:

```
startClassInstanceMoving(myBouncer);
```

If you run Test Movie now, you'll see circle2 bouncing across the stage. Of course, the same goes for the Gravity class—using the following code, you'll have circle3 bouncing with gravity and friction effect on the stage:

```
startClassInstanceMoving(myGravity);
```

There is nothing stopping you from using all three at once; as there are three class instances, they can operate completely independently. Try the following code to see all circle instances on stage moving at the same time:

```
startClassInstanceMoving(myMover);
startClassInstanceMoving(myBouncer);
startClassInstanceMoving(myGravity);
```

As you've probably discovered by now, polymorphism is a very easy principle, but applying it in object-oriented projects does wonders for creating reusable code. Polymorphism allows you to write simple code, even though there might be very complex underlying class interaction. You shouldn't have to know or care about that if you use polymorphic design throughout a project—you could even use classes written by another developer without even opening them once.

Bear in mind that applying this technique is useful only if you use the same name for functions that perform more or less the same task. There is a danger of going overboard with polymorphism and using very generic function names such as "update", "run", and so forth. Doing so isn't good for code readability, and it might even result in more confusion than clarity. Be sure to refer to Chapter 6, which covers best practices, if you're in doubt about how to handle naming conventions.

Implementing polymorphism for application reuse

With encapsulation, inheritance, and polymorphism, you have the tools to make software reuse a reality. The sections that follow present examples demonstrating this concept.

Basic concept of polymorphism

Functional polymorphism occurs when multiple classes implement consistent functions. For example, consider the following classes:

Bored.as

```
package {
  public class Bored {
    public function Bored() {
```

```
    }
    public function doSomething():void {
      trace("I'm bored, let's do something!");
    }
  }
}
```

Tired.as

```
package {
  public class Tired {
    public function Tired() {
    }
    public function doSomething():void {
      this.doNothing();
    }
    private function doNothing():void {
      trace("I'm tired, I don't want to do anything.");
    }
  }
}
```

Hungry.as

```
package {
  public class Hungry {
    public function Hungry() {
    }
    public function doSomething():void {
      this.doLunch();
    }
    private function doLunch():void {
      trace("I'm hungry, let's get lunch!");
    }
  }
}
```


All of these classes implement the doSomething function, so you could write the following in an FLA document located in the same folder:

```
import Tired;
import Bored;
import Hungry;

var bob:Tired = new Tired();
var jill:Bored = new Bored();
var janet:Hungry = new Hungry();
```

```
bob.doSomething();  // Output:  I'm tired, I don't want to do anything.
jill.doSomething();  // Output:  I'm bored, let's do something!
janet.doSomething();  // Output:  I'm hungry, let's get lunch!
```

This is a simple example, and you had to create the objects manually, but what if you could create the objects dynamically? Polymorphism allows you to control dynamic objects without knowing ahead of time which objects you're dealing with.

Functional polymorphism at work

Now let's look at a slightly more useful example of polymorphism. If you were to build a Flash-based tool for a human resources department, a good place to start would be an Employee class, as follows. This base class then holds all properties and methods that are shared by all types of employees the company might have.

Employee.as

```
package {
  public class Employee {

    protected var baseSalary:Number = 1000;

    public function Employee() {
      super();
    }

    public function receivePayment():Number {
      return this.baseSalary;
    }

  }
}
```

The preceding code shows an Employee class with just one property that contains the base salary of an employee, and a `receivePayment` method, because that's what we care about most, no?

With this base class in place, you have a starting point to create any number of employee types. Each employee type is a class that inherits from the Employee class and implements its own `receivePayment` method. For example, the following class defines an Engineer employee type.

Engineer.as

```
package {

  import Employee;
```

```
    public class Engineer extends Employee {

      public function Engineer() {
         super();
      }
      override public function receivePayment():Number {
        return this.baseSalary*2;
      }

    }
  }
```

The Engineer type has its own receivePayment method, but it is still able to use the baseSalary property it inherited from the Employee class. In a real-world situation, calculating the payment for an individual employee isn't as easy as multiplying the base salary by a given number, but you can see the value of this type of approach for calculating end-of-year bonuses, paid leave, and so forth.

The wonderful thing about polymorphism, as you know by now, is that your code doesn't need to know about all employee types that you create. Because they all implement the same set of properties and methods (either overwritten or inherited from the base class), your project remains flexible and you can easily add new types of employees without needing to restructure your application.

To illustrate this, let's create some more employee type classes, as follows:

UnpaidIntern.as

```
package {

  import Employee;

  public class UnpaidIntern extends Employee {

    public function UnpaidIntern() {
       super();
    }

    override public function receivePayment():Number {
      return 0;
    }

  }
}
```

Unpaid interns—a vastly underrated asset for any office when it comes to shifting the blame for missed deadlines—are not surprisingly paid nothing.

Manager.as

```
package {

  import Employee;

  public class Manager extends Employee {

    public function Manager() {
      super();
    }

    override public function receivePayment():Number {
      return baseSalary*3;
    }

  }
}
```

Managers in our wonderful company, on the other hand, are paid triple the base salary for their hard work hiring unpaid interns. Again, these classes just represent a specific employee type and implement their own `receivePayment` method to overwrite the default.

Those classes are all nice to have, but how do you take advantage of this polymorphic design when implementing them in the application? Let's look at a bit of code that you could use to bring together the different employee classes.

Create a new FLA file and save it in the same folder where you have the `Employee.as`, `UnpaidIntern.as`, and `Manager.as` classes stored.

With the FLA open, on the first keyframe of Layer 1 type the following code:

```
import Employee;
import UnpaidIntern;
import Engineer;
import Manager;

function payEmployee(employeeType:Employee):Number {
  return employeeType.receivePayment();
}

trace(payEmployee(new UnpaidIntern())); // outputs 0
trace(payEmployee(new Engineer())); // outputs 2000
trace(payEmployee(new Manager())); // outputs 3000
```

What is interesting about the preceding code snippet is that the payEmployee function actually takes a reference to an Employee instance as its argument (whether it be an Engineer, UnpaidIntern, or Manager). It then runs the `receivePayment` method on it and returns that value.

As a side note, because the instantiated employee type class was not assigned to a reference, it will not remain. It is immediately flushed from Flash Player's memory as soon as that statement has ended.

To test this `payEmployee` function, we create three calls to it, each passing a different employee type class, and have them trace out the values to the Output panel. When you run this code, you'll see the Flash Output panel holds the values 0, 2,000, and 3,000 for the instance of the unpaid intern, engineer, and manager, respectively.

What's next?

The examples in this chapter have given you a glimpse of how polymorphism can be an invaluable tool for your applications. I'm sure you'll be even more convinced of polymorphism's worth when we look at more advanced examples later on in this book.

Encapsulation, inheritance, and polymorphism are the basic building blocks of OOP. ActionScript 3.0, as indeed was the case in ActionScript 2.0, supports *interfaces*, which help implement those building blocks. I'll cover that feature in detail in the next chapter.

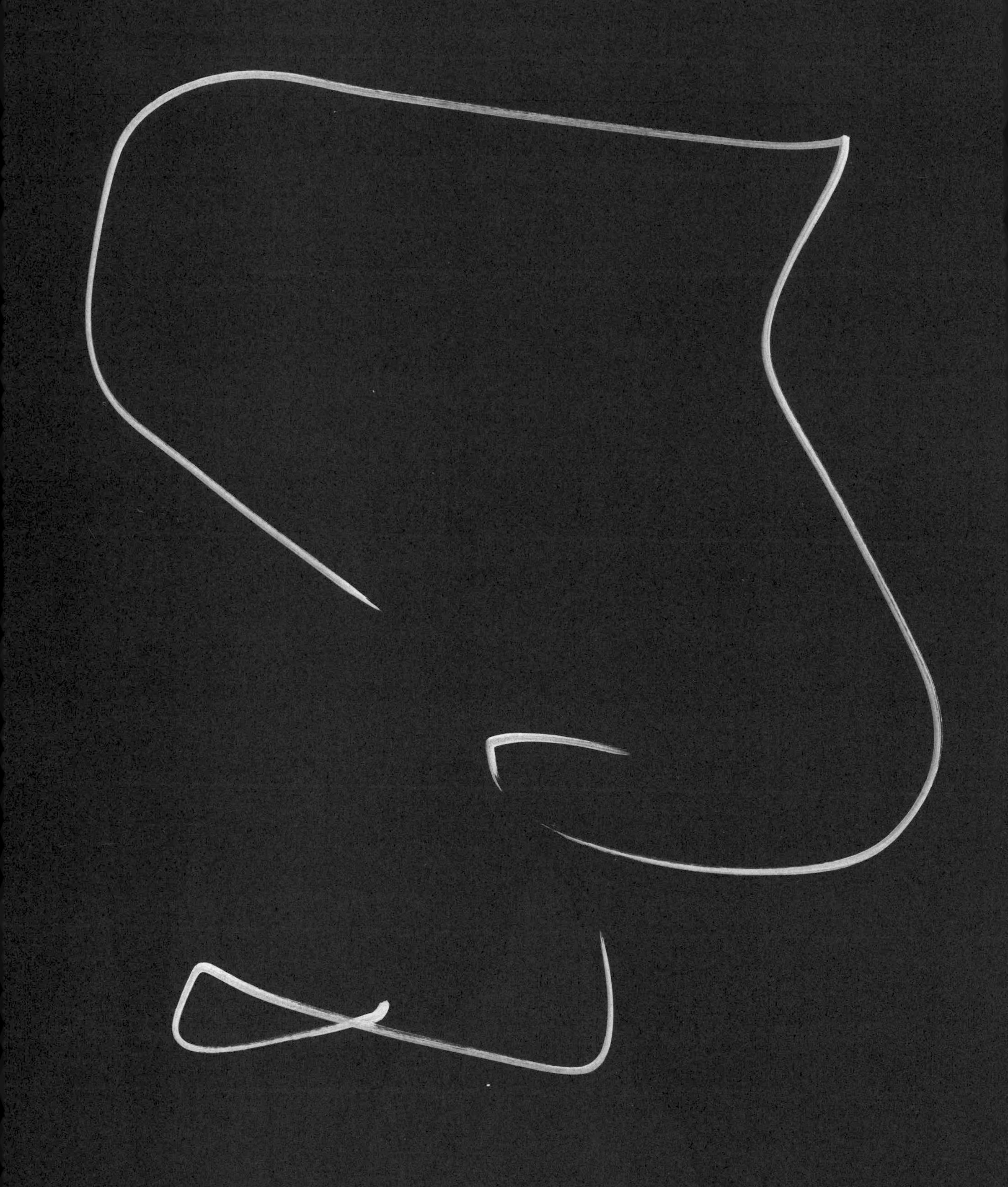

12 INTERFACES

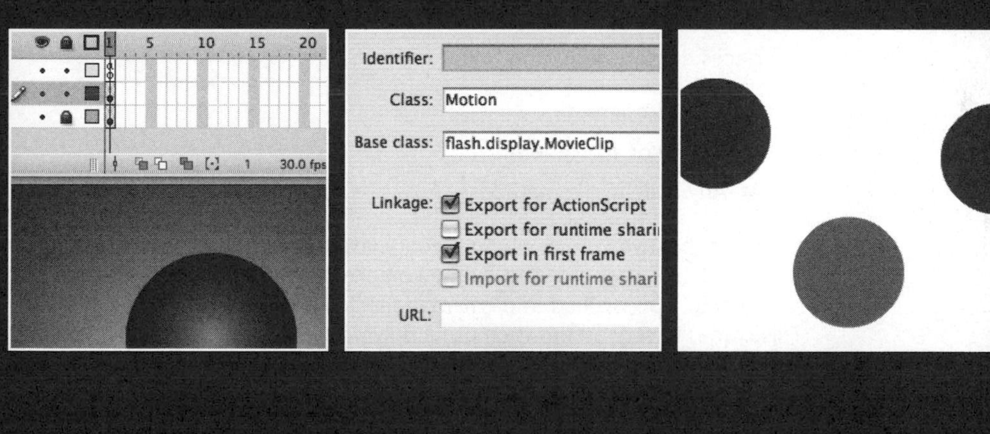

In the last few chapters, we looked at what might be considered the pillars of OOP: encapsulation, inheritance, and polymorphism. With *interfaces*, the topic of this chapter, you're able to bring together those OOP pillars and draw up a template of what your class should look like.

This chapter focuses on what interfaces are, why you should use them, and how to apply them to the code you've written in prior chapters. We'll start by looking at the concept of interfaces and how they're implemented in ActionScript 3.0.

Interfaces overview

Think back to the house-building analogy I used in the first chapter of this book. If you compare a *class* to an architect's blueprint, *class objects* are the houses built from that blueprint, and an *interface* is the contract you sign with the architect. It lists the specifications your house has to conform to and makes it legally binding.

Despite what you may expect, interfaces do not contain any code implementation. Their purpose is to provide a set of methods with corresponding typed parameters and a return datatype that a class must minimally implement to be considered valid. If a class does not conform with the interface(s) it implements, a compile error will be thrown. Interfaces do not, however, support defining properties or private class methods.

Interfaces define the following information for your class:

- The scope of a method (only public is allowed)
- The method name
- The method parameters and their corresponding datatypes
- The method return type

New in ActionScript 3.0 is the ability to define getter/setter methods in interfaces, which is a very welcome addition.

Interfaces do not specify the following:

- Class properties
- Private or static methods
- Any code inside methods

Interfaces help you check whether your classes contain all the methods you need them to have available. They are used by the compiler to validate your code and provide you with a means to plan method implementations and APIs at the planning stage of your project. This comes in very useful when using polymorphism in your classes—as interfaces enforce classes to implement specific methods and use the same naming convention.

What makes interfaces even more powerful is that they can actually serve as a datatype. If you have several classes that extend the same superclass, and you have a method that may need to accept any of these class instances as an argument, you can have them implement an interface and use that interface name as the datatype for the argument. Even better, you can use a concept called *type casting* to convert a generic interface datatype to a specific class implementation. More about this later in this chapter in the section "Implementing an interface."

To quickly familiarize you with interfaces, I'll cover some uses for interfaces and look at a simple example of an interface in the sections that follow.

Interface use cases

Now, why the heck would you want to use interfaces? At first glance, interfaces seem like a lot of extra work for little in return, but once you start looking at the bigger picture, you'll find situations where you'll want to have interfaces in place.

In the previous chapter, which covered polymorphism, I showed that because the Mover, Bouncer, and Gravity classes all inherit the same `startMoving()` method, for all intents and purposes they are completely interchangeable, assuming each instance is typed as the superclass, Mover. You can start movement on any of those classes by calling the same method. You might think since they all need to have the same method implemented these are good candidates for an interface, yet that is not the case. Since all of these classes extend the same superclass, we already know the method is implemented, and the interface would serve little purpose.

A better use case for interfaces is when you're designing an API for a class. Oftentimes in large projects, applications are separated into different code modules, and they all need to provide a specific set of methods to communicate with one another. This is where interfaces come in.

In such situations, interfaces can be used as a virtual checklist to ensure all methods are in place and have the correct datatypes and return values applied. Typically in this setup, you would define interfaces during the project planning process and give them to the team as a template to work with.

Although you can find many situations in which you can use interfaces—and in which interface usage might even be the recommended practice—most of your everyday ActionScript OOP will likely not require you to go to the length of creating interfaces. If your code is part of a larger context and will be extended upon in the future, or if you're working with a strict method structure for your classes, interfaces are definitely the way to go.

What an interface looks like

By now you're probably wondering what an interface looks like. You already know it doesn't define any code and that it simply acts as a template of what a class that implements it should look like. Let's examine a sample interface.

First, just as with ActionScript classes, an interface is saved in its own file with an `.as` extension, and it should be called by the name you assign to the interface.

> *A note on the naming convention of interfaces: most developers like to have interface names start with a capital "I" followed by the either the name of the class + "able"* (`IMoveable`) *if it is a verb or simply the class name if it is a noun* (`IGravity`). *Whatever naming convention you choose for your interfaces, it's a good idea to make sure those interface names are distinguishable from normal class names and that the names are descriptive of the types of methods defined.*

IMyInterface.as

```
package {
  public interface IMyInterface {
    public function myFirstMethod(myProperty:String):void;
    public function mySecondMethod(mySecondProperty:Number):Number;
  }
}
```

The preceding example interface is very simple. You'll notice that it's similar in structure to a class. One of the first noticeable differences is the keyword `interface` where `class` would appear. Inside the interface are two public method declarations: `myFirstMethod()`, which accepts a parameter of datatype `String` named `myProperty` and has a return type `void`, and `mySecondMethod()`, which accepts a `Number` parameter called `mySecondProperty` and returns a `Number` type.

Notice that we aren't using curly braces after the method declaration—it is followed by just a semicolon because, as I stated earlier, interfaces do not need or in fact allow you to specify any code in the method body.

Now that you know what interfaces are used for and look like, let's build some for the classes discussed in the earlier chapters and cover how they're implemented.

Implementing an interface

Let's consider the following situation—we're developing an e-commerce site and want to develop code to handle the checkout process. To do this, we can start by designing the interface of what methods we will need to have implemented.

IProduct.as

```
package {
  public interface IProduct {
    function get price():uint;
    function set price(val:uint):void;
    function get name():String;
    function set name(val:String):void;
    function get description():String;
    function set description(val:String):void;
  }
}
```

Here we have a basic interface all product instances in our e-commerce catalog can implement: price, name, and description through getter/setter methods.

Now that we have this interface, we can create some product classes:

Didgeridoo.as

```
package {
  public class Didgeridoo implements IProduct {
    private var _price:uint = 100;
    private var _name:String = "Handpainted Didgeridoo";
    private var _description:String = "Imported from Australia";

    public function get price():uint {
      return this._price;
    }
    public function set price(val:uint):void {
      this._price = val;
    }

    public function get name():String {
      return this._name;
    }
    public function set name(val:String):void {
      this._name = val;
    }

    public function get description():String {
      return this._description;
    }
    public function set description(val:String):void {
      this._description = val;
    }

  }
}
```

TShirt.as

```
package {
  public class TShirt implements IProduct {

    private var _price:uint = 20;
    private var _name:String = "T-Shirt";
    private var _description:String = "Made in China";

    public function get price():uint {
      return this._price;
    }
    public function set price(val:uint):void {
      this._price = val;
    }

    public function get name():String {
      return this._name;
    }
    public function set name(val:String):void {
      this._name = val;
    }

    public function get description():String {
      return this._description;
    }
    public function set description(val:String):void {
      this._description = val;
    }

  }
}
```

As you can see, we've just created two widely differing products that both implement the same interface. What this means is that in our checkout code, we can simply accept anything with a datatype of IProduct and know it has all the methods we require—but more about that later in this section.

Since we have such varying products we need to support in our e-commerce site, they might need to contain more specific information. It would be nice if we could enforce that through interfaces as well. As you might have guessed, that's possible, and just as with classes achieved through inheritance, interfaces can simply extend each other.

Let's put this into practice and extend the IProduct interface to hold some more getter/setter methods specifically for clothing.

IClothing.as

```
package {
  public interface IClothing extends IProduct {
    function get color():String;
    function set color(val:String):void;
    function get size():String;
    function set size(val:String):void;
  }
}
```

Now we can change our TShirt class to implement the IClothing interface instead of just IProduct.

TShirt.as

```
package {

  public class TShirt implements IClothing {

    private var _price:uint = 20;
    private var _name:String = "T-Shirt";
    private var _description:String = "Made in China";
    private var _color:String = "black";
    private var _size:String = "XXL";

    public function get price():uint {
      return this._price;
    }
    public function set price(val:uint):void {
      this._price = val;
    }

    public function get name():String {
      return this._name;
    }
    public function set name(val:String):void {
      this._name = val;
    }

    public function get description():String {
      return this._description;
    }
    public function set description(val:String):void {
      this._description = val;
    }
```

12

```
    public function get color():String {
      return this._color;
    }
    public function set color(val:String):void {
      this._color = val;
    }

    public function get size():String {
      return this._size;
    }
    public function set size(val:String):void {
      this._size = val;
    }

  }
}
```

As you will have realized, it's not enough to simply change the interface. We of course need to implement these new methods as done earlier to prevent the compiler from throwing errors.

Pretty cool—we now have a base interface that all products in our e-commerce site implement and a more specific interface for items of clothing in the store. Something else that is unique to interfaces is that, unlike inheritance, classes can implement multiple interfaces.

Our e-commerce site might for example support custom prints; these could be on any item—be it clothing, office supplies, and so on. If you think about it, using interface inheritance wouldn't be the most convenient option as it would double the number of interfaces you would need to prepare. What we can do instead is simply define one interface and use this feature of implementing multiple interfaces to our advantage.

ICustomizable.as

```
package {
  public interface ICustomizable {
    function get customPrint():String;
    function set customPrint(val:String):void;
  }
}
```

Then, if we wanted to have our TShirt class allow people to specify a custom print, we can simply use the following syntax:

TShirt.as

```
package {

  public class TShirt implements IClothing, ICustomizable {

    private var _price:uint = 20;
    private var _name:String = "T-Shirt";
    private var _description:String = "Made in China";
    private var _color:String = "black";
    private var _size:String = "XXL";
    private var _customPrint:String;

    public function get price():uint {
      return this._price;
    }
    public function set price(val:uint):void {
      this._price = val;
    }

    public function get name():String {
      return this._name;
    }
    public function set name(val:String):void {
      this._name = val;
    }

    public function get description():String {
      return this._description;
    }
    public function set description(val:String):void {
      this._description = val;
    }

    public function get color():String {
      return this._color;
    }
    public function set color(val:String):void {
      this._color = val;
    }

    public function get size():String {
      return this._size;
    }
    public function set size(val:String):void {
      this._size = val;
    }
```

```
      public function get customPrint():String {
        return this._customPrint;
      }
      public function set customPrint(val:String):void {
        this._customPrint = val;
      }

    }

  }
```

Great, we've got a nice little setup here. Now to move on to the actual checkout code and put the power of interfaces to action. For this, we'll create a new class called Checkout:

Checkout.as

```
package {
  public class Checkout {
    private var _items:Array;

    public function Checkout() {
      this._items = new Array();
    }

    public function addItem(product:IProduct):void {
      this._items.push(product);
    }

    public function calculate():uint {
      var tmp:uint = 0;
      for(var i:uint=0; i<this._items.length; i++) {
        tmp += this._items[i].price;
      }
      return tmp;
    }

  }
}
```

Looking at the preceding code, we have a private property called `_items` that is used to keep track of purchased products, an `addItem` method to add new items to the shopping basket, and a calculate method to figure out the full price of all purchased items.

To do a quick test of this code, we'll create a new blank FLA in Flash CS3 and add the following code to Layer 1 of the timeline:

```
var shoppingBasket:Checkout = new Checkout();
shoppingBasket.addItem(new Didgeridoo());
shoppingBasket.addItem(new TShirt());

trace("The total price is: "+shoppingBasket.calculate());
```

When you run Test Movie on this FLA, you'll see that the Output panel reads as follows: The total price is: 120. This of course is the sum of the default price value stored in the Didgeridoo and TShirt class instances we added to the shopping basket.

Now, what if we wanted to check whether a class implements a certain interface? Let's say there's a surcharge for purchasing a t-shirt with a custom print. The option of type casting, changing an expression of a given type into another type, has been available since ActionScript 2.0.

In the case of interfaces, this comes in very handy as it allows us to check whether a specific class instance has a specific interface implemented. If the type cast fails, it returns a null value, so we know it wasn't compatible; otherwise, we can simply go ahead and use those interface-specific methods.

```
public function calculate():uint {
  var tmp:uint = 0;
  for(var i:uint=0; i<this._items.length; i++) {
    tmp += this._items[i].price;
    if(this._items[i] as ICustomizable != null) {
      if(this._items[i].customPrint != null) {
        tmp += 1;
      }
    }
  }
  return tmp;
}
```

The preceding code shows the calculate method of the Checkout class amended to check whether a particular item in the shopping basket is customizable, in which case a surcharge is added to the product price. Note that type casting using the as operator is new in ActionScript 3.0.

In this particular example, we could just as easily have used the is operator, which returns a Boolean of whether or not the object *is* of the given datatype. The difference with the as keyword is that it returns either the converted datatype or null if the type can't be converted.

Let's give this a final go in that blank FLA we created earlier. First let's try the following:

```
var shoppingBasket:Checkout = new Checkout();
shoppingBasket.addItem(new TShirt());

trace("The total price is: "+shoppingBasket.calculate());
```

You'll notice that running this code gives us the following output: The total price is: 20. Why is that, you might ask? Well, even though the TShirt class instance has ICustomizable implemented, it doesn't specify a custom print, so there is no surcharge.

If we change the code to read as follows, however:

```
var shoppingBasket:Checkout = new Checkout();
var myTShirt:TShirt = new TShirt();
myTShirt.customPrint = "Interface Guru";
shoppingBasket.addItem(myTShirt);

trace("The total price is: "+shoppingBasket.calculate());
```

we will have a custom print message defined for the TShirt instance and, when we compile, the Output panel will read The total price is: 21.

It's not difficult to see how this becomes a very useful feature; imagine using this in the e-commerce site to easily handle different tax rates, shipping methods, and so on while still having the same generic interface to work with.

What's next?

Don't underestimate the power of interfaces once you start extending existing projects. They can help you code more consistently and will save you time you would otherwise spend on debugging applications because you forgot to add a particular method to one of your classes. Interfaces are relatively quick and easy to build, and will prove to be an essential part of your development workflow once you start developing your own extensive ActionScript 3.0 frameworks.

This chapter concludes a series of chapters in which you learned the core topics of OOP. Before moving on to present more examples of ActionScript 3.0 code, I'm going to introduce you to *design patterns*, which are practical programmatic approaches to solving specific problems and which will help you understand the reasoning behind the way code is structured in upcoming chapters.

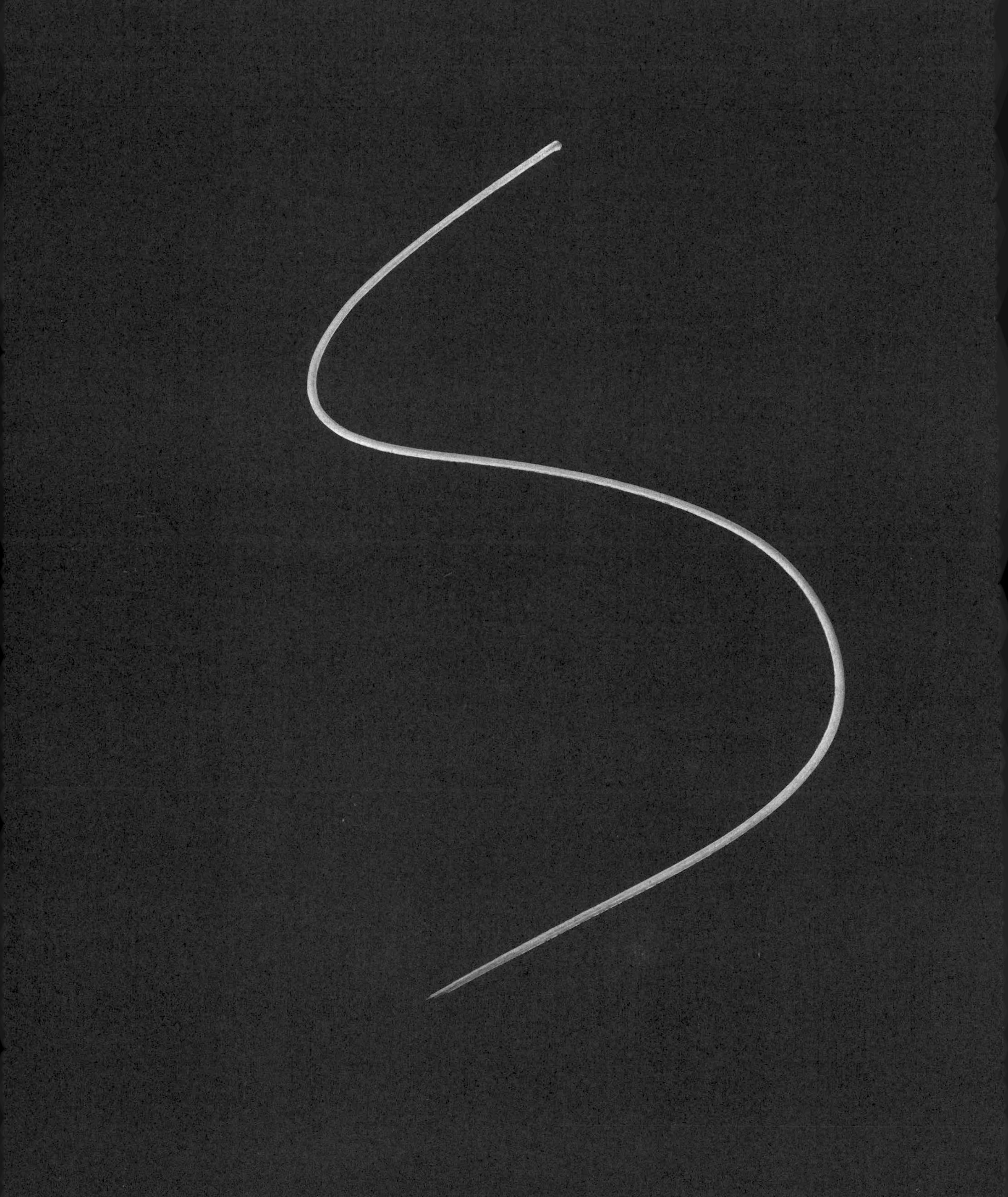

13 DESIGN PATTERNS

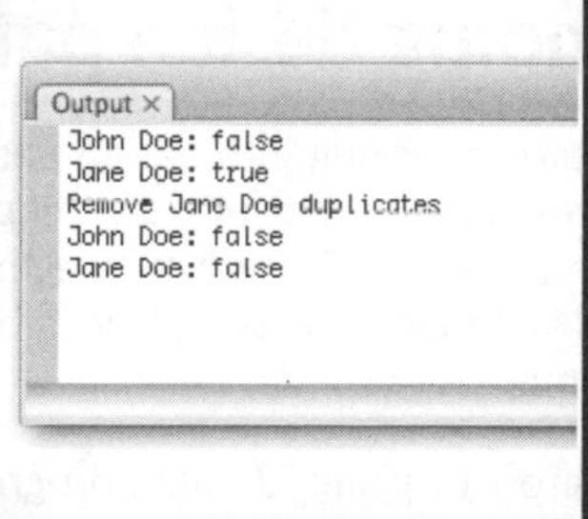

Now that you've read about OOP concepts and best practices, and you've seen OOP applied within some ActionScript 3.0 examples, it's time to get more involved and look at troubleshooting your code and making it more efficient. This is where *design patterns* come in.

> *When talking about design patterns, it's impossible to ignore one of the most authoritative books on the subject,* Design Patterns: Elements of Reusable Object-Oriented Software *by Erich Gamma, Richard Helm, Ralph Johnson, and John Vlissides, who are affectionately called the Gang of Four (GoF). This book, published by Addison-Wesley, first hit the shelves back in 1995 and has contributed tremendously in evangelizing this topic.*

Design patterns provide you with a means to structure your application and streamline communication between classes to effectively deal with common code problems. That being said, there is almost a cult following of developers passionate about the importance and superiority of a very particular implementation of a design pattern. Following the topic of design patterns is actually good entertainment—browse the Web for an afternoon, and you'll find endless heated debates on even the most minor and insignificant details. I take a much more pragmatic approach to design patterns, and feel they help developers handle specific code problems in an efficient and OO-friendly way. Whether you call it apples or pears is not what's important; it just needs to do the job. This is also the approach I'll take when I introduce design patterns for OOP with ActionScript 3.0 in this chapter. Rather than focusing on the technicalities and underlying theory, I'll show you some practical implementations of common patterns.

This chapter covers the Observer, Singleton, Decorator, and Model-View-Controller (MVC) patterns that are among the most useful when building ActionScript 3.0 projects. I advise you to read through each example of a design pattern in full in this chapter, and then sit down and try to apply it to one of your projects. By doing so, you'll soon grasp the concepts and better understand the benefits of using certain design patterns in specific situations.

Understanding design patterns

When I first started looking into design patterns for OOP with ActionScript, I must admit that I had some serious difficulties getting my head wrapped around the topic and its implementation in ActionScript. I'm sure the same thing was happening to a lot of other ActionScript developers who don't have a background in low-level OOP languages (as was the case with me).

There's no reason to panic, though; progress has been made since the ActionScript 1.0 days, and the new object-oriented syntax makes it much easier to "borrow" some implementations of design patterns in Java and port them to ActionScript 3.0. That does not mean that you should get carried away with this—ActionScript 3.0 is not Java, and just because something works well in Java does not mean it will automatically be a good thing to do in ActionScript 3.0. While design patterns can help your project, you have to find the balance between what you need and what you can do with them. Failing that, you're stuck with some convoluted and highly restrictive code that hinders your workflow more than it helps with sorting out programming problems. The best way to learn this balance is through understanding design patterns and the role they play in your application.

Design patterns take an abstract description of a situation and talk about the way to handle this in OOP. Now, the interesting thing is that design patterns don't give you ready-made solutions; rather, they simply discuss the different segments of a pattern and how they relate to each other. It's up to you to find an implementation for the pattern and get it embedded in your project. This is really what many people have difficulty with when starting out with design patterns. It is absolutely essential that you have a complete overview of your project and can visualize the relationships of classes and how they communicate with each other. If you're familiar with UML diagrams, they can help tremendously, but in some more complex projects, I recommend using a method that's a bit unorthodox.

In such situations, I suggest taking pieces of paper, each of which represents a class, and spreading them out on a table. On each piece of paper, you then write the class name, a description of its function, and any important methods it implements, and you start walking through the application. You look at a task that the classes need to perform, and keep track of the different steps and roles that your classes play.

When you do that, you'll probably come across some situations where your code isn't as efficient or straightforward as you'd like it to be. You can label those as possible structural failures in your application design and look at how they can be remodeled to behave better.

You'll likely find that many of those instances of potential failures are good candidates for having a design pattern implemented. You can then focus on those specific trouble spots and see what type of situation you're dealing with. Here are some examples of situations in which you might use the design patterns that we'll discuss in this chapter:

- **Observer pattern**: Multiple classes that all depend on the state of a specific class can subscribe to that class and get automatically notified when its state changes. This pattern can be used to keep various elements that use the same data in a project in sync with each other.
- **Singleton pattern**: Classes require only one instance to be available for your entire application. This pattern allows you to have a single centralized point where all information is managed for a project.
- **Decorator pattern**: A class adds functionality to another class. This pattern can be used as an alternative to class inheritance.
- **MVC pattern**: Classes are defined as the Model, View, and Controller of your application, which allows you to separate data, programming logic, and presentation. Using this pattern, you can easily make changes to the View, for example, without it affecting the rest of the application.

Once you've found a suitable design pattern that addresses the trouble spot in your application design, you can start to look at a way to implement it. That's exactly what we'll do next. I'll introduce you to each of the design patterns just listed and help you work out a good ActionScript 3.0 implementation for it.

Implementing design patterns

There's more than one way to implement design patterns. Finding the best implementation is not just having it adhere to the specifications of the pattern, but also looking at how it best fits in with your project. Even the most useful pattern can become your worst enemy if you're too strict in the way you fit it in. Design patterns shouldn't be looked at as separate from your application, but rather as an integral part of your project model.

In the following sections, we'll look at the design patterns listed earlier and walk through how to apply them to an ActionScript 3.0 project.

Observer pattern

The Observer design pattern is one of the most common patterns you'll find in OOP with ActionScript 3.0 and most other programming languages, for that matter. The theory behind it is simple: class instances can subscribe to a class that uses this Observer pattern and automatically be notified of any changes that occurred. What gives this design pattern its real power is the ability to centralize notifications. Rather than having all classes that rely on a property of a different class continually check for changes, the information is pushed to every subscribing class if and when changes have occurred. This makes the Observer pattern a very efficient way to handle data changes and synchronize events between different classes.

Basic implementation

A basic implementation of the Observer pattern is relatively easy to build. You need an `Array` class property that keeps track of the class instances that subscribed, methods to add and remove subscribers, and a method that sends out the notifications.

The following Observer class is saved in a file called `Observer.as` and shows this basic implementation of the Observer pattern.

Observer.as

```
package {

  public class Observer {

    private var subscribers:Array;

    public function Observer() {
      this.subscribers = new Array();
    }

    public function addSubscriber(classInstance:Object):void {
      this.subscribers.push(classInstance);
    }

    public function removeSubscriber(classInstance:Object):void {
      for(var i:uint=0; i<this.subscribers.length; i++) {
```

```
          if(this.subscribers[i] == classInstance) {
            this.subscribers.splice(i,1);
            break;
          }
        }
      }

      public function notifyChanges():void {
        for(var i:String in this.subscribers) {
          this.subscribers[i].update();
        }
      }

    }

  }
```

You'll notice that there is a private variable of an Array type named `subscribers`, a method called `addSubscriber` that adds subscribers to the `subscribers` array, a `removeSubscriber` method that removes subscribers from the `subscribers` array, and a method called `notifyChanges` that loops through the `subscribers` array and calls an `update` function on all of the instances that subscribed for notifications.

Let's give this class a try and see if it does the trick:

1. Launch Flash CS3.
2. Choose Flash Document from the Create New menu on the Start Page.
3. Save the blank document in the same folder as `Observer.as` with the filename `Observer.fla`.
4. Rename Layer 1 in the timeline to ActionScript.
5. Open to Actions panel (select Window ➤ Development Panels ➤ Actions).
6. Add the following code to Frame 1 of the ActionScript layer:

```
var myObserver:Observer = new Observer();
var myFirstSubscriber:Object = new Object();
var mySecondSubscriber:Object = new Object();

myFirstSubscriber.update = function():void {
  trace("myFirstSubscriber notified by Observer class");
}
mySecondSubscriber.update = function():void {
  trace("mySecondSubscriber notified by Observer class");
}

myObserver.addSubscriber(myFirstSubscriber);
myObserver.addSubscriber(mySecondSubscriber);
myObserver.notifyChanges();
```

7. Save the document (select File ➤ Save).

13

By following these steps, you create a new instance of the Observer class named `myObserver` and two objects named `myFirstSubscriber` and `mySecondSubscriber` that each have an `update` function that traces out a message when called. Then those two object instances are added as subscribers to the Observer class using the `addSubscriber` method, and finally the `myObserver` instance calls the `notifyChanges` method.

If you run Test Movie (Control ➤ Test Movie) now, you should now see both the `myFirstSubscriber` and `mySecondSubscriber` instances having their `update` function called. Congratulations! You've just applied the Observer pattern to some ActionScript 3.0 code (see Figure 13-1).

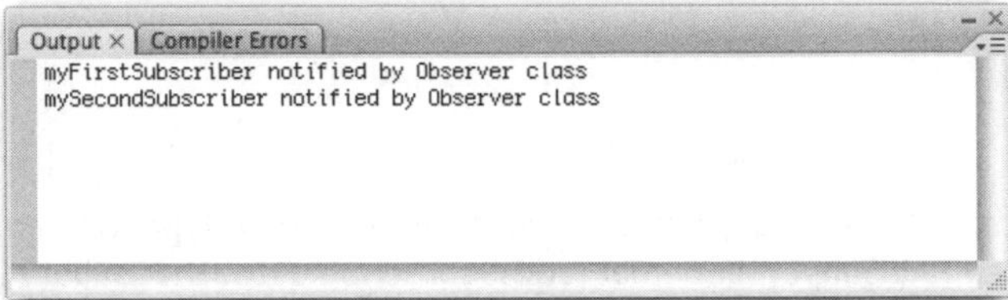

Figure 13-1. Output panel showing the Observer design pattern example

When working with the Observer pattern, it's important to note that a class instance is not automatically removed when it gets deleted. If you delete a class instance and don't remove it as a subscriber, Flash will still attempt to call it every time it sends out a notification. For this reason, be sure to unsubscribe a class instance before you delete it to keep your code optimized.

That's all well and good, but it doesn't look very practical just yet. We'll get to a more practical implementation of the Observer pattern soon, but let's first look at some little tweaks that are required.

The `addSubscriber` method used in this Observer class doesn't check for duplicate entries. Having the same class instance subscribed multiple times is not very efficient and can easily be avoided. What you'll do is check whether the class instance is already added, and if that is the case, you'll return a `false` value; otherwise, you'll add it to the `subscribers` array and return `true`. By returning this Boolean `true`/`false` value, you also have confirmation of whether or not the class instance was added to the `subscribers` array.

```
public function addSubscriber(classInstance:Object):Boolean {
    for(var i:uint=0; i<this.subscribers.length; i++) {
      if(this.subscribers[i] == classInstance) {
        return false;
      }
    }
    this.subscribers.push(classInstance);
    return true;
  }
```

If you changed the code in Observer.as to have the addSubscriber method look like the preceding code, give it a test in Flash. Make sure you change the code in Frame 1 of the ActionScript layer to read as follows:

```
var myObserver:Observer = new Observer();
var myFirstSubscriber:Object = new Object();
var mySecondSubscriber:Object = new Object();

myFirstSubscriber.update = function():void {
  trace("myFirstSubscriber notified by Observer class");
}
mySecondSubscriber.update = function():void {
  trace("mySecondSubscriber notified by Observer class");
}

trace(myObserver.addSubscriber(myFirstSubscriber));
trace(myObserver.addSubscriber(mySecondSubscriber));
trace(myObserver.addSubscriber(myFirstSubscriber));

myObserver.notifyChanges();
```

Here, you've added another call to addSubscriber, again passing myFirstSubscriber as a parameter. With the changes you just made to the Observer class, the addSubscriber method now returns a true or false statement indicating whether or not the instance was added to the subscribers array. This was done to avoid duplicate entries. By using the trace statement with these addSubscriber calls, you get the return values traced out to the Output panel when running Test Movie. Let's do just that and check whether that works (see Figure 13-2).

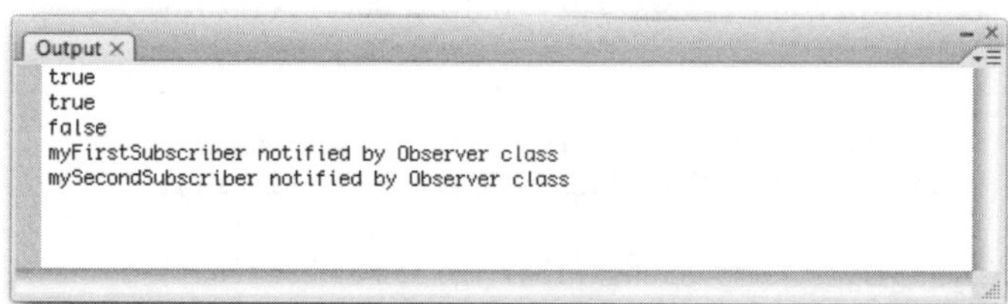

Figure 13-2. Output panel showing the Observer design pattern notification

Great, that seems to work just fine! The first two lines in the Output panel read true, which indicates that myFirstSubscriber and mySecondSubscriber were successfully added to the subscribers array in the Observer class. However, the next line reads false, and if you look at the corresponding line in Frame 1 of the ActionScript layer, that is the result of trying to add myFirstSubscriber to the Observer class again. Finally, you have the last two lines, which you also had last time around, that show that the subscribing instances were notified by the Observer class.

While we're at it, we might as well do the same for the removeSubscriber method. In its current form, this method does not return any value when called. Having it return a

Boolean type would be very handy to know if a subscriber was effectively removed from the subscribers array in the Observer class. The code for this looks as follows:

```
public function removeSubscriber(classInstance:Object):Boolean {
  for(var i:uint=0; i<this.subscribers.length; i++) {
    if(this.subscribers[i] == classInstance) {
      this.subscribers.splice(i,1);
      return true;
    }
  }
  return false;
}
```

Make sure you save Observer.as after applying these changes, and you might want to give it a try in your project. Change the code on Frame 1 of the ActionScript layer to read as follows:

```
var myObserver:Observer = new Observer();
var myFirstSubscriber:Object = new Object();
var mySecondSubscriber:Object = new Object();
var myThirdSubscriber:Object = new Object();

myFirstSubscriber.update = function():void {
  trace("myFirstSubscriber notified by Observer class");
}
mySecondSubscriber.update = function():void {
  trace("mySecondSubscriber notified by Observer class");
}
myThirdSubscriber.update = function():void {
  trace("myThirdSubscriber notified by Observer class");
}

trace(myObserver.addSubscriber(myFirstSubscriber));
trace(myObserver.addSubscriber(mySecondSubscriber));

trace(myObserver.removeSubscriber(myFirstSubscriber));
trace(myObserver.removeSubscriber(myThirdSubscriber));

myObserver.notifyChanges();
```

The code now has a call to the addSubscriber method for the myFirstSubscriber and mySecondSubscriber instances, and a call to the removeSubscriber method, passing myFirstSubscriber as the instance to be removed from the subscribers array in the Observer class. Finally, you've also added a line that tries to remove a myThirdSubscriber subscriber as an observer that was never registered with the Observer class.

If you run Test Movie with this code in place, you'll see the lines shown in Figure 13-3 in the Output panel.

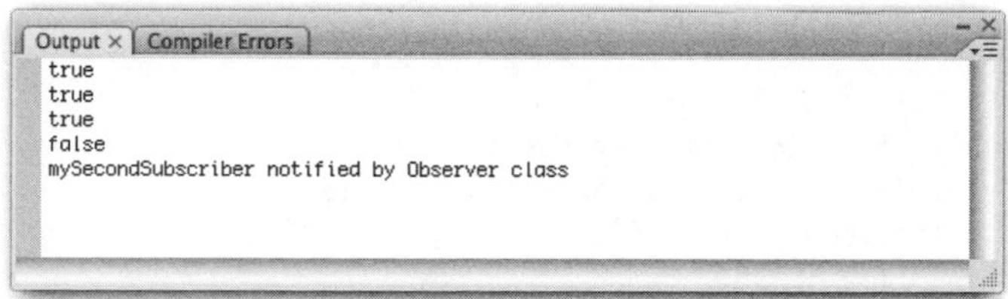

Figure 13-3. Output panel showing addSubscriber and removeSubscriber in action

The first two lines in the Output panel read true, as they correspond with the myFirstSubscriber and mySecondSubscriber instances being added as subscribers to the Observer class. The third line also reads true, which means that the myFirstSubscriber instance was successfully removed from the observers array in the Observer class. The next line reads false because the instance myThirdSubscriber wasn't found in the subscribers array. Now, this is fun! The final line shows you that mySecondSubscriber was notified by the Observer class. Note that the myFirstSubscriber update method was not called, which also confirms that it was removed from the observers array in the Observer class.

So far, so good. With all these tweaks in place, the Observer class now looks as follows:

```
package {

  public class Observer {

    private var subscribers:Array;

    public function Observer() {
      this.subscribers = new Array();
    }

    public function addSubscriber(classInstance:Object):Boolean {
      for (var i:uint=0; i<this.subscribers.length; i++) {
        if (this.subscribers[i] == classInstance) {
          return false;
        }
      }
      this.subscribers.push(classInstance);
      return true;
    }

    public function removeSubscriber(classInstance:Object):Boolean {
      for (var i:uint=0; i<this.subscribers.length; i++) {
        if (this.subscribers[i] == classInstance) {
          this.subscribers.splice(i,1);
          return true;
        }
      }
```

13

```
      return false;
    }

    public function notifyChanges():void {
      for (var i:String in this.subscribers) {
        this.subscribers[i].update();
      }
    }

  }

}
```

Practical implementation

As mentioned earlier, the Observer class isn't very practical as it is used now. For one thing, it needs to have the addSubscriber, removeSubscriber, and notifyChanges functions in place with every class that we want to apply the Observer design pattern to.

By extending the Observer class, we can avoid having to manually add the functions and have a reusable class for our ActionScript 3.0 projects. Next, we'll create an Attendees class that shows how this is done in a typical project.

Attendees.as

```
package {

  public class Attendees extends Observer {

    public var attendeesList:Array;

    public function Attendees() {
      this.attendeesList = new Array();
    }

    public function addAttendee(name:String):Boolean {
      for(var i:uint=0; i<this.attendeesList.length; i++) {
        if(this.attendeesList[i] == name) {
          return false;
        }
      }
      this.attendeesList.push(name);
      super.notifyChanges();
      return true;
    }
```

```
    public function removeAttendee(name:String):Boolean {
      for(var i:uint=0; i<this.attendeesList.length; i++) {
        if(this.attendeesList[i] == name) {
          this.attendeesList.splice(i,1);
          super.notifyChanges();
          return true;
        }
      }
      return false;
    }

    public function getAttendees():Array {
      return attendeesList;
    }

  }

}
```

The Attendees class keeps track of attendees in an Array class property named attendeesList and provides methods to add, remove, and retrieve all attendees. The addAttendee and removeAttendee methods work in much the same way as the Observer class, and because the Attendees class extends this Observer class, it can call the notifyChanges method to send out notifications to subscribing class instances.

Let's see this in action. Save the class in the preceding listing as Attendees.as in the same folder as the Observer class (or get a copy from the downloadable source files on the friends of ED website at www.friendsofed.com) and create a blank FLA called Attendees.fla. With that new blank FLA open, perform the following steps:

1. Rename Layer 1 to ActionScript.
2. Select Frame 1 of the ActionScript layer.
3. Open the Actions panel and add the following code:

```
var myAttendees:Attendees = new Attendees();
var attendeeMonitor:Object = new Object();

attendeeMonitor.update = function():void {
  trace("myAttendees sent notification!");
}

myAttendees.addSubscriber(attendeeMonitor);

myAttendees.addAttendee("John Doe");
myAttendees.removeAttendee("John Doe");
```

If you run Test Movie with this code in place, you'll get the lines in the Output panel shown in Figure 13-4.

13

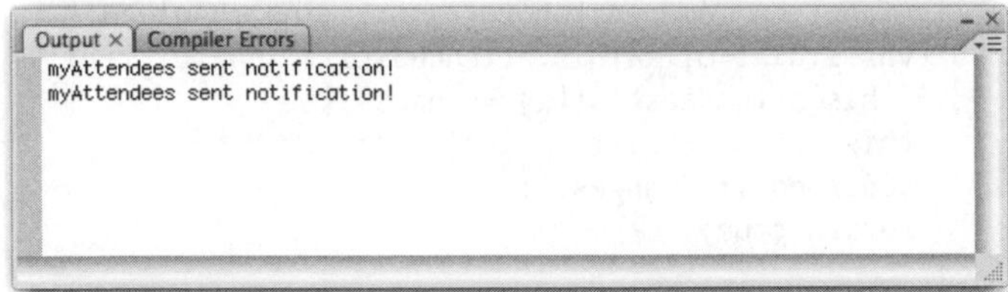

Figure 13-4. Output panel showing the Attendees class example using the Observer pattern

Great, we've just managed to get our custom Attendees class to use the Observer class to implement the Observer design pattern! There's just one problem, though: whenever the `update` function of `attendeeMonitor` is called, we don't know whether it was caused by the addition or removal of an attendee. More complex implementations of the Observer design pattern have ways of dealing with this, but in this situation we'll use the `getAttendees` method to get the latest version of the `attendeeList` array any time it is triggered.

Extending the practical implementation

To do so, we'll make things a bit more interactive and add some controls that allow us to add and remove attendees and show this in a `ListBox` component. Perform the following steps:

1. Insert a new layer in the Timeline panel (select Insert ➤ Timeline ➤ Layer).
2. Rename Layer 2 to Interface.
3. Open the Components panel (select Window ➤ Components).
4. Drag two instances of the `Button` component on the stage in the Interface layer.
5. Drag an instance of the `List` component on the stage in the Interface layer.
6. Drag an instance of the `TextInput` component on the stage in the Interface layer.
7. Position the components on the stage (see Figure 13-5).

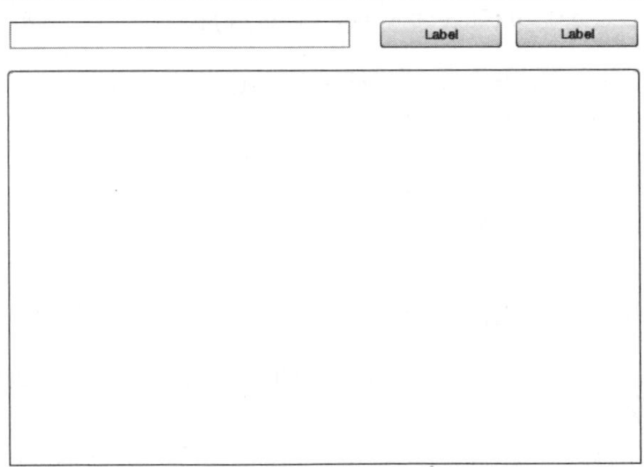

Figure 13-5. Component layout on the stage

8. Open the Properties panel (select Window ➤ Properties).
9. Select the `List` component and give it the instance name `attendees_list`.
10. Select the `TextInput` component and give it the instance name `attendee_txt`.
11. Select the first `Button` component and give it the instance name `add_btn`.
12. Select the second `Button` component and give it the instance name `remove_btn`.
13. With the first `Button` selected, set the label property in the Properties panel to Add (see Figure 13-6).

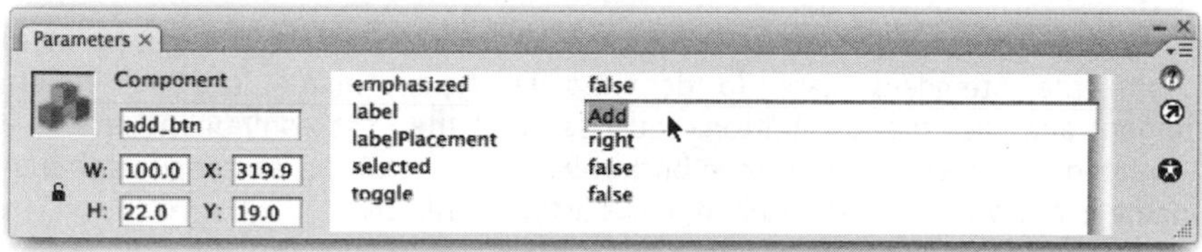

Figure 13-6. Parameters panel for the `add_btn` component instance

14. With the second `Button` selected, set the label property in the Properties panel to Remove.
15. Change the code in Frame 1 of the ActionScript layer to read as follows:

```
import fl.data.DataProvider;

var myAttendees:Attendees = new Attendees();
var attendeeMonitor:Object = new Object();

attendeeMonitor.update = function():void {
  attendees_list.dataProvider = ➥
   new DataProvider(myAttendees.getAttendees());
}

function addPerson(evt:Event):void {
  myAttendees.addAttendee(attendee_txt.text);
}

function removePerson(evt:Event):void {
  myAttendees.removeAttendee(attendee_txt.text);
}

add_btn.addEventListener("click", addPerson);
remove_btn.addEventListener("click", removePerson);

myAttendees.addSubscriber(attendeeMonitor);
```

The code we now have in place on the first frame of the ActionScript layer does a number of things. First, it creates an instance of the Attendees class (remember, this class extends the Observer class) and creates an Object instance named `attendeeMonitor`.

13

This attendeeMonitor object has an update function called by the Attendees class any time an attendee is added or removed from the array. This function sets the dataProvider for attendee_list (the List component on stage) to the array (wrapped up as a DataProvider instance) returned by the getAttendees method of the Attendees class. By doing this, we can always be sure that our list on the stage is up to date with the array in the myAttendees instance of the Attendees class.

The next two functions, addPerson and removePerson, call the addAttendee and removeAttendee methods of the myAttendees instance. Those functions are triggered when the Add or Remove button is clicked.

When you run Test Movie (Control ➤ Test Movie) with all this in place, you get to interact a little with the Attendees class. To demonstrate, type a name into the TextInput component and click the Add button. You'll see that the List component on the stage gets updated. If you click the Remove button with a name in the TextInput component, that name is removed from the List if it was listed there.

We've sure come a long way! Let's see what actually happens when adding an attendee:

1. When the Add button is clicked, the addPerson function gets called.
2. The addPerson function calls the addAttendee method in the myAttendees instance of the Attendees class and passes it the value of the TextInput component.
3. The addAttendee method in the Attendees class adds the attendee to the attendeesList array, if it is not a duplicate, and calls the notifyChanges method of its superclass, Observer.
4. The attendeeMonitor object has subscribed to notifications of myAttendees and so its update function gets called when notifyChanges is triggered.
5. The update function in the attendeeMonitor object updates the dataProvider of the List component with the latest version of the attendeesList array from the Attendees class by calling the getAttendees method.

Whew—that's quite a few steps for simply updating a List component on the stage! Of course, the same goes for removing an attendee from the Attendees class. Now, you might be wondering if it's worth the trouble to code all that to simply generate a list of attendees. If you are thinking that, you do have a point.

There's no real use in applying the Observer pattern when there's just one instance subscribing to the notifications. Imagine the possibilities with the Attendees class, though—without much hassle, you can have a counter that automatically updates the number of attendees every time it receives a notification. You might even have a visual representation of a meeting hall and show the number of seats that are left. That's when things become interesting with the Observer pattern.

As an exercise to try on your own, you might want to add a Label component that automatically shows the number of attendees by subscribing to the Attendees class. You'll find the solution for this exercise in this book's downloadable source files, which you can obtain from the friends of ED website (www.friendsofed.com).

Singleton pattern

The Singleton pattern is used for projects where you want to create classes that can only ever have one instance. "How is that useful?" you may be asking. Well, there are situations in your ActionScript 3.0 projects where you want to have one and only one instance of a class available.

Typically, this pattern will be used for manager-type classes that hold data for your entire project. These classes provide you with a centralized, single point of access that you can reach from anywhere in your project. In that sense, classes that implement the Singleton pattern are often simply used as repositories for holding data or references to other class instances.

Basic implementation

So, how exactly do you create a class with the Singleton pattern implemented? First of all, you need to find a way to limit the number of instances a class can create to one. The obvious approach would be to have a property that keeps track of the number of instances a class has. Doing that, you'll soon come across a practical problem: how can you keep count of the number of instances a class has, when class properties are defined on the class instance and not shared throughout the class?

Defining a class property as `static` makes sure it is shared throughout all instances (in this case, just one instance). Knowing that, we can define a static class property of a `uint` (`unsigned integer`) type and in the class constructor (remember, the constructor always gets called immediately when a class is instantiated) increment it. Let's see how that would work:

Singleton.as

```
package {

  public class Singleton {

    static var instanceCount:uint = 0;

    public function Singleton() {
      instanceCount++;
      if(instanceCount == 1) {
        trace("First Singleton class instance");
      } else {
        trace("Singleton class allows only one instance");
      }
    }

  }

}
```

13

Save the preceding file as `Singleton.as` and create a blank FLA named `Singleton.fla` in the same folder. Double-click `Singleton.fla` to open up Flash and perform the following steps:

1. Rename Layer 1 in the timeline to ActionScript.
2. Select Frame 1 of the ActionScript layer.
3. Open the Actions panel (select Window ➤ Actions).
4. Add the following ActionScript to the Actions panel:

```
var myFirstSingleton:Singleton = new Singleton();
var mySecondSingleton:Singleton = new Singleton();
```

With this code in place, save the FLA and run Test Movie (Control ➤ Test Movie). You should see the result shown in Figure 13-7 in the Output panel.

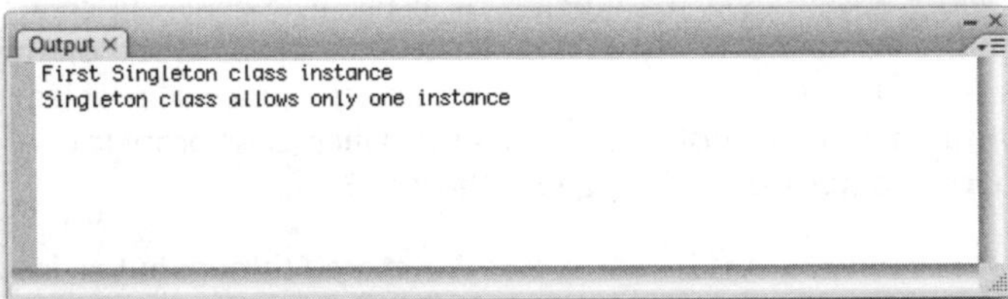

Figure 13-7. Output panel showing the Singleton pattern example

As you can see, the first line of the Output panel reads First Singleton class instance, and the second line reads Singleton class allows only one instance. Great, that looks as though you've managed to keep track of the number of classes the Singleton class has. There are a couple of problems with this approach, though.

If you want to add functionality to this Singleton class, you'll need to have a conditional statement that checks the `instanceCount` property in each and every method. That's not exactly user friendly, as shown in this example:

Singleton.as

```
package {

  public class Singleton {

    static var instanceCount:uint = 0;

    public function Singleton() {
      instanceCount++;
      if(instanceCount == 1) {
        trace("First Singleton class instance");
      } else {
        trace("Singleton class allows only one instance");
```

```
      }
    }

    public function doSomething():void {
      if(instanceCount == 1) {
        // do something;
      } else {
        // do nothing
      }
    }

  }

}
```

Notice that we have exactly the same conditional as in the class constructor in the doSomething method. That's not exactly a great way to implement the Singleton pattern because it doesn't actually prevent creating more than one instance. With this implementation, we can create as many instances of the class as we want; it's just the methods that prevent the code from executing by checking that the number of instances hasn't exceeded one.

Let's try something else. If we were to assign a private scope to the constructor method, that would essentially disable us from creating class instances, right? Unfortunately, this is no longer possible in ActionScript 3.0 like it was in ActionScript 2.0; the constructor cannot be set to private. Dealing with this restriction, a number of attempts in the community were made to find a workaround that still allows the Singleton pattern to be enforced.

Following you'll find the implementation of an enforced Singleton pattern in ActionScript 3.0, originally put forward by Grant Skinner, which I personally like the best:

Singleton.as

```
package {

  public class Singleton {

    private static var instance:Singleton;
    private static var allowInstance:Boolean;

    public function Singleton() {
      if(!allowInstance) {
        throw new Error("use Singleton.getInstance() ➥
        instead of new keyword");
      }
    }

  }
}
```

13

Save the preceding class as Singleton.as, and in the Singleton.fla file open up the Actions panel for Frame 1 of the ActionScript layer and change the code to read as follows:

```
var mySingleton:Singleton = new Singleton();
```

If you run Test Movie (Control ➤ Test Movie) on this code, you'll get what you might expect: an error message (see Figure 13-8).

```
Output
Error: Error: use Singleton.getInstance() instead of new keyword
  at Singleton$iinit()
  at Singleton_fla::MainTimeline/Singleton_fla::frame1()
```

Figure 13-8. Error message when trying to instantiate Singleton class

So how exactly does that code help us with the Singleton pattern? The first attempt allowed multiple instances to be created, and now we can't have any. Not to worry, with a little tweak to that code, we can have a public method in the class control the instantiation of the class.

Singleton.as

```
package {

  public class Singleton {

    private static var instance:Singleton;
    private static var allowInstance:Boolean;

    public function Singleton() {
      if(!allowInstance) {
        throw new Error("Error: use Singleton.getInstance()➥
        instead of new keyword");
      }
    }

    public static function getInstance():Singleton {
      allowInstance = true;
      instance = new Singleton();
      allowInstance = false;
      return instance;
    }

    public function doSomething():void {
      trace("doing something");
    }

  }

}
```

The preceding code uses a public method named `getInstance` to return a new instance of the Singleton class. Because it is called from within the class itself, the instantiation isn't blocked by the private scope attribute of the class. Now, you might be wondering how we'll be able to trigger that `getInstance` method, as we can't create any new instance of the class to call it on. That's where the `static` keyword comes in again. Any methods that are defined as static can be called by simply using the class name, in this case `Singleton.getInstance()`.

Let's see if this code does what we want it to. Open up `Singleton.fla` again and change the code in Frame 1 of the ActionScript layer to read as follows:

```
var mySingleton:Singleton = Singleton.getInstance();
mySingleton.doSomething();
```

If you run Test Movie (Control ➤ Test Movie) using the preceding code, you'll see the results in the Output panel as shown in Figure 13-9.

Figure 13-9. Output panel showing the Singleton class in action

We've been able to get an instance of the Singleton class created, and we've called the `doSomething` method on that instance, which traced out doing something. The only thing that's left to do is add a conditional statement that restricts the number of instances the `getInstance` method returns to one. This time we'll use a slightly different approach. Rather than keeping track of the number of instances that were created, we'll just store a reference to the Singleton class in the property.

Singleton.as

```
package {

  public class Singleton {

    private static var instance:Singleton;
    private static var allowInstance:Boolean;

    public function Singleton() {
      if(!allowInstance) {
        throw new Error("Error: use Singleton.getInstance() ➥
        instead of new keyword");
      }
    }
```

13

```
            public static function getInstance():Singleton {
              if(instance == null) {
                allowInstance = true;
                instance = new Singleton();
                trace("Singleton instance created");
                allowInstance = false;
              } else {
                trace("Singleton instance already exists");
              }
              return instance;
            }

            public function doSomething():void {
              trace("doing something");
            }

          }

        }
```

What the preceding code does differently relates to the class property. We've given it a private scope and static property, so it can't be manipulated from outside the class, and given it a value of undefined. In the getInstance method, we then go on to check whether this class property is undefined, and if so, we create a new Singleton instance. If the instance class property is not null, an instance of Singleton was already created, and the existing instance simply gets returned. I added two trace statements to help you see what's going on. Let's try this out in the Singleton.fla Flash file.

Change the ActionScript code on Frame 1 of the ActionScript layer to read as follows:

```
var myFirstSingleton:Singleton = Singleton.getInstance();
var mySecondSingleton:Singleton = Singleton.getInstance();
```

If you run Test Movie (Control ➤ Test Movie) with this code in place, you'll get the result in the Output panel shown in Figure 13-10.

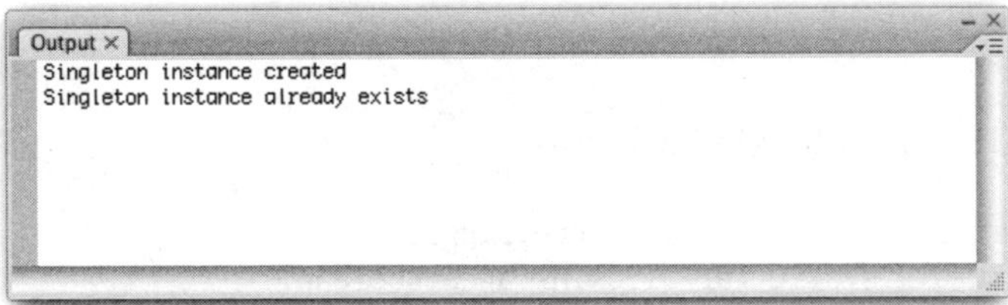

Figure 13-10. Output panel showing the Singleton class's inner workings

The first line of the Output panel reads Singleton instance created, while the second line says Singleton instance already exists. This effectively means that your code to limit the number of instances created using the getInstance method is working properly. If no instance existed, it creates one for you, and if one was already present, it returns a reference to that Singleton instance. Doing that allows you to only ever have one class instance instantiated, and have that instance accessible from anywhere in your application.

Practical implementation

That wasn't too difficult, was it? Now that we've found a good implementation of the Singleton pattern, let's apply it to an ActionScript 3.0 project. Building on the Attendees class we had for the Observer pattern, we'll now work on a MeetingRoomManager class using the Singleton pattern. This class will hold references to MeetingRoom class instances that in turn keep track of the attendees.

The first thing we'll do is use the Singleton class implementation just created as a template for the MeetingRoomManager class.

MeetingRoomManager.as

```
package {

  public class MeetingRoomManager {

    private static var instance:MeetingRoomManager;
    private static var allowInstance:Boolean;

    public function MeetingRoomManager() {
      if (!allowInstance) {
        throw new Error("use Singleton.getInstance() ➥
        instead of new keyword");
      }
    }

    public static  function getInstance():MeetingRoomManager {
      if (instance == null) {
        allowInstance = true;
        instance = new MeetingRoomManager();
        trace("MeetingRoomManager instance created");
        allowInstance = false;
      } else {
        trace("MeetingRoomMananger instance already exists");
      }
      return instance;
    }

  }

}
```

Next, we'll add some methods for us to be able to add, remove, and retrieve meeting rooms from the MeetingRoomManager class. The methods we'll be using are addMeetingRoom, removeMeetingRoom, and getMeetingRoom. To keep track of the meeting rooms in the MeetingRoomManager class, we have the meetingRooms class property that has a datatype of Array.

MeetingRoomManager.as

```
package {

  public class MeetingRoomManager {

    public static var meetingRooms:Array = new Array();

    private static var instance:MeetingRoomManager;
    private static var allowInstance:Boolean;

    public function MeetingRoomManager() {
      if(!allowInstance) {
        throw new Error("use Singleton.getInstance() ➥
        instead of new keyword");
      }
    }

    public static function getInstance():MeetingRoomManager {
      if(instance == null) {
        allowInstance = true;
        instance = new MeetingRoomManager();
        trace("MeetingRoomManager instance created");
        allowInstance = false;
      } else {
        trace("MeetingRoomMananger instance already exists");
      }
      return instance;
    }

    public function addMeetingRoom(meetingRoomName:String):void {
      meetingRooms.push({name:meetingRoomName, ➥
      instance:new MeetingRoom()});
    }

    public function removeMeetingRoom(meetingRoomName:String):void {
      for(var i:uint=0; i<meetingRooms.length; i++) {
        if(meetingRooms[i].name == meetingRoomName) {
          meetingRooms.splice(i,1);
        }
      }
    }
```

```
      public function getMeetingRoom(meetingRoomName:String):➥
      MeetingRoom {
        for(var i:uint=0; i<meetingRooms.length; i++) {
          if(meetingRooms[i].name == meetingRoomName) {
            return meetingRooms[i].instance;
          }
        }
        throw new Error("meeting room not found");
      }

    }

  }
```

That's an interesting piece of code. As you'll notice in the addMeetingRoom method, we accept a parameter that specifies the name of our meeting room. That name, as well as a new anonymous instance of the MeetingRoom class, form the name and instance properties of an object (note the curly brackets shorthand notation) that gets pushed to the meetingRooms array.

The removeMeetingRoom method also takes this meetingRoomName parameter and uses that to loop through the meetingRooms array, looking for an entry where the name attribute is equal to the parameter. If that is the case, it removes that meeting room from the array. That same approach goes for the getMeetingRoom method, but you'll notice that method has a return type of MeetingRoom. It loops through the meetingRooms array looking for a meeting room where the name is equal to the meetingRoomName parameter and, if found, returns the MeetingRoom instance that was created for that entry in the array.

Before you can do any testing on this, you'll have to create a MeetingRoom class. This class will simply extend the Attendees class (which in turn extends the Observer class), so you have access to the addAttendee and removeAttendee functions and can have instances subscribe when the attendees list is updated for that particular MeetingRoom instance.

MeetingRoom.as

```
package {

  public class MeetingRoom extends Attendees {

    public function MeetingRoom() {
    }

  }

}
```

13

That's really all that you have to do! Make sure the files MeetingRoomManager.as, MeetingRoom.as, Attendees.as, and Observer.as are in the same folder as Singleton.fla, and let's look at the class in action. When you have the file Singleton.fla open, change the code in Frame 1 of the ActionScript layer to read as follows:

```
// Get an instance of MeetingRoomManager
var myMeetingRoomManager:MeetingRoomManager = ➥
MeetingRoomManager.getInstance();

// Add meeting rooms to MeetingRoomManager
myMeetingRoomManager.addMeetingRoom("boardroom");
myMeetingRoomManager.addMeetingRoom("ballroom");

// Set up listeners for the meeting rooms
var boardroomListener:Object = new Object();
boardroomListener.update = function():void {
  trace("boardroom attendees: "+➥
  myMeetingRoomManager.getMeetingRoom("boardroom")➥
  .getAttendees());
}

var ballroomListener:Object = new Object();
ballroomListener.update = function():void {
  trace("ballroom attendees: "+ ➥
  myMeetingRoomManager.getMeetingRoom("ballroom")➥
  .getAttendees());
}

// Subscribe to updates from MeetingRoom instances
myMeetingRoomManager.getMeetingRoom("boardroom")
.addSubscriber(boardroomListener);
myMeetingRoomManager.getMeetingRoom("ballroom")
.addSubscriber(ballroomListener);

// Add attendees to MeetingRoom instances
myMeetingRoomManager.getMeetingRoom("boardroom")
.addAttendee("John Doe");
myMeetingRoomManager.getMeetingRoom("ballroom")
.addAttendee("Jane Doe");
```

The preceding code looks pretty complex, but you'll soon see that it's not. The first line of code stores the instance of the MeetingRoomManager class in a variable called myMeetingRoomManager. Remember, the MeetingRoomManager class has the Singleton pattern implemented, so it can have only one instance. Next, we add two meeting rooms (boardroom and ballroom) to the MeetingRoomManager class using the addMeetingRoom method.

Following that, we define two object instances that will act as listeners for the meeting rooms we created. For this to work with our implementation of the Observer pattern, the instances need to have an update function defined, which is called when attendees are added or removed. With those two objects in place, we can now subscribe them to the MeetingRoom instances. This is done through the addSubscriber method.

Finally, we add an attendee for both of the MeetingRoom instances. When you save Singleton.fla with these changes in place, or if you grabbed a copy of the source files available from the friends of ED website, you can run Test Movie (Control ➤ Test Movie) and watch the results in the Output panel (see Figure 13-11).

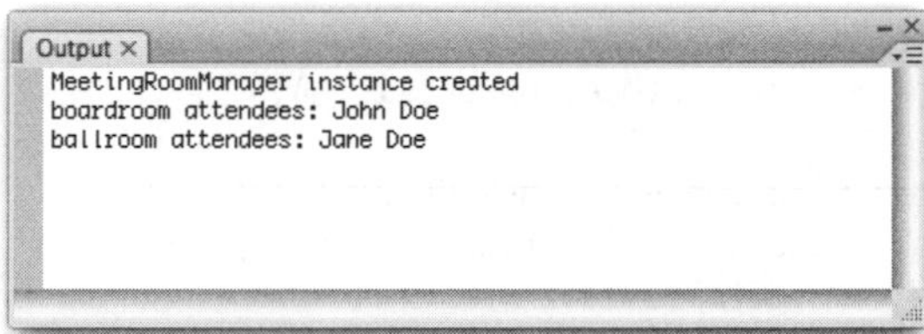

Figure 13-11. Output panel showing the MeetingRoomManager Singleton example

The first line in the Output panel reads MeetingRoomManager instance created, which indicates that there was no earlier instance of the MeetingRoomManager class. The next line, boardroom attendees: John Doe, is the result of notification sent to the boardroomListener update function. The final line in the Output panel, ballroom attendees: Jane Doe, comes from the ballroomListener.

Now, be honest—isn't that some incredibly cool code? One last thing we'll do is build ourselves an interface around this class to add some user interaction.

Building an interface

Get a copy of the file Attendees.fla that was created earlier and rename it to MeetingRoomManager.fla in the folder where all your classes are stored. With MeetingRoomManager.fla open in Flash, perform the following steps:

1. Open the Components panel (select Window ➤ Components).
2. Drag an instance of the ComboBox component to the Interface layer.
3. Give the ComboBox component the instance name meetingrooms_cb (see Figure 13-12).

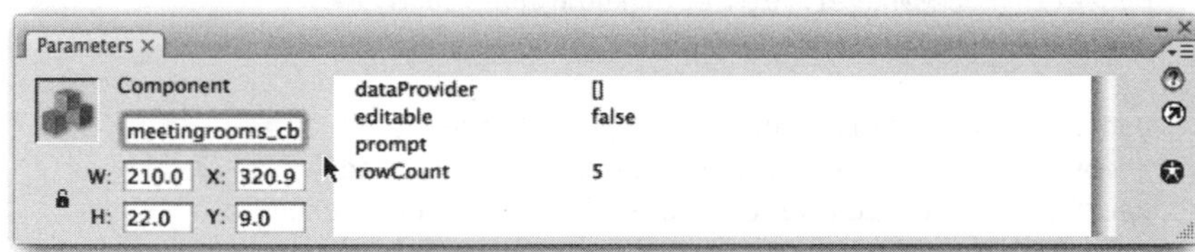

Figure 13-12. Parameters panel showing the ComboBox component

13

4. Change the code in Frame 1 of the ActionScript layer to read as follows:

```
import fl.data.DataProvider;

var myMeetingRoomManager:MeetingRoomManager =➥
MeetingRoomManager.getInstance();

myMeetingRoomManager.addMeetingRoom("boardroom");
myMeetingRoomManager.addMeetingRoom("ballroom");

meetingrooms_cb.dataProvider = ➥
myMeetingRoomManager.getMeetingRoomList();

var attendeeMonitor:Object = new Object();
attendeeMonitor.update = function():void {
  attendees_list.dataProvider =➥
  new DataProvider(myMeetingRoomManager➥
  .getMeetingRoom(meetingrooms_cb.selectedItem.label)➥
  .getAttendees());
}

function addPerson(evt:Event):void {
  myMeetingRoomManager➥
  .getMeetingRoom(meetingrooms_cb.text)➥
  .addAttendee(attendee_txt.text);
}

function removePerson(evt:Event):void {
  myMeetingRoomManager➥
  .getMeetingRoom(meetingrooms_cb.text)➥
  .removeAttendee(attendee_txt.text);
}

function changeRoom(evt:Event):void {
  attendeeMonitor.update();
}

myMeetingRoomManager.getMeetingRoom("boardroom")➥
.addSubscriber(attendeeMonitor);
myMeetingRoomManager.getMeetingRoom("ballroom")➥
.addSubscriber(attendeeMonitor);

add_btn.addEventListener("click", addPerson);
remove_btn.addEventListener("click", removePerson);
meetingrooms_cb.addEventListener("change", changeRoom);
```

5. Add the following method to the MeetingRoomManager class in MeetingRoomManager.as:

```
public function getMeetingRoomList():Array {
  var tmp:Array = new Array();
  for(var i:uint=0; i<meetingRooms.length; i++) {
    tmp.push(meetingRooms[i].name);
  }
  return tmp;
}
```

Once you've completed these steps, save your files and run Test Movie (Control ➤ Test Movie). As with the Observer pattern, you'll now have an interface where you can add and remove attendees. You've just added support for multiple meeting rooms.

The ComboBox component gets filled with the available meeting rooms by assigning the array it gets from the new getMeetingRoomList method you added to its dataProvider. By using the built-in addEventListener method, you can update the List component with attendees as soon as the meeting room in the ComboBox component is changed. The addPerson and removePerson functions that get called when the corresponding Button components are clicked have now been changed to store the attendees in the correct meeting room in the MeetingRoomManager class.

Feel free to play around with this example, just as with the Observer example. You may want to try and add another listener that displays the number of attendees for the selected meeting room. You'll find the solution to this exercise in the downloadable source files that you can obtain from the friends of ED website.

Decorator pattern

The Decorator pattern is one of my favorite design patterns because it's very flexible and a quick-and-easy alternative to subclassing your code. This pattern adds functionality to an existing class by accepting a class instance as an argument in its constructor. One advantage of the Decorator pattern over inheritance is that it allows classes to have functionality added at runtime, a concept called *composition* in OOP. If you read up on the topic, you'll often find the Decorator class gets called the *front-end class* while the decorated class is the *back-end class*.

It's not very difficult to get this pattern to work, so let's start with the basic class structure.

Basic implementation

13

The following code creates a Decorator that accepts an object instance as an argument and stores that in a private variable named decorateInstance:

Decorator.as

```
package {

  public class Decorator {

    private var decorateInstance:Object;

    public function Decorator(decorateObj:Object) {
      this.decorateInstance = decorateObj;
    }

  }

}
```

If you were to "decorate" the Attendees class, the code on the timeline in Flash would look something like this:

```
var myAttendees:Attendees = new Attendees();
var myDecorator:Decorator = new Decorator(myAttendees);
```

Or if you don't need to have a reference to the Attendees instance and just want to work with the Decorator class, an anonymous instance would also work:

```
var myDecorator:Decorator = new Decorator(new Attendees());
```

The way the Decorator pattern works is it defines all additional methods it wants to add to the existing functionality of the `decorateInstance` object and overrides any methods it wants changed. All other method calls to the Decorator class should just be relayed to the `decorateInstance` object. Let's take the Attendees class as an example again and see how that would look.

Decorator.as

```
package {

  public class Decorator {

    private var decorateInstance:Object;

    public function Decorator(decorateObj:Object) {
       this.decorateInstance = decorateObj;
    }

    public function addAttendee(name:String):void {
      this.decorateInstance.addAttendee(name);
    }
```

```
        public function removeAttendee(name:String):void {
          this.decorateInstance.removeAttendee(name)
        }

        public function getAttendees():void {
          this.decorateInstance.getAttendees();
        }

        public function clearAttendees():void {
          this.decorateInstance.attendeesList = new Array();
        }

    }

}
```

As you can see from the preceding code, the Decorator class implements all methods that the decorateInstance object has and relays the methods through to that class instance. In this example, we also added a clearAttendees method that resets that attendees array. By doing this, we can now use the Decorator class and have all the functionality of the Attendees class, as well as being able to use the clearAttendees method. The code on the timeline in Flash to work with this class would look something like this:

```
var myDecorator:Decorator = new Decorator(new Attendees());
myDecorator.addAttendee("John Doe");
myDecorator.clearAttendees();
```

Practical implementation

"Hang on a minute," you may be thinking. "You said this pattern was quick and easy, and how can you possibly call this flexible?" You're absolutely right—even though the preceding code works well, it's not the most convenient way to implement the Decorator pattern. Luckily, ActionScript comes to the rescue and provides us with an invaluable class: flash.utils.Proxy.

This Proxy class, among other things such as retrieving and modifying properties of an object, is a replacement for what used to be __resolve in ActionScript 2.0. What __resolve would do was allow any method not defined in the class to be routed to the __resolve method and capture the method name as an argument.

Now in ActionScript 3.0 with the Proxy class, we need to create a class that extends flash.utils.Proxy, use the flash_proxy namespace (to prevent method name collisions with any methods in your class), and override the callProperty method. Additionally, to prevent the compiler from throwing an error when it notices a method call that is not implemented in the class, we set it to dynamic. This dynamic property of the class means it is not sealed and can have properties and methods added to it at runtime.

Inside the callProperty method, we then reference the decorated class instance and use array notation to trigger the method to be called on it. Using the Function.apply method, we're then able to have it use the scope of the decorated class instance.

Decorator.as

```
package {

  import flash.utils.Proxy;
  import flash.utils.flash_proxy;

  public dynamic class Decorator extends Proxy {

    private var decorateInstance:Object;

    public function Decorator(decorateObj:Object) {
      decorateInstance = decorateObj;
    }

    flash_proxy override function callProperty(name:*, ...rest):* {
      return decorateInstance[name].apply(decorateInstance);
   }

  }

}
```

This is more like it! Create a blank FLA and save it in the same folder as `Decorator.as` and `Attendees.as`. With this file open in Flash, rename Layer 1 in the timeline to ActionScript and add the following code to Frame 1:

```
var myAttendees:Attendees = new Attendees();
var myDecorator:Decorator = new Decorator(myAttendees);

myDecorator.addAttendee("John Doe");
trace(myDecorator.getAttendees());
```

As you can see, in the preceding code snippet we decorate a new instance of the Attendees class, add an attendee, and subsequently read out the attendee list through the Decorator class instance. Let's give this a try by running Test Movie (Control ➤ Test Movie).

Oops, looks like we've got an error happening there (see Figure 13-13). The reason for this is that our implementation of the `callProperty` method of the `flash.utils.Proxy` class does not pass any arguments to the decorated class. The `addAttendee` method expects an argument to get passed, and it doesn't get one.

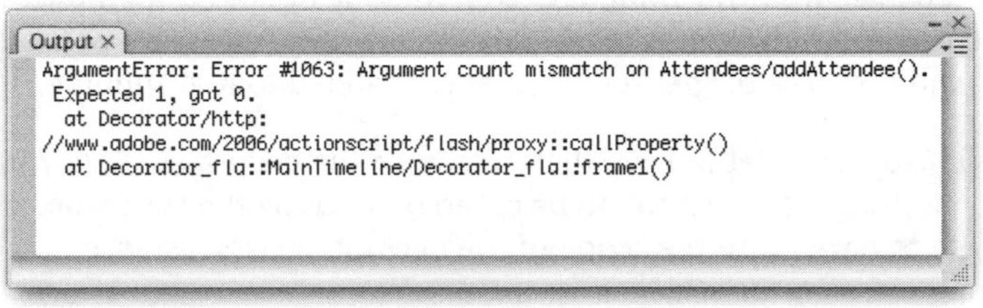

```
Output ×
ArgumentError: Error #1063: Argument count mismatch on Attendees/addAttendee().
 Expected 1, got 0.
  at Decorator/http:
//www.adobe.com/2006/actionscript/flash/proxy::callProperty()
  at Decorator_fla::MainTimeline/Decorator_fla::frame1()
```

Figure 13-13. Output panel showing the error with the Decorator example

Fixing this is not difficult at all; we just need to check the rest parameter defined in the callProperty method. What this rest parameter does is define an array of all additional arguments that got passed to the method. The syntax for this is ...rest, where rest is the name of the variable we want to access the array through. You can decide to use any other name as a convention, for example, ...arguments.

The only thing that needs to happen is to check whether or not any rest arguments were defined and if so pass them. To achieve this, simply update the code as shown here:

```
flash_proxy override function callProperty(name:*, ...rest):* {
  if(rest.length > 0) {
    return decorateInstance[name].apply(decorateInstance, rest);
  } else {
    return decorateInstance[name].apply(decorateInstance);
  }
}
```

Now let's run Test Movie (Control ➤ Test Movie) again (see Figure 13-14) to see if that fixed the problem.

Figure 13-14. Output panel showing the Decorator example in action

That did the trick! We now have a line in the Output panel showing "John Doe" as the only attendee in the attendeeList array of our decorated Attendees class instance.

> *It's important to note that if both the Decorator class and the* decorateInstance *object implement the same method, only the method in the Decorator class will get called.*

Let's try one more example: first we create a new instance of the Decorator class and pass it an instance of the Attendees class to decorate. Then we define a listener object with an update function that traces out the current attendee list. Next, we subscribe this listener object to updates coming from the Decorator class instance and add John Doe and Jane Doe as attendees.

13

```
var myDecorator:Decorator = new Decorator(new Attendees());

var listenObj:Object = new Object();
listenObj.update = function():void {
  trace(myDecorator.getAttendees());
}
```

```
myDecorator.addSubscriber(listenObj);
myDecorator.addAttendee("John Doe");
myDecorator.addAttendee("Jane Doe");
```

Let's try running this example: choose Test Movie (Control ➤ Test Movie). Figure 13-15 shows the results you should see.

Figure 13-15. Output panel showing the attendee list

That's now running like a train: the `listenObj` is now subscribed to the `myDecorator` instance, and its update function gets called any time we run `addAttendee`. With this Decorator implementation in place, we can now have a working copy of the Attendees class and add additional functionality.

So, why exactly is the Decorator pattern more flexible than subclassing? Well, the most important reason is you can extend functionality of a class at runtime by assigning a class instance as an argument for the Decorator class constructor. But be aware that there is a downside to using this technique: it doesn't work on class properties. To decorate class properties, you'll need to create methods that set and retrieve this property. I personally don't have a problem with this, as I quite like to use methods for getting and setting class properties rather than directly manipulating the properties themselves.

Let's apply the Decorator pattern to something useful in ActionScript 3.0. For example, say we want to add some functionality to the Array class.

Array2.as

```
package {

  import flash.utils.Proxy;
  import flash.utils.flash_proxy;

  dynamic class Array2 extends Proxy{

    private var decorateInstance:Object;

    public function Array2(decorateObj:Object) {
      decorateInstance = decorateObj;
    }
```

```
        flash_proxy override function callProperty(name:*, ...rest):* {
           if(decorateInstance[name]) {
             decorateInstance[name].apply(decorateInstance, rest);
           } else {
             trace(name+" method does not exist!");
           }
        }


        public function checkDuplicate(name:String):Boolean {
          var count:uint = 0;
          for(var i:uint=0; i<decorateInstance.length; i++) {
            if(decorateInstance[i] == name) {
              count++;
            }
          }
          if(count > 1) {
            return true;
          } else {
            return false;
          }
        }

        public function removeDuplicate(name:String):void {
          var count:uint = 0;
          for(var i:uint=0; i<decorateInstance.length; i++) {
            if(decorateInstance[i] == name) {
              count++;
              if(count > 1) {
                decorateInstance.splice (i,1);
         }
        }
       }
      }
     }
    }
```

As you can see in the preceding code, the same Decorator template created earlier is used, and the class name and constructor method are simply changed to Array2. Next, we add two new methods, checkDuplicate and removeDuplicate, that loop through the Array instance to which a reference is stored in the decorateInstance class property.

Both methods take an argument that defines what entry they look for in the array and have a local count variable that keeps track of the number of times it encounters that entry. The checkDuplicate method returns a Boolean value indicating whether or not an entry has duplicates in the array. The removeDuplicate method removes any duplicate entries that occur in the array after the first occurrence.

Create a new blank FLA in the same folder where you saved Array2.as and name it Array2.fla. With Array2.fla open in Flash, perform the following steps:

1. Rename Layer 1 in the timeline to ActionScript.
2. Select Frame 1 of the ActionScript layer.
3. Open the Actions panel (select Window ➤ Actions).
4. Add the following ActionScript to the Actions panel:

```
var myArrayDecorator:Array2 = new Array2(new Array());

myArrayDecorator.push("Jane Doe");
myArrayDecorator.push("John Doe");
myArrayDecorator.push("Jane Doe");

trace("John Doe: "+myArrayDecorator.checkDuplicate("John Doe"));
trace("Jane Doe: "+myArrayDecorator.checkDuplicate("Jane Doe"));

trace("Remove Jane Doe duplicates");
myArrayDecorator.removeDuplicate("Jane Doe");

trace("John Doe: "+myArrayDecorator.checkDuplicate("John Doe"));
trace("Jane Doe: "+myArrayDecorator.checkDuplicate("Jane Doe"));
```

If you save Array2.fla and run Test Movie (Control ➤ Test Movie), you'll get the result shown in Figure 13-16.

Figure 13-16. Output panel for the Decorator pattern example

The code we use adds three items to the array: one "John Doe" entry and two "Jane Doe" entries. Using the checkDuplicate method, we check for duplicates of "John Doe" and "Jane Doe" in the array, and the results of this are traced out in the first two lines of the Output panel. For John Doe, the result of this is false and for Jane Doe it's true.

Next, we use the removeDuplicate method to remove all duplicates of "Jane Doe" in the array. We add a trace statement saying Remove Jane Doe duplicates.

Finally, we run the checkDuplicate method again for "John Doe" and "Jane Doe," and watch the result in the Output panel. This time, the checkDuplicate method returns false for both entries, which means there are no more duplicate entries.

That's it! You've just created a working implementation of the Decorator pattern and extended an Array object. Now, have some fun and try adding a couple more methods to the Array2 class. For example, you could have a method that uses the checkDuplicate and removeDuplicate methods to automatically remove all duplicates from the array. You can find the solution to this exercise in the downloadable source files for this chapter on the friends of ED site.

Model-View-Controller pattern

The MVC pattern is, technically speaking, not really a design pattern; rather, it's a collection of various patterns that form an architectural framework. That distinction is not all that important for us at the moment, as we're more interested in what the pattern does and how we can apply it to ActionScript 3.0 code.

Using the MVC pattern, we are able to separate the Model (the class that holds the data of the application), the View (the visual presentation of the application), and the Controller (the class that handles user interaction).

Of course, separating a project into these three entities does not help us all that much. What is important is the way the Model, View, and Controller interact.

The MVC pattern specifies the way the different classes can communicate with each other as follows:

- **Model**: Implements the Observer pattern and sends notifications to the View when there are changes to the data it holds.
- **View**: Holds a reference to the Model and the Controller, and is only allowed to connect to the Model to retrieve information when it receives notification from the Model. When user interaction occurs, the View calls the appropriate method on the Controller.
- **Controller**: Holds a reference to the Model and updates that Model through the methods that are called from the View.

Basic implementation

Knowing these specifications, we can create a class template for the Model, View, and Controller, as follows:

Model.as

```
package {

  public class Model extends Observer {

    public function Model() {
    }

    public function registerView(view:Object):void {
      super.addSubscriber(view);
    }

  }

}
```

The Model class extends our Observer class, so it can add, remove, and notify subscribers when changes occur in the data it holds. Our Model class template also holds a method called registerView, which subscribes that View instance to receive notifications.

View.as

```
package {

  public class View {

    private var model:Object;
    private var controller:Object;

    public function View(model:Object,controller:Object) {
      this.model = model;
      this.controller = controller;
      this.model.registerView(this);
    }

    public function update():void {
    }

  }

}
```

The View class accepts two arguments in its constructor. Those arguments are an instance of the Model class and an instance of the Controller class. A reference to the Model and Controller instances are stored in private class properties called model and controller. Using the model class property, we register this instance of the View class with the Model instance so it subscribes to updates. We defined an empty update function that will be used to respond to notifications sent from the Model.

Controller.as

```
package {

  public class Controller {

    private var model:Object;

    public function Controller(model:Object) {
      this.model = model;
    }

  }

}
```

The Controller class accepts one argument in its constructor: a reference to the Model instance it can modify. A reference to this Model class instance is stored in a private class property called `model`.

With those classes in place, we can use the following code on the timeline in Flash:

```
var myModel:Model = new Model();
var myController:Controller = new Controller(myModel);
var myView:View = new View(myModel,myController);
```

The easiest way to see the MVC pattern in action is to apply it to the example we've been working with for the Observer and Singleton patterns.

Practical implementation

We'll be using the Attendees class as our Model, and we'll write new classes to manage the View (the components on the stage) and the Controller (the user interaction that updates the Model). Let's see what the Attendees class looks like and how we'll be applying our Model class template to it:

```
package {

  public class Attendees extends Observer {

    public var attendeesList:Array;

    public function Attendees() {
      attendeesList = new Array();
    }

    public function addAttendee(name:String):Boolean {
      for(var i:uint=0; i<this.attendeesList.length; i++) {
        if(this.attendeesList[i] == name) {
          return false;
        }
      }
      this.attendeesList.push(name);
      super.notifyChanges();
      return true;
    }

    public function removeAttendee(name:String):Boolean {
      for(var i:uint=0; i<this.attendeesList.length; i++) {
        if(this.attendeesList[i] == name) {
          this.attendeesList.splice(i,1);
          super.notifyChanges();
          return true;
        }
      }
      return false;
    }
```

```
      public function getAttendees():Array {
        return attendeesList;
      }

    }

  }
```

To make the code a little more readable, let's rename the class to AttendeeModel and make the necessary changes to make it fit in with our Model class template.

AttendeeModel.as

```
  package {

    public class AttendeeModel extends Observer {

      public var attendeesList:Array;

      public function AttendeeModel() {
        attendeesList = new Array();
      }

      public function registerView(view:Object):void {
        super.addSubscriber(view);
      }

      public function addAttendee(name:String):Boolean {
        for(var i:uint=0; i<this.attendeesList.length; i++) {
          if(this.attendeesList[i] == name) {
            return false;
          }
        }
        this.attendeesList.push(name);
        super.notifyChanges();
        return true;
      }

      public function removeAttendee(name:String):Boolean {
        for(var i:uint=0; i<this.attendeesList.length; i++) {
          if(this.attendeesList[i] == name) {
            this.attendeesList.splice(i,1);
            super.notifyChanges();
            return true;
          }
        }
        return false;
      }
```

```
    public function getAttendees():Array {
      return attendeesList;
    }

  }

}
```

All code that appears in bold shows you changes or additions made to the class. The tweaks we made to this class now make it conform with the MVC Model class specifications.

For the View, we'll need to create a new class, as we didn't previously use a class to work with the components. Sticking to the same naming convention, we'll call this class AttendeeView.

AttendeeView.as

```
package {

  import flash.display.MovieClip;
  import flash.events.Event;
  import fl.data.DataProvider;

  public class AttendeeView extends MovieClip {

    private var model:Object;
    private var controller:Object;

    public function AttendeeView(model:Object, controller:Object) {
      this.model = model;
      this.controller = controller;
      this.model.registerView(this);

      this.add_btn.addEventListener("click", addPerson);
      this.remove_btn.addEventListener("click", removePerson);
    }

    public function update():void {
      this.attendees_list.dataProvider = new DataProvider(➥
      this.model.getAttendees());
    }

    public function addPerson(evt:Event):void {
      this.controller.addPerson(this.attendee_txt.text);
      this.attendee_txt.text = "";
    }
```

```
        public function removePerson(evt:Event):void {
          this.controller.removePerson(this.attendee_txt.text);
          this.attendee_txt.text = "";
        }

      }

    }
```

In the AttendeeView constructor, we use addEventListener to listen for the click event of add_btn and remove_btn. The update function receives notifications from the Model when data has changed, and this then assigns that new data to the attendees_list data provider. The addPerson and removePerson methods forward the method to the Controller instance and clear the attendee_txt TextInput component.

AttendeeController.as

```
package {

  public class AttendeeController {

    private var model:Object;

    public function AttendeeController(model:Object) {
      this.model = model;
    }

    public function addPerson(name:String):void {
      this.model.addAttendee(name);
    }

    public function removePerson(name:Object):void {
      this.model.removeAttendee(name);
    }

  }

}
```

The AttendeeController class basically just holds a reference to the Model instance that was passed as an argument to its constructor and calls the necessary methods on the Model through the methods that get called by AttendeeViewer.

Bringing together the Model, View, and Controller

OK, so now we have the three necessary classes ready: AttendeeModel, AttendeeView, and AttendeeController. All that's left for us to do is prepare the Flash file. Place the files AttendeeModel.as, AttendeeView.as, AttendeeController.as, and Observer.as in the same folder, and get a copy of the file Attendees.fla you created when building the earlier example of the Observer pattern.

Rename Attendees.fla to AttendeesMVC.fla, open it up in Flash, and make the following changes to Frame 1 of the ActionScript layer:

```
var myAttendeeModel:AttendeeModel = new AttendeeModel();➥
var myAttendeeController:AttendeeController =
new AttendeeController(myAttendeeModel);
var myAttendeeView:AttendeeView = ➥
new AttendeeView(myAttendeeModel,myAttendeeController);

addChild(myAttendeeView);
```

What we'll do next is make the components available for the AttendeeView class to use. Selecting all components on stage, choose Modify ➤ Convert to Symbol. We'll name this new movie clip view and link it up to our AttendeeView class (see Figure 13-17).

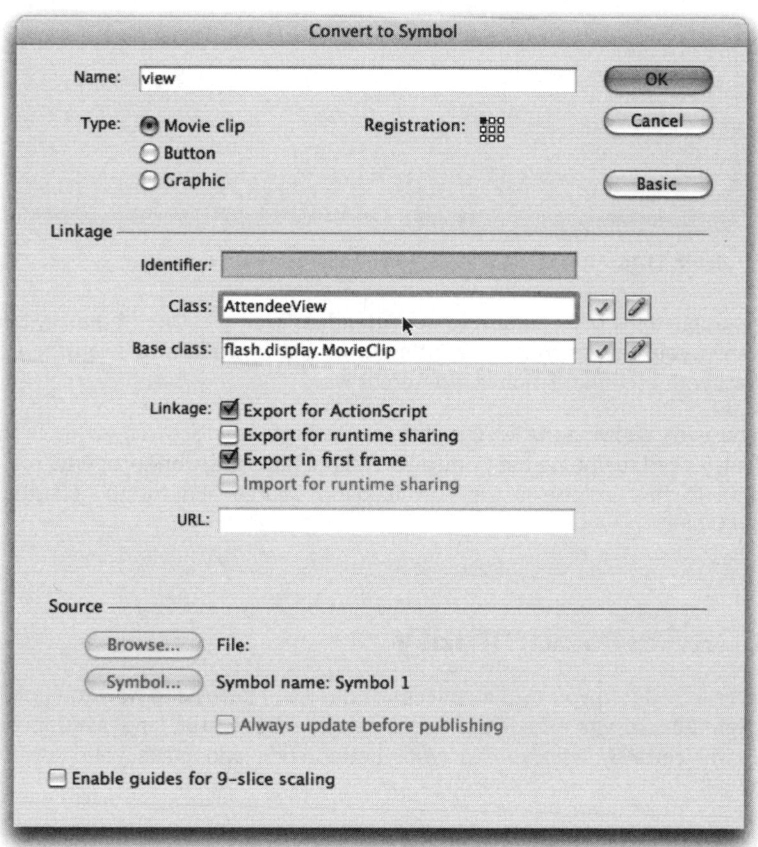

Figure 13-17. Linking view movie clip to AttendeeView class

The final thing we'll do is remove the movie clip instance from the stage since we're instantiating it and calling addChild using ActionScript 3.0 to show it at runtime.

Save `AttendeesMVC.fla` and run Test Movie (Control ➤ Test Movie) to see the MVC example in action (see Figure 13-18).

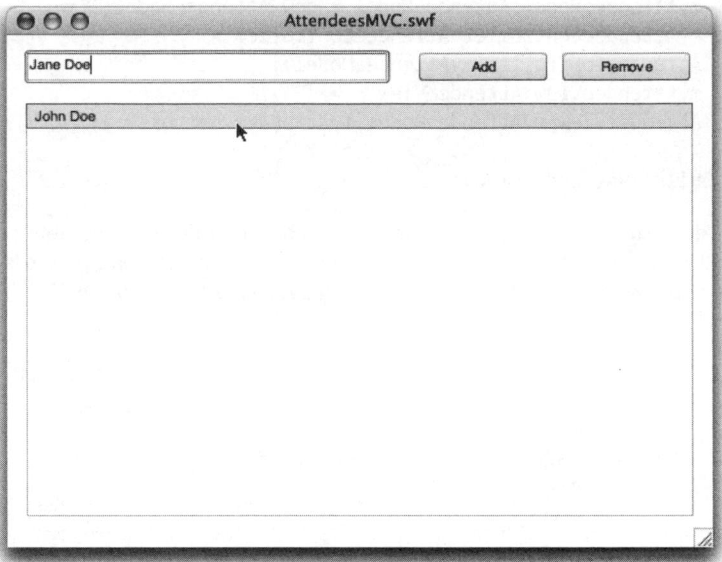

Figure 13-18. Attendee Model-View-Controller pattern example

We've now applied the MVC pattern to our Attendees example. One of the key benefits of this pattern is you can easily assign a different Model to a View, or swap the Controller class to deal with user interaction in a different way.

As an exercise, try applying the MVC pattern to the code we discussed earlier in this chapter. You'll also need to update the Controller class to have this work properly. You can find the solution to this exercise in the downloadable source files for this chapter on the friends of ED site.

Design patterns summary

This chapter introduced you to the concept of design patterns and how to apply them to ActionScript 3.0 projects. The Observer, Singleton, Decorator, and MVC patterns we discussed will certainly help you to write better code and make your projects more manageable.

The important thing to remember when applying any of these design patterns is that they need to become an integral part of your application, and stricter implementations of a pattern don't necessarily mean better implementations. Although design patterns are very useful in making your project more efficient, there is no amount of pattern implementation that can save a badly planned application.

Using design patterns in projects once again boils down to best practices and good planning. If you're looking to implement design patterns in your OOP projects with ActionScript 3.0, read up on best practices and project planning, and with that little extra time you invest I'm sure you'll be pleased with the results.

What's next?

To conclude Part 3 of this book, the final chapter is a case study that walks you through creating an OOP media player. At this point, we've covered OOP concepts in depth, and you'll see them put to action in a real-world project.

The following chapter is highly recommended if you want a recap on what you've learned so far, as moving forward we will introduce you to the ActionScript 3.0 framework and its functionality, which builds on these concepts.

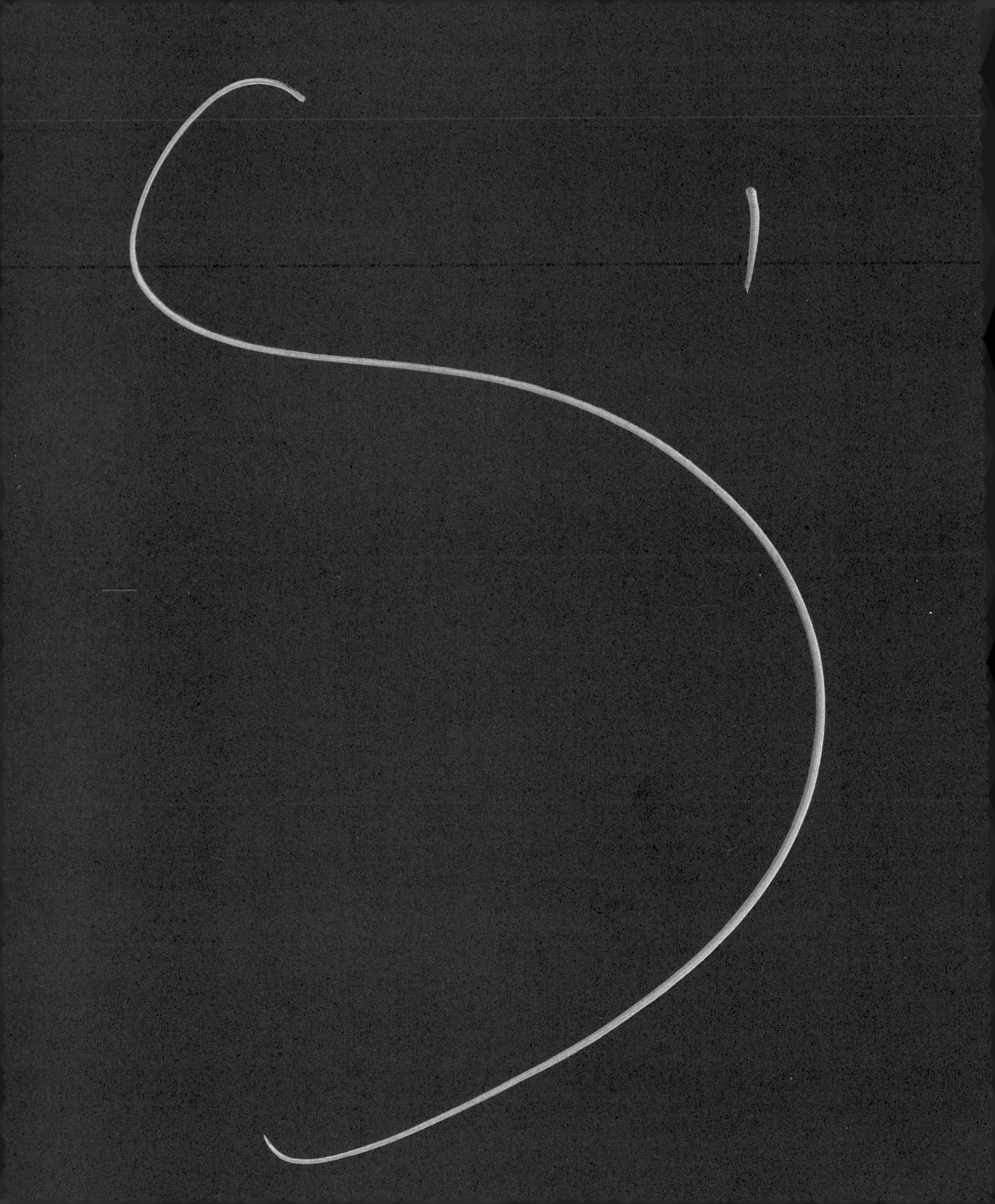

14 CASE STUDY: AN OOP MEDIA PLAYER

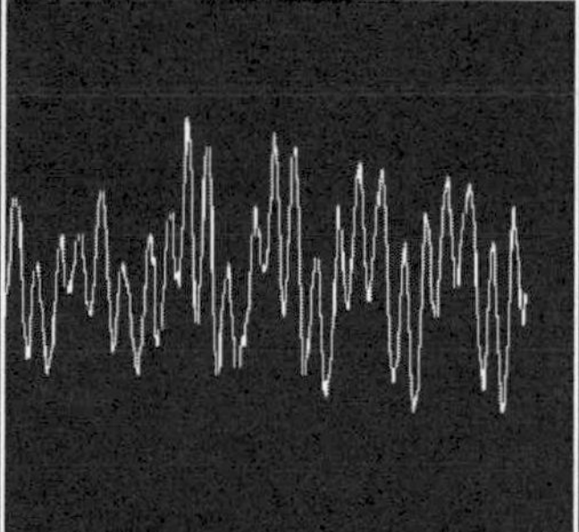

In the previous chapters, we explored many important OOP concepts, including encapsulation, classes, inheritance, polymorphism, interfaces, and design patterns. Conceptualization can only go so far, though, so it's important we solidify these ideas by implementing them in the Flash environment. Many of the previous examples of these concepts have been completely virtual, as is often the case when discussing programming ideas. Since Flash is such a visual tool, however, we'll work through this chapter on a more visual implementation of OOP techniques, namely the building of classes to handle displaying media that can be loaded into Flash, including SWFs, FLVs, and MP3s (all right, the last is hardly visual, but with the introduction of the `SoundMixer` and its `computeSpectrum()` method, it *can* be). As we progress through this chapter, we'll touch on each of the topics discussed in the preceding section, beginning, of course, at the planning stage.

Planning the player

You've learned better than to jump right in and start coding (as tempting as that may seem at the outset!). The best way to begin a project with any scope is to spend a little time planning how to approach it.

Picking a pattern

The media player we'll build in this chapter will utilize a form of the Model-View-Controller framework discussed in Chapter 13, as illustrated in Figure 14-1. In this case, the model will be the media itself that is loaded into Flash. A controller class will be built to manipulate this media by telling it to play, stop, seek a position, set volume, and so on when it's prompted to do so by the view. The view class will display the media as it changes and call methods in the controller class to affect the media. As the media changes, the view is updated.

Guaranteeing methods and datatypes with an interface

Because we wish all three media types to respond to the same methods, it makes sense to create some simple interfaces to define those methods. That way, even though in ActionScript you tell an MP3, FLV, or a SWF to play in different ways, we can trust (and guarantee to those using our classes) that calling a single specified method will play each of the media types the same way. To guarantee this, our media controllers will implement two interfaces: `IPlayable` for controlling playback of media and `IAudible` for controlling audio properties.

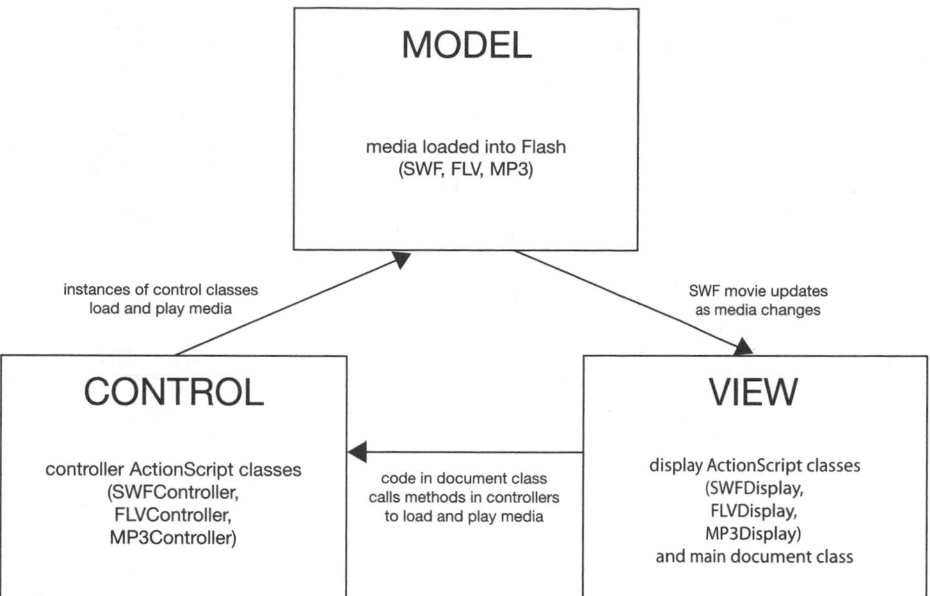

Figure 14-1. The Model-View-Controller interaction for the media player

Examining class structure

A number of classes will be combining to form the finished media player. The built-in `EventDispatcher` will act as the base class for `MediaController`, which will define the common methods and properties for all three of the separate media-type controllers. These three controllers, `SWFController`, `FLVController`, and `MP3Controller`, will inherit these common methods and properties from `MediaController`, but implement the media controller methods (specified in `IPlayable`) in ways appropriate to their media type, acting as a nice example of polymorphism. A developer calling `playMedia()` on any of these three classes can expect that the appropriate media type will play, despite the different ways Flash plays media. The classes will hide the implementation of these methods through encapsulation. For the view, `MediaDisplay` will act as a base class for the display of all three of our media types: `FLVDisplay`, `SWFDisplay`, and `MP3Display` (which can plug in various sound visualizers, all inheriting from the base `SoundVisualizer`). Finally, we will extend `Event` for our special media events by creating, no surprise here, a `MediaEvent` class.

That's the basic breakdown of the classes we'll be building throughout the rest of the chapter. For a better understanding of how it all fits together, be sure to look at the UML diagram in Figure 14-2 detailing the model for the media player. Once you are confident with the structure, open up Flash and prepare to code!

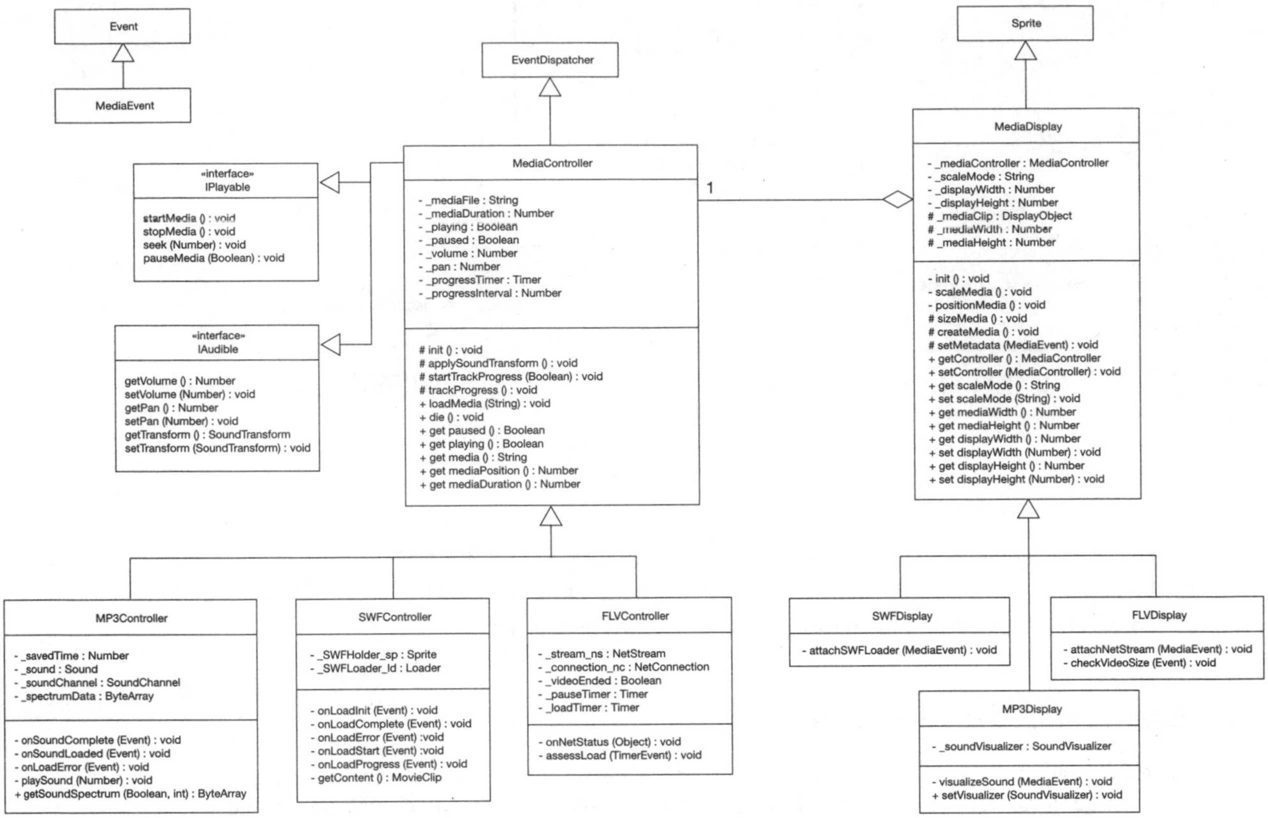

Event
MediaEvent

EventDispatcher

Sprite

«interface»
IPlayable
startMedia () : void
stopMedia () : void
seek (Number) : void
pauseMedia (Boolean) : void

«interface»
IAudible
getVolume () : Number
setVolume (Number) : void
getPan () : Number
setPan (Number) : void
getTransform () : SoundTransform
setTransform (SoundTransform) : void

MediaController
- _mediaFile : String
- _mediaDuration : Number
- _playing : Boolean
- _paused : Boolean
- _volume : Number
- _pan : Number
- _progressTimer : Timer
- _progressInterval : Number
init () : void
applySoundTransform () : void
startTrackProgress (Boolean) : void
trackProgress () : void
+ loadMedia (String) : void
+ die () : void
+ get paused () : Boolean
+ get playing () : Boolean
+ get media () : String
+ get mediaPosition () : Number
+ get mediaDuration () : Number

1

MediaDisplay
- _mediaController : MediaController
- _scaleMode : String
- _displayWidth : Number
- _displayHeight : Number
_mediaClip : DisplayObject
_mediaWidth : Number
_mediaHeight : Number
- init () : void
- scaleMedia () : void
- positionMedia () : void
sizeMedia () : void
createMedia () : void
setMetadata (MediaEvent) : void
+ getController () : MediaController
+ setController (MediaController) : void
+ get scaleMode () : String
+ set scaleMode (String) : void
+ get mediaWidth () : Number
+ get mediaHeight () : Number
+ get displayWidth () : Number
+ set displayWidth (Number) : void
+ get displayHeight () : Number
+ set displayHeight (Number) : void

MP3Controller
- _savedTime : Number
- _sound : Sound
- _soundChannel : SoundChannel
- _spectrumData : ByteArray
- onSoundComplete (Event) : void
- onSoundLoaded (Event) : void
- onLoadError (Event) : void
- playSound (Number) : void
+ getSoundSpectrum (Boolean, int) : ByteArray

SWFController
- _SWFHolder_sp : Sprite
- _SWFLoader_ld : Loader
- onLoadInit (Event) : void
- onLoadComplete (Event) : void
- onLoadError (Event) :void
- onLoadStart (Event) :void
- onLoadProgress (Event) : void
- getContent () : MovieClip

FLVController
- _stream_ns : NetStream
- _connection_nc : NetConnection
- _videoEnded : Boolean
- _pauseTimer : Timer
- _loadTimer : Timer
- onNetStatus (Object) : void
- assessLoad (TimerEvent) : void

SWFDisplay
- attachSWFLoader (MediaEvent) : void

FLVDisplay
- attachNetStream (MediaEvent) : void
- checkVideoSize (Event) : void

MP3Display
- _soundVisualizer : SoundVisualizer
- visualizeSound (MediaEvent) : void
+ setVisualizer (SoundVisualizer) : void

Figure 14-2. The UML diagram for the media player classes

Building the media player

We'll begin this project by defining the packages for our classes. Determine the base directory for your project, and within this directory create a new folder named com. Within com, create another folder named foed, and within foed create two folders named media and events, respectively. See Figure 14-3 for the result. com.foed will be the package for all of the classes we create for the next several chapters.

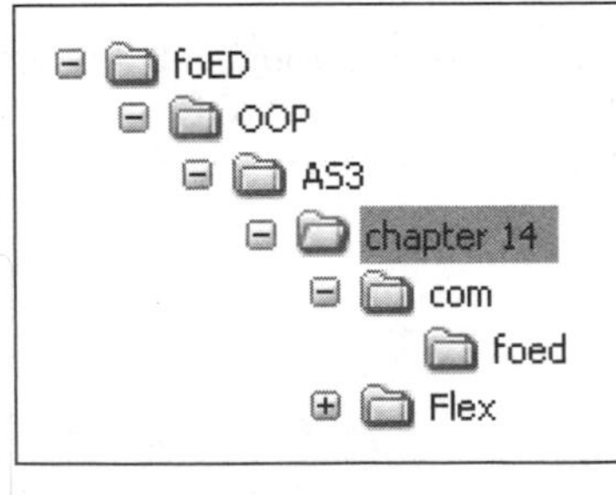

Figure 14-3. A new directory has been added to the Flash Classes directory

Defining the interfaces

Two interfaces will be used by the classes in this tutorial. IPlayable and IAudible will define how media is to be controlled and interacted with. The first, IPlayable, lists four methods for controlling playback of media. Create a new ActionScript file and save it as IPlayable.as in the com/foed/media directory. Enter the following code:

```
package com.foed.media {

  public interface IPlayable {

    function startMedia():void;
    function seek(pOffset:Number):void;
    function stopMedia():void;
    function pauseMedia(pPause:Boolean):void;

  }

}
```

startMedia() will set media playing, stopMedia() will halt its progress and return its position to the beginning, seek() will find a certain point in the media, and pauseMedia() will halt the media's progress but leave its position at the current location.

Moving on to the audio properties of the media, create a new ActionScript file named IAudible.as and save it into the same com/foed/media directory. Enter the following code:

```
package com.foed.media {

  import flash.media.SoundTransform;

  public interface IAudible {

    function getVolume():Number;
    function setVolume(pVolume:Number):void;

    function getPan():Number;
    function setPan(pPan:Number):void;

    function getSoundTransform():SoundTransform;
    function setSoundTransform(pTransform:SoundTransform):void;

  }

}
```

These are the six methods to control the audio component of any media. They are defined here in an interface, since each of the three types of media we'll be controlling (SWF, MP3, and FLV) all implement the control of the media's sound in slightly different ways, and we want to guarantee a consistent interface for all three.

As you work through this tutorial, you might notice that these interfaces are only used within the `MediaController` abstract base class, so some may question the relevance of using interfaces to define these methods. The reason I have included them here is that an interface for playing back media would be useful not only for these controller classes, but also for player classes that interact with these controllers. As an example, I have built applications that dynamically loaded in either a media controller or a complete player (a media controller and a display object, sometimes with a set of controls). In all cases, I needed to interact with this object; however, I could not count on it being a `MediaController` instance, but perhaps a player that contained a media controller. As such, being able to code against the interface, which all these classes implemented, allowed interaction with the media playback object without relying on a concrete class. We do not create more than the controllers in this case study, and so the interfaces conceivably could be left out, but that does not mean the interfaces will not prove useful if you choose to develop these classes further, and so I wanted to show how you might include them from the outset.

Defining events

The media controller classes will use the built-in events as much as possible, but there will be additional events we need to broadcast, and for that purpose we will create a `MediaEvent` class that extends Event. This class will be short and sweet and will consist of the following code:

```
package com.foed.events {

  import flash.events.Event;

  public class MediaEvent extends Event {

    public static const START:String = "mediaStart";
    public static const STOP:String = "mediaStop";
    public static const PROGRESS:String = "mediaProgess";
    public static const COMPLETE:String = "mediaComplete";
    public static const METADATA:String = "mediaMetadata";
    public static const LOAD:String = "mediaLoad";

    private var _width:Number;
    private var _height:Number;
    private var _position:Number;
    private var _duration:Number;

    public function MediaEvent(
      pType:String,
      pPosition:Number=0,
      pDuration:Number=0,
```

```
      pWidth:Number=0,
      pHeight:Number=0,
      pBubbles:Boolean=false,
      pCancelable:Boolean=false
    ) {
      super(pType, pBubbles, pCancelable);
      _position = pPosition;
      _duration = pDuration;
      _width = pWidth;
      _height = pHeight;
    }

    override public function clone():Event {
      return new MediaEvent(
        type,
        _position,
        _duration,
        _width,
        _height,
        bubbles,
        cancelable
      );
    }

    public function get width():Number { return _width; }
    public function get height():Number { return _height; }
    public function get position():Number { return _position; }
    public function get duration():Number { return _duration; }

  }

}
```

Create a new directory, events, in the com/foed directory and save this code into that directory as MediaEvent.as. The static properties at the top of the class give us some nice constants to use for our events. Four private properties then follow for the values we want to hold in a media event. The constructor follows, calling the Event constructor, then setting its unique member properties based on the arguments sent. After that, the clone() method is overridden, as is necessary for Event child classes. Finally, the four getters at the bottom allow public access to the member properties. Piece of cake!

Controlling media

14

With all of the interfaces and events taken care of, we can begin the coding of the media classes to control the playback of media loaded into Flash. MediaController will act as a base class for all the media type controllers and contain the common methods and properties for all.

Defining properties

Create a new directory within the com/foed/media directory and name it controllers. Within this, create a new ActionScript file and save it as MediaController.as. Enter the following code:

```
package com.foed.media.controllers {

  import flash.events.EventDispatcher;
  import flash.events.TimerEvent;
  import flash.events.Event;
  import flash.utils.Timer;
  import flash.media.SoundTransform;
  import com.foed.events.MediaEvent;
  import com.foed.media.IAudible;
  import com.foed.media.IPlayable;

  public class MediaController➥
 extends EventDispatcher➥
 implements IAudible, IPlayable {

    private var _mediaFile:String;
    private var _mediaDuration:Number;
    private var _playing:Boolean;
    private var _paused:Boolean;
    private var _volume:Number;
    private var _pan:Number;
    private var _progressTimer:Timer;

    static private var _progressInterval:Number = 40;

    public function MediaController() {
      init();
    }

  }

}
```

After the package declaration, we start the code by importing the classes we will be referencing within the class. I have the benefit of knowing what these will be beforehand, but generally you would just add these as they become required by your code. We then define the MediaController class, which inherits from the EventDispatcher class and implements the two media control interfaces.

What follows is a list of private properties utilized in the class. With decent naming of properties, it should be evident what each is for.

- _mediaFile holds the name of the file to be loaded.
- _mediaDuration is the total time for the media loaded.

- _playing and _paused define the current status of the media.
- _volume and _pan hold values for the sound properties.
- _progressTimer holds a reference to the Timer instance used to call a method to monitor media playback progress.
- _progressInterval, the static property that follows the main list, resides on the MediaController class itself (not on an instance) and holds the length in milliseconds for repeated interval calls to monitor the progress of media playback.

After the properties are defined, the constructor appears and includes a call to the class's init() method. We'll take care of writing that method next.

One thing to note is that the preceding constructor, like all constructors in ActionScript 3.0, is made public. MediaController, though, is really intended as an abstract class, meaning that there should be no direct instantiation; instead, a concrete child class should be used (i.e., you would instantiate a class like FLVController in your code, never MediaController). However, since ActionScript 3.0 does not include the abstract modifier and does not support private constructors (which was the workaround for creating abstract classes in ActionScript 2.0), we are left with either trusting the class will not be used directly or adding code to each class in order to throw a compile-time or runtime error if the class is instantiated directly. There are some interesting methods you can find to accomplish the latter, but for our purposes, we will use the former solution and trust the developers, in this case us!

Protected methods

Add the following code to the MediaController class:

```
protected function init():void {
  _volume = 1;
  _pan = 0;
  _paused = false;
  _playing = false;
  _progressTimer = new Timer(_progressInterval, 0);
}

protected function startTrackProgress(pStart:Boolean):void {
  if (pStart) {
    dispatchEvent(new MediaEvent(MediaEvent.START,➥
mediaPosition, mediaDuration));
    _progressTimer.addEventListener(TimerEvent.TIMER,➥
trackProgress, false, 0, true);
    _progressTimer.start();
  } else {
    dispatchEvent(new MediaEvent(MediaEvent.STOP,➥
mediaPosition, mediaDuration));
    _progressTimer.removeEventListener(➥
TimerEvent.TIMER, trackProgress);
    _progressTimer.stop();
  }
}
```

14

```
    protected function trackProgress(pEvent:Event):void {
      dispatchEvent(new MediaEvent(MediaEvent.PROGRESS,➥
mediaPosition, mediaDuration));
    }
```

All three of these methods are given the protected modifier, meaning that child classes are free to access and/or override these methods, which we will take advantage of later in the chapter. The `init()` method sets default properties for the controller and initializes the `Timer` instance that will monitor media playback. Passing the `0` as the second parameter enables the timer to run indefinitely.

`startTrackProgress()` is sent a `true` or `false` value depending on whether the media is being started or stopped. If the media is being started, our `_progressTimer` is started and a `START` event is dispatched. The method `trackProgress` will be called every 40 milliseconds (the value for `_progressInterval` passed to `_progressTimer` on instantiation). If the media is being stopped, the timer is stopped and the `STOP` event is dispatched.

> *The parameters we are passing to the* `addEventListener` *method of the* `Timer` *are, in order, the event to register for, the function to call to handle the event, whether to process the event in the capture phase of the event handling, the numeric priority of the event listener, and, the final argument, whether to use a weak reference when adding the listener. It's this final argument that is important to note (we are just using the default values for the* `useCapture` *and* `priority` *arguments), as it ensures the garbage collection can remove references to a function if it only exists as a listener. Generally, you will be passing to the* `addEventListener` *method a function that exists elsewhere within a class (as here, where it is a method), which will be safe from the garbage collection until we delete the instance of the* `MediaController` *class. At that point, if we have not removed the event listeners (which we should try to do anyway) and also have not used weak references when adding listeners, the handlers we passed when adding the listeners will not be deleted as desired. It becomes important then for us to use weak references by default to ensure that resources are managed appropriately in the player. As such, we will be passing weak references in all* `addEventListener` *calls throughout this case study.*

The final protected method, `trackProgress()`, simply dispatches an event to any listeners that wish to know that the media is playing and act accordingly (imagine that this might be used by a playhead progressing, or perhaps a running collection of subtitles that need to be updated as the media progresses).

Public methods

The protected methods defined previously will be used only internally by this class and any class that extends `MediaController`. This next set of methods can be called from any object and will be used to control the properties of the media. Add the following code to the `MediaController` class:

```
    public function loadMedia(pFileURL:String):void {
      _mediaFile = pFileURL;
      _playing = false;
      _paused = false;
    }

    public function startMedia():void {
      _playing = true;
      setVolume(_volume);
      setPan(_pan);
      startTrackProgress(true);
    }

    public function seek(pOffset:Number):void {
      dispatchEvent(new MediaEvent(MediaEvent.PROGRESS,➥
mediaPosition, mediaDuration));
    }

    public function stopMedia():void {
      _playing = false;
      startTrackProgress(false);
    }

    public function pauseMedia(pPause:Boolean):void {
      _playing = !pPause;
      _paused = pPause;
      startTrackProgress(!pPause);
    }
```

The first method listed, loadMedia(), will be called to load an external media file for the controller to play. Since the three types of media are all loaded in separate ways, the actual loading will have to take place in the classes we write to handle those media types. Here in this base class, the file name is saved and _paused and _playing are set to false, which makes sense since the media hasn't yet loaded!

The next four methods are necessary when implementing the IPlayable interface. Again, since the control of different media types is implemented differently, the classes extending MediaController will take care of the brunt of the work. Here, the values for _playing and _paused are set when appropriate, with calls to startTrackProgress() being made when media either stops or starts, and events are broadcast using dispatchEvent() to let registered listeners know the status of the media has changed.

Add these next several methods to the public methods defined earlier (that's between the pauseMedia() method and the class's closing brace):


```
    public function get mediaFile():String { return _mediaFile; }

    public function get mediaPosition():Number { return 0; }
    public function set mediaPosition(pPosition:Number):void {}
```

```
    public function get mediaDuration():Number {➥
return _mediaDuration; }
    public function set mediaDuration(pDuration:Number):void {➥
_mediaDuration = pDuration; }

    public function get paused():Boolean { return _paused; }

    public function get playing():Boolean { return _playing; }
```

These methods we've just added are simply implicit getter/setter methods for other objects to set or retrieve values for the MediaController instance's properties. An implicit getter/setter method allows an object to call the method as if it were a property. This simply means that instead of using

```
var isPlaying:Boolean = mediaController.playing();
```

to retrieve the value of the _playing property, the following must be used instead:

```
var isPlaying:Boolean = mediaController.playing;
```

Setters work similarly to getters, but must receive a value and cannot return anything. A developer would access a setter with

```
mediaController.mediaPosition = 60;
```

Notice for each of the preceding getters, the private property value is simply returned. However, for mediaPosition, the value of 0 is returned. This is because the value will be constantly changing, and the classes extending MediaController will simply return the current position of the media as opposed to storing a value in a property.

For _mediaDuration and _mediaPosition, we are also providing setters. This makes sense for _mediaPosition, as setting this should send the playhead of the media to the specified position, but why do we allow this access for _mediaDuration? Unfortunately, for video it might not always be possible for our controllers to dynamically assess the duration of a video file, as that information must be embedded (and embedded correctly) as metadata in the FLV. Since we cannot guarantee that, we are allowing for this duration to be set manually, so to speak, by the code. For instance, data describing a video file might be pulled from a database or from an XML file, in which case the code that sends the video to the controller to load and manage can also pass the duration.

The next set of public methods will allow objects to set and retrieve values for the sound properties of the media, fulfilling the requirements of the IAudible interface that MediaController is implementing. With them is an empty, abstract method, applySoundTransform(), which will need to be overridden and implemented differently in child classes of MediaController, since each type of media has a different way of applying its soundTransform. Enter the following code below the methods we just defined, but before the class's closing brace:

```
protected function applySoundTransform():void {}

public function getSoundTransform():SoundTransform {
  return new SoundTransform(_volume, _pan);
}
public function setSoundTransform(
  pSoundTransform:SoundTransform
):void {
  _volume = pSoundTransform.volume;
  _pan = pSoundTransform.pan;
  applySoundTransform();
}

public function getVolume():Number { return _volume; }
public function setVolume(pVolume:Number):void {
  _volume = pVolume;
  applySoundTransform();
}

public function getPan():Number { return _pan; }
public function setPan(pPan:Number):void {
  _pan = pPan;
  applySoundTransform();
}
```

These are the necessary methods for classes implementing the IAudible interface. Each sets or retrieves the values for the media's sound. To go with these methods, which are *explicit* getter and setter methods, we'll also define some *implicit* getter and setter methods for easier access to these properties. Add the following below the methods defined previously:

```
    public function get volume():Number { return getVolume(); }
    public function set volume(pVolume:Number):void {➥
setVolume(pVolume); }
    public function get pan():Number { return getPan(); }
    public function set pan(pPan:Number):void { setPan(pPan); }
```

So now the developer can use the methods defined in IAudible or these methods to control the audio.

There is one more getter method for our MediaController class, and that will be used to retrieve the current media being managed by the controller. Since this will change based on the type of controller, we will just return null in the MediaController class and expect this method to be overridden by the child classes. You can place this line directly after the sound methods previously shown:

```
public function get media():Object { return null; }
```

This completes the code for our base MediaController class. Since it was presented in bits, be sure to check your file against the MediaController.as file included with the download files for this chapter.

Controlling FLVs

The first class we'll create to control a specific media type is FLVController. Create a new ActionScript file and save it as FLVController.as into the com/foed/media/controllers directory. Add the following code to the file:

```
package com.foed.media.controllers {

  import flash.utils.Timer;
  import flash.events.Event;
  import flash.events.IOErrorEvent;
  import flash.events.TimerEvent;
  import flash.events.NetStatusEvent;
  import flash.events.ProgressEvent;
  import flash.net.NetConnection;
  import flash.net.NetStream;
  import com.foed.events.MediaEvent;

  public class FLVController extends MediaController {

    private var _stream_ns:NetStream;
    private var _connection_nc:NetConnection;
    private var _videoEnded:Boolean;
    private var _loadTimer:Timer;

  }

}
```

After the package declaration and the importing of all the classes we will be using, we have our class declaration. The FLVController will extend the MediaController class and so inherit all of its methods. The list of properties that follows applies specifically to video clips. _stream_ns holds a reference to a NetStream object. _connection_nc holds a reference to a NetConnection object. Both NetStream and NetConnection instances are necessary to play FLV files. _videoEnded is a Boolean flag to determine whether the end of the FLV has been reached. Rounding out the list is a Timer instance, _loadTimer, which will be used to monitor the load progress of the FLV.

Public methods

Let's begin the body of the FLVController class by looking at the public methods of MediaController we are overriding. These methods in the superclass are fairly generic, as each media type will need to be handled in a different way, so the meat of these methods will lie in the child classes, like FLVController. We'll start with loadMedia().

```
    override public function loadMedia(pFileURL:String):void {
      super.loadMedia(pFileURL);
      _connection_nc = new NetConnection();
      try {
        _connection_nc.connect(null);
        _stream_ns = new NetStream(_connection_nc);
        _stream_ns.addEventListener(NetStatusEvent.NET_STATUS,➥
onNetStatus, false, 0, true);
        _stream_ns.client = this;
        dispatchEvent(new MediaEvent(MediaEvent.LOAD));
        startMedia();
      } catch (e:Error) {}
    }
```

The loadMedia() function will be called to load an FLV and play using an FLVController instance. The file location as a string is sent as an argument. The super.loadMedia() is invoked, a new NetConnection is created, and, within a try block, its connect() method is passed null, which is necessary for playing FLV files progressively over HTTP. Next, a new NetStream instance is created with the _connection_nc passed in the constructor. After adding an event listener for the NetStream's NET_STATUS event (which will inform us of a change in the stream), we set its client to be this, which in this scope means our FLVController instance. The NetStream client property allows you to assign an object as a listener for the NetStream events that are not dispatched using the EventDispatcher, but rather to special event handlers. We will use this to listen for when metadata is detected in the stream. More on that in a moment.

At the end of the try block, we dispatch a LOAD event and immediately call the startMedia() method, which we will define specifically for FLVController shortly. Then following the try block is a single catch block for a generic error. Ideally, we would want to catch and actually handle specific errors that could occur within the try block (the NetStream constructor can throw an error, as well as the NetConnection connect() method, and assigning a client to a NetStream), but for the purposes of this tutorial, we'll simply make sure that errors are caught and our program will proceed.

The loadMedia() method is a good example of polymorphism and encapsulation at work. The developer using the FLVController class doesn't need to know how this method is implemented, nor how the implementation differs from loading a SWF or an MP3. All that a developer needs to know is that loadMedia() will load the specified media file.

Assigning an object as the client for a NetStream instance allows us to set up two special event handlers specifically for NetStream events. These don't follow the same event handling model employed by most of the built-in objects and require specific handlers to be defined. Let's add these two handlers to the class:

```
    public function onCuePoint(pData:Object):void {}

    public function onMetaData(pData:Object):void {
      if (pData.duration > 0) mediaDuration = pData.duration;
      dispatchEvent(new MediaEvent(MediaEvent.METADATA,➥
mediaPosition, mediaDuration, pData.width, pData.height));
    }
```

14

The first handler, onCuePoint(), we will leave empty for our example here, but you could use it to listen for cue points embedded in an FLV. The second handler, onMetaData(), is called when the metadata embedded in the FLV is detected. This metadata usually (but, unfortunately, not always) includes dimensions and duration information. Within the handler, we only set the mediaDuration property if it exists, and then dispatch an event and pass the position, duration, and dimensions (if they are defined). We will soon write a class that handles displaying this media and takes advantage of this event. Notice that we are accessing mediaDuration using the public setter of the super class, and then mediaDuration and mediaPosition using the implicit getters. Because we set these properties as private in MediaController, we cannot directly access them from a derived class and so must use the implicit getters and setters. Keeping these properties private ensures that they cannot be manipulated outside of our base class. This might not always be the desired behavior (I'll show a need to have the superclass use protected properties later in this chapter when we discuss MediaDisplay), but it serves us well here as it nicely contains responsibility for managing these properties within a single class when the child classes do not need direct access.

The next lines of code are another example of polymorphism at work with our media classes. These are the methods defined in IPlayable for controlling playback of the media. We'll start with startMedia(). Add the lines after the loadMedia() method.

```
    override public function startMedia():void {
      _videoEnded = false;
      if (paused) {
        _stream_ns.resume();
      } else {
        try {
          _stream_ns.play(mediaFile);
          if (_stream_ns.bytesLoaded != _stream_ns.bytesTotal➥
&& _stream_ns.bytesTotal > 0) {
            _loadTimer = new Timer(500, 0);
            _loadTimer.addEventListener(TimerEvent.TIMER,➥
assessLoad, false, 0, true);
            _loadTimer.start();
          }
        } catch (e:Error) {}
      }
      super.startMedia();
    }
```

In this method, overridden from the superclass, we initialize the _videoEnded property to false. Next, we check to see whether the stream is currently paused, and if it is, simply resume its playback. If the stream has not yet started, we call the play() method of the NetStream instance within a try..catch block. Again, ideally you would want to catch the errors that might be thrown and do something appropriate, but for our example we'll just make sure the program doesn't come to a complete halt.

You can see that once the stream is started (if no error is thrown) and the FLV has not already been downloaded, we set up another Timer instance to assess the load every half of a second. That handler, assessLoad(), has not been written yet. Before we finish up the IPlayable methods, let's add it in.

```
private function assessLoad(pEvent:TimerEvent):void {
  dispatchEvent(new ProgressEvent(ProgressEvent.PROGRESS,➥
false, false, _stream_ns.bytesLoaded, _stream_ns.bytesTotal));
  if (_stream_ns.bytesLoaded == _stream_ns.bytesTotal) {
    dispatchEvent(new Event(Event.COMPLETE));
    _loadTimer.removeEventListener(TimerEvent.TIMER, assessLoad);
    _loadTimer.stop();
  }
}
```

Here in the assessLoad() method, we first dispatch a PROGRESS event, and then we check to see whether the bytesLoaded is equal to the bytesTotal, and if it is, we stop the timer, remove the listener, and dispatch a COMPLETE event. Not a rough detour, was it?

Back to the IPlayable methods; the following lines of code take care of the three remaining required methods for the interface. You could add these directly below the startMedia() method.

```
override public function seek(pOffset:Number):void {
  _videoEnded = false;
  var pTime:int = Math.round(pOffset*1000)/1000;
  _stream_ns.seek(pTime);
  super.seek(pTime);
}

override public function stopMedia():void {
  _stream_ns.seek(0);
  _stream_ns.pause();
  super.stopMedia();
}

override public function pauseMedia(pPause:Boolean):void {
  if (pPause) {
    _stream_ns.pause();
  } else {
    if (!playing) _stream_ns.resume();
  }
  super.pauseMedia(pPause);
}
```

seek() sends the NetStream instance to a specific time, taking a number that indicates the position to find specified in number of seconds. It rounds this to the thousandths, and then invokes the seek() method of the NetStream instance. We set the _videoEnded Boolean property to false as a flag so that we know any stopping of the video that occurs here is due to the seek and not because the end of the stream has been reached.

For the next two methods, stopMedia() sends the stream back to the beginning and pauses it, and pauseMedia() either pauses the stream or resumes playback, depending on the value sent to the method. There's not much more happening here than that. Again, the beauty is that although the interaction with an FLV is different from interaction with a SWF or an MP3, the fact that all of our controllers will adhere to the same interface will make it easier for us to then interact with the media.

Private and protected methods

We're almost done with this controller class. One method we have already referenced (within the loadMedia() method) but not yet written is the onNetStatus() method, which will be fired whenever there is a netStatus event fired on the NetStream. Place this method with the other private methods in the FLVController class.

```
private function onNetStatus(pEvent:NetStatusEvent):void {
  switch (pEvent.info.level) {
    case "error":
      dispatchEvent(new IOErrorEvent(IOErrorEvent.IO_ERROR));
      break;
    case "status":
      switch (pEvent.info.code) {
        case "NetStream.Play.Start":
          dispatchEvent(new Event(Event.INIT));
          break;
        case "NetStream.Play.Stop":
          _videoEnded = true;
          break;
      }
      break;
  }
}
```

onNetStatus() is sent a NetStatusEvent instance that contains an info level of either "error" or "status." In the case of the former, we simply dispatch an IO_ERROR event to inform any listener that there was a problem. If the level is "status," we then check to see whether a start or a stop event was detected. If a start event was detected, we dispatch an event to inform listeners that the FLV has started streaming in. If instead a stop event was detected, we set the _videoEnded flag to true. We will use this flag in our trackProgress() method as a check to determine whether the stream has completed. More on that next.

Let's add the trackProgress() method, which will monitor the position in the stream as the FLV plays.

```
override protected function trackProgress(pEvent:Event):void {
  if (mediaPosition == mediaDuration || _videoEnded) {
    _videoEnded = false;
    stopMedia();
    dispatchEvent(new MediaEvent(MediaEvent.COMPLETE,➥
mediaPosition, mediaDuration));
```

```
    }
    super.trackProgress(pEvent);
  }
```

As a video file plays, trackProgress() will be called (this was handled in MediaController's startTrackProgress() method). In this method, we check to see whether the mediaPosition has reached the mediaDuration or the _videoEnded flag has been set to true. We set the _videoEnded flag in the onNetStatus() method if the stop status event was fired for the NetStream instance.

Why the extra check? This is just a safeguard since there are times when discrepancies exist between mediaPosition and mediaDuration where a stream might complete, but the position might actually be a half-second less than the duration, in which case the end of the stream will not be detected. By setting the _videoEnded flag to true when the NetStream's stop status event is detected, we can use this as an extra check within trackProgress() when looking for the stream completion. Since trackProgess() is run only while the stream is supposedly playing (and not after the stopMedia() method is called), the only reason that _videoEnded would be true within the trackProgress() method is because the stream stopped by itself.

Once we reset the _videoEnded property, stopMedia() is called. An event is broadcast to listeners informing them that the media is complete. Finally, super.trackProgress() is called to take care of any code that needs to be run in the super object, which takes care of broadcasting a PROGRESS event.

There are two pieces left before the FLVController is complete. First, we need to override some property accessors defined in MediaController for the FLV-specific pieces. You can add these lines to the end of your FLVController class:

```
    override public function get mediaPosition():Number {➥
  return _stream_ns.time; }

    override public function get media():Object { return _stream_ns; }
```

Since mediaPosition is accessed differently for FLVs than for other media, and since the media is unique for an FLV (in this case, the media is referring to the NetStream instance), we override the getters from MediaController.

Controlling sound

The final piece in FLVController is to allow sound to be controlled, as we guaranteed with the IAudible interface. In MediaController, sound values are stored in _volume and _pan properties and can be retrieved individually or through getSoundTransform(). For FLVs, the NetStream includes a soundTransform property that references a SoundTransform instance for the specific NetStream instance. To set this, we will simply override the applySoundTransform() method in MediaController, and also will make sure to call this on a newly created NetStream instance to set its initial sound settings. Add the bold lines to your FLVController class:

```
override protected function applySoundTransform():void {
  _stream_ns.soundTransform = getSoundTransform();
}

override public function loadMedia(pFileURL:String):void {
  super.loadMedia(pFileURL);
  _connection_nc = new NetConnection();
  try {
    _connection_nc.connect(null);
    _stream_ns = new NetStream(_connection_nc);
    _stream_ns.addEventListener(NetStatusEvent.NET_STATUS,➥
onNetStatus, false, 0, true);
    _stream_ns.client = this;
    applySoundTransform();
    dispatchEvent(new MediaEvent(MediaEvent.LOAD));
    startMedia();
  } catch (e:Error) {}
}
```

With that, we have completed the MediaController and FLVController classes. Be sure to check your completed FLVController file with the FLVController.as file included with the download files for this chapter. Now that we have our controller for playing video set up, we can work on actually displaying the video!

Building a video view

So much coding, and yet we have not until this point been able to see a visual demonstration of the media controllers. All the planning and preparation will pay off here, however, as it becomes clear how easy it now is to load and control playback of an FLV.

Create a new ActionScript file and save it as FLVQuickTest.as. Enter the following code, which represents all that will be needed for this test:

```
package {

  import flash.display.Sprite;
  import flash.events.MouseEvent;
  import flash.events.Event;
  import flash.media.Video;
  import flash.net.NetStream;

  import com.foed.media.controllers.FLVController;
  import com.foed.events.MediaEvent;

  public class FLVQuickTest extends Sprite {

    private var _flvController:FLVController;
```

```
    public function FLVQuickTest() {
      init();
    }

    private function init():void {
      _flvController = new FLVController();
      _flvController.addEventListener(Event.INIT, mediaInit,➥
false, 0, true);
      _flvController.addEventListener(MediaEvent.COMPLETE,➥
mediaComplete, false, 0, true);
      _flvController.loadMedia("cyber_minotaur.flv");

      var pDisplay:Video = addChild(new Video()) as Video;
      pDisplay.x = 115;
      pDisplay.y = 80;
      pDisplay.width = 320;
      pDisplay.height = 240;
      pDisplay.attachNetStream(NetStream(_flvController.media));

      stage.addEventListener(MouseEvent.MOUSE_DOWN,➥
mouseDown, false, 0, true);
    }

    private function mediaInit(pEvent:Event):void {
      trace("FLV init");
    }

    private function mediaComplete(pEvent:MediaEvent):void {
      trace("FLV complete");
    }

    private function mouseDown(pEvent:MouseEvent):void {
      _flvController.pauseMedia(!_flvController.paused);
    }

  }

}
```

After importing the necessary classes for the file and within the definition of the FLVQuickTest class, we declare a single private member, `_flvController`. The constructor then simply calls the `init()` method, where most of the functionality lies.

Within the `init()` method, we instantiate an `FLVController` instance and add two listeners, for the `INIT` (when the video loads) and `COMPLETE` (when the video completes playing) events. We then load in the file `cyber_minotaur.flv`.

The next block of lines in the `init()` method creates a Video instance and adds it to the FLVQuickTest instance (which you should note extends Sprite). The video's position and size are set, and then the `NetStream` instance that can be accessed through the

FLVController instance's media property is attached to the video. Finally, we set up a listener for MOUSE_DOWN events on the stage.

When the video starts, the mediaInit() method will be called and a message will be traced. When the video completes playing, the mediaComplete() function will be called and another message will be traced. Whenever the mouse is clicked in the movie, the video will toggle its pause state.

Testing in Flash

Create a new FLA document and save it into the same directory as FLVQuickTest.fla. In the Property inspector, set FLVQuickTest as the Document class for the FLA. If your com package directory does not exist in the same directory as these new files, make sure you set the class path in the FLA to point to where it can find the com directory using File ➤ Publish Settings ➤ Flash, and then clicking the Settings button next to the ActionScript version.

cyber_minotaur.flv is available in the code download for this book, accessible from www.friendsofed.com. Copy it to the same directory as FLVQuickTest.fla. Test the movie to see the video being loaded and controlled by our media classes. The result should appear as in Figure 14-4. If you have trouble with the example, compare the code with FLVQuickTest.as and its supporting classes in the downloadable files.

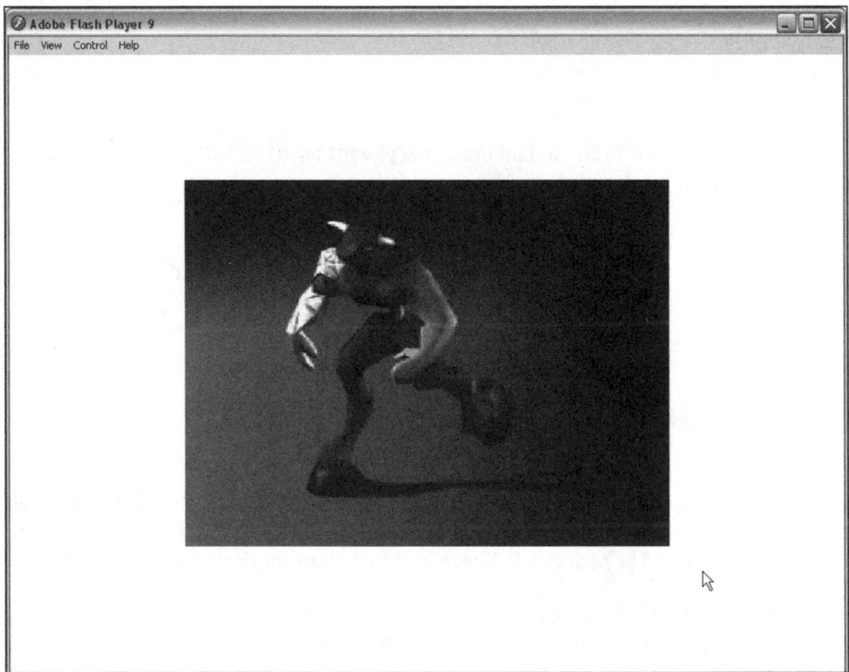

Figure 14-4. The media controller playing back an FLV file

Testing in Flex Builder

Create a new ActionScript project in Flex Builder with FLVQuickTest as the main document class. If the com directory you have been working with is not within the project directory, make sure that it is added as a source for the project.

cyber_minotaur.flv is available in the code download for this book, accessible from www.friendsofed.com. Copy it into the bin directory of your project. Test the movie, and your browser should open to show the video. If you have trouble with the example, compare the code with FLVQuickTest.as and its supporting classes in the downloadable files.

Improving the display

The previous test showed that it is relatively easy to use the FLVController to load and play back media. However, there is a definite area for improvement in how we display that media. In the code in FLVQuickTest, we create a Video instance, and then attach the NetStream instance accessed through the media property of the FLVController instance. This works fine for FLVs, but the implementation for displaying other media, for instance SWFs, will be different, and this difference will require you, or other developers using your classes, to have direct knowledge about those implementations and how different instances of MediaController will need to act. What would be a wonderful addition is an abstract MediaDisplay class we can use to hide this implementation in displaying media in much the same way our MediaController hides how media is loaded and played back. That's what we'll try to accomplish next.

Setting up MediaDisplay

Create a new ActionScript file and save it as MediaDisplay.as into a new directory, displays, within the com/foed/media/ directory (so the path would be com/foed/media/displays/MediaDisplay.as). This class will act as the abstract class for each type of display (FLVs, SWFs, MP3s). Start the class off with the following code:

```
package com.foed.media.displays {

  import flash.display.Sprite;
  import flash.display.DisplayObject;
  import flash.geom.Rectangle;

  import com.foed.events.MediaEvent;
  import com.foed.media.controllers.MediaController;

  public class MediaDisplay extends Sprite {

    private var _mediaController:MediaController;
    private var _scaleMode:String = "showAll";
    private var _displayWidth:Number;
    private var _displayHeight:Number;
    protected var _mediaClip:DisplayObject;
    protected var _mediaWidth:Number;
    protected var _mediaHeight:Number;
```

14

```
    public function MediaDisplay() {
      init();
    }

    private function init():void {
      createMediaClip();
    }

    protected function createMediaClip():void {
      if (_mediaClip != null) removeChildAt(0);
    }

  }

}
```

Within the class definition, we declare several properties, defined in the following list:

- _mediaController will hold the reference to the MediaController instance used by the display.
- _scaleMode determines the way that loaded media will scale within the display.
- _displayWidth and _displayHeight determine the dimensions of the display itself.
- _mediaClip will hold the reference to the DisplayObject instance used to display the media.
- _mediaWidth and _mediaHeight will hold the actual dimensions of the loaded media.

Within the constructor, we call the init(), and within that init() we merely call createMediaClip(), which removes the current media clip in the display (the hard-coded index in removeChildAt() means that we should only ever create and add a single DisplayObject instance to the display).

Before we move on to the rest of the class, let's take care of that scale mode we assigned in the properties. Notice how the value is set to a string. This was very common in ActionScript 2.0, but most of the internal classes in ActionScript 3.0 do away with these "magic strings," as they're called, and use constant values, which helps prevent any bugs that might be caused by typos. We can do the same.

Providing for scale modes

Create a new ActionScript file and save it as ScaleModes.as into the com/foed/media/displays directory. The code for this class is short and sweet:

```
package com.foed.media.displays {

  public class ScaleModes {

    public static const NO_SCALE:String = "noScale";
    public static const EXACT_FIT:String = "exactFit";
```

```
        public static const SCALE_DOWN:String = "scaleDown";
        public static const SHOW_ALL:String = "showAll";

    }

}
```

Here we create a class that defines four constants for the scale modes our displays will allow. All that's needed now is to alter the line in MediaDisplay to use one of these constants:

```
private var _mediaController:MediaController;
private var _scaleMode:String = ScaleModes.SHOW_ALL;
private var _displayWidth:Number;
```

Now there is no fear of typos, as we would get a compile error if SHOW_ALL was undefined.

To use these different scale modes, we will create a new method, sizeMedia(), that accounts for the different types and acts accordingly. Add this after the createMediaClip() method.

```
protected function sizeMedia():void {
  _mediaClip.scrollRect = _mediaClip.getRect(_mediaClip);
  switch (_scaleMode) {
    case ScaleModes.EXACT_FIT:
      _mediaClip.width = _displayWidth;
      _mediaClip.height = _displayHeight;
      break;
    case ScaleModes.NO_SCALE:
      positionMedia();
      if (_mediaWidth > _displayWidth➥
|| _mediaHeight > _displayHeight) {
        _mediaClip.scrollRect =➥
new Rectangle(0, 0, _displayWidth, _displayHeight);
      }
      break;
    case ScaleModes.SCALE_DOWN:
      if (_mediaWidth > _displayWidth➥
|| _mediaHeight > _displayHeight) {
        scaleMedia();
      } else {
        positionMedia();
      }
      break;
    case ScaleModes.SHOW_ALL:
      scaleMedia();
      break;
  }
}
```

In this method, we set up a switch statement to check the current value of _scaleMode. Within each case, we size the media within the display based on that scale mode. For EXACT_FIT, the media is made the exact width and height of the display. For NO_SCALE, we first call positionMedia() (which we will write next, and which will center the media within the display dimensions), and then we set the scrollRect of the clip to be equal to the dimensions of the display, effectively cropping off anything outside of the display. For SCALE_DOWN, scaling is only done if the media is larger than the display, in which case scaleMedia(), which we will also write next, is called. Otherwise, if the media is smaller than the display, we simply center it. Finally, SHOW_ALL always calls scaleMedia(), so any media loaded in, whether larger or smaller than the display, will be scaled proportionally to fit snugly within the display window.

I promised that positionMedia() and scaleMedia() would be written next, so here they are without further ado:

```
    private function positionMedia():void {
      _mediaClip.x = (_displayWidth - _mediaClip.width)/2;
      _mediaClip.y = (_displayHeight - _mediaClip.height)/2;
    }

    private function scaleMedia():void {
      var pRatio:Number;
      if (_displayWidth > _displayHeight) {
        pRatio = _displayHeight/_mediaHeight;
        if (_mediaHeight < _mediaWidth &&➥
_mediaWidth*pRatio > _displayWidth) {
          pRatio = _displayWidth/_mediaWidth;
        }
      } else {
        pRatio = _displayWidth/_mediaWidth;
        if (_mediaWidth < _mediaHeight &&➥
_mediaHeight*pRatio > _displayHeight) {
          pRatio = _displayHeight/_mediaHeight;
        }
      }
      _mediaClip.width = _mediaWidth*pRatio;
      _mediaClip.height = _mediaHeight*pRatio;
      positionMedia();
    }
```

positionMedia() is a simple two-line method that centers the media within the display.

scaleMedia() is more difficult to explain than it actually is. The first thing that is done in the method is a test to see whether the width of the display is greater than the height, as that will determine how the media can be scaled up or down within the boundaries. If the width is greater, we calculate the ratio of the display's height to the media's height. However, if the media's height is less than the media's width and that width multiplied by the calculated ratio will be greater than the width of the display, we need to instead take the ratio of the display height to the media height so that the media, when scaled, isn't made wider than the display.

The else block simply reverses the calculations in the if block. The end result after the if..else is that we have a ratio that, when multiplied to the media's width and height, will scale the media to fit proportionally within the display window without excess space or having anything cropped.

There is only one more method to add to our sizing collection. Place this after the scaleMedia() method shown previously.

```
protected function setMetadata(pEvent:MediaEvent):void {
  if (pEvent.width > 0 && pEvent.height > 0) {
    _mediaWidth = pEvent.width;
    _mediaHeight = pEvent.height;
    sizeMedia();
  }
}
```

setMetadata() will be used to set the width and height of the media when it is accessible. For instance, an FLV might have the dimensions embedded in its actual metadata. For SWFs, the data might have to be determined from the actual width and height of the SWF as it loads. This method can be used to set the actual properties, and then call sizeMedia() to ensure everything is scaled correctly.

Adding the accessors

The final methods for the MediaDisplay class are the getter/setter methods for the display's properties. You can add these to the end of the class definition.

```
public function getController():MediaController {
  return _mediaController;
}
public function setController(pController:MediaController):void {
  _mediaController = pController;
}

public function get scaleMode():String {
  return _scaleMode;
}
public function set scaleMode(pMode:String):void {
  _scaleMode = pMode;
  sizeMedia();
}

public function get mediaWidth():Number {
  return _mediaWidth;
}
public function get mediaHeight():Number {
  return _mediaHeight;
}
```

```
    public function get displayWidth():Number {
      return _displayWidth;
    }
    public function set displayWidth(pWidth:Number):void {
      _displayWidth = pWidth;
    }

    public function get displayHeight():Number {
      return _displayHeight;
    }
    public function set displayHeight(pHeight:Number):void {
      _displayHeight = pHeight;
    }
```

The preceding should be self-explanatory for the most part. I will only point out that the `mediaWidth` and `mediaHeight` exist only as getters, as the value should only be set from the loaded media. Also, the choice to use an explicit getter and setter method for the `_mediaController` property is purely a personal choice. It seemed as if the task of assigning a controller warranted a method (I will often use explicit getter/setters for more complex objects and implicit getter/setters for simple, scalar values), but these could be rewritten as an implicit getter/setter just as easily.

Displaying FLVs

Most of the work for displaying media is taken care of in the `MediaDisplay` class, so all that is left for us is to define the FLV-specific functionality in a child class (and there's not very much to it). Create a new ActionScript file and save it as `FLVDisplay.as` in the `com/foed/media/displays` directory. Add the following code:

```
package com.foed.media.displays {

  import flash.events.Event;
  import flash.media.Video;
  import flash.net.NetStream;

  import com.foed.events.MediaEvent;
  import com.foed.media.controllers.MediaController;

  public class FLVDisplay extends MediaDisplay {

    override protected function createMediaClip():void {
      super.createMediaClip();
      _mediaClip = addChild(new Video());
    }

    override public function setController(
      pController:MediaController
    ):void {
```

```
      super.setController(pController);
      getController().addEventListener(MediaEvent.LOAD,➥
attachNetStream, false, 0, true);
      getController().addEventListener(MediaEvent.METADATA,➥
setMetadata, false, 0, true);
    }

  }

}
```

Here we have defined FLVDisplay as a child class of MediaDisplay and overridden two of its methods. createMediaClip() creates a Video instance and adds it to the display list. setController() adds two listeners to the MediaController. On the load of the media, attachNetStream() will be called (to be written next), and when the FLV metadata is detected, setMetadata(), defined in MediaDisplay, will be called.

These last two methods will complete our FLVDisplay class. I told you there wasn't a lot to it!

```
    private function attachNetStream(pEvent:MediaEvent):void {
      createMediaClip();
      Video(_mediaClip).attachNetStream(➥
NetStream(getController().media));
      addEventListener(Event.ENTER_FRAME,➥
checkVideoSize, false, 0, true);
    }

    private function checkVideoSize(pEvent:Event):void {
      if (_mediaClip.width > 0) {
        removeEventListener(Event.ENTER_FRAME, checkVideoSize);
        _mediaWidth = _mediaClip.width;
        _mediaHeight = _mediaClip.height;
        sizeMedia();
      }
    }
```

attachNetStream() creates a new Video instance, and then grabs the NetStream instance from the FLVController and attaches it to the video. A new listener is then added to the ENTER_FRAME event on the display itself so that it may assess the video's size. The reason we need to do this is that the dimensions embedded in the FLV metadata may not be accurate, if they are even there, which is not guaranteed. Having a polling method set up to assess the size of the media as it first streams in will allow us to accurately detect the original media's size.

That's it for the FLVDisplay. All that is left is to alter the FLVQuickTest.as file we created originally to test the FLV playback to use our new display. Resave the file as FLVTest.as in the same directory. The updated lines are in the following code in bold. Once these are changed, you should be able to test in both Flash and Flex Builder to see the results once you update your project or FLA to point to the new document class.

```
package {

  import flash.display.Sprite;
  import flash.events.MouseEvent;
  import flash.events.Event;
  import flash.media.Video;
  import flash.net.NetStream;

  import com.foed.media.controllers.FLVController;
  import com.foed.media.displays.FLVDisplay;
  import com.foed.events.MediaEvent;

  public class FLVTest extends Sprite {

    private var _flvController:FLVController;
    private var _flvDisplay:FLVDisplay;

    public function FLVTest() {
      init();
    }

    private function init():void {
      _flvController = new FLVController();
      _flvController.addEventListener(Event.INIT,➥
mediaInit, false, 0, true);
      _flvController.addEventListener(MediaEvent.COMPLETE,➥
mediaComplete, false, 0, true);

      _flvDisplay = new FLVDisplay();
      addChild(_flvDisplay);
      _flvDisplay.x = 115;
      _flvDisplay.y = 80;
      _flvDisplay.displayWidth = 320;
      _flvDisplay.displayHeight = 240;
      _flvDisplay.setController(_flvController);

      _flvController.loadMedia("cyber_minotaur.flv");

      stage.addEventListener(MouseEvent.MOUSE_DOWN,➥
mouseDown, false, 0, true);
    }

    private function mediaInit(pEvent:Event):void {
      trace("FLV init");
    }
```

```
    private function mediaComplete(pEvent:MediaEvent):void {
      trace("FLV complete");
    }

    private function mouseDown(pEvent:MouseEvent):void {
      _flvController.pauseMedia(!_flvController.paused);
    }

  }

}
```

It's not any less code in this file itself, but notice that the Video instance instantiation and the NetStream access is now completely hidden. If you look closely, you will see that the lines for the FLVDisplay could be used for a SWFDisplay or an MP3Display or an ImageDisplay. The developer no longer needs to worry about how the FLVController works with its media, as the FLVDisplay handles everything behind the scenes. In fact, all that would be needed for a developer is knowledge of the MediaController and MediaDisplay classes in order to work with any kind of media (well, after those other media classes are written, of course!).

Controlling SWFs

Controlling SWF files is only slightly less involved than controlling FLVs, but you will find that now with the MediaController class complete, creating a new concrete class doesn't take long at all.

Create a new ActionScript file and save it into the com/foed/media/controllers directory as SWFController.as. Add the following code:

```
package com.foed.media.controllers {

  import flash.display.Sprite;
  import flash.display.Loader;
  import flash.display.LoaderInfo;
  import flash.display.MovieClip;
  import flash.net.URLRequest;
  import flash.utils.Timer;
  import flash.events.Event;
  import flash.events.TimerEvent;
  import flash.events.IOErrorEvent;
  import flash.events.ProgressEvent;
  import flash.errors.IOError;

  import com.foed.events.MediaEvent;

  public class SWFController extends MediaController {
```

```
      private var _SWFHolder_sp:Sprite;
      private var _SWFLoader_ld:Loader;

    }

  }
```

Lots of classes to import, but so far not much code. The only properties defined for the class, both private, will hold the main media Sprite instance and the Loader instance used to load the external SWF.

Let's start the main methods with the largest of the lot, loadMedia(), which overrides the method of the superclass so it may load in SWFs.

```
      override public function loadMedia(pFileURL:String):void {
        super.loadMedia(pFileURL);
        _SWFHolder_sp = new Sprite();
        _SWFLoader_ld = new Loader();
        var pLoaderInfo:LoaderInfo = _SWFLoader_ld.contentLoaderInfo;
        pLoaderInfo.addEventListener(Event.COMPLETE, onLoadComplete,➥
  false, 0, true);
        pLoaderInfo.addEventListener(Event.INIT, onLoadInit,➥
  false, 0, true);
        pLoaderInfo.addEventListener(Event.OPEN, onLoadStart,➥
  false, 0, true);
        pLoaderInfo.addEventListener(IOErrorEvent.IO_ERROR, ➥
  onLoadError, false, 0, true);
        pLoaderInfo.addEventListener(ProgressEvent.PROGRESS,➥
  onLoadProgress, false, 0, true);
        _SWFHolder_sp.addChild(_SWFLoader_ld);
        applySoundTransform();
        _SWFHolder_sp.visible = false;
        try {
          _SWFLoader_ld.load(new URLRequest(mediaFile));
          dispatchEvent(new MediaEvent(MediaEvent.LOAD));
        } catch (e:Error) {}
      }
```

After calling the super's implementation of the method, we create a Sprite and a Loader instance. We then add a number of event listeners to the LoaderInfo instance stored in _SWFLoader_ld so that we may monitor load and playback. _SWFLoader_ld is then added as a child to _SWFHolder_sp, _SWFHolder_sp's soundTransform will be set in applySoundTransform(), and the holder is made invisible. The reason a Sprite is used as a container for the Loader is that a Loader does not have a SoundTransform to access, so to manipulate sound for our loaded file, we need to wrap the loader within a class containing a SoundTransform, such as Sprite. Finally, within the try..catch block, we attempt to load the SWF file passed in the method call, catching a generic error (as noted earlier, we would probably want this to catch and handle it for specific error instances).

We may as well continue with the methods we need to override, but first we need to create a helper method for us to use throughout the rest of our SWFController code. Add this above the loadMedia() method:

```
private function getContent():MovieClip {
  return _SWFLoader_ld.content as MovieClip;
}
```

Since the content property of the Loader instance will return a DisplayObject reference, and since we will be calling methods on this property as if it were a movie clip, we create this method to return the content after casting it as a MovieClip instance. You will see how helpful that becomes in the later methods.

This next set is the methods for the IPlayable interface. Their implementation is overridden here so that the specifics of SWFs may be dealt with. Add these below the loadMedia() method.

```
override public function startMedia():void {
  super.startMedia();
  getContent().play();
}

override public function seek(pOffset:Number):void {
  pOffset = Math.round(pOffset);
  if (playing) {
    getContent().gotoAndPlay(pOffset-1);
  } else {
    getContent().gotoAndStop(pOffset);
  }
  super.seek(pOffset);
}

override public function stopMedia():void {
  getContent().gotoAndStop(1);
  super.stopMedia();
}

override public function pauseMedia(pPause:Boolean):void {
  super.pauseMedia(pPause);
  if (paused) {
    super.stopMedia();
    getContent().stop();
  } else {
    startMedia();
  }
  startTrackProgress(!paused);
}
```

In startMedia(), we tell the loaded content to play. seek() uses gotoAndPlay() or gotoAndStop() to send the loaded content's playhead to the appropriate frame. stopMedia() uses gotoAndStop() as well, and pauseMedia() either uses stop() to pause the media or calls startMedia() to unpause the media.

We have three more methods to override, trackProgress() and startTackProgress(), which were defined in MediaController and are used to monitor playback of the media; and applySoundTransform(), to set the sound levels for the Sprite holder and its contents. Add those next.

```
    override protected function applySoundTransform():void {
      _SWFHolder_sp.soundTransform = getSoundTransform();
    }

    override protected function startTrackProgress(
      pStart:Boolean
    ):void {
      if (pStart) {
        dispatchEvent(new MediaEvent(MediaEvent.START,➥
mediaPosition, mediaDuration));
        _SWFHolder_sp.addEventListener(Event.ENTER_FRAME,➥
trackProgress, false, 0, true);
      } else {
        dispatchEvent(new MediaEvent(MediaEvent.STOP,➥
mediaPosition, mediaDuration));
        _SWFHolder_sp.removeEventListener(➥
Event.ENTER_FRAME, trackProgress);
      }
    }

    override protected function trackProgress(pEvent:Event):void {
      if (mediaPosition == mediaDuration) {
        stopMedia();
        getContent().gotoAndStop(mediaDuration);
        dispatchEvent(new MediaEvent(MediaEvent.COMPLETE,➥
mediaPosition, mediaDuration));
      }
      super.trackProgress(pEvent);
    }
```

startTrackProgress() will be different here from its implementation in the superclass, since SWFs use frames instead of time. It makes more sense to use an ENTER_FRAME handler to determine progress instead of a timer, so we override the method here in SWFController. As you can see, when a SWF begins to play, an ENTER_FRAME handler is used to call trackProgress() in the SWFController instance. When the SWF stops, the listener is removed.

trackProgress() is similar to FLVController's implementation. If the current position matches the total duration, the media is stopped and a COMPLETE event is dispatched.

The next block of methods include the handlers for the LoaderInfo events that we subscribed to in the loadMedia() method. You can add these within the class, though I usually place any private methods at the top of the definition.

```
    private function onLoadInit(pEvent:Event):void {
      mediaDuration = getContent().totalFrames;
      startMedia();
      _SWFHolder_sp.visible = true;
      dispatchEvent(new MediaEvent(MediaEvent.METADATA, ➥
mediaPosition, mediaDuration, ➥
_SWFHolder_sp.width, _SWFHolder_sp.height));
      dispatchEvent(pEvent);
    }

    private function onLoadComplete(pEvent:Event):void {
      dispatchEvent(pEvent);
    }

    private function onLoadError(pEvent:Event):void {
      dispatchEvent(pEvent);
    }

    private function onLoadStart(pEvent:Event):void {
      dispatchEvent(pEvent);
    }

    private function onLoadProgress(pEvent:Event):void {
      dispatchEvent(pEvent);
    }
```

As you can see, the latter four methods simply pass the event through to whatever listeners may have subscribed to the controller. onLoadInit(), though, does a little bit more. First, the duration is set based on the frame count of the loaded SWF. Then, after startMedia() is called and the clip is made visible, we dispatch two events. The first is the METADATA event, since the duration is now accessible, and the second is the INIT event that was passed to this handler.

The last pieces to our SWFController are two accessors that we must override from MediaController. You can add these at the end of the class definition.

```
    override public function get mediaPosition():Number {
      return getContent().currentFrame;
    }

    override public function get media():Object {
      return _SWFHolder_sp;
    }
```

The media position will be returned based on the current frame in the loaded SWF, while the media returned will be the Sprite instance containing the Loader instance containing the loaded SWF.

That finishes up all the code for the SWFController class. Once again, you can check your files against the SWFController.as file included with this chapter's download files. With inheritance doing a lot of the heavy lifting for us, that wasn't so bad, now was it?

Building a SWF view

Once again, we get to the fun part of seeing the fruits of all this labor. Let's build the SWF display so we can see what we've accomplished!

Create a new ActionScript file and save it as SWFDisplay.as into the com/foed/media/displays directory. The following represents the entirely of the code for that file:

```
package com.foed.media.displays {

  import flash.display.Sprite;

  import com.foed.media.controllers.MediaController;
  import com.foed.events.MediaEvent;

  public class SWFDisplay extends MediaDisplay {

    private function attachSWFLoader(pEvent:MediaEvent):void {
      createMediaClip();
      Sprite(_mediaClip).addChild(Sprite(getController().media));
    }

    override protected function createMediaClip():void {
      super.createMediaClip();
      _mediaClip = addChild(new Sprite());
    }

    override public function setController(
      pController:MediaController
    ):void {
      super.setController(pController);
      getController().addEventListener(MediaEvent.LOAD,➥
attachSWFLoader, false, 0, true);
      getController().addEventListener(MediaEvent.METADATA,➥
setMetadata, false, 0, true);
    }

  }

}
```

Just as we did in FLVDisplay, we override MediaDisplay's createMediaClip() and setController() so that we may account for the differences when displaying SWFs. createMediaClip() creates and adds a new Sprite instance. setController() adds listeners for the LOAD and METADATA events.

When the LOAD event is fired, the attachSWFLoader() handler is invoked. Here, the SWFController's media is added as a child to the SWFDisplay's media clip.

That's all there is to it. The only thing left is to create a class to put everything together.

Create one more ActionScript file and save it as SWFTest.as into the same directory where you saved FLVTest.as earlier in the chapter. Add the following code, which instantiates a SWFController to load and manage playback of a SWF and SWFDisplay to display that media.

```
package {

  import flash.display.Sprite;
  import flash.events.Event;
  import flash.events.MouseEvent;

  import com.foed.media.controllers.SWFController;
  import com.foed.media.displays.SWFDisplay;
  import com.foed.events.MediaEvent;

  public class SWFTest extends Sprite {

    private var _swfController:SWFController;
    private var _swfDisplay:SWFDisplay;

    public function SWFTest() {
      init();
    }

    private function init():void {
      _swfController = new SWFController();
      _swfController.addEventListener(Event.INIT, mediaInit,➥
false, 0, true);
      _swfController.addEventListener(MediaEvent.COMPLETE,➥
mediaComplete, false, 0, true);

      _swfDisplay = new SWFDisplay();
      addChild(_swfDisplay);
      _swfDisplay.x = 115;
      _swfDisplay.y = 80;
      _swfDisplay.displayWidth = 320;
      _swfDisplay.displayHeight = 240;
      _swfDisplay.setController(_swfController);
```

```
      _swfController.loadMedia("bookworm.swf");

      stage.addEventListener(MouseEvent.MOUSE_DOWN,➥
mouseDown, false, 0, true);
    }

    private function mediaInit(pEvent:Event):void {
      trace("SWF init");
    }

    private function mediaComplete(pEvent:MediaEvent):void {
      trace("SWF complete");
    }

    private function mouseDown(pEvent:MouseEvent):void {
      _swfController.pauseMedia(!_swfController.paused);
    }

  }

}
```

If you compare this code to FLVTest, you will see that the only difference lies in which controller and display are used. We have encapsulated all implementation for loading, managing, and displaying two completely different types of media within our classes, and exposed a common set of polymorphic methods so that any developer can interact with that media in a common way. Not too shabby for a single chapter!

Make sure that bookworm.swf from this chapter's download files is saved into the same directory as this file if you are using the Flash IDE, or into your bin directory if you are using Flex Builder. For Flash users, just as you did for FLVTest.as, you will need to create a new Flash file in the same directory as SWFTest.as and use SWFTest as the main document class. For Flex Builder users, you can use the same project you created for FLVTest, but specify SWFTest as the main application class. Test your movie and see the result! It should resemble what you see in Figure 14-5.

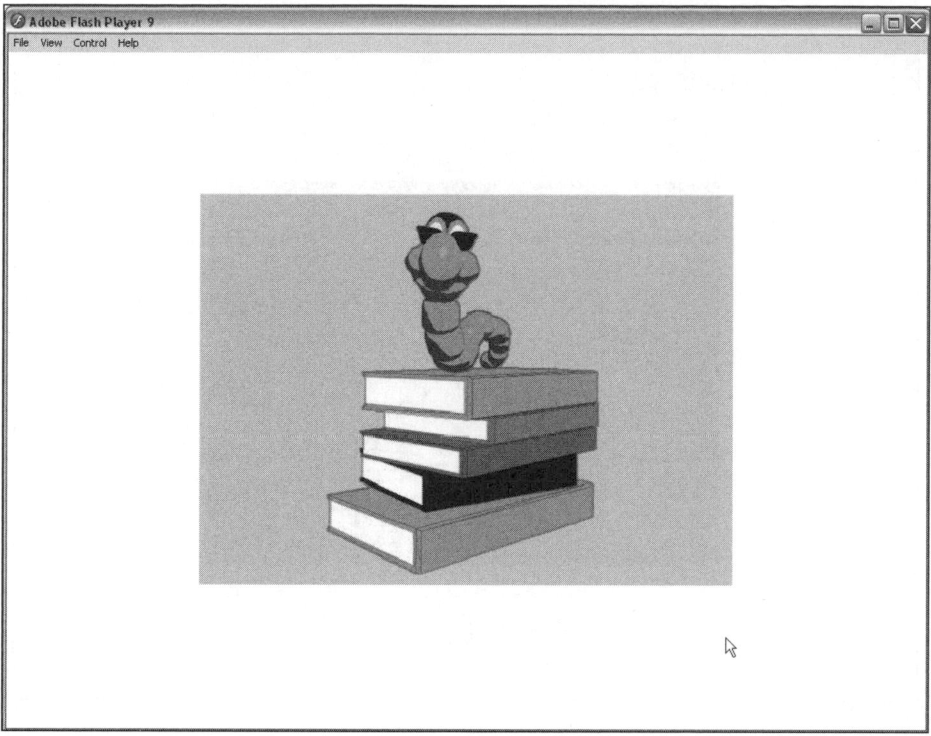

Figure 14-5. The media controller loading and playing back a SWF

Controlling MP3s

There is of course at least one more media type, but as you have already been through two, I think you've probably typed enough! The `MP3Controller` and `MP3Display` classes can be found in the code download, as well as a collection of `SoundVisualizer` classes that can be used to plug in to the `MP3Display` in order to graphically display the sound (a great new feature in ActionScript 3.0). I would encourage you to open these files up and peruse the code, which is all fully commented. The output of these classes can be seen in Figure 14-6.

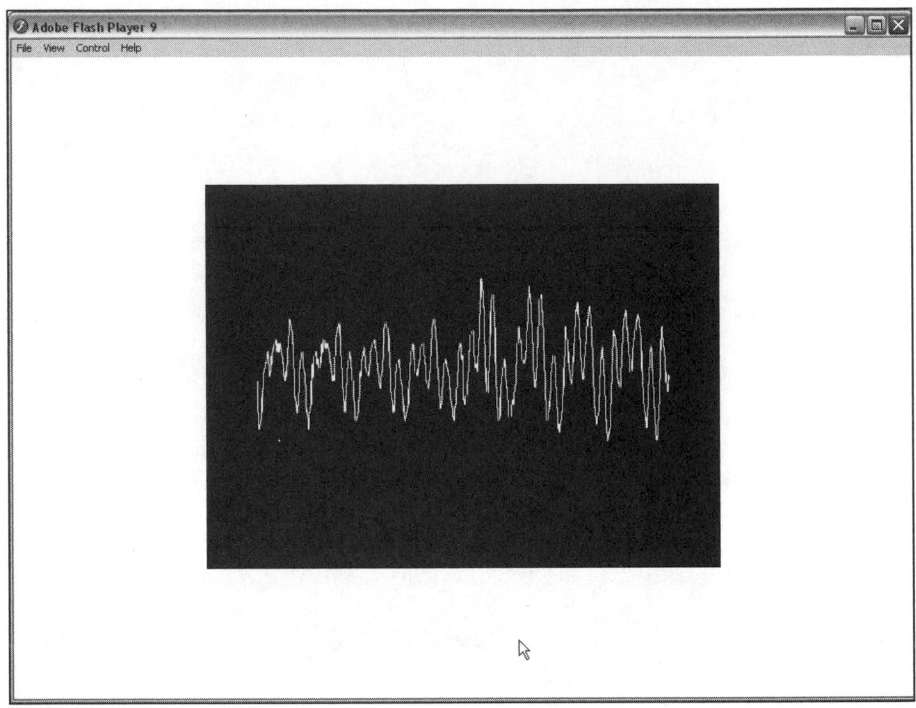

Figure 14-6. The media controller loading and playing back an MP3

The methods used in Flash to load and play MP3 files are very different from what we have used so far with SWFs and FLVs (both of which were different from the other). With MP3s, the Sound object's `load()` method is used to bring the file into the player. `play()` is used to both start and seek, while the new SoundChannel's `stop()` is used to halt playback. `length` on the Sound object and `position` on the `SoundChannel` are used to note time. Sound is controlled by a `SoundTransform` instance passed to the Sound's `play()` method.

What this means is that when dealing with sounds, what's going on behind the scenes would be very different than what occurs for a SWF or FLV. However, to anyone using `MP3Controller`, the same methods used for `FLVController` and `SWFController` (`startMedia()`, `stopMedia()`, `loadMedia()`, etc.) would be implemented. This is the beauty of polymorphism. With it, we can hide the implementation of different methods while exposing the same API.

What's next?

After all of the concepts of the previous section, it's helpful to see a practical and visual demonstration of what you've learned. This case study has walked through the planning and building of classes to control a very important aspect in Flash development—externally loaded media. Interfaces were defined to guarantee that methods to control media would not change from instance to instance. Abstract base classes were built to hold common functionality for all three media type controllers and displays. These controllers and displays then used inheritance to extend the functionality of the base class. All of the methods to load and control the media were encapsulated in these classes, classes that demonstrated polymorphism by overriding in different ways the methods implemented in the superclass, methods originally defined by the `IPlayable` and `IAudible` interfaces. And that is some ActionScript OOP at work!

Now that the general OOP concepts have been discussed, the next part of this book will delve into more Flash-centric ideas on implementing OOP in development, from building components to interacting with live data and web servers. Be prepared for some exciting possibilities!

PART FOUR **BUILDING AND EXTENDING DYNAMIC FRAMEWORKS**

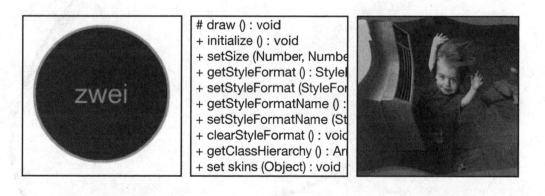

draw () : void
+ initialize () : void
+ setSize (Number, Numbe
+ getStyleFormat () : Stylel
+ setStyleFormat (StyleFor
+ getStyleFormatName () :
+ setStyleFormatName (St
+ clearStyleFormat () : voic
+ getClassHierarchy () : Ar
+ set skins (Object) : void

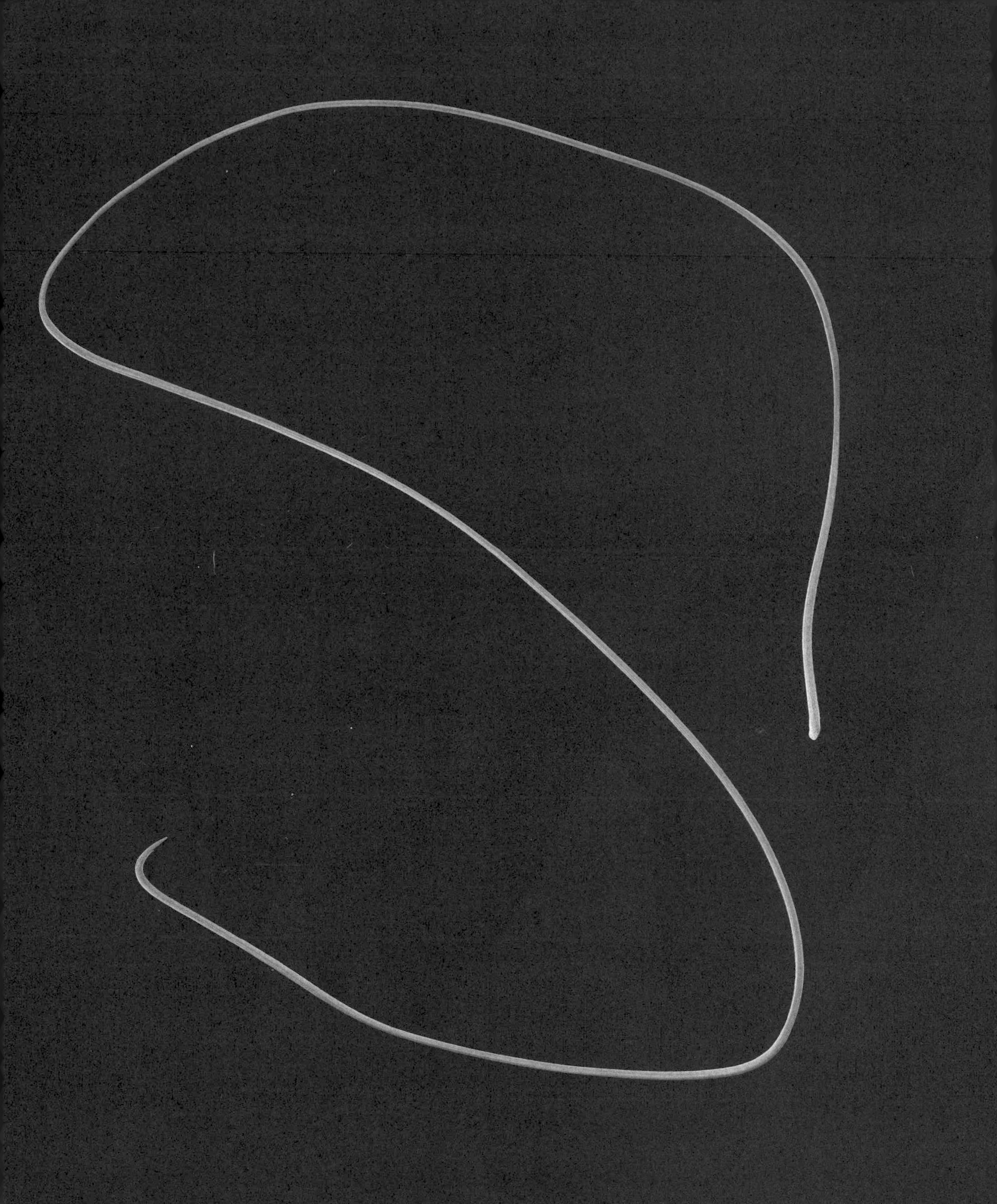

15 MANAGER CLASSES

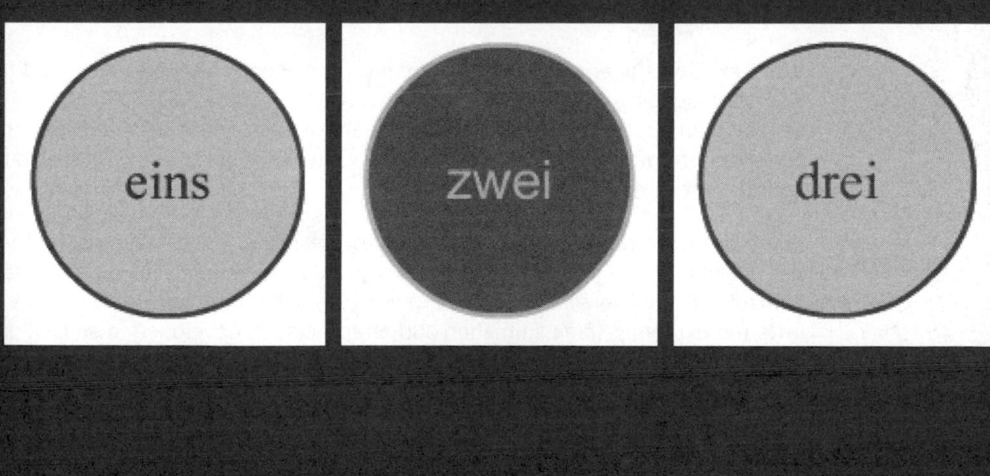

After learning the OOP and design patterns basics and how they apply to a class or small groups of classes, the next logical step is to look at developing a larger framework using an object-oriented methodology. Before we investigate this more closely, I think it's important to know that the term *framework* has become something of an overused—perhaps even abused—buzzword. What exactly defines a framework, and how does it differ from just any old collection of classes?

In the context of this and the next chapter, I describe a framework as a set of logically related classes that provide a solid structure through an API that promotes encapsulation, and consists of one or more base classes that you extend to build your application code on. As such, frameworks often, if not always, use practical design patterns to link together the various classes to create an optimized structure for specific code problems.

A number of ActionScript frameworks are available today. The Flex framework provides many of the classes needed to rapidly produce a next generation of rich Internet applications. Flash users have for several versions now had a component framework that ties drag-and-drop interface widgets with a number of related application classes. Developers can choose to use the components and classes that utilize these frameworks and build new classes to fit within them, or developers can create a unique framework from the ground up on which to build their components. The benefits of using the preexisting frameworks are obvious: the code is already written and thought through, and the components are ready to drag and drop into your interface or reference through code. If you need a quick solution, this is a great way to go, as interface prototypes can be rapidly developed and demonstrated, especially in the case of Flex Builder. However, the greatest benefit of developing your own classes from scratch is that you will have a deep understanding of what each class can do and how to extend it with new functionality. This is obviously possible with any open source framework, but not without a lot of work scrutinizing others' code. If work is to be invested, why not work to build something you have complete control over and can more easily extend and modify? This and the next two chapters will show you how to begin.

Planning the framework

What exactly is needed to build a working framework? Although we could jump right in and start building a button, which is arguably the simplest Flash widget to create, if we instead plan a solid course of action for an entire component set, we'll save time in further development of more complex components (and save ourselves from inevitably having to rework that same simple button).

The framework we'll explore in the next few chapters, just to get your feet wet, will consist broadly of widgets (the UI controls visible on the stage), manager classes (classes to control specific overall functionality of widgets or the interface), and utilities (we'll have a little fun exploring some animation and effects classes developed in an OOP manner). The next chapter concentrates on interface widgets and the one that follows that on utility classes. This chapter focuses on the classes to manage an entire collection of widgets in an interface or application.

What to manage

When considering manager classes, imagine the tasks that you'll need performed throughout the interface or for the entirety of the interface where having a single class instance accessible from any other class in the framework will ease development and/or allow for centralized modifications. What classes could we create to centralize our tasks?

One great candidate for a manager class of UI elements is a `StyleManager`. Multiple interfaces utilizing components will require different styles (colors for widget elements for different states), and having a centralized class to handle styles for all components will only speed later development as components are appropriated in new interfaces. In addition, if ever styles should be defined by values from an external file or database, having the styles stored within a single class or instance will allow for smoother integration with the back-end.

For similar reasons, a `SoundManager` is a good candidate for a manager class as well. Many widgets can be enhanced by sounds (a button click is the most obvious example), and instead of coding event listeners to play sounds for every instance, we can build into our components an interface with a global `SoundManager`. Within this `SoundManager` would be the definitions for all event sounds and the `Sound` objects to create those sounds.

Another helpful manager would be a `LabelManager`, to maintain a list of all common labels, such as button and input field labels and dialog titles. This would be enormously helpful to have centralized if a single label ever needed to be changed across a whole application (for instance, changing a lowercase "ok" to uppercase). In addition, the class could manage internationalization of an interface, swapping languages without other classes within the application having to contain that logic.

Additional managers that would fit nicely within a component framework for building interfaces in Flash, and ones we won't directly explore here, are a `FocusManager` to handle tab navigation within views, perhaps a `ContextMenuManager` to handle creating right-click context-sensitive menus in nested elements, and a `ToolTipManager` for creating pop-up tooltips for components that can float above all other elements in the interface. As applications grow and become more complex, a `DragManager` to handle drag-and-drop functionality and a `PopUpManager` to handle the creation of pop-up dialog boxes would be great development aids. In each of these manager class examples, it's cleaner to have a centralized class where visual definitions, behavior, and functionality reside that individual components or timelines could call. This will keep the individual component code slimmer and more manageable.

Diagramming the classes

As always, it's helpful to map out classes before beginning to code. We've discussed UML diagrams and used them to describe classes in earlier chapters, so you should be starting to feel more comfortable taking in such a diagram and referring to it as a blueprint. Peruse Figures 15-1 and 15-2 for the classes we'll explore in this chapter, and look back to them for reference as we begin to code.

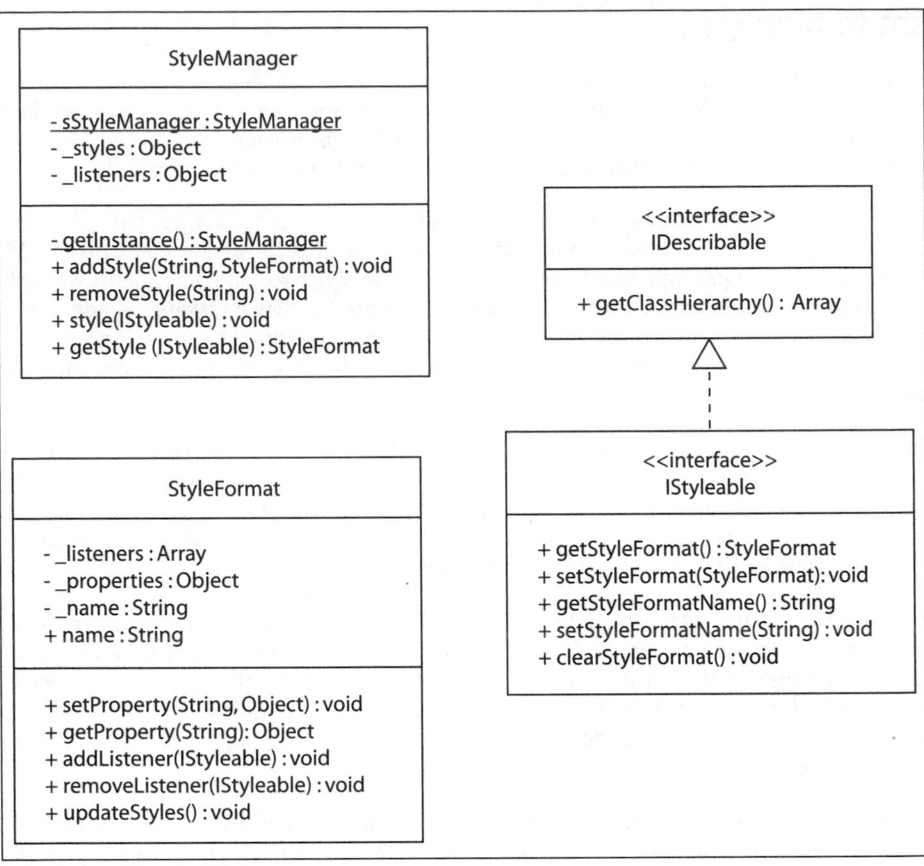

Figure 15-1. UML diagrams for `StyleManager` and associated classes

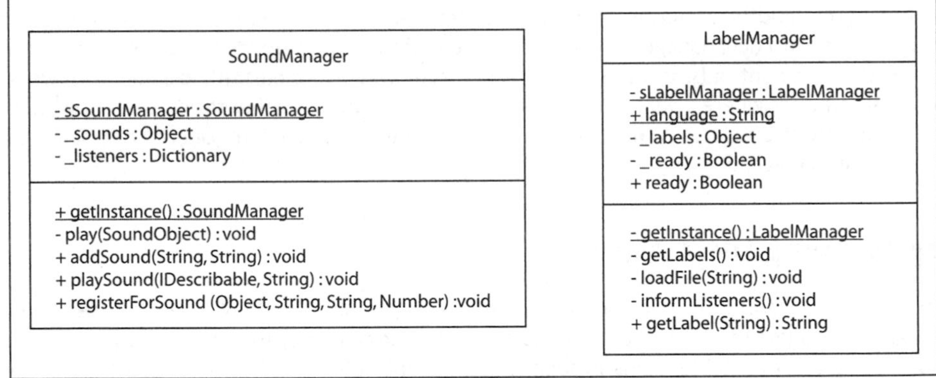

Figure 15-2. UML diagrams for `SoundManager` and `LabelManager` classes

We'll continue to build within the package structure we created in Chapter 14's case study. As you can see in the diagram, we'll be adding three classes to the `com.foed.managers` package: `StyleManager`, `SoundManager`, and `LabelManager`. The `StyleManager` itself will be managing multiple instances of style formats, so we create a `StyleFormat` class for this purpose within a new `com.foed.graphic` package, as well as two new interfaces, `IStyleable` and `IDescribable`, which will define how the `StyleManager` will interact with styleable classes.

Once you're comfortable with the structure proposed in the class diagram, fire up Flash or Flex Builder and get ready for some framework coding!

Building managers

Individual component widgets are all well and good, but it's the centralized means of controlling the look and feel of those widgets that can make working with components a breeze (as well as speed up the creation of new and unique applications!). These three manager classes, two interfaces, and the `StyleFormat` class will go a long way in making components reusable from application to application without making everything appear the same.

IDescribable and IStyleable

Before we code the classes to apply and receive styles, let's create the two interfaces that define the methods for an object that should be able to be styled. The first, `IDescribable`, defines a single method that will allow an object to be queried for its class hierarchy. This will be used in our style code in order to select the proper styles for an object based on its class, but it could conceivably be useful for other purposes (as you will see with the `SoundManager`), and so we separate it out into its own interface. Save the following code as `IDescribable` into a `com.foed` directory, which you can use from the code developed in the last chapter's case study.

```
package com.foed {

  public interface IDescribable {

    function getClassHierarchy():Array;

  }

}
```

`IStyleable` will then extend this interface, as any object that needs to be styled should also provide access to the array of classes that `IDescribable` guarantees. Here is the entirety of the code for `IStyleable`, saved into the `com/foed/graphic` directory, which is a new directory you'll have to create.

```
package com.foed.graphic {

  import com.foed.IDescribable;

  public interface IStyleable extends IDescribable {

    function getStyleFormat():StyleFormat;

    function setStyleFormat(pFormat:StyleFormat):void;

    function getStyleFormatName():String;

    function setStyleFormatName(pName:String):void;

    function clearStyleFormat():void;

  }

}
```

Knowing that we will be building a StyleFormat class, and that any object that should be styled will have a StyleFormat applied, we first include the obvious getStyleFormat() and setStyleFormat() methods. getStyleFormatName() and its counterpart setStyleFormatName() will allow the names of formats to be passed to and retrieved from objects as opposed to the StyleFormats directly, which I have found useful when loading in styles dynamically since the StyleFormat instances might not be compiled into an application. clearStyleFormat() would remove whatever StyleFormat instance has been applied.

StyleFormat

The next class we'll create to manage the look of our components is StyleFormat, which we referred to in the preceding interface. Instances of this class will hold values for a number of visual properties for components and will be used to assign a style to a component instance, a whole class, or the entire set of components. In a larger framework, such a class may go beyond colors or TextFormats, as we will use it here, and might also define animation properties (the length for transitions, the type of effects for rollover, etc.) or behavior (where StyleFormat instances could be used to enable tooltips or right-click menus). Here, we'll keep it simple and define color and text properties.

To begin, create a new ActionScript file and save it into the com/foed/graphic class directory as StyleFormat.as. Enter the following code into the file:

```
package com.foed.graphic {

  public class StyleFormat {

    private var _name:String;

    public function StyleFormat(pName:String) {
      init(pName);
    }

    private function init(pName:String):void {
      _name = pName;
    }

    public function get name():String {
      return _name;
    }

  }

}
```

To start off, we have a class that we will pass a name to in the constructor, and that can be retrieved at any time through the implicit getter. The next item we will want to add is the ability to set and retrieve specific properties for the instance. The following bold code does just that:

```
package com.foed.graphic {

  public class StyleFormat {

    private var _name:String;
    private var _properties:Object;

    public function StyleFormat(pName:String) {
      init(pName);
    }

    private function init(pName:String):void {
      _properties = {};
      _name = pName;
    }

    public function setProperty(pKey:String, pValue:Object):void {
      _properties[pKey] = pValue;
    }
```

```
    public function getProperty(pKey:String):Object {
      return _properties[pKey];
    }

    public function get name():String {
      return _name;
    }

  }

}
```

The bold lines in the preceding code add a `_properties` member to the class, which can be added to using `setProperty()` and retrieved from using `getProperty()`. We don't define the types of properties that can be used by this class, but keep this open ended, which will enable the class to be dynamic and be useful for many different purposes. The immediate power of this class in our framework will come when component instances register themselves with a `StyleFormat` instance and update their graphical look to match its style values, which can be set through these two methods. It just remains to add the ability for component instances to register to receive data and updates from a `StyleFormat`, which we will do next.

```
package com.foed.graphic {

  public class StyleFormat {

    private var _name:String;
    private var _listeners:Array;
    private var _properties:Object;

    public function StyleFormat(pName:String) {
      init(pName);
    }

    private function init(pName:String):void {
      _listeners = [];
      _properties = {};
      _name = pName;
    }

    public function setProperty(pKey:String, pValue:Object):void {
      _properties[pKey] = pValue;
    }

    public function getProperty(pKey:String):Object {
      return _properties[pKey];
    }
```

```
    public function addListener(pObj:IStyleable):void {
      var pFormat:StyleFormat = pObj.getStyleFormat();
      if (pFormat != null) {
        pFormat.removeListener(pObj);
      }
      pObj.setStyleFormat(this);
      for each (var i:IStyleable in _listeners) {
        if (i == pObj) return;
      }
      _listeners.push(pObj);
    }

    public function removeListener(pObj:IStyleable):void {
      var pLength:uint = _listeners.length;
      for (var i:uint = 0; i < pLength; i++) {
        if (_listeners[i] == pObj) {
          _listeners.splice(i, 1);
          break;
        }
      }
      pObj.clearStyleFormat();
    }

    public function updateStyles():void {
      for each (var i:IStyleable in _listeners) {
        i.setStyleFormat(this);
      }
    }

    public function get name():String {
      return _name;
    }

  }

}
```

The new methods include an addListener() and removeListener() method, which simply add or remove a component instance to a list of listeners stored in a StyleFormat class instance. addListener() takes care of removing the object passed in as a listener for any previous StyleFormat instance, and it also ensures that the object has not yet been added as a listener to this StyleFormat. Notice that both methods are expected to be passed an object that implements the IStyleable interface.

updateStyles() is where the true power lies, as all of the listeners can be easily updated with changes to the StyleFormat instance. Using this class alone, you could assign styles to any object that implements the IStyleable interface and its setStyleFormat() method and so control the look of multiple graphic objects. However, it will require using addListener() for every single instance you want to assign a format to. That means if there are 20 buttons in your interface and you want them all to look the same, you'll need to add 20 addListener() calls. What would help immensely is a class that manages this process for all the components. Which brings us nicely to the next topic . . .

StyleManager

The StyleManager will handle the registering and format assignment for all components in our framework. The concept is that a single StyleManager instance will hold references to all the StyleFormat instances in a movie. Component instances that we create will automatically "check in" with the StyleManager to see which format they should apply. Let's step through the code to see how to create this.

Create a new ActionScript file in the com/foed/managers directory and name it StyleManager.as. Add the following code:

```
package com.foed.managers {

  import com.foed.graphic.StyleFormat;
  import com.foed.graphic.IStyleable;

  public class StyleManager {

    private static var sStyleManager:StyleManager;

    private var _styles:Object = {};
    private var _listeners:Object = {};

    static public function getInstance():StyleManager {
      if (sStyleManager == null) sStyleManager = new StyleManager();
      return sStyleManager;
    }

  }

}
```

These lines set up the StyleManager class. Two private properties, _styles and _listeners, hold references to StyleFormat instances and components, respectively. Next, we provide a getInstance() method to return a single instance of the StyleManager to any class that calls it. Only the first time this method is called will the instance be created. All other calls will return the previously created instance.

This is an example of one way to use the Singleton pattern for a global manager class. With this class, there should only ever be one instance present and used. It is not a foolproof method, as another instance can still be created through use of the new operator, and certain techniques can be employed to try to ensure only a single instance is created by throwing either a compile-time or runtime error, but these have their downsides as well, and for our purposes, where we are managing our own code, this method will work fine for us.

Now, let's continue and add the methods that will allow StyleFormats to be added to this manager for, well, management. The new lines are in bold.

```
package com.foed.managers {

  import com.foed.graphic.StyleFormat;
  import com.foed.graphic.IStyleable;

  public class StyleManager {

    private static var sStyleManager:StyleManager;

    private var _styles:Object = {};
    private var _listeners:Object = {};

    static public function getInstance():StyleManager {
      if (sStyleManager == null) sStyleManager = new StyleManager();
      return sStyleManager;
    }

    public function addStyle(pName:String, pFormat:StyleFormat):void {
      _styles[pName] = pFormat;
    }

    public function removeStyle(pName:String):void {
      delete _styles[pName];
    }

  }

}
```

In the addStyle() method, the format passed in is placed in the _styles object property under the key name passed in. removeStyle() simply deletes this value for the object.

The final two methods take care of assigning StyleFormat instances to individual components.

```
package com.foed.managers {

  import com.foed.graphic.StyleFormat;
  import com.foed.graphic.IStyleable;

  public class StyleManager {

    private static var sStyleManager:StyleManager;

    private var _styles:Object = {};
    private var _listeners:Object = {};
```

```
        static public function getInstance():StyleManager {
          if (sStyleManager == null) sStyleManager = new StyleManager();
          return sStyleManager;
        }

        public function addStyle(pName:String, pFormat:StyleFormat):void {
          _styles[pName] = pFormat;
        }

        public function removeStyle(pName:String):void {
          delete _styles[pName];
        }

        public function style(pObj:IStyleable):void {
          var pFormat:StyleFormat = getStyle(pObj);
          pFormat.addListener(pObj);
          pObj.setStyleFormat(pFormat);
        }

        public function getStyle(pObj:IStyleable):StyleFormat {
          var pStyleFormatName:String = pObj.getStyleFormatName();
          if (pStyleFormatName != null) {
            for (var j:String in _styles) {
              if (_styles[j].name == pStyleFormatName) {
                return _styles[j];
              }
            }
          }
          var pClasses:Array = pObj.getClassHierarchy();
          for (var i:int = pClasses.length-1; i > -1; i--) {
            if (_styles[pClasses[i]] != undefined) {
              return _styles[pClasses[i]];
            }
          }
          return _styles["default"];
        }

      }

    }
```

style() will be called by every component internally. style() in turn calls getStyle(), which determines which of the StyleFormat instances should be applied to the object passed in. The way this is determined is broken down into the following steps:

1. If the object has a specific style format name value and that refers to a StyleFormat instance stored in the StyleManager, use that style.
2. Otherwise, if the object belongs to a class and that class has an associated StyleFormat instance stored in the StyleManager, use that style.
3. If neither of the previous cases is true, use the default StyleFormat instance, which you will note is stored under the key "default".

When we build UI classes in the next chapter, we'll plug them into these classes and interfaces to better illustrate how the style hierarchy works. However, we can test out the concept without having to create full component classes. The next section demonstrates how.

Coding with style

To try out the three classes explored in the previous section, we'll create a simple class that implements IStyleable to take its color values from a StyleFormat. Create a new ActionScript file and save it as Ellipse.as. Add the following code, representing the entirety of the class, which simply draws an ellipse with a variable width and height and uses the StyleManager to control its coloring. The relevant style code is in bold.

```
package {

  import flash.display.Sprite;

  import com.foed.graphic.StyleFormat;
  import com.foed.graphic.IStyleable;

  public class Ellipse extends Sprite implements IStyleable {

    private var _styleFormat:StyleFormat;
    private var _styleFormatName:String;
    protected var _width:Number;
    protected var _height:Number;

    public function Ellipse(
      pWidth:Number,
      pHeight:Number=0,
      pStyleFormatName:String=null
    ) {
      init(pWidth, pHeight, pStyleFormatName);
    }

    protected function init(
      pWidth:Number,
      pHeight:Number,
      pStyleFormatName:String
    ):void {
```

15

```
      if (pHeight < 1) pHeight = pWidth;
      _width = pWidth;
      _height = pHeight;
      _styleFormatName = pStyleFormatName;
      StyleManager.getInstance().style(this);
    }

    protected function draw():void {
      var pBorder:uint = _styleFormat.getProperty("border") as uint;
      var pFace:uint = _styleFormat.getProperty("face") as uint;
      graphics.clear();
      graphics.lineStyle(2, pBorder, 1);
      graphics.beginFill(pFace, 1);
      graphics.drawEllipse(0, 0, _width, _height);
      graphics.endFill();
    }

    public function getStyleFormat():StyleFormat {
      return _styleFormat;
    }

    public function setStyleFormat(pFormat:StyleFormat):void {
      _styleFormat = pFormat;
      draw();
    }

    public function getStyleFormatName():String {
      return _styleFormatName;
    }

    public function setStyleFormatName(pName:String):void {
      _styleFormatName = pName;
    }

    public function getClassHierarchy():Array {
      return ["Ellipse"];
    }

    public function clearStyleFormat():void {
      _styleFormat = null;
    }

  }

}
```

You can see that the majority of the methods are those that are required by the IStyleable interface. getStyleFormat() and getStyleFormatName() simply return instance properties, while setStyleFormat() and setStyleFormatName() set the same, with setStyleFormat() also calling the draw() method when the StyleFormat instance changes. The final two IStyleable methods are clearStyleFormat(), which nulls the reference to the StyleFormat, and getClassHierarchy(). This last method returns an array of classes that make up the inheritance chain of this class. For our purposes here in this short example, we just pass the string "Ellipse", letting the StyleManager know that this is the name of the class, but this method will be used more fully when we build UI objects in the next chapter.

The two remaining methods, excepting the constructor, which just passes the arguments to the init() method, are init() and draw(). init() sets the initial variables based on the arguments passed in, and then calls the style() method of the StyleManager, which applies the appropriate StyleFormat instance to this Ellipse instance. This class code does not need to know what StyleFormat is being applied, as all of that code and logic is contained in the StyleManager. All that needs to happen here is a single call to style() to have the necessary StyleFormat applied.

After that, when draw() is called (which occurs in the setStyleFormat() method, which the StyleManager will call to apply the StyleFormat instance), the color values for the fill and border can be obtained from the StyleFormat and an ellipse can be drawn. We will next create a document class that will demonstrate how Ellipse instances can be created and managed with the StyleManager.

Create a new ActionScript file and save it as StyleTest.as. Enter the following code:

```
package {

  import flash.display.Sprite;

  import com.foed.managers.StyleManager;
  import com.foed.graphic.IStyleable;
  import com.foed.graphic.StyleFormat;

  public class StyleTest extends Sprite {

    public function StyleTest() {
      init();
    }

    private function init():void {
      createStyles();
      draw();
    }

    private function createStyles():void {
      var pStyleManager:StyleManager = StyleManager.getInstance();
      var pFormat:StyleFormat = new StyleFormat("default");
      pFormat.setProperty("face", 0x0000FF);
      pFormat.setProperty("border", 0xFF0000);
      pStyleManager.addStyle("default ", pFormat);
```

15

```
      pFormat = new StyleFormat("Ellipse");
      pFormat.setProperty("face", 0xCCCCCC);
      pFormat.setProperty("border", 0x333333);
      pStyleManager.addStyle("Ellipse", pFormat);
    }

    private function draw():void {}

  }

}
```

In the init() method of this class, we first call createStyles(), which creates two separate StyleFormat instances. One is saved as "default" and the other is saved as "Ellipse". Any Ellipse instance that we create will use the "Ellipse" StyleFormat instance by default, since in the getClassHierarchy() method the string "Ellipse" is passed to the StyleManager. This can be overridden only by an Ellipse instance having a styleFormatName that points to a different StyleFormat. In the draw() method that we will fill in next, we will show how this is done.

Add the following bold code to the draw() method:

```
    private function draw():void {
      var pRadius:uint = 100;
      var pY:Number = (stage.stageHeight-pRadius)/2;

      var pEllipse:Ellipse = new Ellipse(pRadius);
      pEllipse.x = 50;
      pEllipse.y = pY;
      addChild(pEllipse);

      pEllipse = new Ellipse(pRadius, pRadius, "default");
      pEllipse.x = 225;
      pEllipse.y = pY;
      addChild(pEllipse);

      pEllipse = new Ellipse(pRadius);
      pEllipse.x = 400;
      pEllipse.y = pY;
      addChild(pEllipse);
    }
```

Here three Ellipse instances are created. The second Ellipse, the one placed in the center, is passed the styleFormatName "default" in its constructor, whereas the other two are not given a styleFormatName. To test the results, in Flash create a new Flash document and assign StyleTest as the document class, making sure to save the FLA in the same directory as the StyleTest.as file, and then select Control ➤ TestMovie. To test in Flex Builder, create a new ActionScript project in Flex Builder with StyleTest.as as the main source file and make sure that the com directory of the class files is added as a source for the project. Then run the movie.

You should see three circles, with the two outside circles taking one StyleFormat instance and the center circle taking another, as shown in Figure 15-3. Remember that the Ellipses themselves did not contain the logic to decide how they would be styled. That logic was in our main file and managed in the StyleManager.

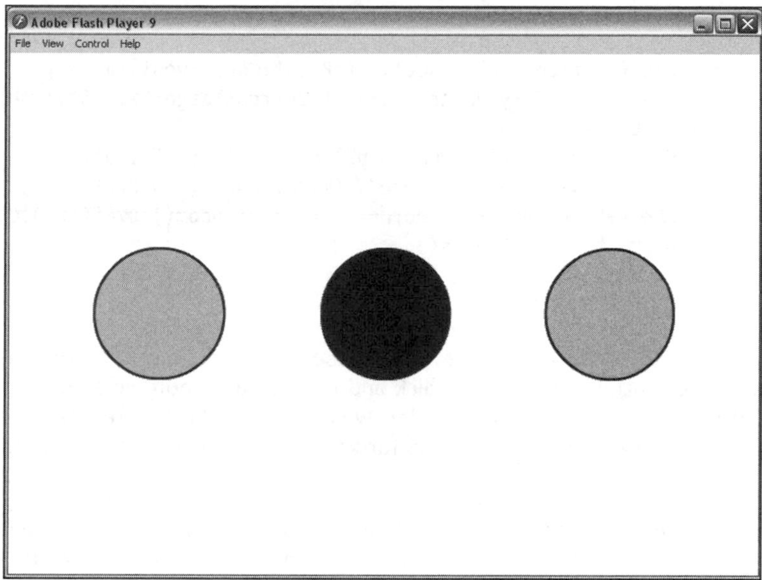

Figure 15-3. The circle instances with StyleFormats applied (though grayscale doesn't do it justice)

Imagine if these circles represented button instances. In a few simple lines of code, we could recolor every single instance, or instances individually. To see how easy it is to change these StyleFormats and have the instances update accordingly, add the following bold lines to the code:

```
private function draw():void {
  var pRadius:uint = 100;
  var pY:Number = (stage.stageHeight-pRadius)/2;

  var pEllipse:Ellipse;
  pEllipse = new Ellipse(pRadius);
  pEllipse.x = 50;
  pEllipse.y = pY;
  pEllipse.addEventListener(MouseEvent.MOUSE_DOWN, onEllipseClick);
  addChild(pEllipse);

  pEllipse = new Ellipse(pRadius, pRadius, "default");
  pEllipse.x = 225;
  pEllipse.y = pY;
  pEllipse.addEventListener(MouseEvent.MOUSE_DOWN, onEllipseClick);
  addChild(pEllipse);
```

```
    pEllipse = new Ellipse(pRadius);
    pEllipse.x = 400;
    pEllipse.y = pY;
    pEllipse.addEventListener(MouseEvent.MOUSE_DOWN, onEllipseClick);
    addChild(pEllipse);
  }

  private function onEllipseClick(pEvent:MouseEvent):void {
    var pElement:IStyleable = pEvent.currentTarget as IStyleable;
    if (pElement != null) {
      var pFormat:StyleFormat = pElement.getStyleFormat();
      pFormat.setProperty("face", (Math.random()*0xFFFFFF)|0);
      pFormat.setProperty("border", (Math.random()*0xFFFFFF)|0);
      pFormat.updateStyles();
    }
  }
```

Also, be sure to import flash.events.MouseEvent at the top of the class. onEllipseClick() handles the mouse click and chooses a random color for the border and face of the Ellipse. Within this function, we can cast to the IStyleable interface, so conceivably such a handler could be used for any class implementing this interface, not just Ellipse.

When you test the movie again, you should be able to click any of the Ellipse instances to change the associated StyleFormat. Notice that when you click either of the outside ellipses, the colors of the others change as well. This is because both are listening to the same StyleFormat, so when this StyleFormat is changed by one of the ellipses, the other is notified as well. Imagine how easy it would be then to have an entire interface update based on style changes, perhaps when a new CSS is loaded. By separating this logic into our style classes, we have made that process much easier to implement! What we've created is a centralized means of managing the styles for all aspects of an interface, which is a powerful demonstration of the usefulness of a global managing class.

In the previous version of this book, when demonstrating the style classes outside of UI widgets, we drew graphics within a symbol and placed code on the timeline to color those graphics based on the StyleFormat*. This was done not only because it was a quick-and-dirty way to see this code in action without having to create more classes, but also to demonstrate that it was just as easy, if not easier, to use styling with predrawn vector or bitmap graphics as it was with code-drawn graphics.*

We avoid using this technique in this edition of the book because we want to provide examples that can be implemented by those using Flex Builder as well as those using Flash. In addition, because of the IStyleable *interface employed in this edition, to accomplish this with graphic symbols in the library would still require creating external classes that implemented the interface to recolor the timeline graphics. However, it should be stressed that there is nothing in these classes that would prevent implementation with timeline graphics, if that is the course required by an application. Old-school Flash users, OOP doesn't mean you have to abandon the timeline!*

SoundManager

With the appearance of widgets being controlled by a centralized manager class, our next step will be to create a similar manager for sounds in the interface. In much the same way that the StyleManager holds references to StyleFormats, the SoundManager will hold references to Sound object instances. Individual objects can then request a sound to play for a certain event. Using this concept, we'll be able to limit the number of Sound object instances—if all buttons should produce the same click when pressed, why create multiple Sound object instances when one will suffice? All that's necessary is a way to manage this for an entire interface, which is where the SoundManager comes in.

Create a new ActionScript file and save it into the com/foed/managers directory as SoundManager.as. Enter the following code in the file:

```
package com.foed.managers {

  import flash.events.IOErrorEvent;
  import flash.media.Sound;
  import flash.media.SoundTransform;
  import flash.net.URLLoader;
  import flash.net.URLRequest;
  import flash.utils.Dictionary;

  import com.foed.IDescribable;

  public class SoundManager {

    private static var sSoundManager:SoundManager;
    private var _sounds:Object;
    private var _listeners:Dictionary;

    public function SoundManager() {
      init();
    }

    public static function getInstance():SoundManager {
      if (sSoundManager == null) sSoundManager = new SoundManager();
      return sSoundManager;
    }

    private function init():void {
      _sounds = {};
      _listeners = new Dictionary();
    }

}
```

This is just the beginnings of the class, which imports all necessary external classes, creates two private properties and a static private property, and provides a getInstance() method for access to a single instance. Yep, we have another example here of a Singleton class, a class that should only ever have one instance available in the application at any time.

The two private properties hold references to the sounds to load (_sounds) and the objects listening for these sounds (_listeners). The init() method that follows assigns a new Object instance to the _sounds property and creates a new Dictionary instance to store in _listeners. The reason for using a Dictionary will be explained shortly.

Now let's fill in some additional methods so that we can see how these two properties are used and how classes will interact with the SoundManager. Add this code within the class definition:

```
    private function onIOError(pEvent:IOErrorEvent):void {
      trace("error loading sound");
    }

    public function addSound(
      pSoundName:String,
      pSoundPath:String
    ):void {
      _sounds[pSoundName] = pSoundPath;
    }

    public function registerForSound(
      pID:Object,
      pSoundName:String,
      pEvent:String,
      pVolume:Number=1
    ):void {
      var pSound:Sound = new Sound();
      var pPath:String = _sounds[pSoundName] + ".mp3";
      try {
        pSound.addEventListener(IOErrorEvent.IO_ERROR, onIOError);
        pSound.load(new URLRequest(pPath));
        if (_listeners[pID] == null) _listeners[pID] = {};
        _listeners[pID][pEvent] = new SoundObject(pSound, pVolume);
      } catch (e:Error) {}
    }

  }
```

The addSound() method will be used to add sounds to the list to be managed. This simply stores the name of the path to the sound by the name used to reference the sound.

registerForSound() is the workhorse of this class. For arguments it takes the name of the object listening for the sound, the name of the sound to receive, the event for which to receive the sound, and the volume at which the sound should be played. A new Sound instance is created in which to load the specified MP3. The path to that MP3 is found in the _sounds array (which would have previously been added to using the addSound() method). Within a try..catch block we then add the onIOError handler to listen for an error in loading the file and attempt to load the MP3.

The if conditional that appears at the end of registerForSound() checks to see whether the pID object passed in has already registered for a previous sound. This might occur, for instance, if a button registered for a rollover sound and then a press sound. If the pID has not previously been passed in, a new object is created and stored in the _listeners dictionary using that pID as the key. The reason a dictionary is used here as opposed to a standard object is so the pID passed to registerForSound() can be either a string or a reference to a specific object since a dictionary can store object instances as separate keys, unlike a standard object. What the SoundManager then allows is for sounds to be registered for an entire class by using the name of the class (like "Button"), as well as individual instances to be passed in to register for sounds. In this way, all buttons could have a sound assigned to their press event by passing in "Button" as a pID, but this could be overridden by single button instances that needed different sounds. You will see how this works when we write the play() method in a moment.

Once a dictionary entry has been created for the pID, the event key is used to store a reference to a new SoundObject, which holds the reference to the Sound to play as well the desired volume. This SoundObject is a custom class that we will write next.

To create the SoundObject, we could create a new class file, but the class is actually fairly limited and will never be used outside of the context of the SoundManager. For this reason, let's add the SoundObject directly to the SoundManager.as file. You can add the code in bold to the end of the SoundManager.as file, after the closing brace for the SoundManager package definition. The code that is nonbold has been truncated, and is included here merely so you may more easily see where to add the SoundObject code.

```
package com.foed.managers {

  public class SoundManager {

    public function SoundManager() {
      init();
    }

  }

}

import flash.media.Sound;

class SoundObject {

  private var mSound:Sound;
  private var mVolume:Number;
```

15

```
    public function SoundObject(pSound:Sound, pVolume:Number) {
      mSound = pSound;
      mVolume = pVolume;
    }

    public function get sound():Sound { return mSound; }
    public function get volume():Number { return mVolume; }

  }
```

You can see that the SoundObject merely saves a reference to the Sound and the volume, and provides implicit getter methods for these properties. We just as easily left this class out and used a line like this in the registerForSound() method:

```
_listeners[pID][pEvent] = {sound:pSound, volume:pVolume};
```

However, making this internal class gives us the benefit of type checking, both at runtime and compile time, as well as compile-time syntax checking.

There are two methods left before we can test our new manager. These will allow objects at runtime to ask the SoundManager if a sound needs to be played for a certain event. Add the following bold lines to the class body. Once again, the surrounding code has been truncated and is only included to help show placement of the new lines.

```
package com.foed.managers {

  public class SoundManager {

    public function SoundManager() {
      init();
    }

    private function play(pSoundObj:SoundObject):void {
      Sound(pSoundObj.sound).play(0, 0,➥
new SoundTransform(Number(pSoundObj.volume)));
    }

    public function playSound(pObj:IDescribable, pEvent:String):void {
      var pListener:Object = _listeners[pObj];
      var pSoundObj:SoundObject;
      if (pListener != null) {
        pSoundObj = pListener[pEvent] as SoundObject;
        if (pSoundObj != null) {
          play(pSoundObj);
          return;
        }
      }
      var pClasses:Array = pObj.getClassHierarchy();
      for (var i:int = pClasses.length-1; i > -1; i--) {
        pListener = _listeners[pClasses[i]];
```

```
            if (pListener != null) {
              pSoundObj = pListener[pEvent] as SoundObject;
              if (pSoundObj != null) {
                play(pSoundObj);
                return;
              }
            }
          }
        }

      }

    }
```

playSound() will be called by all of the object instances (such as components) when they wish to play a sound, and as you see they must implement the IDescribable interface. The method will be sent a reference to the object as well as the event for the sound. Using these parameters, and in a similar way to how the StyleManager returned style formats to objects, the SoundManager first checks to see whether there is a sound for that event specifically stored for the instance calling, and if so, it calls play() for that SoundObject instance. If, however, no sound exists for that listener and that event, the listener's classes are checked, using the getClassHierarchy() defined in the IDescribable interface, to see whether there are sounds registered for those particular classes. In this way, we can assign a single sound to all button clicks, all window pop-ups, all check box toggles, and so on.

The play() method that is called from within playSound() accepts a SoundObject instance as an argument. The Sound instance stored by the SoundObject is played and passed a new SoundTransform to set the volume. Let's see how this all fits together by building on our test file from the previous section.

Sounding off

Open StyleTest.as and resave it as SoundTest.as. Add the following bold lines to the code:

```
package {

  import flash.display.Sprite;
  import flash.events.MouseEvent;

  import com.foed.managers.SoundManager;
  import com.foed.managers.StyleManager;
  import com.foed.graphic.IStyleable;
  import com.foed.graphic.StyleFormat;
  import com.foed.IDescribable;

  public class SoundTest extends Sprite {
```

15

```
    public function SoundTest() {
      init();
    }

    private function init():void {
      createStyles();
      setSounds();
      draw();
    }

    private function setSounds():void {
      var pSoundManager:SoundManager = SoundManager.getInstance();

      pSoundManager.addSound("kiss", "CLICK2");
      pSoundManager.addSound("click", "CLICK8");

      pSoundManager.registerForSound("Ellipse", "kiss",➥
MouseEvent.MOUSE_DOWN);
    }

    private function createStyles():void {
      var pStyleManager:StyleManager = StyleManager.getInstance();
      var pFormat:StyleFormat = new StyleFormat("default");
      pFormat.setProperty("face", 0x0000FF);
      pFormat.setProperty("border", 0xFF0000);
      pStyleManager.addStyle("default", pFormat);

      pFormat = new StyleFormat("Ellipse");
      pFormat.setProperty("face", 0xCCCCCC);
      pFormat.setProperty("border", 0x333333);
      pStyleManager.addStyle("Ellipse", pFormat);
    }

    private function draw():void {
      var pRadius:uint = 100;
      var pY:Number = (stage.stageHeight-pRadius)/2;

      var pEllipse:Ellipse;
      pEllipse = new Ellipse(pRadius);
      pEllipse.x = 50;
      pEllipse.y = pY;
      pEllipse.addEventListener(MouseEvent.MOUSE_DOWN, onEllipseClick);
      addChild(pEllipse);

      pEllipse = new Ellipse(pRadius, pRadius, "default");
      pEllipse.x = 225;
      pEllipse.y = pY;
      pEllipse.addEventListener(MouseEvent.MOUSE_DOWN, onEllipseClick);
```

```
      SoundManager.getInstance().registerForSound(pEllipse,➥
"click", MouseEvent.MOUSE_DOWN, .3);
      addChild(pEllipse);

      pEllipse = new Ellipse(pRadius);
      pEllipse.x = 400;
      pEllipse.y = pY;
      pEllipse.addEventListener(MouseEvent.MOUSE_DOWN, onEllipseClick);
      addChild(pEllipse);
    }

    private function onEllipseClick(pEvent:MouseEvent):void {
      var pElement:IStyleable = pEvent.currentTarget as IStyleable;
      if (pElement != null) {
        var pFormat:StyleFormat = pElement.getStyleFormat();
        pFormat.setProperty("face", (Math.random()*0xFFFFFF)|0);
        pFormat.setProperty("border", (Math.random()*0xFFFFFF)|0);
        pFormat.updateStyles();
      }
      if (pElement is IDescribable) {
        SoundManager.getInstance().playSound(➥
IDescribable(pElement), pEvent.type);
      }
    }

  }

}
```

You can see that the code to add sounds to our ellipses is easy and fairly limited, with all of the logic for loading and managing the sounds delegated to the SoundManager. In the init() method, the setSounds() method is now called. This setSounds() method adds two sound paths to the SoundManager; CLICK2, which we save using the key "kiss"; and CLICK8, which we save using the key "click". The last line of this method tells the SoundManager that all Ellipse instances, when the MOUSE_DOWN event in called, should play the sound stored under the key "kiss".

In the draw() method, the only line added registers the single Ellipse instance for the "click" sound on mouse down, set at a volume of .3. This line will override the sound set in the previous step only for this one instance.

Finally, in the onEllipseClick() handler, we check to see whether the target for the event implements the IDescribable interface. If it does, we pass it to the SoundManager so that its sound for that event, if any, will be played.

Test your movie to see—or rather hear—the result. Let's hear it for the SoundManager!

LabelManager

The last manager class we will explore in this chapter is a Singleton class to centralize all labels to not only make it easier to edit common labels (for instance, if an OK label on all dialog boxes needed to become Yes), but also simplify localization of applications by the runtime swapping of languages. We will accomplish this with the LabelManager class by having all classes that require text fields to query the manager for the proper text to display. The manager will load the appropriate labels based on the user's browser language settings unless it is overridden by the application (meaning you).

Let's start by creating four XML files for four different languages: English (english.xml), Spanish (spanish.xml), French (french.xml), and German (german.xml). Here is the english.xml file in full:

```
<?xml version="1.0" ?>
<labels>
  <label key="one">one</label>
  <label key="two">two</label>
  <label key="three">three</label>
</labels>
```

As you can see, each label has a key by which to access it and a value for that key, which is the text node value. For the English file, the keys and values match up here, but that might not always be the case (the key might be truncated; for instance, the key "welcome" might contain a long welcome message). The Spanish file looks like this:

```
<?xml version="1.0" ?>
<labels>
  <label key="one">uno</label>
  <label key="two">dos</label>
  <label key="three">tres</label>
</labels>
```

The German and French files would then substitute the values for their respective translations (the files are available to download with this chapter's files).

Now for the ActionScript to utilize these files. Start off by creating a new ActionScript file and saving it as LabelManager.as in your com/foed/managers directory. Add the following code:

```
package com.foed.managers {

  import flash.events.IOErrorEvent;
  import flash.events.SecurityErrorEvent;
  import flash.events.ErrorEvent;
  import flash.events.Event;
  import flash.events.EventDispatcher;
  import flash.net.URLLoader;
  import flash.net.URLRequest;
  import flash.system.Capabilities;
```

```
public class LabelManager extends EventDispatcher {

  static private var sLabelManager:LabelManager;
  static private var ENGLISH_LABELS:String = "english.xml";
  static private var SPANISH_LABELS:String = "spanish.xml";
  static private var FRENCH_LABELS:String = "french.xml";
  static private var GERMAN_LABELS:String = "german.xml";

  static public var language:String;
  static public var ENGLISH:String = "en";
  static public var SPANISH:String = "es";
  static public var FRENCH:String = "fr";
  static public var GERMAN:String = "de";

  private var _labels:Object;
  private var _ready:Boolean;

  public function LabelManager() {
    _labels = {};
    _ready = false;
    getLabels();
  }

  static public function getInstance():LabelManager {
    if (sLabelManager == null) sLabelManager = new LabelManager();
    return sLabelManager;
  }

}

}
```

After the necessary class imports, including EventDispatcher, which this class extends, we establish a number of static properties. The private static properties hold references to the single LabelManager instance (remember, this will be a Singleton) as well as the paths to each of the XML files containing the labels. The public static properties will allow external classes to set the language that the LabelManager should load by providing an accessible property (language) as well as a constant value for each language.

Additionally, there are two private instance properties, _labels and _ready. _labels will hold all of the labels loaded from the XML, and _ready will be a flag to inform classes looking to access labels if those labels have been loaded.

Finally, we have the constructor, which initializes _labels and calls an as-yet-undefined method, getLabels(), and the getInstance() method, which allows access to the Singleton instance of the class.

15

The next bit of code, which can be added to the body of the class, retrieves the labels from the XML.

```
private function getLabels():void {
  switch (LabelManager.language || Capabilities.language) {
    case SPANISH:
      loadFile(SPANISH_LABELS);
      break;
    case FRENCH:
      loadFile(FRENCH_LABELS);
      break;
    case GERMAN:
      loadFile(GERMAN_LABELS);
      break;
    default:
      loadFile(ENGLISH_LABELS);
  }
}

private function loadFile(pFile:String):void {
  var pLoader:URLLoader = new URLLoader();
  pLoader.addEventListener(Event.COMPLETE, onLoadComplete);
  pLoader.addEventListener(IOErrorEvent.IO_ERROR, onLoadError);
  pLoader.addEventListener(SecurityErrorEvent.SECURITY_ERROR,➥
onLoadError);
  try {
    pLoader.load(new URLRequest(pFile));
  } catch (e:Error) {
    onError(e.message);
  }
}
```

In the getLabels() method, a switch statement is set up to call loadFile() with a file based on the value of the static language property, if it is set, or else it defaults to the user's Capabilities.language setting. In loadFile(), a URLLoader is instantiated to load the specified XML file, which it does within a try..catch block after the necessary listeners are added. So at this point we have a Singleton manager class that instantiates and loads an XML file based on the language settings. The preceding code includes a number of handlers that need defining, so we'll take care of that next.

The following code can be added within the body of the LabelManager class:

```
private function onLoadComplete(pEvent:Event):void {
  var pContent:XML = new XML(URLLoader(pEvent.target).data);
  var pLabels:XMLList = pContent.child("label");
  for each (var pLabel:XML in pLabels) {
    _labels[pLabel.@key] = pLabel.valueOf();
  }
  informListeners();
}
```

```
private function onLoadError(pEvent:ErrorEvent):void {
  onError(pEvent.type + ": " + pEvent.text);
}

private function onError(pError:String):void {
  trace(pError);
  informListeners();
}
```

onLoadComplete() creates a new Flash XML object using the text data loaded from the file. It then utilizes the new E4X syntax to iterate through all the label nodes within the XML, assigning the appropriate values to each key, before calling informListeners(), a method we will write next.

onLoadError() will be called when there is a problem loading the required file. In such a case, the onError() method is called (the same method that was called from within the catch block in the previous step), which, at this point, merely traces the error and calls the same informListeners() method.

Seems like this informListeners() might be important! Let's finish the class with that. Add the following to the body of the LabelManager class and we'll be all set:

```
private function informListeners():void {
  _ready = true;
  dispatchEvent(new Event(Event.COMPLETE));
}

public function get ready():Boolean {
  return _ready;
}

public function getLabel(pKey:String):String {
  return _labels[pKey] || pKey;
}
```

As you can see, informListeners() sets the _ready flag to true, signifying that there has been an attempt, whether successful or not, to load the XML file. Then, dispatchEvent() is called to notify any classes awaiting the loading of labels. The final two methods are an implicit getter method to return the current values of the _ready flag, and getLabel(), which returns the value of the specified key. The || within the return statement ensures that if the value for the key does not exist, because there was an error in loading the XML, the key was not defined in the XML, or the XML hasn't yet loaded, the key is returned back.

That's it for the LabelManager class. Next, you'll see how to utilize this new functionality.

LabelEllipse

To demonstrate the application of the LabelManager, we will extend the Ellipse class used in earlier examples so it displays a text field. The following is the entirety of the code for the class, which should be saved in the same directory as Ellipse.as. The relevant lines using the LabelManager have been marked in bold.

```
package {

  import flash.events.Event;
  import flash.text.TextField;
  import flash.text.TextFieldAutoSize;
  import flash.text.TextFormat;
  import flash.text.TextFormatAlign;

  import com.foed.managers.LabelManager;

  public class LabelEllipse extends Ellipse {

    private var _label:String;
    private var _labelKey:String;
    private var _field:TextField;

    public function LabelEllipse(
      pLabel:String,
      pWidth:Number,
      pHeight:Number=0,
      pStyleFormatName:String=null
    ) {
      _labelKey = pLabel;
      super(pWidth, pHeight, pStyleFormatName);
    }

    override protected function draw():void {
      super.draw();
      if (_labelKey != null) label = _labelKey;
    }

    private function drawLabel():void {
      _label = LabelManager.getInstance().getLabel(_labelKey);
      if (_field == null) {
        _field = new TextField();
        _field.selectable = false;
        _field.autoSize = TextFieldAutoSize.LEFT;
        addChild(_field);
      }
      _field.embedFonts = getStyleFormat().getProperty("embedFonts")➥
as Boolean;
```

```
      _field.defaultTextFormat = getStyleFormat().getProperty➥
("textFormat") as TextFormat;
      if (_label != null) _field.text = _label;
      _field.x = (_width-_field.width)/2;
      _field.y = (_height-_field.height)/2;
    }

    private function onLabelsLoaded(pEvent:Event):void {
      LabelManager.getInstance().removeEventListener(➥
Event.COMPLETE, drawLabel);
      drawLabel();
    }

    public function get label():String {
      return _label;
    }

    public function set label(pLabel:String):void {
      _labelKey = pLabel;
      if (LabelManager.getInstance().ready) {
        drawLabel();
      } else {
        LabelManager.getInstance().addEventListener(➥
Event.COMPLETE, onLabelsLoaded);
      }
    }

  }

}
```

This class is passed a desired label in its constructor, which is saved as _labelKey. In the draw() method, overridden from the superclass, the implicit setter label is called if the _labelKey exists. In this setter, the LabelManager is queried to see whether it is ready with the loaded labels. If it is, drawLabel() is immediately called. However, if the labels are not yet loaded, this instance is added as a listener to the LabelManager's complete event, which we know is dispatched once the labels load. onLabelsLoaded() handles this event, removing the instance as an event listener and calling drawLabel().

drawLabel() creates a text field the first time it is called and adds it as a child. The TextFormat for the field is retrieved from the styleFormat (and so the StyleManager), and the text for the field is retrieved from the LabelManager using its getLabel() method.

In the end, we have an ellipse that draws a label. However, that label is retrieved from a centralized class that handles the loading and managing of multilingual labels. The LabelEllipse instances don't need to know where the text comes from, and the parent application doesn't need to keep track of copy changes or language. All text changes can go directly into the external XML files (a further enhancement might be to externalize the supported languages and XML file paths as well, so the LabelManager itself does not even need to know this information).

We have all the pieces. The only remaining step is to plug them into our test application.

Slap on a label

Open SoundTest.as from the earlier example and save it as LabelTest.as. Make the following additions in bold:

```
package {

  import flash.display.Sprite;
  import flash.events.MouseEvent;
  import flash.text.TextFormat;

  import com.foed.managers.SoundManager;
  import com.foed.managers.StyleManager;
  import com.foed.graphic.IStyleable;
  import com.foed.graphic.StyleFormat;
  import com.foed.IDescribable;

  public class LabelTest extends Sprite {

    public function LabelTest() {
      init();
    }

    private function init():void {
      createStyles();
      setSounds();
      draw();
    }

    private function setSounds():void {
      var pSoundManager:SoundManager = SoundManager.getInstance();

      pSoundManager.addSound("kiss", "CLICK2");
      pSoundManager.addSound("click", "CLICK8");

      pSoundManager.registerForSound("Ellipse", "kiss",➥
MouseEvent.MOUSE_DOWN);
    }

    private function createStyles():void {
      var pStyleManager:StyleManager = StyleManager.getInstance();
      var pFormat:StyleFormat = new StyleFormat("default");
      pFormat.setProperty("face", 0x0000FF);
      pFormat.setProperty("border", 0xFF0000);
      pFormat.setProperty("textFormat", new TextFormat("Arial", 20));
      pFormat.setProperty("embedFonts", true);
      pStyleManager.addStyle("default", pFormat);
```

```
      pFormat = new StyleFormat("Ellipse");
      pFormat.setProperty("face", 0xCCCCCC);
      pFormat.setProperty("border", 0x333333);
      pFormat.setProperty("textFormat",➥
new TextFormat("Times New Roman", 20, 0x333333));
      pFormat.setProperty("embedFonts", true);
      pStyleManager.addStyle("Ellipse", pFormat);
    }

    private function draw():void {
      var pRadius:uint = 100;
      var pY:Number = (stage.stageHeight-pRadius)/2;

      var pEllipse:LabelEllipse
      pEllipse = new LabelEllipse("one", pRadius);
      pEllipse.x = 50;
      pEllipse.y = pY;
      pEllipse.addEventListener(MouseEvent.MOUSE_DOWN, onEllipseClick);
      addChild(pEllipse);

      pEllipse = new LabelEllipse("two", pRadius, pRadius, "default");
      pEllipse.x = 225;
      pEllipse.y = pY;
      pEllipse.addEventListener(MouseEvent.MOUSE_DOWN, onEllipseClick);
      SoundManager.getInstance().registerForSound(pEllipse,➥
"click", MouseEvent.MOUSE_DOWN, .3);
      addChild(pEllipse);

      pEllipse = new LabelEllipse("three", pRadius);
      pEllipse.x = 400;
      pEllipse.y = pY;
      pEllipse.addEventListener(MouseEvent.MOUSE_DOWN, onEllipseClick);
      addChild(pEllipse);
    }

    private function onEllipseClick(pEvent:MouseEvent):void {
      var pElement:IStyleable = pEvent.currentTarget as IStyleable;
      if (pElement != null) {
        var pFormat:StyleFormat = pElement.getStyleFormat();
        pFormat.setProperty("face", (Math.random()*0xFFFFFF)|0);
        pFormat.setProperty("border", (Math.random()*0xFFFFFF)|0);
        var pTextFormat:TextFormat = pFormat.getProperty➥
("textFormat") as TextFormat;
        pTextFormat.color = pFormat.getProperty("border") as uint;
        pFormat.setProperty("textFormat", pTextFormat);
        pFormat.updateStyles();
      }
      if (pElement is IDescribable) {
        SoundManager.getInstance().playSound(➥
```

```
IDescribable(pElement), pEvent.type);
            }
        }

    }

}
```

The preceding changes include adding textFormat and embedFonts properties to the StyleFormats, and instantiating LabelEllipses instead of Ellipses, passing in a label key to the constructor. In the onEllipseClick handler, the TextFormat for the clicked instance has its color changed to match the new border color.

Before you can test your movie, you will need to embed the necessary fonts. If you are using the Flash IDE, open the Library and select New Font from its menu. Name the font Times New Roman and select Times New Roman from the Font drop-down list. Click OK. Now right-click the item in the Library and select Linkage, check the Export in ActionScript check box, and click OK (the fields that fill in by default will be exactly what you need). Now run through the same steps for Arial (creating the menu item and then setting its linkage), and you will be ready to test.

If you are using Flex Builder, you will need to embed the fonts in your SWF. Add the following directives to your LabelTest.as ActionScript file within the class definition:

```
[Embed(source="arial.ttf", fontName="Arial",➥
mimeType="application/x-font")]
public var ArialFont:Class;
[Embed(source="times.ttf", fontName="Times New Roman",➥
mimeType="application/x-font")]
public var TimesFont:Class;
```

You will then need to find the two fonts on your system (on Windows, fonts are located in C:\WINDOWS\Fonts) and copy them to your project root directory.

If you test your application now in either environment, you should see the three ellipses with labels, as in Figure 15-4.

If you want to force the language of the labels, you would add the following line:

```
LabelManager.language = LabelManager.GERMAN;
```

Remember to import LabelManager into the file in order to use this line. If you test your movie again, the labels will be switched to German, as shown in Figure 15-5, with the ellipses themselves being none the wiser, and all logic to swap out each label contained within the LabelManager. Not bad output for only a few, but powerful, manager classes!

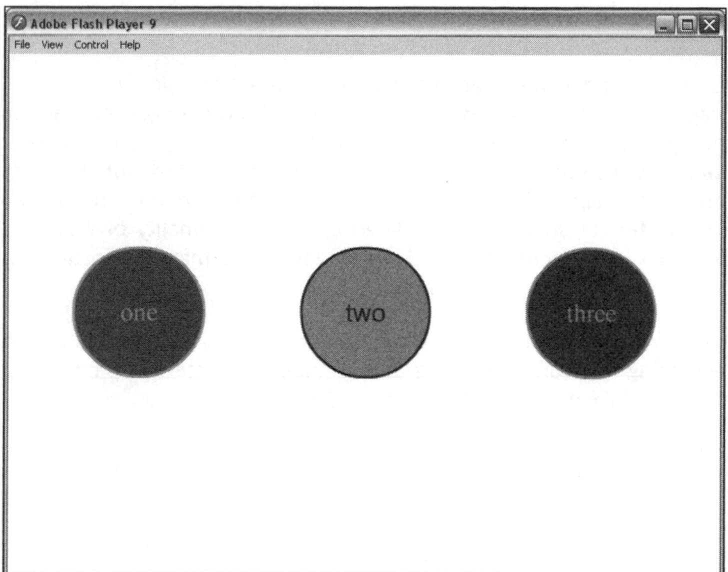

Figure 15-4. The circle instances with labels retrieved from the `LabelManager` and external XML

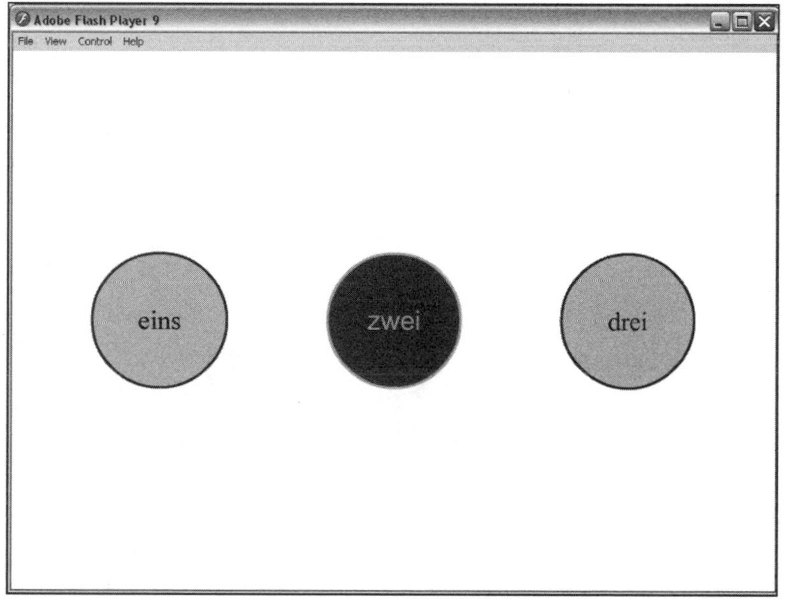

Figure 15-5. Language is swapped without any change to the buttons themselves.

What's next?

This chapter explored manager classes for an ActionScript component framework. I hope that this chapter has demonstrated how useful centralized manager classes can be when handling multiple components. This will become even more apparent as you build actual visual components and use them in an interface. By having the functionality common to all widgets stored within and referenced in a single class, you have much more control of the overall look and feel of an application. Altering that functionality or changing an interface's appearance then becomes a cinch, as updating the manager instance propagates changes throughout the entire component set.

The next chapter examines how to build visual components to handle standard UI functionality, leveraging the work done here on the manager classes. To paraphrase Al Jolson, you ain't seen nothin' yet!

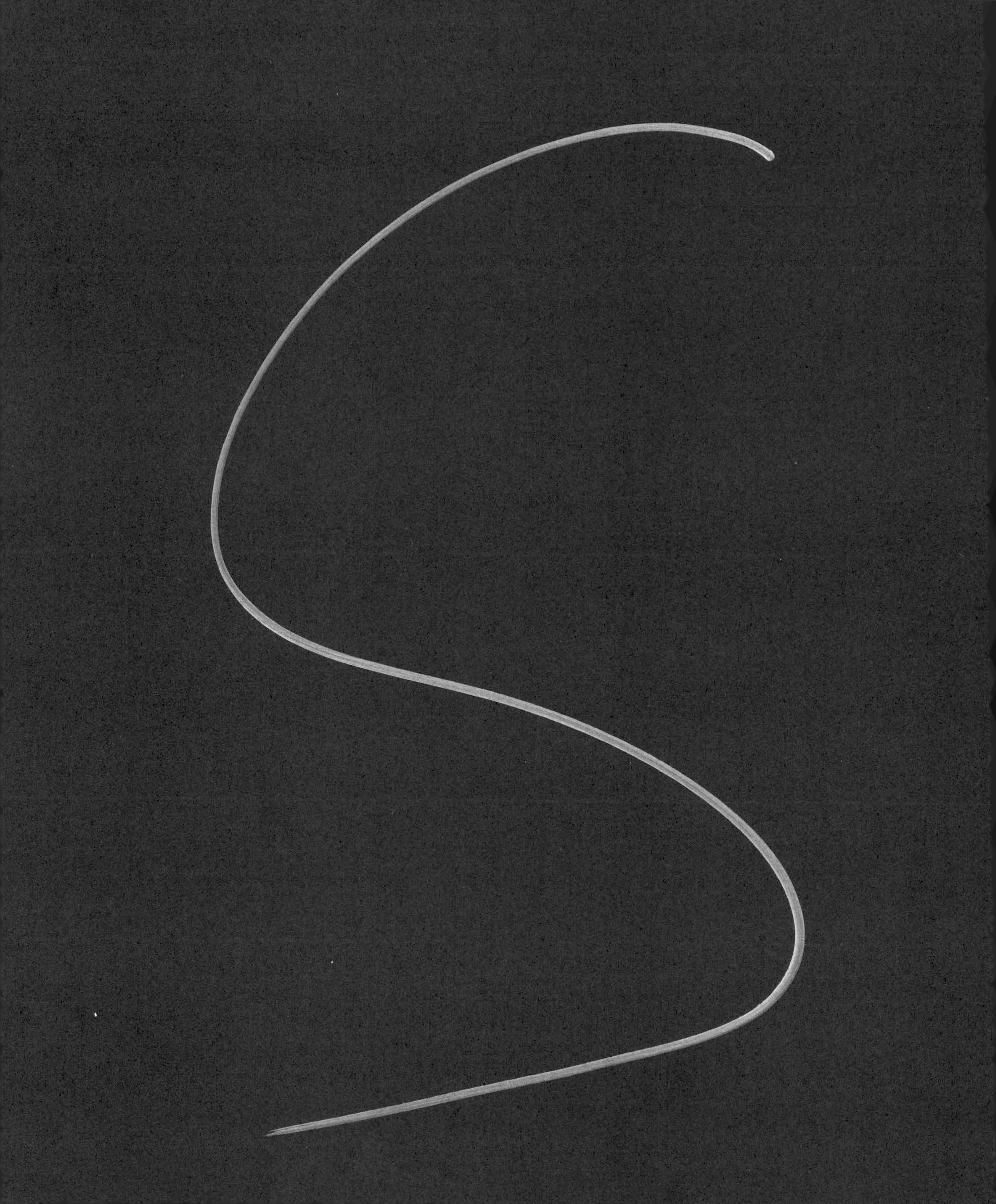

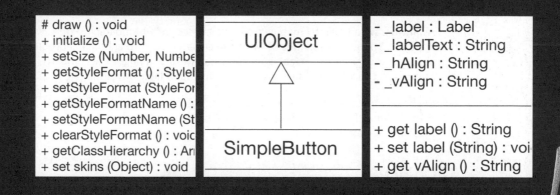

16 UI WIDGETS

draw () : void
+ initialize () : void
+ setSize (Number, Numbe
+ getStyleFormat () : StyleI
+ setStyleFormat (StyleFor
+ getStyleFormatName () :
+ setStyleFormatName (St
+ clearStyleFormat () : voic
+ getClassHierarchy () : Ar
+ set skins (Object) : void

UIObject

SimpleButton

- _label : Label
- _labelText : String
- _hAlign : String
- _vAlign : String

+ get label () : String
+ set label (String) : voi
+ get vAlign () : String

When it comes to a user interface, the most obvious components are the visual *widgets* that allow the user to interact with the application. These include, to name but a few in their simplest form, labels, buttons, and sliders. Individually, each can be created rather easily and quickly using the built-in tools in Flash (if that is your application of choice) or through ActionScript, but how do you create a set of these widgets that can seamlessly work within and integrate into the architecture of an entire application? To do this requires some OOP forethought and the creation of classes that standardize how widgets may be interacted with, through inheritance and polymorphism.

In this chapter, I'll show you what it takes to lay down the foundation for a framework containing UI widgets and how OOP can help create a structure that allows for common code interfaces with these widgets. Together, we'll build upon the work begun in the previous chapter with our manager classes to start a component library that could be used for a multitude of applications.

It should be noted once more that there already exists a number of components and component frameworks, including the component framework that comes bundled with Flash or the Flex framework with Flex Builder. We are building from the ground up instead of using a prebuilt set for a number of reasons. First, it'll allow you to more easily go in and add or modify the code to do exactly what you need without having to wade through others' code, when that's even possible. Second, you can ensure the functionality is exactly what you need in your own projects and optimize the code for that purpose. Third, if changes need to be made for any reason, it's far easier to go in and alter your own code than that of others, where changing functionality might have more of a ripple effect than you may suspect. Finally, this is a book about learning and using OOP in your own Flash platform projects. There is no better way to learn than to get in and code the object-oriented interaction from scratch.

Diagramming the classes

As always, we'll begin by mapping out the classes we'll be building before we start in on the code. This gives us an idea of what is necessary, brings to light initial problems we must address, and gives us a clear goal for what we are trying to accomplish. A few extra moments at the start will save a world of frustration later down the line!

We'll start by looking at the base `UIObject` class, `Block`, and `SimpleButton`. So as not to overwhelm with diagrams, we'll save `Label` and its associated classes till after we complete these initial classes.

UIObject

Let's consider some of the properties and methods that will be important for all visual UI elements. We can place this common functionality into a superclass from which all of our widgets will inherit, `UIObject`.

The purpose, at this phase, is not to envision every possible method and property that would ever be needed and lock it down, but to come up with a plan on how to approach coding a base class for all UI widgets. Our goal here is to break down the problem into its smallest blocks and solve those blocks. We want to code a class that can be used for visual UI widgets, so what issues will be common to all visual user interaction elements?

For our framework, we will begin with a simple `UIObject` that does little more than implement the methods of the interfaces required to work with our managers from the last chapter, specifically the `IStyleable` interface, which in turn inherits from the `IDescribable` interface. These methods, `getStyleFormat()`, `setStyleFormat()`, `getStyleFormatName()`, `setStyleFormatName()`, `clearStyleFormat()`, and `getClassHierarchy()`, will allow `UIObject` to work with both the `StyleManager` and `SoundManager`. Properties to support these methods will include `_styleFormat`, `_styleFormatName`, and `_classes`.

To aid with setting the visual appearance of components, we'll add the implicit setter for a `_skins` property that will hold an object made up of skin properties and the graphic classes that will draw them, so for a component to determine what its background should be, it might look to `skins.background`. This will save us having to create a setter for every single skin property of more complex components (a scrollpane, for instance, could contains dozens of skins for different internal elements). A companion to this will be a `setSkin()` method to set an individual skin.

In order for a component to determine how skins should be drawn using which classes, we'll add a `getSkin()` method, which will first look to the instance's skins property, and then to `resolveSkin()`. `resolveSkin()` will determine how skins will be drawn based on the class if the instance doesn't have a skin set, and if the class doesn't have a setting, it will work up the inheritance chain for the component. These two methods will allow us to create a complex method of determination for how individual components, classes of components, collections of classes, and an entire application is drawn. We'll look at it more in depth when we implement this in the "Managing skins" section.

For sizing, we'll add the old standby, `setSize()`, which will accept both width and height parameters. We'll also override the default `width` and `height` implicit setters so that a component can determine how it is resized by using the `setSize()` method and not be scaled.

Finally, we'll add a protected `init()` method, which will set up a component with defaults, a public `initialize()`, which will be called when a component's settings have been added and will set a Boolean `_initialized` flag, and `draw()`, which will draw the component. This last method will be left empty here in `UIObject`, as there is nothing to be drawn in this base class, which really is an abstract class, but the `draw()` method should be overridden by the concrete classes derived from `UIObject`.

Of course, additional properties and methods may come to light as you program (better positioning methods, perhaps, or a `getEnabled()` and `setEnabled()` pair?), and this class may continue to grow as it's used and built upon. The functionality we've addressed here is a good starting place, though, so let's start with our diagram, shown in Figure 16-1.

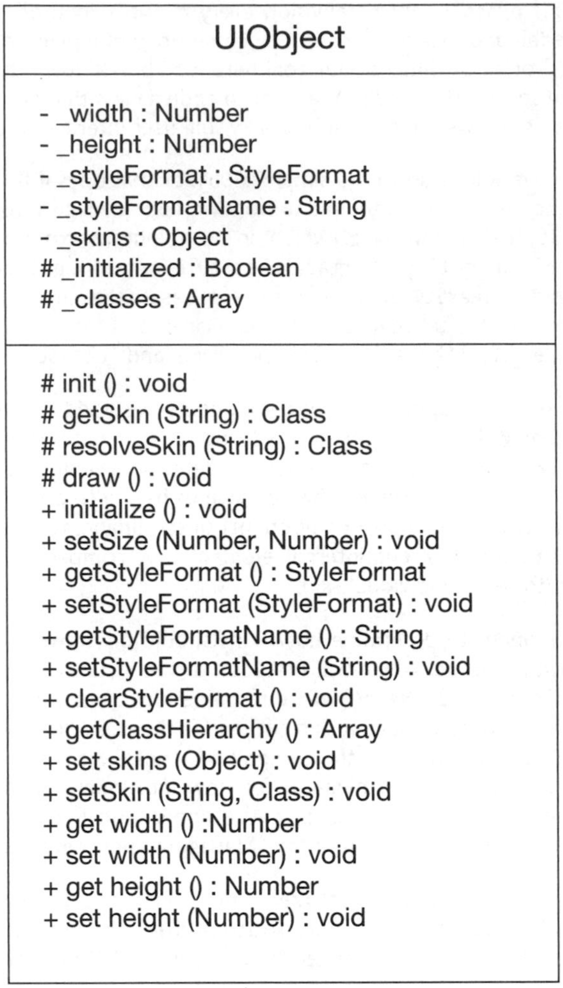

UIObject
- _width : Number - _height : Number - _styleFormat : StyleFormat - _styleFormatName : String - _skins : Object # _initialized : Boolean # _classes : Array
init () : void # getSkin (String) : Class # resolveSkin (String) : Class # draw () : void + initialize () : void + setSize (Number, Number) : void + getStyleFormat () : StyleFormat + setStyleFormat (StyleFormat) : void + getStyleFormatName () : String + setStyleFormatName (String) : void + clearStyleFormat () : void + getClassHierarchy () : Array + set skins (Object) : void + setSkin (String, Class) : void + get width () :Number + set width (Number) : void + get height () : Number + set height (Number) : void

Figure 16-1. The class diagram for `UIObject`

Block

Once our base class, `UIObject`, is created, we can easily extend it to other classes. The first and most useful class will be the simplest graphic form used by all other widgets. We can call this `Block`, and it'll serve as the graphic aspect of all other components. For instance, a button would attach a single `Block` instance to serve as its graphic. A slider might attach a `Block` instance for its slider well and another for its slider button. As long as we program a way for a `Block` instance to take different skins, it could be used anywhere a graphic is required. Putting all the graphic-attaching code into a single class will make managing styles and skins so much easier when we come to it, since it'll all be handled within a single class.

So what methods might Block have in addition to those of UIObject? Again, let's keep it simple to begin with. We'll definitely need to override draw(), since that is Block's main purpose, as well as setSize(). It would then also be useful for a single Block to support multiple states (for instance, a single Block could be used to represent all states of a button). For this, we will add a changeState() and implicit getter/setters for state. The _state property will store this current state of the Block, and finally _skin will hold the graphic class used for drawing. Keeping the actual drawing code in a separate class is what will allow us to have a single Block class used for all graphics drawn in an application. Block will determine the size, position, and current state for the skin, which will then draw itself based on these settings. Each Block might then have a different skin. As for a skin, we'll also add an ISkin interface to establish the required methods for a class interacting with Block, which will also allow us to type the skin within Block as ISkin. Figure 16-2 shows the diagram of this class.

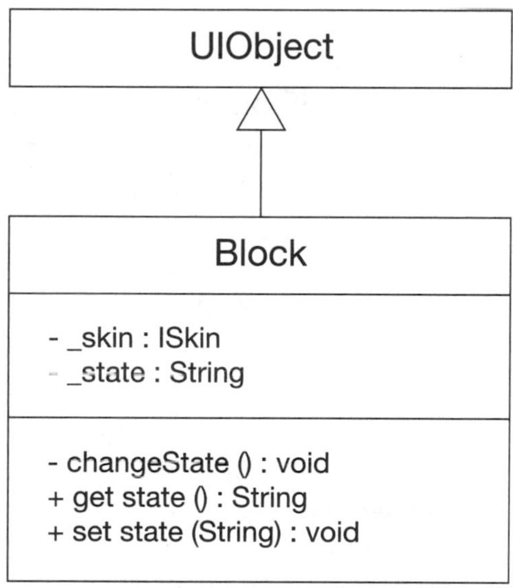

Figure 16-2. The class diagram for Block

Not too bad, is it? With UIObject taking on so much useful functionality, child classes become much easier to write.

SimpleButton

The final class in this section we'll be looking at for our component foundation is for the simplest user interaction widget, the button. That said, a button can actually be fairly complex, with toggling capability and label and icon placement, so we'll create a simpler button named SimpleButton, as that seems appropriate, that will handle changing visual states based on user interaction.

For SimpleButton, the actual button events rollOutButton(), rollOverButton(), pressButton(), releaseButton(), and releaseOutsideButton() will be the most important methods that will be called by handlers for the mouse events. Adding listeners for these events will be taken care of in a setEvents() method. Since SimpleButton will have states and a single skin, we could have it inherit from Block, but it was a personal choice to have Block act as the single class that attaches skins, and having SimpleButton inherit from that would cause some muddiness in this clear intention. Whenever possible, it is good to keep the number of responsibilities at a minimum for a class (some would suggest a single responsibility, or purpose, for a class). As an example, here we have Block handling the attaching of a skin, a skin handling drawing, and SimpleButton handling user interaction.

We'll have to override a few of UIObject's methods, like draw() and setSize(), but we'll leave these out of the diagram and focus only on the new methods. The diagram is shown in Figure 16-3.

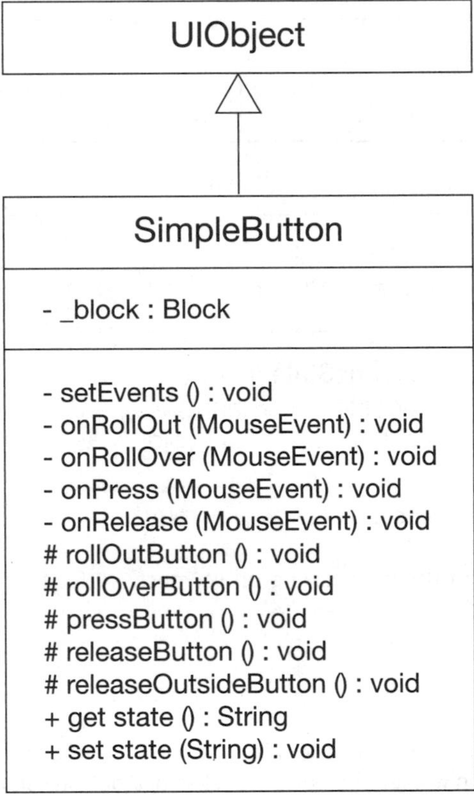

Figure 16-3. The class diagram for SimpleButton

Making the foundation

With these initial classes diagrammed, we can now get into the ActionScript needed to code our component foundation. Open Flash or Flex Builder or your ActionScript editor of choice, create a new ActionScript file named UIObject.as, and save it into the com/foed directory you used in the previous two chapters. Add the following code, which is the start of our base class:

```
package com.foed {

  import flash.display.Sprite;
  import flash.events.Event;
  import flash.utils.getQualifiedClassName;

  import com.foed.graphic.StyleFormat;
  import com.foed.graphic.IStyleable;

  public class UIObject extends Sprite implements IStyleable {

    static public const CLASS:String = getQualifiedClassName(UIObject);

    protected var _classes:Array;

    private var _styleFormat:StyleFormat;
    private var _styleFormatName:String;

    public function UIObject() {
      init();
    }

    protected function init():void {
      _classes = [UIObject.CLASS];
    }

    public function getStyleFormat():StyleFormat {
      return _styleFormat;
    }

    public function setStyleFormat(pFormat:StyleFormat):void {
      _styleFormat = pFormat;
    }

    public function getStyleFormatName():String {
      return _styleFormatName;
    }

    public function setStyleFormatName(pName:String):void {
      _styleFormatName = pName;
    }
```

```
        public function getClassHierarchy():Array {
          return _classes;
        }

        public function clearStyleFormat():void {
          _styleFormat = null;
        }

      }

    }
```

As you can see from the class definition, the UIObject will inherit from the Sprite class, which means it'll have all of the properties and methods belonging to Sprite. Also note that UIObject implements the IStyleable interface, which in turn inherits from the IDescribable interface, and you'll see that the majority of the current code is to include the methods required by these interfaces. Each method merely sets or returns the corresponding private property.

The only other piece in the preceding code is the constructor, which calls a protected init() method. All that occurs in the init() method at this time is that the fully qualified class name is pushed into a _classes array, the same array that will be returned in the getClassHierarchy() call. To get the class name and package, we take advantage of getQualifiedClassName(), which will return the value in the form of "package::class" and set a static variable that any instance will be able to retrieve after it's initially set.

Next we'll override a few methods of Sprite in order to better control sizing and how event listeners are handled. You can add the following code anywhere within the UIObject class definition:

```
        override public function addEventListener(
          pType:String,
          pListener:Function,
          pUseCapture:Boolean=false,
          pPriority:int=0,
          pUseWeakReference:Boolean=true
        ):void {
          super.addEventListener(
            pType,
            pListener,
            pUseCapture,
            pPriority,
            pUseWeakReference
          );
        }

        override public function get width():Number {
          return _width;
        }
```

```
override public function set width(pWidth:Number):void {}

override public function get height():Number {
  return _height;
}

override public function set height(pHeight:Number):void {}
```

Here we override the default implementation of addEventListener() so that we can change the default value for useWeakReference from false to true. In general, we will want to use weak references, for reasons explained in the focus point (which appears in a shaded box) in Chapter 14, and by setting that as the default here, we won't have to worry about setting it each time when working with UIObject instances.

We also override the width and height getter/setters since we want complete control over how a component is redrawn when it is resized. For the setters, we do nothing here, and the getters simply return the value of the private property. Alternatively, we could have the setters call the setSize() method, though I tend to avoid that as setSize() operations can sometimes be expensive, and yet it could be called twice by a developer calling both the width and height back to back. To prevent this, there is the possibility of creating an invalidation strategy that delays operations like setSize() until the rendering in the following frame, but I have often found these more problematic than the issues they are trying to fix. As such, for these examples we will simply prevent developers from calling width and height directly to set the size. Of course, those properties should be added to the listing at the top:

```
static public const CLASS:String = getQualifiedClassName(UIObject);

protected var _classes:Array;

private var _styleFormat:StyleFormat;
private var _styleFormatName:String;
private var _width:Number;
private var _height:Number;
```

We'll also add that setSize() method so that a component can be resized by passing in both a width and height. For UIObject, that method will look like the following, once again added within the class definition:

```
public function setSize(pWidth:Number, pHeight:Number):void {
  _width = pWidth;
  _height = pHeight;
  dispatchEvent(new Event(Event.RESIZE, true));
}
```

The setSize() method sets the private _width and _height properties. It'll be up to the classes that inherit from UIObject to redraw themselves when setSize() is called. You'll see this implemented shortly in both Block and SimpleButton. Notice that we also dispatch a bubbling RESIZE event here since it's an event that other objects might need to be aware of.

The next group of methods will allow for components to be skinned by providing a way for skins to be set for individual properties, whatever those properties might be for a class, as well as a way at runtime for an individual instance to determine the appropriate skin to draw with. Add these methods to the body of UIObject, and we'll look at them more in depth.

```
protected final function resolveSkin(pProp:String):Class {
  // determine if skin was set for class or ancestor classes
}

protected final function getSkin(pProp:String):Class {
  return (_skins[pProp] || resolveSkin(pProp));
}

public function setSkin(pKey:String, pSkin:Class):void {
  _skins[pKey] = pSkin;
}

public function set skins(pSkins:Object):void {
  _skins = pSkins;
}
```

The two public methods allow for a group of skins to be set (the implicit skins setter) as well as a single skin (the setSkin() method). When a component needs to determine which skin to use, it would call the protected getSkin() method. This method looks to the _skins property and, if the skin was set there, uses that. If the skin was not set, it returns the result of the resolveSkin() method. resolveSkin() right now contains nothing but a comment, but we will in a moment add code that will return a skin based on the class instance calling the method.

Of course, since we are now accessing a _skins property, we must add it to the list of declarations at the top, and we'll initialize it within the init() method.

```
static public const CLASS:String = getQualifiedClassName(UIObject);

protected var _classes:Array;

private var _styleFormat:StyleFormat;
private var _styleFormatName:String;
private var _width:Number;
private var _height:Number;
private var _skins:Object;

public function UIObject() {
  init();
}

protected function init():void {
  _classes = [UIObject.CLASS];
  _skins = {};
}
```

The final piece to add is the code that will draw the component for the first time. There are a number of ways that we might handle this. What we do know is that we will instantiate the class by using the new operator. After that, we will generally be setting whatever properties need to be set for that instance, and then we will most likely be attaching that instance using addChild(). Since we don't want a UIObject to run any drawing routines upon instantiation before properties have been set, we want to delay the initial drawing until a later point in time. We could have the component wait until it is added to the display list for this to occur. We could set up an enterFrame handler to draw itself on the next frame after instantiation, or we could introduce a method that would be manually called to tell the component to draw itself initially. It is this last option we will opt for here, as it will give us the most flexibility.

To that end, let's add a public initialize() method. We'll also add an _initialized property so that internal methods can check the current state when necessary.

```
import com.foed.managers.StyleManager;
import com.foed.graphic.StyleFormat;
import com.foed.graphic.IStyleable;

public class UIObject extends Sprite implements IStyleable {

  static public const CLASS:String = getQualifiedClassName(UIObject);

  protected var _classes:Array;
  protected var _initialized:Boolean;

  private var _styleFormat:StyleFormat;
  private var _styleFormatName:String;
  private var _width:Number;
  private var _height:Number;
  private var _skins:Object;

  public function UIObject() {
    init();
  }

  protected function init():void {
    _classes = [UIObject.CLASS];
    _skins = {};
  }

  public function initialize():void {
    StyleManager.getInstance().style(this);
    _initialized = true;
    draw();
  }

  protected function draw():void {
    throw new Error("draw() method must be overridden.");
  }
```

In the initialize() method, we first call the style() method of the StyleManager Singleton instance. It is only at this point that a StyleFormat can be accurately determined based on the class hierarchy of an instance since the _classes array won't be fully populated with all child classes within the init() method of UIObject.

After the StyleFormat is assigned, the _initialized flag is set to true, and the draw() method is called. For UIObject, it doesn't make sense to actually implement the draw() method, as each UIObject child class will require a different drawing routine, so we just add a method that must be overridden or an error will be thrown.

And that's it! Since the UIObject code was pieced together as we went along, be sure to take a look at the finished class available in this chapter's download files and check it against your own code.

Managing skins

One piece that we left off in the previous section was the way to find the proper skin for each component property if it wasn't set directly on a component instance. Imagine that you have 20 buttons, and each one will have the same skin applied to the skin property we define, graphic. You could set this individually on each instance as follows:

```
button0.setSkin("graphic", SomeSkin);
button1.setSkin("graphic", SomeSkin);
button2.setSkin("graphic", SomeSkin);
etc.
```

It is obvious that this would quickly become unmanageable. One solution is that we have another centralized class through which we can set skins for entire classes. So we might instead set

```
manager.setSkin(SimpleButton, "graphic", SomeSkin);
```

In this way, we could set this in one line, making it less code to manage and more centralized. Individual instances might override this default value, but for those instances that did not need to override this, the default could be determined easily.

We will accomplish this with a new SkinManager class. Create a new ActionScript file and save it as SkinManager.as into your com.foed.managers directory. The following is the entirety of the class:

```
package com.foed.managers {

  import com.foed.IDescribable;

  public class SkinManager {

    private static var sManager:SkinManager;
    private var _skins:Object;
```

```
        public function SkinManager() {
          _skins = {};
        }

        static public function getInstance():SkinManager {
          if (sManager == null) sManager = new SkinManager();
          return sManager;
        }

        public function setClassSkins(pClass:String, pSkins:Object):void {
          _skins[pClass] = pSkins;
        }

        public function getSkin(pObj:IDescribable, pProp:String):Class {
          var pClasses:Array = pObj.getClassHierarchy();
          var pClass:String;
          var i:int = pClasses.length;
          while (--i > -1) {
            pClass = pClasses[i];
            if (_skins[pClass] != null) {
              if (_skins[pClass][pProp] != null) {
                return _skins[pClass][pProp];
              }
            }
          }
          return null;
        }

      }

    }
```

This once more is a Singleton manager class, so we provide the standard getInstance() access. The setClassSkins() method would be used to set a group of skins for a single component class. The getSkin() method works in a very similar way to the getStyle() method of the StyleManager. IDescribable's getClassHierarchy() is called to obtain a list of the calling instance's classes. This array is run through backwards until a class is found that has had skins set in the manager. Once a class is found, the value for the particular property being asked for is checked. If it exists for that class, it is returned. If not, the checking continues all the way up the class hierarchy. If no skin is ever found, null is returned.

To plug this into UIObject, return to UIObject.as and replace the contents of the resolveSkin() method with the following:

```
protected final function resolveSkin(pProp:String):Class {
  return SkinManager.getInstance().getSkin(this, pProp);
}
```

Also, be sure to import the SkinManager at the top of your class. Now, if a UIObject does not have an instance skin set, it will call resolveSkin(), which in turn will query the SkinManager. The SkinManager will look at the classes of the calling instance and return the appropriate skin, if available.

We will see this working shortly, but let's take a look how this might be applied. Let's say we have three buttons, bn0, bn1, and bn2. The first two buttons are instances of com.foed.ui.buttons.SimpleButton. The third button is an instance of com.foed.ui.buttons.Button, which inherits from SimpleButton. To set the exact same graphic skin for all three instances using a single line of code, we would write the following:

```
SkinManager.getInstance().setClassSkins(➥
  SimpleButton.CLASS, {graphic:SimpleSkin});
```

When buttons one and two are initialized, they will call their getSkin() method to look for the value of graphic. Since the value was not set on either instance's _skins property, resolveSkin() is called. The SkinManager is then queried for the value of graphic for both instances. SkinManager uses getClassHierarchy() to access the classes of the instances, and sees that each is first an instance of com.foed.ui.buttons.SimpleButton. Since that class has skin settings (added by our preceding line of code) and the graphic property exists, the value SimpleSkin is returned to the two buttons so they can draw themselves.

For bn2, the third button, a similar process occurs. Since no instance _skins values have been set, resolveSkin() is called. The SkinManager sees that the button is first an instance of com.foed.ui.buttons.Button. No skin settings exist for that class, so it next looks at the superclass, SimpleButton. Skins have been set for that class, so ultimately SimpleSkin will be returned to bn2 as well.

Now if you wanted bn0 to have its own special skin, no worries. All that is required is to use the following line:

```
bn0.setSkin("graphic", SpecialSkin);
```

Now, when the instance's getSkin() method is invoked, the value graphic *has* been set in the instance's _skins property, so that is used to draw and resolveSkin() never needs to be called. The end result is that with a few lines of code we have enabled hierarchies of classes to have similar skin settings, with child classes able to override their ancestor classes' skins, and instances being able to override their class's skins. That's pretty powerful stuff! Now we just need to code the graphic classes that will make it all come to life.

Basic building block

The previous section had plenty of code, but we as of yet haven't been able to see any result. This is because we don't yet have any visual component for the UIObject, which only serves as a superclass for all the visual widgets, but doesn't have any visual elements itself (which makes sense, seeing as how all visual elements will require different graphic aspects). In this section, we'll look at Block, which will serve as the graphic building block for all widgets. With one class handling the instantiation and rendering of skins, making components skinnable will be much easier.

We'll start out the Block class with some bare bones code, with all the methods present but not yet filled in. Create a new ActionScript file, save it as Block.as into the com/foed directory, and enter the following code:

```
package com.foed {

  import flash.utils.getQualifiedClassName;

  import com.foed.graphic.StyleFormat;
  import com.foed.UIObject;

  public class Block extends UIObject {

    static public const CLASS:String = getQualifiedClassName(Block);

    private var _state:String;

    override protected function init():void {
      super.init();
      _classes.push(Block.CLASS);
    }

    override protected function draw():void {
    }

    private function changeState(pState:String):void {
      _state = pState;
    }

    override public function setSize(
      pWidth:Number,
      pHeight:Number
    ):void {
      super.setSize(pWidth, pHeight);
    }

    override public function setStyleFormat(
      pStyleFormat:StyleFormat
    ):void {
      super.setStyleFormat(pStyleFormat);
    }

    public function get state():String {
      return _state;
    }
```

```
    public function set state(pState:String):void {
      changeState(pState);
    }

  }

}
```

There's nothing too surprising yet. We start with the class declaration, which as you can see has Block inheriting from UIObject. We initialize a static property to hold the name of the class, just as we did with UIObject, and then push this value into the _classes array in the init() method after calling the superclass's init(). For Block instances, this will result in the _classes array having the value ["com.foed::UIObject","com.foed::Block"]. Next we override the draw() method, but as yet don't do anything within it. For setSize() and setStyleFormat(), we also override the super's implementation, but invoke the superclass's method within each method. We will add lines in a moment that will redraw the skin if the size or style changes, which is why these methods needed to be overridden. Finally, to allow a Block instance to have multiple states, we have added the property _state to keep track of the current state, the implicit getter/setters for this property, as well as a private changeState() method, which will also cause our skin to redraw, once we have that implemented.

So as it stands, Block does little right now but keep track of the current state. All of the drawing will occur within a skin, which could possibly be different for each Block instance. As such, we need Block to be able to communicate with a skin without it mattering which skin it is using. We need some common methods for skin classes that will be the same no matter the skin. Now, if you have already guessed that an interface for skins is exactly what we are looking for, you really have been paying attention. If we could provide gold stars with the download files, your link would be on its way!

Let's diverge from Block for a moment and create a new interface, ISkin, to be used by any class that can be used for a skin with Block. We have already seen that a skin will need to be resized, restyled, and have its state changed. A simple interface could then be the following, which you can save as ISkin.as into a new com/foed/graphic/skins directory (graphic already existed from last chapter, but you will need to create the skins subdirectory).

```
package com.foed.graphic.skins {

  import com.foed.graphic.StyleFormat;

  public interface ISkin {

    function setSize(pWidth:Number, pHeight:Number):void

    function changeState(pState:String):void
```

```
    function styleElements(pStyleFormat:StyleFormat):void

  }

}
```

Now we can have Block type its skin to the ISkin interface in order to communicate with it, and as long as the skins it employs implement ISkin and these methods, it won't matter the skin used.

Head back to Block.as and add the following bold lines to the file:

```
import flash.display.DisplayObject;
import flash.utils.getQualifiedClassName;

import com.foed.graphic.skins.ISkin;
import com.foed.graphic.StyleFormat;
import com.foed.UIObject;

public class Block extends UIObject {

  static public const CLASS:String = getQualifiedClassName(Block);
  static public const GRAPHIC:String = "graphic";

  private var _skin:ISkin;
  private var _state:String;

  override protected function init():void {
    super.init();
    _classes.push(Block.CLASS);
  }

  override protected function draw():void {
    var pSkin:Class = getSkin(GRAPHIC);
    _skin = addChild(DisplayObject(new pSkin())) as ISkin;
    setSize(width, height);
    changeState(_state);
    setStyleFormat(getStyleFormat());
  }
```

After importing the new ISkin interface and DisplayObject (which we need in order to add the skin to the display list), we set a new constant to hold the name of the skin property "graphic", as well as declare a new _skins property and type it as ISkin. Within the draw() method, we use UIObject's getSkin() method to return the class that should be used for the skin. We instantiate an instance of the resulting class and cast it as a DisplayObject so that it may be passed to the addChild() method. Since addChild() returns a reference to the added child, we put that reference directly into the _skin property, but first we must recast to ISkin since that is what _skin expects.

Once the skin has been instantiated and added in this way, we call the setSize(), changeState(), and setStyleFormat() methods so that the new skin can update based on the Block's settings. We just need to add to these methods now so that the values are passed through to the skin.

Add the bold lines to the Block code to finish up the class:

```
private function changeState(pState:String):void {
  _state = pState;
  if (!_initialized) return;
  _skin.changeState(_state);
}

override public function setSize(
  pWidth:Number,
  pHeight:Number
):void {
  super.setSize(pWidth, pHeight);
  if (!_initialized) return;
  _skin.setSize(width, height);
}

override public function setStyleFormat(
  pStyleFormat:StyleFormat
):void {
  super.setStyleFormat(pStyleFormat);
  if (!_initialized) return;
  _skin.styleElements(getStyleFormat());
}
```

As you can see, each of these three methods passes its arguments into the _skin, which we know exists since the _skin must implement ISkin. How a skin might implement the methods is irrelevant to Block. Of course, we cannot pass values through unless the _skin is instantiated, so we must first check that the class has been properly initialized.

That's the class, folks! It's nice seeing that once you have laid the foundation properly, as we did with UIObject, and then taken advantage of inheritance, creating new classes really can be quick and painless. Here we've created a new graphic class that can be used within any visual component, and we kept it around 50 lines of code. So now let's test it out.

A simple skin

Now that we have a UIObject base class and a Block class to handle skin instantiation, we need to create a skin that actually draws something to the display. Many skins we create will contain a common number of methods, so let's create an abstract base class that different skins can inherit from. The purpose of this class will be to save changes that need to be made to the skin (like size or state) and cause the skin to be redrawn on the next screen refresh.

Create a new ActionScript file and save it as Skin.as into the com/foed/graphic/skins directory with ISkin. Add the following code:

```
package com.foed.graphic.skins {

  import flash.display.Sprite;

  import com.foed.graphic.StyleFormat;

  public class Skin extends Sprite implements ISkin {

    protected var _state:String;
    protected var _width:Number;
    protected var _height:Number;
    protected var _styleFormat:StyleFormat;
    protected var _formatChanged:Boolean = true;
    protected var _stateChanged:Boolean = true;
    protected var _sizeChanged:Boolean = true;

    protected function draw():void {
    }

    public function changeState(pState:String):void {
      _stateChanged = _state != pState;
      _state = pState;
      draw();
    }

    public function styleElements(pStyleFormat:StyleFormat):void {
      _formatChanged = true;
      _styleFormat = pStyleFormat;
      draw();
    }

    public function setSize(pWidth:Number, pHeight:Number):void {
      _sizeChanged = (_width != pWidth || _height != pHeight);
      _width = pWidth;
      _height = pHeight;
      draw();
    }

  }

}
```

This class currently contains four methods. changeState(), styleElements(), and setSize() are the three methods required by ISkin. Each of these sets a Boolean flag for _stateChanged, _formatChanged, and _sizeChanged, respectively; saves the values passed to the method; and then calls the draw() method, which is currently empty. By setting these flags, we can have the skin intelligently redraw based on what values have changed. The draw() method will take care of pushing the actual drawing to the next frame so that the redraw only happens once per frame.

Add the bold lines to the file to enable this next frame redraw:

```
package com.foed.graphic.skins {

  import flash.display.Sprite;
  import flash.events.Event;

  import com.foed.graphic.StyleFormat;

  public class Skin extends Sprite implements ISkin {

    protected var _state:String;
    protected var _width:Number;
    protected var _height:Number;
    protected var _styleFormat:StyleFormat;
    protected var _formatChanged:Boolean = true;
    protected var _stateChanged:Boolean = true;
    protected var _sizeChanged:Boolean = true;

    private var _redrawing:Boolean;

    protected function draw():void {
      if (!_redrawing) {
        addEventListener(Event.ENTER_FRAME, drawNextFrame);
      }
      _redrawing = true;
    }

    protected function redraw():void {
      _sizeChanged = false;
      _stateChanged = false;
      _formatChanged = false;
      _redrawing = false;
    }

    private function drawNextFrame(pEvent:Event):void {
      removeEventListener(Event.ENTER_FRAME, drawNextFrame);
      redraw();
    }
```

draw() sets a _redrawing flag so that only the first time this method is called in a frame will the skin be added as a listener to the ENTER_FRAME event. When drawNextFrame() is invoked the next frame, the skin is removed as a listener and the redraw() method is called. In this abstract class, the flags are all reset to false, and it will be up to the concrete classes inheriting from Skin to actually draw their graphics.

For states of the Block and its corresponding skins, we will use strings that correspond to the button states that Flash developers are used to, _Up, _Down, and _Over, but instead of worrying about typos, let's follow the example of the built-in AS3 classes in the Flash Player and define these as constants in a separate class. Create a new ActionScript file and save it as SkinStates.as into the same com/foed/graphic/skins directory as Skin and ISkin. Enter the following code:

```
package com.foed.graphic.skins {

  public class SkinStates {

    public static const UP:String = "_Up";
    public static const DOWN:String = "_Down";
    public static const OVER:String = "_Over";
    public static const DISABLED:String = "_Disabled";

  }

}
```

Now because these are constants defined in this class, we don't have to worry about typos that don't throw errors. Return the Skin class and enter the following bold lines to complete the class:

```
import com.foed.graphic.StyleFormat;
import com.foed.graphic.skins.SkinStates;

public class Skin extends Sprite implements ISkin {

  protected var _state:String;
  protected var _width:Number;
  protected var _height:Number;
  protected var _styleFormat:StyleFormat;
  protected var _formatChanged:Boolean = true;
  protected var _stateChanged:Boolean = true;
  protected var _sizeChanged:Boolean = true;

  private var _redrawing:Boolean;

  public function Skin() {
    _state = SkinStates.UP;
  }

  protected function draw():void {
    if (!_redrawing) {
      addEventListener(Event.ENTER_FRAME, drawNextFrame);
    }
    _redrawing = true;
  }
```

A skin will now default to the UP state unless a new state is passed in by Block.

Of course, Skin gave us an abstract class to house common methods, but that means we will need to build concrete classes that handle the actual drawing. The simplest skin we could create is a class that draws a solid rectangle of a flat color, which we will name SimpleRect. Since Skin takes care of so much, SimpleRect simply needs to take care of the drawing routines.

Create a new ActionScript file and save it into the com/foed/graphic/skins directory as SimpleRect.as. The following is the entirety of the code:

```
package com.foed.graphic.skins {

  public class SimpleRect extends Skin {

    protected function drawFace():void {
      if (_formatChanged || _sizeChanged || _stateChanged) {
        var pColor:uint;
        switch (_state) {
          case SkinStates.OVER:
            pColor = _styleFormat.getProperty("rolloverFace") as uint;
            break;
          case SkinStates.DOWN:
            pColor = _styleFormat.getProperty("selectedFace") as uint;
            break;
          default:
            pColor = _styleFormat.getProperty("face") as uint;
            break;
        }
        graphics.clear();
        graphics.beginFill(pColor, 1);
        graphics.drawRect(0, 0, _width, _height);
        graphics.endFill();
      }
    }

    override protected function redraw():void {
      drawFace();
      super.redraw();
    }

  }

}
```

When redraw() is called before the screen refresh, SimpleRect calls its drawFace() method, which finds the appropriate color value in its StyleFormat based on its current state, and then uses the drawRect() method of the Graphics class to draw a solid rectangle. In this case, if any of the three Boolean flags are true, the skin is redrawn, but in other cases a skin might only need to redraw if its size changes, or if its style changes, or it might need to perform different routines for each.

In this chapter, we have already created UIObject, SkinManager, Block, ISkin, Skin, SkinStates, and SimpleRect, and these work in conjunction with the classes from the last chapter. With these complete, all that is left is to create a document class that pulls these all together to demonstrate how much configurability we have already built in to our framework.

Block party

Now is the time to demonstrate a little bit what we have accomplished thus far with our custom class framework. We will create a document class that creates three Block instances and have the skins, styles, and states all set within the document class, with the Blocks simply redrawing based on these settings. Create a new ActionScript document named BlockTest.as and enter the following code:

```
package {

  import flash.display.Sprite;

  import com.foed.graphic.StyleFormat;
  import com.foed.graphic.skins.SkinStates;
  import com.foed.graphic.skins.SimpleRect;
  import com.foed.managers.SkinManager;
  import com.foed.managers.StyleManager;
  import com.foed.Block;

  public class BlockTest extends Sprite {

    public function BlockTest() {
      init();
    }

    private function init():void {
      createStyles();
      draw();
    }

    private function createStyles():void {
      var pStyleManager:StyleManager = StyleManager.getInstance();

      var pFormat:StyleFormat = new StyleFormat("default");
      pFormat.setProperty("face", 0x999999);
      pFormat.setProperty("rolloverFace", 0xCCCCCC);
      pFormat.setProperty("selectedFace", 0x333333);
      pStyleManager.addStyle("default", pFormat);
    }
```

```
        private function draw():void {
        }

    }

}
```

BlockTest extends Sprite since it will serve as our document class. The constructor calls the init() method, in which we call setStyles() and draw(). setStyles() grabs an instance of the Singleton StyleManager and creates a single StyleFormat instance, setting three color properties (which you may recall match the properties referenced in SimpleRect for the different states). We will fill in draw() next:

```
private function draw():void {
  var pSkins:Object = {};
  pSkins[Block.GRAPHIC] = SimpleRect;
  SkinManager.getInstance().setClassSkins(Block.CLASS, pSkins);

  var pBlock:Block;
  pBlock = new Block();
  pBlock.x = 100;
  pBlock.y = 50;
  pBlock.setSize(100, 50);
  pBlock.initialize();
  addChild(pBlock);

  pBlock = new Block();
  pBlock.x = 100;
  pBlock.y = 150;
  pBlock.state = SkinStates.OVER;
  pBlock.setSize(100, 50);
  pBlock.initialize();
  addChild(pBlock);

  pBlock = new Block();
  pBlock.x = 100;
  pBlock.y = 250;
  pBlock.state = SkinStates.DOWN;
  pBlock.setSize(100, 50);
  pBlock.initialize();
  addChild(pBlock);
}
```

At the beginning of the method, we use the setClassSkins() method of the Singleton SkinManager instance to assign SimpleRect as the skin class to be used for Block's GRAPHIC property. Then, we create three Block instances, leaving the first instance to use its default state while setting a different state for each of the other two.

If you are using Flash, create a new FLA and set BlockTest as the document class in the Property inspector. Make sure that you have the com class directory that we have been using set in the class paths for the FLA. If you are using Flex Builder, create a new ActionScript project and use BlockTest as the main document class, also making sure that the project settings include our com directory in the class path. Test your movie (in either environment), and you should see a result like Figure 16-4.

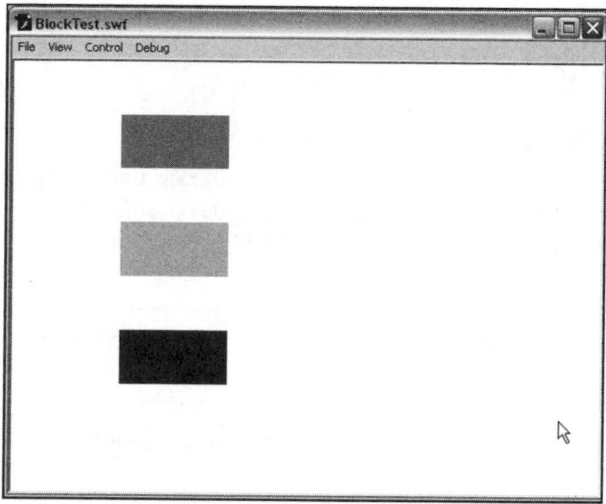

Figure 16-4. BlockTest draws three Block instances, with their skins, styles, and states set in the document class.

Adding interactivity with SimpleButton

OK, so drawing three rectangles of different color doesn't in itself inspire awe. But what we have established will allow for so much ease of configurability as we move into more complex widgets. We'll start off by creating a SimpleButton class that adds interactivity to our framework. This class will include a Block instance to handle all the drawing of skins, and will layer on top of it handlers for standard mouse events.

Create a new ActionScript file and save it as SimpleButton.as into a new directory, com/foed/buttons. Enter the following code to start off the class:

```
package com.foed.buttons {

  import flash.events.MouseEvent;
  import flash.utils.getQualifiedClassName;

  import com.foed.UIObject;

  public class SimpleButton extends UIObject {

    static public const CLASS:String = ➥
getQualifiedClassName(SimpleButton);
```

```
    override protected function init():void {
      super.init();
      _classes.push(SimpleButton.CLASS);
      setEvents();
    }

    override protected function draw():void {
    }

    private function setEvents():void {
      addEventListener(MouseEvent.ROLL_OVER, onRollOver);
      addEventListener(MouseEvent.ROLL_OUT, onRollOut);
      addEventListener(MouseEvent.MOUSE_DOWN, onPress);
    }

    private function onRollOut(pEvent:MouseEvent):void {
    }

    private function onRollOver(pEvent:MouseEvent):void {
    }

    private function onPress(pEvent:MouseEvent):void {
    }

    override public function setSize(
      pWidth:Number,
      pHeight:Number
    ):void {
      super.setSize(pWidth, pHeight);
    }

    override public function setStyleFormat(
      pStyleFormat:StyleFormat
    ):void {
      super.setStyleFormat(pStyleFormat);
    }

  }

}
```

The class begins much like Block did, by overriding the protected init() method and pushing the SimpleButton's class name into the _classes array. It then calls setEvents(), which adds itself as an event listener for when the mouse rolls over, rolls off, or is clicked while over the instance. The handlers for these mouse events are currently empty. Finally, we override the superclass's draw(), setSize(), and setStyleFormat() methods, but do not do much yet other than call the superclass's implementation, at least for the latter two.

Next, let's add the code that will instantiate and add a Block instance to handle the skins in SimpleButton. Add the following bold lines to the SimpleButton.as file:

```
package com.foed.buttons {

  import flash.events.MouseEvent;
  import flash.utils.getQualifiedClassName;

  import com.foed.Block;
  import com.foed.UIObject;
  import com.foed.graphic.StyleFormat;

  public class SimpleButton extends UIObject {

    static public const CLASS:String = ➥
getQualifiedClassName(SimpleButton);
    static public const GRAPHIC:String = "graphic";

    private var _block:Block;

    override protected function init():void {
      super.init();
      _classes.push(SimpleButton.CLASS);
      setEvents();
    }

    override protected function draw():void {
      _block = new Block();
      _block.setSize(width, height);
      _block.setSkin(Block.GRAPHIC, getSkin(GRAPHIC));
      _block.setStyleFormatName(getStyleFormat().name);
      _block.initialize();
      addChild(_block);
    }

    private function setEvents():void {
      addEventListener(MouseEvent.ROLL_OVER, onRollOver);
      addEventListener(MouseEvent.ROLL_OUT, onRollOut);
      addEventListener(MouseEvent.MOUSE_DOWN, onPress);
    }

    private function onRollOut(pEvent:MouseEvent):void {
    }

    private function onRollOver(pEvent:MouseEvent):void {
    }
```

```
    private function onPress(pEvent:MouseEvent):void {
    }

    override public function setSize(
      pWidth:Number,
      pHeight:Number
    ):void {
      super.setSize(pWidth, pHeight);
      if (!_initialized) return;
      _block.setSize(width, height);
    }

    override public function setStyleFormat(
      pStyleFormat:StyleFormat
    ):void {
      super.setStyleFormat(pStyleFormat);
      if (!_initialized) return;
      _block.setStyleFormat(getStyleFormat());
    }

    public function get state():String {
      return _block.state;
    }

    public function set state(pState:String):void {
      _block.state = pState;
    }

  }

}
```

At the top we import the Block class and declare a private property _block to store a reference to a Block instance within SimpleButton. In the draw() method, we instantiate a Block instance, set its size, skin, and style, and then initialize it and add it to the display list. Down in the setSize() and setStyleFormat() methods, we pass the values directly into the Block instance, much as we did within Block for the skin. Finally, we provide getters/setters for the skin state, which we pass directly in or retrieve directly from the Block instance.

To finish up SimpleButton, we need to fill in those mouse event handlers. Add the following bold lines to the SimpleButton class:

```
    private function onRollOut(pEvent:MouseEvent):void {
      if (!pEvent.buttonDown) rollOutButton();
    }
```

```
private function onRollOver(pEvent:MouseEvent):void {
  if (!pEvent.buttonDown) rollOverButton();
}

private function onPress(pEvent:MouseEvent):void {
  stage.addEventListener(MouseEvent.MOUSE_UP, onRelease);
  pressButton();
}

private function onRelease(pEvent:MouseEvent):void {
  stage.removeEventListener(MouseEvent.MOUSE_UP, onRelease);
  if (hitTestPoint(pEvent.stageX, pEvent.stageY)) {
    releaseButton();
  } else {
    releaseOutsideButton();
  }
}

protected function rollOutButton():void {
  state = SkinStates.UP;
}

protected function rollOverButton():void {
  state = SkinStates.OVER;
}

protected function pressButton():void {
  state = SkinStates.DOWN;
}

protected function releaseButton():void {
  dispatchEvent(new MouseEvent(MouseEvent.ROLL_OVER));
}

protected function releaseOutsideButton():void {
  dispatchEvent(new MouseEvent(MouseEvent.ROLL_OUT));
}
```

Building buttons is a bit more complex in AS3 than it was for AS2, so let's look at the preceding code piece by piece so you can fully understand what's going on. First, the handlers `onRollOut()` and `onRollOver()` make sure to call only the `rollOutButton()` and `rollOverButton()` methods, respectively, when the mouse button is not currently depressed. These two methods take care of updating the `_block` state, and the behavior that is expected based on previous versions of Flash is that if you click off of a button and then drag over it, this would not register a `rollOver` event, but a `dragOver` event (which no longer exists, since these cases are now both covered by `rollOver`). The same applies to clicking a button and dragging the mouse off. This now registers a `rollOut` event, though the expected behavior is that a button will remain in the depressed state until the mouse is released. The two conditionals in the onRollOut() and onRollOver() ensure that the behavior of our button will match previous versions of Flash.

Next, the onPress() handler calls a pressButton() method, but before that adds a listener to the stage's MOUSE_UP event. This is because a MOUSE_UP on the button itself will only register if the mouse is over the button when it is released. If the user clicks down on a button, drags off, and then releases, the button will never receive a MOUSE_UP event. For this reason, we instead listen for a MOUSE_UP on the stage itself, which because of event bubbling will occur no matter where the mouse is released.

In the onRelease() handler for the stage's MOUSE_UP, we remove the SimpleButton instance as a listener, and then, by using hitTestPoint(), determine whether the mouse was released over the button (in which case releaseButton() is called) or outside of the button (in which case releaseOutsideButton() is called).

In the rollOutButton(), rollOverButton(), and pressButton(), we set the state of the _block instance based on the event. The releaseButton() dispatches a ROLL_OVER event so that the SimpleButton instance will redraw itself in its rollOver state. releaseOutsideButton() dispatches the ROLL_OUT event.

Be sure to import com.foed.graphic.skins.SkinStates at the top of your class since we utilized its constants in the last bit of code.

We could end our class here, but by adding three more lines of code, we can enable sounds for button events using the SoundManager we built last chapter. First, import the SoundManager at the top of the class:

```
import com.foed.Block;
import com.foed.UIObject;
import com.foed.graphic.skins.SkinStates;
import com.foed.graphic.StyleFormat;
import com.foed.managers.SoundManager;
```

Then, in the rollOverButton() and pressButton() methods, add the following lines:

```
protected function rollOverButton():void {
  state = SkinStates.OVER;
  SoundManager.getInstance().playSound(this, MouseEvent.ROLL_OVER);
}

protected function pressButton():void {
  state = SkinStates.DOWN;
  SoundManager.getInstance().playSound(➥
this, MouseEvent.MOUSE_DOWN);
}
```

Now, we can assign sounds to the SimpleButton class for these two events, and all instances will be able to play them, or we can assign sounds to individual instances. We'll do just that in the next section, when we create another document class to see how our SimpleButton class holds up.

From block to button

We will create a document class to test SimpleButton just as we did for Block. In fact, you can take the BlockTest.as file and resave it as SimpleButtonTest.as. The following bold code is all that you need to change:

```
package {

  import flash.display.Sprite;
  import flash.events.MouseEvent;

  import com.foed.buttons.SimpleButton;
  import com.foed.graphic.StyleFormat;
  import com.foed.graphic.skins.SimpleRect;
  import com.foed.managers.SkinManager;
  import com.foed.managers.SoundManager;
  import com.foed.managers.StyleManager;
  import com.foed.Block;

  public class SimpleButtonTest extends Sprite {

    public function SimpleButtonTest() {
      init();
    }

    private function init():void {
      assignSounds();
      createStyles();
      draw();
    }

    private function assignSounds():void {
      var pSoundManager:SoundManager = SoundManager.getInstance();

      pSoundManager.addSound("kiss", "CLICK2");
      pSoundManager.addSound("click", "CLICK8");

      pSoundManager.registerForSound(SimpleButton.CLASS,➥
"kiss", MouseEvent.ROLL_OVER, .4);
      pSoundManager.registerForSound(SimpleButton.CLASS,➥
"click", MouseEvent.MOUSE_DOWN);
    }

    private function createStyles():void {
      var pStyleManager:StyleManager = StyleManager.getInstance();

      var pFormat:StyleFormat = new StyleFormat("default");
      pFormat.setProperty("face", 0x999999);
      pFormat.setProperty("rolloverFace", 0xCCCCCC);
```

```
      pFormat.setProperty("selectedFace", 0x333333);
      pStyleManager.addStyle("default", pFormat);
    }

    private function draw():void {
      var pSkins:Object = {};
      pSkins[Block.GRAPHIC] = SimpleRect;
      SkinManager.getInstance().setClassSkins(Block.CLASS, pSkins);

      var pBlock:SimpleButton;
      pBlock = new SimpleButton();
      pBlock.x = 100;
      pBlock.y = 50;
      pBlock.setSize(100, 50);
      pBlock.initialize();
      addChild(pBlock);

      pBlock = new SimpleButton();
      pBlock.x = 100;
      pBlock.y = 150;
//      pBlock.state = SkinStates.OVER;
      pBlock.setSize(100, 50);
      pBlock.initialize();
      addChild(pBlock);

      pBlock = new SimpleButton();
      pBlock.x = 100;
      pBlock.y = 250;
//      pBlock.state = SkinStates.DOWN;
      pBlock.setSize(100, 50);
      pBlock.initialize();
      addChild(pBlock);
    }

  }

}
```

Other than swapping SimpleButton for Block and commenting out the state settings, the only addition is the new assignSounds() method, which is called from the init(). This new method adds two sounds to the Singleton SoundManager, and then registers one to the SimpleButton's ROLL_OVER event and the other to the MOUSE_DOWN event.

To test this movie, if you are using Flash, create a new Flash document and set SimpleButtonTest as the document class and make sure to point to the com directory for your ActionScript class path. You will also need to have the CLICK2.mp3 and CLICK8.mp3 files in the same directory as your FLA (these are available in this chapter's download files, as well as the download files from last chapter where you used the same sounds). For Flex Builder, create a new ActionScript project with SimpleButtonTest as the main document class. Make sure that you include the com directory in the project's class path, and that the two MP3 files are in the project's bin directory.

Test your file, and you should see a result like Figure 16-5, which is similar to the Block test, but now rolling over and off the rectangles, and clicking and releasing, will cause the states to change and sounds to be heard. See how it's all starting to come together?

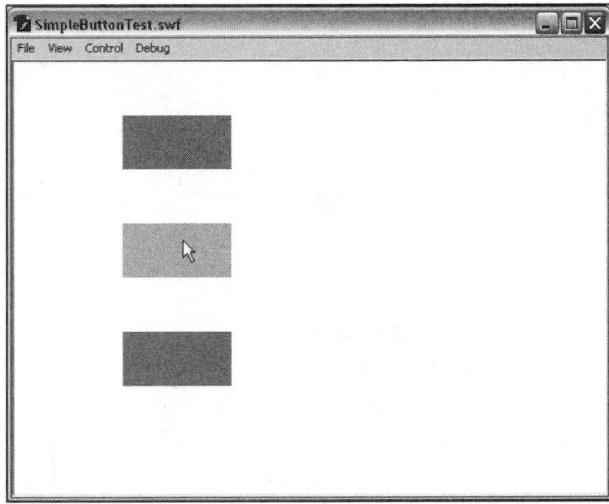

Figure 16-5. SimpleButtonTest showing user interaction with our components

Mapping out some new classes

Well, we have a whole slew of classes now serving as the foundation for a component framework. Before this chapter is complete, I want to tie in the last manager that we created in the last chapter, LabelManager, and show how that might interact with the classes we have created. To that purpose, let's spend a little time mapping out two new classes that we will develop to tie everything together, Label and LabelButton.

Label

A label is one of the simplest controls you can have in an application, but we can offer a degree of configurability and control that will make it so much more useful than a simple text field. For our demonstration here, we will create a Label that draws itself based on our current styling system and offers nine different alignment permutations. In addition, we will plug our Label component into last chapter's LabelManager so that the language for the text might be swapped out easily without any additional coding in the application.

Figure 16-6 shows the UML diagram for the class. _vAlign and _hAlign will hold values for the alignment, and we'll provide implicit getter/setters for these values, along with getter/setters for the private _text property. setTextFormat() will apply a TextFormat instance to the text. Private methods will include a positionLabel() for positioning and a makeLabel() to create the text field used, which will be stored in the private property _field. addText() will be the method used to add the text string to a label, which may be called when text changes or when the LabelManager loads labels from an external file, at which point onLabelsLoaded() would be called.

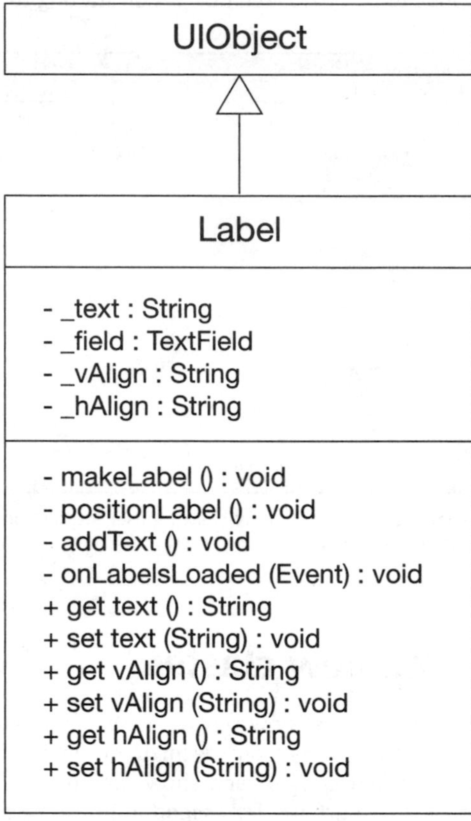

Figure 16-6. The UML diagram for the Label class

LabelButton

LabelButton will add label functionality to our SimpleButton class. The only new methods that will be needed are implicit getter/setters for _vAlign, _hAlign, and _labelText. _label will hold a reference to a Label instance. There will be additional methods to override from the superclass, but we will leave the diagram to display only the additions to the methods (see Figure 16-7).

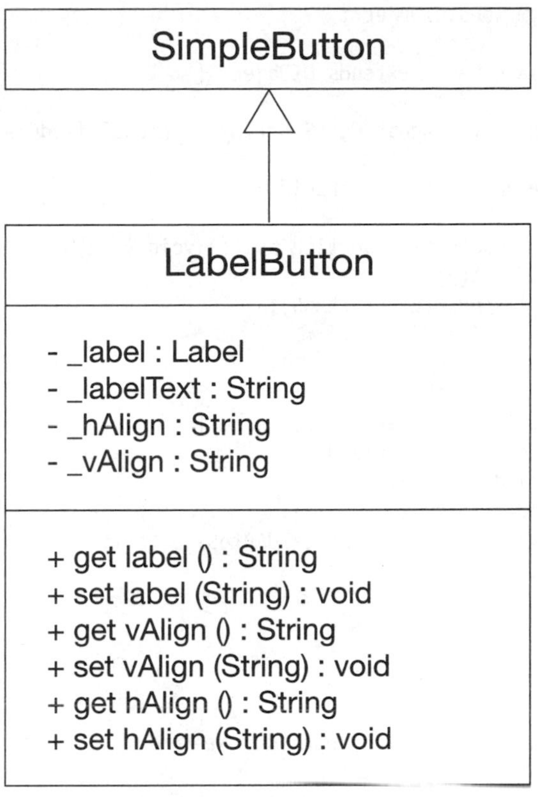

Figure 16-7. The UML diagram for the LabelButton class

So much more than a text field

Believe it or not, the Label class has more code than many of the classes we've already coded. The code in itself is not terribly complex, in fact you will recognize a bit of it from last chapter's LabelEllipse, but there are a number of things that need to occur in order to draw and style a text field and position it properly, not to mention tie it in with the LabelManager. Let's begin with the bare bones.

Create a new ActionScript class and save it as Label.as into a new com/foed/text directory. Add the following code:

```
package com.foed.text {

  import flash.text.TextField;
  import flash.text.TextFieldAutoSize;
  import flash.utils.getQualifiedClassName;
```

```
    import com.foed.UIObject;

    public class Label extends UIObject {

      private static const CLASS:String = getQualifiedClassName(Label);

      private var _field:TextField;

      override protected function init():void {
        super.init();
        _classes.push(Label.CLASS);
        makeLabel();
      }

      private function makeLabel():void {
        _field = new TextField();
        addChild(_field);
        _field.selectable = false;
        _field.autoSize = TextFieldAutoSize.LEFT;
      }

    }

  }
```

At this point, we have a similar init() method as we've seen with Block and SimpleButton, with the super's init() being called, and then the class name being pushed into the _classes array. Next, makeLabel() is called, in which a field is created and added to the display list, with its selectable and autoSize properties set.

Before we look at positioning of the field within the component, it makes sense for us to define some constants for alignment in another class, just as we did with SkinStates earlier this chapter. Take a moment and create a new ActionScript file and save it as Alignment.as into the com/foed directory. The complete code follows:

```
package com.foed {

  public class Alignment {

    public static const LEFT:String = "left";
    public static const CENTER:String = "center";
    public static const RIGHT:String = "right";
    public static const TOP:String = "top";
    public static const MIDDLE:String = "middle";
    public static const BOTTOM:String = "bottom";

  }

}
```

With these constants defined, we can add the alignment properties to the Label class. Return to Label.as and add the following bold lines:

```
package com.foed.text {

  import flash.text.TextField;
  import flash.text.TextFieldAutoSize;
  import flash.utils.getQualifiedClassName;

  import com.foed.Alignment;
  import com.foed.UIObject;

  public class Label extends UIObject {

    private static const CLASS:String = getQualifiedClassName(Label);

    private var _field:TextField;
    private var _vAlign:String;
    private var _hAlign:String;

    override protected function init():void {
      super.init();
      _classes.push(Label.CLASS);
      _vAlign = Alignment.TOP;
      _hAlign = Alignment.LEFT;
      makeLabel();
    }

    private function makeLabel():void {
      _field = new TextField();
      addChild(_field);
      _field.selectable = false;
      _field.autoSize = TextFieldAutoSize.LEFT;
    }

    private function positionLabel():void {
      switch (_vAlign) {
        case Alignment.BOTTOM:
          _field.y = (height - _field.height)|0;
          break;
        case Alignment.MIDDLE:
          _field.y = ((height - _field.height)/2)|0;
          break;
        default:
          _field.y = 0;
      }
      switch (_hAlign) {
        case Alignment.RIGHT:
          _field.x = (width - _field.width)|0;
```

```
          break;
        case Alignment.CENTER:
          _field.x = ((width - _field.width)/2)|0;
          break;
        default:
          _field.x = 0;
      }
    }

    public function get vAlign():String {
      return _vAlign;
    }

    public function set vAlign(pAlign:String):void {
      _vAlign = pAlign;
      if (_initialized) positionLabel();
    }

    public function get hAlign():String {
      return _hAlign;
    }

    public function set hAlign(pAlign:String):void {
      _hAlign = pAlign;
      if (_initialized) positionLabel();
    }

  }

}
```

We initialize the _hAlign and _vAlign properties in the init() method to default values that can then be overridden. At the bottom of the code are the getter/setters for these properties, with the setters calling positionLabel() if the component is initialized. positionLabel() aligns first vertically, and then horizontally, calculating position based on the size of the text field in relation with the size of the component. The |0 added to the end of each positioning line is a bitwise OR operation that works the same as a call to Math.floor(), but one that I've found worked slightly faster in previous versions of Flash.

Of course, the most important aspect of Label is the text displayed, so it's time we add that piece. These methods are similar to ones we coded in LabelEllipse in the last chapter. Add the following lines to the Label definition:

```
    private function addText():void {
      _field.text = LabelManager.getInstance().getLabel(_text);
      positionLabel();
    }
```

```
    private function onLabelsLoaded(pEvent:Event):void {
      LabelManager.getInstance().removeEventListener(➥
Event.COMPLETE, onLabelsLoaded);
      addText();
    }

    public function get text():String {
      return _text;
    }

    public function set text(pText:String):void {
      _text = pText;
      if (!_initialized) return;
      var pLabelManager:LabelManager = LabelManager.getInstance();
      if (pLabelManager.ready) {
        addText();
      } else {
        pLabelManager.addEventListener(Event.COMPLETE, onLabelsLoaded);
      }
    }
```

And to allow for the classes and properties used previously, add these bold lines to the top of the file:

```
  import flash.events.Event;
  import flash.text.TextField;
  import flash.text.TextFieldAutoSize;
  import flash.utils.getQualifiedClassName;

  import com.foed.Alignment;
  import com.foed.UIObject;
  import com.foed.managers.LabelManager;

  public class Label extends UIObject {

    private static const CLASS:String = getQualifiedClassName(Label);

    private var _text:String;
    private var _field:TextField;
    private var _vAlign:String;
    private var _hAlign:String;
```

When text is set for a Label instance, the first thing that occurs is the _text property is set. Then, if the component is initialized, the LabelManager is checked to see whether it has labels loaded and ready. If so, addText() is immediately called. If not, the Label instance is added as a listener for the LabelManager's COMPLETE event. The handler for this event is onLabelsLoaded(), which in turn calls addText(). The result of all of this is that addText() is called once labels are loaded and ready in the LabelManager, whether this occurred immediately, or after a delay when the labels are loaded. addText() adds the appropriate text string as returned by the LabelManager, and then repositions itself.

Just as we did with Block and SimpleButton, we'll have to override some UIObject methods for sizing and restyling, since we will need to apply these settings to the text field as well. Add these lines to the Label class:

```
override public function setSize(
  pWidth:Number,
  pHeight:Number
):void {
  super.setSize(pWidth, pHeight);
  if (_initialized) positionLabel();
}

override public function setStyleFormat(
  pStyleFormat:StyleFormat
):void {
  super.setStyleFormat(pStyleFormat);
  if (_initialized) draw();
}

public function setTextFormat(
  pNewFormat:TextFormat,
  pBeginIndex:Number=-1,
  pEndIndex:Number=-1
):void {
  if (!_initialized) return;
  _field.setTextFormat(pNewFormat, pBeginIndex, pEndIndex);
  _field.defaultTextFormat = pNewFormat;
  if (_text.length > 0) positionLabel();
}
```

We override both setSize() and setStyleFormat() and, if the component is initialized, call positionLabel() and draw(), respectively. We will need to override draw() as well in the next step since the superclass's draw() method is actually an empty implementation.

setTextFormat() allows for a TextFormat to be passed to the instance to be used, but only if the component has been initialized. If so, setTextFormat() and defaultTextFormat are called on the text field and positionLabel() is called again as well, since a restyling of the text would undoubtedly require a repositioning of the field.

Since StyleFormat is used in the preceding code, make sure to import com.foed.graphic.StyleFormat at the top of your class. You will also need to import flash.text.TextFormat since that is used as well.

There are only two methods left for our Label to be complete. Add the following lines to your class:

```
override public function initialize():void {
  super.initialize();
  if (_text != null) text = _text;
}
```

```
    override protected function draw():void {
      _field.embedFonts = getStyleFormat().getProperty(➥
"embedFonts") as Boolean;
      setTextFormat(getStyleFormat().getProperty(➥
"textFormat") as TextFormat);
    }
```

Here we override the UIObject's initialize() method so that once the component is initialized, the text, if any, can be applied to the field. In the draw() method, which we also override from the superclass, we set whether the text field should use embedded fonts by looking at a property in the StyleFormat instance. If we do not set this to true through the StyleFormat, Flash will use system fonts for the text field. Then, we call setTextFormat() to apply the necessary TextFormat to the text field, looking to the StyleFormat instance in this case as well for a textFormat property value.

Lots of code there, but a pretty powerful label in the end, allowing for centralized styling, easy localization, and multiple alignment options. Let's create a test class to see how it's all working.

Slapping on a label

We will create a document class similar to the SimpleButtonTest and BlockTest classes in the previous sections in order to test our code. Create a new ActionScript file, and add the following, saving the result as LabelTest.as:

```
package {

  import flash.display.Sprite;
  import flash.text.TextFormat;

  import com.foed.Alignment;
  import com.foed.graphic.StyleFormat;
  import com.foed.managers.StyleManager;
  import com.foed.text.Label;

  public class LabelTest extends Sprite {

    public function LabelTest() {
      init();
    }

    private function init():void {
      createStyles();
      draw();
    }

    private function createStyles():void {
      var pStyleManager:StyleManager = StyleManager.getInstance();
```

```
      var pFormat:StyleFormat = new StyleFormat("default");
      pFormat.setProperty("textFormat", new TextFormat("Arial", 14));
      pFormat.setProperty("embedFonts", true);
      pStyleManager.addStyle("default", pFormat);

      pFormat = new StyleFormat("redLabel");
      pFormat.setProperty("textFormat", new TextFormat(➥
"Times New Roman", 20, 0xFF0000));
      pFormat.setProperty("embedFonts", true);
      pStyleManager.addStyle("redLabel", pFormat);
    }

    private function draw():void {
      var pLabel:Label;
      pLabel = new Label();
      pLabel.x = 100;
      pLabel.y = 50;
      pLabel.text = "one";
      pLabel.setSize(100, 50);
      pLabel.initialize();
      addChild(pLabel);

      pLabel = new Label();
      pLabel.x = 100;
      pLabel.y = 150;
      pLabel.text = "two";
      pLabel.setSize(100, 50);
      pLabel.hAlign = Alignment.RIGHT;
      pLabel.vAlign = Alignment.BOTTOM;
      pLabel.setStyleFormatName("redLabel");
      pLabel.initialize();
      addChild(pLabel);

      pLabel = new Label();
      pLabel.x = 100;
      pLabel.y = 250;
      pLabel.text = "three";
      pLabel.setSize(100, 50);
      pLabel.hAlign = Alignment.CENTER;
      pLabel.vAlign = Alignment.MIDDLE;
      pLabel.initialize();
      addChild(pLabel);

      graphics.lineStyle(1);
      graphics.drawRect(100, 50, 100, 50);
      graphics.drawRect(100, 150, 100, 50);
      graphics.drawRect(100, 250, 100, 50);
    }

  }

}
```

Once again, we have our init() call a createStyles() and draw() method. In createStyles(), we create two StyleFormat instances and add them to the StyleManager Singleton. Each instance has only a single style property, textFormat, in which we place a different TextFormat instance.

In the draw() method, we create three Label instances and assign a different text string and alignment to each. After we create these instances, we draw three rectangles to demonstrate how the alignment works with each label's space.

To test your file in the Flash IDE, you will need to create a new Flash document and save it into the same directory as the LabelTest class. Use the Properties panel to set LabelTest as the FLA's document class. Make sure that the com directory we have been using for our classes is included in the FLA's ActionScript class path. Next you will need to embed a font in the FLA, exporting it from the Library as a symbol in the standard way. Open the Library (Window ➤ Library) and use the drop-down menu in the upper right of the panel to add a new font. Set Arial as the name and navigate to Arial in the font drop-down list. Click OK, and then right-click the Arial font symbol in the Library and select Linkage. In the dialog box that opens, select Export for ActionScript and accept the default settings in the fields by clicking OK. Now repeat the process to embed Times New Roman as well. Finally, you will need to make sure the language XML files that were used last chapter (and are also available with this chapter's download files) are in the same directory as our FLA.

To test your file in Flex Builder, create a new ActionScript project and point to LabelTest as your main document class. Make sure that the com directory for classes is included in the class paths for your project. To embed a font, add the following lines to LabelTest:

```
    [Embed(source="arial.ttf", fontName="Arial",➥
mimeType-"application/x font")]
    public var ArialFont:Class;
    [Embed(source="times.ttf", fontName="Times New Roman",➥
mimeType="application/x-font")]
    public var TimesFont:Class;
```

You will have to find the necessary font files on your system (for Windows users, they can be found in c:\windows\fonts) and place the files in your project's root directory. Also make sure that you have the language XML files in your bin directory (available in either this or last chapter's download files) and that the two font files are in the same directory as your main class.

If you test your movie in either application, the result should be something like that shown in Figure 16-8, with labels aligning in each of their individual spaces and the middle label taking on the redFormat StyleFormat.

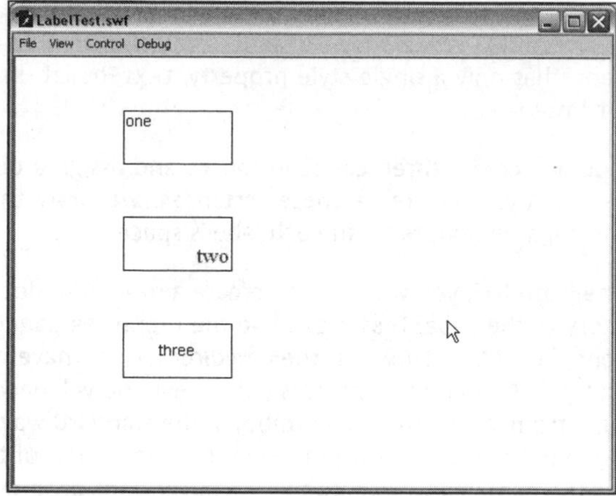

Figure 16-8. Label instances aligning and styling

Putting it all together

We have our base UIObject, we have our graphic Block, we have a SimpleButton, and we have a Label. We have managers to handle skins, styles, sounds, and labels, and a number of supporting classes and interfaces. Now is the time to put every single piece together and see how it all works as a unit so we can truly call it (the beginnings of) a framework.

In this last section, we will extend SimpleButton to create LabelButton, adding (as you might suspect) labels to our interactive buttons. These widgets will be passed keys for labels for which to retrieve values from LabelManager. They will be skinned and styled using SkinManager and StyleManager, respectively, with a class implementing ISkin and extending Skin handling all the drawing, and a StyleFormat holding all TextFormat and color information for the skin. Clicking one of these buttons will produce a sound, as managed by our SoundManager. All in all, we will utilize all of the classes we have explored in this and the last chapter to create a simple application that demonstrates the interaction of classes in an OOP framework.

LabelButton

LabelButton takes most of its functionality from its superclass, SimpleButton. As such, we only need a number of new public methods that allow the setting of values for a label. Create a new ActionScript file and save it as LabelButton.as into the com/foed/buttons directory with SimpleButton.as. Let's start with the following code:

```
package com.foed.buttons {

  import flash.utils.getQualifiedClassName;

  import com.foed.Alignment;
  import com.foed.text.Label;

  public class LabelButton extends SimpleButton {

    static public const CLASS:String = ➥
getQualifiedClassName(LabelButton);

    private var _label:Label;
    private var _labelText:String;
    private var _hAlign:String;
    private var _vAlign:String;

    override protected function init():void {
      super.init();
      _classes.push(LabelButton.CLASS);
      _vAlign = Alignment.MIDDLE;
      _hAlign = Alignment.CENTER;
    }

    override protected function draw():void {
      super.draw();
      _label = new Label();
      _label.hAlign = _hAlign;
      _label.vAlign = _vAlign;
      _label.setSize(width, height);
      _label.setStyleFormatName(getStyleFormat().name);
      _label.text = _labelText;
      _label.initialize();
      addChild(_label);
    }

  }

}
```

Here, the init() method hold no surprises, with the superclass's init() first being called, the class name being pushed into the _classes array, and then alignment settings getting their defaults. We then override SimpleButton's draw() method, which you may recall takes care of creating a Block instance, invoke the super's method so that it may still create the Block instance, create a Label instance, and add it to the display list after giving it values and initializing it.

Next we add the methods needed to set the new properties for our class. Add these to the body of LabelButton:

```
public function get label():String {
  return _labelText;
}

public function set label(pLabel:String):void {
  _labelText = pLabel;
  if (_initialized) _label.text = _labelText;
}

public function get hAlign():String {
  return _hAlign;
}

public function set hAlign(pAlign:String):void {
  _hAlign = pAlign;
  if (_initialized) _label.hAlign = _hAlign;
}

public function get vAlign():String {
  return _vAlign;
}

public function set vAlign(pAlign:String):void {
  _vAlign = pAlign;
  if (_initialized) _label.vAlign = _vAlign;
}
```

We provide getter/setters for hAlign, vAlign, and label (the latter sets and retrieves the private _labelText property). For the setters, if the component has been initialized, the values are also passed to the Label instance.

Finish the LabelButton class off with the following methods, overridden from the superclass:

```
override protected function rollOutButton():void {
  super.rollOutButton();
  _label.setTextFormat(getStyleFormat().➥
getProperty("textFormat") as TextFormat);
}

override protected function rollOverButton():void {
  super.rollOverButton();
  _label.setTextFormat(getStyleFormat().➥
getProperty("rolloverTextFormat") as TextFormat);
}
```

```
    override protected function pressButton():void {
      super.pressButton();
      _label.setTextFormat(getStyleFormat().➥
getProperty("selectedTextFormat") as TextFormat);
    }

    override public function setSize(
      pWidth:Number,
      pHeight:Number
    ):void {
      super.setSize(pWidth, pHeight);
      if (!_initialized) return;
      _label.setSize(width, height);
    }

    override public function setStyleFormat(
      pStyleFormat:StyleFormat
    ):void {
      super.setStyleFormat(pStyleFormat);
      if (!_initialized) return;
      _label.setStyleFormat(getStyleFormat());
    }
```

For the mouse event handlers, we want to change the Label instance's TextFormat based on the event, so that the text color can change on rollover, rollout, and click. We can use Label's setTextFormat() and pass a value retrieved from the LabelButton instance's StyleFormat, making sure to cast the result as a TextFormat as required by setTextFormat(). setSize() and setStyleFormat() both pass values on to the Label instance if the component has been initialized.

To complete the class, you will need to add the newly referenced classes at the top in the import statements. Add the bold lines to your file:

```
package com.foed.buttons {

  import flash.text.TextFormat;

  import com.foed.Alignment;
  import com.foed.text.Label;
  import com.foed.graphic.StyleFormat;

  public class LabelButton extends SimpleButton {
```

Since Label and SimpleButton take care of most of the functionality we need, this class was a relatively painless addition. You will find that if you have created a strong foundation and modularity to your classes, adding new classes is quick work.

Not-so-SimpleRect

We have been using a SimpleRect skin in our tests thus far, but with the work that we've done to enable skinning, creating a new, much more interesting skin is a piece of cake. In fact, here's all the code for a new beveled, gradient, rounded rectangle skin given to you in one fell swoop. Add this class to your com/foed/graphic/skins directory as BeveledGradientRoundedRect.as (yep, that pretty much describes it!):

```
package com.foed.graphic.skins {

  import flash.display.GradientType;
  import flash.filters.BevelFilter;
  import flash.geom.Matrix;

  public class BeveledGradientRoundedRect extends Skin {

    protected function drawFace():void {
      if (_formatChanged || _sizeChanged || _stateChanged) {
        var pColors:Array;
        switch (_state) {
          case SkinStates.OVER:
            pColors = _styleFormat.getProperty("rolloverFace")➥
as Array;
            filters = [new BevelFilter(4)];
            break;
          case SkinStates.DOWN:
            pColors = _styleFormat.getProperty("selectedFace")➥
as Array;
            filters = [new BevelFilter(4, 235)];
            break;
          default:
            pColors = _styleFormat.getProperty("face") as Array;
            filters = [new BevelFilter(4)];
            break;
        }
        var pAlphas:Array = _styleFormat.getProperty("faceAlpha")➥
as Array;
        var pRatios:Array = _styleFormat.getProperty("faceRatios")➥
as Array;
        var pRotation:Number =➥
_styleFormat.getProperty("faceRotation") as Number;
        var pMatrix:Matrix = new Matrix();
        pMatrix.createGradientBox(_width, _height, pRotation);
        graphics.clear();
        graphics.beginGradientFill(GradientType.LINEAR,➥
pColors, pAlphas, pRatios, pMatrix);
        graphics.drawRoundRect(0, 0, _width, _height, 15);
        graphics.endFill()
      }
    }
```

```
    override protected function redraw():void {
      drawFace();
      super.redraw();
    }

  }

}
```

When redraw() is called by the superclass, Skin, this class calls its drawFace() method. Within drawFace(), the local variable pColors is filled with an array value retrieved from the StyleFormat instance based on the current state of the skin. A BevelFilter is applied for the OVER and default states to give a raised look, while the DOWN state gets a depressed look. Additional values for alphas, ratios, and rotation are also retrieved from the StyleFormat instance, and then all of these values are used to draw a rounded rectangle with a gradient fill. All pretty much handled in a single method.

Final test

To tie it all together, we need a new document class. Since so much of this class is similar to the SimpleButtonTest.as file we created earlier this chapter, you can take that file and resave it as LabelButtonTest.as and make the following changes in bold:

```
package {

  import flash.display.Sprite;
  import flash.events.MouseEvent;
  import flash.text.TextFormat;

  import com.foed.buttons.SimpleButton;
  import com.foed.buttons.LabelButton;
  import com.foed.graphic.StyleFormat;
  import com.foed.graphic.skins.BeveledGradientRoundedRect;
  import com.foed.managers.SkinManager;
  import com.foed.managers.SoundManager;
  import com.foed.managers.StyleManager;
  import com.foed.Block;

  public class LabelButtonTest extends Sprite {

    public function LabelButtonTest() {
      init();
    }

    private function init():void {
      assignSounds();
      createStyles();
      draw();
    }
```

```
    private function assignSounds():void {
      var pSoundManager:SoundManager = SoundManager.getInstance();

      pSoundManager.addSound("kiss", "CLICK2");
      pSoundManager.addSound("click", "CLICK8");

      pSoundManager.registerForSound(SimpleButton.CLASS,➥
"kiss", MouseEvent.ROLL_OVER, .4);
      pSoundManager.registerForSound(SimpleButton.CLASS,➥
"click", MouseEvent.MOUSE_DOWN);
    }

    private function createStyles():void {
      var pStyleManager:StyleManager = StyleManager.getInstance();

      var pFormat:StyleFormat = new StyleFormat("default");
      pFormat.setProperty("face", [0x999999, 0xAAAAAA, 0x999999]);
      pFormat.setProperty("rolloverFace",➥
[0xCCCCCC, 0xFFFFFF, 0xCCCCCC]);
      pFormat.setProperty("selectedFace",➥
[0x333333, 0x454545, 0x333333]);
      pFormat.setProperty("faceAlpha", [1, 1, 1]);
      pFormat.setProperty("faceRatios", [50, 100, 150]);
      pFormat.setProperty("faceRotation", Math.PI/2);
      pFormat.setProperty("textFormat",➥
new TextFormat("Arial", 18, 0x333333));
      pFormat.setProperty("rolloverTextFormat",➥
new TextFormat("Arial", 18, 0x000000));
      pFormat.setProperty("selectedTextFormat",➥
new TextFormat("Arial", 18, 0xCCCCCC));
      pFormat.setProperty("embedFonts", true);
      pStyleManager.addStyle("default", pFormat);
    }

    private function draw():void {
      var pSkins:Object = {};
      pSkins[Block.GRAPHIC] = BeveledGradientRoundedRect;
      SkinManager.getInstance().setClassSkins(Block.CLASS, pSkins);

      var pBlock:LabelButton;
      pBlock = new LabelButton();
      pBlock.x = 100;
      pBlock.y = 50;
      pBlock.setSize(100, 50);
      pBlock.label = "one";
      pBlock.initialize();
      addChild(pBlock);
```

```
            pBlock = new LabelButton();
            pBlock.x = 100;
            pBlock.y = 150;
            pBlock.setSize(100, 50);
//          pBlock.state = SkinStates.OVER;
            pBlock.label = "two";
            pBlock.initialize();
            addChild(pBlock);

            pBlock = new LabelButton();
            pBlock.x = 100;
            pBlock.y = 250;
//          pBlock.state = SkinStates.DOWN;
            pBlock.setSize(100, 50);
            pBlock.label = "three";
            pBlock.initialize();
            addChild(pBlock);
        }

    }

}
```

The changes we have made here are primarily to create a new style, assign a new skin, and change the class we are instantiating. The StyleFormat instance we create now has arrays passed as values for its color properties, since that is what our gradient skin requires. We also include TextFormat properties for the three different button states.

To test this movie, you will need to embed the font Arial into your movie. Follow the steps from the last section on the Label component test to embed the font in either the Flash IDE or in your class using Flex Builder. You will also need to make sure the languages XML and MP3 files are in the same directory as your LabelButtonTest.fla (Flash) or your bin directory (Flex Builder). Then test your movie. The result should look like Figure 16-9.

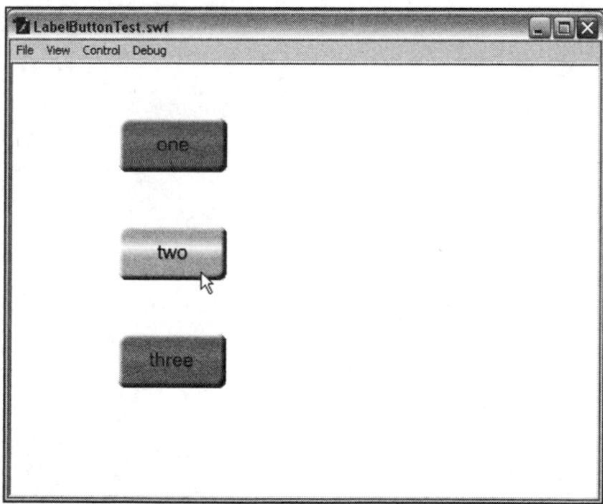

Figure 16-9. The LabelButton instances in all their glory!

Make sure to click the buttons to see the state changes and hear the sounds. Then try swapping fonts, languages, colors, or sounds to see how easy it is to manage changes to the application. Try creating a new skin, perhaps an ellipse that glows on rollover, to test how quickly an interface might be reskinned with a different look and feel. The steps we have taken in this chapter and the last have produced a group of classes that already give you a remarkable level of configurability and modularity, developed with an OOP mindset to keep objects and responsibilities separate and encapsulated, taking advantage of established design patterns (Singleton, Observer), and using class inheritance to our advantage and interfaces to establish common methods for interaction. How's that for applying lessons learned in previous chapters?

What's next?

Well, that was a pretty full chapter! We've covered developing UI components from humble diagrams through to skinnable, stylable, configurable, broadcasting (both events and sound!), full-fledged widgets. Building on the knowledge from throughout this book, we've applied practical OOP to create a basic framework for developing an entire component library, separating function from the visuals as much as possible. Although in the end a simple button with a label might seem a small prize at the completion of so much work, realize that this merely demonstrates the process now by which all other visual widgets may be developed. With all of the hard work already completed, building visual widgets of any complexity is made that much easier. Abstract where you can (does a button need to know how it's colored or what sounds it makes?), and the work can be broken up into smaller pieces—much more easier to deal with than the whole.

We spent this chapter developing UI components that are themselves elements in the display list. In the next chapter, we explore classes that don't have a visual component, but instead alter the visuals of `DisplayObjects` using effects and image manipulation available through ActionScript. There are so many great graphic capabilities, and we'll use OOP to help organize and manage these capabilities so we may more easily apply them to great effect (and great fun!).

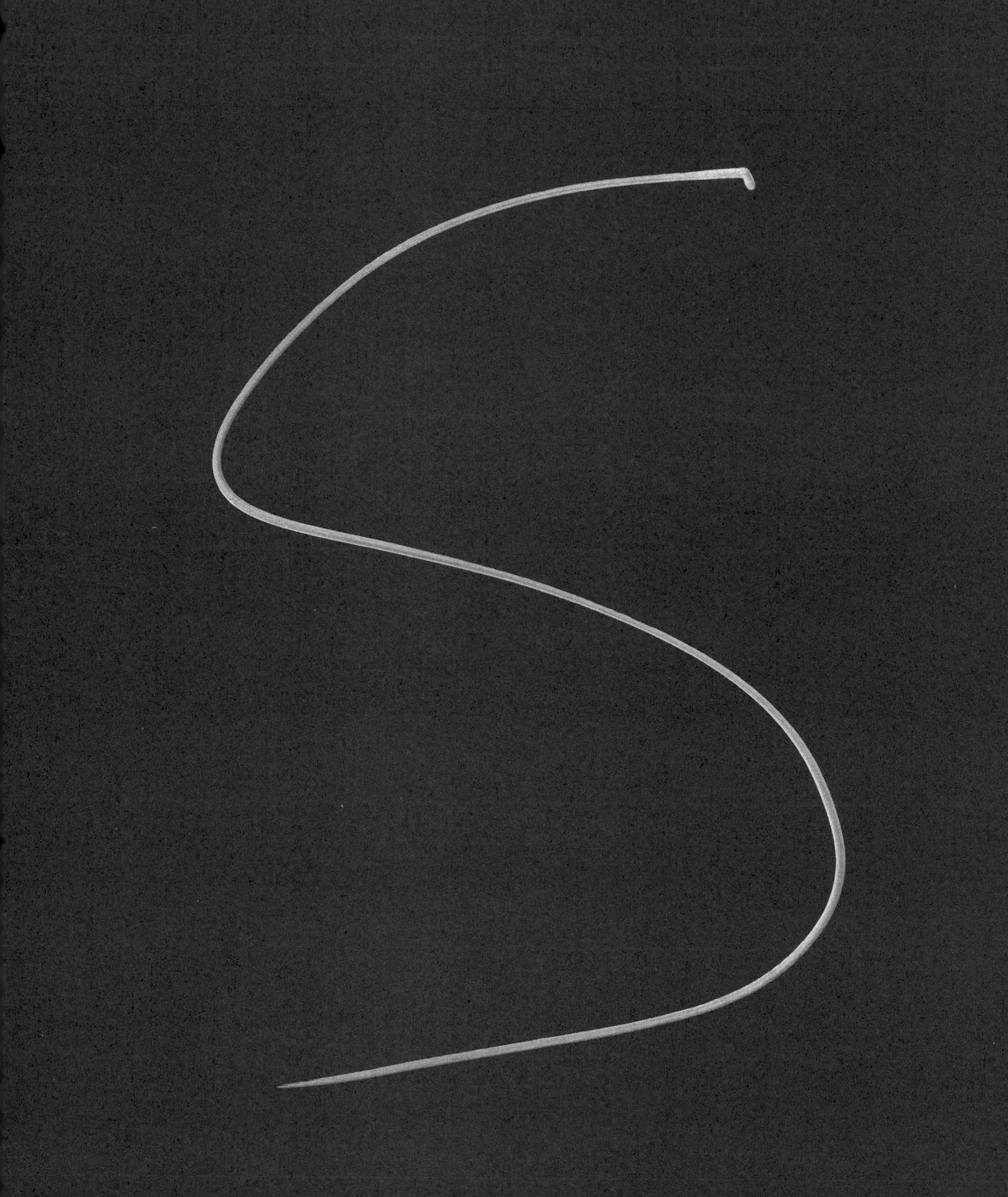

17 OOP ANIMATION AND EFFECTS

The original purpose of Flash was animation. Using the timelines, animators either drew frame-by-frame graphics to simulate motion or used Flash's tweening capabilities to create animation between keyframes. With the addition of ActionScript, animation did not go out the window. In fact, ActionScript proved to be just another tool, like the timeline, that developers could use to create animation. By altering visual properties of movie clips through code, fluid and complex animation could be created without timelines. But how exactly can we apply OOP to this process of animation in order to make it easier, more modular, and more manageable?

The first thing to consider is that in the case of animation classes, most likely these classes won't themselves be visible, but will instead handle the animation of other visual objects. For instance, a sprite class that can tween its position would be extremely useful, but more useful would be a class outside of that sprite class that could handle the tweening animation. This tweening class could then be applied to other objects as well, not just the single sprite class. If we think of these animation classes as handling animation as opposed to visually animating themselves, we can focus in on the useful pieces that would comprise such classes.

Events being fired when an animation begins, is occurring, or ends would be the most important feature, and this can be handled using the built-in `EventDispatcher`. This could serve as the base class for all of our animation classes. Generally, if we have a class that can broadcast when it's animating and we can pass that class a reference to a display object that we wish to animate, we have the basis for any animation class. How the class handles the animation of the sprite through some looping mechanism like a `Timer` would be up to each animation class individually.

In this chapter, we'll explore a number of different classes to control the animation of display objects in an object-oriented manner, playing a bit with the functionality of filters and bitmap manipulation. Making a break from the process of previous chapters, we'll dive right into the code without spending too much time in the planning stages here in the text. Instead, I'll present the UML diagram for the classes we will be creating for you to examine. Have a look at Figures 17-1 and 17-2, and when you are comfortable with the structure, fire up your application of choice.

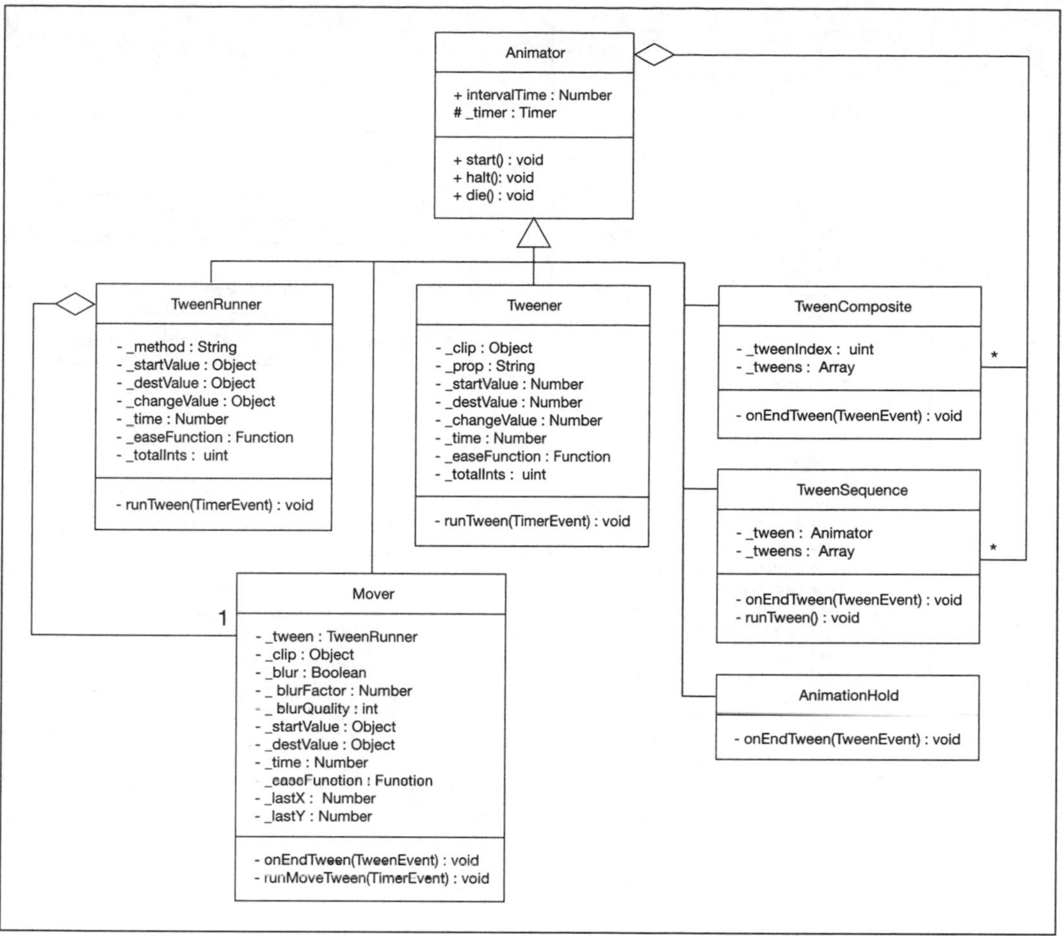

Figure 17-1. The class diagrams for the tweening classes presented in this chapter

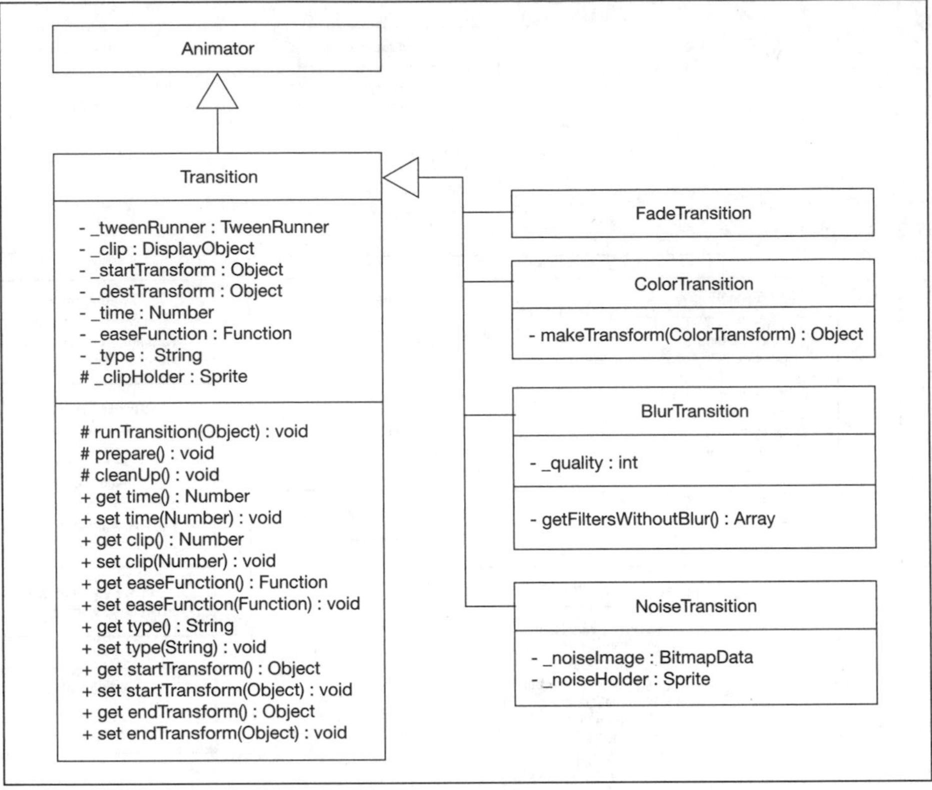

Figure 17-2. The class diagrams for the transition classes presented in this chapter

Preparing for animation

The base class of the animators we create will use `EventDispatcher` in order to broadcast events to listeners detailing when an animation begins, is occurring, and ends. As we won't know any additional information about the type of animation in this superclass, there won't be too much code we need to add.

Animator

Create a new ActionScript file in Flash, Flex Builder, or your text editor and save it as `Animator.as` into a new `com/foed/animation` directory. Add these lines, which will be the entirety of our class:

```
package com.foed.animation {

  import flash.events.EventDispatcher;
  import flash.utils.Timer;
```

```
  public class Animator extends EventDispatcher {

    public static var intervalTime:Number = 30;
    protected var _timer:Timer;

    override public function addEventListener(
      pType:String,
      pListener:Function,
      pUseCapture:Boolean=false,
      pPriority:int=0,
      pUseWeakReference:Boolean=true
    ):void {
      super.addEventListener(pType, pListener, pUseCapture,➥
pPriority, pUseWeakReference);
    }

    public function start():void {}

    public function halt():void {}

    public function die():void {
      halt();
      _timer = null;
    }

  }

}
```


As I said, there's not much to add to this class on top of the EventDispatcher functionality. You can see from the code that it simply inherits from EventDispatcher and then overrides the addEventListener() so that useWeakReference can be set by default to true, as we did for UIObject in the last chapter. Three other methods exist within this class, but two of them, start() and halt(), are empty. The third, die(), acts as a manual destructor, calling halt() and then setting an instance property to null to clean up the class before it is removed.

Two properties are also included. The first, intervalTime, is a static property that holds the number of milliseconds between timer calls. The second, _timer, is an instance property that stores a reference to a Timer that will be running on that interval. This Timer instance is what will be used to alter values over time.

This class is another example of an abstract class like we saw in the last chapter with UIObject and Skin. Like those classes, an Animator should never be instantiated directly, but only through concrete child classes derived from Animator. The functionality is almost so limited that we could have used an interface to define the Animator methods, but since we wanted to override the addEventListener() method, an abstract base class is used instead.

Tweening properties and values

With the base class coded, it's time to get into some actual animation. The first thing we'll look at is how to tween simple display object properties in order to create movement. We can contain this functionality in a single class, named Tweener, which will handle taking an object and changing a specific value for that object over the course of time.

Tweener

Create a new ActionScript file and save it as Tweener.as into the com/foed/animation directory. Let's begin with its basic blueprint.

```
package com.foed.animation {

  import flash.events.TimerEvent;
  import flash.utils.Timer;

  public class Tweener extends Animator {

    private var _clip:Object;
    private var _prop:String;
    private var _startValue:Number;
    private var _destValue:Number;
    private var _changeValue:Number;
    private var _time:Number;
    private var _totalInts:uint;

    public function Tweener(
      pClip:Object,
      pProp:String,
      pStartValue:Number,
      pDestValue:Number,
      pTime:Number
    ) {
      _clip = pClip;
      _prop = pProp;
      _startValue = pStartValue;
      _destValue = pDestValue;
      _changeValue = _destValue - _startValue;
      _time = pTime;
      _totalInts = Math.floor(_time/Animator.intervalTime);
    }

    private function runTween(pEvent:TimerEvent):void {
    }
```

```
        override public function start():void {
          _clip[_prop] = _startValue;
          _timer = new Timer(Animator.intervalTime, _totalInts);
          _timer.addEventListener(TimerEvent.TIMER,➥
    runTween, false, 0, true);
          _timer.start();
        }

        override public function halt():void {
          _timer.removeEventListener(TimerEvent.TIMER, runTween);
          _timer.stop();
        }

        override public function die():void {
          super.die();
          if (_timer && _timer.running) _timer.stop();
          _clip = null;
        }

      }

    }
```


For a tween, we would expect a number of properties in order to perform the animation, and these we ask for in the constructor and are all mapped to private properties of the Tweener class. These include _clip, which is the object that is having some property value altered, _prop, the property being altered during the animation, the _startValue and _destValue, which are the values of the property at either end of the tween, and _time, the length of the animation in milliseconds.

Using these values passed to the constructor, we can calculate _changeValue, which is the amount the property will change during the course of the animation, and _totalInts, which is the total number of intervals that the Timer instance will call in order to perform the tween. How is this _totalInts calculated exactly? First, you'll see that it uses the static property of Animator, intervalTime, which will dictate the frequency with which a TimerEvent is fired by _timer, in this case every 30 milliseconds. With that in mind, we can see that if a time of 3 seconds, or 3000 milliseconds, is passed to the Tweener, the total number of intervals will be 100 (i.e., 3000/30). That means that the handler for our TimerEvent function should be called a total of 100 times in order to perform the animation.

Although all of the properties are set in the constructor, the Tweener won't actually do anything until it is told. To start a tween, the aptly named start() will be called. Within this method, the animated property of _clip is set to the start value and then a new Timer instance is created with the interval time and the total number of intervals passed in. We add runTween() as the handler to the TIMER event and call start() on the Timer instance itself. As _timer runs, runTween() will be called. Right now, we have left that method empty, but we will fill that in next so that the _clip's property is altered each interval of the animation.

The halt() method would be used to stop a tween. This merely stops _timer and removes its event listener. The die() method acts as a destructor, stopping the timer if it's running and clearing the reference to _clip.

All that's left now is to determine how the tween will be performed in runTween(). To start off easily, we'll perform a linear tween, meaning that the value of the clip's property will change an equal amount each interval. Let's add this to the runTween() method and see how it works.

```
public function runTween(pEvent:TimerEvent):void {
  _clip[_prop] = _startValue + ➥
((_changeValue/_totalInts)*_timer.currentCount);
  if (_timer.currentCount >= _totalInts) {
    _clip[_prop] = _destValue;
    halt();
  }
}
```

Here, the property on _clip is given a new value based on the currentCount of the Timer instance. This formula works by taking the amount the property needs to change each interval call (_changeValue/_totalInts) and multiplying it by the current count, adding this to the initial value of the property. It's perhaps a bit easier to see how this formula works by plugging in numbers. For instance, if we were tweening a sprite's x position from 50 to 450 over the course of 2 seconds, the _changeValue value would be 400 and the _totalInts would be 66 (2000 milliseconds / Animator.intervalTime rounded down). This means after 1 second has passed, the count would be 33 (half of the total 2 seconds worth of 66 intervals). The formula would then become, after substitution

```
clip.x = 50 + ((400/66)*33);
```

So the clip would be placed at 250, halfway between 50 and 450.

The conditional that follows just checks to see whether the current count equals or exceeds the allotted number of intervals for the animation (we could also look to the Timer instance's repeatCount property). If so, the clip's property is given the destination value and halt() is called.

That's the bare bones of our Tweener class, so let's try it out to see how it performs. We'll first create a base class that we can use for all of our subsequent animation tests. Create a new ActionScript class and save it as AnimationTest.as into a root project directory (not into the class directories we have been using in com/foed). Add the following code:

```
package {

  import flash.display.Sprite;

  public class AnimationTest extends Sprite {

    protected var _testSprite:Sprite;
```

```
    public function AnimationTest() {
      init();
    }

    protected function init():void {
      attachGraphics();
    }

    private function attachGraphics():void {
      _testSprite = new Sprite();
      _testSprite.x = stage.stageWidth/2;
      _testSprite.y = stage.stageHeight/2;
      _testSprite.graphics.beginFill(0xFF, 1);
      _testSprite.graphics.drawRect(-25, -25, 50, 50);
      _testSprite.graphics.endFill();
      addChild(_testSprite);
    }

  }

}
```


This class merely draws a rectangle on the stage and positions it at center. Now we'll create a child class for specifically testing Tweener. Create another ActionScript file and save it into the same directory as AnimationTest.as. Save this file as TweenerTest.as and add the following code:

```
package {

  import com.foed.animation.Tweener;

  public class TweenerTest extends AnimationTest {

    private var _tweener:Tweener;

    override protected function init():void {
      super.init();
      _tweener = new Tweener(
        _testSprite,
        "x",
        50,
        450,
        2000
      );
      _tweener.start();
    }

  }

}
```

In the init(), we create a new Tweener instance and pass in the values to tween _testSprite's x property from 50 to 450 over the course of 2 seconds. To test your movie, if you are using Flash, create a new Flash document and set TweenerTest as the document class, making sure that you include the com directory in your ActionScript class path. In Flex Builder, create a new ActionScript project with TweenerTest as the main document class, making sure the com directory is in your project's class path. In either case, you should see a blue square moving in a linear motion across the screen, as shown in Figure 17-3.

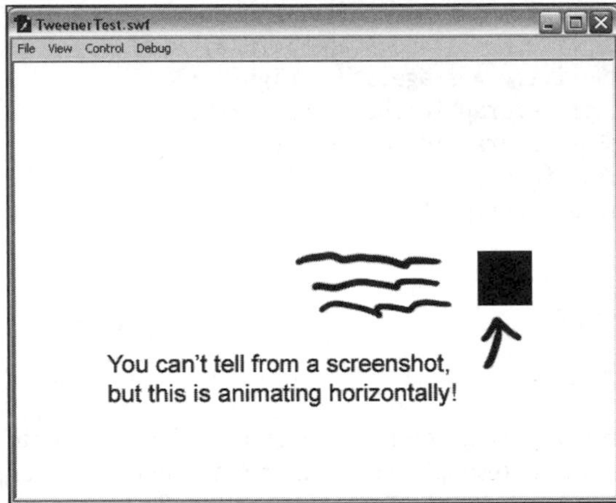

Figure 17-3. A programmatic tween applied to a blue rectangle

So we got a sprite to move. What is missing, however, is any type of organic feel to the movement. We can add that in by using a bit of easing, or acceleration/deceleration, to the animated movement.

Easing values

It just so happens that someone has already spent the time to write the ActionScript equations that can be used to create easing movement, similar to what we did earlier with the linear animation equation. Robert Penner (www.robertpenner.com) has provided open source easing equations for several versions of ActionScript now, equations you can download from www.robertpenner.com/easing/. These were written in ActionScript 1.0 and ActionScript 2.0, and now have been incorporated into Adobe's own libraries. If you are using Flash, you can find the code files in your Flash configuration directory under ActionScript 3.0/Classes/fl/motion/easing. If you are using Flex Builder, the classes are built into the framework and are in the mx.effects.easing package. We'll leverage this useful and excellent code to provide more interesting animation possibilities without a large amount of excess work, but to make it easier for me to provide samples that will work for readers using either Flash or Flex Builder, we'll use a new easing directory that contains these equations as adapted from the original ActionScript 2.0 open source.

You will need to copy the com/foed/animation/easing classes from this chapter's download files into the same directory as your current class files. Let's take a look at one of these easing classes, Cubic.

```
package com.foed.animation.easing {

  public class Cubic {

    static public function easeIn(➥
t:Number, b:Number, c:Number, d:Number):Number {
      return c*(t/=d)*t*t + b;
    }

    static public function easeOut(➥
t:Number, b:Number, c:Number, d:Number):Number {
      return c*((t=t/d-1)*t*t + 1) + b;
    }

    static public function easeInOut(➥
t:Number, b:Number, c:Number, d:Number):Number {
      if ((t/=d/2) < 1) return c/2*t*t*t + b;
      return c/2*((t-=2)*t*t + 2) + b;
    }

  }

}
```

Here you can see that a single easing equation type (Cubic) has three different static methods, easeIn(), easeOut(), and easeInOut(). Let's make some modification to our Tweener class so that we may use these equations in our animations.

Go back to the Tweener.as file and add the following bold lines. Note that some methods (start() and halt()) are excluded from this listing since no changes to those methods need to be made, though the methods should remain in your code.

```
package com.foed.animation {

  import flash.events.TimerEvent;
  import flash.utils.Timer;

  import com.foed.animation.easing.Linear;

  public class Tweener extends Animator {

    private var _clip:Object;
    private var _prop:String;
    private var _startValue:Number;
    private var _destValue:Number;
    private var _changeValue:Number;
```

```
      private var _time:Number;
      private var _easeFunction:Function;
      private var _totalInts:uint;

      public function Tweener(
        pClip:Object,
        pProp:String,
        pStartValue:Number,
        pDestValue:Number,
        pTime:Number,
        pEaseFunction:Function=null
      ) {
        _clip = pClip;
        _prop = pProp;
        _startValue = pStartValue;
        _destValue = pDestValue;
        _changeValue = _destValue - _startValue;
        _time = pTime;
        _totalInts = Math.floor(_time/Animator.intervalTime);
        _easeFunction = pEaseFunction||Linear.easeNone;
      }

      private function runTween(pEvent:TimerEvent):void {
        _clip[_prop] = _easeFunction(_timer.currentCount,➥
  _startValue, _changeValue, _totalInts);
        if (_timer.currentCount >= _totalInts) {
          _clip[_prop] = _destValue;
          halt();
        }
      }

      // NO CHANGES to start() and halt() from previous implementation

      override public function die():void {
        super.die();
        if (_timer && _timer.running) _timer.stop();
        _clip = null;
        _easeFunction = null;
      }

    }

  }
```

Here you can see that we now accept another parameter in the constructor, a function for the ease. We might wish in the future to modify the easing equations to inherit from a single Ease class or implement an expected interface so that we could type this argument accordingly, but for now we'll type it as Function. Within the constructor, we check to see whether a function has been passed in and, if not, we use the Linear.easeNone method, which you'll notice if you look at that particular method is the linear equation we originally coded ourselves.

Within runTween(), we use this new equation to calculate the new value for _clip's property. In the die() method, we make sure to clear the reference to this function as well.

Go back to your TweenerTest.as and pass in an easing function to see how it works. Here we try Elastic.easeInOut so that the square appears to both wind up before the movement and wind down after.

```
package {

  import com.foed.animation.Tweener;
  import com.foed.animation.easing.Elastic;

  public class TweenerTest extends AnimationTest {

    private var _tweener:Tweener;

    override protected function init():void {
      super.init();
      _tweener = new Tweener(
        _testSprite,
        "x",
        50,
        450,
        2000,
        Elastic.easeInOut
      );
      _tweener.start();
    }

  }

}
```

Adding events

The last thing we will do to our Tweener is plug it into the event broadcasting model available through the EventDispatcher, so that classes using Tweener can listen for events like when a tween has completed its animation. Animator extended EventDispatcher, so the capability is already there, we just need to decide where and what events to dispatch.

Instead of trying to determine how an animation's events might map to some of the standard events, we will create an event class specifically for animations, which we'll call TweenEvent. This class, which will extend Event, will contain constants for event types corresponding to the start of a tween, the end of a tween, and each iteration of a tween.

Create a new ActionScript class and save it into a com/foed/events directory as TweenEvent.as. The following is the entirety of the code for the TweenEvent class:

```
package com.foed.events {

  import flash.events.Event;

  import com.foed.animation.Animator;

  public class TweenEvent extends Event {

    public static const START:String = "tweenEnd";
    public static const END:String = "tweenStart";
    public static const CHANGE:String = "tweenChange";

    private var _animator:Animator;

    public function TweenEvent(
      pType:String,
      pAnimator:Animator,
      pBubbles:Boolean=false,
      pCancelable:Boolean=false
    ) {
      super(pType, pBubbles, pCancelable);
      _animator = pAnimator;
    }

    override public function clone():Event {
      return new TweenEvent(type, _animator, bubbles, cancelable);
    }

    public function get animator():Animator {
      return _animator;
    }

  }

}
```

Other than the constants for each event type, the class defines an instance property, _animator, which holds a reference to the Animator instance firing the event, and a getter method for that same property. The class also overrides Event's clone() method, a necessary action when subclassing Event. It is not enforced by the compiler, but can cause runtime errors if you do not.

With this class created, we can now dispatch the appropriate events in Tweener. Return to Tweener.as and add the following bold lines. Note that nothing should be *removed* from the code. The following listing only shows the affected portions. All other methods and properties should be left as is.

```
package com.foed.animation {

  import flash.events.TimerEvent;
  import flash.utils.Timer;

  import com.foed.animation.easing.Linear;
  import com.foed.events.TweenEvent;

  public class Tweener extends Animator {

    private function runTween(pEvent:TimerEvent):void {
      _clip[_prop] = _easeFunction(_timer.currentCount,➥
_startValue, _changeValue, _totalInts);
      if (_timer.currentCount >= _totalInts) {
        _clip[_prop] = _destValue;
        halt();
        dispatchEvent(new TweenEvent(TweenEvent.END, this));
      } else {
        dispatchEvent(new TweenEvent(TweenEvent.CHANGE, this));
      }
    }

    override public function start():void {
      _clip[_prop] = _startValue;
      _timer = new Timer(Animator.intervalTime, _totalInts);
      _timer.addEventListener(TimerEvent.TIMER,➥
runTween, false, 0, true);
      _timer.start();
      dispatchEvent(new TweenEvent(TweenEvent.START, this));
    }

  }

}
```

Grouping animations

We can now subscribe to events broadcast by a Tweener instance. To test this, we will create several more animation classes that take advantage of this event dispatching, TweenSequence, TweenComposite, and AnimationHold. These classes, combined with Tweener, will allow for some fairly complex animations with limited code, demonstrating a take on a common and useful design pattern, the Composite pattern (not to be confused with composition). This pattern, in a nutshell, is defined by an instance that implements an interface (or that is a concrete class derived from an abstract base class) that may contain other instances that implement the same interface, and through polymorphic methods a controller class may interact with that instance whether it contains other instances or not. These instances are like nodes in a tree hierarchy, where a node can be a leaf (has no children) or a branch (has children).

OK, that's a big nutshell, so perhaps an example would best illustrate. In our case, we have an abstract base class in Animator. This class should never be instantiated directly, but should instead be instantiated through child classes, like Tweener. However, no matter the child class, we know that the methods start() and halt() will be available in the child class since these are actually established in Animator. Because of this, if we have *any* class that is derived from Animator, we can safely call start() to begin its animation. The compiler will like it, the player will like it, and all will be grand.

Right now, we only have Tweener as a concrete class, but in this section we will add a new class, TweenComposite. TweenComposite is a branch node in our Composite pattern, as it will take a number of Animator instances and run them all simultaneously, whereas Tweener is a leaf, since it does not contain children. Our main document class will instantiate one Animator instance and call start(). Whether that class instantiated is Tweener or TweenComposite won't matter. We will simply call start() and expect the animation to run.

For a TweenComposite instance, when start() is called it will iterate through all of its children and call start() on each instance. Its children may be Tweeners or TweenComposites, but it won't matter since we know that either will have a start() method. If one of the children happens to be a TweenComposite, it will call start() on its own children, etc. The end result is that each of the Animators called may perform an animation itself, or may call other nested Animators to perform animations, and this nesting can continue to any reasonable depth. This nested structure is common for the Composite pattern, and such a structure is what allows us to create complex animations, and then start them with a single start() call to the top-level Animator instance.

Whew! Enough of theory and words, words, words. Let's turn to code, code, code to demonstrate the preceding. We will create three classes, TweenComposite, TweenSequence, and AnimationHold. The first, as was previously explained, will group a number of Animators together and run them simultaneously. TweenSequence will also group Animators, but will instead run them in a sequence, starting an animation after the previous one completes, which is now enabled, thanks to our inclusion of the event broadcasting. Finally, AnimationHold is sort of an anti-animation. It will hold all animations for a specified period of time. This will allow a sequence to contain a number of animations with pauses between different sequences.

Each of these classes is relatively small, so the next sections will present the code for each in its entirety and comment on the important aspects.

TweenComposite

Save the following class into the com/foed/animation directory. A TweenComposite instance will group a number of Animator instances together and run their animations simultaneously.

```
package com.foed.animation {

  import com.foed.events.TweenEvent;

  public class TweenComposite extends Animator {
```

```
        private var _tweenIndex:uint;
        private var _tweens:Array;

        public function TweenComposite(pTweens:Array) {
          _tweens = pTweens;
        }

        private function onEndTween(pEvent:TweenEvent):void {
          if (++_tweenIndex >= _tweens.length) {
            dispatchEvent(new TweenEvent(TweenEvent.END, this));
          }
        }

        override public function halt():void {
          for each (var i:Animator in _tweens) {
            i.removeEventListener(TweenEvent.END, onEndTween);
            i.halt();
          }
        }

        override public function start():void {
          _tweenIndex = 0;
          for each (var i:Animator in _tweens) {
            i.addEventListener(TweenEvent.END, onEndTween);
            i.start();
          }
        }

        override public function die():void {
          super.die();
          _tweens = null;
        }

      }

    }
```


TweenComposite accepts an array of Animators in its constructor. When start() is called, all the animators are looped through and told to start(). Note that we type everything here to the abstract base class, so as long as Animator is extended for each instance in the array, we can start any type of animation in this way. This is the beauty of polymorphism, since an animator might be a Tweener, another TweenComposite, or any other type that we can define (a Mover, a Scaler, a Shaker, etc.). All we need to worry about is calling start(). halt() does something similar, as you can see, iterating through the _tweens, removing the event listener, and calling halt() on each animator.

onTweenEnd() handles the completion of individual animators. When this is invoked, we increment the _tweenIndex that we initialized to zero in the start() method. Once we reach the total number of animators, we know the TweenComposite is complete and dispatch an END event. For clean up, the last method, die(), removes all references to stored animators.

TweenSequence

The next class, TweenSequence, is very similar to TweenComposite, but instead of running all animations at once, the animations are run back to back in a sequence. Let's take a look at how that's done. Save the following class into the same com/foed/animations directory as well.

```
package com.foed.animation {

  import com.foed.events.TweenEvent;

  public class TweenSequence extends Animator {

    private var _tween:Animator;
    private var _tweens:Array;

    public function TweenSequence(pTweens:Array) {
      _tweens = pTweens;
    }

    private function onEndTween(pEvent:TweenEvent):void {
      _tween.removeEventListener(TweenEvent.END, onEndTween);
      runTween();
    }

    private function runTween():void {
      _tween = (_tweens.shift() as Animator);
      if (_tween == null) {
        dispatchEvent(new TweenEvent(TweenEvent.END, this));
      } else {
        _tween.addEventListener(TweenEvent.END, onEndTween);
        _tween.start();
      }
    }

    override public function halt():void {
      _tween.removeEventListener(TweenEvent.END, onEndTween);
      _tween.halt();
    }

    override public function start():void {
      runTween();
    }

    override public function die():void {
      super.die();
```

```
        _tweens = null;
      }

    }

  }
```


You can see here that when start() is called, it immediately invokes runTween(), which is also called from onEndTween() when any of the child animations completes. runTween() uses Array's shift() operation to remove the next animation in the sequence. If the animation exists, an event listener is added for its END event, and the animation is told to start(). Otherwise, we know all animations have completed, and we can dispatch an END event for the whole TweenSequence.

AnimationHold

The final Animator child class, AnimationHold, allows for pauses in a sequence of animations and will work hand in hand with TweenSequence in order to create complex animations. This should go into the com/foed/animations directory with TweenComposite.as and TweenSequence.as.

```
package com.foed.animation {

  import flash.events.TimerEvent;
  import flash.utils.Timer;

  import com.foed.events.TweenEvent;

  public class AnimationHold extends Animator {

    public function AnimationHold(pTime:Number) {
      _timer = new Timer(pTime, 1);
      _timer.addEventListener(TimerEvent.TIMER_COMPLETE,➥
onEndTween, false, 0, true);
    }

    private function onEndTween(pEvent:TimerEvent):void {
      halt();
      dispatchEvent(new TweenEvent(TweenEvent.END, this));
    }

    override public function halt():void {
      if (_timer.running) _timer.stop();
    }

    override public function start():void {
      dispatchEvent(new TweenEvent(TweenEvent.START, this));
      _timer.start();
    }
```

```
    override public function die():void {
      _timer.removeEventListener(TimerEvent.TIMER_COMPLETE,➥
onEndTween);
      super.die();
    }

  }

}
```

When an AnimationHold instance is created, it is passed a time in milliseconds for which it will pause a sequence of animations using the Timer instance, _timer. When start() is called, _timer is started. When the _timer dispatches its TIMER_COMPLETE event, AnimationHold in turn dispatches an END event. Short and sweet, but potentially very useful when creating animations.

Testing animation sequences and composites

To test out our new animation classes, we will create another child class of AnimationTest. In this document class, we will create a sequence of animations to tween our rectangle to different points on the screen in a continuous loop, animating both position and rotation with pauses in between each sequence, and we'll do it all with a small amount of code, benefiting from the encapsulation of functionality in our Animator classes and our use of the Composite pattern.

Create a new ActionScript file and save it as TweenCompositeTest.as into your root project directory. Add the following code:

```
package {

  import flash.geom.Point;

  import com.foed.animation.*;
  import com.foed.animation.easing.*;
  import com.foed.events.TweenEvent;

  public class TweenCompositeTest extends AnimationTest {

    private var _tweener:TweenSequence;
    private var _positions:Array;
    private var _tweenCount:uint;

    override protected function init():void {
      super.init();
      _positions =
        [
        new Point(100, 100),
        new Point(stage.stageWidth-100, stage.stageHeight-100),
        new Point(stage.stageWidth-100, 100),
        new Point(100, stage.stageHeight-100)
```

```
        ];
        _tweenCount = 0;
        startNextTween();
      }

      private function startNextTween():void {
        var pPosition:Point = _positions[_tweenCount] as Point;
        _tweener = new TweenSequence(
          [
          new TweenComposite(
            [
            new Tweener(_testSprite, "rotation", 0,➥
90, 800, Quad.easeInOut),
            new Tweener(_testSprite, "x", _testSprite.x,➥
pPosition.x, 800, Quad.easeIn),
            new Tweener(_testSprite, "y", _testSprite.y,➥
pPosition.y, 800, Quad.easeOut)
            ]
          ),
          new AnimationHold(1000)
          ]
        );
        _tweener.addEventListener(TweenEvent.END, onEndTween);
        _tweener.start();
        if (++_tweenCount >= _positions.length) _tweenCount = 0;
      }

      private function onEndTween(pEvent:TweenEvent):void {
        startNextTween();
      }

    }

  }
```

In the `init()` method, we create an array of four positions on the stage, initialize a counter, and call `startNextTween()`. `startNextTween()` is the workhorse of our class. In this method, we get the current position in the `_positions` array using the current count, and then we create a new `TweenSequence` instance. This sequence consists, at the top level, of only two animations. The first is a composite of tweens, and the second is an `AnimationHold` instance that pauses the animations for one second. The composite consists of three separate animations, one for `rotation`, one for `x` position, and one for `y` position. The end effect is that the sequence will animate the square's position and rotation, and then will pause for one second. Once that second is complete, the `TweenSequence` will be complete and so `onEndTween()` will be called. That handler merely calls `startNextTween()` again, and a new `TweenSequence` is set up for the next position in the `_positions` array. This continues on until all positions have been animated to, then the counter is reset and the whole process begins again.

Test the movie in either Flash or Flex Builder using the same process detailed earlier for TweenerTest and you will see the square performing a number of complex tweens about the stage, all managed by our animation classes and created with about 50 lines of code. Play with the animations, adding new properties to animate, trying new easing equations, and nesting further sequences and composites. The combinations and effects are really endless. And yet we have only just begun!

Introducing TweenRunner

A common need for animation in Flash is tweening the position of display objects on the stage, which obviously involves changing not one, but two variables over the course of the animation. To accomplish this, the TweenComposite class could be used (as we did in the previous exercise), but it would be helpful to have a class that handled specifically the tweening of position. We'll do this in a moment with a new Mover class.

In order to create the Mover class, we'll first need to create a new type of general animator that will prove useful for not only Mover, but for any other type on animation that involves the changing of multiple properties over time. Tweener is limited to altering one property per call. When more complex properties need to be changed, like a ColorTransform object or even a multidimensional structure, the Tweener would not be sufficient. What we need then is a class that can handle multiple and diverse values over the course of an animation. We'll accomplish this with the TweenRunner class, whose purpose is merely to calculate easing values for any type of object passed in and then broadcast an event as these values change over the course of a timed animation. In this way, we'll open up endless possible uses, from tweening a sprite's position to altering ColorTransforms to even performing 3D transformations.

Create a new ActionScript class and save it into com/foed/animation as TweenRunner.as. Add the following code to begin:

```
package com.foed.animation {

  import flash.events.TimerEvent;
  import flash.utils.Timer;

  import com.foed.animation.easing.Linear;
  import com.foed.events.TweenEvent;

  public class TweenRunner extends Animator {

    private var _startValue:Object;
    private var _destValue:Object;
    private var _changeValue:Object;
    private var _currentValue:Object;
    private var _time:Number;
    private var _easeFunction:Function;
    private var _totalInts:uint;
```

```
    public function TweenRunner(
      pStartValue:Object,
      pDestValue:Object,
      pTime:Number,
      pEaseFunction:Function=null
    ) {
      _startValue = pStartValue;
      _destValue = pDestValue;
      _time = pTime;
      _totalInts = Math.floor(_time/Animator.intervalTime);
      _easeFunction = pEaseFunction||Linear.easeNone;
      _changeValue = {};
      for (var i:String in _startValue) {
        _changeValue[i] = _destValue[i] - _startValue[i];
      }
    }

    private function runTween(pEvent:TimerEvent):void {
    }

    override public function start():void {
      _timer = new Timer(Animator.intervalTime, _totalInts);
      _timer.addEventListener(TimerEvent.TIMER, runTween,➥
false, 0, true);
      _timer.start();
      _currentValue = _startValue;
      dispatchEvent(new TweenEvent(TweenEvent.START, this));
      runTween(new TimerEvent(TimerEvent.TIMER));
    }

    override public function halt():void {
    }

    override public function die():void {
    }

    public function get value():Object {
      return _currentValue;
    }
  }

}
```

The arguments passed to the constructor are very similar to those passed to Tweener. The changes to note are that there is no clip or property to alter passed to the TweenRunner. Also, _startValue and _destValue are typed as Object as opposed to Number.

In the constructor, after the instance properties are set based on the arguments passed in and the total intervals are calculated in the same way they were for Tweener, the _changeValue object is populated by running through each item in _startValue and calculating its difference from _destValue. At this point, the TweenRunner instance will wait until start() is invoked to begin the transforming of values.

Within start(), a new _timer is set up to invoke TweenRunner's runTween() method each iteration in order to transform the animation values over the course of time. Then runTween() is invoked immediately so that properties on an animating object might be set up to start the animation. Of course, we need to fill in runTween() in order to perform the animation. This is the method that will be called every interval when the TweenRunner is started. In this method, the multiple values stored will have their new values calculated, and the _currentValue will be set based on these new values, which will be retrievable through the value intrinsic getter method.

Add the following bold code to your TweenRunner class to add this functionality:

```
private function runTween(pEvent:TimerEvent):void {
  if (_timer.currentCount >= _totalInts) {
    _currentValue = _destValue;
    halt();
    dispatchEvent(new TweenEvent(TweenEvent.CHANGE, this));
    dispatchEvent(new TweenEvent(TweenEvent.END, this));
  } else {
    _currentValue = {};
    for (var i:String in _changeValue) {
      _currentValue[i] = _easeFunction(_timer.currentCount,➥
_startValue[i], _changeValue[i], _totalInts);
    }
    dispatchEvent(new TweenEvent(TweenEvent.CHANGE, this));
  }
}
```

Within the method, we first check to see whether the current count of _timer has reached the total number of intervals. If that is the case, we set the current value to be equal to the destination value and halt our TweenRunner, dispatching both a CHANGE and an END event. If the animation has not completed, the values within _changeValue are run through, and the easing equation is used to calculate their new values, which are assigned to _currentValue. Once that is complete, we dispatch a CHANGE event.

All that is left to fill in are our halt() and die() methods. Just as in Tweener, the former stops an animation while the latter cleans up the TweenRunner by clearing references to properties stored.

```
override public function halt():void {
  _timer.removeEventListener(TimerEvent.TIMER, runTween);
  _timer.stop();
}

override public function die():void {
  super.die();
```

```
      _startValue = null;
      _destValue = null;
      _easeFunction = null;
      _changeValue = null;
      _currentValue = null;
    }
```


Mover

Now that we have added TweenRunner, creating unique animators that can handle complex objects is pretty simple. Take for instance the Mover class discussed at the beginning of the last section. Let's look at the code necessary to create such a class using the new TweenRunner.

Create a new ActionScript file and save it as Mover.as into the com/foed/animation directory where TweenRunner.as resides. Add the following lines of code, which is the entirety of a simple Mover class:

```
package com.foed.animation {

  import flash.display.DisplayObject;
  import flash.geom.Point;

  import com.foed.events.TweenEvent;

  public class Mover extends Animator {

    private var _tween:TweenRunner;
    private var _clip:DisplayObject;
    private var _startValue:Object;
    private var _destValue:Object;
    private var _time:Number;
    private var _easeFunction:Function;

    public function Mover(
      pClip:DisplayObject,
      pStartValue:Point,
      pDestValue:Point,
      pTime:Number,
      pEaseFunction:Function=null
    ) {
      _clip = pClip;
      _startValue = {x:pStartValue.x, y:pStartValue.y};
      _destValue = {x:pDestValue.x, y:pDestValue.y};
      _time = pTime;
      _easeFunction = pEaseFunction;
    }
```

```
    private function onEndTween(pEvent:TweenEvent):void {
      halt();
      dispatchEvent(new TweenEvent(TweenEvent.END, this));
    }

    private function onChangeTween(pEvent:TweenEvent):void {
      var pChangedValues:Object = _tween.value;
      _clip.x = pChangedValues.x;
      _clip.y = pChangedValues.y;
      dispatchEvent(new TweenEvent(TweenEvent.CHANGE, this));
    }

    override public function halt():void {
      _tween.removeEventListener(TweenEvent.CHANGE, onChangeTween);
      _tween.removeEventListener(TweenEvent.END, onEndTween);
      _tween.halt();
    }

    override public function start():void {
      _tween = new TweenRunner(➥
_startValue, _destValue, _time, _easeFunction);
      _tween.addEventListener(TweenEvent.CHANGE, onChangeTween);
      _tween.addEventListener(TweenEvent.END, onEndTween);
      _tween.start();
      dispatchEvent(new TweenEvent(TweenEvent.START, this));
    }

  }

}
```

As you can see, with TweenRunner handling the calculations of multiple values over the course of an animation, creating a class like Mover that handles transforming multiple values on an object is pretty simple. Here, the constructor takes the same arguments we used for Tweener, except the start and end values will be Point instances instead of scalar values. However, even though these values will be passed in as Points, we need to transform them into Object instances, as the TweenRunner uses a for..in loop to run through the object properties, and the x and y values of a Point instance are not able to be iterated over using this technique.

In the start() method, we create a new TweenRunner instance, add the Mover instance as a listener, and then start the TweenRunner. As the animation runs, onChangeTween() will be called. Within this method, Mover will retrieve the current value of the TweenRunner to set the position of the animated clip. onEndTween() is called upon the completion of the TweenRunner's time, and halt() can always be called to stop the animation in progress.

That's it! The simple Mover class is complete, so let's try it out. Create a new ActionScript file and save it into the same directory as AnimationTest.as as MoverTest.as. Add the following code:

```
package {

  import flash.events.MouseEvent;
  import flash.geom.Point;

  import com.foed.animation.Mover;
  import com.foed.animation.easing.*;

  public class MoverTest extends AnimationTest {

    private var _mover:Mover;

    override protected function init():void {
      super.init();
      stage.addEventListener(MouseEvent.MOUSE_DOWN, moveToMouse);
    }

    private function moveToMouse(pEvent:MouseEvent):void {
      if (_mover != null) _mover.halt();
      _mover = new Mover(
        _testSprite,
        new Point(_testSprite.x, _testSprite.y),
        new Point(pEvent.stageX, pEvent.stageY),
        600,
        Circ.easeInOut
        );
      _mover.start();
    }

  }

}
```

Since AnimationTest, if you recall, draws a square on the stage, MoverTest simply has to decide how to move it about. In the init() method, we set up a handler for when the mouse is clicked on the stage. This handler, moveToMouse(), creates a new Mover instance (after first halting a previous Mover if it exists) to tween _testSprite from its current position to the point clicked on the stage in 600 milliseconds using the Circ.easeInOut easing equation.

Test the movie in Flash or Flex Builder using the methods laid out for TweenerTest and click the stage to see the rectangle tween to the clicked position. Not bad! What would be great now is if we could add a little dynamic blur to the fast-moving object in order to create a little more realistic movement. Turns out that with the BlurFilter, we can!

Motion blur

With the BlurFilter, we can add a bit of motion blur to our objects as they move across the stage, a cool little effect with minimal additional work. This won't be a true directional motion blur, but a close approximation. When things are moving fast across the screen in a blur, it will be hard to tell the difference anyway!

What we'll do is calculate the distance an object has traveled since the last interval call and use the distance on each axis to set the blur on each axis, properties of the BlurFilter. Therefore, if an object moves more vertically than horizontally, the blur on the y axis will be greater than the blur on the x axis.

The first thing we'll add to our Mover.as file is the code to import the BlurFilter class and set up properties specifically for blurring, allowing those properties to be set in the constructor. Add the following bold lines to Mover:

```
package com.foed.animation {

  import flash.display.DisplayObject;
  import flash.filters.BlurFilter;
  import flash.geom.Point;

  import com.foed.events.TweenEvent;

  public class Mover extends Animator {

    private var _tween:TweenRunner;
    private var _clip:DisplayObject;
    private var _useBlur:Boolean;
    private var _blurAmount:Number;
    private var _blurQuality:int;
    private var _blurFilter:BlurFilter;
    private var _startValue:Point;
    private var _destValue:Point;
    private var _time:Number;
    private var _easeFunction:Function;
    private var _lastPosition:Point;

    public function Mover(
      pClip:DisplayObject,
      pStartValue:Point,
      pDestValue:Point,
      pTime:Number,
      pEaseFunction:Function=null,
      pUseBlur:Boolean=false,
      pBlurAmount:Number=1,
      pBlurQuality:int=1
    ) {
      _clip = pClip;
      _startValue = {x:pStartValue.x, y:pStartValue.y};
      _destValue = {x:pDestValue.x, y:pDestValue.y};
      _time = pTime;
      _easeFunction = pEaseFunction;
      _useBlur = pUseBlur;
```

```
      _blurAmount = pBlurAmount;
      _blurQuality = pBlurQuality;
    }
```

_useBlur will determine whether the Mover uses the BlurFilter on its tweened clip, turned off by default. _blurAmount will be used to help determine the blurX and blurY values for the BlurFilter (higher values will produce more blur), and _blurQuality will be passed to the BlurFilter as its quality property, controlling how many blur calculations are performed on the object. Higher quality obviously produces better results, but at the cost of more processing cycles. Finally, _lastPosition will be used to store the previous position of the object so that the amount of blur to a new position can be calculated based on distance.

The next step is to add a BlurFilter to the tweened clip when a tween starts (and when blur is set to true). Add these lines to the start() method:

```
    override public function start():void {
      _tween = new TweenRunner(➥
_startValue, _destValue, _time, _easeFunction);
      _tween.addEventListener(TweenEvent.CHANGE, onChangeTween);
      _tween.addEventListener(TweenEvent.END, onEndTween);
      if (_useBlur) {
        _lastPosition = new Point(_clip.x, _clip.y);
        var pFilters:Array = _clip.filters || [];
        _blurFilter = new BlurFilter(0, 0, _blurQuality);
        pFilters.push(_blurFilter);
        _clip.filters = pFilters;
      }
      _tween.start();
      dispatchEvent(new TweenEvent(TweenEvent.START, this));
    }
```

If _useBlur is set to true, we store the current position of the clip and then grab either the filters array currently assigned to the object or, if it doesn't yet exist, create a new array. Then, we create a new instance of a BlurFilter, which we will use throughout the animation to apply to the clip. Finally, we push this new BlurFilter instance into the filters array and reassign this modified array back as the clip's filters. We are now ready to tween!

Now that the BlurFilter is prepared on the tweened clip, we can alter its values each frame to create the motion blur. This will all occur in the onChangeTween() method.

```
    private function onChangeTween(pEvent:TweenEvent):void {
      var pChangedValues:Object = _tween.value;
      _clip.x = pChangedValues.x;
      _clip.y = pChangedValues.y;
      if (_useBlur) {
        var pFactor:Number = _blurAmount/10;
        _blurFilter.blurX = Math.abs((pChangedValues.x-➥
_lastPosition.x)*pFactor);
```

```
      _blurFilter.blurY = Math.abs((pChangedValues.y-➥
_lastPosition.y)*pFactor);
      var pFilters:Array = _clip.filters.slice(0, -1);
      _clip.filters = pFilters.concat(_blurFilter);
      _lastPosition = new Point(pChangedValues.x, pChangedValues.y);
    }
    dispatchEvent(new TweenEvent(TweenEvent.CHANGE, this));
  }
```

Here is the logic applied to create our blur. Each frame, the Mover looks to the _lastPosition property, which will hold the last screen position of the clip on each axis so it can check the difference of these values and the current position of the clip and use this to calculate the blur. How exactly is that calculated? A pFactor variable is determined based on the _blurAmount property of Mover. The movement on each axis is multiplied by this factor to determine the blur amount, so the larger the factor and the greater the movement, the larger the blur. By default, _blurAmount is set to 1, which makes pFactor resolve to 0.1. Therefore, with these settings, a movement of 50 pixels on the x axis will set the BlurFilter's blurX value to 5. This calculation occurs every time this method is called during a tween to create a dynamic blur.

The last step would be to remove the blur upon completion of the tween. This is taken care of in the halt() method.

```
override public function halt():void {
  if (_useBlur) {
    _clip.filters = _clip.filters.slice(0, -1);
  }
  _tween.removeEventListener(TweenEvent.CHANGE, onChangeTween);
  _tween.removeEventListener(TweenEvent.END, onEndTween);
  _tween.halt();
}
```

Once the tween is complete, the BlurFilter, last in the list of filters for the clip, is removed.

To test this in action, return to the MoverTest.as file and set the Mover instance's useBlur property to true.

```
private function moveToMouse(pEvent:MouseEvent):void {
  if (_mover != null) _mover.halt();
  _mover = new Mover(
    _testSprite,
    new Point(_testSprite.x, _testSprite.y),
    new Point(pEvent.stageX, pEvent.stageY),
    600,
    Circ.easeInOut,
    true
    );
  _mover.start();
}
```

Test your movie, and you should see a subtle blur as you click the stage and tween the clip. To get a more distinct blur (less distinct?), try raising the blurAmount.

```
private function moveToMouse(pEvent:MouseEvent):void {
  if (_mover != null) _mover.halt();
  _mover = new Mover(
    _testSprite,
    new Point(_testSprite.x, _testSprite.y),
    new Point(pEvent.stageX, pEvent.stageY),
    600,
    Circ.easeInOut,
    true,
    3
    );
  _mover.start();
}
```


The result of this new value can be seen in Figure 17-4. With just a little bit of code encapsulated in an animation class, we've now enabled the ability to tween the position of any movie clip object in our movies and have a motion blur applied!

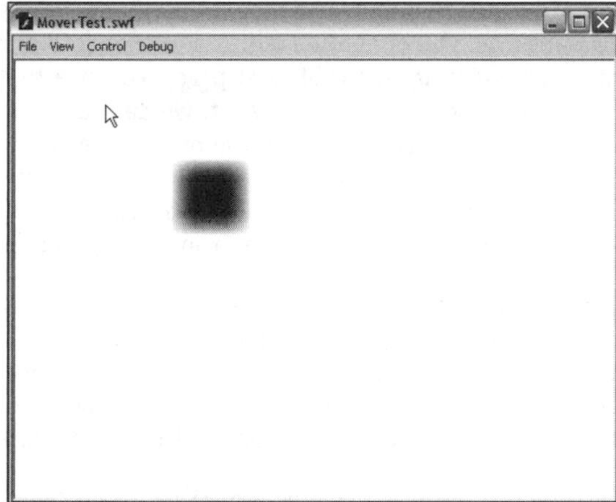

Figure 17-4. The Mover class applying a motion blur to a moving clip

Transitioning views

With this next group of classes, we'll explore the transitioning of visual objects from one state to another. By abstracting these transition classes out from the objects themselves, they may be reused over and over from one project to another with little to no additional work. For instance, if you were developing an image slideshow and you wanted a simple fade in/out of all the images, you might consider making a function that uses an ENTER_FRAME handler or a timer to change the alpha of one image till it disappeared, and then tweens up the opacity of another image to bring it into view. This sort of transition is fairly easy to accomplish and might even be something that you have already copied and pasted from one project to another. How much easier would it be, even for this simple function, to create a transition instance, pass it the clip to be transitioned, and just tell it to start. Once completed, an event would be broadcast so you could have another transition tween in the new image. It becomes more obviously useful when dealing with more complex transitions, as we'll create through the rest of this chapter, using some of the bitmap manipulation available in ActionScript. By separating the transition code from the graphic objects themselves, these classes can be reused in any project with little fuss.

Transition

All transitions will have similar needs, so it makes sense to have an abstract base class from which all transitions will inherit. This class will establish the common properties and the start and end events for transitions, as well as prepare objects for transitioning. Transitions will take advantage of the `TweenRunner` class to transform one or multiple properties over time and will utilize the new display list hierarchy in ActionScript 3.0.

The display list allows objects to be "reparented," which means that we can at runtime change the parent of an object. In previous versions of ActionScript, an object was tied to the movie clip it was initially attached to, which meant that if you needed to add new clips in order to perform a transition, you either needed to add clips to the transitioning object itself or to its parent, which went against OOP best practices since that required altering an object's state directly. But with the new display list, we can take a transitioning object and replace it in its parent's display hierarchy with the objects we need to perform a transition. In this way, a parent's hierarchy does not get added to (it just has a new object swapped in seamlessly), and we do not need to alter the display list of the transitioning object either. All of this will be handled in our base `Transition` class.

Before we create `Transition`, let's first make a class that will hold constants for a type of transition, which for our samples will simply be `IN` and `OUT`. An `IN` transition will transform the view of an object from a `Transition`'s start values to its end values, while an `OUT` transition will reverse these values (so a `FadeTransition` set to `OUT` will tween an object to 0% opacity, while an `IN` `FadeTransition` will fade an object from 0 to 100% opacity).

Create a new ActionScript class file and save it as `TransitionType.as` into a new directory, `com/foed/animation/transitions`. Enter the following code, which is the class in its entirety:

```
package com.foed.animation.transitions {

  public class TransitionType {

    public static const IN:String = "in";
    public static const OUT:String = "out";

  }

}
```

Ah, if only all classes could be that straightforward and simple! That's a nice, ironic segue to Transition. Create another new ActionScript class and save it as Transition.as into the same transitions directory. Enter the following code to get started:

```
package com.foed.animation.transitions {

  import flash.display.DisplayObject;
  import flash.display.DisplayObjectContainer;
  import flash.display.Sprite;

  import com.foed.animation.Animator;
  import com.foed.animation.easing.*;
  import com.foed.animation.TweenRunner;
  import com.foed.events.TweenEvent;

  public class Transition extends Animator {

    protected var _clipHolder:Sprite;

    private var _tweenRunner:TweenRunner;
    private var _time:Number;
    private var _clip:DisplayObject;
    private var _easeFunction:Function;
    private var _type:String;
    private var _startTransform:Object;
    private var _endTransform:Object;

    public function Transition(
      pClip:DisplayObject=null,
      pTime:Number=1000,
      pStartTransform:Object=null,
      pEndTransform:Object=null,
      pType:String=null,
      pEaseFunction:Function=null
    ) {
      _clip = pClip;
      _time = pTime;
      _easeFunction = pEaseFunction || Linear.easeNone;
      _type = pType || TransitionType.IN;
      startTransform = pStartTransform;
      endTransform = pEndTransform;
    }

  }

}
```

Once again, at the top of the class we import the other necessary classes for the code. Transition will inherit from Animator, so it will have all the event dispatching functionality.

In the properties declarations, we have the _tweenRunner that will be performing the interval calculations, and a number of properties that you should be familiar with from their counterparts in Tweener and TweenRunner. The only new property is _type, which will be one of the TransitionType constants we just created.

In the constructor, we set the instance properties based on the arguments passed in. As you can see, all of the properties are optional, so we'll want to provide getter/setters to set these after instantiation. For _easeFunction, we default to Linear.easeNone if no function is passed in. For _type, we default to an IN transition. The other properties will remain null if not passed in.

Since we have already identified the need for getter/setters, let's go ahead and add those next. Include the following code in the body of the Transition class:

```
public function get time():Number {
  return _time;
}

public function set time(pTime:Number):void {
  _time = pTime;
}

public function get clip():DisplayObject {
  return _clip;
}

public function set clip(pClip:DisplayObject):void {
  _clip = pClip;
}

public function get easeFunction():Function {
  return _easeFunction;
}

public function set easeFunction(pFunction:Function):void {
  _easeFunction = pFunction;
}

public function get type():String {
  return _type;
}

public function set type(pType:String):void {
  _type = pType;
}

public function get startTransform():Object {
  return _startTransform;
}
```

```
        public function set startTransform(pObject:Object):void {
          _startTransform = pObject;
        }

        public function get endTransform():Object {
          return _endTransform;
        }

        public function set endTransform(pObject:Object):void {
          _endTransform = pObject;
        }
```


I hope at this point nothing here is surprising! Each of these methods either sets or returns the respective property. Now we need to do something with these properties. As with all animators, a developer would initiate a transition by calling its start() method. We will add this next, along with methods that will support it.

```
        private function onEndTween(pEvent:TweenEvent):void {
          cleanUp();
          dispatchEvent(new TweenEvent(TweenEvent.END, this));
        }

        private function onChangeTween(pEvent:TweenEvent):void {
          runTransition(_tweenRunner.value);
          dispatchEvent(new TweenEvent(TweenEvent.CHANGE, this));
        }

        protected function runTransition(pChangeValues:Object):void {
        }

        protected function prepare():void {
        }

        protected function cleanUp():void {
        }

        override public function start():void {
          prepare();
          if (_type == TransitionType.IN) {
            _tweenRunner = new TweenRunner(➥
      _startTransform, _endTransform, _time, _easeFunction);
          } else {
            _tweenRunner = new TweenRunner(➥
     _endTransform, _startTransform, _time, _easeFunction);
          }
          _tweenRunner.addEventListener(TweenEvent.CHANGE, onChangeTween);
          _tweenRunner.addEventListener(TweenEvent.END, onEndTween);
          dispatchEvent(new TweenEvent(TweenEvent.START, this));
          _tweenRunner.start();
        }
```

When start() is called, we call a protected prepare() method, which will perform any necessary preparations that need to be run before the transition begins. We will fill this in shortly, but we leave it protected so that child classes can also have the ability to prepare in their own necessary ways. Next in the start() method, we create a TweenRunner instance to transform from _startTransform to _endTransform, or vice versa depending on the transition type. We set up listeners for the TweenRunner instance's CHANGE and END events and invoke its start() method after first dispatching a START event.

As the TweenRunner instance runs, it will call the onChangeTween handler inside Transition. Within that method, we merely call runTransition() and dispatch a CHANGE event. Since this base class does not know how a transition will need to be performed, there is not much else to do, and it will be up to concrete child classes to override the runTransition() method and fill in the necessary operations.

When the transition is complete, as reported by the TweenRunner instance, the onEndTween handler will be called, at which point we call a currently empty cleanUp() method (again, that we leave protected so that child classes can override it and perform their own clean up if necessary) and dispatch an END event.

At the beginning of this section, I presented how we can utilize the new display list functionality in ActionScript 3.0 in order to perform transitions more seamlessly. This is handled in the prepare() and cleanUp() methods, which we fill in next.

```
protected function prepare():void {
  _clipHolder = new Sprite();
  _clip.visible = true;
  var pParent:DisplayObjectContainer = _clip.parent;
  var pDepth:int = pParent.getChildIndex(_clip);
  pParent.removeChild(_clip);
  pParent.addChildAt(_clipHolder, pDepth);
  _clipHolder.addChild(_clip);
}

protected function cleanUp():void {
  if (_clipHolder == null || _clip.parent != _clipHolder) return;
  var pParent:DisplayObjectContainer = _clipHolder.parent;
  var pDepth:int = pParent.getChildIndex(_clipHolder);
  pParent.removeChild(_clipHolder);
  pParent.addChildAt(_clip, pDepth);
  _clipHolder = null;
  _clip.visible = true;
}
```

In the prepare() method, we create a new Sprite instance and reference it with _clipHolder. We then find the depth at which the transitioning clip is positioned within its parent and save a reference both to that and the parent container. At this point, we can remove the clip from its parent and add _clipHolder in its place. The clip can then be added as a child to _clipHolder. In this way, we have nested _clip within _clipHolder at the same depth within the parent container that _clip was previously positioned. We are now free to add additional objects to _clipHolder without disturbing the display list hierarchy of either _clip or its (previous) parent container.

In the cleanUp() method, we reverse this process. We remove _clipHolder from the parent container and add _clip back into that position, clearing the reference to _clipHolder so it may be disposed of during garbage collection.

The only methods left for Transition are those we expect for every Animator, a halt() and a die() method (I must have been a bad mood when those were named!).

```
    override public function halt():void {
      if (_tweenRunner != null) {
        _tweenRunner.removeEventListener(TweenEvent.CHANGE,➥
onChangeTween);
        _tweenRunner.removeEventListener(TweenEvent.END, onEndTween);
        _tweenRunner.halt();
        _tweenRunner = null;
      }
      if (clip != null)
        runTransition((_type == TransitionType.IN) ?➥
_endTransform : _startTransform);
      cleanUp();
    }

    override public function die():void {
      super.die();
      cleanUp();
      _clip = null;
      _startTransform = null;
      _endTransform = null;
      _easeFunction = null;
    }
```

When halt() is called, we stop _tweenRunner from running, if it exists. We then call runTransition() with either the start or end values of the transition passed in so that a clip isn't stuck halfway through a transition and perform the necessary clean up. In the die() method, we also perform our clean up, and then clear any references to objects stored in the transition.

Now, this class in and of itself won't do anything, being an abstract base class. Next, we'll build a class that extends Transition in order to perform a visual effect. You will see that since so much functionality has been included in Transition, child classes can be relatively small since they only need to control how a transition must be applied.

FadeTransition

Now that we have the base class functionality, each transition that builds off it merely needs to concern itself with code specific to performing its unique transition. We'll start with one of the easiest examples, an alpha fading transition.

Create a new ActionScript class and save it as FadeTransition.as into the com/foed/animation/transitions directory. The following is the entire class listing, with explanation to follow:

```
package com.foed.animation.transitions {

  import flash.display.DisplayObject;

  public class FadeTransition extends Transition {

    public function FadeTransition(
      pClip:DisplayObject=null,
      pStartTransform:Number=0,
      pEndTransform:Number=1,
      pTime:Number=1000,
      pType:String=null,
      pEaseFunction:Function=null
    ) {
      super(pClip, pTime, pStartTransform,➥
pEndTransform, pType, pEaseFunction);
    }

    override protected function runTransition(
      pChangeValues:Object
    ):void {
      clip.alpha = pChangeValues.alpha as Number;
      super.runTransition(pChangeValues);
    }

    override protected function cleanUp():void {
      clip.alpha = 1;
      super.cleanUp();
    }

    override public function set startTransform(pObject:Object):void {
      super.startTransform = {alpha:Number(pObject)};
    }

    override public function set endTransform(pObject:Object):void {
      super.endTransform = {alpha:Number(pObject)};
    }

  }

}
```

Every method in this class is simply an overridden method of the superclass. The first items to note are the setters for startTransform and endTransform. These take care of wrapping number values passed to the transition inside of objects with an alpha property. Why is this necessary? This is because the TweenRunner expects values inside of complex objects as opposed to scalar values, like numbers. However, since it makes sense for a FadeTransition to be passed alpha values for its transforms, we take care of the wrapping of these values inside the class to make it easier (and more intuitive) when using the class. Take a moment to go back and have a look at the constructor for Transition, and you will see that the implicit setters are invoked there:


```
public function Transition(
  pClip:DisplayObject=null,
  pTime:Number=1000,
  pStartTransform:Object=null,
  pEndTransform:Object=null,
  pType:String=null,
  pEaseFunction:Function=null
) {
  _clip = pClip;
  _time = pTime;
  _easeFunction = pEaseFunction || Linear.easeNone;
  _type = pType || TransitionType.IN;
  startTransform = pStartTransform;
  endTransform = pEndTransform;
}
```

So when the Transition constructor is called (from within the FadeTransition constructor), the overridden methods are called in FadeTransition, which take care of the boxing of these scalar values in complex objects.

Next, in the runTransition() method of FadeTransition, the alpha of the transitioning clip is set based on the changed values passed from the TweenRunner instance. cleanUp() takes care of setting the alpha to 1, if it has been transformed during the transition.

That's it! Transition has done all the heavy lifting, so FadeTransition is pretty painless by comparison. Of course, we still have to test it out.

Testing transitions

We now have a base Transition class and a FadeTransition inheriting from it, so it's time to see the fruits of our labors and watch a transition! Of course, what that means is we need to prepare a document class with some object to transition. This class will run through all transitions that we store in an array, which we can add to as we create more transitions. The class will also load in an external PNG that we can use for the transitions.

Create a new ActionScript class in the root directory of your project and save it as TransitionTest.as, adding the following code to start it off:

```
package {

  import flash.display.Loader;
  import flash.display.LoaderInfo;
  import flash.display.Sprite;
```

```
  import flash.events.Event;
  import flash.events.MouseEvent;
  import flash.filters.DropShadowFilter;
  import flash.net.URLRequest;

  import com.foed.animation.transitions.*;
  import com.foed.events.TweenEvent;

  public class TransitionTest extends Sprite {

    private var _image:Loader;
    private var _imageHolder:Sprite;
    private var _transition:Transition;
    private var _transitionList:Array;
    private var _transitionCount:uint;
    private var _transitioning:Boolean;

    public function TransitionTest() {
      init();
    }

    private function init():void {
      _transitionList =
        [
        FadeTransition
        ];
      _transitionCount = 0;
      _image = new Loader();
      _image.contentLoaderInfo.addEventListener(Event.COMPLETE,➥
onImageLoaded);
      _image.load(new URLRequest("Audrey.png"));
    }

    private function onImageLoaded(pEvent:Event):void {
      _imageHolder = addChild(new Sprite()) as Sprite;
      _imageHolder.filters = [new DropShadowFilter(➥
10, 45, 0x000000, .4, 5, 5, .7)];
      _imageHolder.x = (stage.stageWidth-_image.width)/2;
      _imageHolder.y = (stage.stageHeight-_image.height)/2;
      _imageHolder.addChild(_image);
      stage.addEventListener(MouseEvent.MOUSE_DOWN,➥
transitionImageOut);
      transitionImageIn();
    }

  }

}
```

This is the first half of the class to test the transitions. After the class imports and property declarations, which will be explained in the actual methods, we begin with the init() method. In this, we create a new Array instance named _transitionList, which will hold all transitions to test. Right now, there is only one, FadeTransition. The current transition (the one that will occur next) has its index stored in the _transitionCount variable. The next several lines use the new Loader class to load in an external image. For our examples, I will be loading in the file Audrey.png, which is included in the download files for this chapter, but you can substitute whatever image you wish (although I can't imagine why you'd want to!).

onImageLoaded() is called when the image completes its load, as you might expect. At that point, we add a new Sprite, _imageHolder, and give it a drop shadow. We position this Sprite instance so that once the image is added, it will be centered on the stage. The reason we are nesting like this is so the transitions will only be performed on the image, not the holder (and its drop shadow).

Once the image is added, we set transitionImageOut() to be called whenever the stage is clicked and immediately call transitionImageIn(), which will start the first transition.

These next functions, completing TransitionTest, define the transition functions. Add these to the class:

```
    private function transitionImageIn():void {
      _transitioning = true;
      var pClass:Class = _transitionList[_transitionCount] as Class;
      _transition = new pClass(_image) as Transition;
      _transition.addEventListener(TweenEvent.END, onEndTransition);
      _transition.start();
    }

    private function transitionImageOut(pEvent:Event):void {
      if (_transitioning) return;
      _transitioning = true;
      _transition.type = TransitionType.OUT;
      _transition.start();
      if (++_transitionCount >= _transitionList.length) {
        _transitionCount = 0;
      }
    }

    private function onEndTransition(pEvent:TweenEvent):void {
      if (_transition.type == TransitionType.IN) {
        _transitioning = false;
      } else {
        transitionImageIn();
      }
  }
```

When transitionImageIn() is called, we set a Boolean flag to true so that another transition may not be called until the transition is complete. Then we create a new transition instance, using the current _transitionCount to access a class from the _transitionList array. This instance is cast to Transition, as that class holds all the common methods and properties for all transitions, and a reference to _image is passed in the constructor. We do not pass any additional parameters, so the default values will be used. Next, we add this class as a listener to the new transition and tell the transition to start().

When the transition is complete, it will call the onEndTransition() handler. At that time, if the current transition was going out, we call transitionImageIn() to transition the image in using the next transition in the list. However, if the transition was coming in, we simply set the transitioning flag to false, meaning that clicking the mouse will start the next transition.

That logic is defined in the transitionImageOut() method, which you'll recall was the MOUSE_DOWN handler. This changes the current transition's type to OUT and starts it up. _transitionCount is then incremented to move on to the next transition. If the maximum number of transitions has been reached, the count is set back to 0.

Time to test the code! If you are using Flash, create a new Flash document in the same directory as TransitionTest.as and set TransitionTest as the document class. Make sure that Audrey.png is in the same directory and that you are pointing to the com directory in your ActionScript class path. For Flex Builder users, create a new ActionScript project with TransitionTest as the main document class. Make sure that you have the com directory in the class path for your project settings and that Audrey.png is in your bin directory.

Test your movie in either environment, and the image should begin transitioning in immediately, as you see in Figures 17-5 and 17-6. Once the transition is complete, click with your mouse to see the image fade out, and then fade back in. This will continue to loop as long as you keep clicking your mouse. Although this end result might seem paltry after all that code, the beauty of it is that the transition itself now can be accomplished with two little lines of code:

```
var pTransition:FadeTransition = new FadeTransition(myImage);
pTransition.start();
```

This small snippet can be used in any project, and you can expect it to work the same. Plus, since you can configure the time, type, and easing function, you have a number of possible transitions at your disposal.

Figure 17-5. The transition test base image between each transition

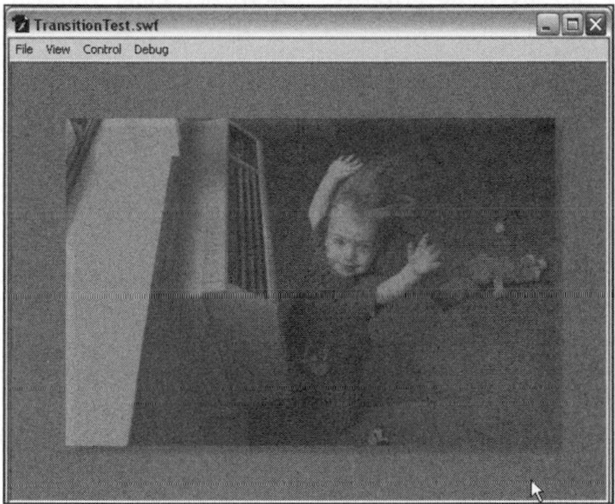

Figure 17-6. The FadeTransition applied to the image

ColorTransition

The next transition we code will also offer many different ways it can be configured. With the `ColorTransition`, any `ColorTransform` can be used to transform in and out of the view of a clip. This means that an image might transition in from white or black or hot pink. It also means that different color effects might be transitioned through, like a transform from a negative of the image to a positive. The transition can change completely based on whatever is passed in as the `startTransform` and `endTransform`. Let's take a look at the code, represented here in its entirety:

```
package com.foed.animation.transitions {

  import flash.display.DisplayObject;
  import flash.geom.ColorTransform;

  public class ColorTransition extends Transition {

    public function ColorTransition(
      pClip:DisplayObject=null,
      pStartTransform:ColorTransform=null,
      pEndTransform:ColorTransform=null,
      pTime:Number=1000,
      pType:String=null,
      pEaseFunction:Function=null
    ) {
      pStartTransform = pStartTransform ||➥
new ColorTransform(0, 0, 0, 1, 255, 255, 255, 0);
      pEndTransform = pEndTransform || new ColorTransform();
      super(pClip, pTime, pStartTransform, pEndTransform,➥
pType, pEaseFunction);
    }

    private function makeTransform(pTransform:ColorTransform):Object {
      var pObject:Object = {
        ra:pTransform.redMultiplier,
        rb:pTransform.redOffset,
        ga:pTransform.greenMultiplier,
        gb:pTransform.greenOffset,
        ba:pTransform.blueMultiplier,
        bb:pTransform.blueOffset,
        aa:pTransform.alphaMultiplier,
        ab:pTransform.alphaOffset
      };
      return pObject;
    }

    override protected function runTransition(
      pChangeValues:Object
    ):void {
      clip.transform.colorTransform = new ColorTransform(
        pChangeValues.ra,
        pChangeValues.ga,
        pChangeValues.ba,
        pChangeValues.aa,
        pChangeValues.rb|0,
        pChangeValues.gb|0,
        pChangeValues.bb|0,
        pChangeValues.ab
      );
```

```
      super.runTransition(pChangeValues);
    }

    override protected function cleanUp():void {
      clip.transform.colorTransform = new ColorTransform();
      super.cleanUp();
    }

    override public function set startTransform(pObject:Object):void {
      super.startTransform = makeTransform(ColorTransform(pObject));
    }

    override public function set endTransform(pObject:Object):void {
      super.endTransform = makeTransform(ColorTransform(pObject));
    }

  }

}
```


The ColorTransition tweens the color properties stored in the two transforms, either end determined by the type of transition, IN or OUT. The default transforms in the constructor, which are assigned if no ColorTransform instances are passed in, will have a clip transition from absolute white (with the offsets for all three channels set to 255) to an identity transform, which effectively means no transform applied.

You can see in the overridden startTransform and endTransform setters that we take an object that is passed in, which we expect to be a ColorTransform instance, and pass this to the makeTransition() method in order to translate it into an object with properties to correspond to the properties in ColorTransform. Why is this done exactly? If you recall, TweenRunner uses a for..in loop to iterate through all properties in the transforming objects in order to calculate changed values. However, ColorTransform properties cannot be iterated through in this way. Therefore, we take the ColorTransform instances passed in and make these into objects that can be iterated over, and by encapsulating this requirement within the class, we simplify the API to use the class since a ColorTransform can be passed in to define the end points in the transition.

The flip side of this is that when these values in our object are recalculated each iteration of the animation, we have to turn them back into a ColorTransform in order to apply them to a clip. This is handled in the runTransition() method. The only other method defined is the overridden cleanUp(), which assigns an identity transform to the clip in order to clear any color transformations.

That's a pretty simple implementation for tweening colors (considering we can even use easing functions to make it more interesting)! This is because we have spent the time laying the groundwork elsewhere in the Transition and TweenRunner classes. We are now getting to the fun part of implementing new effects with very little elbow grease.

To see how this works, add the ColorTransition to your TransitionTest class.

```
    private function init():void {
      _transitionList =
        [
        FadeTransition,
        ColorTransition
        ];
      _transitionCount = 0;
      _image = new Loader();
      _image.contentLoaderInfo.addEventListener(Event.COMPLETE,➥
onImageLoaded);
      _image.load(new URLRequest("Audrey.png"));
    }
```

Test the movie and, after the opacity fade transition, you'll see the image perform a color transition from white to its normal colors. Figure 17-7 gives you an idea of how this will look.

Figure 17-7. The `ColorTransition` applied to the image

BlurTransition

This next transition utilizes the `BlurFilter` we already worked with in the `Mover` class. The transition will be from a blurred image to crisp, or vice versa. Once more, the class is fairly small, smaller than `ColorTransition`, since a lot of the work is taken care of elsewhere, so the following represents the complete listing, with explanation to follow.

```
package com.foed.animation.transitions {

  import flash.display.DisplayObject;
  import flash.filters.BlurFilter;

  public class BlurTransition extends Transition {
```

```
    private static var DEFAULT_BLUR:Number = 25;
    private var _quality:int = 1;
    private var _blurFilter:BlurFilter;

    public function BlurTransition(
      pClip:DisplayObject=null,
      pStartTransform:Object=null,
      pEndTransform:Object=null,
      pTime:Number=1000,
      pType:String=null,
      pEaseFunction:Function=null
    ) {
      pStartTransform = pStartTransform ||➥
{blurX:DEFAULT_BLUR, blurY:DEFAULT_BLUR};
      pEndTransform = pEndTransform || {blurX:0, blurY:0};
      super(pClip, pTime, pStartTransform, pEndTransform,➥
pType, pEaseFunction);
    }

    override protected function runTransition(
      pChangeValues:Object
    ):void {
      _blurFilter.blurX = pChangeValues.blurX;
      _blurFilter.blurY = pChangeValues.blurY;
      var pFilters:Array = clip.filters.slice(0, -1);
      clip.filters = pFilters.concat(_blurFilter);
      super.runTransition(pChangeValues);
    }

    private function getFiltersWithoutBlur():Array {
      var pFilters:Array = clip.filters || [];
      if (pFilters[pFilters.length-1] is BlurFilter) {
        pFilters = pFilters.slice(0, -1);
      }
      return pFilters;
    }

    override protected function prepare():void {
      super.prepare();
      var pFilters:Array = getFiltersWithoutBlur();
      _blurFilter = new BlurFilter(0, 0, _quality);
      pFilters.push(_blurFilter);
      clip.filters = pFilters;
    }

    override protected function cleanUp():void {
      super.cleanUp();
      var pFilters:Array = getFiltersWithoutBlur();
      clip.filters = pFilters;
```

```
                _blurFilter = null;
            }

        }

    }
```

Much of this bears a striking resemblance to what we already coded in the Mover class. When the prepare() method is called when the transition is about to begin, a new BlurFilter instance is pushed into the clip's filters array, but first we ensure that the last filter applied is *not* a BlurFilter instance by calling getFiltersWithoutBlur(), which removes a final BlurFilter from the filters array if it exists.

The runTransition(), which is called by onChangeTween() every interval with new values, removes the last filter in the clip's filters array (which will be the previously added BlurFilter) and adds back in the modified BlurFilter instance with new values, reapplying this modified array to the clip.

cleanUp() in this transition removes the final filter from the clip if it is a BlurFilter by calling the same getFiltersWithoutBlur() method employed in the prepare() method.

To test, once again return to TransitionTest.as and add the BlurTransition to the _transitionList.

```
        private function init():void {
          _transitionList =
            [
            FadeTransition,
            ColorTransition,
            BlurTransition
            ];
          _transitionCount = 0;
          _image = new Loader();
          _image.contentLoaderInfo.addEventListener(Event.COMPLETE,➥
    onImageLoaded);
          _image.load(new URLRequest("Audrey.png"));
        }
```

Test the movie with this change and see all three transition types playing together (Figure 17-8 shows what the BlurTransition looks like). That's three complete transition effects, each between 40 to 70 lines of code, demonstrating the powers of abstraction, inheritance, and polymorphism. But we can still do more!

Figure 17-8. The BlurTransition applied to the image

NoiseTransition

The NoiseTransition takes advantage of the BitmapData object and its noise() method, which fills an image with pixel noise. We'll use this to create a sort of TV snow effect, as if a television channel is coming into focus (you know, from the days we still had knobs on our TVs). The code is once again less than 60 lines, so here is the full listing, with its explanation to follow:

```
package com.foed.animation.transitions {

  import flash.display.Bitmap;
  import flash.display.BitmapData;
  import flash.display.DisplayObject;
  import flash.display.Sprite;
  import flash.utils.getTimer;

  import com.foed.events.TweenEvent;

  public class NoiseTransition extends Transition {

    private var _noiseImage:BitmapData;
    private var _noiseHolder:Sprite;
    private var _fade:FadeTransition;

    public function NoiseTransition(
      pClip:DisplayObject=null,
      pStartTransform:Object=null,
      pEndTransform:Object=null,
      pTime:Number=1000,
      pType:String=null,
      pEaseFunction:Function=null
```

```
    ) {
      super(pClip, pTime, 0, 1, pType, pEaseFunction);
    }

    override protected function runTransition(
      pChangeValues:Object
    ):void {
      _noiseImage.noise(getTimer(), 0, 255, 7, true);
      super.runTransition(pChangeValues);
    }

    override protected function prepare():void {
      super.prepare();
      _noiseImage = new BitmapData(➥
clip.width, clip.height, true, 0x00FFFFFF);
      var pNoise:Bitmap = new Bitmap(_noiseImage);
      _noiseHolder = new Sprite();
      _noiseHolder.addChild(pNoise);
      _clipHolder.addChild(_noiseHolder);
    }

    override protected function cleanUp():void {
      super.cleanUp();
      _noiseImage.dispose();
      _noiseImage = null;
      _fade = null;
    }

    override public function start():void {
      super.start();
      _fade = new FadeTransition();
      _fade.clip = _noiseHolder;
      _fade.type = ((type == TransitionType.IN) ?➥
TransitionType.OUT : TransitionType.IN);
      _fade.easeFunction = easeFunction;
      _fade.time = time;
      _fade.start();
    }

  }

}
```

When the transition's prepare() is called, a new transparent BitmapData object is created to match the clip's dimensions. Then, a new Sprite, _noiseHolder, is created and has a Bitmap instance containing the BitmapData added as a child. _noiseHolder is then added as a new child of _clipHolder (here is the first time we are taking advantage of the _clipHolder to nest new objects). ActionScript 3.0 requires a little more nesting here than you might expect, but a Bitmap instance is needed in order to draw the BitmapData and display it on the display list. This in turn needs to be nested within a Sprite instance since we want to tween the opacity of the noise image, and this is not something that can be done with a Bitmap instance (but can with a Sprite). All of this is added to _clipHolder so that the noise image can be placed above the transitioning clip.

To have the noise fade in or out once the transition begins in the start() method, we'll reuse the FadeTransition we created earlier (see how it all fits together nicely now?), passing _noiseHolder as its clip to transition. The type will be the opposite of NoiseTransition's type—for instance, if the NoiseTransition is to transition in, we want the noise itself to fade out.

If you look to runTransition(), it's a single line in addition to the invocation of the superclass's method. The noise() method of BitmapFilter simply applies noise to the image. By passing in a different seed value each time (the first parameter—getTimer() ensures that this will never be the same value), the noise is changed each frame, creating the snow animation. When the FadeTransition instance completes its transition, cleanUp() is called, which disposes of the noise image since it is no longer needed.

Return to TransitionTest and add the NoiseTransition into the list of transitions to test.

```
    private function init():void {
      _transitionList =
        [
        FadeTransition,
        ColorTransition,
        BlurTransition,
        NoiseTransition
        ];
      _transitionCount = 0;
      _image = new Loader();
      _image.contentLoaderInfo.addEventListener(Event.COMPLETE,➥
onImageLoaded);
      _image.load(new URLRequest("Audrey.png"));
    }
```

Test the movie to see all the transitions in action! Figure 17-9 shows how the NoiseTransition appears.

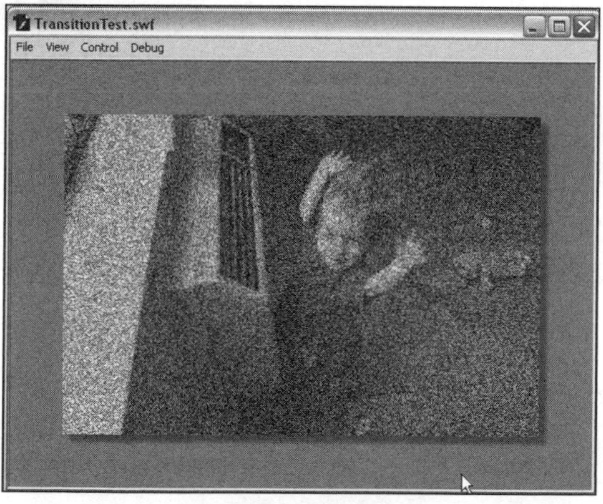

Figure 17-9. The NoiseTransition applied to the image

DissolveTransition and WaterTransition

Included with this chapter's download files to further inspire you are two more transitions that are a bit more complex, using more bitmap manipulation features. You can copy these files into your class directory and test them in the same TransitionTest class by adding them to the _transitionList array.

The DissolveTransition uses the pixelDissolve() method of the BitmapData class to dissolve an image from a solid image, breaking it down into smaller clumps of pixels, and vice versa. The WaterTransition uses the powerful DisplacementMapFilter and the perlinNoise() method of the BitmapData class to create a water-like effect, rippling the image into a static position. Since we will not explore this code in depth, I won't include it here, but I would invite you to open up the files to see how you might create more transition effects, and add them to your TransitionTest class to see them in action. Although they are certainly more complex than the earlier transitions, they are still less than 100 lines of code apiece.

Figure 17-10 shows how the DissolveTransition should look when you test it.

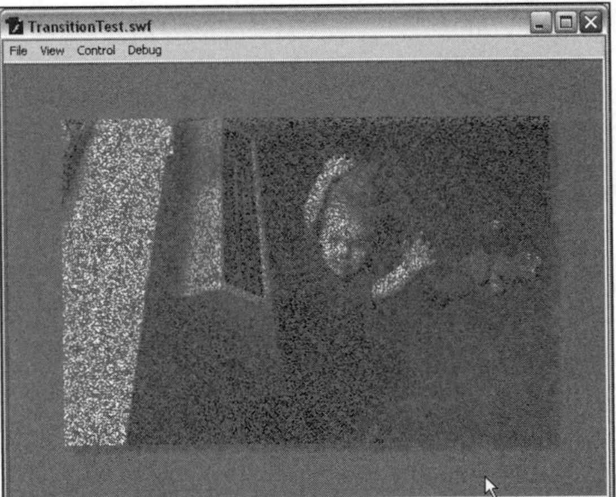

Figure 17-10. The DissolveTransition applied to the image

The WaterTransition will appear as shown in Figure 17-11 when you test it.

Figure 17-11. The `WaterTransition` applied to the image

What's next?

That's another hefty chapter behind you with a lot of good practice creating classes in an OOP manner, utilizing encapsulation to house functionality within the animation classes that can now be reused in many projects, inheritance to extend base classes to allow for more specific functionality (`EventDispatcher` to `Animator` to `Transition` to `FadeTransition`), composition to build functionality onto base classes, as in the case of `Mover` containing a `TweenRunner` instance, and polymorphism to enable multiple transitions to respond to the same method calls in their own unique ways, with the implementation hidden from the user. You developed several animation classes that abstracted the animation from the objects to be animated, making for a powerful and robust animation code library with a multitude of applications.

The next chapter starts our exploration of data integration by delving into data binding as a means of sharing content between components. We'll work through several examples that demonstrate how to create both scripted and visual bindings, exploring related topics such as formatters along the way.

PART FIVE **DATA INTEGRATION**

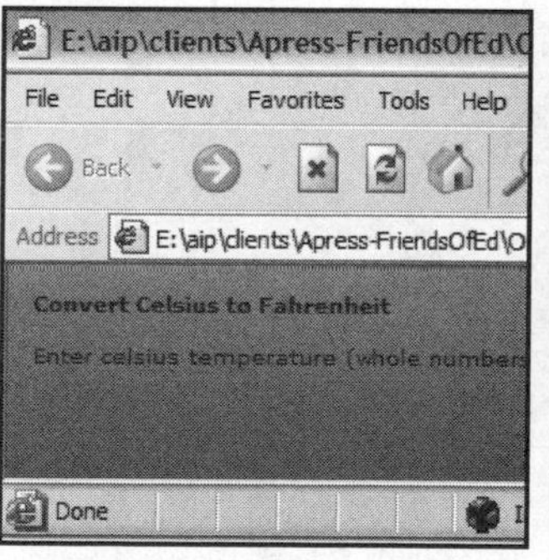

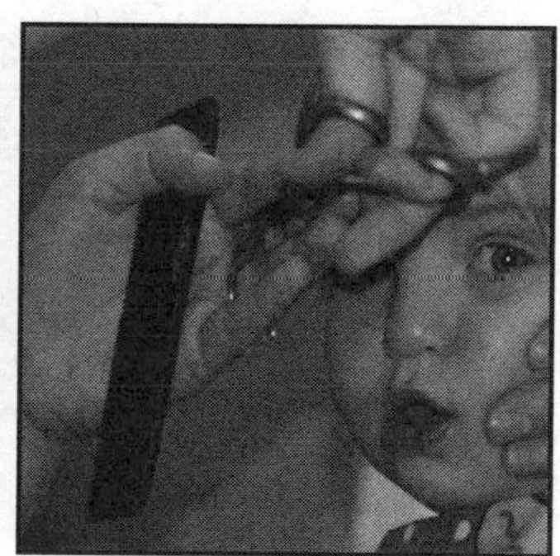

18 EXCHANGING DATA BETWEEN COMPONENTS

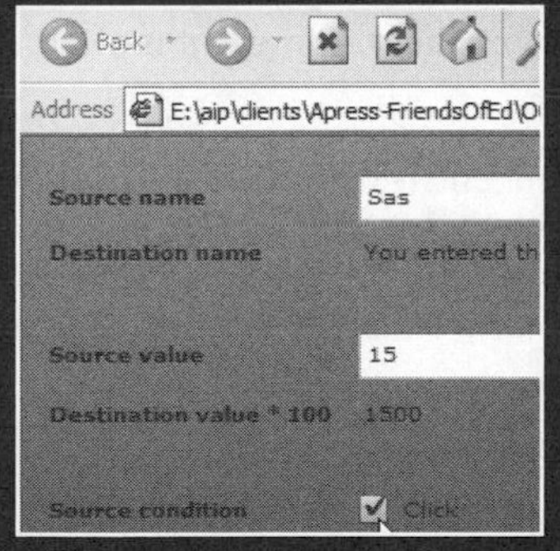

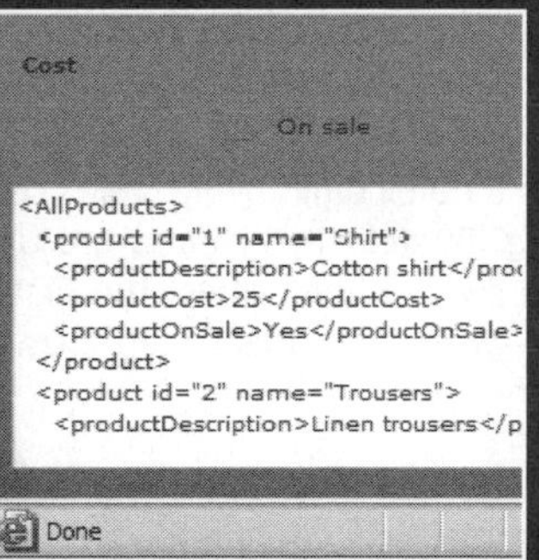

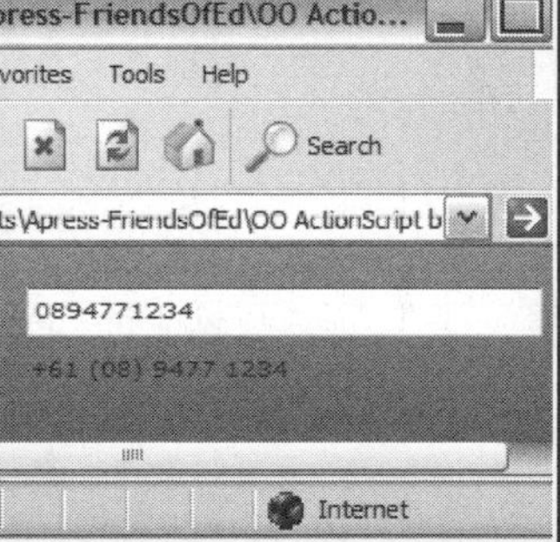

In this chapter, you'll learn how components interact with each other. Specifically, you'll see how you can share data between components using data binding. Within data binding, a property from one component, the *source* component, is bound to the property of another, the *destination* component. Whenever the source property is updated, the source component shares the new value with the destination component.

You can bind data between different UI controls and also between UI controls and data requests. For example, you can bind two `TextInput` controls so that their `text` properties are always synchronized. You could also share the `result` from a service request made by using the `<mx:HTTPService>` component. You'll see examples of both of these types of data binding within this chapter.

During the binding process, you can apply a formatter to transform the bound content. For example, you could transform a number so that it appears as a zip code or telephone number. You can take advantage of several built-in formatters, and you can also create your own.

A discussion of data binding in ActionScript 3 can't take place without reference to Flex components as the two are interrelated—data binding is a part of the Flex framework. You can use any of the following approaches to bind data:

- Use braces, {}, when setting a property value in Flex.
- Use the `<mx:Binding>` tag in Flex.
- Use the `BindingUtils` ActionScript methods.

Within this chapter, we'll look at all three approaches, starting with an overview of the data binding process.

Data binding

Data binding allows you to associate a bindable property from one component with a bindable property in another component. Some kind of triggering event indicates when the property should be updated in the target component. This event is often the updating of the bound property in the first component.

The process of data binding involves two components—the source and destination points for the binding. By default, bindings are one-way—one component affects another, but changes in the second don't affect the first component. It is also possible to create two-way bindings—both components can change each other so that their bound properties remain synchronized.

In order to set up a binding, you need to specify a bindable property from each component. For example, you could specify the `result` from a service request or the `text` property of a `TextArea`. You can also specify a path within a property, for example, a specific property within the `result`.

As mentioned, you can implement data binding using the curly braces syntax within Flex components or by using the <mx:Binding> tag. You can also implement the binding entirely through ActionScript using the BindingUtils methods.

We'll start with a look at data binding within Flex using curly braces.

Using curly braces syntax

Using curly braces provides the simplest way to bind data between two components. You can use curly braces around any bindable component property to indicate that the value should be bound to a property within another component. Using this approach, Flex will automatically update the bound property whenever the source property changes.

You can use the following approaches with curly braces:

- Direct binding between components
- Binding using an ActionScript expression
- Binding XML content using an E4X expression
- Using an ActionScript function in the binding

I'll work through each of these approaches, starting with direct binding.

Using direct binding

You can create a direct binding by using curly braces within the relevant property on the destination component. The curly braces need to refer to the id of the source component and the bound property as shown here:

```
<mx:TextInput id="sourceTI" />
<mx:TextInput id="destinationTI" text="{sourceTI.text}"/>
```

The following MXML code shows a very simplistic example of this approach:

```
<?xml version="1.0"?>
<mx:Application xmlns:mx="http://www.adobe.com/2006/mxml"
  layout="absolute">
  <mx:HBox x="10" y="10">
    <mx:VBox>
      <mx:Label text="Source control" fontWeight="bold"/>
      <mx:Label text="Destination control" fontWeight="bold"/>
    </mx:VBox>
    <mx:VBox>
      <mx:TextInput id="sourceTI" width="229"/>
      <mx:Text text="{sourceTI.text}" width="300" height="20"/>
    </mx:VBox>
  </mx:HBox>
</mx:Application>
```

In this simple example, the text property of a TextInput control provides the value for display in the text property of a Text control. There is a direct, one-way binding between the two controls. Whenever the TextInput receives new content, the updated value displays within the Text control as shown in Figure 18-1.

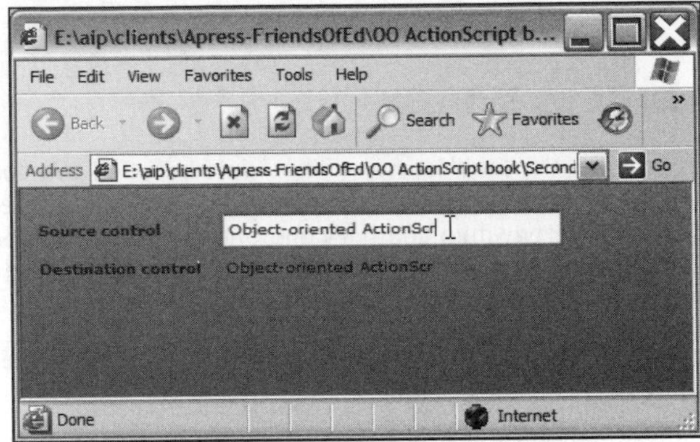

Figure 18-1. The output from simple binding within Flex

As you type within the TextInput control, you'll notice that the Text control updates accordingly. Each new letter that you enter appears within the destination control.

If you need to make alterations to the bound property as part of the binding process, you can use an ActionScript expression rather than a direct binding.

Using ActionScript expressions

ActionScript expressions allow you to apply a transformation to the bound property. For example, you could include calculations, concatenation, and conditional expressions as shown in the following code block:

```
<?xml version="1.0"?>
<mx:Application xmlns:mx="http://www.adobe.com/2006/mxml"
  layout="absolute">
  <mx:VBox x="10" y="10">
    <mx:HBox>
      <mx:VBox width="150">
        <mx:Label text="Source name" fontWeight="bold"/>
        <mx:Label text="Destination name" fontWeight="bold"/>
      </mx:VBox>
      <mx:VBox>
        <mx:TextInput id="sourceName" width="230"/>
        <mx:Text text="You entered the name {sourceName.text}"/>
      </mx:VBox>
    </mx:HBox>
```

```
      <mx:Spacer height="20"/>
      <mx:HBox>
        <mx:VBox width="150">
          <mx:Label text="Source value" fontWeight="bold"/>
          <mx:Label text="Destination value * 100" fontWeight="bold"/>
        </mx:VBox>
        <mx:VBox>
          <mx:TextInput id="sourceValue"  width="230"/>
          <mx:Text text="{Number(sourceValue.text)*100}" width="300"/>
        </mx:VBox>
      </mx:HBox>
      <mx:Spacer height="20"/>
      <mx:HBox>
        <mx:VBox width="150">
          <mx:Label text="Source condition" fontWeight="bold"/>
          <mx:Label text="Destination condition" fontWeight="bold"/>
        </mx:VBox>
        <mx:VBox>
          <mx:CheckBox label="Click" id="sourceCondition"/>
          <mx:Text text="{(sourceCondition.selected) ? 1 : 0 }"
            width="300"/>
        </mx:VBox>
        </mx:HBox>
    </mx:VBox>
  </mx:Application>
```


In the first example, we create a simple concatenation in a Text control using the expression

```
text="You entered the name {sourceName.text}"
```

The second example casts the text property as a number before multiplying it by 100.

```
text="{Number(sourceValue.text) * 100}"
```

The third example uses an if expression to display a value of either 0 or 1, depending on whether or not the CheckBox control is checked.

```
text="{(sourceCondition.selected) ? 1 : 0 }"
```

Figure 18-2 shows the resulting output when this application runs.

If you need to apply the same type of transformation repeatedly, for example, displaying a number as a zip code, a better approach is to use a formatter. You'll see how to do this in the "Adding a formatter to a binding" section of this chapter.

In applications, it is common to load an XML document to provide data for display in UI components. You can use data binding to bind specific parts of the XML content for display in Flex controls.

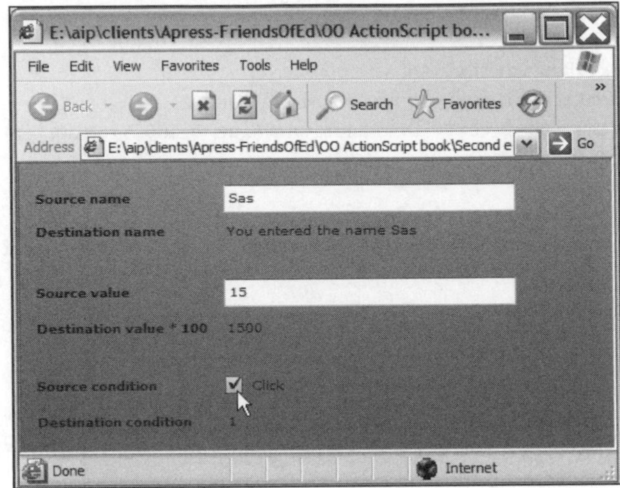

Figure 18-2. Simple bindings can include ActionScript statements within Flex.

Using an E4X expression

You can use an E4X expression to bind a specific part of an XML document to other components. E4X is the ECMAScript standard for working with XML content. You can find out more about the E4X specification at `www.ecma-international.org/publications/standards/Ecma-357.htm`.

Before you can bind a component to the XML document, it's important to ensure that the property is bindable. You will need to add the `[Bindable]` tag to the property in your code.

The following code block provides a simple demonstration of binding to XML. For simplicity, I'm not loading the XML content from an external document. You'll see an example of this a little later in the chapter in the section called "Working through a binding example."

```
<?xml version="1.0"?>
<mx:Application xmlns:mx="http://www.adobe.com/2006/mxml"
  layout="absolute">
  <mx:Script>
    <![CDATA[
      [Bindable]
      private var productXML:XML = <product id="1" name="Shirt">
          <productDescription>Cotton shirt</productDescription>
          <productCost>25</productCost>
        </product>;
    ]]>
  </mx:Script>
  <mx:HBox x="10" y="10">
    <mx:VBox>
```

```
        <mx:Label text="Product name" fontWeight="bold"/>
        <mx:Label text="Product description" fontWeight="bold"/>
        <mx:Label text="Cost" fontWeight="bold"/>
      </mx:VBox>
      <mx:VBox>
        <mx:Text width="300" id="productName"
          text="{productXML.@name}"/>
        <mx:Text width="300" id="productDescription"
          text="{productXML.productDescription}"/>
        <mx:Text width="300" id="productCost"
          text="${productXML.productCost}"/>
      </mx:VBox>
    </mx:HBox>
  </mx:Application>
```


In this example, the source for the bound text properties comes from nodes within the productXML variable (i.e., the XML document tree). The nodes in the document are targeted using dot notation. You can see two types of examples: the first targeting an attribute with productXML.@name and the second targeting the text within a node using productXML.productDescription and productXML.productCost.

It's worth noting that where the destination for the binding is a String property, the toString() method is called automatically as part of the binding process.

Figure 18-3 shows the output from running the application.

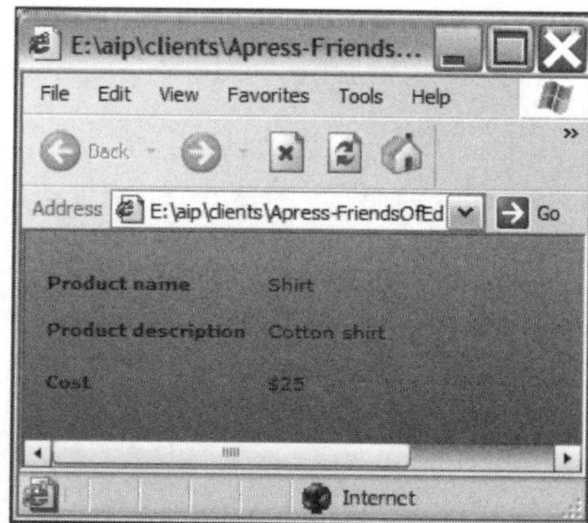

Figure 18-3. Bound XML displays in user interface controls

You can further refine the binding process with the application of an ActionScript function.

Binding with an ActionScript function

You might use an ActionScript function where you want to apply a complicated transformation to a bound property as part of the binding process. The transformation may include a type conversion or adding formatting to the bound property.

In the following example, the selected property of a CheckBox is set during binding using an ActionScript function. The function returns a value of true or false, depending on whether or not the productOnSale node has a value of Yes.

```
<?xml version="1.0"?>
<mx:Application xmlns:mx="http://www.adobe.com/2006/mxml"
  layout="absolute">
  <mx:Script>
    <![CDATA[
      [Bindable]
      private var productXML:XML = <product id="1" name="Shirt">
          <productDescription>Cotton shirt</productDescription>
          <productCost>25</productCost>
          <productOnSale>No</productOnSale>
        </product>;
      private function checkSaleStatus(onSale:String):Boolean {
        if (onSale == "Yes") {
          return true;
        }
        else {
          return false;
        }
      }
    ]]>
  </mx:Script>
  <mx:HBox x="10" y="10">
    <mx:VBox>
      <mx:Label text="Product name" fontWeight="bold"/>
    </mx:VBox>
    <mx:VBox>
      <mx:Text width="300" id="productName"
        text="{productXML.@name}"/>
      <mx:CheckBox label="On Sale" id="sourceCondition"
        selected="{checkSaleStatus(productXML.productOnSale)}"/>
    </mx:VBox>
  </mx:HBox>
</mx:Application>
```

Notice that the checkSaleStatus() function call passes the value of the selected XML node. Running this application produces the output shown in Figure 18-4.

You can check that this approach works correctly by changing the value in the productOnSale node to Yes in the code. The CheckBox should appear checked when you run the application.

Another approach to binding data is to use the <mx:Binding> tag in Flex.

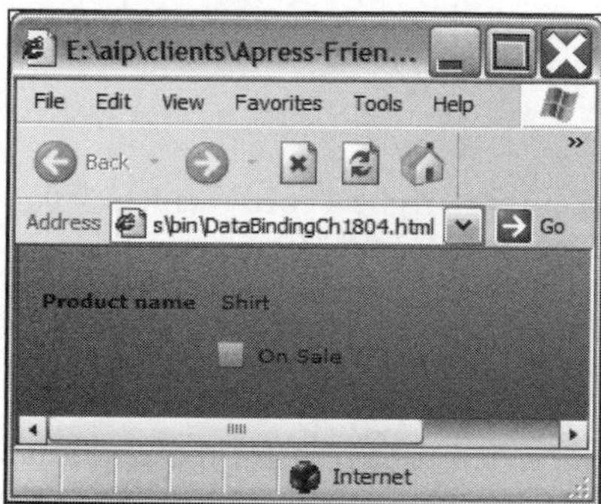

Figure 18-4.
Bound XML is transformed with an ActionScript function.

Using the <mx:Binding> tag

An alternative approach to binding components is to use the `<mx:Binding>` tag instead of curly braces. One advantage is that you can use this tag to separate the bindings from the user interface. You might want to do this if your application uses Model-View-Controller (MVC) architecture. You can also specify two-way bindings.

As with curly braces, you can use the following approaches:

- Direct binding
- Binding using an ActionScript expression
- Binding XML content using an E4X expression
- Using an ActionScript function in the binding

We'll start with a look at direct binding.

Using direct binding

You can create a direct binding with the `<mx:Binding>` tag. All you need to do is to provide a source and destination for the binding using the `source` and `destination` properties.

```
<mx:Binding source="src.property" destination="dest.property"/>
```

The following example shows a binding that uses this approach:

```
<?xml version="1.0"?>
<mx:Application xmlns:mx="http://www.adobe.com/2006/mxml"
  layout="absolute">
  <mx:Binding source="sourceTI.text"
    destination="destinationText.text" />
  <mx:VBox x="10" y="10">
    <mx:HBox>
```

```
      <mx:Label text="Source" fontWeight="bold" width="100"/>
      <mx:TextInput id="sourceTI" width="230"/>
    </mx:HBox>
    <mx:HBox>
      <mx:Label text="Destination" fontWeight="bold" width="100"/>
      <mx:Text width="230" id="destinationText"/>
    </mx:HBox>
  </mx:VBox>
</mx:Application>
```

In this simple example, the source and destination properties of the <mx:Binding> tag create the binding. Running the application produces the same output shown in Figure 18-1 as the two examples are equivalent.

Creating multiple bindings with the same controls

You can add more than one binding tag to specify the bindings within an application. Simply add a new <mx:binding> tag for each binding that you need.

You can also bind more than one source to a single destination, but it's not possible to do this using only the curly braces notation. You'll need to use the <mx:Binding> tag if you need this functionality in your application.

In the following example, two different sources are bound to the same destination. Updating either source control will update the destination control.

```
<?xml version="1.0"?>
<mx:Application xmlns:mx="http://www.adobe.com/2006/mxml"
    layout="absolute">
  <mx:Binding source="source1.text" destination="destination.text"/>
  <mx:Binding source="source2.text" destination="destination.text"/>
  <mx:VBox x="10" y="10">
    <mx:HBox>
      <mx:Label text="Source 1" fontWeight="bold" width="100"/>
      <mx:TextInput id="source1" width="230"/>
    </mx:HBox>
    <mx:HBox>
      <mx:Label text="Source 2" fontWeight="bold" width="100"/>
      <mx:TextInput id="source2" width="230"/>
    </mx:HBox>
    <mx:HBox>
      <mx:Label text="Destination" fontWeight="bold" width="100"/>
      <mx:Text id="destination" width="300"/>
    </mx:HBox>
  </mx:VBox>
</mx:Application>
```

Running the application shows the output that appears in Figure 18-5.

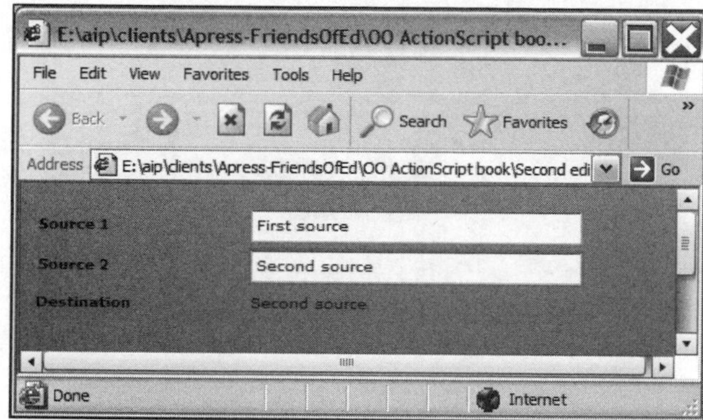

Figure 18-5. Updating a single destination control from two source controls

The next code block shows a single source control bound to more than one destination control.

```
<?xml version="1.0"?>
<mx:Application xmlns:mx="http://www.adobe.com/2006/mxml"
  layout="absolute">
  <mx:Binding source="source.text" destination="destination1.text"/>
  <mx:Binding source="source.text" destination="destination2.text"/>
  <mx:VBox x="10" y="10">
    <mx:HBox>
      <mx:Label text="Source" fontWeight="bold" width="100"/>
      <mx:TextInput id="source" width="230"/>
    </mx:HBox>
    <mx:HBox>
      <mx:Label text="Destination 1" fontWeight="bold" width="100"/>
      <mx:Text id="destination1" width="230"/>
    </mx:HBox>
    <mx:HBox>
      <mx:Label text="Destination 2" fontWeight="bold" width="100"/>
      <mx:Text id="destination2" width="230"/>
    </mx:HBox>
  </mx:VBox>
</mx:Application>
```

When you update the source control, both destination controls are updated by the direct bindings specified in the `<mx:Binding>` tags.

Figure 18-6 shows the effect of running this application.

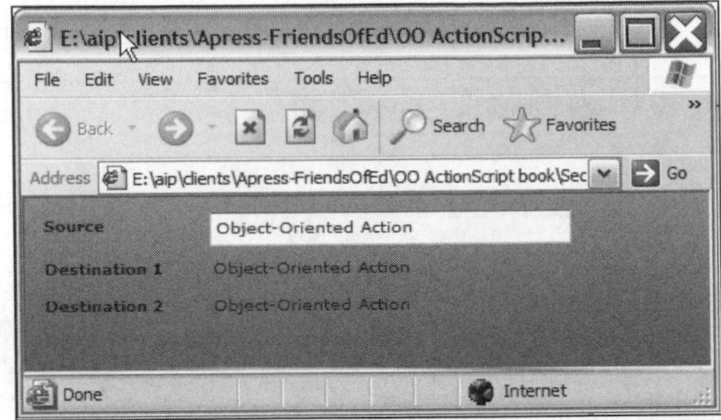

Figure 18-6. Updating multiple destination controls from a single source control

You can also use ActionScript expressions in <mx:Binding> tags.

Using ActionScript expressions

An <mx:Binding> tag can also include ActionScript expressions and even curly braces notation. You use the latter to create concatenated content. ActionScript expressions in the <mx:Binding> tag work much the same as they do within curly braces. You can use them to include concatenated content, calculations, and conditional content.

The following example illustrates the use of three <mx:Binding> tags to create bound data:

```
<?xml version="1.0"?>
<mx:Application xmlns:mx="http://www.adobe.com/2006/mxml"
  layout="absolute">
  <mx:Binding source="You entered the name {sourceName.text}"
    destination="destinationName.text"/>
  <mx:Binding source="String(Number(sourceValue.text) * 100)"
    destination="destinationValue.text"/>
  <mx:Binding source="String((sourceCondition.selected) ? 1 : 0)"
    destination="sourceConditionText.text"/>
  <mx:VBox x="10" y="10">
    <mx:HBox>
      <mx:VBox width="150">
        <mx:Label text="Source name" fontWeight="bold"/>
        <mx:Label text="Destination name" fontWeight="bold"/>
      </mx:VBox>
      <mx:VBox>
        <mx:TextInput id="sourceName" width="230"/>
        <mx:Text id="destinationName" width="300"/>
      </mx:VBox>
    </mx:HBox>
    <mx:Spacer height="20"/>
    <mx:HBox>
```

```
      <mx:VBox width="150">
        <mx:Label text="Source value" fontWeight="bold"/>
        <mx:Label text="Destination value * 100" fontWeight="bold"/>
      </mx:VBox>
      <mx:VBox>
        <mx:TextInput id="sourceValue" width="230"/>
        <mx:Text id="destinationValue" width="300"/>
      </mx:VBox>
    </mx:HBox>
    <mx:Spacer height="20"/>
    <mx:HBox>
      <mx:VBox width="150">
        <mx:Label text="Source condition" fontWeight="bold"/>
        <mx:Label text="Destination condition" fontWeight="bold"/>
      </mx:VBox>
      <mx:VBox>
        <mx:CheckBox label="Click" id="sourceCondition"/>
        <mx:Text id="sourceConditionText" width="300"/>
      </mx:VBox>
    </mx:HBox>
  </mx:VBox>
</mx:Application>
```


The example shows a concatenation,

```
You entered the name {sourceName.text}
```

a calculation,

```
Number(sourceValue.text) * 100
```

and a conditional expression:

```
(sourceCondition.selected) ? 1 : 0
```

If you run this application, you'll get the result shown in Figure 18-2, as the examples are equivalent.

Using an E4X expression

As with curly braces, you can use E4X expressions in an <mx:Binding> tag. The following code block illustrates the use of E4X expressions:

```
<?xml version="1.0"?>
<mx:Application xmlns:mx="http://www.adobe.com/2006/mxml"
  layout="absolute">
  <mx:Script>
    <![CDATA[
      [Bindable]
      private var productXML:XML = <product id="1" name="Shirt">
```

```
        <productDescription>Cotton shirt</productDescription>
        <productCost>25</productCost>
      </product>;
    ]]>
  </mx:Script>
  <mx:Binding source="productXML.@name"
    destination="productName.text"/>
  <mx:Binding source="productXML.productDescription"
    destination="productDescription.text"/>
  <mx:Binding source="${productXML.productCost}"
    destination="productCost.text"/>
  <mx:HBox x="10" y="10">
    <mx:VBox>
      <mx:Label text="Product name" fontWeight="bold"/>
      <mx:Label text="Product description" fontWeight="bold"/>
      <mx:Label text="Cost" fontWeight="bold"/>
    </mx:VBox>
    <mx:VBox>
      <mx:Text width="300" id="productName"/>
      <mx:Text width="300" id="productDescription"/>
      <mx:Text width="300" id="productCost"/>
    </mx:VBox>
  </mx:HBox>
</mx:Application>
```

In this example, three `<mx:Binding>` tags target three different parts of the `productXML` variable. When you run the application, your application should look like the screenshot shown in Figure 18-3, as this example is equivalent.

Binding with an ActionScript function

You can include an ActionScript function as part of an `<mx:Binding>` tag just as you did previously with the curly braces syntax. The following example is equivalent to that shown in Figure 18-4:

```
<?xml version="1.0"?>
<mx:Application xmlns:mx="http://www.adobe.com/2006/mxml"
  layout="absolute">
  <mx:Script>
    <![CDATA[
      [Bindable]
      private var productXML:XML = <product id="1" name="Shirt">
        <productDescription>Cotton shirt</productDescription>
        <productCost>25</productCost>
        <productOnSale>Yes</productOnSale>
      </product>;
      private function checkSaleStatus(onSale:String):Boolean {
        if (onSale == "Yes") {
          return true;
```

```
        }
        else {
          return false;
        }
      }
    ]]>
  </mx:Script>
  <mx:Binding source="productXML.@name"
    destination="productName.text"/>
  <mx:Binding source="{checkSaleStatus(productXML.productOnSale)}"
    destination="sourceCondition.selected"/>
  <mx:HBox x="10" y="10">
    <mx:VBox>
      <mx:Label text="Product name" fontWeight="bold"/>
    </mx:VBox>
    <mx:VBox>
      <mx:Text width="300" id="productName"/>
      <mx:CheckBox label="On Sale" id="sourceCondition"/>
    </mx:VBox>
  </mx:HBox>
</mx:Application>
```


In this example, the <productOnSale> node is bound to the selected property of the CheckBox. The checkSaleStatus() function returns the Boolean value for this property.

Working through a binding example

Before we move on to creating bindings in ActionScript, it might be useful to see a more detailed example of data binding within Flex. In this example, we'll load an external XML document and bind data within the document to a ComboBox control. When we choose an item from the ComboBox, other controls in the application will update with details of the selected item. We'll also load the entire XML document into a TextArea so you can see the full XML content.

The XML document that we'll load is called products.xml, and you can download it with the other resources for the chapter from www.friendsofed.com. The structure of the file follows. For brevity, I've only included one product.

```
<?xml version="1.0" encoding="UTF-8"?>
<AllProducts>
  <product id="1" name="Shirt">
    <productDescription>Cotton shirt</productDescription>
    <productCost>25</productCost>
    <productOnSale>Yes</productOnSale>
  </product>
</AllProducts>
```

If you have a copy of Flex Builder, feel free to create a new project and work through the code that follows. Otherwise, you can find the finished file saved as DataBindingExample1.mxml with the downloaded files.

1. After you've created your Flex project, start by creating the interface. Add a VBox to the stage containing four HBox containers. To the first HBox, add a Label with the text Product and a ComboBox with an ID of productCBO. Add a Label with the text Description and a Text control without any text to the second HBox. To the third, add a Label with the text Cost and another Text control without any text. Finally, add a Spacer with a width of 100, a disabled CheckBox without a label, and a Label with the text On sale to the fourth HBox. Below this HBox, add a TextArea with the ID of showXML. My layout is shown in Figure 18-7.

   The code for the interface should look like the following:

```
<?xml version="1.0"?>
<mx:Application xmlns:mx="http://www.adobe.com/2006/mxml"
  layout="absolute">
  <mx:VBox x="10" y="10">
    <mx:HBox>
     <mx:Label text="Product" fontWeight="bold" width="100"/>
     <mx:ComboBox id="productCBO">
    </mx:HBox>
    <mx:HBox>
      <mx:Label text="Description" fontWeight="bold" width="100"/>
      <mx:Text width="330"/>
    </mx:HBox>
    <mx:HBox>
      <mx:Label text="Cost" fontWeight="bold" width="100"/>
      <mx:Text id="productCost" width="330"/>
    </mx:HBox>
    <mx:HBox>
      <mx:Spacer width="100"/>
      <mx:CheckBox enabled="false"/>
      <mx:Label text="On sale"/>
    </mx:HBox>
    <mx:TextArea width="440" height="130" id="showXML"/>
  </mx:VBox>
</mx:Application>
```

2. Add an <mx:HTTPService> tag above the first VBox. Give it the ID of allProducts and the URL of the XML document. Mine is in an assets folder, so the URL is assets/products.xml. Specify that the resultFormat is e4x and that when the result from the service is received, it calls the processProducts() function, passing the event object as a parameter. We'll create this function shortly.

```
<mx:HTTPService id="allProducts" url="assets/products.xml"
  result="processProducts(event)" resultFormat="e4x"/>
```

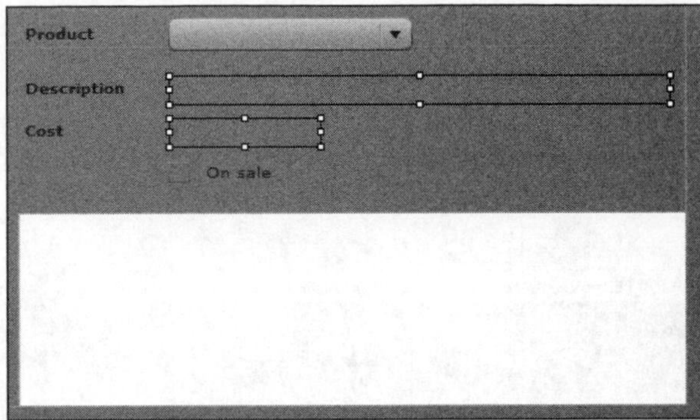

Figure 18-7. The interface for the example application

3. We will send off this request with the send method when the interface has finished building. When the interface is finished, it dispatches the creationComplete event, so add the following attribute to the opening <mx:Application> tag:

```
creationComplete="allProducts.send()"
```

4. Add the following script block below the opening <mx:Application> tag. We start by importing the ResultEvent class. We need to reference this class because the HTTPService dispatches a ResultEvent when it receives a result. We then create a private variable called productXML to store the loaded XML document. Most importantly, we've made this variable bindable by adding the [Bindable] metadata tag. This tag allows the variable to be bound to interface components.

```
<mx:Script>
  <![CDATA[
    import mx.rpc.events.ResultEvent;
    [Bindable]
    private var productXML:XML;
  ]]>
</mx:Script>
```

5. Next we need to add the processProducts() function to the script block. This function receives the ResultEvent event object as a parameter, and we can use the result property of that object to find the value returned by the allProducts request. We then assign the result to the productXML variable. Notice that we had to specify the data type of XML because the returned result property is actually an object. The function also displays the String value of the XML content in the showXML TextArea. I've done this so you can check what's been loaded from the XML document.

```
private function processProducts(event:ResultEvent):void {
  productXML = event.result as XML;
  showXML.text = productXML.toString();
}
```

6. Save and run the application. You should see the TextArea component displaying the XML content from the external file as shown in Figure 18-8.

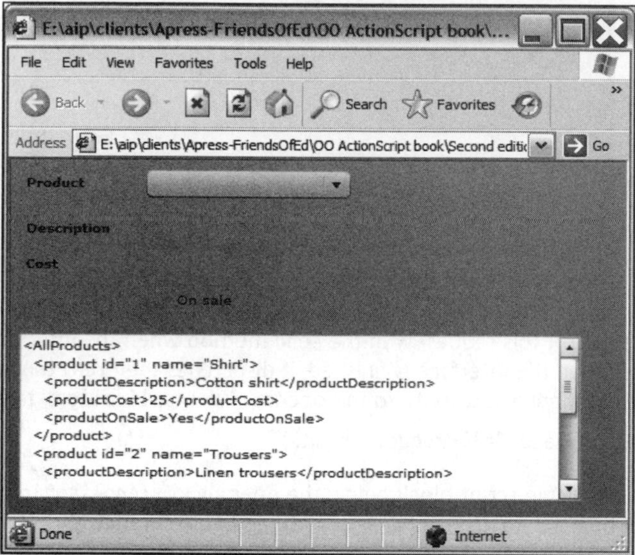

Figure 18-8. The loaded XML content displayed in the interface

7. The next step is to populate the ComboBox component from the XML variable. We'll do this by binding the dataProvider attribute of the ComboBox to the product node from the XML document. Modify the ComboBox as shown in the following bold code. We'll also need to set the labelField so that the ComboBox knows which value to display for the label.

```
<mx:ComboBox x="105" y="8" id="productCBO"
  dataProvider="{productXML.product}" labelField="@name"/>
```

8. Run the application again, and you should see the ComboBox populated with the three products: Shirt, Trousers, and Jacket.

9. The dataProvider for the ComboBox contains all of the data from the XML document below the root node. We'll bind the selectedItem property from the ComboBox so we can display the description and cost of the item as well as whether it is currently on sale. Modify the MXML tags as shown in bold:

```
<mx:VBox x="10" y="10">
  <mx:HBox>
    <mx:Label text="Product" fontWeight="bold" width="100"/>
    <mx:ComboBox id="productCBO"
      dataProvider="{productXML.product}" labelField="@name"/>
  </mx:HBox>
  <mx:HBox>
    <mx:Label text="Description" fontWeight="bold" width="100"/>
  <mx:Text width="330"
    text="{productCBO.selectedItem.productDescription}"/>
  </mx:HBox>
```

```
<mx:HBox>
  <mx:Label text="Cost" fontWeight="bold" width="100"/>
  <mx:Text id="productCost" width="330"
    text="${productCBO.selectedItem.productCost}"/>
</mx:HBox>
<mx:HBox>
  <mx:Spacer width="100"/>
  <mx:CheckBox enabled="false"
   selected="{processOnSale(productCBO.selectedItem.➥
  productOnSale)}"/>
  <mx:Label text="On sale"/>
</mx:HBox>
<mx:TextArea width="440" height="130" id="showXML"/>
</mx:VBox>
```


10. Before we run the application, we need to add the following processOnSale() function to the script block at the top of the file. This function returns a Boolean value that determines whether or not the CheckBox should be checked.

```
private function processOnSale(onSale:String):Boolean {
  if (onSale == "Yes") {
    return true;
  }
  else {
    return false;
  }
}
```

11. Run the application, and you should see the interface shown in Figure 18-9. You should be able to choose different items from the ComboBox component and see the bound controls update their content.

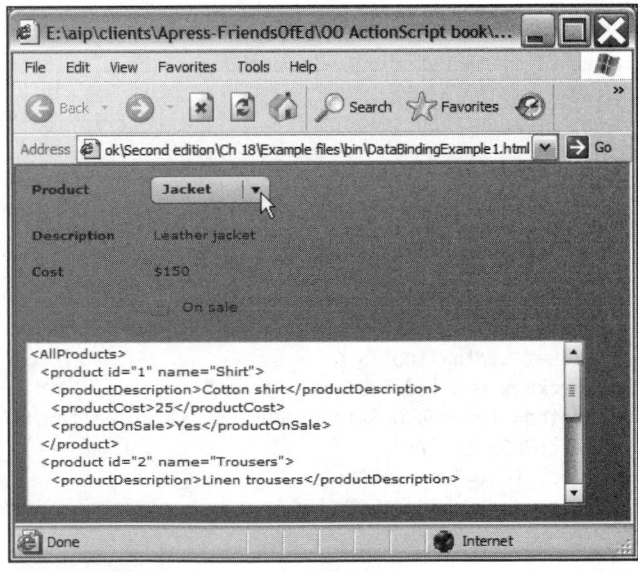

Figure 18-9. The completed application

12. The complete code for the application follows.

```
<?xml version="1.0"?>
<mx:Application xmlns:mx="http://www.adobe.com/2006/mxml"
  layout="absolute" creationComplete="allProducts.send()">
  <mx:Script>
    <![CDATA[
      import mx.rpc.events.ResultEvent;
      [Bindable]
      private var productXML:XML;
      private function processProducts(event:ResultEvent):void {
        productXML = event.result as XML;
        showXML.text = productXML.toString();
      }
      private function processOnSale(onSale:String):Boolean {
        if (onSale == "Yes") {
          return true;
        }
        else {
          return false;
        }
      }
    ]]>
  </mx:Script>
  <mx:HTTPService id="allProducts" url="assets/products.xml"
    result="processProducts(event)" resultFormat="e4x"/>
  <mx:VBox x="10" y="10">
    <mx:HBox>
      <mx:Label text="Product" fontWeight="bold" width="100"/>
      <mx:ComboBox id="productCBO"
        dataProvider="{productXML.product}" labelField="@name"/>
    </mx:HBox>
    <mx:HBox>
      <mx:Label text="Description" fontWeight="bold" width="100"/>
      <mx:Text width="330"
        text="{productCBO.selectedItem.productDescription}"/>
    </mx:HBox>
    <mx:HBox>
      <mx:Label text="Cost" fontWeight="bold" width="100"/>
      <mx:Text id="productCost" width="330"
        text="${productCBO.selectedItem.productCost}"/>
    </mx:HBox>
    <mx:HBox>
      <mx:Spacer width="100"/>
      <mx:CheckBox enabled="false"
        selected="{processOnSale(productCBO.selectedItem.➥
        productOnSale)}"/>
      <mx:Label text="On sale"/>
    </mx:HBox>
```

```
        <mx:TextArea width="440" height="130" id="showXML"/>
      </mx:VBox>
    </mx:Application>
```

This example shows a range of different binding techniques, all using curly braces notation. The example loads an external XML document and uses it as the dataProvider for a ComboBox. When a value is selected in the ComboBox, the bindings in the application select the relevant fields from the dataProvider using the selectedItem property.

So far, we've seen bindings that are created in Flex partly using ActionScript. It's also possible to create bindings entirely in ActionScript, and that's the topic for the next section.

Using the BindingUtils class in ActionScript

Another way to define bindings is to use the mx.binding.utils.BindingUtils ActionScript 3.0 class. You can use the static bindProperty method to create a binding to a property or the static bindSetter method to bind to a property value set with a setter method. We'll look at both approaches here. Whichever you choose, you'll need to make sure you import the BindingUtils class with the following statement:

```
import mx.binding.utils.BindingUtils;
```

Binding to a property

You can use the bindProperty() method to bind one property to another within ActionScript. This method is equivalent to creating a direct binding. The bindProperty() method has the following structure:

```
bindProperty(site:Object, prop:String, host:Object, chain:Object,➥
  commitOnly:Boolean - default is false):ChangeWatcher
```

You would normally use this method in the following way:

```
BindingUtils.bindProperty(destControlID, "text", srcControlID, "text");
```

Most of the parameters in this method are self-explanatory, but the chain and commitOnly parameters need a little more explanation. The chain parameter specifies the source for the bound value, and it can be set in three different ways. By far the most common approach is to use a string value that specifies the name of the bound source property.

The parameter can also be specified as an object that uses the following structure:

```
{name: propertyName, getter:function(host) {return host[name]}}
```

Finally, you can specify the parameter using an array of chained bindable properties from the source, and you'll see this in a later example in the section "Working through a scripted binding example." This value can be specified as an array of String properties. For example, the property src.a.b.c would be defined as ["a" " "b", "c"]. This approach can be useful for drilling down into a hierarchy of properties.

In most cases, you are unlikely to need the last parameter, commitOnly. This parameter allows you to specify which events cause the event handler to be called. If the parameter value is set to true, the handler is called on committing change events. Otherwise, both committing and noncommitting change events will call the handler. Noncommitting change events are specified with the [NonCommittingChangeEvent(<event-name>)] metatags.

The bindProperty() method returns a ChangeWatcher object, which allows you to define an event handler to detect and respond when the binding occurs.

In the following code block, ActionScript creates the binding between a TextInput and Text control. Notice that the binding is created on the initialize event of the application by calling the createBinding() function. The initialize event is a FlexEvent that is dispatched when all children of the container, in this case the application, have been attached, but before the interface is positioned or sized.

```
<?xml version="1.0"?>
<mx:Application xmlns:mx="http://www.adobe.com/2006/mxml"
  layout="absolute" initialize="createBinding();">
  <mx:Script>
    <![CDATA[
      import mx.binding.utils.BindingUtils;
      private function createBinding():void {
        BindingUtils.bindProperty(destinationText, "text", sourceTI, ➥
          "text");
      }
    ]]>
  </mx:Script>
  <mx:HBox x="10" y="10">
    <mx:VBox>
      <mx:Label text="Source control" fontWeight="bold"/>
      <mx:Label text="Destination control" fontWeight="bold"/>
    </mx:VBox>
    <mx:VBox>
      <mx:TextInput id="sourceTI" width="229"/>
      <mx:Text id="destinationText" width="300" height="20"/>
    </mx:VBox>
  </mx:HBox>
</mx:Application>
```

Running this application would show the same outcome as seen in Figure 18-1. This example is equivalent to the direct binding example shown in that screenshot.

Binding to a method

Another alternative approach to scripted bindings is to use a method that sets the value of the destination property and reference it within the bindSetter() method. The bindSetter() method is constructed in the following way:

```
bindSetter(setter:Function, host:Object, chain:Object, ➥
  commitOnly:Boolean - default is false):ChangeWatcher
```

Again, you would normally use this method in the following way:

```
BindingUtils.bindSetter(setterFunction, srcControlID, "text");
```

The chain and commitOnly parameters work in the same way as with the bindProperty() method. The bindSetter() method also returns a ChangeWatcher object, and you'll see how it's used in a later example in the section "Working through a scripted binding example."

The sample code that follows shows a simple binding between a TextInput and Text control created with the bindSetter() method. This example is equivalent to the one that demonstrates the bindProperty() method. Again, the binding is initialized in the <mx:Application> tag.

```
<?xml version="1.0"?>
<mx:Application xmlns:mx="http://www.adobe.com/2006/mxml"
  layout="absolute" initialize="createBinding();">
  <mx:Script>
    <![CDATA[
      import mx.binding.utils.*;
      private function setTextValue(textValue:String):void {
        destinationText.text = textValue;
      }
      private function createBinding():void {
        var watcherSetter:ChangeWatcher = BindingUtils.bindSetter(➥
          setTextValue, sourceTI, "text");
      }
    ]]>
  </mx:Script>
  <mx:HBox x="10" y="10">
    <mx:VBox>
      <mx:Label text="Source control" fontWeight="bold"/>
      <mx:Label text="Destination control" fontWeight="bold"/>
    </mx:VBox>
    <mx:VBox>
      <mx:TextInput id="sourceTI" width="229"/>
      <mx:Text id="destinationText" width="300" height="20"/>
    </mx:VBox>
  </mx:HBox>
</mx:Application>
```

Notice that in this example, we imported the entire mx.binding.utils.* package, as it also contains the ChangeWatcher class.

The private method called setTextValue() sets the value of the text property in the destination Text control. The createBinding() function uses the bindSetter() method to create the binding between the TextInput and Text controls. This method specifies the function setTextValue(), which is called when the value of the text property in the sourceTI control changes.

Working through a scripted binding example

We'll work through an example of scripted binding so you can see how it all hangs together. I'll rework the previous example where we loaded an external XML document and bound it to the dataProvider of a ComboBox control. You'll be able to see how to use both the bindProperty() and bindSetter() methods.

If you didn't previously download the resource file products.xml, you will need to do so now from www.friendsofed.com. As a refresher, the file contains the following structure, although it includes three product nodes:

```
<?xml version="1.0" encoding="UTF-8"?>
<AllProducts>
  <product id="1" name="Shirt">
    <productDescription>Cotton shirt</productDescription>
    <productCost>25</productCost>
    <productOnSale>Yes</productOnSale>
  </product>
</AllProducts>
```

You can find the finished file saved as DataBindingExample2.mxml with the downloaded files.

1. Create a new Flex project and add a VBox to the stage containing four HBox containers. The first HBox should contain a Label with the text Product and a ComboBox with an ID of productCBO. The second HBox should contain a Label with the text Description and a Text control. Add a Label with the text Cost and another Text control without any text to the third HBox. Finally, add a Spacer with a width of 100, a disabled CheckBox without a label, and a Label with the text On sale to the fourth HBox. Add a TextArea with the ID of showXML below the last HBox. You can see my layout in Figure 18-7, shown with the previous example.

   The code for the interface follows.

```
<?xml version="1.0"?>
<mx:Application xmlns:mx="http://www.adobe.com/2006/mxml"
  layout="absolute">
  <mx:VBox x="10" y="10">
    <mx:HBox>
     <mx:Label text="Product" fontWeight="bold" width="100"/>
     <mx:ComboBox id="productCBO"/>
    </mx:HBox>
    <mx:HBox>
      <mx:Label text="Description" fontWeight="bold" width="100"/>
      <mx:Text id="descriptionText" width="330"/>
    </mx:HBox>
    <mx:HBox>
      <mx:Label text="Cost" fontWeight="bold" width="100"/>
      <mx:Text id="productCost" width="330"/>
    </mx:HBox>
    <mx:HBox>
```

```
      <mx:Spacer width="100"/>
      <mx:CheckBox id="onSaleChk" enabled="false"/>
      <mx:Label text="On sale"/>
    </mx:HBox>
    <mx:TextArea width="440" height="130" id="showXML"/>
  </mx:VBox>
</mx:Application>
```

2. Add an `<mx:HTTPService>` tag above the first VBox container. Give it the ID of `allProducts` and the URL of the `products.xml` document. I stored my XML document in an assets folder in the project, so I used the URL `assets/products.xml`. Specify that the `resultFormat` is e4x and the result calls the `processProducts()` function, which we'll create soon.

```
<mx:HTTPService id="allProducts" url="assets/products.xml"
  result="processProducts(event)" resultFormat="e4x"/>
```

3. We need to request the XML document after the interface is built. Add the following attribute to the opening `<mx:Application>` tag:

```
creationComplete="allProducts.send()"
```

4. Import the relevant classes in a script block below the opening `<mx:Application>` tag. We need to import the `ResultEvent` class and the `BindingUtils` class.

```
<mx:Script>
  <![CDATA[
    import mx.rpc.events.ResultEvent;
    import mx.binding.utils.BindingUtils;
  ]]>
</mx:Script>
```

5. We'll use a private variable called `productXML` to store the loaded XML document. Because we need to bind the variable to the `dataProvider` of the ComboBox, we must mark it as bindable. Add the variable declaration to the script block below the `import` statements.

```
[Bindable]
private var productXML:XML;
```

6. When the XML document loads, the `processProducts()` function assigns the `result` property of the `allProducts` request to the `productXML` variable. We also need to call the `createBindings()` function to create the bindings between the controls. Add this function now as well as the empty function `createBindings()`.

```
private function processProducts(event:ResultEvent):void {
  productXML = event.result as XML;
  showXML.text = productXML.toString();
  createBindings();
}
private function createBindings():void {
}
```

18

7. If you run the application now, you'll see the TextArea component displaying the XML content from the external file as shown earlier in Figure 18-8.

8. We need to bind the dataProvider attribute of the ComboBox to the product node from the loaded XML document. Modify the createBindings() function as shown in bold. We also need to set the labelField for the ComboBox so that we know which value to display as the label.

```
private function createBindings():void {
  BindingUtils.bindProperty(productCBO, "dataProvider", productXML,
  ➥"product");
  productCBO.labelField = "@name";
}
```

9. If you run the application, you'll see the ComboBox populated with three products: Shirt, Trousers, and Jacket.

10. We need to bind the remaining items to display the details associated with the selected item in the ComboBox. We'll start with the product description. Add the following line to the createBindings() function. Notice that we needed to specify a chain of bound properties from the ComboBox using array notation.

```
BindingUtils.bindProperty(descriptionText, "text", productCBO, ➥
  ["selectedItem", "productDescription"]);
```

11. We'll bind the product cost and on sale CheckBox a little differently, using the bindSetter method. This approach will allow us to specify methods that can transform the bound values. Start by adding the following lines of code to the createBindings() function:

```
BindingUtils.bindSetter(setCost, productCBO, ["selectedItem", ➥
  "productCost"]);
BindingUtils.bindSetter(setOnSale, productCBO, ["selectedItem", ➥
  "productOnSale"]);
```

12. We'll now need to add the two methods setCost() and setOnSale() to the script block. The setCost() method concatenates a dollar sign with the numeric cost, while the setOnSale() sets the value of the selected property of the CheckBox depending on the variable value.

```
private function setCost(theCost:String):void {
  productCost.text = "$" + theCost;
}
private function setOnSale(onSale:String):void {
  if (onSale == "Yes") {
    onSaleChk.selected = true;
  }
  else {
    onSaleChk.selected = false;
  }
}
```

13. Test the application, and you should see the same result as that displayed previously in Figure 18-9. When you select a new value in the ComboBox, the other controls should update accordingly. The complete code for the application follows:

```
<?xml version="1.0"?>
<mx:Application xmlns:mx="http://www.adobe.com/2006/mxml"
  layout="absolute" creationComplete="allProducts.send()">
  <mx:Script>
    <![CDATA[
      import mx.rpc.events.ResultEvent;
      import mx.binding.utils.*;
      [Bindable]
      private var productXML:XML;
      private function setCost(theCost:String):void {
        productCost.text = "$" + theCost;
      }
      private function setOnSale(onSale:String):void {
        if (onSale == "Yes") {
          onSaleChk.selected = true;
        }
        else {
          onSaleChk.selected = false;
        }
      }
      private function processProducts(event:ResultEvent):void {
        productXML = event.result as XML;
        showXML.text = productXML.toString();
        createBindings();
      }
      private function createBindings():void {
        BindingUtils.bindProperty(productCBO, "dataProvider", ➥
          productXML, "product");
        productCBO.labelField = "@name";
        BindingUtils.bindProperty(descriptionText, "text", ➥
          productCBO, ["selectedItem", "productDescription"]);
        BindingUtils.bindSetter(setCost, productCBO, ["selectedItem",➥
          "productCost"]);
        BindingUtils.bindSetter(setOnSale, productCBO, ➥
          ["selectedItem", "productOnSale"]);
      }
    ]]>
  </mx:Script>
  <mx:HTTPService id="allProducts" url="assets/products.xml"
    result="processProducts(event)" resultFormat="e4x"/>
  <mx:VBox x="10" y="10">
    <mx:HBox>
      <mx:Label text="Product" fontWeight="bold" width="100"/>
      <mx:ComboBox id="productCBO"/>
    </mx:HBox>
    <mx:HBox>
```

```
        <mx:Label text="Description" fontWeight="bold" width="100"/>
        <mx:Text id="descriptionText" width="330"/>
      </mx:HBox>
      <mx:HBox>
        <mx:Label text="Cost" fontWeight="bold" width="100"/>
        <mx:Text id="productCost" width="330"/>
      </mx:HBox>
      <mx:HBox>
        <mx:Spacer width="100"/>
        <mx:CheckBox enabled="false" id="onSaleChk"/>
        <mx:Label text="On sale"/>
      </mx:HBox>
      <mx:TextArea width="440" height="130" id="showXML"/>
    </mx:VBox>
  </mx:Application>
```

In this example, we used bindings created in ActionScript and both the `bindProperty()` and `bindSetter()` methods. You saw how we could bind a loaded XML document to the `dataProvider` property of a `ComboBox` control. You also saw how we could bind various properties of the `selectedItem` of the `ComboBox` to other controls using the static methods `bindProperty()` and `bindSetter()`.

Now that we've worked through the various types of bindings, it's time to look at how formatters work with bound content.

Adding a formatter to a binding

A *formatter* is a Flex component that formats data into strings. Flex includes several built-in formatters that change the way bound data appears in a target component. Formatters apply after the bound data is sent from the source component but before it is received by the target. To use a formatter, you create it in MXML code and then call it with the `format()` method. You can also create the formatter in ActionScript, but we'll focus on MXML tags here.

Using built-in formatters

The `mx.formatters.Formatter` class is the base class for the following built-in formatters:

- `CurrencyFormatter`: Formats a valid number with a currency symbol
- `DateFormatter`: Creates date and time strings from a string or date object
- `NumberFormatter`: Formats a valid number using decimals, the thousands separator, and a negative sign
- `PhoneFormatter`: Formats a valid number into a telephone format
- `ZipCodeFormatter`: Formats a valid number into one of a number of predetermined formats

You can also create your own custom formatters, and we'll look at that a little later. In the meantime, we'll work through each of the built-in formatters.

Using the CurrencyFormatter

The CurrencyFormatter allows you to rewrite a number using a currency format, including a currency symbol, thousands separator, rounding, and the negative symbol. You can create the format with the following syntax:

```
<mx:CurrencyFormatter
    alignSymbol="left|right"
    currencySymbol="$"
    decimalSeparatorFrom="."
    decimalSeparatorTo="."
    precision="-1"
    rounding="none|up|down|nearest"
    thousandsSeparatorFrom=","
    thousandsSeparatorTo=","
    useNegativeSign="true|false"
    useThousandsSeparator="true|false"/>
```


The following code block shows a simple example of applying a CurrencyFormatter during the binding process:

```
<?xml version="1.0"?>
<mx:Application xmlns:mx="http://www.adobe.com/2006/mxml"
  layout="absolute">
  <mx:CurrencyFormatter id="AUDFormatting" precision="2"
    currencySymbol="$" decimalSeparatorFrom="."
    decimalSeparatorTo="." useNegativeSign="true"
    useThousandsSeparator="true" alignSymbol="left"/>
  <mx:HBox x="10" y="10">
    <mx:VBox>
      <mx:Label text="Number" fontWeight="bold"/>
      <mx:Label text="Currency" fontWeight="bold"/>
    </mx:VBox>
    <mx:VBox>
      <mx:TextInput id="sourceNumber" width="230"/>
      <mx:Text text="{AUDFormatting.format(sourceNumber.text)}"
        width="300"/>
    </mx:VBox>
  </mx:HBox>
</mx:Application>
```

Figure 18-10 shows the effect of this formatter.

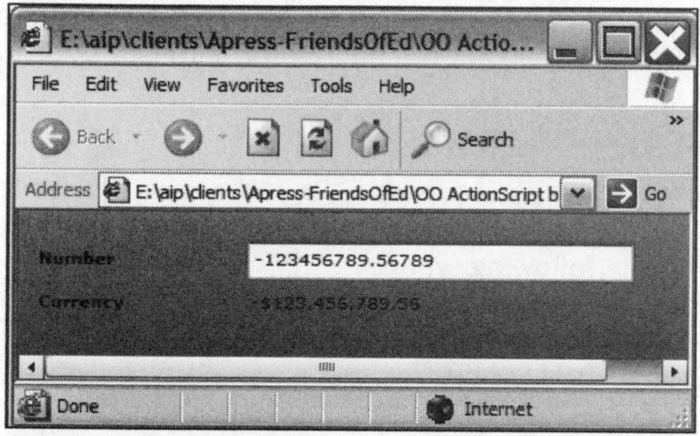

Figure 18-10. Applying a CurrencyFormatter during binding

Using the DateFormatter

The DateFormatter allows you to specify a date format using a string. This might be useful if you were passing a value that included a time and you only wanted to include the date portion. You can use the following to create the format:

```
<mx:DateFormatter
  formatString="Y|M|D|A|E|H|J|K|L|N|S"/>
```

In the following code block, the DateFormatter converts a US date in MM/DD/YYYY format to an Australian-style date in DD-MM-YYYY format:

```
<?xml version="1.0"?>
<mx:Application xmlns:mx="http://www.adobe.com/2006/mxml"
  layout="absolute">
  <mx:DateFormatter id="USToAUSDate"
    formatString="DD-MM-YYYY"/>
  <mx:HBox x="10" y="10">
    <mx:VBox>
      <mx:Label text="Date (mm/dd/yyyy)" fontWeight="bold"/>
      <mx:Label text="Australian date" fontWeight="bold"/>
    </mx:VBox>
    <mx:VBox>
      <mx:TextInput id="sourceDate" width="230"/>
      <mx:Text width="300" height="20"
        text="{USToAUSDate.format(sourceDate.text)}"/>
    </mx:VBox>
  </mx:HBox>
</mx:Application>
```

Running the application gives the results shown in Figure 18-11.

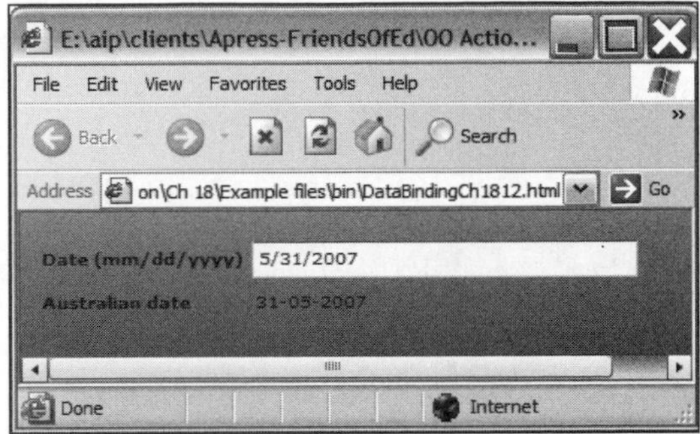

Figure 18-11. Applying a DateFormatter during binding

Using the NumberFormatter

The NumberFormatter allows you to choose the number of decimal places and set the thousands separator as well as the negative sign. It's similar to the CurrencyFormatter, and you can create the format with the following syntax:

```
<mx:NumberFormatter
  decimalSeparatorFrom="."
  decimalSeparatorTo="."
  precision="-1"
  rounding="none|up|down|nearest"
  thousandsSeparatorFrom=","
  thousandsSeparatorTo=","
  useNegativeSign="true|false"
  useThousandsSeparator="true|false"/>
```

In the following code example, the formatter displays the number with four decimal places, a negative sign, and a comma as the thousands separator:

```
<?xml version="1.0"?>
<mx:Application xmlns:mx="http://www.adobe.com/2006/mxml"
  layout="absolute">
  <mx:NumberFormatter id="myNumberFormat"
    precision="4"
    useThousandsSeparator="true"
    useNegativeSign="true"/>
  <mx:HBox x="10" y="10">
    <mx:VBox>
      <mx:Label text="Number" fontWeight="bold"/>
      <mx:Label text="formatted" fontWeight="bold"/>
    </mx:VBox>
    <mx:VBox>
      <mx:TextInput id="sourceNumber" width="230"/>
      <mx:Text width="300"
        text="{myNumberFormat.format(sourceNumber.text)}" />
```

```
    </mx:VBox>
  </mx:HBox>
</mx:Application>
```

You can see the result in Figure 18-12.

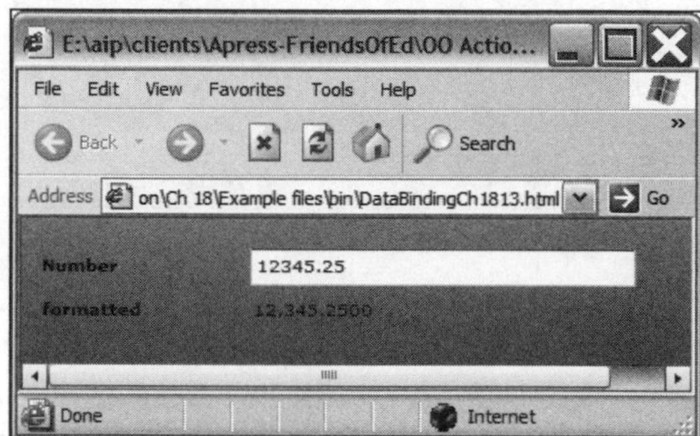

Figure 18-12. Applying a NumberFormatter during binding

Using the PhoneFormatter

You can use the PhoneFormatter to format a number into one of many different phone formats using the following syntax:

```
<mx:PhoneFormatter
    areaCode="-1"
    areaCodeFormat="(###)"
    formatString="(###) ###-####"
    validPatternChars="+()#-. "/>
```

In the following example, the PhoneFormatter formats a ten-digit number into the Australian international phone format +61 (##) #### ####:

```
<?xml version="1.0"?>
<mx:Application xmlns:mx="http://www.adobe.com/2006/mxml"
  layout="absolute">
  <mx:PhoneFormatter id="AusPhoneFormat"
    areaCode="-1"
    areaCodeFormat="(##)"
    formatString="+61 (##) #### ####"
    validPatternChars="+61 ()#"/>
  <mx:HBox x="10" y="10">
    <mx:VBox>
      <mx:Label text="Number" fontWeight="bold"/>
      <mx:Label text="Australian phone" fontWeight="bold"/>
    </mx:VBox>
    <mx:VBox>
      <mx:TextInput id="sourceNumber" width="230"/>
      <mx:Text width="300"
```

```
        text="{AusPhoneFormat.format(sourceNumber.text)}" />
    </mx:VBox>
  </mx:HBox>
</mx:Application>
```

Figure 18-13 shows the resulting format.

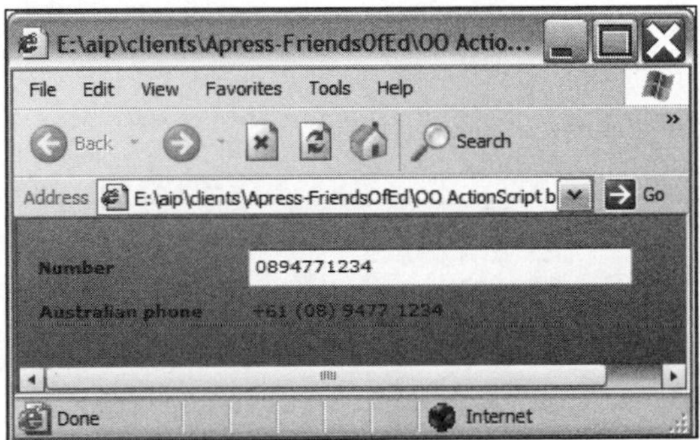

Figure 18-13. Applying a PhoneFormatter during binding

Using the ZipCodeFormatter

The last built-in formatter is the ZipCodeFormatter, which allows you to apply one of the following zip code formats:

- #####-####
- ##### ####
- #####
- ### ###

You'll notice that this formatter only deals with five-, six-, or nine-digit zip codes, and you must match the length of your input with the chosen format. The formatter uses the following syntax:

```
<mx:ZipCodeFormatter
  formatString="#####-####|##### ####|#####|### ###"/>
```

The following example formats a nine-digit number as a nine-digit zip code separated with a hyphen:

```
<?xml version="1.0"?>
<mx:Application xmlns:mx="http://www.adobe.com/2006/mxml"
  layout="absolute">
  <mx:ZipCodeFormatter id="myZipFormatter"
    formatString="#####-####"/>
  <mx:HBox x="10" y="10">
    <mx:VBox>
      <mx:Label text="Number" fontWeight="bold"/>
```

```
      <mx:Label text="Zip code" fontWeight="bold"/>
    </mx:VBox>
    <mx:VBox>
      <mx:TextInput id="sourceNumber" width="230"/>
      <mx:Text width="300"
        text="{myZipFormatter.format(sourceNumber.text)}" />
    </mx:VBox>
  </mx:HBox>
</mx:Application>
```

You can see the applied format in Figure 18-14.

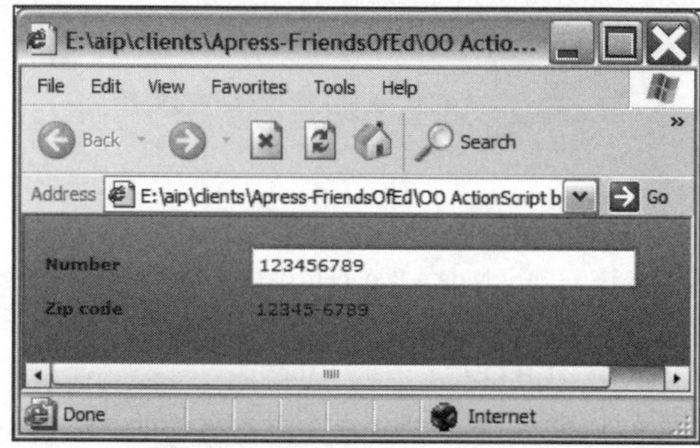

Figure 18-14. Applying a ZipCodeFormatter during binding

Detecting formatter errors

If you don't provide the correct bound input for a formatter, it will return an empty string. This response is by design so you can detect an error more easily and deal with it in ActionScript.

In the following example, we'll use the ZipCodeFormatter from the previous section and see how we can handle the situation where the user enters an incorrect number of digits. We'll choose a nine-digit format and see what happens when the user enters a different number of digits.

```
<?xml version="1.0"?>
<mx:Application xmlns:mx="http://www.adobe.com/2006/mxml"
  layout="absolute">
  <mx:Script>
    <![CDATA[
      private function applyFormat(source:String):String {
        var zipCode:String = myZipFormatter.format(source);
        if (zipCode == "") {
          if (myZipFormatter.error != null ) {
            zipCode = "A zip code must have 9 digits";
          }
        }
```

```
            return zipCode;
          }
        ]]>
      </mx:Script>
      <mx:ZipCodeFormatter id="myZipFormatter"
        formatString="#####-####"/>
      <mx:HBox x="10" y="10">
        <mx:VBox>
          <mx:Label text="Number" fontWeight="bold"/>
          <mx:Label text="Zip code" fontWeight="bold"/>
        </mx:VBox>
        <mx:VBox>
          <mx:TextInput id="sourceNumber" width="230"/>
          <mx:Text width="300"
            text="{applyFormat(sourceNumber.text)}" />
        </mx:VBox>
      </mx:HBox>
    </mx:Application>
```

When you run the application, you'll notice that the error message appears once you start typing. This occurs because at the beginning, you've typed less than the required number of digits. The error message persists until you enter the correct number of digits. By default, this is either five or nine digits, so the error message will appear at all other times. Notice that the error message disappears when you get to five digits in the zip code and reappears afterward until you get to nine digits.

Figure 18-15 shows the result from running the application.

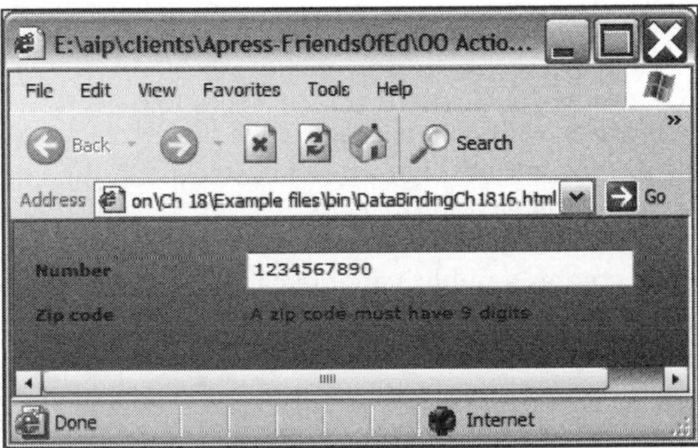

Figure 18-15. Detecting formatting errors during binding

Working with custom formatters

Custom formatters are ActionScript 3.0 classes that extend the `mx.formatters.Formatter` base class or any of the built-in formatters. The class must contain a public `format()` method that takes an argument (the input) and returns a string (the formatted output). You can use a `formatString` property if you need to pass a pattern for the formatted output.

The following code block shows a custom formatter class called CustomZipCode. It formats a four-digit number so that it appears in brackets. Pretend it's the way a zip code is written in an imaginary country!

```
package customFormatters {
  import mx.formatters.Formatter;
  public class CustomZipCode extends Formatter {
    public var formatString:String = "(####)";
    public function CustomZipCode(){
      super();
    }
    override public function format(value:Object):String {
      if(value.length == 0) {
        error="Zero Length String";
        return "";
      }
      if (value.length !=4) {
        error="Zip code must be 4 digits";
        return "";
      }
      if (formatString == "(####)") {
        return "(" + value+ ")";
      }
      else {
        error="Invalid Format String";
        return "";
      }
    }
  }
}
```

This custom formatter exists within a package called customFormatters. The package starts by importing the mx.formatters.Formatter base class. It then declares a class called CustomZipCode that extends the Formatter class.

The CustomZipCode class creates a public variable called formatString that we set to contain the default value of (####). The class also creates a call to the superclass within its constructor using the super() method.

The custom formatter overrides the format() method from the superclass, taking the value to be formatted as an argument. It first checks to see whether this argument has a zero-length value and, if this is the case, it sets the error message and returns a zero-length string. It also checks to see whether the length of the value is anything other than four characters and again sets up the appropriate error handling.

Finally, the value of the formatString is checked, and if it matches (####), an appropriate value is returned. Otherwise, the method sets an appropriate error message and returns a zero-length string. At this point, you could include a switch statement with a range of alternative values for the formatString. For simplicity, I haven't done so.

The following application uses this custom formatter:

```
<?xml version="1.0"?>
<mx:Application xmlns:mx="http://www.adobe.com/2006/mxml"
  layout="absolute" xmlns:cust="customFormatters.*">
  <cust:CustomZipCode id="myCustomZipCode"
    formatString="(####)"/>
  <mx:HBox x="10" y="10">
    <mx:VBox>
      <mx:Label text="Number" fontWeight="bold"/>
    <mx:Label text="Zip code" fontWeight="bold"/>
    </mx:VBox>
    <mx:VBox>
      <mx:TextInput id="sourceNumber" width="230"/>
      <mx:Text width="300"
        text="{myCustomZipCode.format(sourceNumber.text)}" />
    </mx:VBox>
  </mx:HBox>
</mx:Application>
```

Note that the package is referred to using the prefix cust to indicate that it comes from the customFormatters namespace specified in the <mx:Application> tag. Namespaces allow us to refer to custom components that we create in our own packages. The application can then call the format() method of the custom formatter, and the resulting output appears in Figure 18-16.

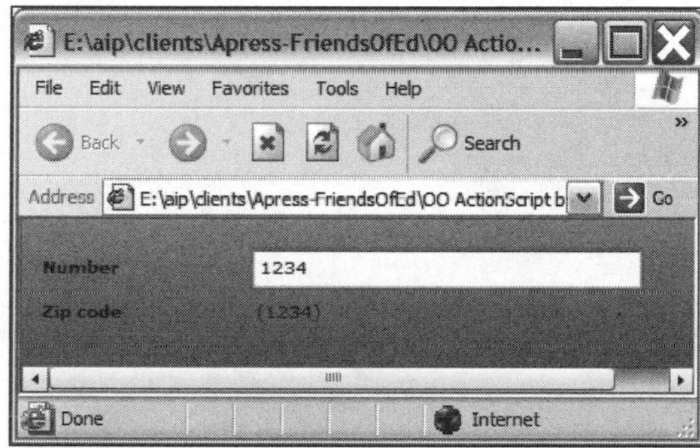

Figure 18-16. Detecting formatting errors during binding

You can find the class file saved as CustomZipCode.as with the other resources for the chapter.

While this is a simplistic example, it demonstrates how you can easily create a custom formatter for use during data binding.

What's next

In this chapter, I introduced the different ways to bind data between components in Flex and ActionScript. I covered binding with curly braces syntax, the use of the `<mx:Binding>` tag, and binding with ActionScript. We worked through two detailed examples that bound loaded XML content to UI controls such as a `ComboBox`, `Text`, and `CheckBox` control.

I covered the use of formatters to change the display of data during the binding process. We worked through each of the built-in formatters, and I showed you how to detect formatting errors. I finished the section by creating a custom formatter.

This chapter only touches the surface of the topic of data binding using Flex and ActionScript 3. Within a single chapter, it's not possible to cover the range of situations that you might encounter. For example, I didn't get a chance to introduce data models and validation. Hopefully, you've seen enough in this chapter to get you started, and what you've read will encourage you to experiment further.

In the next chapter, we'll look at how we can use ActionScript 3.0 to communicate with a web browser. We'll explore the interaction between JavaScript and ActionScript. We'll also have a look at the FABridge code library included with the LiveCycle Data Services 2.5 Beta.

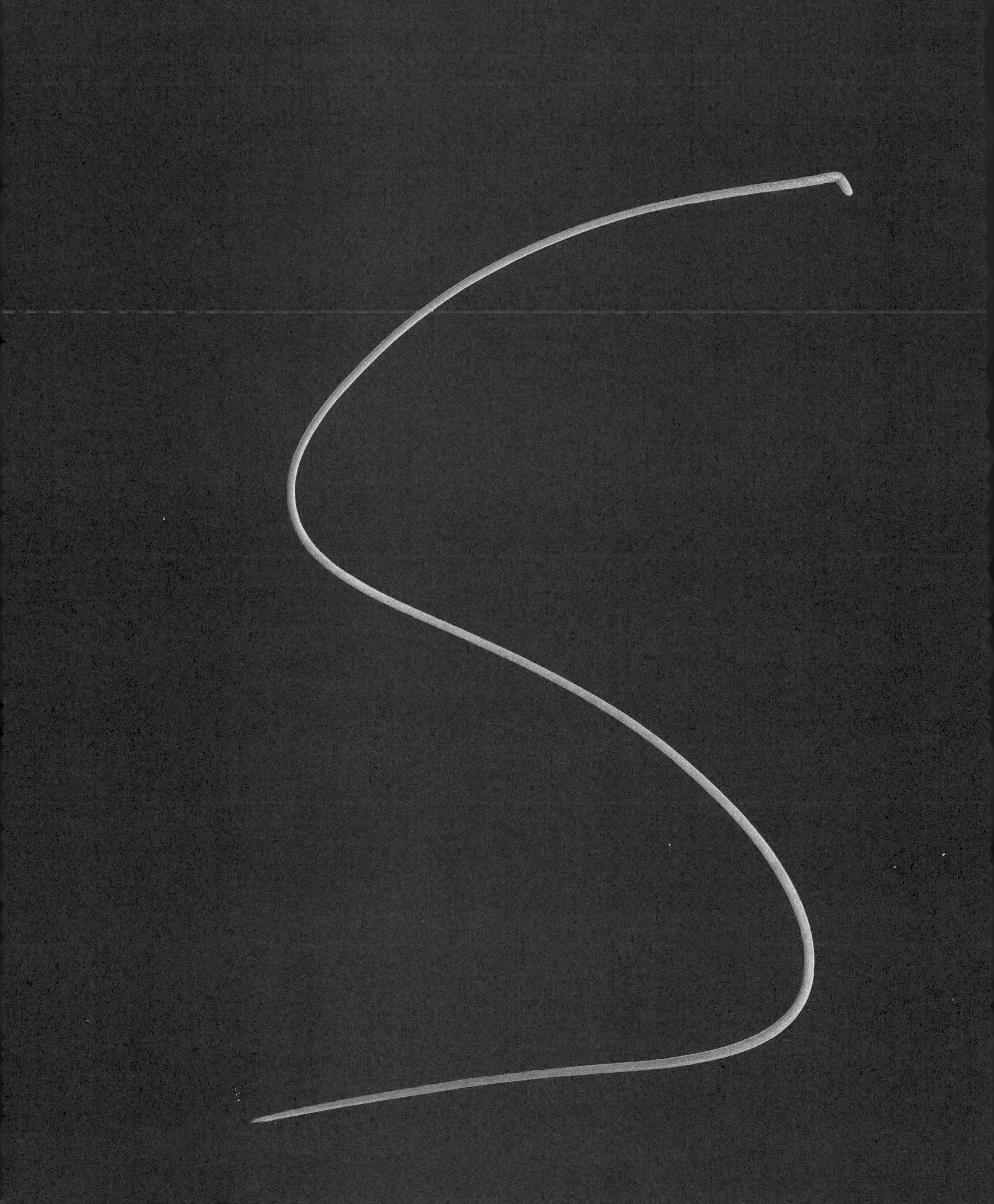

19 COMMUNICATION BETWEEN FLASH AND THE BROWSER

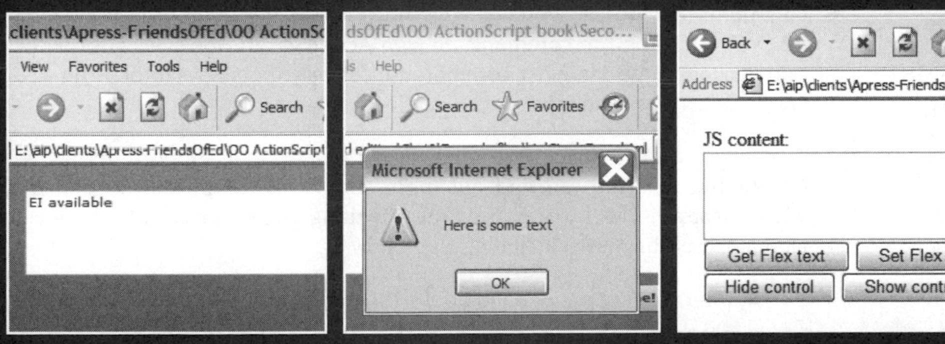

A common requirement for developers is allowing Flash movies to communicate with the hosting web page. Perhaps the Flash movie needs to send values to an HTML form or receive information from a JavaScript function. The Flash movie may need to redirect the browser to a different website or receive authentication information from the hosting page.

There are different ways that developers can achieve this communication, depending on the version of the Flash Player that they are targeting. For Flash Player 7 and below, developers can use FlashVars or JavaScript to send content into Flash. A Flash movie can also call JavaScript functions with `getURL()` or `fscommand()`, optionally sending variables from Flash into the function. Flash Player 8 introduced another alternative—the `ExternalInterface` class, also called the External API. ActionScript 3.0 has updated this class for use with Flash Player 9.

The `ExternalInterface` class allows for communication between a Flash movie and the Flash Player container—usually a web page or desktop application. The class provides similar functionality to the ActionScript `fscommand()` or FlashVars. The communication can occur in either direction—from the container to a Flash movie or from the Flash movie back to the container. However, unlike other methods, the calls are synchronous—they can wait for and receive a response.

The External API is recommended for all communication between JavaScript and ActionScript. A JavaScript function can call an ActionScript function in the Flash movie. The ActionScript function can return a value to the calling JavaScript function. The reverse is possible so that an ActionScript function can call a JavaScript function in the web page hosting the Flash movie, passing arguments as required and receiving a return value from the JavaScript function.

When working with ActionScript 3.0, the method you choose for browser communication will depend on which Flash Player you're targeting. If you're targeting Flash Player 9 with ActionScript 3.0, you'll need to use the External API provided by the AS3 `ExternalInterface` class. If you need to target a player earlier than Flash Player 9, you'll need to use the ActionScript 2.0.

ActionScript 3.0 isn't limited to communicating with a web browser. Flash Player 9 can communicate with any container that hosts a SWF file so you can use a language like C#, VB .NET, or Python to communicate with ActionScript. However, as browser communication is likely to be the most common use for developers, we'll focus on ActionScript and JavaScript in this chapter.

The `ExternalInterface` class requires a browser that supports either ActiveX or the NPRuntime API. You can find out more about this API at `www.mozilla.org/projects/plugins/npruntime.html`. At the time of writing, the `ExternalInterface` class works with all major web browsers, including the following:

- Internet Explorer 5.0 and above for Windows
- Firefox 1.0 and above for both Windows and Macintosh
- Mozilla 1.7.5 and above for both Windows and Macintosh
- Netscape 8 and above for both Windows and Macintosh
- Safari 1.3 and above for Macintosh

Note that you can't use the External API with web pages hosted in Opera, as Opera doesn't support the NPRuntime API or ActiveX controls.

In this chapter, we'll look at how a SWF movie can communicate

- With a web browser using `fscommand()`
- With a web browser using the External API
- Using the Flex-Ajax Bridge
- With other container applications

You can download the resource files for this chapter from `www.friendsofed.com`.

We'll start with a brief look at the `fscommand()` function. You'd use this for Flash/JavaScript communication with Flash Players earlier than version 8.

Communicating using fscommand()

The `fscommand()` function has been available since the first version of ActionScript. In ActionScript 3.0, the function has been repackaged into the `flash.system` package. Not much has really changed though, as the function is still used in much the same way as in previous versions of ActionScript.

The `fscommand()` function allows ActionScript 2.0 and below to communicate with a web browser using JavaScript. You can also use the `fscommand()` to communicate with other container applications. Other than a brief overview, that topic is beyond the scope of this chapter.

Flash Player 9 implements the same security model for loading external data as in Flash Player 8. This security model has some implications for using `fscommand()`.

Understanding Flash Player Security

When it comes to implementing the `fscommand()` function, different releases of the Flash Player have different security rules. Before you can use the `fscommand()` function with Flash Player 7 and above, the `allowScriptAccess` setting in the `<object>` or `<embed>` section of a web page has to be set to `always` or `sameDomain`. The `always` setting means that outbound scripting always succeeds, whereas the `sameDomain` setting only allows communication with scripts that exist in the same domain as the SWF movie.

In Flash Player 8 and above, the default value for the `allowScriptAccess` setting is `sameDomain` if it is not otherwise specified. In Flash Player 7, the default setting is `always`. You don't need to worry about this restriction for earlier Flash Players as their security model is not as strict as in later versions.

You also need to consider security sandboxes. Depending on their location when loaded, Flash Player allocates SWF files to different sandboxes for security purposes. SWF files that originate on the Internet are placed into separate remote sandboxes where they can only access content from the same remote sandbox. They can access other remote sandboxes with permissions such as through a cross-domain policy file and the Security.allowDomain method. SWF files in a remote sandbox cannot access local files.

Flash Player can also allocate SWF files to one of three types of local sandboxes: the local-with-filesystem sandbox, the local-with-networking sandbox, and the local-trusted sandbox. The first is the default for all local SWF files, and these SWF files can load local resources but cannot communicate with the network. In the second case, the SWF file is published with network access. These files cannot access local resources but can communicate with the network. Network-based permissions must be granted to these files. Local SWF files can be registered as trusted to be placed in the local-trusted sandbox. This can be done by users or by an installer program. These files can interact with any other SWF files either locally or remotely.

For a local SWF file to be trusted, it has to appear in a list of trusted content stored on the local computer. This can occur in one of two ways: first, using the Global Security Settings panel, and second, through an installation process.

The Global Security Settings panel runs on your local computer accessed from and displayed within the Adobe website at www.macromedia.com/support/documentation/en/flashplayer/help/settings_manager04.html. You can manage the trusted locations in the Edit locations drop-down box. When you install software, the publisher of the software can automatically register the content as trusted.

The sandbox security system has implications for the use of fscommand(). You can't use the fscommand() function with Flash Player 9 if the calling SWF file is in the local-with-filesystem or local-with-network sandbox and the HTML page container is in an untrusted sandbox.

Now that you understand the security implications affecting the use of fscommand(), it's time to see it in action.

Using the fscommand() function

The fscommand() action takes two arguments—the name of the command to execute and the parameters or arguments to be sent to the JavaScript function:

```
fscommand("CommandToExecute", "Parameters");
```

It's possible for Flash to include multiple fscommand() actions, sending different parameters each time. By sending through a command name, the receiving JavaScript function can distinguish between each action.

The JavaScript function is named using the ID (<object> tag) or the name (<embed> tag) of the Flash movie. The suffix _DoFSCommand is added to the function name as shown:

```
<script language ="JavaScript">
function FlashMovieNameOrID_DoFSCommand(command, args) {
  //do something;
}
</script>
```

As there can only be a single JavaScript function with that name within the web page, Flash can specify which command to execute:

```
fscommand("Command1", "Parameters1");
fscommand("Command2", "Parameters2");
fscommand("Command3", "Parameters3");
```

The JavaScript function can then act according to the command name:

```
< script language ="JavaScript">
function FlashMovieNameOrID_DoFSCommand (command, args) {
  if(command == "Command1"){
    //do something;
  }
  else if(command == "Command2"){
    //do something else
  }
  else if(command == "Command3"){
    //do something else
  }
}
</script>
```


Internet Explorer also requires some VBScript in addition to the JavaScript function. The VBScript subroutine is named in a similar way to the JavaScript function, appending _FSCommand to the name. It then calls the JavaScript function, passing in the arguments from Flash:

```
<script language ="VBScript">
Sub FlashMovieNameOrID_FSCommand(ByVal command, ByVal args)
  call FlashMovieNameOrID_DoFSCommand(command, args)
end sub
</script>
```

The only other requirement to enable fscommand() communication is that if you're using the <embed> tag, you'll need to set the attribute swLiveConnect to true:

```
<embed swLiveConnect="true"... />
```

One disadvantage of using fscommand() to call a JavaScript function is that ActionScript doesn't receive a response letting the SWF movie know of the outcome of the function call. It's possible for the communication to fail silently without any notification to the user. Luckily, this shortcoming is addressed in the ExternalInterface class.

Understanding the ExternalInterface class

The ExternalInterface class allows a SWF movie to communicate with the container hosting the Flash Player. Because it's a static class, you don't need to instantiate it first before you can start calling methods. The class has two methods and two properties that we'll explore further in the remainder of this chapter.

The ExternalInterface class offers several advantages over other methods of communication with JavaScript:

- The class creates synchronous calls so you can receive an immediate response from the function that is called.
- You can call any JavaScript function from within a Flash movie. When using the fscommand(), you can only call a single function.
- There are no limits to the number of arguments that you can send to a JavaScript function. With the fscommand(), you must send the command and parameters arguments.
- You can preserve primitive datatypes such as Boolean, Number, and String during function calls.

You can only use the ExternalInterface ActionScript 3.0 class if you're targeting Flash Player 9. In the majority of cases, you'll probably use this class for JavaScript communication, although it's possible to use it with other types of containers.

The web browser that hosts the Flash Player must support either ActiveX or the NPRuntime API, and you can make sure that the class is available for use by checking the available property:

```
ExternalInterface.available;
```

This read-only property returns a Boolean value. If the property returns a false value, you'll have to use an alternative method of communicating with the container or let the user know that some functionality is unavailable using their current Flash Player.

The ExternalInterface class also has an objectID property that allows ActionScript access to the identifier of the Flash Player instance. This identifier corresponds to the id attribute of the <object> tag or the name attribute of the <embed> tag. This property returns null for containers other than web browsers.

The ExternalInterface class has two methods, call() and addCallback(). The addCallback() method allows an ActionScript function to be registered for JavaScript communication, while the call() method allows ActionScript to call a JavaScript function. We'll start by looking at the call() method.

Using the call() method

The call() method allows a Flash movie to call a function in the container, usually a JavaScript function. You can optionally pass parameters to the called function as shown:

```
call(functionName:String, [parameter1:Object, parameter2:Object]);
```

The `call()` method returns an object—either the value returned by the container function or `null` if the container function is not available. In the case of JavaScript communication, the method looks for a function in the `<script>` tag:

```
<script type="text/javascript" language="javascript">
```

If you are using some other type of container for the Flash movie, the `call()` method fires the `FlashCall` ActiveX event named with the `functionName` parameter to the container for processing.

Let's work through an example to see how a Flash movie can call a JavaScript function. I'll use Flex Builder 2 to create the interface and associated SWF and HTML files. We'll enter text into a `TextArea` control and send it through to a JavaScript function. The JavaScript function will display the entered text in an alert box and send a response back to Flash. We'll display the response within the Flash movie. It's a fairly abstract example, but hopefully it will demonstrate how the communication occurs.

Start by creating a new Flex application and add a `Label`, `TextArea`, and `Button` to a Canvas control. Figure 19-1 shows the interface.

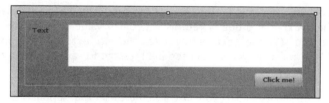

Figure 19-1. The Flex interface

The MXML code that creates the interface follows:

```
<?xml version="1.0" encoding="utf-8"?>
<mx:Application xmlns:mx="http://www.adobe.com/2006/mxml"
  layout="absolute">
  <mx:VBox x="10" y="10">
    <mx:Label text="Text"/>
    <mx:TextArea width="370" height="70" id="swfText"/>
    <mx:HBox width="100%">
      <mx:Spacer width="100%"/>
      <mx:Button label="Click me!"/>
    </mx:HBox>
  </mx:VBox>
</mx:Application>
```

First, we'll display a message in the `TextArea` control indicating whether the External API is available. We'll do this by calling a function when the application initializes. Modify the `<mx:Application>` tag as shown in bold.

```
<mx:Application xmlns:mx="http://www.adobe.com/2006/mxml"
  layout="absolute" initialize="showEIAvailability(event)">
```

The application calls the showEIAvailability function when it initializes. This function also passes a FlexEvent event object.

We'll add the showEIAvailability function in a script block below the opening <mx:Application> tag.

```
<mx:Script>
  <![CDATA[
    import mx.events.FlexEvent;
    private function showEIAvailability(e:FlexEvent):void {
      if (ExternalInterface.available) {
        swfText text = "EI available";
      }
      else {
        swfText.text =  "EI not available";
      }
    }
  ]]>
</mx:Script>
```

The function checks to see whether the External API is available using ExternalInterface.available. The available property returns a Boolean value. The function checks the returned value and sets the text property for the swfText control appropriately. If the External API is available, you should see the message EI available in the TextArea component.

Run this application and, providing you have a web browser that supports the External API, you should see something similar to Figure 19-2.

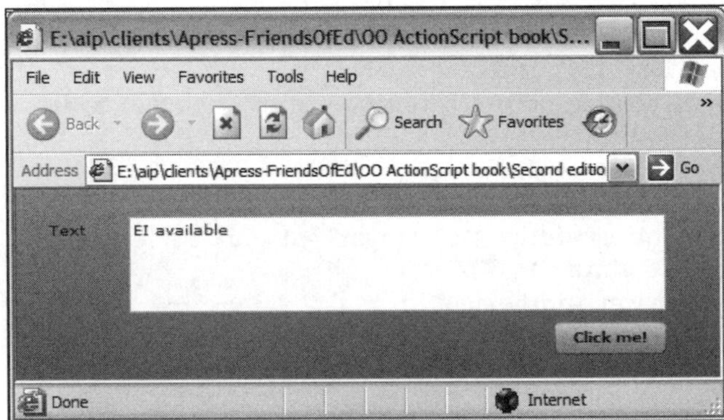

Figure 19-2. Testing that the External API is available

We now need to enable the Click me! button so that clicking it calls a JavaScript function. Change the <mx:Button> tag as shown in bold.

```
<mx:Button x="360" y="83" label="Click me!" click="sendToJS(event)"/>
```

Clicking the button will call the sendToJS() function. Add this function within the script block.

```
private function sendToJS(e:MouseEvent):void {
  if (swfText.text.length > 0 && ExternalInterface.available) {
    var response:Object = ExternalInterface.call("showSWFString",➥
       swfText.text);
    swfText.text = response.toString()+ " from " + ExternalInterface.➥
       objectID;
  }
}
```

The sendToJS() function starts by checking that the user has entered something into the swfText TextArea control and that the External API is available. If both conditions are met, the function then calls a JavaScript function in the container application called showSWFString(). The function call sends the text property of the TextArea as an argument.

Because this communication is synchronous, ActionScript pauses until it receives a response from the called JavaScript function. The response from the call() method is assigned to the response variable. The datatype of the returned value is object. The sendToJS() function then displays a string representation of the response in the TextArea component along with the id or name of the SWF object. We find that value using ExternalInterface.objectID.

Before we can run this application, we need to add the showSWFString() JavaScript function to the hosting web page. Once you've run the application from Flex, you can find the relevant HTML page in the bin folder of your application along with the compiled SWF file.

So you can't accidentally overwrite the HTML file next time you save and run the Flex application, create a copy of it and open it in an HTML editor. Add the following JavaScript function:

```
function showSWFString(theString) {
    alert(theString);
    return "Thanks for the text";
  }
```

This simple JavaScript function receives a parameter called theString, which equates to the text property of the Flex TextArea control. It then displays the value in an alert box. The function returns the text Thanks for the text to the SWF file. The ActionScript function sendToJS() will display this text in the TextArea component.

Run the application from Flex and change the URL of the loaded HTML page so it loads the page you just modified. You should see something similar to Figure 19-3 when you click the Click me! button.

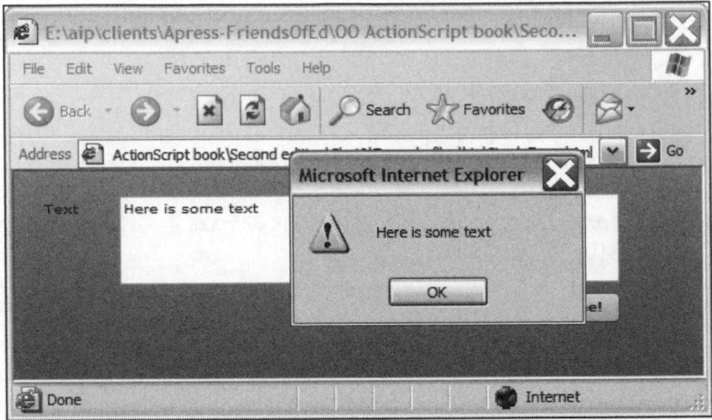

Figure 19-3. Running that application

The text entered in the TextArea control appears in the alert box thanks to the JavaScript function. When you click the OK button in the JavaScript alert, the TextArea control in the SWF movie will update to say Thanks for the text. It should also include the text from and the name or ID of the SWF movie from the HTML page.

In this example, you saw how a SWF file can call a JavaScript function and receive a response synchronously. The example is a simple one, but hopefully it illustrates how easy it is to facilitate ActionScript to JavaScript communication.

You can find the files associated with the example in the resource folder 19-1 with the other chapter resources. You'll need to import them into your Flex application before you can run them on your computer.

> *Caution: The help documentation states that you can't include any JavaScript operators in the ID given to the SWF object in Internet Explorer. This condition means that you can't include characters such as -, +, /, \ in the object ID; otherwise,* `ExternalInterface` *calls from ActionScript won't work.*
>
> *In addition, you can't include* `<object>` *and* `<embed>` *tags in an HTML form if you want to use the External API in your application.*

You've seen one type of the communication, where ActionScript calls a JavaScript function. Now it's time to look at the other type, where JavaScript makes a call to an ActionScript function. You can do this by using the addCallback() method of the External API.

Using the addCallback() method

If you want to call an ActionScript function from the Flash Player container, you need to do two things:

1. Register the function in ActionScript using the addCallback() method.
2. Call the function from the container, most commonly using JavaScript.

The addCallback() method makes an ActionScript function available to be called from the container application. For example, you could use this method to register an ActionScript function so that a JavaScript function in an HTML page can call it, optionally passing parameters. The JavaScript function needs to know the id (in the case of the <object> tag) or name (in the case of the <embed> tag) of the Flash movie to reference it correctly.

The addCallback() ActionScript method takes the following arguments and returns nothing:

```
addCallback (functionName:String, closure:Function);
```


The functionName parameter is the name that JavaScript will use to refer to the ActionScript function. The closure is the name of same function in ActionScript. It is the ActionScript representation of the function called by JavaScript using the functionName argument.

You use the addCallback() method in the following way:

```
ExternalInterface.addCallback("functionName", asFunctionName);
```

You need to make sure that you've set up the closure function so that there is an ActionScript response to the JavaScript call. Good practice means that this function should be given the same name as that used in the functionName parameter. However, this isn't a requirement.

After registering the callback in ActionScript, you can then call the ActionScript function from within the container hosting the SWF movie. Most developers will do this using JavaScript on an HTML page. JavaScript calls the function as if it's a method of the SWF object.

```
flashObjectNameOrID.JSfunctionName(parametersForAS);
```

An example function call follows:

```
function callAS() {
  flashMovieID.asFunctionName(params);
}
```

We'll work through a simple example where we enter a value in an HTML form and send it through to an ActionScript function. The ActionScript function will then return a string to the HTML page for display in an alert box.

Start by creating a new Flex application with the interface shown in Figure 19-4. It contains a Label and TextArea control.

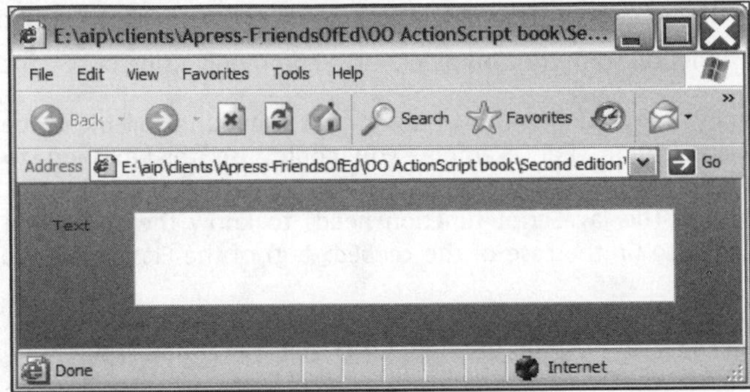

Figure 19-4. The starting interface for the application

I created the interface using the following code:

```
<?xml version="1.0" encoding="utf-8"?>
<mx:Application xmlns:mx="http://www.adobe.com/2006/mxml"
  layout="absolute">
  <mx:HBox x="10" y="10">
    <mx:Label text="Text"/>
    <mx:TextArea width="370" height="70" id="JSText"/>
  </mx:HBox>
</mx:Application>
```

This time, when I initialize the application, I want to set up the ActionScript callback. Modify the `<mx:Application>` tag as shown in bold to call the `addCallback()` function.

```
<mx:Application xmlns:mx="http://www.adobe.com/2006/mxml"
  layout="absolute" initialize="addCallback(event)">
```

When the application is initialized, it calls the `addCallback()` function. Add that function to a script block below the `<mx:Application>` tag.

```
<mx:Script>
  <![CDATA[
    import mx.events.FlexEvent;
    private function addCallback(e:FlexEvent):void{
      if (ExternalInterface.available) {
        ExternalInterface.addCallback("sayHiToAS",showGreeting);
        JSText.text = "EI available"
      }
      else {
        JSText.text = "EI not available"
      }
    }
  ]]>
</mx:Script>
```

Note that I would normally keep the two function names the same in the addCallback() method. However, in this case I didn't do so because I wanted you to be able to tell the source for each function easily by their different names.

The addCallback() function first checks to see that the ExternalInterface class is available, If this is the case, the function adds a callback to the ActionScript function called showGreeting(). Note that we still need to add this function in ActionScript. JavaScript will call this function using the name sayHiToAS, the first argument passed in the addCallback() method. As in the previous example, the addCallback function also displays whether or not the ExternalInterface class is available by displaying appropriate text in the JSText TextArea control.

We now need to add the showGreeting() ActionScript function. Enter the following code into the <mx:Script> block:


```
private function showGreeting(theName:String):String {
  JSText.text = "Hello " + theName + ". Welcome to the External API";
  return "ActionScript says hello";
}
```

This simple function receives a string from JavaScript and displays it with some other text in the TextArea. The function returns the text ActionScript says hello.

Run the application to generate the SWF and HTML files in the bin folder. Before we can test this application, we need to add some JavaScript to the container HTML page.

Save a copy of the generated HTML page in the bin folder under a different name so you can't accidentally overwrite it when you make changes to the Flex file. Open the new HTML page in an HTML editor and add the following form within the <body> section of the page:

```
<form id="JSAS">
  <p>Name: <input type="text" id="txtName"/>
  <input type="button" onclick="communicate();" value="Click me!"></p>
</form>
```

The form includes an input box with the text Name: to the left and a button showing the text Click me!. When we click the button, we'll call the communicate JavaScript function, which will in turn call the ActionScript function showGreeting, which we registered as sayHiToAS for use in JavaScript.

Add the communicate() function to the <head> section of the HTML document. The function that follows assumes that the SWF object has an id and name of simpleForm2:

```
function communicate() {
  var theName = document.getElementById("txtName").value;
  var response = simpleForm2.sayHiToAS(theName);
  alert(response);
}
```

The complete JavaScript block for the HTML page follows:

```
script language="javascript" type="text/javascript">
<!--
// -----------------------------------------------------------------
// Globals
// Major version of Flash required
var requiredMajorVersion = 9;
// Minor version of Flash required
var requiredMinorVersion = 0;
// Minor version of Flash required
var requiredRevision = 0;
// -----------------------------------------------------------------
// -->
function communicate() {
  var theName = document.getElementById("txtName").value;
  var response = simpleForm2.sayHiToAS(theName);
  alert(response);
}
</script>
```

Run the application from Flex and modify the path to point to your new HTML page. The page doesn't look that great, but you can easily tell where the HTML elements are compared with the Flex elements. If you are using a recent web browser, you should see the words EI available in the Flex TextArea control.

Enter a name into the HTML input control and click the Click me! button. You should see the SWF movie TextArea control update with new content including the name you entered in the input control. You should also see a JavaScript alert box displaying the ActionScript response as shown in Figure 19-5.

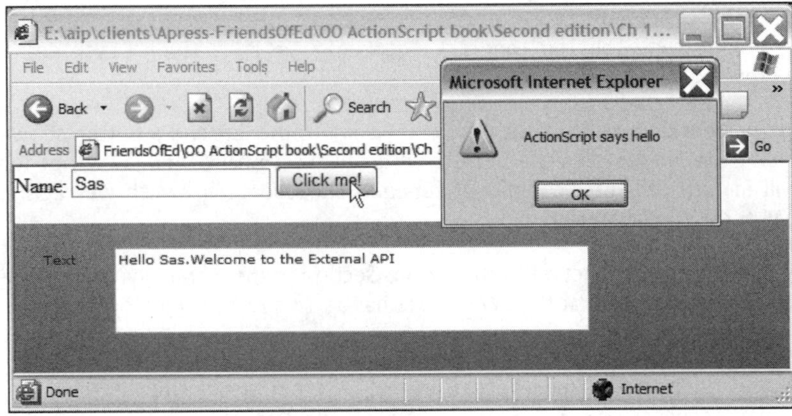

Figure 19-5. The finished application

This simple example is not pretty, but it shows how you can use JavaScript to call an ActionScript function. It also shows how JavaScript can deal with the ActionScript response. You can find these files saved in the folder 19-2 with your resources. You'll need to import these files into a Flex application before you can work with them.

So far in this chapter, we've worked through two examples that show one-way communication, either ActionScript calling a JavaScript function or JavaScript calling an ActionScript function. It's possible to combine these approaches so that the HTML container and SWF file can enjoy two-way communication. We'll work through an example.

Create a new Flex application that uses the following interface:

```
<?xml version="1.0" encoding="utf-8"?>
<mx:Application xmlns:mx="http://www.adobe.com/2006/mxml"
  layout="absolute">
  <mx:VBox x="10" y="10">
    <mx:CheckBox label="External interface available"
      id="chkEIAvailable"/>
    <mx:HBox x="10" y="10">
      <mx:Label text="Text"/>
      <mx:TextArea width="370" height="70" id="sharedText"/>
    </mx:HBox>
    <mx:HBox width="100%">
      <mx:Spacer width="100%"/>
      <mx:Button label="Click me!"/>
    </mx:HBox>
  </mx:VBox>
</mx:Application>
```


Figure 19-6 shows the interface for the application.

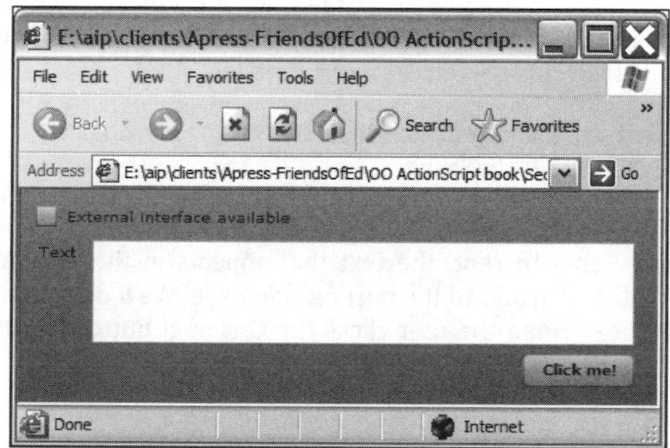

Figure 19-6. The application interface

We'll configure the CheckBox so that it reflects whether the ExternalInterface is available. Add a script block containing the following code underneath the opening <mx:Application> tag:

```
<mx:Script>
  <![CDATA[
    import mx.events.FlexEvent;
    private function showEIAvailability(e:FlexEvent):void{
      chkEIAvailable.selected = ExternalInterface.available;
    }
  ]]>
</mx:Script>
```

The showEIAvailability() function checks the chkEIAvailable control if the ExternalInterface is available. I also imported the FlexEvent class as I'll call this function in the initialize attribute of the <mx:Application> tag. Modify that tag now as shown in bold.

```
<mx:Application xmlns:mx="http://www.adobe.com/2006/mxml"
  layout="absolute" initialize="showEIAvailability(event)">
```

If you run the application again in a browser, you'll see that the CheckBox control is checked, assuming your browser supports the External API.

We'll modify the showEIAvailability() function to add a callback so that JavaScript can access an ActionScript function. Add the lines shown in bold to this function.

```
private function showEIAvailability(e:FlexEvent):void{
  chkEIAvailable.selected = ExternalInterface.available;
  if (ExternalInterface.available) {
    ExternalInterface.addCallback("showGreeting",showGreeting);
  }
}
```

If the ExternalInterface is available, we'll be able to call the showGreeting() ActionScript function using the name showGreeting. The function will receive text from the hosting web page and display it within the Flex TextArea component with the id of sharedText. Add the following showGreeting() function:

```
private function showGreeting(theName:String):void {
  sharedText.text = theName;
}
```

We'll also need to be able to send the text that appears in the TextArea to an HTML <textarea> control that we'll add to the hosting web page. We'll do this in the sendToJS() function, which we'll call when the user clicks the Click me! button. Add this function to the script block:

```
private function sendToJS(e:MouseEvent):void {
   if (sharedText.text.length > 0 && ExternalInterface.available) {
    var response:Object = ExternalInterface.call("showSWFString", ➥
      sharedText.text);
  }
}
```

The function uses the call() method to call the JavaScript function showSWFString(), passing the text from the sharedText TextArea control. You'll need to call this function with the following click handler in the Button control.

```
<mx:Button label="Click me!" click="sendToJS(event)"/>
```

Run the application to generate the SWF and HTML files in the bin folder. Open the HTML file in a text editor and save it under a different name. Add the following HTML form immediately underneath the opening <body> tag:

```
<form id="JSAS">
  <p>Name: <textarea id="txtName" rows="4" cols="60"></textarea>
  <input type="button" onclick="communicate();" value="Click me!"></p>
</form>
```


This simple form displays an HTML <textarea> control and a button. When the button is clicked, it calls the JavaScript communicate() function. Add this function in the <script> block:

```
function communicate() {
  var theName = "From JavaScript: " + ➥
    document.getElementById("txtName").value;
  var response = simpleForm3.showGreeting(theName);
}
```

The function creates a string from the text From JavaScript: and adds the value showing in the txtName control. It then calls the showGreeting() ActionScript function, passing this text.

We also need to add the JavaScript function that we'll call from the SWF file. This function will receive a string from the SWF file. Add the following function:

```
function showSWFString(theString) {
  document.getElementById("txtName").value = "From ActionScript: "➥
    + theString;
}
```

This simple function displays the passed value from the SWF file along with the text From ActionScript: in the <textarea> control.

Open the modified web page in a web browser. Enter some text in each text box and click the relevant Click me! button. You should be able to see that the messages pass between ActionScript and JavaScript as shown in Figure 19-7.

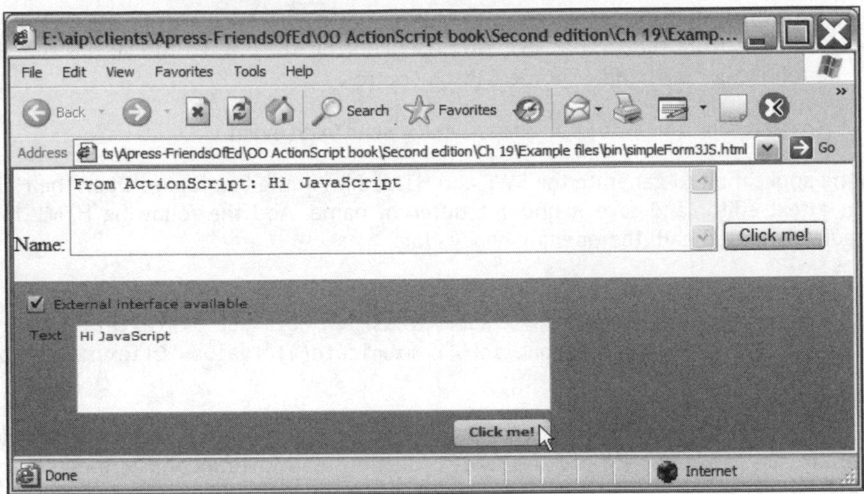

Figure 19-7. Two-way communication between JavaScript and ActionScript

This simple example shows two-way communication between JavaScript and ActionScript. You can find the files used in this example saved in the 19-4 folder with the other resources.

While the External API is very useful, it does have some limitations.

Understanding the limitations of the ExternalInterface class

The External API offers significantly more functionality than that provided within the `fscommand()` function; however, it still has some limitations. From the two examples that we worked through, you should notice that you had to write both JavaScript and ActionScript code in order to enable even one-way communication between the SWF movie and HTML page. This means that a developer needs to have skills in ActionScript as well as JavaScript to be able to use the External API successfully.

In addition, you can only pass certain datatypes between ActionScript and JavaScript. With the External API, you're limited to primitive datatypes, arrays, and simple objects. You can't use your own ActionScript classes in the communication or carry out more complicated types of communication, such as dynamically changing the SWF movie interface.

An alternative approach to ActionScript/JavaScript communication is to use the Flex-Ajax Bridge. This code library essentially allows you to write JavaScript that controls a SWF movie. It is included with the beta version of LiveCycle Data Services 2.5 at `http://labs.adobe.com/downloads/livecycle_dataservices2_5.html`.

Understanding the Flex-Ajax Bridge

While you can use the `ExternalInterface` class for ActionScript and JavaScript communication, an alternative approach is to use the Flex-Ajax Bridge (FABridge). The FABridge allows you to write JavaScript in the container HTML page to control your SWF movie.

The FABridge is a small code library that you can add to a Flex application to allow it to be controlled with browser scripting. You can access any control within a Flex application as well as its properties and methods by writing JavaScript within the HTML page. One advantage of this approach is that you don't need to add script to control the interaction in two different places. This allows the FABridge to streamline the way you write code for your application.

Getting started with the Flex-Ajax Bridge

To get started with the FABridge, you need to install the LiveCycle Data Services 2.5 Beta. On a Windows computer, the FABridge code library is included at `C:\lcds\resources\FABridge\`. You'll see that this folder contains a `src` folder and a `samples` folder. Place the `src` folder in your ActionScript classpath and add a reference to this folder in your Flex application.

You can do this by right-clicking your application and choosing Properties. Select the Flex Build Path option and add a reference to the `src` folder. When you click OK, you should see the project updated with a `[source path] src` folder.

You'll also need to make sure that the `FABridge.js` file from the `src` folder is accessible to the HTML file hosting the Flex application. You will need to add it to the bin folder in your Flex application. You'll also need to make sure that you add an appropriate `<script>` tag so that you include the `FABridge.js` file in the HTML file.

You can include the FABridge library in your Flex application by adding the following tag below your `<mx:Application>` tag:

```
<fab:FABridge xmlns:fab="bridge.*" />
```

You can then script any control in your Flex application using JavaScript in the hosting web page.

Writing FABridge JavaScript

With any JavaScript that you write, your first step is to set a reference to the FABridge using the following code:

```
var flexApp = FABridge.flash.root();
```

You can then use the variable `flexApp` as the starting point for the rest of your JavaScript code.

The FABridge allows you to retrieve the value of any attribute within a Flex control by referring to the control name and attribute name in a path from the FABridge variable. Make sure you add brackets to both the control name and property name as shown here:

```
var controlProperty = flexApp.controlID().propertyName();
```

You can set the property of a control using a similar approach. You need to use the command set combined with the property name, for example, `setPropertyName`. If you were setting the `text` property of a Flex control, you'd need to use `setText()`. Notice that the first letter of the property is capitalized.

```
flexApp.controlID().setPropertyName(someValue);
```

You can also call object methods using the following code:

```
flexApp.controlID().methodName(methodArgs);
```

You can even pass functions to ActionScript and use JavaScript to create Flex controls dynamically. See the FABridge sample at `http://flexapps.macromedia.com/flex2beta3/fabridge/samples/FABridgeSample.html` for examples of more advanced functionality that is available through the FABridge.

To get you started, we'll work through a simple example where we enable two-way communication between a Flex TextArea control and an HTML `textarea` control.

Working through a simple example

In this example, our HTML page will host an HTML form containing a `textarea` control. The HTML page will also host a Flex application containing a `TextArea` control. We'll use HTML buttons with the FABridge to get and set the value in the Flex TextArea. We'll also use HTML buttons to show and hide the `TextArea` control in the SWF movie. It's another simplistic example, but it will serve as an introduction to the FABridge. The style of coding takes a little practice, but once you've been introduced, you'll probably want to explore further.

Create a new Flex application and add the classpath to the `src` folder in the FABridge code library as described earlier in this section. Add the `FABridge.js` file to the `bin` folder of the application.

Create an interface that looks like the one shown in Figure 19-8. It contains a `Label` control and a `TextArea`. I've removed the background color so that the HTML form and SWF file blend better.

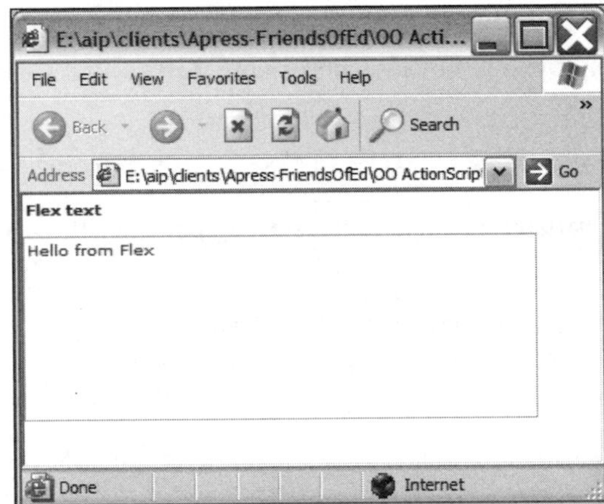

Figure 19-8. The Flex interface for the FABridge application

The MXML code to create this interface follows:

```
<?xml version="1.0" encoding="utf-8"?>
<mx:Application xmlns:mx="http://www.adobe.com/2006/mxml"
  layout="absolute" backgroundGradientColors="[#ffffff, #ffffff]">
  <fab:FABridge xmlns:fab="bridge.*"/>
  <mx:VBox x="10" y="10" id="canvasControl">
    <mx:Label text="Flex text" fontWeight="bold"/>
    <mx:TextArea width="340" height="120"
      id="txtContent" text="Hello from Flex"/>
  </mx:VBox>
</mx:Application>
```


Notice that we include the line

```
<fab:FABridge xmlns:fab="bridge.*"/>
```

to enable to FABridge code library.

The Flex application file doesn't need any more content because we'll control it entirely through ActionScript.

Run the Flex application to create the SWF and HTML files in the bin folder. Make a copy of the HTML file in the bin folder and save it under a different name. Open the new file in your favorite HTML editor. We'll start by adding an HTML form.

Add the following form after the <body> tag in the HTML file:

```
<form id="JSAS">
  <p>JS content:<br/>
    <textarea id="txaContent" rows="4" cols="40"></textarea><br/>
    <input type="button" onclick="getFlexText();" ➥
      value="Get Flex text">
    <input type="button" onclick="setFlexText();" ➥
      value="Set Flex text"><br/>
    <input type="button" onclick="visibleTextArea(false);" ➥
      value="Hide control"/>
    <input type="button" onclick="visibleTextArea(true);" ➥
      value="Show control"/>
  </p>
</form>
```

The form consists of a textarea control and four buttons. We've set click event handlers for each button, and we'll create them shortly.

Run the Flex application and change the path of the HTML page to the one you've just modified. You should see an interface similar to the one shown in Figure 19-9. I purposely haven't styled the HTML elements, so it's obvious which section comes from Flex and which is created in HTML.

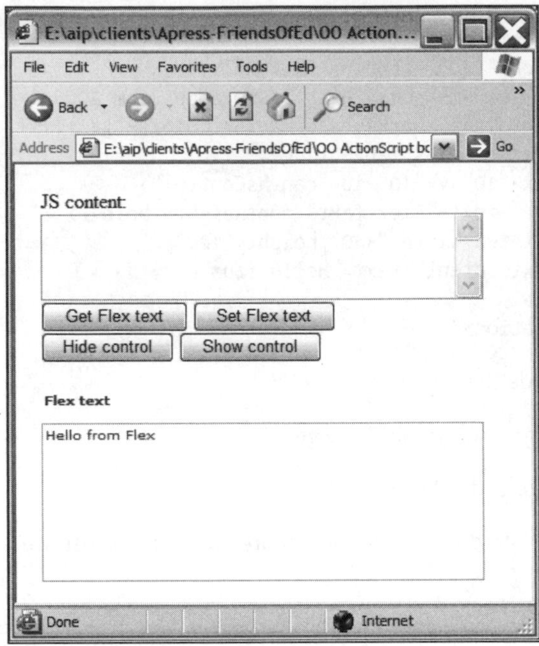

Figure 19-9. The HTML interface

We now need to add the click handlers to a new <script> block in the <head> section. We'll add them one at a time so I can explain the functionality of each as we go along.

We'll start with the getFlexText() handler. Add it to the <head> section in a new <script> block.

```
function getFlexText() {
  var flexApp = FABridge.flash.root();
  var flexText = flexApp.txtContent().text();
  var textareaControl = document.getElementById("txaContent");
  textareaControl.value = flexText;
}
```

The getFlexText() function starts by obtaining a reference to the Flex application and then accesses the text property of the txtContent component using

```
flexApp.txtContent().text();
```

The function then locates the HTML textarea control using document.getElementById("txaContent") and sets its value property to the text property of the Flex TextArea control.

Save the HTML file and reload the web browser. When you click the Get Flex text button, you should see the HTML textarea populated with the contents from the Flex TextArea control.

The setFlexText() handler sets the text displayed in the Flex TextArea control using the value from the HTML textarea. Add the function that follows to the <script> block:

```
function setFlexText() {
  var flexApp = FABridge.flash.root();
  var textareaContent = document.getElementById("txaContent").value;
  flexApp.txtContent().setText(textareaContent);
}
```

Again, the function sets a reference to the Flex application and then retrieves the value from the HTML textarea control. It sets the text property of the txtContent control using

```
flexApp.txtContent().setText(textareaContent);
```


Save and reload the HTML page. When you click the Set Flex text button, you should be able to set the text in the Flex TextArea control to whatever currently appears in the HTML textarea control.

The final two buttons use the same click handler function, although they pass a different parameter each time. The visibleTextArea() function calls the Flex TextArea control's visible property. This function acts as a toggle, showing and hiding the Flex TextArea control in the SWF file interface. Add it to the <script> block.

```
function visibleTextArea(show) {
  var flexApp = FABridge.flash.root();
  flexApp.txtContent().setVisible(show);
}
```

This function starts by referencing the FABridge, and then it calls the TextArea's visible property to hide and show the txtContent control. The Boolean value show comes from the function call in the two button click handlers. When you save and reload the HTML page, clicking the Hide control and Show control buttons should hide and show the Flex TextArea in the SWF file.

Hopefully, this simple example demonstrates that it's easy to implement ActionScript-JavaScript communication with the FABridge. Once you get used to the style of scripting, you may find it easier than working with the ExternalInterface class in ActionScript 3.0. You can find the finished files saved in the 19-3 folder with the other chapter resources. You'll need to import these files into a Flex project before you can work with them.

At the time of writing, the FABridge was in pre-alpha stage and had only been tested on Firefox 1.5 and Internet Explorer 6 (SP 2). It hadn't been tested on any Macintosh or Linux browsers. However, it's worthwhile keeping an eye on this approach as it promises to simplify ActionScript-JavaScript communication greatly, especially for developers who like to work in JavaScript.

In the last section of this chapter, I'd like to look at ActionScript communication with languages other than JavaScript.

ActionScript communication with other languages

So far in the book, you've seen how ActionScript can call JavaScript functions. As I mentioned earlier, the External API can also communicate with other languages in applications that host the Flash Player. Although it is beyond the scope of this chapter to explore this area in any detail, it's worth mentioning how non-JavaScript communication takes place.

When you use the External API to communicate with an ActiveX container application, function calls and return values are sent by the Flash Player in a specific XML format. The Flash Player expects that the same XML format will be used for function calls and return values from the container application. Once you understand this XML vocabulary, you can use it to facilitate any type of SWF movie/container communication. The External API uses one approach to make function calls and another to deal with parameters and return values from function calls.

Making function calls

The process of making function calls involves passing an XML string between ActionScript and the container application. The following XML code block shows how to make a function call:

```
<invoke name="functionName" returntype="xml">
  <arguments>
    (individual argument values)
    </arguments>
</invoke>
```

Notice that the root node is called `<invoke>`. This node has two attributes. The `name` attribute shows the name of the function being called, and the `returntype` attribute must always have a value of `xml`. Any parameters sent with the function call are contained within a child `<arguments>` node.

Each of the parameters or return values sent with the function call has to be formatted in a specific way, according to its datatype. Table 19-1 provides a summary showing the XML vocabulary that is required for each datatype.

Table 19-1. XML formatting required for parameter and return values

Datatype	Format
Null	`<null/>`
Boolean `true`	`<true/>`
Boolean `false`	`<false/>`
String	`<string>Some text/string>`
Number, int, uint	`<number>15</number>`

Datatype	Format
Array (can contain mixed elements)	<array> <property id="0"> <number>15</number> </property> <property id="1"> <string>Hello world</string> </property> </array>
Object	<object> <property id="name"> <string>Sas Jacobs</string> </property> <property id="location"> <string>Australia</string> </property> </object>

Note that you can't send any datatypes other than those listed in Table 19-1 to the container application.

Providing you use the correct XML structures, you can send and receive data between a SWF movie and a container application. Given the wide range of possible container applications, it's beyond the scope of this chapter to explore the topic in detail, but hopefully this section will give you enough information to get started.

What's next?

In this chapter, you've seen how a SWF movie can communicate with the Flash Player container. We spent the majority of the chapter looking at ActionScript and JavaScript communication as that is likely to be the focus of most developers' work. We examined how you can call a JavaScript function from within Flash and how you can use JavaScript to access an ActionScript function.

As an alternative, you saw that it was possible to use the FABridge code library to simplify the communication process. This approach allowed you to control the interaction from the HTML page, using only JavaScript. Finally, you also saw that it's possible for Flash Player 9 to work with other container languages such as C#, VB .NET, and Python.

Within the chapter, we covered different approaches to ActionScript-JavaScript communication. The bulk of the chapter focused on the ActionScript 3.0 External API, which is available to Flash Player 9. One of the key advantages of this approach is the ability to make synchronous function calls. This isn't possible where you're targeting earlier Flash Players using `fscommand()`, although you can make synchronous calls with Flash 8 and the ActionScript 2.0 `ExternalInterface` class. Hopefully, you'll have seen that the External API offers a streamlined and functional approach to communication with the Flash Player.

In the next chapter, we'll explore how Flash communicates with data sources across server connections. Specifically, we'll focus on two efficient means of undertaking server communication in Flash: XML and Web Services. Of course, you'll also want to ensure your data exchanges are secure, and the next chapter shows you how.

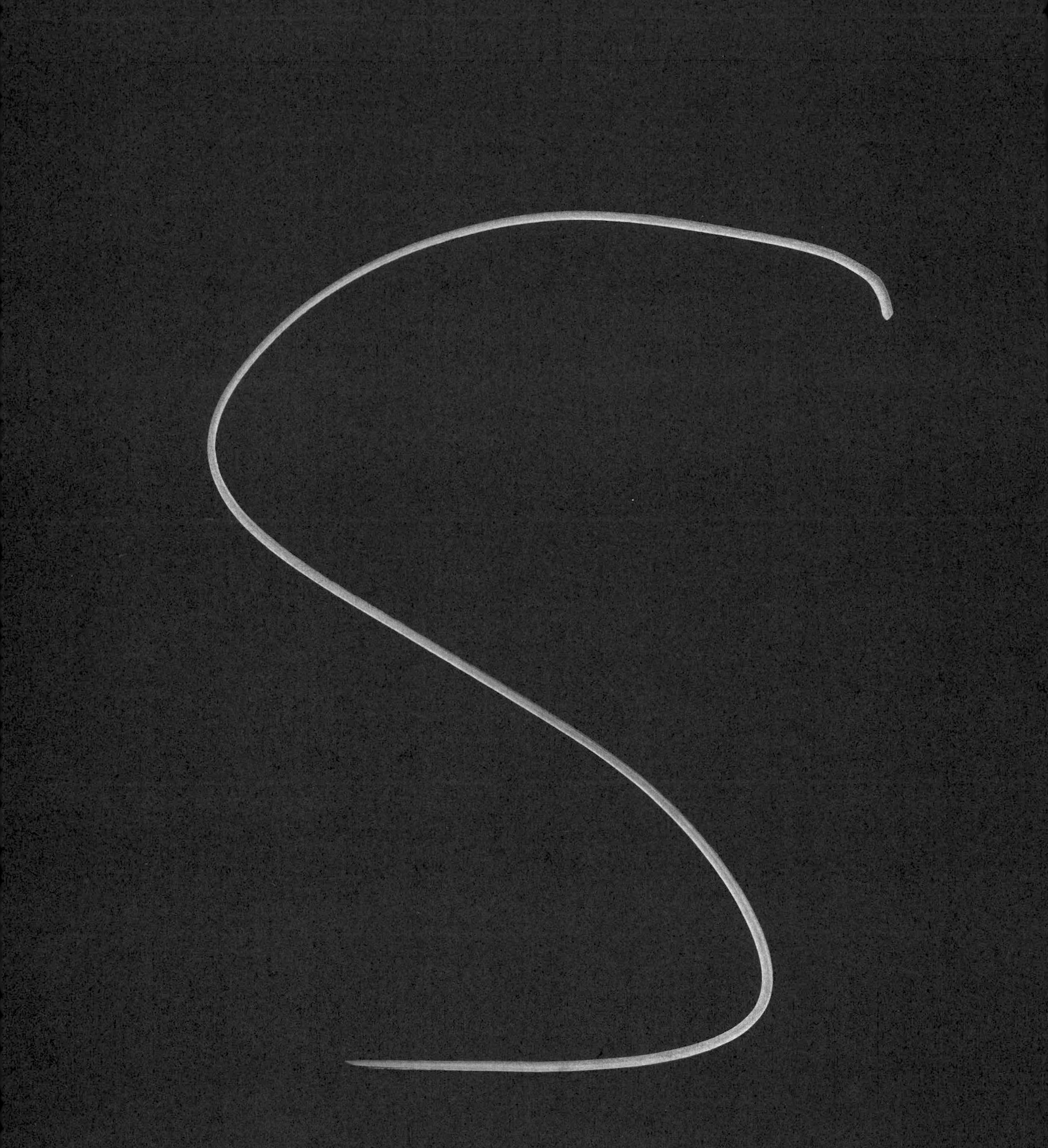

20 SERVER COMMUNICATION (XML AND WEB SERVICES)

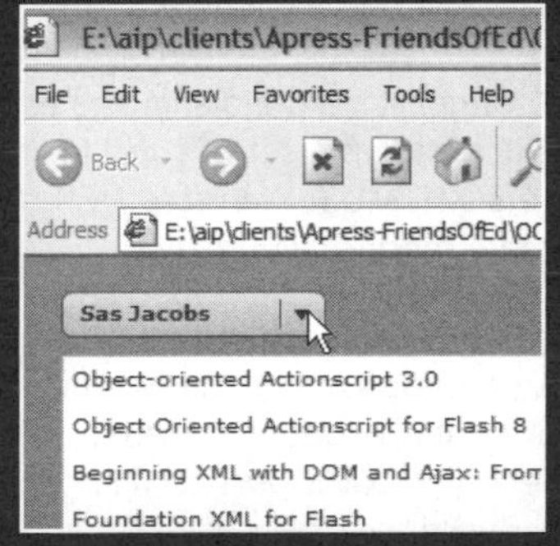

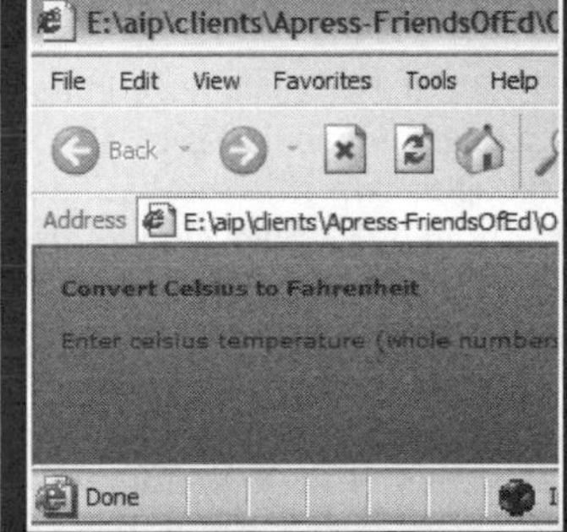

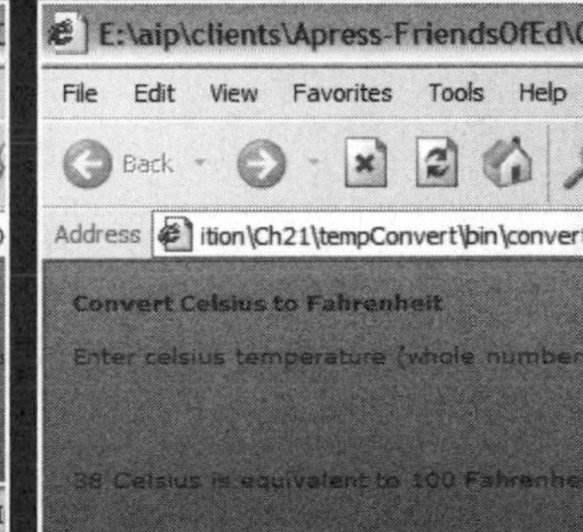

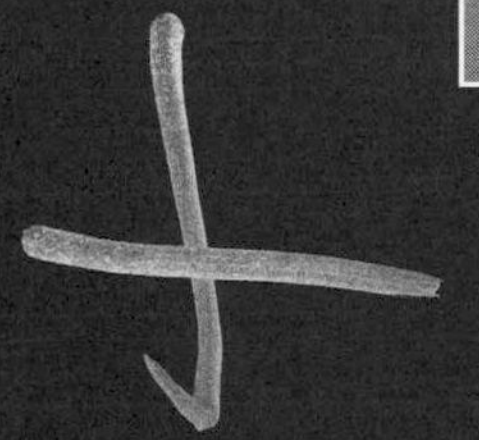

There are many different ways that Flex applications can work with external data. They can load text information, name-value variable pairs, and XML content. One of the most popular of these formats is XML. XML allows for the storage of data in a text format so it can be read by both computers and humans.

XML content comes from a range of sources: static XML documents, server-side pages that generate XML structured data, requests to databases returned in XML format, RSS feeds, and requests for Web Services. You can use ActionScript 3.0 to load, process, and update content stored this way.

If you're familiar with earlier versions of ActionScript, you'll find that things have changed quite a lot when it comes to locating content in XML documents. ActionScript 3.0 includes a new XML class based on the ECMAScript for XML (E4X) specification. You can find out more about this standard at `www.ecma-international.org/publications/standards/Ecma-357.htm`. One of the benefits to developers is that it's now much easier to find your way around an XML document.

In this chapter, I want to start by giving you an overview of XML so you can understand its role in the world of web development. I also want to introduce you to E4X expressions and spend some time working through the new XML class. The second part of the chapter will focus on Web Services, and I'll show you how to use the WebService class. We'll work through several examples, so you can put theory into practice.

Let's start with an introduction to XML.

Understanding XML

In many ways XML, or *eXtensible Markup Language*, defines the Web as we know it today. XML documents store data in a structured way using a text-based format and descriptive tags to mark up the content. Providing an XML document sticks to a set of construction rules, it can use pretty much any approach to describe data, data structures, and data relationships, so it's very flexible. Being a text-based format, XML is also platform independent.

So what is XML? XML is not a language in itself, rather it's a metalanguage used to create other languages, called vocabularies of XML. XML provides a set of rules for how to write these other languages, and it is the basis for the XHTML (*eXtensible Hypertext Markup Language*) that is used by web developers to create modern web pages.

XML documents are designed to be read by both humans and software packages. They are often called self-describing because they can use descriptive tag names. This makes it easier for developers to determine the type of information contained within the document. Software packages that read XML content are called *XML parsers*. Flex Builder 2 and Flash 9 both contain an XML parser as did earlier versions of Flash.

If you've worked with XHTML, you'll be familiar with XML documents. The content in an XHTML document is marked up using a predefined set of tags. For example, an XHTML document has an element called `<html>` that contains all content for the web page. Within this element, there are two other elements, the <head> element that contains information about the page and the <body> element that contains the content to display on the page.

In XML, we refer to these elements or tags, as *nodes*. There are a range of rules describing how these nodes come together to form an XML document. One of the first rules is that every XML document has a single root node containing all other content. As you've just seen in an XHTML page, that's the <html> element.

The root node can optionally contain other nodes, and again you can see this rule in practice in an XHTML page with the <head> and <body> elements. These two nodes contain other nodes in a hierarchical arrangement. For example, <meta> tags appear in the <head> element, and tags such as <p>, <h1>, and <img> can occur in the <body> element. Using XHTML as an example, it's easy to see how the hierarchy develops.

XHTML is one example of an XML vocabulary, and many groups have come together to create their own vocabularies, for example, Chemical Markup Language (CML), Small and Medium-Sized Business XML (smbXML), and MathML. These groups can use a Document Type Definition (DTD) or XML schema document to describe how their markup language works. These descriptions allow other people to write XML documents that are valid for the specific vocabulary.

20

In addition to predetermined XML vocabularies, developers can make up their own node structures and tag names. This approach makes it easy to describe just about any type of data that you can imagine. The following block shows an example:

```
<book>
  <bookTitle>Object-Oriented ActionScript 3.0</bookTitle>
  <author>Todd Yard</author>
  <author>Peter Elst</author>
  <author>Sas Jacobs</author>
  <chapter>1</chapter>
  <chapter>2</chapter>
</book>
```

It's easy to see that this block of markup describes a book by including <bookTitle> and <author> elements. These elements contain text. The markup also describes two of the book chapters, although not in very much detail. If we wanted to learn more about each chapter, we could rewrite the markup as follows:

```
<book>
  <bookTitle>Object-Oriented ActionScript 3.0</bookTitle>
  <author>Todd Yard</author>
  <author>Peter Elst</author>
  <author>Sas Jacobs</author>
  <chapter id="1">
    <title>Introduction to OOP</title>
  </chapter>
  <chapter id="2">
    <title>Programming concepts</title>
  </chapter>
</book>
```

We have two <chapter> nodes that include an attribute id indicating the chapter number. They also include a child <title> element. Attributes generally provide further information about a node. In this case, because we have nodes with the same name, attributes help to distinguish between them. We could also use the same approach with the <author> nodes.

Another way to write the same block of markup follows:

```
<book>
  <bookTitle>Object-Oriented ActionScript 3.0</bookTitle>
  <author>Todd Yard</author>
  <author>Peter Elst</author>
  <author>Sas Jacobs</author>
  <chapter>
    <chapterNumber>1</chapterNumber >
    <title>Introduction to OOP</title>
  </chapter>
  <chapter>
        <chapterNumber>1</chapterNumber >
    <title>Programming concepts</title>
  </chapter>
</book>
```

In this case, we've rewritten the attributes as child nodes, and both approaches are acceptable. Providing we follow the construction rules set down by XML, we'll have a *well-formed* XML document.

Understanding well-formed documents

When a document follows all of the XML construction rules, it is called a well-formed document. Well-formed documents meet the following criteria:

- The document contains one or more elements or nodes.
- The document contains a single root node, which may contain other nested elements.
- Each element closes properly.
- Elements nest correctly.
- Attribute values are contained in quotes.

If you've worked with XHTML, you are probably familiar with many of these rules, especially those about closing and nesting elements correctly. For example, the following block of XHTML code is well formed:

```
<strong><em><span class="norm">Some text</span>
<br/>More text</em></strong>
```

while this block isn't:

```
<em><strong><span class=norm>Some text</span>
<br>More text</em></strong>
```

The second block of code doesn't nest elements correctly. The </strong> tag should appear before the </em> tag. In addition, the value for the class attribute in the <span> element isn't enclosed in quotes.

Writing comments

It can be useful to include comments in an XML document to provide explanations about the content. Comments in XML documents are not usually read by an XML parser, and they use a format that is identical to XHTML comments. They start with the characters `<!--` and finish with `-->`.


```
<!-- This is an XML comment -->
```

You can include comments just about anywhere in an XML document, providing they don't cause the document to lose its well-formed status. For example, a comment should not hide a closing tag.

There's one more thing to consider about XML documents, and that's the inclusion of special characters.

Adding special characters

Certain characters are reserved for an internal use in XML documents. These include less than (<) and greater than (>) signs, which mark the beginning and end of tag names. If you need to include reserved characters in text within an XML node, you'll either have to use an HTML entity to represent the character or enclose the block containing the characters in a CDATA declaration.

Table 20-1 shows the reserved characters and their entities.

Table 20-1. Reserved characters and their HTML entities

ASCII Character	Description	Escape Code
>	Greater than	>
<	Less than	<
'	Single quote	'
"	Double quote	"
&	Ampersand	&
%	Percentage	%

If you need to use a string containing a less-than sign (<) in the text inside a node, you could do it as follows:

```
<example>
  <comparison>5 &lt; 10</comparison>
</example>
```

This text inside the node is equivalent to `5 < 10`.

You could also enclose the content in a CDATA declaration. This declaration tells the XML parser that the contents of the block are not to be treated as XML elements.

```
<example>
  <comparison><![CDATA[5 < 10]]></comparison>
</example>
```

A `CDATA` declaration starts with the characters `<![CDATA[` and ends with `]]>`. Everything written between those characters is treated as text rather than XML content. You could use the same approach to include XHTML tags in a text block so that they're not interpreted as XML tags.

```
<example>
  <name><![CDATA[<strong>Sas Jacobs</strong>]]></name>
</example>
```

You can use entities inside attribute values, but `CDATA` declarations can only be included around text blocks inside nodes.

XML declarations

So far, I haven't mentioned XML declarations. An XML declaration is an optional line at the start of an XML document indicating that the document is of the type XML. If you work with Flex, for example, you'll notice that all MXML documents start with the following XML declaration:

```
<?xml version="1.0" encoding="utf-8"?>
```

The XML declaration is optional when working with XML documents in ActionScript 3.0.

An XML declaration tells the XML parser that it is working with an XML document and provides information about what version of XML the document uses, its character encoding, and whether or not it is a stand-alone file.

The most basic XML declaration looks like this:

```
<?xml version="1.0" ?>
```

The declaration tells the XML parser that it is working with an XML 1.0 document. An encoding attribute can be added to show what type of character encoding is used, for example, Unicode.

```
<?xml version="1.0" encoding="UTF-8" ?>
```

This is more important when working with European and Asian languages.

The `standalone` attribute determines whether or not an external DTD is associated with the document.

```
<?xml version="1.0" encoding="UTF-8" standalone="yes" ?>
```

This attribute is optional, but if included, it must appear after the encoding attribute. In fact, the attributes must appear in the order listed in the preceding code block.

This section of the chapter doesn't aim to provide a comprehensive introduction to XML, so if you're an XML expert, don't worry that I've left something out. Rather, I've aimed to provide an overview of the main points that you need to understand when working with XML. So, now that you understand them, it's time to move on to using ActionScript 3.0 to work with XML content.

Using ActionScript 3.0 with XML

If you've worked with XML in earlier versions of ActionScript, you'll need to forget what you've learned so far. The new E4X approach used in ActionScript 3.0 uses different methods for navigating in XML documents. Developers who are used to writing paths like

```
theXML.firstChild.childNodes[0].childNodes[1].firstChild.nodeValue;
```

to access XML content will be very relieved to know that they can use more descriptive paths. They can create a path of node names separated by dots and use node index numbers as well as the attribute operator `@`. Dot notation allows for much more descriptive paths such as

```
theXML.book.chapter[1].title;
```

In other words, this expression refers to the title of the second `<chapter>` child element of the `<book>`element.

E4X is a useful approach because it makes it easier to understand the paths within XML documents. Compare the two preceding examples to see the difference.

Let's find out a little more about how this E4X standard works.

Understanding E4X

E4X is the acronym used for the ECMAScript for XML specification, also known as ECMA-357. This specification is relatively new and is still evolving, so you may not find much support for it in current web browsers.

To get you used to the E4X approach, I thought I'd show you some simple methods for navigating XML documents.

Navigating XML documents with E4X

You can navigate an XML document using a path created with dot notation and the names of nodes. You can also use the @ operator to indicate an attribute within a node. For the purposes of this example, let's assume that we have assigned the XML content we'll use to a variable called theXML. In ActionScript 3.0, this would look like the following code block:

```
var theXML:XML = <book>
  <bookTitle>Object-Oriented ActionScript 3.0</bookTitle>
  <author>Todd Yard</author>
  <author>Peter Elst</author>
  <author>Sas Jacobs</author>
  <chapter id='1'>
    <title>Introduction to OOP</title>
  </chapter>
  <chapter id='2'>
    <title>Programming concepts</title>
  </chapter>
</book>
```

Notice that I've used single quotes around the attribute values, although I could just have easily used double quotes. In fact, the two are interchangeable.

Table 20-2 shows how we can use dot notation to access different parts of the XML document. You might want to do this so you can retrieve the values of nodes or attributes or assign new values. Note that the expression theXML is equivalent to the root node of the XML document.

Table 20-2. Targetting XML document content with dot notation

Content	Expression	Returns
Book title	`theXML.bookTitle`	Object-Oriented ActionScript 3.0
Second author	`theXML.author[1]`	Peter Elst
First chapter title	`theXML.chapter[0].title`	Introduction to OOP
First chapter title	`theXML..title[0]`	Introduction to OOP
The id of the second chapter	`theXML.chapter[1].@id`	2
Title of the chapter with id of 2	`theXML.chapter.(@id==2).title`	Programming Concepts

If you've worked with XPath before, you'll notice that these expressions seem familiar. For those who aren't familiar with XPath, it is a W3C recommendation for how to address different parts of an XML document, and it includes a range of built-in functions.

We use dot notation to create a path from higher-level nodes down to their children. We can use the shorthand `@` operator to target attributes and the `..` operator to target descendants of a node. Notice that nodes in each collection are numbered from 0 onwards. In the final example, we were able to filter the content using the expression `@id==2`.

> *In ActionScript 3.0, all text and attribute values are treated as strings regardless of any datatype listed in the XML document. That means you may need to cast the value to a different type in ActionScript. For example, if you need to process the content as a number, you will need to use the* `Number` *function to return a numeric value.*

As well as targeting individual pieces of content, you can use E4X expressions to return a collection of nodes. For example, the expression `theXML.author` returns all three author nodes from the XML document. Once you'd returned this collection, you could then use ActionScript to loop through it and retrieve each of the individual author names.

```
var theAuthors:XMLList = theXML.author;
for (var i:Number=0; i<theAuthors.length();i++) {
  //do something with each author using author[i]
}
```

We'll see more of this approach in one of our examples a little later on.

E4X with ActionScript

ActionScript treats nodes, attributes, comments, processing instructions, and text inside elements as XML objects. Processing instructions are just instructions from the XML document to the XML parser. They might tell the XML document to open in a specific package, for example.

XML objects come in two flavors: simple and complex. Nodes that have children are complex, while attributes, comments, and text are simple XML objects.

E4X defines a set of classes for working with XML content, and ActionScript 3.0 includes the `XML`, `XMLList`, `QName`, and `Namespace` classes. In this section, I want to focus on the `XML` and `XMLList` classes in ActionScript 3.0.

> *Note: ActionScript 2.0 worked with the* `XML` *class. This class is different from the ActionScript 3.0* `XML` *class, so the version 2.0 class has been renamed to* `XMLDocument`*. AS3 also includes the* `XMLNode`*,* `XMLParser`*, and* `XMLTag` *classes in the* `flash.xml` *package for backward compatibility.*

Understanding the XML class

The XML class is a top-level class for working with XML content. It implements the E4X standard for working with XML documents.

Properties of the XML class

The XML class has five static properties. Because they are static properties, they need to be accessed using the class name rather than an XML object as shown here:

```
XML.propertyName
```

Table 20-3 shows the static properties of the XML class.

Table 20-3. Static properties of the XML class

Property	Type	Explanation	Default Value
ignoreComments	Boolean	Determines whether to ignore comments in the XML document	true
ignoreProcessingInstructions	Boolean	Determines whether to ignore processing instructions in the XML document	true
ignoreWhitespace	Boolean	Determines whether to ignore whitespace in the XML document	true
prettyIndent	Int	Determines the amount of indenting in spaces when prettyPrinting is set to true	2
prettyPrinting	Boolean	Determines whether white space is preserved when the XML document displays with the toString or toXMLString methods	True

These properties act as global settings for the XML object in ActionScript 3.0.

Methods of the XML class

The XML class has several methods for identifying XML content as well as creating new content and modifying existing content. In this section, I'll work through the most common methods. Table 20-4 shows the methods that allow you to work with content in an XML document. These methods also apply to the `XMLList` class.

Table 20-4. Methods of the XML class for identifying XML content

Method	Explanation
`attribute`	Returns the value of a specified attribute.
`attributes`	Returns a list of attribute values for a specified node.
`child`	Lists all children of a specified node.
`childIndex`	Identifies the position of the child within its parent node, starting from zero.
`children`	Returns all children of the specified node.
`comments`	Returns all comments.
`descendants`	Returns all descendants of an `XML` object.
`elements`	Lists the elements of an `XML` object.
`hasComplexContent`	Determines whether an `XML` object contains complex content.
`hasSimpleContent`	Determines whether an `XML` object contains simple content.
`nodeKind`	Returns the node kind: `text`, `attribute`, `comment`, `processing-instruction`, or `element`.
`parent`	Returns the parent of the specified `XML` object.
`processingInstructions`	Returns all processing instructions.
`text`	Returns all text nodes.
`toString`	For complex content, returns XML content as a string containing all tags. Returns text only for simple content.
`toXMLString`	Returns all XML content as a string, including all tags.
`XML`	Constructor method. Creates a new `XML` object.

Table 20-5 shows the methods that allow you to modify XML content in ActionScript. These methods also apply to the `XMLList` class.

Table 20-5. Methods of the XML class for modifying XML content

Method	Explanation
appendChild	Inserts a child node at the end of the child nodes collection of the specified node
copy	Creates a copy of a node
insertChildAfter	Inserts a child node after a specified child node
insertChildBefore	Inserts a child node before a specified child node
prependChild	Inserts a child node at the beginning of the child nodes of the specified node
replace	Replaces a specified property with a value
setChildren	Replaces children of an XML object with specified content

Understanding the XMLList class

The `XMLList` class represents an ordered collection of XML objects. This collection might be all of the children of the current node or the attributes in an element. An `XMLList` containing a single object is treated in the same way as an XML object.

`XMLList` objects are returned by the following `XML` class methods:

- `attribute`
- `attributes`
- `child`
- `children`
- `descendants`
- `elements`
- `parent`

You might return an `XMLList` object so you can work through the collection in order and deal with each item separately.

Now that you've seen how the `XML` and `XMLList` classes work, how do we get the XML content into ActionScript in the first place?

Creating XML content

There are several approaches to creating XML objects in ActionScript 3.0. These include

- Assigning content directly
- Assigning a string to the XML constructor
- Loading an external XML document from either a static or server-side file, or from a Web Service

We'll work through each of these approaches.

Assigning XML content to an XML object

In a previous example, you saw how easy it was to assign XML content directly to an XML object. We were able to use the following approach:

```
var theXML:XML = <message>Hello world</message>
```

If you're new to AS3, you'll see that this is quite a different approach from the one used in earlier versions of ActionScript. Previously, you had to create a string variable and pass that into the constructor function. This approach is still available in ActionScript 3.0.

Passing string content to the XML constructor

I could also have assigned the XML content to a string variable and then used the XML constructor function to create the XML object.

```
var strXML:String = "<message>Hello world</message>"
var theXML:XML = new XML(strXML);
```

Note that you'll get a runtime error if the content is not well formed, for example, if your tags don't nest correctly or you've left out closing tags. You'll also have to make sure that you use single quotes for attribute values if your string is created with double quotes, and vice versa.

Even though these two approaches are available, the most common approach is to load the XML content from an external source.

Loading XML content from an external source

You can load XML content from an external source such as a static XML file or XML generated by making a call to a server-side file. To do this, you can use either the `URLLoader` or `HTTPService` class. If you want to create a socket connection, you can also use the `XMLSocket` class. In this section, I want to cover the `URLLoader` and `HTTPService` approaches.

Understanding the URLLoader class

The `URLLoader` class loads the text from an external document so you can parse it with an XML object. The following code shows how to request information from an external file called `books.xml` and access the content through an XML object called `theXML`.

```
var theXML:XML;
var loader:URLLoader = new URLLoader();
loader.addEventListener(Event.COMPLETE, processXML);
loader.load(new URLRequest("books.xml"));
```

```
function processXML (e:Event):void {
  theXML = new XML(e.target.data);
}
```

The code creates a new URLLoader object and adds an event listener that listens for the complete event. When the event is dispatched, the processXML() function is called. The load() method loads a new URLRequest for the file books.xml.

The processXML function can use the passed Event argument to access the XML content via the data property of the event target. I'll show you this in more detail a little later.

An alternative approach is to use the HTTPService class to load the external document.

Understanding the HTTPService class

The HTTPService class allows you to access a URL that returns XML content. It makes a GET or a POST request to the server for the URL. The URL of the XML content can be located relative to the current file, for example, as a static XML document. It can also be located on a completely different server, for example, as the result of a call to a URL-based Web Service like an RSS feed. If you are loading data from another domain, you'll need to consider Flash Player security issues, and I'll cover that a little later in the chapter in the section called "Working with Flash Player security."

The following code shows how you can access the books.xml file using the HTTPService class. In this case, we reference the loaded XML content with an XML object called theXML.

```
var theXML:XML;
var service:HTTPService = new HTTPService();
service.url = "books.xml";
service.resultFormat = "e4x";
service.addEventListener("result", processXML);
service.send();
function processXML(e:ResultEvent):void {
  theXML= new XML(e.target.data);
}
```

The code creates a new HTTPService object called service and assigns the url property to the filename for the book. It specifies that the format for the results is e4x. This indicates that the returned value uses an XML format that can be accessed with E4X expressions.

The code assigns a handler for the result event, and we could also capture the fault event in the same way. Finally, the code block uses the send() method to request the file from the server. At this point, we could send through any extra parameters for the request inside the send() method. The preceding code block doesn't do this. The processXML() function accesses the loaded XML content using the data property of the event target. This content is assigned to the XML object.

I'll take you through an example that uses the URLLoader class to load an external XML document. Afterwards, I'll show you a simple example using the <mx:HTTPService> tag in a Flex application.

Working through an example with the URLLoader class

You'll learn a bit more about working with an external XML document with the URLLoader class as I walk you through a simple example. We'll create a Flex Builder 2 application that displays author names from a loaded XML document in a ComboBox control. When we choose an author from the ComboBox, the books that they've published will appear in a List control. It's a simple example, but it will show you how to load XML content from an external file and how to locate information within an XML document.

The XML document that we'll use for this example has the following structure:

```
<?xml version="1.0" encoding="UTF-8"?>
<book>
  <author>
    <authorName><!-- Multiple authors --></authorName>
    <bookTitle><!--Multiple book titles per author--></bookTitle>
  </author>
</book>
```


Start by creating a new Flex project with File ➤ New ➤ Flex project. Give it the name Books and save it anywhere on your hard drive. You can accept the default location if you like. Click the Finish button to create the project.

Create a new folder in the Flex project by right-clicking it in the Navigator view and choosing New ➤ Folder. Assign the folder the name assets. If you haven't already done so, you'll need to download the chapter resources from www.friendsofed.com. They contain the authorBooks.xml file that we'll use for the example.

Right-click the assets folder in the Navigator view and choose Import. Select the File System option and click Next. Click the Browse button to navigate to the location where you unzipped the downloaded chapter resources. Check the file authorBooks.xml and click the Finish button. You should see the file inside the assets folder in the Navigator view.

We'll create an interface for the application in the Books.mxml file. Add a VBox control containing a ComboBox and List control. We'll load the author names into the ComboBox control. When we select an author, we'll load a list of his or her books into the List control. My MXML file contains the following code:

```
<mx:VBox x="10" y="10">
  <mx:ComboBox id="cboAuthors"/>
  <mx:List id="booksList" height="154" width="427"/>
</mx:VBox>
```

Figure 20-1 shows the appearance of this file when it runs in a web browser.

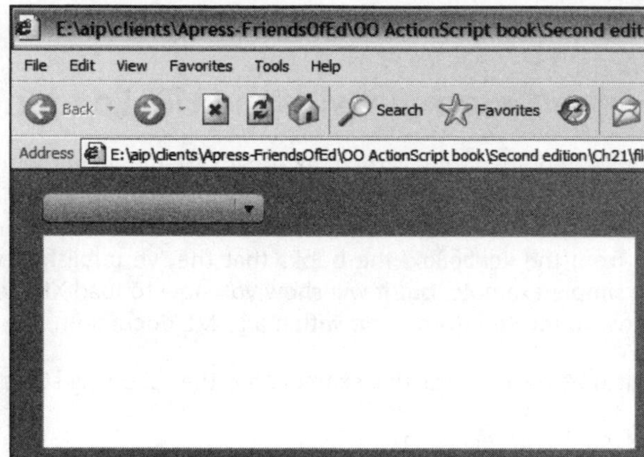

Figure 20-1. The application interface

Before we populate the interface, we'll create an ActionScript 3.0 class to handle the loading and data management from the XML document. Choose File ➤ New ➤ ActionScript class.

Create the class in the com.aip package. Enter the name ManageXML for the class. Click Finish and you should see that a file called ManageXML.is created in the folder com/aip containing the following code:

```
package com.aip {
  public class ManageXML {
  }
}
```

We'll start by creating the private variables we'll need within the class. In this example, we only need one variable to store the loaded XML content. We'll call the variable __books, and it is of the type XML. Add the following line below the class declaration:

```
private var __books:XML;
```

We need to add a constructor function to the class file. Our Flex application will call the constructor, passing in the URL of the XML document to load. Add the following function to the class file:

```
public function ManageXML(urlToLoad:String) {
  loadXMLFromFile(urlToLoad);
}
```

This function calls another function called loadXMLFromFile(). I find it useful to separate out the functionality for loading XML into a separate function at this point so I can call it from other functions if necessary.

We now need to add the private function loadXMLFromFile().

```
private function loadXMLFromFile(urlToLoad:String):void {
  var theLoader:URLLoader = new URLLoader();
  theLoader.addEventListener(Event.COMPLETE, processXML);
  theLoader.load(new URLRequest(urlToLoad));
}
```

The function takes the URL of the XML document as a parameter and returns nothing. It creates a new `URLLoader` object called `theLoader`. It adds an event listener that listens for the `COMPLETE` event and then calls the `processXML()` function. Finally, it loads a new `URLRequest` object using the URL of the XML document.

We will need to import the following classes below the class declaration because we haven't used fully qualified names. Flex does this automatically, so check that your class file includes the following declarations at the top of the document:

```
import flash.events.*;
import flash.net.*;
```


If you're not familiar with the `URLLoader` class, it loads content from a URL and can work with text and XML documents. You need to make sure that the URL being loaded is in the same subdomain as the SWF file, or else you'll hit the Flash Player security restrictions. I'll cover a little more about that later in the chapter in the section "Working with Flash Player security."

You'll notice we haven't yet created the `processXML()` function that will deal with the loaded XML document. We'll do so now. Let's start by performing a simple trace of what we've loaded. Add the following private function to your class file:

```
private function processXML(e:Event):void {
  __books = new XML(e.target.data as String);
  e.target.removeEventListener(Event.COMPLETE, processXML);
  trace (__books.toXMLString());
}
```

The function simply accesses the loaded content by using the `data` property of the `URLLoader`. We accessed this using `e.target.data`, which we cast as a string. We also removed the event listener. The final line displays a string representation of the loaded XML content using the `trace()` method. We can only see the output from this action in the Console view when we debug instead of running the application.

Switch back to the MXML file and add an `<mx:Script>` block below the opening `<mx:Application>` element. Create a new instance of the `ManageXML` class with the following code:

```
<mx:Script>
  <![CDATA[
    import com.aip.ManageXML;
    private var bookDetails:ManageXML = ➥
       new ManageXML("assets/authorBooks.xml");
  ]]>
</mx:Script>
```

In order to see the results from the trace() method, we'll need to click the Debug button on the toolbar. Do this now and switch back to Flex Builder after the web browser opens. The Console view should show the contents from the XML document as you see in Figure 20-2.

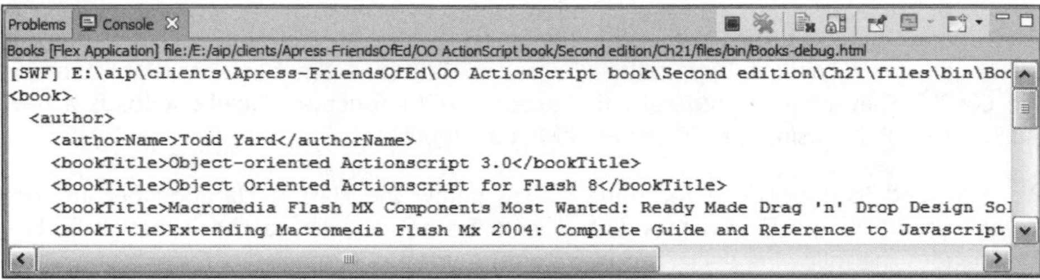

Figure 20-2. The Console view displaying the loaded XML content

Now that we know we've got the XML document loaded correctly, we can use it to populate the ComboBox control with a list of author names. We'll create a public method called getAuthorNameArray() to handle this functionality in our class file.

Switch back to ManageXML.as and add the following public method:

```
public function getAuthorNameArray():Array {
  var theAuthors:XMLList = __books..authorName;
  var arrAuthors:Array = new Array();
  for (var i:Number=0; i<theAuthors.length();i++) {
    arrAuthors.push(theAuthors[i]);
  }
  arrAuthors.sort();
  return arrAuthors;
}
```

This method accepts no parameters and returns an array of all of the authors, sorted into alphabetical order. It starts by declaring an XMLList variable called theAuthors, which is a collection of all <authorName> elements. We create the collection using the E4X expression __books..authorName. This expression finds any <authorName> elements that are descendants of the __books XML object. We then create a new array called arrAuthors, and this array will contain the return values. We'll be able to assign it directly to the dataProvider property of the ComboBox control.

The method uses a for loop to work through each of the authors in the XMLList and adds them to the array. After the loop finishes, it sorts the authors into alphabetical order. The final line returns the array.

We'll call this method in the creationComplete event in the <mx:Application> tag in the MXML file. Switch back to this file and modify the element as shown in bold:

```
<mx:Application xmlns:mx="http://www.adobe.com/2006/mxml"
  layout="absolute" creationComplete=" populateCombo(event)">
```

The line calls the populateCombo() function, which we'll add to the MXML file now.

```
private function populateCombo(e:FlexEvent):void {
  cboAuthors.prompt = "Choose author";
  cboAuthors.dataProvider = bookDetails.getAuthorNameArray();
}
```

Check that entering this function has added the following import statement to the file:

```
import mx.events.FlexEvent;
```

This function sets the prompt for the ComboBox control as well as the dataProvider property. We use the array returned by the call to the getAuthorNameArray() public method for the value of the second property.

Run the application now, and you should see that ComboBox is populated with author names, as shown in Figure 20-3, including the first line, Choose author.

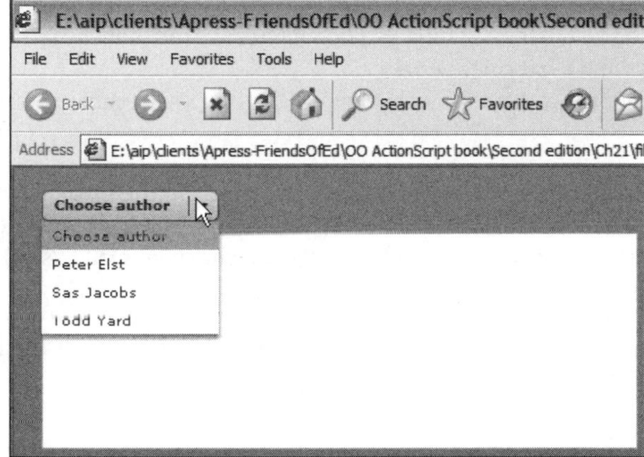

Figure 20-3. The ComboBox component is populated from the loaded XML document.

The next task is to show a list of books when we select an author from the ComboBox. We'll do this in response to the change event for the ComboBox control. Modify the <mx:ComboBox> element as shown in bold in the following line:

```
<mx:ComboBox x="10" y="6" id="cboAuthors" change="showBooks()"/>
```

The showBooks() function will need to access a list of all books for the selected author. We'll need to add a new public method to the class file so we can identify these books from a specified author name. The method will need to take the author name as a parameter and return an array. Add the following public method to the class file:

```
public function returnAuthorBooksXMLList(theAuthorName:String) ➥
  :XMLList {
  var theAuthorBooks:XMLList = __books.author.(authorName == ➥
```

```
      theAuthorName).bookTitle;
    return theAuthorBooks;
  }
```

The returnAuthorBooksXMLList() method starts by creating an array variable called theAuthorBooks, which it will return. It creates an XMLList of relevant books using the following E4X expression:

```
__books.author.(authorName == theAuthorName).bookTitle
```

This expression finds the relevant author by navigating to the author elements and filtering them using the author name passed to the function. The expression then locates the child bookTitle nodes relevant to this author to create the collection and returns the XMLList.

We'll call this method in the showBooks() function that we call in the change event of the ComboBox control. Switch back to the MXML file and add this function now.

```
private function showBooks():void {
  var selectedAuthor:String = cboAuthors.selectedLabel;
 booksList.dataProvider = ➥
      bookDetails.returnAuthorBooksXMLList(selectedAuthor);
}
```

The function starts by identifying which author is selected in the ComboBox and storing it in the selectedAuthor variable. It sets the dataProvider property of the booksList control to the returned XMLList from a call to the returnAuthorBooksXMLList() method of the bookDetails object.

Run the application, and you should be able to select an author from the list to see his or her list of books. Figure 20-4 shows the resulting application.

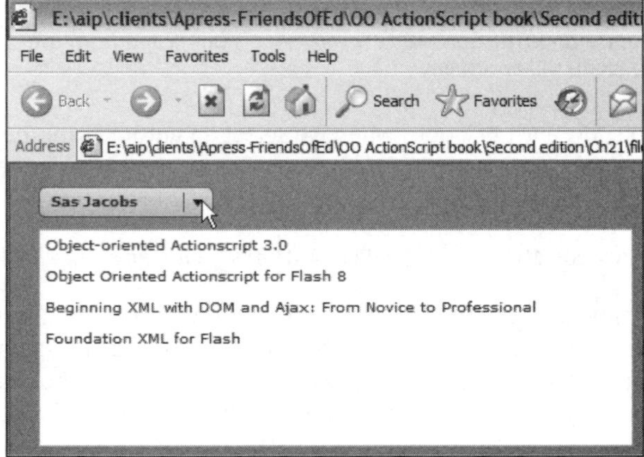

Figure 20-4. The completed application

While this example is simplistic, it shows how you can load content from an external XML document and add it to the interface of a Flex application. It also demonstrates some techniques for navigating through a loaded XML document using E4X expressions. You can find my finished files saved with the resources as ManageXML.as and Books.mxml.

Let's work through a simplified version of this example using a tag-based approach. This time, we'll use the <mx:HTTPService> tag to load books by Sas Jacobs from the file sasjacobsBooks.xml.

Working through an example with the <mx:HTTPService> tag

In this example, we'll load a list of book titles from an XML document into a List control using the <mx:HTTPService> tag. We'll use the resource file sasjacobsBooks.xml, so you should import it into the assets folder of your Flex project. The instructions for importing files appear in the previous example. This XML document has the same structure as the one in the previous example except that it only contains books for a single author.

Create a new MXML file by choosing File ➤ New ➤ MXML Application. Call the document SingleAuthorBooks.mxml and add the following MXML tags:

```
<mx:VBox x="10" y="10">
  <mx:Label text="Books by Sas Jacobs"
    fontWeight="bold" fontSize="14"/>
  <mx:List id="booksList" width="427" height="154" />
</mx:VBox>
```

Figure 20-5 shows how the interface appears when the application is run.

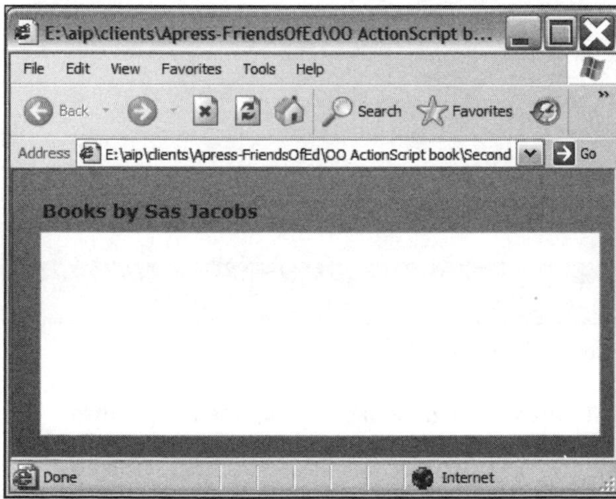

Figure 20-5. The application interface

Add the following <mx:HTTPService> tag below the <mx:Application> tag:

```
<mx:HTTPService id="booksXML" url="assets/sasjacobsBooks.xml"
  resultFormat="e4x" />
```

This tag loads the file sasjacobsBooks.xml from the assets folder and sets a format for the results of e4x. We'll call the send method to actually make the request for the XML document. We can do this in the creationComplete handler inside the <mx:Application> tag. Modify it as shown in bold here:

```
<mx:Application xmlns:mx="http://www.adobe.com/2006/mxml"
  layout="absolute" creationComplete="booksXML.send()">
```

The final step is to bind the dataProvider property for the List control to the contents of the XML file. We can do that by changing the <mx:List> control code as shown:

```
<mx:List x="10" y="36" width="427" id="booksList" height="154"
  dataProvider="{booksXML.lastResult.author.bookTitle}"/>
```

In this case, we've used the curly braces syntax for data binding to select the lastResult property of the booksXML object. We traverse the XML content with the E4X expression author.bookTitle.

When you run the application, you should see something very similar to Figure 20-6.

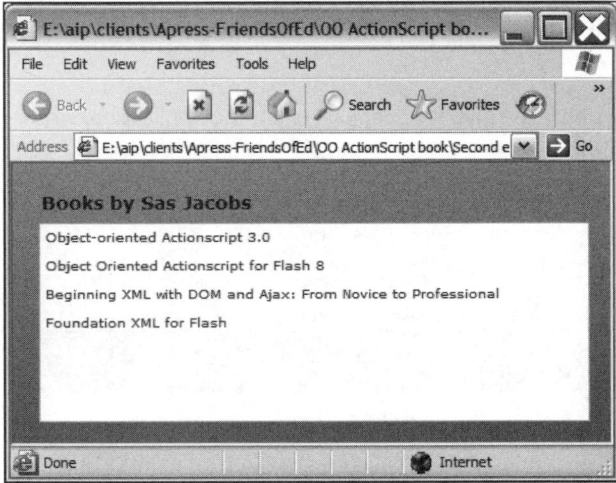

Figure 20-6. The completed example

Obviously, I haven't written enough books to fill up the List control!

You can see that this approach is much simpler than using an ActionScript-based approach, but it gives you less flexibility than we had in the class file. You can find the completed application file saved under the name SingleAuthorBooks.mxml with your downloaded resources.

Now that you've seen two approaches for working with XML documents, let's turn our attention to Web Services. I want to give you an understanding of what they are before showing you how to work with them in ActionScript.

Understanding Web Services

Web Services have really been hyped over the last few years as the must-have technology for businesses, and there is definitely some truth to that assertion. A Web Service allows you to communicate with a remote server, although it could technically also be your own, to call a remote method or procedure, and receive results back in XML format. Requesting information in this way is called *consuming* a Web Service.

There are many different types of Web Services, and an RSS feed could really be considered to be a simple Web Service. One of the most common methods for working with Web Services is Simple Object Access Protocol (SOAP). This protocol uses an XML format to send calls back and forward between the different servers. Messages are usually sent over the HTTP or HTTPS protocol on port 80, which means it shouldn't have any problems passing through firewalls. Because all communication uses an XML format, it is completely platform independent. Any software package capable of understanding XML can use the results returned by the Web Service. Humans can also read the contents.

You might be wondering how people know what they can do with each Web Service. Web Services define the methods that are available, the parameters they require, and the format for results in a WSDL (Web Services Description Language) file—pronounced *whiz dull*. This language is not meant to be read by humans, so I won't look at it in any further detail. It's enough to know that these files exist. Instead, let's take a closer look at the SOAP protocol and see the role it plays in Web Services.

Understanding SOAP

As mentioned earlier, SOAP messages are sent in an XML format. The structure of a SOAP message is simple—it consists of an envelope that contains a header and a body. The header is optional, but could contain information such as authentication for the Web Service and other information about the service call. The structure of the message depends on whether you're working with SOAP 1.1 or 1.2. The following example shows a SOAP 1.1 message:

```
<?xml version="1.0" ?>
<env:Envelope xmlns:env="http://schemas.xmlsoap.org/soap/envelope/">
   <env:Body>
     <yd:getEmployeeDetails xmlns:yd="http://www.yourdomain.com/">
       <yd:employeeID>108</yd:employeeID>
     </yd:getEmployeeDetails>
   </env:Body>
 </env:Envelope>
```

The SOAP 1.2 version of the second line appears here:

```
<env:Envelope xmlns:env="http://www.w3.org/2003/05/soap-envelope">
```

This is about the most basic SOAP call you could imagine—it's just the envelope and the body. The SOAP message calls the method getEmployeeDetails() and passes an argument called employeeID that contains a value of 108.

One thing you'll notice here is that SOAP message uses XML namespaces. We use one namespace for the SOAP elements and another for the calls to the remote procedure. The XML namespace in the Envelope node refers to the XML schema for the SOAP protocol, and the namespace in the getEmployeeDetails node indicates that this part of the XML message is not defined in the SOAP schema. It indicates the domain where the Web Service is deployed.

When the Web Service receives this message, it processes the request by calling the method, passing any arguments. It then sends back another SOAP message containing the results from the method.

```
<?xml version="1.0" ?>
<env:Envelope xmlns:env="http://schemas.xmlsoap.org/soap/envelope/">
   <env:Body>
     <yd:getEmployeeDetailsResponse
       xmlns:yd ="http://www.yourdomain.com/">
      <yd:getEmployeeDetailsResult>
         <yd:employeeID>108</yd:employeeID>
         <yd:employeeName>John Doe</yd:employeeName>
         <yd:employeeDepartment>Marketing</yd:employeeDepartment>
       </yd:getEmployeeDetailsResult>
     </yd:getEmployeeDetailsResponse>
   </env:Body>
 </env:Envelope>
```

The result message isn't much more complicated. The method name that we called is sent back with the text Response appended to indicate that it is a SOAP response. In getEmployeeDetailsResponse, there is another node that contains the results, in this case the method name with Result appended. Inside getEmployeeDetailsResult is every property that the method returned after it was called.

We can also access errors that occur when making SOAP requests. Let's say the getEmployeeDetails method didn't pass the employeeID parameter. In this case, the Web Service would send back a SOAP message with information about the fault that occurred.

```
<?xml version="1.0" ?>
<env:Envelope xmlns:env="http://schemas.xmlsoap.org/soap/envelope/">
  <env:Body>
    <env:Fault>
      <env:faultcode>Client</env:faultcode>
      <env:faultstring>employeeID parameter is missing
```

```
        </env:faultstring>
      </env:Fault>
    </env:Body>
  </env:Envelope>
```

These are obviously very basic examples, and SOAP is a complex and extensive topic to discuss. You can find out more about the most recent version of SOAP, SOAP 1.2, in the primer at the W3C website—www.w3.org/TR/2003/REC-soap12-part0-20030624/. You can also see the messaging framework at www.w3.org/TR/2003/REC-soap12-part1-20030624/ and the adjuncts at www.w3.org/TR/2003/REC-soap12-part2-20030624/.

In the next section, I want to show you how ActionScript works with SOAP Web Services.

Consuming Web Services

Flex and Flash applications can consume SOAP Web Services providing that the applications can access a WSDL file for the service. The WSDL file is usually provided at a remote URL.

One of the difficulties in accessing Web Services is the Flash Player security sandbox. Basically, a Flex application can't access data from a domain or subdomain other than its own, unless it has permission. This causes a bit of a problem with Web Services as they are normally located at different domains from the calling SWF file. I'll cover the security implications of this in the next section, but in the interim, we'll assume it isn't an issue.

While you can consume a Web Service using the <mx:WebService> element in Flex, I want to focus on achieving the same thing with the WebService class. After we've achieved that, I'll show you the same example using the <mx:WebService> element.

Understanding the WebService class

You can use the WebService class to consume SOAP Web Services. You need to instantiate a WebService object and pass the URL of a WSDL file. You also need to create an AbstractOperation object before you can create the call to the Web Service. The AbstractOperation object represents the remote method that you're calling on the Web Service, and you can add arguments that are passed with the object when the call is made.

The process can be quite confusing, and I have found the help documentation in this area to be scant. At the time of writing, it didn't include any useful examples. I thought the best approach in this chapter would be to work through an example and then explain the relevant properties and methods of the WebService class afterwards.

I'll show you an example that connects to a simple SOAP Web Service to convert temperatures from Celsius to Fahrenheit. You can find the WSDL file at http://developerdays.com/cgi-bin/tempconverter.exe/wsdl/ITempConverter. We'll call the CtoF method, which returns the Fahrenheit temperature when you specify the Celsius temperature.

Working through a scripted example

Let's start our example in Flex by creating the application interface. Create a new Flex project with File ➤ New ➤ Flex Project. Call the project TempConvert and choose any location.

We'll add the following interface below the opening `<mx:Application>` element:

```
<mx:NumberValidator id="wholeNumValidator"
source="{txtTemp}" property="text"
trigger="{btnConvert}" triggerEvent="click"
precision="0" required="true"
invalid="txtConvertedTemp.text='Please enter a whole number'" ➥
valid="callWS(event)"/>
<mx:VBox x="10" y="10">
  <mx:Label text="Convert Celsius to Fahrenheit" fontWeight="bold"/>
  <mx:HBox>
    <mx:Label text="Enter celsius temperature (whole numbers only)"/>
    <mx:TextInput id="txtTemp" width="50"/>
  </mx:HBox>
  <mx:HBox width="100%">
    <mx:Spacer width="100%"/>
    <mx:Button label="Convert" id="btnConvert"/>
  </mx:HBox>
  <mx:Text id="txtConvertedTemp"/>
</mx:VBox>
```

You can see that I've taken advantage of the VBox and HBox layout containers to simplify the positioning of my user interface elements. I've also included a NumberValidator to check for a valid entry. Figure 20-7 shows how the interface appears at this point.

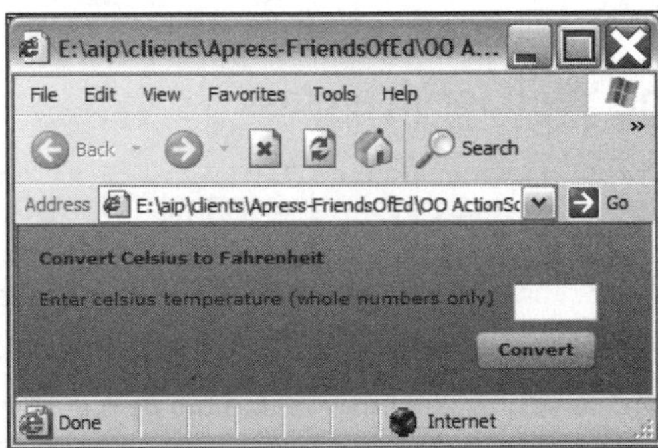

Figure 20-7. The temperature converter interface

We'll display the result in the `txtConvertedTemp` `Label` control.

Now we need to create the `TempConvert` class file that will drive the application. The class file will provide a public method called `findFTemp()` that consumes the Web Service. Create a new ActionScript class file by choosing File ➤ New ➤ ActionScript Class. Add it to package com.aip and give it the name TempConvert.as. You should see the following code block in your class file:

```
package com.aip {
  public class TempConvert
  }
}
```

We'll start by declaring the private variables that we need. Add the following lines underneath the class declaration:

```
private var __tempConvertWS:WebService;
private var __WSOperation:AbstractOperation;
private var __WSOperationArguments:Object;
private var __convertedTemp:int;
```

Theses variables respectively reference the Web Service, the operation of the Web Service, an object to store the arguments to be sent with the operation call, and the converted Fahrenheit temperature as an integer.

Check to see which import statements have been added at the top of the package. Make sure the list includes the following:

```
import mx.rpc.AbstractOperation;
import mx.rpc.soap.WebService;
```

We'll start by creating the constructor function for the class. Add the following code to the class declaration. It creates the constructor, which in turn calls a private method, initWS().

```
public function TempConvert() {
  initWS();
}
```

The initWS method will set up the Web Service call, so add it to the class file.

```
private function initWS():void {
  __tempConvertWS = new WebService();
  __WSOperationArguments = new Object();
  __tempConvertWS.loadWSDL("http://developerdays.com/cgi-bin/➥
    tempconverter.exe/wsdl/ITempConverter");
  __tempConvertWS.useProxy = false;
  __WSOperation = __tempConvertWS["CtoF"];
  __tempConvertWS.addEventListener("result", resultHandler);
  tempConvertWS.addEventListener("fault", faultHandler);
}
```

The method starts by creating a new WebService object that we'll reference with __tempConvertWS. It also creates an object that we'll use to store the arguments to send with the Web Service call. We need to pass the Celsius temperature to the CtoF() method, and we'll get that value from the TextInput control in the MXML file.

The code block also uses the loadWSDL() method to request and download the WSDL document from the Web Service. We set the useProxy property to false, as we're not using the Flex proxy service, and we set the operation to the CtoF() remote method on the Web Service. Finally, we add event listeners for the result and fault events. We'll add those private methods next.

The result and fault event handlers for the Web Service call receive a ResultEvent and FaultEvent argument, respectively. Add them to the class file.

```
private function resultHandler(e:ResultEvent):void {
  __convertedTemp = e.target.CtoF.lastResult as int;
  dispatchEvent(new Event("result"));
}
private function faultHandler(fault:FaultEvent):void {
  dispatchEvent(new Event("fault"));
}
```

Add the following public method:

```
public function findFTemp(cTemp:int):void {
  __WSOperationArguments.temp = cTemp;
  __WSOperation.arguments = __WSOperationArguments;
  __WSOperation.send();
}
```

The method receives the Celsius temperature as an argument and returns nothing. It assigns the temperature to the temp property of the __WSOperationArguments object. It then assigns that object to the arguments property of the Web Service operation and calls the send method to make the request.

We need to add one more method to this class file, and that's the getter method that returns the Fahrenheit temperature. The method simply returns the __convertedTemp variable.

```
public function get fTemp():int {
  return __convertedTemp;
}
```

We'll make the class bindable so that all getters and setters can be bound in the application file. Add the following meta tag above the class definition:

```
[Bindable]
public class TempConvert {
```

The complete code for the TempConvert class follows:

```
package com.aip {
  import mx.rpc.AbstractOperation;
  import mx.rpc.soap.WebService;
  import mx.rpc.events.ResultEvent;
  import mx.rpc.events.FaultEvent;
```

```
    [Bindable]
    public class TempConvert {
      private var __tempConvertWS:WebService;
      private var __WSOperation:AbstractOperation;
      private var __WSOperationArguments:Object;
      private var __convertedTemp:int;
      public function TempConvert() {
        initWS();
      }
      public function get fTemp():int {
        return __convertedTemp;
      }
      public function findFTemp(cTemp:int):void {
        __WSOperationArguments.temp = cTemp;
        __WSOperation.arguments = __WSOperationArguments;
        __WSOperation.send();
      }
      private function initWS():void {
        __tempConvertWS = new WebService();
        __WSOperationArguments = new Object();
        __tempConvertWS.loadWSDL("http://developerdays.com/cgi-bin/➥
          tempconverter.exe/wsdl/ITempConverter");
        __tempConvertWS.useProxy = false;
        __WSOperation = __tempConvertWS["CtoF"];
        __tempConvertWS.addEventListener("result", resultHandler);
        __tempConvertWS.addEventListener("fault", faultHandler);
      }
      private function resultHandler(e:ResultEvent):void {
        __convertedTemp = e.target.CtoF.lastResult as int;
        dispatchEvent(new Event("result"));
      }
      private function faultHandler(e:FaultEvent):void {
        dispatchEvent(new Event("fault"));
      }
    }
  }
```


We have a couple of modifications to make to the application, so switch back to the MXML file. First, we need to create an instance of the TempConvert class in a script block at the top of the application file. Start by adding a script block and importing the class file.

```
<mx:Script>
  <![CDATA[
    import com.aip.TempConvert;
  ]]>
</mx:Script>
```

Declare the following variable called theTempConvert:

```
private var theTempConvert:TempConvert;
```

We need to create an instance of the TempConvert class, and we'll do this in a function called setupWS(). We'll call this function in the creationComplete event of the application. Add the function now.

```
private function setupWS(e:FlexEvent):void {
  theTempConvert = new TempConvert();
  theTempConvert.addEventListener("result", resultHandler);
  theTempConvert.addEventListener("fault", faultHandler);
}
```

The function creates an instance of the TempConvert class and adds event listeners for the result and fault events dispatched by the class file. It takes a FlexEvent as an argument as this is passed from the creationComplete event.

Modify the opening <mx:Application> tag as shown:

```
<mx:Application xmlns:mx="http://www.adobe.com/2006/mxml"
  layout="absolute" creationComplete="setupWS(event)">
```

We'll need to add the resultHandler() and faultHandler() functions as well as the callWS() function that calls the public findFTemp() method. Add the following functions:

```
private function callWS(e:ValidationResultEvent):void{
  theTempConvert.findFTemp(int(txtTemp.text));
  txtConvertedTemp.text = "Making request";
}
private function resultHandler(e:Event):void {
  txtConvertedTemp.text = txtTemp.text + " Celsius is equivalent to "➥
    + theTempConvert.fTemp.toString() + " Fahrenheit";
}
private function faultHandler(e:Event):void {
  txtConvertedTemp.text = "Error contacting Web Service";
}
```

The first function, callWS(), receives a ValidationResultEvent as an argument as it's called when the valid event is dispatched by the validator. This function calls the findFTemp() public method of the TempConvert class, passing the entry from the txtTemp control cast as an int. It displays the text Making request in the txtConvertedTemp control.

The resultHandler() function responds to the result event from the TempConvert class. It displays the converted value along with some text. Notice that it calls the fTemp() getter method, converting it for display with the toString() method. The faultHandler() method displays a simple error message in the txtConvertedTemp control.

Check that the import statements at the top of the script block include the following:

```
import com.aip.TempConvert;
import mx.events.FlexEvent;
import mx.events.ValidationResultEvent;
```

The complete code for the MXML file follows:

```
<?xml version="1.0" encoding="utf-8"?>
<mx:Application xmlns:mx="http://www.adobe.com/2006/mxml"
  layout="absolute" creationComplete="setupWS(event)">
  <mx:Script>
    <![CDATA[
      import com.aip.TempConvert;
      import mx.events.FlexEvent;
      import mx.events.ValidationResultEvent;
      private var theTempConvert:TempConvert;
      private function setupWS(e:FlexEvent):void {
        theTempConvert = new TempConvert();
        theTempConvert.addEventListener("result", resultHandler);
        theTempConvert.addEventListener("fault", faultHandler);
      }
      private function callWS(e:ValidationResultEvent):void{
        theTempConvert.findFTemp(int(txtTemp.text));
        txtConvertedTemp.text = "Making request";
      }
      private function resultHandler(e:Event):void  {
        txtConvertedTemp.text = txtTemp.text + " Celsius is ➥
          equivalent to " + theTempConvert.fTemp.toString() ➥
          + " Fahrenheit";
      }
      private function faultHandler(e:Event):void {
        txtConvertedTemp.text = "Error contacting Web Service";
      }
    ]]>
  </mx:Script>
  <mx:NumberValidator id="wholeNumValidator"
    source="{txtTemp}" property="text"
    trigger="{btnConvert}" triggerEvent="click"
    precision="0" required="true"
    invalid="txtConvertedTemp.text='Please enter a whole number'"
    valid="callWS(event)"/>
  <mx:VBox x="10" y="10">
    <mx:Label text="Convert Celsius to Fahrenheit" fontWeight="bold"/>
    <mx:HBox>
      <mx:Label text="Enter celsius temperature (whole numbers only)"/>
      <mx:TextInput id="txtTemp" width="50"/>
    </mx:HBox>
    <mx:HBox width="100%">
      <mx:Spacer width="100%"/>
      <mx:Button label="Convert" id="btnConvert"/>
    </mx:HBox>
    <mx:Text id="txtConvertedTemp"/>
  </mx:VBox>
</mx:Application>
```

The last step is to run the application to make sure it actually works. Enter a Celsius temperature and click the Convert button. You should initially see the text Making request appear in the Label control. If you wait for a minute or two, you should see the converted temperature displaying as shown in Figure 20-8. If the request fails, you'll see the error message.

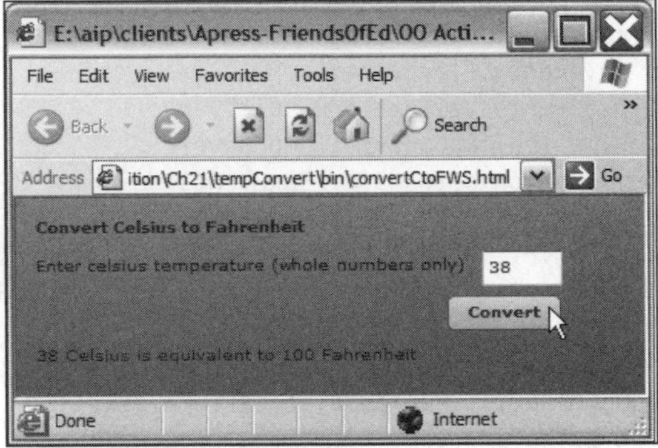

Figure 20-8. The completed application

This simple example shows how to consume a Web Service and access the results in ActionScript 3.0. You can find the completed examples in the files TempConvert.as and convertCtoFWS.mxml with the downloaded resources.

It's worth looking a little more closely at the methods and properties of the WebService class. We'll then re-create the same example using the <mx:WebService> element.

Properties of the WebService class

The WebService class is based on the AbstractService class. It's this class that manages the Web Service operations. You can use the WebService class with Flex Data Services, but that's beyond the scope of this chapter. Table 20-6 shows the most common properties of the WebService class.

Table 20-6. Properties of the WebService class

Property	Type	Explanation
description	String	The description of the Web Service.
headers	Array	The list of SOAP headers registered with the Web Service.
makeObjectsBindable	Boolean	Set this to true to force the returned objects to bindable objects.
port	String	Specifies the port that the Web Service should use.
requestTimeout	Int	Determines the timeout in seconds for messages sent to Web Services.

Property	Type	Explanation
rootURL	String	The base URL that the Web Service should use when calculating relative URLs.
service	String	The service to be used within the WSDL document.
useProxy	Boolean	Specifies whether to use the Flex proxy service.
wsdl	String	The location of the WSDL document for the Web Service.

Methods of the WebService class

Table 20-7 shows the public methods of the WebService class. The default values of the parameters are shown in brackets.

Table 20-7. The public methods of the WebService class

Method	Parameters	Explanation
addHeader	header: SOAPHeader	Adds the specified SOAP header for all operations of the Web Service
addSimpleHeader	qnameLocal: String, qnameNamespace: String, headerName: String, headerValue: String	Adds the specified SOAP header for all operations of the Web Service
canLoadWSDL		Returns a Boolean value indicating whether the WSDL document can be loaded
clearHeaders		Clears all SOAP headers that apply to all operations of the Web Service
disconnect		Disconnects from the Web Service and removes and pending requests
getHeader	qname: String, headerName: String (null)	Returns the SOAPHeader that matches the specified qname

Continued

Table 20-7. The public methods of the WebService class *(continued)*

Method	Parameters	Explanation
getOperation	name: String	Returns an operation of the given name
loadWSDL	uri: String (null)	Tells the Web Service to load the WSDL document
logout		Logs the user out of the destination
removeHeader	qname: String, headerName: String (null)	Removes the specified SOAP header from all operations of the Web Service
setRemoteCredentials	remoteUsername: String, remotePassword: String	Provides the username and password required to access the Web Service
toString		Returns the Web Service as a String representation
WebService	destination: String (null), rootURL: (null)	Constructor returning a new WebService object

Events dispatched by the WebService class

The WebService class dispatches the events summarized in Table 20-8. Most of the events are inherited from the AbstractService class.

Table 20-8. Events dispatched by the WebService class

Event	Defined by	Explanation
fault	AbstractService class	Dispatched when the call to the Web Service fails
invoke	AbstractService class	Dispatched when an operation of the Web Service is invoked
load	WebService class	Dispatched when the WSDL document has successfully loaded
result	AbstractService class	Dispatched when the call to the Web Service successfully returns data

Now that you know how to script the WebService class, let's now see how we could have consumed the Web Service we saw in the previous example using the <mx:WebService> element.

Using the <mx:WebService> element

The <mx:WebService> tag allows you to communicate with a Web Service without much scripting at all. It works with the <mx:operation> tag, which specifies the name of the operation to call. If parameters need to be passed with the call, we can use the <mx:request> tag as well.

The <mx:WebService> tag has the following structure:

```
<mx:WebService
  concurrency="multiple|single|last"
  destination="No default."
  id="No default."
  serviceName="No default."
  showBusyCursor="false|true"
  makeObjectsBindable="false|true"
  useProxy="false|true"
  wsdl="No default."
  fault="No default."
  result="No default."
/>
```

20

One useful attribute here is the ability to show a busy cursor while the Web Service request is being made. You can't do this as a property of the WebService class in ActionScript.

Let's re-create the previous example using the <mx:WebService> tag. Add a new MXML application to your project by choosing File ➤ New ➤ MXML Application. We'll use the same interface as before.

```
<?xml version="1.0" encoding="utf-8"?>
<mx:Application xmlns:mx="http://www.adobe.com/2006/mxml"
  layout="absolute">
  <mx:NumberValidator id="wholeNumValidator"
    source="{txtTemp}" property="text"
    trigger="{btnConvert}" triggerEvent="click"
    precision="0" required="true"
    invalid="txtConvertedTemp.text='Please enter a whole number'"
    valid="callWS(event)"/>
  <mx:VBox x="10" y="10">
    <mx:Label text="Convert Celsius to Fahrenheit"➥
      fontWeight="bold"/>
    <mx:HBox>
      <mx:Label text="Enter celsius temperature (whole numbers ➥
        only)"/>
```

```
      <mx:TextInput id="txtTemp" width="50"/>
    </mx:HBox>
    <mx:HBox width="100%">
      <mx:Spacer width="100%"/>
      <mx:Button label="Convert" id="btnConvert"/>
    </mx:HBox>
    <mx:Text id="txtConvertedTemp"/>
  </mx:VBox>
</mx:Application>
```

The interface is identical to the one we created in the previous example. If we validate the entered Celsius temperature, we'll call the callWS() method.

We'll add the following <mx:WebService> tag below the opening <mx:Application> tag:

```
<mx:WebService id="tempConvertWS"
  wsdl="http://developerdays.com/cgi-bin/tempconverter.exe/wsdl/➥
  ITempConverter"
  useProxy="false"
  showBusyCursor="true"
  result="showResult(event)">
  <mx:operation name="CtoF">
    <mx:request>
      <temp>{int(txtTemp.text)}</temp>
    </mx:request>
  </mx:operation>
</mx:WebService>
```

This tag has the id tempConvertWS and starts by setting the wsdl property. It doesn't use the Flex proxy and shows the busy cursor when the call is in progress. The tag sets the result event handler to the showResult() ActionScript function.

The preceding code also includes the <mx:operation> tag, which specifies the name of the operation to call on the Web Service, in this case CtoF(). The request sends the <temp> element, which is bound to the text property of the txtTemp control. Notice that the value is cast as an int.

To create the showResult() function, add an <mx:Script> block below the opening <mx:Application> tag. Add the following function:

```
<mx:Script>
  <![CDATA[
    private function showResult(e:Event):void {
      txtConvertedTemp.text = txtTemp.text + " Celsius is equivalent➥
        to " + e.target.CtoF.lastResult.toString() + " ➥
        Fahrenheit";
    }
  ]]>
</mx:Script>
```

The function sets the text property of the txtConvertedTemp control to the returned value from the lastResult of the call, including some addition text.

The validator calls the callWS() function if the entered number is valid. Add this function to the script block.

```
private function callWS(e:ValidationResultEvent):void {
  tempConvertWS.CtoF.send();
}
```

This function calls the send() method of the CtoF() operation to make the request. Make sure that the ActionScript block includes the following import statement:

```
import mx.events.ValidationResultEvent;
```

Run the application now, and you should see results of your request. In fact, the results will appear the same as in Figure 20-8. You can find my finished file convertCtoFWSTag.mxml saved with your resources.

The completed MXML file follows:

```
<?xml version="1.0" encoding="utf-8"?>
<mx:Application xmlns:mx="http://www.adobe.com/2006/mxml"
  layout="absolute">
  <mx:Script>
    <![CDATA[
      import mx.events.ValidationResultEvent;
      private function showResult(e:Event):void {
        txtConvertedTemp.text = txtTemp.text + " Celsius is➥
          equivalent to " + e.target.CtoF.lastResult➥
          .toString() + " Fahrenheit";
      }
      private function callWS(e:ValidationResultEvent):void {
        tempConvertWS.CtoF.send();
      }
    ]]>
  </mx:Script>
  <mx:WebService id="tempConvertWS"
    wsdl="http://developerdays.com/cgi-bin/tempconverter.exe/wsdl/➥
      ITempConverter"
    useProxy="false"
    showBusyCursor="true"
    result="showResult(event)">
    <mx:operation name="CtoF">
      <mx:request>
        <temp>{int(txtTemp.text)}</temp>
      </mx:request>
    </mx:operation>
  </mx:WebService>
  <mx:NumberValidator id="wholeNumValidator"
```

```
    source="{txtTemp}" property="text"
    trigger="{btnConvert}" triggerEvent="click"
    precision="0" required="true"
    invalid="txtConvertedTemp.text='Please enter a whole number'"
    valid="callWS(event)"/>
  <mx:VBox x="10" y="10">
    <mx:Label text="Convert Celsius to Fahrenheit"➥
      fontWeight="bold"/>
    <mx:HBox>
      <mx:Label text="Enter celsius temperature (whole numbers➥
        only)"/>
      <mx:TextInput id="txtTemp" width="50"/>
    </mx:HBox>
    <mx:HBox width="100%">
      <mx:Spacer width="100%"/>
      <mx:Button label="Convert" id="btnConvert"/>
    </mx:HBox>
    <mx:Text id="txtConvertedTemp"/>
  </mx:VBox>
</mx:Application>
```

In this section, you've seen how to access a SOAP-based Web Service using ActionScript and the <mx:WebService> tag. As Web Services are normally located on different domains, you need to be aware of the security restrictions imposed by the Flash Player. That's the topic of the final section of this chapter.

Working with Flash Player security

Since Flash Player 6, there has been an increase in security surrounding the way external data is included in SWF files. This is referred to as the *security sandbox*. One reason for this interest is to stop the chance of malicious code being run.

The sandbox is the environment where the SWF file runs, and where data is located in a different sandbox from the SWF file, certain security rules apply. There aren't any issues if you are loading data from the same subdomain, but as soon as you need to access content from another server or subdomain, you need explicit permissions. External data relates to any SWF content, including XML files and anything else loaded into the Flash Player at runtime.

The rules vary according to the Flash Player version. Flash Player 8 and onward recognize several different sandboxes, including local and remote sandboxes. You can find where the Flash Player has allocated a SWF file using the `Security.sandboxType` property.

Local sandboxes can be divided into the following:

- **local-with-filesystem**: The default sandbox for local content, where SWF files can read local content but can't communicate with the network.
- **local-with-networking**: Occurs when network access is granted when publishing, and SWF files can access the network with appropriate permissions but not local files.
- **local-trusted**: SWF files are registered as trusted by users or programs and can interact with any data either local or remote.

Remote SWF files can access data from other domains, excluding local sources, by

- Explicit website and author permissions
- Cross-domain policy files
- Using `Security.allowDomain`

Let's start by looking at the `Security.allowDomain` method.

Security.allowDomain

The `Security.allowDomain` method sets all domains that are granted access to a resource. Let's say we have a file called `abc.swf` hosted on `www.mydomain.com`, and a file called `xyz.swf` hosted on `www.myotherdomain.com` that contains a doSomething function. If the file `abc.swf` loads in the file `xyz.swf`, it has no access to the doSomething function. To grant access to this file, `xyz.swf` needs to have `Security.allowDomain("www.mydomain.com")` in place. It could also use `Security.allowDomain("*")` to grant permission to all other domains and subdomains.

This method has a related method, `Security.allowInsecureDomain`, that does the same thing but between HTTPS and HTTP resources. When the method is called from a secure protocol or from HTTPS, this method allows access by the insecure protocol or from HTTP.

The downside of using the `Security.allowDomain` method is that it requires you to recompile your SWF file any time you need to provide another domain with access.

Cross-domain policy files

The second way to grant permission for content to be loaded from a different domain is to use a *cross-domain policy file*. Obviously, XML files and other data formats don't have the option of using the `Security.allowDomain` method, so they need to use this approach.

A cross-domain policy file is an XML file called `crossdomain.xml` located in the root of the server that hosts the external content. The file specifies which domains can access that content. You can use another location for the file or a different filename with the `Security.loadPolicyFile` method.

The cross-domain policy file looks like this:

```
<?xml version="1.0"?>
<!DOCTYPE cross-domain-policy SYSTEM➥
  "http://www.macromedia.com/xml/dtds/cross-domain-policy.dtd">
<cross-domain-policy>
  <allow-access-from domain="www.mydomain.com" />
</cross-domain-policy>
```

In the preceding example, the `crossdomain.xml` file would be saved in the root of the domain `www.myotherdomain.com`.

When you request content from a different domain or subdomain, the Flash Player checks for the existence of this cross-domain file. If it finds the file, it checks to see whether your domain, subdomain, or IP address is present. Where Flash Player can't find this cross-domain file, it checks the SWF file for the `Security.allowDomain` method. If neither of these are available, access will be denied. The same happens if the Flash Player finds the cross-domain file but can't locate a suitable domain, subdomain, or IP address.

It's important to note that the approach changed slightly between Flash Player 6 and Flash Player 7 and upward. In Flash Player 6, subdomains were allowed to access all files on the same domain, so for example `mysite.mydomain.com` could access content from `yoursite.mydomain.com`. Since Flash Player 7 this is no longer the case, and subdomains also need to be granted permission explicitly. In Flash Player 7 and above, `www.mydomain.com` and `mydomain.com` can't load data from each other.

You can solve the issue of different subdomains by using the following cross-domain policy:

```
<?xml version="1.0"?>
<!DOCTYPE cross-domain-policy SYSTEM ➥
  "http://www.macromedia.com/xml/dtds/cross-domain-policy.dtd">
<cross-domain-policy>
  <allow-access-from domain="*.mydomain.com" />
</cross-domain-policy>
```

This example uses the wildcard character to allow all subdomains of `mydomain.com` to access content from the server. You can limit the access to `www.mydomain.com` and `mydomain.com` with the following file:

```
<?xml version="1.0"?>
<!DOCTYPE cross-domain-policy SYSTEM ➥
  "http://www.macromedia.com/xml/dtds/cross-domain-policy.dtd">
<cross-domain-policy>
  <allow-access-from domain="mydomain.com" />
  <allow-access-from domain="www.mydomain.com" />
</cross-domain-policy>
```

You can also use a wildcard to grant access to all domains and subdomains as shown here:

```
<?xml version="1.0"?>
<!DOCTYPE cross-domain-policy SYSTEM ➥
  "http://www.macromedia.com/xml/dtds/cross-domain-policy.dtd">
<cross-domain-policy>
  <allow-access-from domain="*" />
</cross-domain-policy>
```

Specifying an IP address will only grant access to SWF files loaded from that IP address when using IP syntax. Access isn't granted to SWF files loaded from a domain name that resolves to the same IP address.

Using a server-side proxy script

Finally, there is one other method that allows users to load external data—the use of a server-side script to proxy the file locally. You might use this if you can't add a cross-domain policy file to the server root.

By using a scripting language such as PHP or ASP .NET, you can create a local copy of the external data that the Flash Player considers to be in the same sandbox. Adobe includes examples of these files at `www.adobe.com/cfusion/knowledgebase/index.cfm?id=tn_16520`.

For things like a basic XML file, this is easy enough to do:

```
<?php
  fpassthru($_POST["proxy_url"]);
?>
```

Let's say you save this PHP code as `proxy.php` on your local server and call `proxy.php?proxy_url=http://www.myotherdomain.com/myfile.xml` when loading in XML content. Since the Flash Player doesn't know where the script gets its data from, it loads the XML content as if it were local so no security measures apply.

This approach isn't quite as easy for a SOAP Web Service, which needs to send and receive SOAP messages, but it's very appropriate for consuming RSS feeds.

It's important to consider these additional security settings whenever working with content located on a different server. While they can be annoying, the measures are important, as they allow the Flash Player to protect itself from loading malicious code.

What's next?

In this chapter, I showed you some different approaches to loading XML content and Web Services into applications. I started with an overview of XML, and you should bear in mind that the chapter didn't provide a complete guide to the topic. XML is a perfect format for hooking up applications to data from a database or other back-end system.

I showed you how to navigate XML documents using the new E4X approach in ActionScript 3.0. We examined the new XML class and looked at the different ways to work with XML content. We finished the topic by looking at two different ways to load external data. First, we used ActionScript with the URLLoader class and second, we used the Flex <mx:HTTPService> element.

The next topic for the chapter was Web Services. These are commonly used for communicating with remote servers and often use the SOAP protocol. I showed you how to script the WebService class as well as how to use the <mx:WebService> element in Flex. I finished with a look at Flash Player security settings, which apply when the application needs to load content from a different domain or subdomain.

We've covered so much information in the chapters so far, you're probably already feeling dizzy. Sit back and relax with a cup of coffee because in the final chapter, we will put it all together in a complete real-world case study to get you inspired to create your own object-oriented ActionScript applications. A great way to recap everything we've discussed so far!

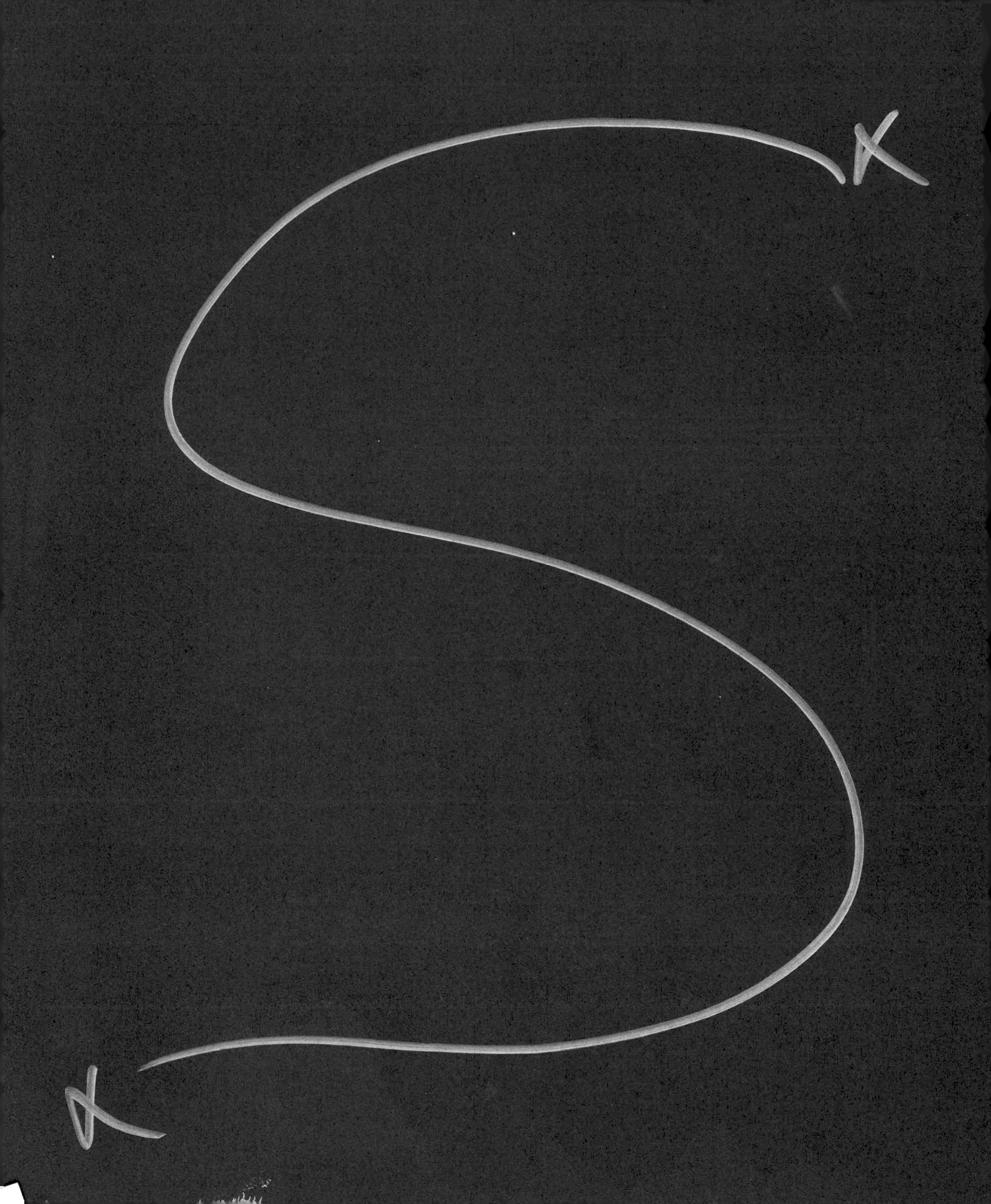